Buying and Selling

Library of the Written Word

VOLUME 72

The Handpress World

Editor-in-Chief

Andrew Pettegree (*University of St Andrews*)

Editorial Board

Ann Blair (*Harvard University*)
Falk Eisermann (*Staatsbibliothek zu Berlin – Preußischer Kulturbesitz*)
Earle Havens (*Johns Hopkins University*)
Ian Maclean (*All Souls College, Oxford*)
Alicia Montoya (*Radboud University*)
Angela Nuovo (*University of Milan*)
Helen Smith (*University of York*)
Mark Towsey (*University of Liverpool*)
Malcolm Walsby (*University of Rennes*)
Arthur der Weduwen (*University of St Andrews*)

VOLUME 55

The titles published in this series are listed at *brill.com/lww*

Buying and Selling

The Business of Books in Early Modern Europe

Edited by

Shanti Graheli

BRILL

LEIDEN | BOSTON

Cover illustration: *Galerie du Palais*, Abraham Bosse, 1637–1638. © Rijksmuseum, Amsterdam, RP-P-OB-42.103.

The Library of Congress Cataloging-in-Publication Data is available online at http://catalog.loc.gov

Typeface for the Latin, Greek, and Cyrillic scripts: "Brill". See and download: brill.com/brill-typeface.

ISSN 1874-4834
ISBN 978-90-04-34032-9 (hardback)
ISBN 978-90-04-34039-8 (e-book)

Copyright 2019 by Koninklijke Brill NV, Leiden, The Netherlands.
Koninklijke Brill NV incorporates the imprints Brill, Brill Hes & De Graaf, Brill Nijhoff, Brill Rodopi, Brill Sense, Hotei Publishing, mentis Verlag, Verlag Ferdinand Schöningh and Wilhelm Fink Verlag.
All rights reserved. No part of this publication may be reproduced, translated, stored in a retrieval system, or transmitted in any form or by any means, electronic, mechanical, photocopying, recording or otherwise, without prior written permission from the publisher.
Authorization to photocopy items for internal or personal use is granted by Koninklijke Brill NV provided that the appropriate fees are paid directly to The Copyright Clearance Center, 222 Rosewood Drive, Suite 910, Danvers, MA 01923, USA. Fees are subject to change.

This book is printed on acid-free paper and produced in a sustainable manner.

PRINTED BY DRUKKERIJ WILCO B.V. - AMERSFOORT, THE NETHERLANDS

Contents

Editorial Conventions   IX
Figures and Tables   X
Notes on Contributors   XVI

1   How to Lose Money in the Business of Books: Commercial Strategies in the First Age of Print   1
  Andrew Pettegree and Shanti Graheli

PART 1
Debt Economies and Bookselling Risks

2   Early Book Printing and Venture Capital in the Age of Debt: the Case of Michel Wenssler's Basel Printing Shop (1472–1491)   23
  Lucas Burkart

3   Venetian Incunabula for Florentine Bookshops (ca. 1473–1483)   55
  Lorenz Böninger

4   Book Prices in Early Modern Europe: an Economic Perspective   72
  Jeremiah Dittmar

5   Privileging the Common Good: the Moral Economy of Printing Privileges in the Seventeenth-Century Dutch Republic   88
  Marius Buning

PART 2
Day to Day Practices of Book Buying and Selling

6   The Business of Browsing in Early Modern English Bookshops   111
  Philip Tromans

7   Printing for the Pilgrims: Krakow Seventeenth-Century Guidebooks   136
  Justyna Kiliańczyk-Zięba

8   Book Lotteries as Sale Events for Slow-Sellers: the Case of Amsterdam in the Late Eighteenth Century   154
        Daniel Bellingradt

PART 3
Selling Strategies

9   Neither Scholar nor Printer: Luxembourg de Gabiano and the Financial Structure of Merchant-Publishing in Sixteenth-Century Lyon   181
        Jamie Cumby

10   Editing the *Thesaurus Linguae Latinae*: Robert Estienne's Dream and Nightmare   208
        Martine Furno

11   'Large Volumes that Are Bought by the Few': Printing and Selling Postils in Early Modern Poland   223
        Magdalena Komorowska

12   Buying and Selling in One Trip: Book Barter in Times of Trouble for Francesco Ciotti's Printing and Bookselling House   246
        Domenico Ciccarello

13   The State of Scottish Bookselling circa 1800   261
        Vivienne Dunstan

14   Cashing in on Counterfeits: Fraud in the Reformation Print Industry   276
        Drew Thomas

PART 4
List and Inventories

15   'Men and Books under Watch': the Brussels' Book Market in the Mid-Sixteenth Century through the Inquisitorial Archives   303
        Renaud Adam

CONTENTS VII

16 'Beautiful Intellects Should not Hide': The Bookshop of Luciano Pasini, Bookseller and Publisher between Perugia and Venice in the Second Half of the Sixteenth Century   322
    Natale Vacalebre

17 Early Modern Shelf Lives: the Context and Content of Georg Willer's Music Stock Catalogue of 1622   353
    Amelie Roper

18 Religion, Learning and Commerce: Daniel Delerpinière, a Protestant Bookseller in Saumur, 1661   380
    Jean-Paul Pittion

PART 5
New Markets

19 Turning News into a Business: the Commerce of Early Newspaper Publishing   397
    Jan Hillgärtner

20 Booksellers, Newspaper Advertisements and a National Market for Print in the Seventeenth-Century Dutch Republic   420
    Arthur der Weduwen

21 'Without Being Denounced or Humiliated': the Purchase of Books for Religious Communities in New Spain   448
    Idalia Garcia

22 Advertising and Selling in Cromwellian Newsbooks   467
    Jason McElligott

PART 6
Modern Book Market

23 Book Bitch to the Rich—the Strife and Times of the Revd. Dr. Thomas Frognall Dibdin (1776–1847)   489
    John A. Sibbald

24   Lost in Transaction: 'Discollecting' Incunabula in the Nineteenth and
     Twentieth Centuries   522
       Falk Eisermann

Modern Authors' Index   540
Subject Index   542
Alphabetical Index   546

Editorial Conventions

Foreign currencies have been expressed in Roman type throughout the volume.

Wherever possible, we have endeavoured to translate or summarize sources in foreign languages.

Figures and Tables

Figures

2.1	*Haus zem Lufft* where Wenssler moved his workshop to in 1479	24
2.2	Gasparino Barzizza, *Epistolae* [Michel Wenssler, Friedrich Biel], Basel 1472. Copy: Universitätsbibliothek Basel, Handschriftenmagazin, Inc 581:3, fol. 2	29
2.3	Aurelius Augustinus, *De civitate Dei* [Bernard Richel, Michel Wenssler], Basel 1479. Copy: Universitätsbibliothek Basel, Handschriftenmagazin, Inc 608	32
2.4	Sixtus IV, *Letter of indulgences* for Freiburg i. Br. [Michel Wenssler], Basel 1479. Copy: Kungliga Bibilioteket—Sveriges Nationalbibliotek Stockholm, Inkunabel 1398	33
2.5	Nicolò de Tudeschi, *Lectura super quinque libros Decretalium* [M. Wenssler, B. Ruppel, B. Richel], Basel 1477. Copy: Universitätsbibliothek Basel, Handschriftenmagazin, Np I 4	34
2.6	Overall printing output of Michel Wenssler's workshop (based on the GW)	40
2.7	Progression of Michel Wenssler's debts from 1472 to 1491 (based on *Vergichtbücher*)	48
2.8	Aggregated view of progression of output and debts (lb) of Wenssler's Basel workshop between 1472 and 1491	50
2.9	Imprints published by Wenssler according to page format	52
2.10	Non-datable imprints according to page format	53
4.1	Cities in Hernando Colón's book purchases	78
4.2	Distribution of book prices in Colón's purchases	79
4.3	The subject matter of Colón's purchases compared to the USTC	81
4.4	Book prices 1460 through 1618	83
4.5	Prices for 25 sheets	84
5.1	Gerardus Ioannes Vossius, *De theologia gentili et physiologia christiana* (Amsterdam: Blaeu, 1668). Bayerische Staatsbibliothek München, 2 Dogm. 354-1/2	104
5.2	Gerardus Ioannes Vossius, *De theologia gentili et physiologia christiana* (Amsterdam: Blaeu, 1668). Austrian National Library, scanned by Google	105
5.3	Willem Baudartius, *Les gverres de Nassav* (Amsterdam: M. Colin, 1616). National Library of the Netherlands, 357F36	106
5.4	Lambertus Hortensius, *Het Boeck D. Lamberts Hortensii* [...] *Van den*	

FIGURES AND TABLES   XI

            oproer der Weder-Dooperen (Enchuysen: J.L. Meyn, 1614). National Library
            of the Netherlands, 942A14:2   107
6.1   A still-bolted quarto showing the location of selected pre-purchase
            pleas   120
6.2   A still-bolted octavo showing the location of selected pre-purchase
            pleas   122
6.3   The pre-purchase plea in Gabriel Harvey's *The Trimming of Thomas
            Nashe*, A1ᵛ, from RB 61318, The Huntington Library, San Marino,
            California   130
7.1   *Przewodnik, abo Kościołów krakowskich i rzeczy w nich widzenia i
            wiedzenia godnych krotkie opisanie* (Krakow: Jakub Siebeneicher, 1603).
            Warsaw, Biblioteka Narodowa, SD XVII.1.1154   138
7.2   *Przewodnik, abo Kościołów krakowskich i rzeczy w nich widzenia i
            wiedzenia godnych krotkie opisanie* (Krakow: Jakub Siebeneicher, 1603).
            Warsaw, Biblioteka Narodowa, SD XVII.1.1154   148
7.3   *Przewodnik, abo Kościołów krakowskich i rzeczy w nich widzenia i
            wiedzenia godnych krotkie opisanie* (Krakow: Jakub Siebeneicher, 1603).
            Warsaw, Biblioteka Publiczna miasta stołecznego Warszawy,
            XVII.1.85   149
7.4   *Stołecznego miasta Krakowa kościoły i klejnoty* (Krakow: Franciszek
            Cezary, 1647). Warsaw, Biblioteka Narodowa, SD XVII.3.2521   151
7.5   *Klejnotów duchownych Stołecznego Miasta Krakowa Aukcyja Znamienita*
            (Krakow: Franciszek Cezary młodszy, post 1711). Krakow, Biblioteka
            Naukowa PAU i PAN, PAU st. Dr. 529 adl.   153
9.1   Average annual growth rate (in number of editions)   183
9.2   Most popular genres in Lyon by decade   186
9.3   Cash flow by industry   188
9.4   *Livre de Raison*: total funds by industry   189
9.5   Chronological distribution of the inventory   191
9.6   Number of printing contracts with recorded funds   192
9.7   Total funds recorded from printing contracts   192
9.8   Land use patterns for rural holdings of Lyon residents, ca. 1518   200
9.9   Urban vs. rural land-related documents   202
10.1   Robert Estienne, *Thesaurus Linguae Latinae* (Paris: Robert Estienne,
            1543), Blickling Hall, f. 621r. Reproduced with the authorization of the
            National Trust of England, Blickling Estate   216
10.2   Robert Estienne, *Thesaurus Linguae Latinae* (Paris: Robert Estienne,
            1543), Blickling Hall, f. 622r. Reproduced with the authorization of the
            National Trust of England, Blickling Estate   217
10.3   Robert Estienne, *Thesaurus Linguae Latinae* (Paris: Robert Estienne,

	1543), Blickling Hall, f. 177r. Reproduced with the authorization of the National Trust of England, Blickling Estate 218
10.4	Robert Estienne, *Thesaurus Linguae Latinae* (Paris: Robert Estienne, 1543), Blickling Hall, f. 482r. Reproduced with the authorization of the National Trust of England, Blickling Estate 220
11.1a–b	Title pages of Martin Luther, *Haußpostil*, Nürnberg 1549 (Bayerische Staatsbibliothek München, 889210 2 Hom. 283, urn=urn:nbn:de:bvb:12-bsb10144042-5) and Mikołaj Rej, *Świętych słów a spraw Pańskich, które tu sprawował Pan a Zbawiciel nasz (…) kronika albo Postylla*, Krakow, 1557 (Biblioteka Jagiellońska, Krakow, Cim.F.8295) 230
11.2a–b	Title pages of Martin Luther, Hauspostil, Wittenberg 1552 (Bayerische Staatsbibliothek München, sign. 889211 2 Hom. 284, urn=urn:nbn:de:bvb:12-bsb10144043-1) and the Polish translation of this work by Hieronim Malecki, *Postylla domowa*, Królewiec, 1556 (Zakład Narodowy im. Ossolińskich, Wrocław, shelf mark XVI.F.4177) 231
11.3	A page from the first edition of Jakub Wujek's 'bigger postil' or *Postylla katoliczna większa*, Krakow, 1573 (Zakład Narodowy im. Ossolińskich, Wrocław, XVI.F.4120). The printer used a woodblock originally designed for a prayer book. 232
11.4	A woodcut by Jost Amman from the second edition of Jakub Wujek's 'bigger postil' or *Postylla katoliczna większa*, Krakow, 1584 (Zakład Narodowy im. Ossolińskich, shelf mark XVI.F.4156) 234
11.5a–b	Pages from the Calvinist postil by Mikołaj Rej printed in Krakow in 1571 (*left*) and Jakub Wujek's counter-reformational *Postylla katoliczna mniejsza* or the 'smaller postil' printed in the same city but by a different printer in 1590 (*right*) (Biblioteka Jagiellońska, Krakow, Cim.F.8295 and Muzeum Narodowe, Krakow, VIII–XVI.93) 235
11.6a–b	The first edition of *Postylla katoliczna mniejsza* or the 'smaller postil' by Jakub Wujek, in quarto (Zakład Narodowy im. Ossolińskich, Wrocław, XVI.Qu.1735) 236
11.7	Piotr Skarga, *Kazania na niedziele i święta*, Krakow 1595 (Zakład Narodowy im. Ossolińskich, Wrocław, XVI.F.4286) 238
11.8a–b	Title pages of *Kazania dwojakie* by Franciszek Rychłowski published in Krakow in 1672. The title page dated in 1695 is pasted over the original title (Biblioteka Jagiellońska, Krakow, Aug. 6112 and Cam.E.xv.6) 240
12.1	Partial reproduction of the act signed before notary Mariano Zapparrata of Palermo on 12 October 1628, concerning a contract between Francesco Ciotti and Leonardo Paulini for sale and bartering of books in Naples and elsewhere in Italy. Biblioteca Municipale, Treviso, ms. 1492, s. 2 255
12.2	Naples, 1628. Account of travelling costs. Biblioteca Municipale, Treviso, ms. 1492, s. 7 256

FIGURES AND TABLES   XIII

12.3   Naples, 1628: "Book bartering with Pietro Paulo Gallo"—"Books received in exchange". Biblioteca Municipale, Treviso, ms. 1492, s. 8   258

12.4   Naples, 1628: Value measurement for book bartering by printed sheets. A sample entry. Biblioteca Municipale, Treviso, ms. 1492, s. 8   259

12.5   Rome, 1628: Final account of the bookselling trip to central Italy, including various expenses and money sent to Ciotti in Palermo; profit of book sales in Naples and Rome; unsold books. Biblioteca Municipale, Treviso, ms. 1492, s. 15   259

13.1   Herman Moll's *The Shires of Fife and Kinros* (1732). Reproduced by permission of the National Library of Scotland   268

13.2   Newspaper advertisement for sale of goods of bankrupt bookseller. *The Scotsman*, 8 January 1825   274

14.1   False by association. Wittenberg split over two lines. Bayerische Staatsbibliothek, Munich (BSB), 4 Hom. 1158. USTC 610282   279

14.2   False by association. Wittenberg on its own line. BSB, 4 Hom. 1185. USTC 610357   281

14.3   False by implication. A false Wittenberg imprint from Strasbourg with a truthful colophon. BSB, Hom. 2098 z. USTC 647263   282

14.4   False by implication. A false Wittenberg imprint from Haguenau with a truthful colophon. BSB, H.ref. 92. USTC 624444   283

14.5   Simple counterfeit. A counterfeit from Basel (left) compared to the Wittenberg original. BSB, Res/4 Polem. 1885#Beibd.1 and Res/4 Th.u. 103,V,8. USTC 703267 and 703265   284

14.6   Simple counterfeit. A false Wittenberg imprint from Augsburg. BSB, 4 Exeg. 484. USTC 633613   285

14.7   Simple counterfeit. A false Wittenberg imprint from Augsburg. BSB, 4 Polem. 1871. USTC 627551   287

14.8   Advanced counterfeit. A counterfeit from Augsburg (left) next to the Wittenberg original. BSB, Res/4 Th.u. 103,XIV,10 and Universitäts- und Landesbibliothek Sachsen-Anhalt, urn:nbn:de:gbv:3:1-108767. USTC 700033 and 700034   288

14.9   Advanced counterfeit. A false imprint and copied border from Nuremberg (left) next to the original border from Wittenberg. BSB, Res/4 Th.u. 103,XXVI,23 a and Res/4 Th.u. 104,VII,37. USTC 700131 and 655628   290

14.10   A Wittenberg border featuring the Luther rose. BSB, 4 Polem. 1893#Beibd.1. USTC 626862   291

14.11   Copied borders by Ulhart in Augsburg. BSB, Res/4 Th.u. 103,I,1 and 4 Asc. 605. USTC 706627 and 609762   292

14.12   A border by Gutknecht in Nuremberg featuring the Luther rose. BSB, Res/4 Th.u. 103,XXXII,17. USTC 656115   293

14.13	The geographic distribution of Wittenberg counterfeits	294
15.1	Michiel van Hamont's bookshop by literary category	311
15.2	Michiel van Hamont's bookshop by language	311
15.3	Prohibited books in Hamont's bookshop by literary category	318
15.4	Prohibited books in Hamont's bookshop by language	319
17.1	Georg Willer's *Catalogus librorum musicalium variorum authorum* (Augsburg: David Franck, 1622), title page (a) and first page (b). Bayerische Staatsbibliothek, Res/4 Cat. 45 (12) [urn:nbn:de:bvb:12-bsb10888116-9]	356
17.2	Portrait of Georg Willer the Elder (ca. 1515–ca. 1594), ca. 1591. Staats- und Stadtbibliothek Augsburg, Graphiksammlung 19/629	360
17.3a–3b	Comparison of the music section of Willer's spring 1621 fair catalogue and the 1622 music stock catalogue. Figure 17.3a (top): Spring 1621 book fair catalogue, Bayerische Staatsbibliothek, Res/4 Cat. 45 (10) [urn:nbn:de:bvb:12-bsb10888114-8]. Figure 17.3b (bottom): Entries 30 to 32 of the 1622 music stock catalogue, Bayerische Staatsbibliothek, Res/4 Cat. 45 (12) [urn:nbn:de:bvb:12-bsb10888116-9]	365
17.4	*Ein newe Rähterschafft* (Augsburg: Daniel Manasser, [1621]), 350 × 242 mm. Herzog August Bibliothek Wolfenbüttel, IE 187	368
19.1	Newspapers published in Germany, 1609–1650	401
19.2a–b	Longevity and disruption in the newspaper business, 1630–1639	407
19.3	The output of Germany's most prolific print centres, 1600–1650	412
19.4	The publishing program of Thomas von Wiering	417
20.1	Advertisers in Amsterdam newspapers, 1636–1645. Each circle represents a city or town. The number in the circle represents the number of advertising booksellers and publishers from that location. The map is an extract of Johannes Janssonius, *Belgii Foederati Nova Descriptio* (Amsterdam: Johannes Janssonius, 1658). Wikimedia Commons	436
23.1	*The Revd. T.F. Dibdin*, engraved by James Thomson after Thomas Phillips, from Dibdin's *Continental tour*, 2nd ed. 1829, privately owned	491
23.2	*The Bibliographical Decameron*, vol. III, p. 123	502
23.3	*Bibliomania*, 1811. Privately owned	504
23.4	*Dr Syntax at an auction*, by Thomas Rowlandson. Privately owned	507
23.5	*The Gateway to St Andrews*, from Dibdin's *Northern Tour*. Privately owned	514
24.1	Halle's first surviving letter to the GW, 27 September 1924. Staatsbibliothek zu Berlin—Preußischer Kulturbesitz, GW archive	527
24.2	Letter from Halle to the GW announcing an unrecorded *Articella* edition, 14 November 1927. Staatsbibliothek zu Berlin—Preußischer Kulturbesitz, GW archive	530

FIGURES AND TABLES   XV

24.3   Broadsheet *Titel des türkischen Kaisers*, imprint: [München: Johann
       Schobser, c. 1500]; whereabouts of unique copy unknown.
       Staatsbibliothek zu Berlin—Preußischer Kulturbesitz, GW archive   533
24.4   *Ars moriendi* [German]. [Strasbourg: Johann Mentelin, not after 1468],
       fol. 1a; whereabouts of unique copy unknown. Staatsbibliothek zu
       Berlin—Preußischer Kulturbesitz, GW archive   535

Tables

9.1   Movable goods   195
11.1 Polish vernacular postils published in the years 1556–1700   225
15.1 Brussels bookshops inspected by the Council of Troubles, 1569   308
16.1 Structure of Pasini's bookshop inventory   333
19.1 Newly established newspapers, 1610–1660   408
19.2 Table of regional book and newspaper production, 1609–1650   414
20.1 Amsterdam Newspapers, 1639   427
20.2 1639 Book Advertisement Genres   430
20.3 Advertising booksellers in Amsterdam newspapers, 1636–1645   435
20.4 The Dutch book trade in relation to Amsterdam newspaper advertisements,
      1636–1645   437
20.5 The number of advertising booksellers and publishers in the newspapers of Jan
      van Hilten and Broer Jansz, 1636–1645   439
20.6 Booksellers and publishers advertising in Amsterdam newspapers,
      1636–1645   442

Notes on Contributors

Renaud Adam

is Marie Skłodowska-Curie Research Fellow (2017–) at LE STUDIUM, Loire Valley Institute of Advanced Studies (Orléans), in residence at the 'Centre d'études supérieures de la Renaissance' in Tours, and Lecturer at the University of Liège, where he teaches History of the Book in the Renaissance (2012–). Previously, he was a postdoctoral researcher with the Fund for Scientific Research (FNRS) in Belgium (2014–2017). From 2002–2013, he worked at the Rare Book Department of the Royal Library of Belgium in Brussels and in the University Library Moretus Plantin in Namur (2014). He has published books and papers dedicated to the history of the book in the Southern Low Countries from the fifteenth through seventeenth centuries, and to the history of libraries and uses of the book since the late Middle Ages to the mid-nineteenth century.

Daniel Bellingradt

is a historian of early modern Europe. He earned his PhD in 2010 at the Free University of Berlin, Germany. In 2014 he became professor of Book Studies at the University of Erlangen-Nuremberg. Bellingradt is the author of *Flugpublizistik und Öffentlichkeit um 1700. Dynamiken, Akteure und Strukturen im urbanen Raum des Alten Reiches* (Stuttgart 2011), co-editor of the journal *Jahrbuch für Kommunikationsgeschichte*, and has published several articles on aspects of media and communication history, and book history. In 2017, he co-edited the volume *Books in Motion in Early Modern Europe. Beyond Production, Circulation and Consumption* (with Jeroen Salman and Paul Nelles), and co-authored *Magical Manuscripts in Early Modern Europe. The Clandestine Trade in Illegal Book Collections* (with Bernd-Christian Otto). He is currently completing a monograph on the paper trade in early modern Amsterdam. In 2018, Daniel Bellingradt was awarded the "Maria-Weber-Grant" (Hans Böckler Foundation) for outstanding postdoctoral scholars.

Lorenz Boeninger

is an independent scholar based in Florence. He has edited two volumes of the critical edition of Lorenzo de' Medici's *Lettere* (Florence, 2010 and 2011) and, more recently, that of the *Ricordanze* of the humanist scribe Lorenzo di Francesco Guidetti (Rome, 2014). For Brill he has published the monograph *Die deutsche Einwanderung in Florenz im Spätmittelalter* (2006). In 2014, together with Paolo Procaccioli, he organized a congress on the printing of Cristoforo Landino's "Comento" to Dante's Divine Comedy (1481); the proceedings have now been published. He is currently working on a biography of the Florentine printer Niccolò di Lorenzo della Magna.

Marius Buning
received his PhD in History and Civilization from the European University Institute (2013) with a dissertation on the making of a patent system in the early Dutch Republic. Marius has held fellowships at Harvard University, the Netherlands Institute for Advanced Study, and the Max Planck Institute for the History of Science. He is currently a DRS Fellow at the Dahlem Humanities Center of the Free University of Berlin. His research interests focus on the origins of intellectual property; the relationship between science and technology; how experiment bears upon theory; and the part played by the early modern state in defining these respective fields.

Lucas Burkart
has been Professor of Medieval and Renaissance History at the University of Basel since 2012. His research interests encompass social, cultural and economic history, the history of visual and material culture, and the history of historiography. His latest publications include 'Aus dem Rahmen. Jacob Burckhardt als Bildregisseur', recently published in *Zeitschrift für Ideengeschichte* (2018) and the two co-edited volumes *Sites of Mediation. Connected Histories of Places, Processes, and Objects in Europe and Beyond, 1450–1650* (2016) and *Mythen, Körper, Bilder: Ernst Kantorowicz zwischen Historismus, Emigration und Erneuerung der Geisteswissenschaften* (2015). He has published widely on various themes of medieval and Renaissance history and culture, including medieval treasuries and treasure hoarding, the politics of imagery and the culture of science in Baroque Rome. Currently, he is overseeing the completion of the critical edition of the works by Jacob Burckhardt.

Domenico Ciccarello
is a librarian at the University of Palermo, Italy. He graduated in Librarianship at the University of Rome "La Sapienza" in 2001, and was awarded an MPhil in Studies on Early Printed Books in 2004. He has participated in academic research projects on sixteenth-century booklists of Italian monastic libraries, and on the mobility of Italian publishers, printers, and booksellers between the fifteenth and seventeenth centuries. His PhD (Siena) consisted of a bibliography of seventeenth-century editions printed in Sicily. He has conducted post-doctoral research on printing and the book trade in Sicily in the seventeenth century. He has been an invited speaker to Library and Information Studies (LIS) conferences in Italy and abroad, and has published several essays

and articles in the field. He participates in the editorial teams of LIS journals in Italy. He has recently become a member of the Italian Society for Bibliography and Librarianship.

Jamie Cumby
is an Associate Editor on Preserving the World's Rarest Books. She has been affiliated with the USTC project since beginning her PhD in 2014. Her doctoral thesis focused on the development of the *Compagnie des libraires* in Lyon before the Wars of Religion, and explored practices of incorporation and risk avoidance in early modern publishing. She first came to St Andrews for an MLitt in Book History, after receiving her BA from Wellesley College with honours in philosophy. She is also St Andrews' contributor to the Material Evidence in Incunabula database.

Jeremiah Dittmar
is Assistant Professor of Economics at the London School of Economics. He received a PhD in Economics from UC Berkeley (2009). His research exploits historical data to document the institutional and technological roots of economic growth.

Vivienne Dunstan
is an independent historian, specialising in Scottish social, cultural, urban and reading history, primarily in the seventeenth, eighteenth and nineteenth centuries. She holds an honorary research fellowship in History at the University of Dundee and has published articles in various academic journals. Her PhD researched reading habits in Scotland circa 1750–1820, using evidence for reading from contemporary accounts, library borrowings and records of book ownership.

Falk Eisermann
has been head of the Gesamtkatalog der Wiegendrucke (Union Catalogue of Incunabula) at the Berlin State Library since 2007. After receiving his PhD in Medieval German Literature at Göttingen University (1995), he held postdoctoral positions at the Universities of Münster (Germany) and Groningen (The Netherlands), where he worked on a three-volume catalogue of fifteenth-century broadsides (published in 2004). From 2002 to 2007, he catalogued German Mediaeval manuscripts at Leipzig University Library. He has published on the transmission of vernacular texts in the later Middle Ages, on manuscripts, incunabula and early printing, and on medieval and early modern epigraphy.

NOTES ON CONTRIBUTORS

Martine Furno
has been Professor of Latin Languages and Literature at Stendhal University in Valence (Drôme) since 2002. Her *habilitation* thesis studied the mental representation of Antiquity in the Renaissance, and her currents (and old) interests focus on the history of the book, especially on erudite and scholastics printers during the sixteenth century, on lexicography and history of Latin language teaching. She is a regular collaborator of the Gabriel Naudé Centre and the ENSSIB in Lyon.

Idalia Garcia
is a researcher at the Library Science and Information Research Institute, National Autonomous University of Mexico (UNAM). She is currently pursuing a doctoral degree in History at the Universidad Nacional de Educación a Distancia. She is the author of various monographs, including *Miradas aisladas, visiones conjuntas: defensa del patrimonio documental mexicano* (2001), *Legislación sobre bienes culturales muebles: protección del libro antiguo* (2002), and *Secretos del Estante* (CUIB, 2011). She also edited a number of volumes, including *Complejidad y materialidad: reflexiones del Seminario del Libro Antiguo* (2009), *El Patrimonio documental en México* (2009, with Bolfy Cotton), *Leer en tiempos de la Colonia* (2010), *El libro en circulación en la América colonial. Producción, circuitos de distribución y conformación de bibliotecas en los siglos XVI al XVIII* (the last two with Pedro Rueda). She is currently researching a project on 'Permanence and transference of Books in New Spain: Second Hand Book Trade in the 17th and 18th century' (2014–2019).

Shanti Graheli
is Lord Kelvin Adam Smith Fellow in Comparative Literature and Translation at the University of Glasgow, where she is pursuing a project entitled 'A European Bestseller: The *Orlando furioso* and Its Readers'. She is a long-term collaborator to the Universal Short Title Catalogue project at St Andrews. Her PhD thesis (St Andrews, 2015) explored the circulation and collection of Italian printed books in France in the sixteenth century; it under contract with Brill, as a monograph entitled *Italian Books and the French Renaissance* (2019). She is the author of various published studies of Italian and French Renaissance print culture.

Jan Hillgärtner
is a lecturer in German at Leiden University. His work focusses on the spread of the newspaper in seventeenth-century Germany and modes of reporting in the periodical press. Before obtaining a PhD in modern History from the University of St Andrews, he graduated from the University of Marburg with a BA in

Germanic Studies and has an MA from the University of Erlangen Nuremberg in Book Studies. He is currently working on a bibliography of German newspapers printed between 1605 and 1650.

Justyna Kiliańczyk-Zieba
is assistant professor at the Jagiellonian University in Krakow, Poland. Her recent published work includes a monograph on printers' devices in early modern Poland-Lithuania (*Sygnety drukarskie w Rzeczypospolitej XVI wieku. Źródła ikonograficzne i treści ideowe*, Krakow 2015) and an edition of a sixteenth-century book on fortune-telling (Stanisław z Bochnie Kleryka, *Fortuna abo Szczęście*, Krakow 2015).

Magdalena Komorowska
is an adjunct at the Faculty of Polish Studies, Jagiellonian University. She is interested in the book culture of early modern Krakow and her current research focuses on print house of the Piotrkowczyk family, active in the years 1574–1674. She also has experience in scholarly editing of sixteenth- and seventeenth-century Polish literature. In 2012, she published a book discussing editorial problems in the writings of a renowned Polish Jesuit preacher Piotr Skarga; she also took part in the preparation of a critical edition of his works.

Dr Jason McElligott
Jason McElligott is the Director of Marsh's Library, Dublin. He is currently working on a history of book-theft in the eighteenth century, a study of Bram Stoker's interest in early modern history, and the 1820 plot to assassinate the British cabinet known as the Cato Street Conspiracy.

Andrew Pettegree
is Professor of Modern History at the University of St Andrews and Director of the Universal Short Title Catalogue. He is the author of over a dozen books in the fields of Reformation history and the history of communication including *Reformation and the Culture of Persuasion* (Cambridge University Press, 2005), *The Book in the Renaissance* (Yale University Press, 2010) and *The Invention of News* (Yale University Press, 2014). His most recent book, *Brand Luther: 1517, Print and the Making of the Reformation* (Penguin USA) was published in October 2015. His new projects include a study of Newspaper Advertising in the Low Countries and 'Preserving the World's Rarest Books', a collaborative project with libraries funded by the Andrew W. Mellon Foundation.

NOTES ON CONTRIBUTORS   XXI

Jean-Paul Pittion
studied at the École Normale Supérieure, Paris and at Trinity College, Dublin. He is Fellow emeritus from Trinity College, Dublin and was Professor at the Centre d'Études Supérieures de la Renaissance, Tours. His main interests are in the intellectual and cultural history of French Protestantism during the early modern period. Recent publications include a history of the French reformed Académie of Saumur (on line) and a book on 'Le livre à la Renaissance'. He is currently working on a monograph on the Saumur Protestant book trade.

Amelie Roper
is Research Development Manager at the British Library. She recently completed a PhD at the University of St Andrews on the culture of music printing in sixteenth-century Augsburg. She has published on the music output of Nuremberg printer Johannes Petreius and the production of song pamphlets and broadsheets in early modern Germany. She is more broadly interested in the material culture of the book, and, in her previous role as College Librarian at Christ's College Cambridge, regularly oversaw exhibitions in the Old Library. Her current research focuses on digital sheet music publishing and the application of digital humanities techniques to the study of sixteenth-century pamphlets.

John Sibbald
is a long-term associate of the St Andrews University Universal Short Title Catalogue project and has given papers at two of its annual conferences. His paper on the *Heinsiana* was published in M. Walsby and N. Constantinidou (eds.), *Documenting the Early Modern Book World: Inventories and Catalogues in Manuscript and Print* (2013). He acquired his first work on The Revd Dr Thomas Frognall Dibdin, *An introduction to the Greek and Latin classics*, at the thoroughly unhealthy age of thirteen. He is a former Librarian of the Advocates Library in Edinburgh and has been involved with the rare book business off and on for over forty years. He is currently editing the medical section of the *Heinsiana*.

Drew Thomas
is a Postdoctoral Research Assistant for the Universal Title Catalogue at the University of St Andrews. He received a BA in theology and philosophy from Saint Louis University, his Master of Theological Studies from Harvard University, and his PhD in history from the University of St Andrews. His doctoral research focused on the rise of the Wittenberg printing industry during Martin Luther's Protestant Reformation. He is the Project Manager of the Caroline Minuscule

Mapping Project hosted by the University of Pennsylvania's Schoenberg Institute for Manuscript Studies.

Philip Tromans
is a Research Fellow at De Montfort University, where he completed his thesis, 'Advertising America: The Printing, Publication, and Promotion of English New World Books, 1553–1600', and won the university thesis prize for 2016. A revised version of part of one of the thesis's chapters appeared in *The Papers of the Bibliographical Society of America* as 'Thomas Hacket's Publication of Books about America in the 1560s' in 2015, and he is currently preparing a contribution to Stanford University Press's forthcoming *The Book Index* (expected 2018) on how Richard Hakluyt indexed his pro-colonial publications of the 1580s. The contribution to this volume reflects his wider interests in the production and retailing of early modern English books, as does his 'The Collation of John Hawkins's *Troublesome Voyage* (1569), and its Wraparound Blank', published by *The Library* in 2017.

Natale Vacalebre
received his PhD in Bibliography and Book History from the University of Udine in 2015. A former Research Fellow of the Bibliographical Society of America, Vacalebre is currently a Benjamin Franklin Fellow in Italian Studies at the University of Pennsylvania in Philadelphia, where he is pursuing a project entitled: '"The Book and He Who Wrote It". Reading Practices and Material Reception of Dante's Commedia in Renaissance Europe'. He has studied the history of books and libraries for many years, with a special interest in ancient collections of religious orders, and the production and commerce of Italian books in the Early Modern age. His latest book, *Come le armadure e l'armi* (2016), is the first detailed account of the history of Early Modern Jesuit libraries. He is the editor of the Open Access journal *Bibliotheca Dantesca*, as well as a member of the editorial board of *L'Almanacco bibliografico* and an active correspondent of the Boston College Jesuit Bibliography. He is also the editor of the book *Five Centuries Later. Aldus Manutius: Culture, Typography and Philology* (2018).

Arthur der Weduwen
is a researcher at the University of St Andrews and the author of *Dutch and Flemish Newspapers of the Seventeenth Century* (2 vols., Brill, 2017). An earlier version of this work won the St Andrews University's Gray prize, and the Elzevier–De Witt prize in the Netherlands. His PhD (2018) is a study of government attempts to shape public opinion in the seventeenth-century Dutch Republic. He is a long-term associate of the Universal Short Title Catalogue

project. His most recent book, *The Bookshop of the World. Making and Trading Books in the Dutch Golden Age* (co-authored with Andrew Pettegree), will appear in 2019 with Yale University Press (in English) and Atlas Contact (in Dutch).

CHAPTER 1

How to Lose Money in the Business of Books: Commercial Strategies in the First Age of Print

Andrew Pettegree and Shanti Graheli

In 1524, the Leipzig town council appealed to George, Duke of Saxony on behalf of their local printers. They were, they said, facing destitution: the publishers of a city that had until recently been the foremost printing city of Germany, were now in danger of losing 'house, home and all their livelihoods'. They asked, in desperation, to be allowed

> to print or sell anything new that is made in Wittenberg or elsewhere. For that which one would gladly sell and for which there is demand they are not allowed to have or sell. But what they have in over-abundance [Catholic treatises] are desired by no-one and cannot even be given away.[1]

We do not always need to take too seriously appeals made on behalf of an economic interest group in early modern Europe, but in this case what they said was quite literally true: the Leipzig printing industry was in total collapse, as we can now confirm by statistics of production.

In 1519 and 1520, the Leipzig presses had turned out respectively 190 and 188 editions, a higher level of production than they would reach at any subsequent time in the sixteenth century. Production halved in 1521 and 1522, and in 1523 and 1524 collapsed altogether. In 1524, Leipzig's once mighty printing houses turned out only 25 editions between them.[2] The publishers were really facing a desperate situation. Some were forced to sell the gracious homes they had bought in happier times; others closed shop altogether. More than one left Leipzig; another, enterprising or daring, even set up a branch office in tiny villages some way out of town to print the sought-after evangelical texts.[3] But

---

1 Felicien Gess (ed.), *Akten und Briefe zur Kirchenpolitik Herzog Georgs von Sachsen. I: 1517–1524* (Leipzig: Teubner, 1905), p. 641. Quoted Edwards, *Printing, Propaganda, and Martin Luther* (Berkeley-Los Angeles-Oxford: University of California Press, 2004), p. 14.
2 Figures from the USTC.
3 In Grimma, and then in Eilenburg. Christoph Reske, *Die Buchdrucker des 16. und 17. Jahrhunderts im Deutschen Sprachgebiet* (Wiesbaden: Harrassowitz, 2007), pp. 314, 516–517 and USTC.

these responses, however enterprising, could not change the hard unyielding fact, that Leipzig had been cut out of the most lucrative market available at the time, Reformation *Flugschriften*. Leipzig printing would not truly recover until the death of Duke George in 1539 and the conversion of Ducal Saxony to Lutheranism.

There are several things that are interesting about this petition to, as it turned out, an unyielding Duke George. First, incunabulists will catch an unmistakable echo of the famous incident when the two Rome printers Sweynheym and Pannartz petitioned the Pope in 1472. They claimed they had thus far manufactured over 10,000 copies, but could not sell them. Their workshop, they said, was 'full of printed sheets, empty of necessities'.[4] Rome in 1472, Leipzig in 1524. We are reminded that the crisis of print was not a specific historical problem, that could be solved, but a recurrent experience that returned each time print entered a new phase or evolved a new market. We see the same experience repeated with the introduction of the newspapers in the seventeenth century: as Jan Hillgärtner recalls in his essay a large proportion of the newspapers started in Germany in the 1630s lasted less than a year; the same was true of serials that emerged from the great upsurge of print in England in the 1640s.[5]

In consequence the airwaves would be filled over the first two centuries of print by lamenting printers, disgruntled publishers and whining authors. And the evidence of business failures can be seen not just in this sort of correspondence, but in inventories of printing stock, the statistics of production, and the mounting number of court cases as desperate disappointed partners tried to recover their money from former friends and business associates on the verge of bankruptcy. Each of these newly discovered pieces of evidence is one more blow to the bright-eyed optimism of the Elizabeth Eisenstein school, with her *Printing Revolution*. In this milestone book Elizabeth Eisenstein charted the triumph of print in much the same terms as its fifteenth-century boosters. This was *The Printing Press as an Agent of Change*, an instrument of enlightenment and empowerment.[6] In view of what we now know

---

4 Victor Scholderer, 'The petition of Sweynheym and Pannartz to Sixtus IV', *The Library*, 3rd s., 6 (1915), pp. 186–190; Eric M. White, 'A census of print runs for fifteenth-century books' (2012–2013), published online on https://www.cerl.org/ (last accessed: 14 May 2018), pp. 3–4.
5 See the article by Jan Hillgärtner in this volume.
6 Elizabeth Eisenstein, *The Printing Press as an Agent of Change: Communications and Cultural Transformations in Early Modern Europe* (Cambridge: Cambridge University Press, 1979); Eisenstein, *The Printing Revolution in Early Modern Europe* (Cambridge: Cambridge University Press, 1983).

about the actual early history of the press, a story of repeated failure and re-invention, this interpretation of print history now begins to look decidedly flawed.

The examples to which we have alluded—pamphlets and newspapers—complicate the picture considerably. These, after all, are normally seen as the salvation of the industry, not the location of further risk. But there is little doubt that the greatest peril lay in books that demanded the greatest investment. Here—in the inventories conducted after a publisher's death, or, not infrequently, bankruptcy—one sees the repeated evidence of business failure in the millions of sheets piling up uselessly in warehouses, some of stock fifty or more years old: useful only for waste paper.[7] The systematic re-issuing of old printed sheets under the cover of a new title page, a staple of many shrewd businessmen and women, is symptomatic of this widespread situation. In the second half of the eighteenth century the ingenious Dutch came up with a new way to clear some space in the over-flowing warehouses: lotteries where the prizes would be hundreds of books. Just who might be drawn to purchase of a ticket by the prospect of 100 books in an unknown selection is hard to say—but it does demonstrate that even in this most commercial of societies, widely seen as the centre of the European book trade in this era, the business of buying and selling books still generated many casualties.[8]

The Problem of Sales

How could one succeed in the business of books? We propose to address this problem in two stages. Firstly, we will address the issue of why selling the new printed books proved to be so problematic. For this was not a difficulty that was anticipated by those who greeted the new art of print with such rapture. Nor was it apparent as print spread with such speed to almost every corner of the continent. At some point in the fifteenth century printing was established in over two hundred places in different parts of Europe. So powerful was this motive force, and this expanding geography, that it has indeed been argued that familiarity with print played a critical role in constructing the very notion of what it meant to be European, or a part of Christendom.[9]

---

7 Ian Maclean, 'Murder, debt and retribution in the Italico-Franco-Spanish book trade: the Beraud-Michel-Ruiz affair, 1586–1591', in his *Learning and the Market Place* (Leiden: Brill, 2009), pp. 227–272.
8 See the article by Daniel Bellingradt in this volume.
9 José María Pérez Fernández, 'Andrés Laguna: translation and the early modern idea of Europe', *Translation and Literature*, 21 (2012), pp. 299–318.

We now know that this expansion was driven essentially by technological fascination, and a desire not to be left behind in the rush to have this new accoutrement of civilization. It was this sentiment that drew in investment capital in quantities that could hardly be justified by the likelihood of commercial return. By the time it was recognised that printed books were a harder sell than anyone had really imagined, the fascination with the new was beginning to wear off. One key group of investors, Europe's rulers and bishops, found new ways of demonstrating their taste for the better things in life: libraries were no longer the display of opulence that they were when manuscript books were both expensive and hard to come by.[10] The result of this confluence of unexpected problems was a drastic retrenchment of the industry.

This first crisis of print bears distinct similarities with the dot.com boom and bust of the 1990s.[11] Here again massive investment was driven by the sense that this was the future: start-ups grew to an absurd multiple of their real stock value. It was only when people realised that insufficient thought had been given to how this could be made to pay—how digital content could be monetised—that the bottom dropped out of the cybermarket and fortunes were lost.

It bears emphasis that the problems of print were not essentially technological. To a quite remarkable degree, the basic technical problems of mechanical production of books had been solved by Gutenberg: the casting of type; the design of the press; the provision of suitable paper and ink, these had all been accomplished, soon followed by the all-important printing by formes. The only really substantial innovation over the next forty years were the two-pull press and the title-page. To this can be added solving the specific problems of specialised type in niche markets like music publishing.

The major problems all occurred in the area of sales: how to tell customers what was now available; how to get the books to them; how to judge the size of the market; how to arrange payment; which other artisan tradesmen needed to be involved to this process. This was one area in the business of books where the manuscript trade offered no useful guidance to the purveyors of the new printed books. The manuscript trade was personal, intimate and by and large retail. The whole process—the provision of texts, a process

---

10   Andrew Pettegree, 'The Renaissance library and the challenge of print', in Alice Crawford (ed.), *The Meaning of the Library* (Princeton: Princeton University Press, 2015), pp. 72–90.
11   John Cassidy, *dot.con* (London: Allen Lane, 2002).

in which the intending purchaser was likely to be personally involved, working with a single text and a single scribe—this was totally different from the developing purchase model of printed books: destined for distant customers who might not even know that they desired the text on offer until they saw it on a bookstall. But it went deeper than that. The idea that printed books were an improvement on the manuscript book market was hard-wired into the rhetoric of fifteenth-century boosters of print, and has been taken as a given pretty much ever since. But it was by no means as obvious to owners of the existing manuscripts.

The new printed books were almost universally admired, but not instinctively loved. Because there were several features of the familiar hand-written books that the new technology found it extremely difficult to replicate. The manuscript book was often full of colour. Print is essentially monochrome. To customers this was difficult to sell as a great step forward. Members of that generation that knew black and white television can often still remember as one of the most vivid moments of childhood coming home to find a colour TV installed. It would today be unthinkable to imagine inviting clients of modern media to accept a step in the opposite direction, of moving from colour to black and white. Yet that is what was involved in the business of books.

Producers recognised this as a problem, and they attempted solutions. One was double or triple impression printing.[12] But this is extremely difficult to carry off successfully. A tiny error of placement can wreck the whole effect. Two or three colour printing added hugely to the time in the print shop and led to far greater wastage from spoiled sheets. Except for title-pages, single-sheet calendars and liturgical books it was soon largely abandoned. The other solution was hand-illumination: the pages of printed text would be handed over to an illuminator for decoration, either by the customer or before sale. Printer-publishers like Antoine Vérard in Paris attempted to tailor their business towards a printed book that would serve as a surrogate for manuscripts. The result of these ventures were copies printed on vellum and illuminated: beautiful volumes, produced for important patrons.[13] These and similar practices rather undercut the whole point of economy of scale and again, greatly increasing the cost. They are largely a feature of a transitional age when printed books were seen as pseudo-manuscripts rather than as a fully independent form.[14]

---

12   Ad Stijnman and Elizabeth Savage, *Printing Colour, 1400–1700* (Leiden: Brill, 2015).
13   Mary Beth Winn, *Anthoine Vérard: Parisian Publisher 1485–1512: Prologues, Poems, and Presentations* (Geneva: Droz, 1997).
14   David McKitterick, *Print, Manuscript and the Search for Order, 1450–1830* (Cambridge: Cambridge University Press, 2003).

The second reason for customer reticence is more subtle, but nevertheless profound. A manuscript books was often a very personal possession: not one single text, but a collection of texts. The owners would have control not only of which texts they wished to gather together but also which portions of texts they wished to include. Miscellany, in other words, was the natural state of the book. Print threatened to eliminate much of this choice. Texts would take on a settled form, indeed the search for a true text was one of the major ideological drivers of the humanist engagement with the classics. It has always been taken as a given that this fixity, claimed as a major aspect of the *Printing Revolution* by Eisenstein, though contested by Adrian Johns, was a huge step forward.[15] For contemporary purchasers we have to understand that it was often quite the opposite. They were used to customising their texts. The reluctance to give up this established aspect of book collecting can be seen in the enduring habit of binding texts together in one book, either multiple printed works or a promiscuous mixture of print and manuscript; though this latter phenomenon has been largely obscured by the well-meaning vandalism of nineteenth-century libraries in dis-binding these miscellanies.

This reflection on the unwelcome fixity of printed texts cuts against the widely assumed advantage of the transition from manuscript to print—that print offered customers a vastly increased choice. This is seen as one of the great glories of print, a vision encapsulated by the mythical scene with two humanist friends wandering down the Merceria in Venice, one lost for hours among the profusion of books available.[16] This was how it was meant to be, and this is the humanist agenda to which printers responded. But the result was that printers reached for the same limited range of texts when choosing what to print: by and large the same books that had been popular in the manuscript era. The result was that the market was soon flooded with multiple editions of the same books. This was to some extent manageable when the books were short—dealing with multiple copies of texts that were used in school, for instance. The more expensive the book, the more delicate the market.

This was an area of the market where a single overbold decision could prove catastrophic. Perhaps this is what lay behind the catastrophic failure of the Basel printer Michel Wenssler.[17] For two decades between 1472 and 1492 Wenssler was a commanding presence in the Basel book world. He turned out over 150 books, including many works of great magnificence. His clientele was

---

15   Adrian Johns, *The Nature of the Book. Print and Knowledge in the Making* (Chicago: University of Chicago Press, 1998).
16   Andrew Pettegree, *The Book in the Renaissance* (London: Yale University Press, 2010), p. xii.
17   See the article by Lucas Burkart in this volume.

mostly scholarly and professional: some 85% of his books were works of religious instruction or jurisprudence, and 65% in the large folio format. But sometime in 1492 his business suffered catastrophic failure. Whether as a result of unwise investment or other cause, Wenssler's indebtedness rose exponentially. When it became clear that his creditors could not be held at bay, Wenssler felt he had no choice but to flee the city, rather ingloriously leaving his wife and children behind him.

Wenssler now joined the ranks of itinerant printers, working first in Cluny, then at Mâcon and finally moving to Lyon. He printed only a handful of further books, and never recovered his former eminence. This experience of recurrent disappointment in a peripatetic career was also far from uncommon.[18] Indeed such cases are so integral to early modern print culture that a recent encyclopaedic project was created to list all itinerant printers, publishers and booksellers in Renaissance Italy.[19] In Wenssler's case it is by no means certain what had occurred: it would be nice to be able to identify the project or projects that brought his business to its knees, but the sources do not help us. But that such a catastrophe was an ever-present danger is evident in the efforts that even Europe's most substantial publishers applied to avoid a rival spoiling their market. In 1485 Johann Amerbach of Basel was contemplating an edition of the so-called *Glossa ordinaria*. This was a massive book of around 1,200 leaves, and Amerbach knew it well since he had supplied the type of an earlier edition, published as a collaboration with the Strasbourg printer Adolf Rusch, and the Nuremberg entrepreneur Anton Koberger.[20] He was stopped in his tracks by an urgent letter from Rusch, warning him that Rusch still had stock in hand from this 1480 edition. In fact, Rusch rather brazenly confessed that he had published 100 copies on his own account over and above his obligation to Koberger.[21] Rather than engage in potentially ruinous competition with this remaining stock, Amerbach drew back. Perhaps he had no wish to cross a valued business associate, or perhaps he was simply not sure of his market. Either way, he turned to other projects. At this point all three of those involved in this project, Amerbach, Rusch and Koberger, were wealthy men. They functioned at

---

18   Pettegree, *The Book in the Renaissance*; Philippe Nieto, 'Géographie des impressions européennes du xve siècle', *Revue française d'histoire du livre*, 118–121 (2004), pp. 125–173.
19   Rosa Marisa Borraccini, Giuseppe Lipari, Carmela Reale, Marco Santoro and Giancarlo Volpato (eds.), *Dizionario degli editori, tipografi, librai itineranti in Italia tra Quattrocento e Seicento* (3 vols., Pisa: Fabrizio Serra, 2014).
20   USTC 740091.
21   Barbara C. Halporn, *The Correspondence of Johann Amerbach* (Ann Arbor: University of Michigan, 2000), pp. 20–21.

the very top of the market. That they nevertheless did everything they could to minimise competition in such large projects speaks volumes for the sensitivity of the market at this level of the business.

In these two instances, the ruin of Wenssler and the prudence of Amerbach, we see two of the problems facing the business of books, one general in the early modern economy, the other particular to this industry. The general problem was the early modern reliance on credit. In early modern Europe one could simultaneously own all the trappings of prosperity and be massively over-borrowed. For example, it was common practice that no payments should take place at the Lyon fairs for current transactions. Accounts would be settled at the following fairs throughout the year, creating a delay of three to nine months before debts had to be paid.[22] Initial capital was key to hopes of success; but not, it appears, sufficient to avoid bankruptcy if things took a wrong turn. A single catastrophic event could not only cause a major problem of liquidity, but also set off a creditor panic of the sort that dooms a modern day bank. We see in Wenssler's precipitate fall from grace how easily an apparently flourishing venture could tip into disaster. For a businessman in any trade, loss of reputation was the first step to destruction: once reputation was compromised, it was hard to put the process into reverse.

The other problem is more specific to print, and that is this: for in printing what constituted success was not so simple a matter as for a cloth merchant, a brewer or a cobbler. Making money and providing for a family were all well and good, but too many publishers hankered for more: to leave a monument; to create a signature edition; to play the intellectual. This confusion of purpose often spelled disaster, as Gutenberg had demonstrated. Unfortunately, his experience proved not a cautionary tale but a model for emulation.

Customers

Any publisher, however lofty, had to learn that customers were fickle and merciless. There was no safety net for poor decision-making. So, let us turn now to the customers. A few years ago, when the rail services in Britain were attracting fairly constant criticism, they faced another catastrophic disruption when the UK was hit by what was by any standards a relatively modest snowfall. Asked why continental railway networks in places like Finland or Austria could keep

---

22 Richard Gascon, 'La France du mouvement: Les commerces et les villes', in Fernand Braudel and Ernest Labrousse (eds.), *Histoire économique et sociale de la France* (2 vols., Paris: Presses Universitaires de France, 1970–1980), I: *De 1450 à 1660*, pp. 231–479: 281–285.

a service going whereas we could not, the hapless spokesman replied, 'we are having particular problems with the type of snow'; to which the interviewer replied, 'Oh, I see, it was the wrong kind of snow'. In the cruel way of modern media, this phrase, 'the wrong type of snow' was immediately attributed, quite inaccurately, to the spokesman himself: the redolent phrase was too good not to use, and it captured the essential truth of the exchange.[23] Printing suffered the same problem—in this case the wrong sort of customers.

The humanists who offered the first rhetorical definitions of the new world of print were extremely influential drivers of the expansion of the book world. But they were far too few, and their pockets too shallow, to provide an adequate market. Their high-minded agenda of serving existing markets better—that is of more and cheaper books for themselves—did not work. Humanist authors found themselves far more invested in the production process than they may have anticipated: providing a cash subsidy, supplying the paper, taking responsibility for selling a large proportion of the edition. The best strategy for extracting some benefit from their authorial or editorial efforts may, indeed, have been to invest heavily in gifting copies to the rich and the powerful, in the hope that they might express their gratitude with a reciprocal gift, or better, a place at court funded by a valuable sinecure. Scholars have often cited examples of such successful deployment of gift-giving, as in the case of John Harington's English translation of the Italian poem *Orlando furioso* (1591), where the high number of large-paper or hand-coloured gift-copies indicates that the edition was clearly designed as a catalyst for social relations.[24] However, the place of complimentary copies within the early modern marketplace of print is one that has never been systematically addressed. The Accademia Veneziana, for example, reserved at least five per cent of each print run to be distributed free of charge, possibly more.[25] Françoise de Louvain, widow of Abel L'Angelier, used gift copies as a strategy to maintain a network of authors around her boutique in Paris—a shrewd strategy that made her perhaps even more effective at business than her husband had been before her.[26] Humanist correspondences as a whole provide a glimpse of quite how many free copies must have circulated

---

23 11 February 1991, The Today Programme (BBC Radio 4).
24 Jason Scott Warren, *Sir John Harington and the Book as Gift* (Oxford and New York: Oxford University Press, 2001).
25 Shanti Graheli, 'Reading the history of the Academia Venetiana through its booklists', in Malcolm Walsby and Natasha Constantinidou (eds.), *Documenting the Early Modern Book World: Inventories and Catalogues in Manuscript and Print* (Leiden: Brill, 2013), pp. 283–319: 307.
26 Jean Balsamo and Michel Simonin, *Abel L'Angelier et Françoise de Louvain* (Geneva: Droz, 2002).

in Renaissance Europe, both as payments in kind and as a means of building reputation—a phenomenon that is perhaps comparable to the dynamics of academic printing today.

To survive, printers had to develop new markets, and crucially expand the range of the book-owning public. It took some time to develop these strategies. But in due course publishers recognised that profit could most easily be found in serving local markets, and particularly in a close relationship with the local power. Rather than the scholars whose appetite for books often outran their purse, a good relationship with the local government, or the local church powers, was by far the best guarantee of financial stability.

The speculative and especially the long-distance Latin trade had many hazards even if the publisher correctly gauged the market for a new edition. Even if readers were there, they were often widely dispersed: essentially one transnational reading community dispersed around all of Europe. To reach this market was extremely costly, involving radiating circles of other middlemen and market specialists all of whom took their own cut, and stripped another layer out of the profit. Often books could only be disposed of by exchange, taking consignments of another publisher's books in return, adding to their own inventory.

Printing an ordinance for the local government, or the church, was a different matter altogether. Here the client was likely to take the whole edition and pay cash. No wonder printers, even printers who undertook far more complex projects, were eager to take on such work, and actively pursued the most cooperative relationship possible with the local authorities. This of course is very far from the Eisenstein thesis, which treats print as an instrument of intellectual liberation. But printers had to put bread on the table, and the best way to do this was through taking easy jobbing work whenever it became available.

Strategies for Survival

With this we are edging towards the core of the question: how to avoid the shoals and pitfalls of the early print world. How could one make money in the business of books? This is a question that has obviously attracted comment from other scholars. For James Raven, in his study of English print, *The Business of Books*, the essentials of success were these: market appraisal, promotion, availability of financial assets, productive versatility.[27] It is also clear that the shape of a sustainable business model emerged only gradually. As Lotte

---

27   James Raven, *The Business of Books* (London: Yale University Press, 2007), p. 17.

Hellinga, the world-leading scholar of the incunabula age, has observed, it only gradually dawned that the invention of printing entailed further inventions, such as publishing and marketing, to which we would add distribution.[28] Ian Maclean, the leading expert on seventeenth-century scholarly print is more pessimistic. For him, success was measured not by profit but by mere survival.[29]

What then to do? Can we, based on what we know of this book world, and not least based on the contributions to this volume, chart a route to survival and prosperity? How could one make a secure living from selling books? Did publishers have to have a coherent business plan? If so, what was the best strategy: innovation or caution; individuality or collaboration; specialism or diversity?

In the first years of print, publishers, as it well known, were extremely cautious in their choice of texts. This led to a massive over-supply of familiar texts. This in turn stimulated a welcome, and ultimately necessary drive to diversify the reader base. But printers remained extremely wary of getting ahead of the market—innovation, in design and genre, remained a cautious matter of incremental steps. One bold strategy was to develop a reputation for a particular type of book: that is, a specialisation. That this became an attractive possibility owed a great deal to the reputational success of Aldus Manutius. Aldus was one of the first in the business to create a brand. A latecomer to the world of printing, Aldus took up printing as a second profession, having been a private teacher until a mature age. He had a clear understanding of pedagogy and of the gaps in the availability of classical texts. At the end of the fifteenth century, Aldus moved to Venice and secured the necessary capital from Andrea Torresano (later to become his father-in-law) and Pier Francesco Barbarigo. Various innovations followed swiftly: the patent for his new italic type; the production of books as part of a series; the creation of the first book catalogues to be distributed to customers.[30] Aldus intuitively understood how to shape the brand. Soon, and certainly in his own lifetime, Aldines, as the books became known, were the must-have item in any distinguished collection. The privileged place they still occupy in the antiquarian book market is a legacy of this.

---

28   Lotte Hellinga, 'Sale advertisements for books printed in the fifteenth century', in Robin Myers, Michael Harris and Giles Mandelbrote (eds.), *Books for Sale. The Advertising and Promotion of Print since the Fifteenth Century* (London: British Library, 2009).

29   Ian Maclean, *Scholarship, Commerce, Religion. The Learned Book in the Age of Confessions, 1560–1630* (Cambridge, Mass.: Harvard University Press, 2012), pp. 5, 109.

30   For a recent list of Aldus's 'firsts', see Neil Harris, 'Aldus and the making of the myth (or what did Aldus really do?)', in Mario Infelise (ed.), *Aldo Manuzio: la costruzione del mito. Aldus Manutius: The Making of the Myth* (Venice: Marsilio, 2016), pp. 346–385.

The power of this reputation may be illustrated by a rather extraordinary episode from the early years of the library of the Elector of Saxony in Wittenberg. Alongside all the other accoutrements of scholarly sophistication that Frederick the Wise required for his capital, naturally he desired to build a library. His secretary Georg Spalatin was entrusted with the task of enhancing the collection, and considerable sums were made available for this purpose.[31] In March 1512, emboldened by the Elector's generosity, Spalatin wrote directly to Aldus Manutius in Venice, asking that Manutius send a catalogue of his books in print. But securing the books from faraway Venice proved difficult. Spalatin's enquiry and then a second letter failed to elucidate a response, so a third was despatched, this time signed personally by the Elector. This explained the sort of library that Frederick wanted to create, and the important part the products of this famous shop would play in building its reputation. A follow-up letter from Spalatin shrewdly asked Aldus to note with a cross the books in his catalogue he kept in stock at his branch office in Frankfurt, from where they could be more cheaply transported to Wittenberg. It is rather extraordinary that despite this battery of correspondence it would be March 1514 before Aldus would reply, rather unconvincingly pleading that earlier letters had vanished in the post. The order was placed and the books supplied. The Aldines were the jewel in an increasingly precious collection, a priceless resource to the local professors and a standing rebuke to the quality of the local press. The survival of the early Aldine catalogues is in itself evidence of the high esteem in which the firm was held by the rulers and nobles of Europe. All three catalogues known to have been printed during Aldus's lifetime (in 1498, 1503 and 1513) are preserved in the MS Grec 3064 at the Bibliothèque nationale de France, a legacy of the French Royal Library, where they were retained as valuable lists of desiderata.[32] As for why the catalogues had been devised in the first place, Aldus himself declared it quite candidly: he was much too busy to reply to the many individual enquiries about the availability of his editions.

Few publishers could have afforded to be this offhand with distinguished and well-healed customers. Aldus was a very special case. Print grew by imitation and adaptation—the development of specialist markets was, to some extent the endless search for the new Aldine: a niche where an individual pub-

---

31 Maria Grossmann, *Humanism in Wittenberg, 1485–1517* (Nieuwkoop: De Graaf, 1975), pp. 100–112.

32 Shanti Graheli, 'Aldo, i suoi lettori e il mercato internazionale del libro', in Tiziana Plebani (ed.), *Aldo al Lettore. Viaggio intorno al mondo del libro e della stampa in occasione del V Centenario della morte di Aldo Manuzio* (Milan/Venice: Unicopli and Biblioteca Nazionale Marciana, 2016), pp. 151–172: 154–155.

lisher could command a wide market, where reputation produced its own price premium. It never worked again quite as it did for Aldus Manutius; but the search went on.

Specialisation had its advantages. High initial investment costs discouraged competition: the best examples are the market in Books of Hours, music printing, and lavishly illustrated books. The large-format illustrated editions of the *Orlando furioso* produced by Gabriele Giolito and Vincenzo Valgrisi, for example, were not challenged by competitors. The high production cost incurred in making fifty individual full-page illustrations meant that imitation was unappealing, despite the obvious success of the poem with the reading public. Other Venetian printers and publishers such as the Guerra brothers, Francesco Rampazetto, or Domenico Farri, contented themselves with producing smaller illustrations that suited both quarto editions and pocket-size formats. Even a powerful publisher like Giolito endeavoured to make the best of such an investment, by recycling them in related publications like Laura Terracina's *Discorso sopra il principio di tutti i canti d'Orlando furioso*.

Specialism thus brought protection, but over-specialised publishers made themselves especially vulnerable to shifts in taste: the canny choice was to reinvest the initial fruits of success in one market in more diverse ventures. This could take two forms: diversification within the industry, or into other types of trade. It is notable that the most successful publishers of seventeenth-century newspapers seldom published only newspapers. They re-invested their profits in other forms of news publication; very often their newspaper was only one part of a larger enterprise. Here we can contrast the success of Broer Jansz, publisher of one of the two first Amsterdam newspapers, with the cautionary tale of Abraham Verhoeven of Antwerp. When Broer Jansz first began publishing his weekly newspaper, probably in 1618, he was already an experienced publisher of news pamphlets, and he continued to make new associations in the book industry in the course of a long career, branching out, for instance, into the publication of bibles. By the time of his death in 1652 he had published some 380 books. When Abraham Verhoeven began his *New Tidings*, a vigorous and dynamic news serial, he too was an experienced business man, but for the ten years of its publication he published little else. On the face of it, this was the more successful enterprise, appearing three times a week. But when he lost official favour he had nothing to fall back on, and he died a pauper. In England we note the contrasting fortunes of the partners in London's first newspaper, Bourne and Butter. Nicolas Bourne diversified and flourished. Butter, the inveterate newsman, did not.

It would be interesting to apply these reflections to other forms of specialist publication. One such was musical publications, one of the more arcane specialisms that required considerable investment in special fonts of type. It would be interesting in this case to explore more systematically how large a role music publishing played in printers' repertoire. Early indications are that German publishers did not specialise exclusively in musical editions, whereas in France and Italy the market for musical part books was dominated by a very small number of publishers who issued little else, such as Antonio Gardane in Venice, or the Le Roy-Ballard partnership in Paris. But it is also the case that merely counting editions will not tell us whether a publisher made money. Verhoeven and Jansz were both almost equally prolific, but only one built a stable business.

The shrewdest publishers often re-invested their profits outside the industry, often in landed property or urban real estate. Lucas Cranach, a major investor in Wittenberg printing as well as court painter, accumulated a portfolio of seven houses in Wittenberg.[33] Christoph Egenolff of Frankfurt, who made a fortune publishing cheap books for a mass readership, owned sixteen. On the other side we have the example of Luxembourg de Gabiano of Lyon, who salted his money away in rural estates.[34] These men all conserved the fruits of publishing extremely effectively; though what it tells us about the book industry, that the best form of diversification was outside the industry, is in itself rather sobering.

Most publishers were not specialists: they remained generalists, publishing in a variety of genres and forms. They adopted different forms of self-protection. Mostly they reached for the familiar weapons of trade regulation. The first of these was monopoly. This was a mechanism favoured by both producers and regulators, though for different reasons. For Europe's rulers, qualified monopolies (or privileges, as they were usually called) were a means of supporting the industry without direct investment. A printer, publisher or author would be granted the exclusive right to publish a text or body of texts for a stipulated period of years. France had by far the most elaborated scheme of privileges, developed in the years surrounding the turn of the fifteenth and sixteenth centuries.[35] Those looking to protect a market for a particular text were required to make a case, based on the unusual cost or special utility of an

---

33   Ralf Klittig-Altmann, 'Archäologische Funde von Grundstücken der Familie Cranach in Wittenberg', in Heiner Lück, Enno Bünz, Leonhard Helten, Armin Kohnle, Dorothée Sack and Hans-Georg Stephan (eds.), *Das ernestinische Wittenberg: Spuren Cranachs in Schloss und Stadt* (Petersberg: Imhof, 2015), pp. 363–399.
34   See the article by Jamie Cumby in this volume.
35   Elizabeth Armstrong, *Before Copyright. The French Book-Privilege System* (Cambridge: Cambridge University Press, 1990).

edition. This petition was then often reproduced in the printed text, usually on the reverse of the title-page or the final leaf.

These published privileges reveal that the penalties for infringement were often quite severe. Whether the law was enforced in the way envisaged—confiscation of pirate copies and destruction of the offending press, along with a heavy fine—is another matter. Perhaps they did not need to be, for the deterrent effect of such privileges seems to have been very powerful. It was very much in the interests of the established members of the publishing fraternity in France that these market protections should be upheld, so the system was for the most part well policed by the publishers themselves.

The instinct for monopoly was strong. It is not always remembered that in 1469 the city of Venice gave the first person who approached them a monopoly on all printing in the city—a disastrous decision from which they were rescued only by the fact that the holder died within a year. The downside of privileges was that they were difficult to obtain, and only valid in the jurisdiction in which they were granted. It was hard to prevent a new edition spoiling a market if they were published elsewhere: a particularly acute problem in the international Latin market. Monopolies and privileges were also controversial because they could cause dissension in the industry, and were increasingly resented by those who did not have them. It may well have been the case, as Marius Buning suggests, that the climate of opinion became more hostile to monopolies in the seventeenth century.[36] This was certainly the case in general economic terms in England, where there was a widespread belief that the granting of monopolies had become an easy way for an impecunious crown to reward courtiers.[37]

A much more sophisticated and successful instrument of market protection was the cartel. This took different forms in different parts of Europe. The best known and most stable form of cartel was the Company: a formally incorporated association of printers established as a permanent or extended business partnership. The most famous examples were established in Lyon in the first half of the sixteenth century, and Paris in the second. They normally involved well-established members of the local print fraternity, and functioned well as a means of raising investment capital for expensive projects. In Lyon, in particular, this played an instrumental role in securing a dominant position in the international market in law books. A regulatory body could also form a very effective cartel. In London, the Stationers' Company was set up to regulate output. In the course of performing this role, it was also able to secure control of

---

36   See the article by Marius Buning in this volume.
37   Joan Thirsk, *Economic Policy and Projects: The Development of a Consumer Society in Early Modern England* (Oxford: Oxford University Press, 1978).

the domestic market for a small elite of publishers. This was a classic example of where a collusive relationship between the trade and government was advantageous to both parties.

One can also see the instinct for cartel played out in more informal, traditional mechanisms. A small number of powerful families established themselves across different territories, ensuring the creation of a trustworthy network of production and distribution. The most prominent such example is represented by the Giunta family, originally from Florence, but soon expanding to the core locations of Venice, Rome, Lyon, as well as establishing a foothold in the Spanish market through Seville, Madrid and Burgos.[38] Warehouses were later established in Paris, Antwerp, Frankfurt, Medina del Campo, Salamanca, Zaragoza and Lisbon. Such a business model was inspired by the great families of international bankers, and in the book trade too it was the province of those equipped with substantial capital. It also served as a powerful mechanism for the distribution of bulky Latin editions, which could not be absorbed by a local or even a national market alone.

Even more frequent was the persistent pattern of intermarriage between publishing families. This proved to be a particularly successful means of preserving the market position of established printing families in Paris, one of the largest and therefore potentially most lucrative print markets. Here, the close-knit group of major firms proved remarkably successful, despite the turmoil of the French Wars of Religion, in preventing significant competition from newcomers to the industry. Over the course of centuries this became institutionalised in French governmental strategy for controlling print, so that in eighteenth-century France the crown established quotas of permitted publishers for all printing towns.[39] It became almost impossible for an apprentice to establish an independent shop unless they could snare a printer's daughter or widow and inherit the business. The result was guaranteed profits for the fortunate few and Europe's most conservative publishing industry: a cosy cartel dissolved only by the French Revolution.

---

38   William Pettas, *A Sixteenth-Century Spanish Bookstore: The Inventory of Juan de Junta* (Philadelphia: American Philosophical Society, 1995); Pettas, 'The Giunti and the book trade in Lyon', in Istituto di Biblioteconomia e Paleografia Università degli Studi, Parma (ed.), *Libri, tipografi e biblioteche. Ricerche storiche dedicate a Luigi Balsamo* (2 vols., Florence: Leo S. Olschki, 1997), I, pp. 169–192.

39   Jane McLeod, *Licensing Loyalty. Printers, Patrons and the State in Early Modern France* (Philadelphia: Penn State, 2011).

Selling

All these mechanisms were essentially conservative: intended in one way or another to restrict or inhibit newcomers. They also inhibited market innovation. This is of course the very opposite of what is meant to be happening in the Eisenstein model of expansive innovation. If all of this did not work; if it proved impossible to break into the increasingly closed and defensive world of publishing; if profit proved elusive: there was one other solution. One could always become a bookseller. This seems to have been the most successful part of the market. There were many reasons why this could have been so. Bookselling was versatile; one could have a shop, or rely on a market stall. It was far easier to down-size or upscale. Even established businesses made much use of ambient peddlers.[40] With a book-shop it was far easier to control stock; one could buy retail, in small numbers, and then re-stock as necessary. Others preferred barter to making up-front payments, as in the case of the bilateral partnership between Giovanni Giolito in Trino and Vincenzo Portonaris in Lyon, or the example of Francesco Ciotti described by Domenico Ciccarello in this volume. Booksellers never faced the publisher's dilemma of having to dispose of several hundred unwanted copies.

This was still a debt and credit economy, and booksellers could still get into trouble. But booksellers were in a stronger position than publishers with regard to debt. They often owed publishers money (and books were often supplied on terms of sale or return), but these debts could be hard to call in. It was difficult for publisher to pursue booksellers if this risked driving them out of business, because this risked throttling their own conduit to the public. The most radical solution was that adopted by one bookman at the Frankfurt Fair, who told a friend that he had given up on selling books altogether—instead he was doing a roaring trade selling spectacles to visitors peering at the books at the fair.

So, who won? Our spectacle seller gives us the clue: that the main beneficiaries of all this trade were the customers. They benefited from this massive speculative investment, with the availability of literally millions of books—perhaps 700 million copies in the first two centuries of print; these too, were books tailored with increasing sophistication to the readers' actual tastes; and they often came with hidden subsidies that ensured that they sold at below their true market value.

---

40 Jeroen Salman, *Pedlars and the Popular Press. Itinerant Distribution Networks in England and the Netherlands, 1600–1850* (Leiden: Brill, 2014).

Here the book market anticipated the trajectory of that other sensational media development, television. As was the case with the invention of printing, television initially offered a highly restricted supply of a limited range of product intended to make us better people. In this scenario BBC executives played the role of fifteenth-century humanists: this high-minded sense of communication as improvement is explicitly laid out in the BBC's royal charter: the corporation existed, it is stated, to instruct, educate and (only thirdly) to entertain.[41] In the later twentieth century, as television entered a more deregulated multi-channel world, intellectuals continued to lament the negative effect of market forces and the debasement of society that came from catering to lowbrow tastes—the same sentiments had found many sympathisers in Renaissance Italy. The idea that books should be a force for cultural enrichment proved remarkably enduring, from the sixteenth-century Perugia bookseller Luciano Pasini's celebration of books as the outlet for 'beautiful intellects' to Eisenstein's print revolution. But the 'beautiful intellects', alas, were not sufficiently numerous to put bread on the table, as the grand projects of idealists like Robert Estienne demonstrate only too well.[42] Instead, customers benefited from greater choice, from books that were affordable, amusing or useful. They also benefited from the increasingly sophisticated mechanisms of sale and distribution.

We want though to end this series of cautionary tales with the story of a book market that worked, and worked spectacularly well. This is the story of Wittenberg.[43] At the beginning of the sixteenth century Wittenberg was like any other small-scale failing market. Printing only reached Wittenberg in 1502: the incunabula age passed it by altogether. And for fifteen years production remained tiny. Four printers came and went: servicing the parochial needs of the university was not much of a living, and in all likelihood the industry survived only through direct subsidy of the local ruler, Frederick the Wise. This was an absolutely typical tale of business failure: the press in Wittenberg was established more as a status symbol than through economic necessity. Wittenberg was on the outer periphery of the European print market, and its needs could effectively be supplied from nearby Leipzig. Between 1502 and 1517 Wittenberg turned out a paltry 125 books, an average of 9 a year. Taking into account their length, printing all of these books would have occupied a single press for less than thirty days a year.

---

41   Ian McIntyre, *The Expense of Glory. A Life of John Reith* (London: Harper/ Collins, 1993).
42   See the article by Martine Furno in this volume.
43   This follows Andrew Pettegree, *Brand Luther. 1517, Printing and the Making of the Reformation* (New York: Penguin, 2015).

From 1517 all that changed. By 1522 Wittenberg had outstripped Leipzig, and it never looked back. The influx of investment capital transformed the city, and the transformation was permanent. By the second half of the sixteenth century Wittenberg was Germany's largest centre of printing.[44] The secret of Wittenberg's success is not hard to discern. Wittenberg had one unique product: Martin Luther. Luther was not a career author, indeed he had published nothing at all until 1516, by which point he was in his mid-thirties. Yet by 1521 he was Europe's most published living figure: indeed the most published author in the history of the printed book.

The Reformation transformed both the German print industry and the reading public. Yet there was no inherent reason why all of these books should have been published in Wittenberg. Indeed, in the first years they were not. In 1517 Wittenberg had one not very capable printer, Johannes Rhau-Grunenberg. At this point Luther's works were swiftly republished around Germany in all of the main centres of production. It required deliberate steps to reserve a larger proportion of this market for Wittenberg. In this Luther himself played an instrumental part. Luther was no disconnected intellectual: he had a highly developed business sense. He chafed at the incompetence of Rhau-Grunenberg's shop, and the crudity of its production. So, he determined to do something about it. In 1519 he entered into negotiation with the established Leipzig printer Melchior Lotter to bring to Wittenberg a second print shop. Lotter sent his son, Melchior junior, to establish a branch office, and the look of Wittenberg books improved immediately.

But this was essentially the Leipzig look—there was nothing distinctly Wittenberg about them. This was addressed by a crucial partnership between Luther and Lucas Cranach. Cranach is mostly known as one of the greatest painters of Renaissance Germany, but in fact he was also deeply involved in the printing industry. For the new books of the Reformation he created a new look—a brand—that made the most of the movement's greatest assets: Luther and Wittenberg. The huge demand for Luther's writings drew new printers and new investment capital into the city, but this could not be a free for all. The market was carefully regulated, not in this case by the state but by the moral authority of Martin Luther. Luther ensured compliance with his wishes by managing the publishing of his own works. They were never supplied exclusively to one favoured printer, but carefully apportioned to each of Wittenberg's print shops. And within the capacious domain of Luther's output each was allowed a speciality. Joseph Klug had the German songbook and scholarly works of the uni-

---

44   Figures from the USTC.

versity community. Nicolas Schirlentz enjoyed the local monopoly of the small catechism; Georg Rhau was allocated the Large Catechism and the Confession of Augsburg. Hans Lufft, the owner of the largest shop published the bibles; Luther shared his own works between all four.

The result was that the print shops established in Wittenberg in the mid-1520s were surprisingly long lived. All survived for twenty years or more, and that of Hans Lufft sixty. The Wittenberg industry was not only buoyant, but remarkably stable. Wittenberg was a special case, with an extraordinary asset, but its success was not pre-ordained. It required a remarkably mature business sense to ensure boom did not turn into bust. The printers accommodated themselves to Luther's regulatory regime with great ease, enjoying the fruits of an informal cartel.

Perhaps Wittenberg benefitted from its late start: there was so much business failure from which to learn. But the enduring, resilient buoyancy of print demonstrates one other thing: the extraordinary availability of venture capital through successive cycles of boom and bust. It is probably no coincidence that print developed most rapidly in capital rich societies: Italy in the fifteenth century, Germany in the sixteenth, the Dutch Republic and England in the seventeenth. Indeed, by sucking up this otherwise mischievous surplus capital they may have had a generally stabilising effect on these economies. Better books than overvalued tulips.[45] People lost money in the business of books partly because there was so much money that people were prepared to lose. The book industry is perhaps the ultimate demonstration that a product that has social cachet that goes beyond its true economic value can have an extraordinarily long career as a loss leader.

---

45 Anne Goldgar, *Tulipmania. Money, Honor and Knowledge in the Dutch Golden Age* (Chicago: Chicago University Press, 2007).

PART 1

Debt Economies and Bookselling Risks

∴

CHAPTER 2

Early Book Printing and Venture Capital in the Age of Debt: the Case of Michel Wenssler's Basel Printing Shop (1472–1491)

Lucas Burkart

At the beginning of 1491, the bailiffs of the city council of Basel searched the house of Michel Wenssler, one of the most important printers in town. His renowned workshop was located in the so-called *Haus zem Lufft*, a building that would come to have an iconic status in the history of Basel culture: later, it housed Froben's workshop and was therefore the domicile of Erasmus of Rotterdam.[1] The official's mission, however, failed and the outcome was sobering. According to the documentation, they found the house mostly empty, and likewise the print shop contained only the presses and their associated wooden components. Printing frames, skillets and types, however, were all gone, as was master Michel himself, although in several trolleys they found faulty books and printed sheets in disarray.[2] Wenssler had arrived in Basel in the late 1460s, and climbed to the zenith of the new printing industry. Now, it was clear, he had fled the city in some haste. The circumstances of his escape must have been dramatic, since he even left behind his pregnant wife.

It is unclear what exactly led to such tragic choices. They were however preceded by several events that precipitated the slow demise of a successful master

---

1   Down to the present day it is remembered as a milestone of humanist Basel, to which the city occasionally chooses to refer as its most renowned moments in history. The connection to books is close even today for the building on Bäumleingasse 18 harbours a renowned antiquarian bookshop. Discussions and help from colleagues and friends were extremely helpful in writing this article. I am particularly indebted to Jan Alessandrini, Falk Eisermann, Andreas Gehringer, Shanti Graheli, Benjamin Hitz and Andrew Pettegree for sharing their thoughts and expertise so generously with me. I owe a special debt of gratitude to Leah R. Clark for her generous support in the preparation of this chapter.

2   "[…] in den kammeren oben in dem huß da standen ettlich Spanbett, on bettgewandt, sunder ler funden; deßglichen in siner Slaffkamer standen kasten und trög gantz ler und nützit darinn, und sye nit mer dann ein Spanbett mit einem bett und pfulwen [*Unterkissen*] und küssy gestanden. In der Truckstuben syent nit mer, den allein die bressen und was von hultzem geschirr darzu gehört, aber die Ramen, Tygel und geschrifte sye alles hin und enweg. […] in ettlichen kaeren ligen defect bücher und vil solichs gedruckten bappirs underainander geworfen". Staatsarchiv Basel-Stadt (StABS), Gerichtsarchiv A 39, 7 July 1491.

FIGURE 2.1 *Haus zem Lufft* where Wenssler moved his workshop to in 1479

in this most innovative economic sector in late fifteenth-century Basel, printing. In this chapter, it is argued that Wenssler's misfortune presents more than just the personal shortcomings of a late medieval entrepreneur going bankrupt. On the contrary, his case is symptomatic of the early printing industry and economy. Gutenberg's invention profoundly changed the book and the culture that went with it; that cannot be disputed. Nevertheless, it is necessary to inquire further and in detail how this paradigm shift actually took place and what immediate consequences it had on its protagonists—both the producers and consumers.

Here we will rely on two very different set of sources: the character and output of Wenssler's printing shop on the one hand and the documentation of his debt recorded by the urban civil court on the other. It will be clear that early printing was deeply embedded in the city's society and economy. Basel's favourable geographic location created a suitable environment both for the settlement of printing within the city's landscape of urban industry and its rapid development up to 1500. At the same time, our investigation challenges the traditional historiography of printing that has placed undue emphasis on the close alliance between the technological invention of printing and humanism, and specifically the humanist concern for the accuracy of the texts published.³ This perspective concentrates on humanists as the protagonists of printing and its triumph in European culture while printers and their economic and entrepreneurial decisions are somehow bypassed.⁴ This proves especially problematic for the first phase of printing when most printers were apparently not humanists themselves. In other words, the historiographical fusion of printer, editor, publisher and humanist is misleading forasmuch as it reduces the history of printing to a history of thought. In contrast to such an interpretation, this chapter foregrounds both the economic features and practices and the social network that characterized early printing in order to come to a more comprehensive understanding of how printing emerged within the late medieval urban economy, society and culture.

The Establishment of Printing in Basel

Originally from Strasbourg, Michel Wenssler moved to Basel in the 1460s. He was enrolled in the University's register in 1462 but never gained a degree.⁵ There are no further traces of him until 1472 when he appears as the publisher of the *Epistolae* by Gasparino Barzizza, a collection of object lessons following classical rhetoric that were widely used in Latin schools and universities to teach students to compose elegant Latin prose. We do not know how or where Wenssler acquired his knowledge in the art of printing. It may have been in his hometown Strasbourg or in the workshop of Berthold Ruppel, Gutenberg's former assistant, who first opened a printing shop in Basel between 1468 and 1470.⁶ In any case, Wenssler belongs to the first generation of printers in Basel

---

3 For this position see Elizabeth L. Eisenstein, *The Printing Press as an Agent of Change. Communications and Cultural Transformations in Early Modern Europe* (Cambridge and New York: Cambridge University Press, 1979); Eisenstein, *The Printing Revolution in Early Modern Europe* (Cambridge: Cambridge University Press, 1983). For the discussion of Eisenstein's approach see among others Peter F. McNally (ed.), *The Advent of Printing. Historians of Science Respond to Elizabeth Eisenstein's "The Printing Press as an Agent of Change"* (Montreal: Graduate School of Library and Information Studies, McGill University, 1987).
4 With focus to Basel see Traugott Geering's description of the whole city's printing industry guided by 'humanist consciousness': "[Die Drucker] waren tief durchdrungen von dem echt humanistischen Bewusstsein, an einer grossen Culturaufgabe der Menschheit in unmittelbarster Weise zu arbeiten". Traugott Geering, *Handel und Industrie der Stadt Basel. Zunftwesen und Wirtschaftsgeschichte bis zum Ende des 17. Jahrhunderts* (Basel: Schneider, 1886), p. 323.
5 Wackernagel, Hans Georg (ed.), *Die Matrikel der Universität Basel* (5 vols., Basel: Verlag der Universitätsbibliothek, 1951–1980), I, 32.
6 Victor Scholderer has assumed that Wenssler acquired his printing knowledge in Strasbourg whereas van der Haegen favored that he did so in Basel, probably with Ruppel. See Victor

and in scholarship his workshop is usually listed third after those of Berthold Ruppel and Bernhard Richel.

The establishment of printing in Basel was the result of many factors, but for the purpose of this study, five will be outlined here. First, the topographical position of Basel at a significant crossroads connecting Italy and South-western France with Europe's north, allowed the city to develop as a significant commercial centre from the fourteenth century onwards. For the distribution of printed books, this favourable geographical position proved to be crucial.[7] Second, several paper mills had been established in Basel in the 1430s and 1440s just outside the city walls benefitting from a pre-existing system of water canals.[8] Third, the General Council that was held in Basel between 1431 and 1449 had a profound impact on the city's economic, cultural and intellectual development. In these years the urban economy boomed; the members of the Council generated an unprecedented demand for goods and services. The paper industry, for instance, grew considerably in order to satisfy the council's demand for writing paper. The consumption habits of the cardinals, bishops, diplomats and their respective entourages gathered in the city required access to ready money to an extent the urban economy could not guarantee. In 1433, Cardinal Cesarini, who presided over the Council, authorized the opening of a branch office of the Medici bank in the city.[9] Fourthly, in the very same year the Council decided to open for its members a *studium generale*. This decision proved to be far-reaching for the city because both teachers and students involved in the *studium generale* played a major role in founding the university in 1460. The council's former secretary, the humanist Enea Silvio Piccolomini, now pope Pius II, executed the deed of foundation.

Finally, the city council promoted the settlement of a printing industry in various ways. Experts of this new craft were received in the city with open arms, granted right of residence, and later, frequently naturalization. The city's commercial policy was also favourably disposed towards printing. As was gen-

---

Scholderer, 'Michael Wenssler, and his press at Basel', in Dennis E. Rhodes (ed.), *Fifty Essays in Fifteenth- and Sixteenth-Century Bibliography* (Amsterdam: Menno Hertzberger & Co., 1966), pp. 46–60. Pierre Louis van der Haegen, *Der frühe Basler Buchdruck. Ökonomische, soziopolitische und informationssystematische Standortfaktoren und Rahmenbedingungen* (Basel: Schwabe, 2001), p. 22.

7   Franz Ehrensperger, *Basels Stellung im internationalen Handelsverkehr des Spätmittelalters* (Zürich: [s.n.], 1972).

8   Gerhard Piccard, *Papiererzeugung und Buchdruck in Basel bis zum Beginn des 16. Jahrhunderts. Ein wirtschaftsgeschichtlicher Beitrag* (Frankfurt am Main: Buchhändler-Vereinigung, 1966).

9   Kurt Weissen, 'Die Bank von Cosimo und Lorenzo de' Medici am Basler Konzil (1433–1444)', *Vierteljahrschrift für Sozial- und Wirtschaftsgeschichte*, 82 (1995), pp. 350–396.

erally the case, the new industry was not subject to guild regulations. Moreover, printers were repeatedly granted commercial privileges that respected the specificities of the industry. For instance, the council decreed that the import of printing paper did not have to go through the merchants' house as was the case with all other commodities traded in the city.

Basel is generally ranked ninth among the cities in which European printing culture evolved.[10] The city's reputation, however, does not result so much from the early establishment of printing but from the second generation of printers who developed the close relationship between printing culture and humanism. The most famous names associated with print were Johannes Amerbach, Johannes Petri and Johannes Froben, and with humanism, Johannes Heynlin, Beatus Rhenanus and, most of all, Erasmus of Rotterdam. However, neither the standard of printing nor the intellectual contribution associated with these great names characterized the first generation of Basel printers, or correctly identified the motivation for the establishment of printing.

While humanists have become the main protagonists in the established history of printing, the choices printers had to make in order to run their business have largely been neglected. By making a case for a more sophisticated study of early printing in Basel this chapter does not categorically deny the mutual connection between humanism and printing or the productivity of this alliance but tries to understand it rather as the result of historical change over approximately fifty years. In this sense, the case of Michel Wenssler is paradigmatic; he illuminates both how printing was deeply rooted in the late medieval urban economy and society and how much it contributed to cultural innovation and historical change.

Opening a Workshop and Facing Market Expectations

Wenssler's edition of Barzizza's *Epistolae* was the first humanist text printed in Basel.[11] It seems that Johannes Heynlin played an instrumental role in this project. After living for two years in Basel, where he possibly first met Wenssler, Heynlin left for Paris in 1466. Here he embarked on what became an outstanding academic career, becoming first prior of the Sorbonne, and in 1469 rector

---

10   Van der Haegen, *Der frühe Basler Buchdruck*, p. 20.
11   For all Incunabula printed in Basel see Pierre Louis van der Haegen, *Basler Wiegendrucke. Verzeichnis der in Basel gedruckten Inkunabeln mit ausführlicher Beschreibung der in der Universitätsbibliothek Basel vorhandenen Exemplare* [Schriften der Universitätsbibliothek Basel 1] (Basel: Schwabe, 1998).

of the university of Paris. Together with his predecessor in office, Guillaume Fichet, he also ran a printing shop. Heynlin was a wealthy man and used his private resources to bring three printers from the Upper Rhine to the Seine: Ulrich Gering, Martin Crantz and Michael Friburger. It was from this successful association that in 1470 emerged the first book ever printed in France, the *Epistolae Gasparini*. In 1474, Heynlin returned to Basel, and one can assume that he re-established his former connections. It seems likely that Heynlin himself suggested printing the *Epistolae* to Wenssler. Such an assumption seems to be further reinforced by the fact that his personal copy of the book has survived in Basel. The volume was originally given to the Carthusian Library, and is now preserved in the University Library.[12]

Wenssler's edition of Barzizza's *Epistles* opens with a short poem in distichs, reproduced here as Figure 2.2. The poem is reminiscent of classical poetry, but also makes explicit references to the present. In particular, Basel is praised as a centre of printing: "Artem pressurae quamquam moguncia finxit | E limo traxit hanc basilea tamen": "Although Mainz invented the art of printing | Basel pulled it out of the mud". In addition, the poem also mentions he who was responsible for the publication: "Mihahel cognomine wentzler". Both the choice of the text and the opening verses recall humanist attitudes and bestow honour to Basel as an outstanding centre of print culture.

It would be misleading to read too much of a programmatic statement into the book's opening poem; as a printer Wenssler was not mainly interested in classical or humanist texts or their distribution by print. In fact, after Barzizza's *Epistolae* he edited just two other humanist works in the strict sense of the word: Franciscus Niger's *Grammatica* and Andrés Gutierrez' *Grammatica* were published by Wenssler's workshop in 1485 and 1486 respectively. Both works were reprints from earlier editions, the former published in Venice in 1480, the latter in Burgos in 1485. Wenssler engaged very little in the printing of the classics. In fact, he edited just one classical author: Cicero, whose *De officiis* he published between 1475 and 1479.[13]

This choice is particularly revealing as to how Wenssler ran his workshop. Cicero's text was well known in the Middle Ages, and widely used in teaching and education. So, to publish the *De officiis* was not an innovative decision but rather one that targeted a well-defined group of customers: Latin schools and

---

12   Universitätsbibliothek Basel, Handschriftenabteilung Inc. 700:1. For more on Heynlin's role for printing in Basel, see Lucas Burkart, 'Gelehrte und Buchdrucker. Oder: Wie der italienische Humanismus in Basel ins gedruckte Buch fand', in *Sprezzatura. Geschichte und Geschichtserzählung zwischen Fakt und Fiktion* (Göttingen: Wallstein, 2016), pp. 230–237.
13   See Gesamtverzeichnis der Wiegendrucke (GW) 06945, Incunabula Short Title Catalogue (ISTC) ic00585500.

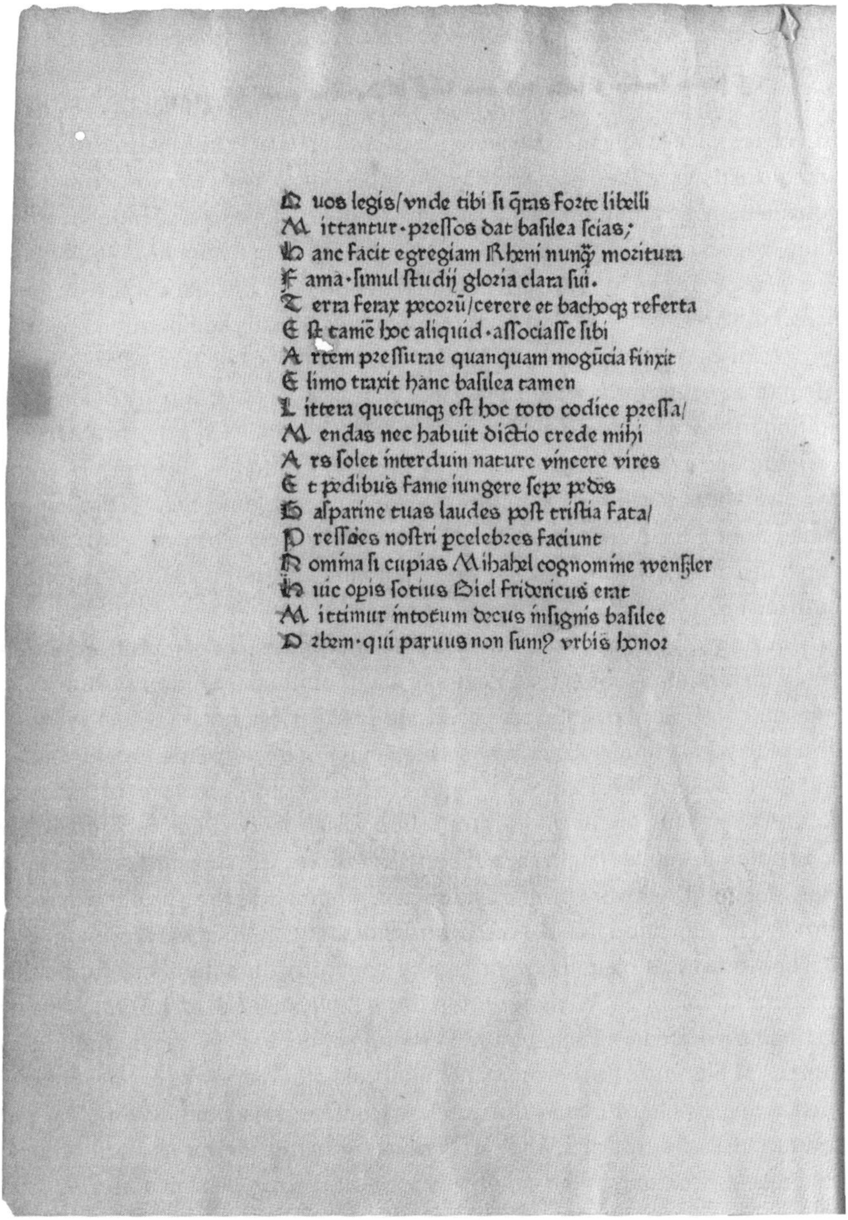

Q uos legis/vnde tibi si q̃ns forte libelli
M ittantur·pressos dat basilea scias;
H anc facit egregiam Rheni nunq̃ mozitum
F ama·simul studij glozia clara sui.
T erra ferax pecozu/cerere et bachoq; referta
E st tamẽ hoc aliquid·associasse sibi
A rtem pressurae quanquam mogũcia finxit
E limo traxit hanc basilea tamen
L ittera quecunq; est hoc toto codice pressa/
M endas nec habuit dictio crede mihi
A rs solet interdum nature vincere vires
E t pedibus fame iungere sepe pedes
H aspartine tuas laudes post tristia fata/
P ressoes nostri pcelebzes faciunt
N omina si cupias Mihahel cognomine wenssler
H uic opis socius Biel fridericus erat
M ittimur in totum decus insignis basilee
D ztem·qui paruus non sum? vrbis honoz

FIGURE 2.2 Gasparino Barzizza, *Epistolae* [Michel Wenssler, Friedrich Biel], Basel 1472
COPY: UNIVERSITÄTSBIBLIOTHEK BASEL, HANDSCHRIFTENMAGAZIN, INC 581:3, FOL. 2

universities both in Basel and beyond. Moreover, for two of the editions singled out above, the *Epistolae* and the *De officiis*, there is clear evidence that Johannes Heynlin was involved in some way. Even if we do not know exactly when this eminent humanist first met Wenssler, his role in the dissemination of humanist books and learning in Basel is widely acknowledged.[14] Even if we cannot say what exactly gave Wenssler the idea of publishing Niger's *Grammatica*, it can convincingly be argued that the work by Andrés Gutierrez was brought to his knowledge by his former associate Friedrich Biel, with whom he co-edited the *Epistolae Gasparini* in 1472. Biel migrated to Burgos in the 1480s where he published the first edition of Gutierrez' *Grammatica* in 1485 and became the most important German printer in Spain, known as Fadrique de Basilea or Federigo Aleman. It is more than plausible that Wenssler received a copy of the 1485 edition from his former associate Biel and simply published a reprint as he did with the *Epistolae Gasparini*, following the Paris edition by Johannes Heynlin. In other words, for three of four humanist or classical works that Wenssler published during his career as a printer in Basel, his choice of works was largely dependent on close social ties rather than following a specific programme of humanist culture.

This impression is confirmed by a scrutiny of the workshop's overall output, which demonstrates that Wenssler paid minimal attention to humanist texts and to the authors of classical antiquity. The Gesamtkatalog der Wiegendrucke (GW) attributes 167 editions, the Incunabula Short Title Catalogue 163, and the Universal Short Title Catalogue 150 editions to Wenssler's workshop in Basel. The production of the printing-shop was broadly conceived and rather conventional, and we can clearly distinguish two types of customers to whom Wenssler's editions were primarily directed: members of the Church and those involved in education in both the Latin schools and at university level.

The workshop's overall output can be structured in a number of different categories. First of all, Wenssler printed the Bible and theological treatises by distinguished medieval scholars such as Augustine, Thomas Aquinas and Antoninus of Florence; furthermore, he published familiar works of hagiography such as the *Legenda aurea* by the Genoese Dominican Jacobus de Voragine and several titles of devotional and recreational literature. Sermons and liturgical manuals (*officia, antiphonaria, breviaria, psalteria, vigilia*) for both the local

---

14 Beat von Scarpatetti, 'Heynlin, Johannes, de Lapide (von Stein)', in Gundolf Keil, Kurt Ruh, Werner Schröder, Burghart Wachinger and Franz Josef Worstbrock (eds.), *Die deutsche Literatur des Mittelalters: Verfasserlexikon* (11 vols., Berlin: de Gruyter 1980), III, Sp. 1213–1219. Beat von Scarpatetti, 'Die Büchersammlung des Johannes de Lapide (gest. 1496)', *Gazette du livre médiéval*, 34 (1999), pp. 37–43.

and the trans-local market made up a considerable proportion of Wenssler's publications. He released, for instance, no fewer than fourteen *breviaria* that reflected the specific needs of local liturgical calendars for places including Basel, Cologne, Constance, Mainz, Rome, Salisbury, Salzburg, Speyer and Utrecht.

Secondly, he provided his customers with legal textbooks, such as the standard reference work *Vocabularius utriusque iuris* by Jodocus of Erfurt, which he printed in six editions between 1473 and 1490. In this field, moreover, he edited collections of both canon and civil law, such as the *Decretum Gratiani* (three editions between 1481 and 1486 with the commentary by Johannes Teutonicus and Bartholomeus Brixiensis), the *Liber Sextus* by pope Bonifacius VIII (four editions between 1476 and 1486 with the gloss by Johannes Andreae), the *Iustiniani Institutiones* (six editions between 1476 and 1487 with the *glossa ordinaria* by Accursius) or finally Emperor Justinian's *Novellae* from 1478. Wenssler published not only traditional legal texts but also contemporary interpretations of canon law. Together with Berthold Ruppel and Bernhard Richel, he co-edited the *Lectura super quinque libros Decretalium* by Nicolò de Tudeschi (1386–1445), archbishop of Palermo and a visitor to the Basel council. Wenssler's textbooks however did not cover only legal education but were directed to the arts as well. They encompassed standard grammars of medieval artistic learning such as Donatus Aelius' *Ars minor* that underwent no fewer than five editions between 1480 and 1490, compilations as the *Disticha Catonis* and philosophical texts such as Boethius' *De consolatione philosophiae* (1473 or 1474). Among the printed matter, Wenssler also produced broadsheets; these include papal bulls and indulgences, an invitation to a "shooting match" or a call to fight the Turks from 1480, released by the archbishop of Mainz.

Analysis of Wenssler's production also reveals an astonishing variety of printed matter in different formats. His output includes all formats from folio to sexto-decimo, and different forms from single sheet items up to volumes of more than 500 pages; they display various layouts, comprising one-column imprints as well as more complex arrangements. In his editions of legal texts, for instance, the source text was placed in the centre of the page and the respective commentaries and glosses set around it as was common in manuscript culture since the thirteenth century. His editions encompass "cheap prints" such as a bull issued by Pope Sixtus IV in 1479 (Figure 2.4) as well as more representative works such as the richly decorated *Lectura super quinque libros Decretalium* by the learned Benedictine Nicolò de Tudeschi, that consisted of three volumes in folio and more than 3,000 pages.[15] With regard to both con-

---

15 Wenssler, Ruppel and Richel printed the *Lectura* as a joint venture; scholarship assumes that Wenssler's contribution was roughly a third, i.e. around 275 sheets.

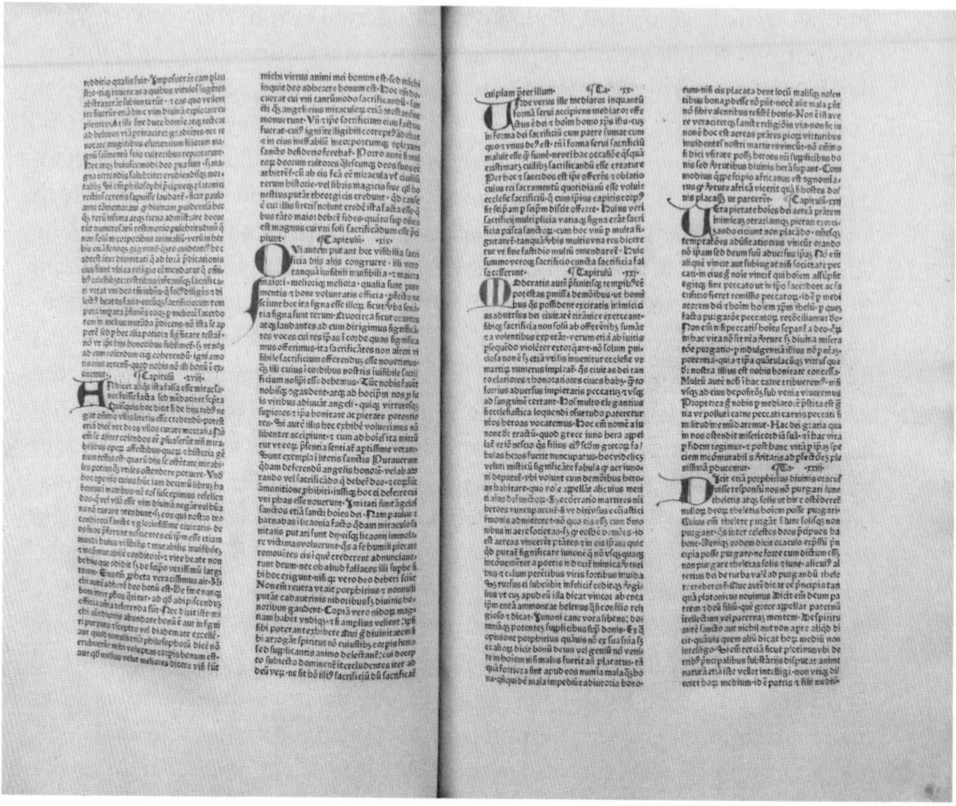

FIGURE 2.3   Aurelius Augustinus, *De civitate Dei* [Bernard Richel, Michel Wenssler], Basel 1479
COPY: UNIVERSITÄTSBIBLIOTHEK BASEL, HANDSCHRIFTENMAGAZIN, INC 608

tent and form, Wenssler's selection of printed works was mostly conventional, and addressed well-established consumption habits that were not altered by the invention of printing. By doing so, he satisfied the wide-ranging demand for books including both objects of conspicuous consumption and means of quick and far-reaching dissemination of information. As a consequence, the major part of what had been printed in Wenssler's Basel workshop belonged either to the well-established literature of the late medieval syllabus or religious literature.[16]

---

16   In this context it is significant that the first generation of printers published almost exclusively Latin, with very few vernacular texts. Whereas research until recently understood this as an expression of the humanist tendencies of early printing, this chapter argues that it reflected rather market expectations and sales opportunities.

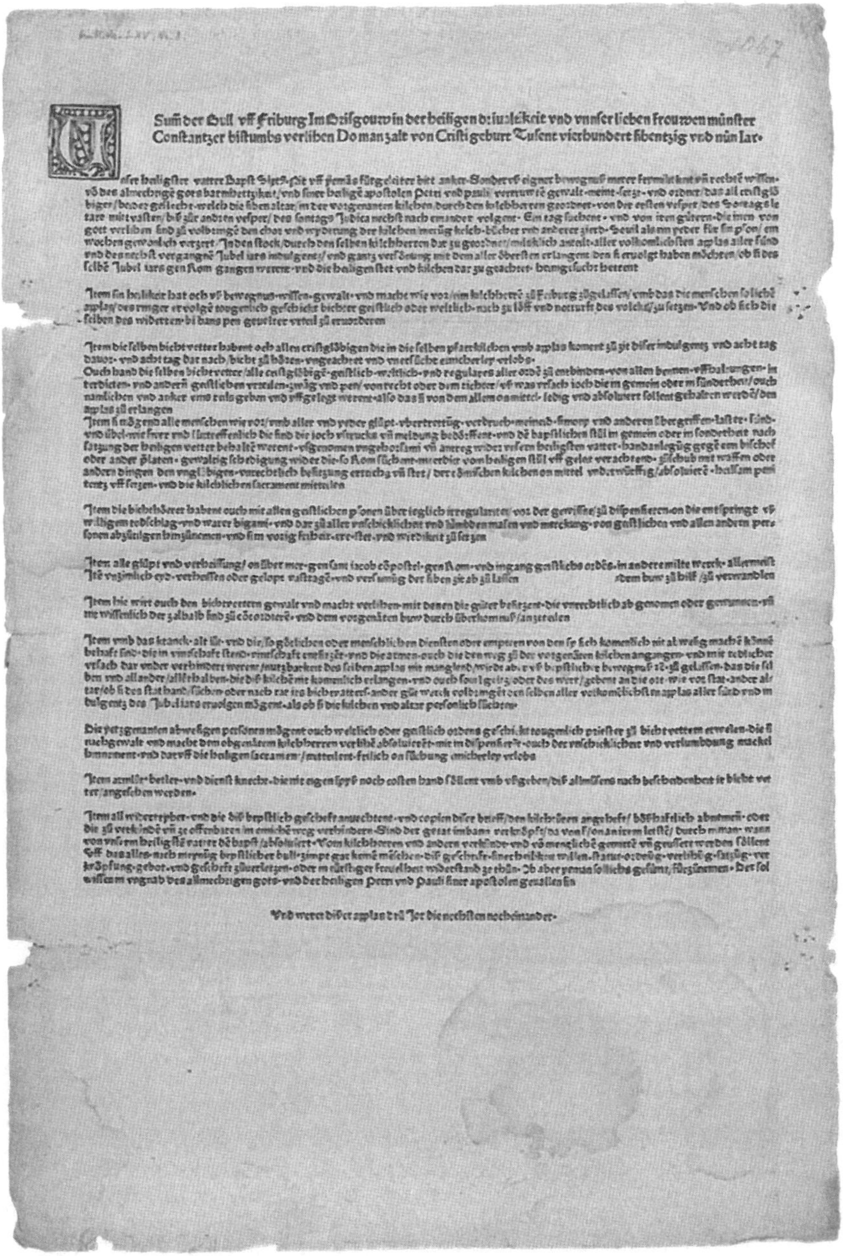
Sum der Bull vff Friburg Im Brisgouw in der heiligen dryualtikeit vnd vnnser lieben frouwen münster Constantzer bistumbs verlihen Do man zalt von Cristi geburt Tusent vierhundert sibentzig vnd nün Jar.

Vnd weret diser applas drü Jor die nechsten nacheinander.

FIGURE 2.4 Sixtus IV, *Letter of indulgences* for Freiburg i. Br. [Michel Wenssler], Basel 1479
COPY: KUNGLIGA BIBILIOTEKET—SVERIGES NATIONALBIBLIOTEK STOCKHOLM, INKUNABEL 1398

FIGURE 2.5   Nicolò de Tudeschi, *Lectura super quinque libros Decretalium* [M. Wenssler, B. Ruppel, B. Richel], Basel 1477
COPY: UNIVERSITÄTSBIBLIOTHEK BASEL, HANDSCHRIFTENMAGAZIN, NP I 4

The conventional character of Wenssler's printing shop is reflected in the way he printed too. Throughout his production he used the *Gotische Bastarde* and never the humanist *antiqua*, introduced in Basel only in 1486 by Johannes Amerbach. These observations apply not only to Wenssler but also to the first generation of printers in general. They were innovative inasmuch as they established a new technology for the production and proliferation of books; but in so doing, they were not necessarily guided by the programmatic ideology of humanist renewal and philological criticism based on the paradigmatic model of classical authors.

Urban Economy, the Landscape of Crafts and Entrepreneurial Skills

Understanding the first age of incunabula less as a profound revolution and more as a process of transformation requires a shift in our analytical framework and a reconsideration of established historiographical narratives. To this end, this chapter shifts attention from the humanists as the presumed protagonists of printing history to focus on economic and societal aspects of production and distribution. The figure of the printer thus appears in a different light: not necessarily a humanist in the idealistic sense of the term but someone who executed a craft and ran a business. This business had several features relatively unfamiliar to medieval craft society. First of all, the craft was fairly new and thus an experienced labour force was not easily or obviously available. Moreover, compared to other crafts of the time printing was characterized by a considerable degree of labour division, which led to a relatively high overhead. Secondly, printing was capital-intensive and marked by a very long return on investment. Indeed, a considerable amount of time would pass between the initial investments in infrastructure, raw material and labour force, and the moment the first books were sold. Finally, for early publishers it was almost impossible to make predictions about market expectations. Local markets normally were quite restricted, whereas trans-regional markets were hard to read; moreover, it was necessary to travel to fairs in order to promote the product.

As mentioned above, printing was not part of the traditional guild system—neither in Basel nor elsewhere. This left considerable room for entrepreneurial initiative, more so than in other industrial sectors that were governed by restrictive guild regulations. Labour division, capital intensity and the "freedom of entrepreneurial initiative" have led some economic historians to consider printing as closely related to the system of sub-contracting work, which in turn challenged the organizational framework of the medieval urban economy. The combination of these aspects has been interpreted as the essential feature of proto-capitalism, with printing seen as one of its biggest catalysts.[17] Such a perspective conveniently integrates printing into a historiographical narrative of modernization that has characterised book history.[18] Although each part of this analysis deserves serious discussion, such a narrative presents an ideological perspective rather than doing justice to the history of early printing. Just as is the case if we overemphasize the relationship between printing and humanism, an exclusive concentration on proto-capitalistic structural development does not illuminate the history of early printing.[19]

For the case of Basel, the exemption of printing from the guild structure proved to be decisive. Its primary importance, however, was not so much that it contributed paradigmatically to economic developments that have been described as proto-capitalist but rather in opening the industry for foreigners. This turned out to be a significant difference in comparison to other crafts organized in guilds open only to citizens. The emerging printing industry in Basel was heavily based on migration; among the early printers only Martin Flach was born in Basel. The others were all immigrants and this remained the dominant model well into the sixteenth century. Between 1470 and 1500, around 70 printing shops were opened in the city—that is a remarkable figure.[20] It can hardly

---

17 The interpretation of late medieval economy as the cradle of capitalism goes back to Werner Sombart's description of symbiosis between capital owners and industrial producers that he observed emerging in the contemporary urban societies. See for a general perspective for example: Hans-Jörg Gilomen, *Wirtschaftsgeschichte des Mittelalters* (Munich: C.H. Beck, 2014), p. 121. For a more recent discussion of the question: Martha C. Howell, *Commerce Before Capitalism in Europe, 1300–1600* (Cambridge: Cambridge University Press, 2010). Specifically for the Basel printing industry see Van der Haegen, *Der frühe Basler Buchdruck*, p. 22.

18 Even Michael Giesecke takes that very same line in his otherwise ground-breaking study on the communicative change of paradigm that went along with printing in early modern times. See Michael Giesecke, *Der Buchdruck in der frühen Neuzeit: eine historische Fallstudie über die Durchsetzung neuer Informations- und Kommunikationstechnologien* (Frankfurt am Main: Suhrkamp, 1991), p. 181.

19 The discourse of innovation is astonishingly dominant for printing and applies equally for intellectual, economic and artisanal aspects. For the latter, however, it is important to remember that printing benefitted from the knowledge of many crafts including xylography, making of almanacs and images of saints that were established branches in urban industries. This emphasizes that printing in its first phase rather integrated and continued knowledge and experts of traditional crafts than ousted them. As a consequence, contemporaries perceived printing not primarily as a revolution or a threat to existing urban professions but rather as a new form within this framework.

20 See Gewerbemuseum Basel (ed.), *Johannes Froben und der Basler Buchdruck des 16. Jahr-*

be explained by the policies of the city council towards foreign printing-experts alone.[21] Another crucial prerequisite for the evolution of print culture was the availability of capital. In the middle of the fifteenth century, Basel was a flourishing city dominated by merchants; thus, private wealth was nothing rare and people were ready to invest capital in new ventures.

For this situation, the case of Michel Wenssler is exemplary. After his arrival from Strasbourg, he teamed up with an associate, Friedrich Biel, for his first enterprise as a printer: the *Epistolae Gasparini*. Although Biel would later become the most eminent German printer in Spain there is no evidence whatsoever that he participated in printing before this—neither in Basel nor anywhere else.[22] As the son of a Basel-based moneychanger, however, he seems to have provided funding for their common undertaking. Within this framework Michel Wenssler made it to the top of the local printing industry. After a modest start in 1472 and 1473, when he released three editions a year, his business took off. In 1474 he produced eight editions, a number he maintained over the following two years. In the first five years of his activity, Wenssler published almost 30 titles. This is an impressive output, and it seems to have paid off. In 1475 his fortune is recorded in the city's tax list at a staggering 1,400 guilders, a sum that positions him among the wealthiest citizens of his time.[23] For the following years up to 1480, Wenssler maintains an impressive presence in the city's

---

hunderts. *Ausstellung im Gewerbemuseum Basel aus Anlass der 500-Jahrfeier der Universität Basel 19. Juni bis 24. Juli 1960* (Basel: Schwabe, 1960), p. 60.

21   For a general overview of the magistrate's policy towards printers see Rudolf Wackernagel, *Geschichte der Stadt Basel* (4 vols., Berlin: Weidmann'sche Buchhandlung, 1907–1924), II, part 2, pp. 603–618.

22   Josef Benzing, 'Biel, Friedrich', in *Neue Deutsche Biographie* (25 vols., Berlin: Duncker & Humboldt, 1971–2013), II, 225. Carlos Gilly, 'Fadrique de Basilea (Friedrich Biel)', in *Historisches Lexikon der Schweiz* (13 vols., Basel: Schwabe, 2002–2014) [henceforth *HLS*], II, 59 or see online http://www.hls-dhs-dss.ch/textes/d/D42843.php, last accessed on 4 May 2016. Ferdinand Geldner, 'Die deutschen Inkunabeldrucker. Ein Handbuch der deutschen Buchdrucker des XV. Jahrhunderts nach Druckorten' (2 vols., Stuttgart: 1968–1970), I, 109–111; II, 297–301.

23   StABS, Steuern B19, Margzal St. Alban 1475/1476. The entry reads clearly a taxable estate of 1,400 [Rhenish guilders] and a tax amount of 5 lb. 8 ß. Nevertheless, in scholarship Wenssler's wealth is repeatedly reported to be 1,700 Rhenisch guilders; this assumption, advanced for instance by Piccard, is based on the tax amount paid by Wenssler from which Piccard extrapolates a taxable estate of 1,700 Rhenish guilder because it seems to be overproportional compared to other entries, for instance to Hans von Hall who for the same year paid 2 lb. 6 ß for a taxable estate of 1,000 Rhenish guilder; this however alters the palaeographic finding and excludes the possibility of a progressive taxation system. See Gerhard Piccard, *Papiererzeugung und Buchdruck*, p. 212.

tax lists even if his payments decrease marginally: 1,600 fl. in 1477/1478, 1,200 fl. (?) in 1478/1479[24] and 1,000 fl. in each of the years 1479/1480 and 1480/1481.

Counting the editions Wenssler published each year might give an impression of his activity but it does not offer a solid analytical base. In order to understand how Wenssler ran his workshop and what economic choices he made, the broad scope of his output must be taken into account. To print a letter of indulgence or a legal commentary were two very different things. In what follows I propose a model that allows for a quantitative perspective of the workshop's activity over almost twenty years.[25] As in all economic or scientific models, complexity needs to be reduced and uncertainties neglected in order to gain an analytical perspective. It goes, therefore, without saying that these figures give just approximate values. In the model, two assumptions had to be made. Firstly, in order to integrate the different formats of printed books in an overview perspective, the sheet has been assumed as a standard measure of all the printed matter.[26] Secondly, since in Wenssler's case we have no information on how many copies of each edition were published, the model relies exclusively on this standard measure of the size of each project.[27]

---

24   This entry is only partially readable for an inkspot. See StABS Steuern B19, Margzal St. Alban 1478/1479.

25   This approach includes an understanding of what has survived from Wenssler's overall printing production. The number of surviving copies of one edition is usually quite a reliable indicator for the "survival" of a workshop's original editions. In Wenssler's case a fair share of his editions does survive in a considerable number of copies. Thus, it could be argued that the 167 surviving editions recorded in the GW represent a number quite close to his entire production.

26   The model is auxiliary. Whereas it might offer a reasonable base for the paper needed in the workshop it does not do so with regard to the amount of time spent setting up pages of different formats and serves therefore at best for an approximate estimate of labour. Nevertheless, the model is appropriate in terms of cost sensitivity since in late medieval economy costs of material were generally higher than those of labour.

27   Occasionally we do have information about print runs, but not for Wenssler, unless we extrapolate from the numbers of surviving copies which, however, provides only indirect and by necessity inaccurate evidence. For early printing scholarship generally assumes a figure between 100 and 300 copies. See for example: Reinhard Wittmann, *Geschichte des deutschen Buchhandels* (Munich: C.H. Beck, 1991), p. 27. The calculation for the model is based on Wenssler's prints listed in the Gesamtkatalog der Wiegendrucke (GW) as the most complete collection of his work and follows the publication dates determined there. The latter are frequently uncertain and based on indirect information as hand-written notes, stylistic estimation of types etc. The model contains many blurs; among others it computationally underestimates the role of "cheap printing" (single sheets, broadsheet, letter of indulgences) in comparison to printed books. Moreover, the corpus of data is by necessity incomplete; from the 167 prints that the GW attributes to Wenssler's Basel workshop 17 are not datable, as often the case in early incunabula printing. Because of the lack

EARLY BOOK PRINTING AND VENTURE CAPITAL IN THE AGE OF DEBT

The diagram obtained from such an approach shows Wenssler's overall printing output between 1472 and 1491. We can clearly observe that after a rather modest start the workshop's activity exploded. While he printed around 190 sheets in his first two years, production skyrocketed to an impressive 775 sheets in 1474 and 1475. After a slight downturn in 1476, Wenssler printed at this production level, and even raised his output in the next two years to almost 1,000 and 925 sheets respectively. Assuming a very modest average of 150 copies of each edition and 280 working days a year in these years Wenssler's shop printed between 305 (1476), 400 (1474/75), over 500 (1477) and around 480 (1478) sheets every day.[28] These are rather remarkable figures for this time. Both the number of edited works and the quantity of printed sheets exceeded the production of all other Basel workshops, by far. It is obvious that an appropriate infrastructure was required: at least two, maybe three or even more printing presses were necessary to allow for such an output. If we consider labour division in the early printing industry, Wenssler appears to have been the head of a sizeable workshop, employing twenty or more assistants and employees. Based on the so called *Schillingsteuer*, a tax applied to wide sections and all strata of the urban population, it has been calculated that Wenssler's workshop had twice if not three times as many employees as that of Berthold Ruppel, for instance.[29] In the light of these figures, we have to think of Wenssler's workshop as the biggest publishing house in the city. It therefore comes as no surprise that Wenssler moved his workshop to a new location, the impressive *Haus zem Lufft*, in 1479, after years of dynamic printing activity (Figure 2.6).[30]

---

of such information, integrating them in the corpus of data would lead to untenable assertions; hence, the decision to leave them out albeit they sum up to considerable printing production. The sheets of the un-datable prints aggregate to an amount of 1235, most of them ecclesiastical prints such as several *breviaria, missalia* or *vigilia defunctorum*.

28   Included in this figure are a few assumptions worth discussing. The assumption, for instance, that all sheets of a book are printed in the year the book came out is neither compelling nor particularly convincing. Taking such aspects into consideration would affect the figure in the same way, namely flattening or smoothening it. The dispersion of the almost 1250 sheets from the not datable prints over the twenty years of Wenssler's printing activity (additional 60 sheets per year) would equally alter the figure. However, these considerations do not affect the overall statement of this chapter. It does not rely on sharp ups and downs or peaks in the figure for the conclusions it draws.

29   Based on the amount of tax paid by 'Michel der trucker' Piccard assumed that he employed more than 21 assistants, in 1479/1480 even a maximum of 29. See Piccard, *Papiererzeugung und Buchdruck*, pp. 204 and 213. Unfortunately, this series of tax lists (*Schillingsteuer*) has not survived for St. Alban, the parish Wenssler used to live in, for the years of Wenssler's hyper-production in 1485, 1486 and 1488.

30   StABS, Gerichtsarchiv B 10, 27 April 1479.

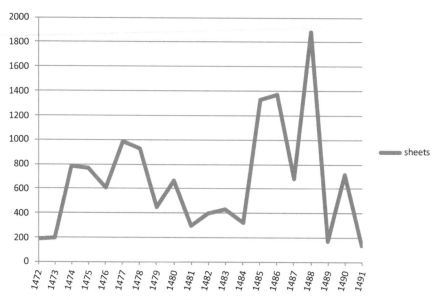

FIGURE 2.6 Overall printing output of Michel Wenssler's workshop
BASED ON THE *GW*

Early printing, however, was a volatile business; many factors influenced its course. Pursuing the workshop's printing activity, we can observe different, yet contradictory developments including a slight decrease, erratic increase, collapse and recovery. All through this entrepreneurial turmoil, Wenssler always continued printing.[31] The development of the following five years is hard to read; overheated hyper-production is twice interrupted by a dramatic collapse.

It is hard to imagine how a printing workshop could materially print in such quantities. In 1485 the output aggregate of 1,300 sheets that year and—applying the above made assumptions of 150 copies and 280 working days—more than 700 printed sheets every day—how was this possible? The questions also arise because in the following years this output was even exceeded; in 1486 it amounted to 1,375 sheets a year corresponding to an estimate of 775 sheets every day, in 1488 even to 2,020 sheets a year and 1,080 sheets every day. We simply have no idea how Wenssler could have organised such a production. It seems more than reasonable to assume that he co-operated with other printers. In the early years Wenssler repeatedly collaborated with other printers, mainly

---

31   It must be added that eight of eleven single sheet imprints that have survived from the workshop were published exactly in these years but do not find their adequate way into the quantitative analysis that records only sheets but not printed sheets. So, the intensified printing of single sheets would actually smooth out at least partially the decrease in these years.

Berthold Ruppel and Bernhard Richel but between 1479 and 1488 we do not have much evidence of this.[32]

Growth and increasing output, however, were by no means the strategy all printers of the first generation pursued. Early printing still had to be established and integrated into urban industry and economy and, different models seem to have been followed.[33] Ruppel and Richel published less than their transient associate master Michel; for Berthold Ruppel the GW records 29 editions published between 1468 and 1480, for Bernhard Richel 49 editions for the years between 1471 and 1486.[34] For the whole incunabula age very diverse business models co-existed in Basel and beyond. These encompassed both large workshops with more than one printing press as well as jobbing printers like Lienhart Ysenhut, for whom we only have 23 known editions from 1480 to 1500. These observations suggest that we need to reconsider our understanding of how early printing as an industry was organised. As indicated above, Wenssler was most probably able to produce such an output only by gathering know-how, a labour force and infrastructure from beyond his own workshop. Given both the high overhead cost of setting up a printing press and the time pressure under which the industry operated suggests that the early printing industry was regularly organised collaboratively between several workshops. Although we have very little direct evidence for any such kind of organizational structure of the printing industry in Basel, it could at least help to understand the inconsistent career of a printer such as Michel Wenssler.

The evidence advanced so far suggests that early printing was organized by workshops that needed to rely on co-operation far more than has been assumed by scholars. This was motivated by economic considerations in a double sense. Firstly, printers needed to produce large amounts of printed matter in a very short time in order to satisfy market demand. Secondly, the high overhead costs of the printing industry and the need to capitalize these costs prompted printers to publish not only in their own name but to work on editions of other workshops as well. Given the lack of circulating currency in late medieval society, we can even assume that these mutual services were not nec-

---

32   In these years Wenssler only printed two works in cooperation with other printers: St Augustine's *De civitate Dei* with Richel, and Roberto Caracciolo's *Sermones* with Ruppel, both published in 1479.

33   See Ursula Rautenberg, 'Buchhändlerische Organisationsformen in der Inkunabel- und Frühdruckzeit', in Vorstand der Maximilian-Gesellschaft and Barbara Tiemann (eds.), *Die Buchkultur des 15. und 16. Jahrhunderts* (Hamburg: Maximilian-Gesellschaft, 1999), pp. 339–376. For Basel see van der Haegen, *Der frühe Basler Buchdruck*, p. 58 and following.

34   The attribution to Ruppel of editions dating from the late 1480s that the GW proposes is based on indirect evidence.

essarily paid for in money, but through some form of barter or credit/debit economy. Moreover, considering the size of the industry it seems plausible that in most cases this sort of collaboration between printing workshops might have occurred without leaving any traces in written sources—neither in the printed books nor in the workshop's account books from this period.

This chapter argues that casual printing for other workshops was essential in order to keep the workshop running. This economic back-coupling not only underpinned the business model of the early printing industry but affected its cultural impact. This socio-economic entanglement reinforced the traditional and conventional character of most of the workshop's output; it solidified bonds between printers, and shaped a cultural dynamic characterised by entrepreneurial spirit, artisanal expertise and a decent education including a fair knowledge of Latin. An industry so deeply embedded in such a social strata and a dynamic economic setting was not primarily inspired by an agenda that followed the preferences of humanism (and humanists). Instead, what the printing industry and humanism shared was the interest in and the capability to circulate not only more texts but more accurate texts.

Cultural Innovation and the Debt Economy

The activity of Wenssler's workshop was ultimately characterised not only by its impressive output but also by the dramatic collapses that occurred in 1487 and 1489. It is difficult to draw unambiguous conclusions from this observation. Yet, the short-term fluctuation in business underlines, once again, the volatility and insecurities that characterized the early printing industry. Insecurity, however, not only refers to production and market expectation but also affected the way printing had been financed. Scholarship has repeatedly emphasized that printing was capital intensive and marked by a very long return on investment. Thus, printers depended heavily on investors. In consequence, opening up a printing shop in the fifteenth century was first of all a matter of financing.[35]

Print shops obtained this capital in three main ways. First, the printer himself had sufficient spending power, in other words the enterprise was based on equity capital; in early printing this scenario was rather exceptional. The easiest access to money in late medieval societies was through professional moneylending. However, this business, often executed by Jews, was not only

---

35 For a general perspective see for instance Carl Wehmer, 'Zur Beurteilung des Methodenstreits in der Inkunabelkunde', *Gutenberg Jahrbuch*, 8 (1933), pp. 250–325: 278. For Basel see Piccard, *Papiererzeugung und Buchdruck*, pp. 25–322, a study somewhat outdated but still rich in material.

morally precarious but also very expensive because interest rates were high. The third option was for printers and investors to undertake printing tasks as a joint venture, whereby the enterprise was based on debt capital. This model would become the most common in early printing; the prerequisite here, however, was the availability of ample investment capital.[36]

These observations apply to Basel in general and to Michel Wenssler in particular. Late medieval Basel was economically characterized by commerce. The city's merchants were organised in three guilds, the so-called *Herrenzünfte* (*Safran, Schlüssel, Hausgenossen*) that were involved in trading a wide range of goods and commodities as well as banking and finance. From the beginning of the fifteenth century, members of these guilds started also to function as corporative trading societies putting together large capital and expanding their business activities to most of Western and Central Europe.[37] It is generally acknowledged that Basel was a wealthy city due to commerce and was a place where private investment capital was readily available. In the course of the 1470s, merchants resident in Basel discovered printing as an attractive field of investment. Merchants involved financially in incunabula printing included well-known names in the city's trade history such as Andreas Bischoff, Ulrich Meltinger, Ludwig Zschekapürlin, Konrad and Heinrich David as well as Jakob von Kilchen or Jakob Steinacher.[38]

Michel Wenssler seems to have run his business from the beginning based on debt capital. The written evidence provided by various offices of the city's civil jurisdiction offers us a better understanding of how a printing workshop was actually run in the 1470s and 1480s.[39] Indeed, already for the period of his

---

36   See Severin Corsten, 'Der frühe Buchdruck und die Stadt', in Ludger Grenzmann, Bernd Moeller, Hans Patze and Karl Stackmann (eds.), *Studien zum städtischen Bildungswesen des späten Mittelalters und der frühen Neuzeit* (Göttingen: Vandenhoeck & Ruprecht, 1983), pp. 123–148.

37   In general see Franz Ehrensperger, *Basels Stellung im internationalen Handelsverkehr des Spätmittelalters*. Martin Illi, 'Handelsgesellschaften', in HLS VI, pp. 88–89. Stefan Hess, 'Halbisen-Gesellschaft', in HLS VI, pp. 48–49. Matthias Steinbrink, *Ulrich Meltinger. Ein Basler Kaufmann am Ende des 15. Jahrhunderts* (Stuttgart: Steiner, 2007). Steinbrink's study on Ulrich Meltinger gives a very good impression of the versatility of these merchants active on very different fields of trade and investment.

38   For this group of merchant bankers see Paul Koelner, *Die Zunft zum Schlüssel in Basel* (Basel: B. Schwabe, 1953), *passim*. Moreover Mario Sabatino, 'Bischoff, Andreas', in HLS II, p. 462. Steinbrink, *Ulrich Meltinger. passim*. Bischoff, Zschekapürlin and Meltinger were associates in the so-called "Grosse Gesellschaft", a trading consortium active from 1481 until 1495 when the city council in Basel prohibited this kind of business associations. Steinbrink, *Ulrich Meltinger*, p. 184.

39   In the 1880s Karl Stehlin published registers from the archives that report all cases from the

first enterprise, the *Epistolae Gasparini*, he is mentioned in the so-called *Vergichtbücher*, a register of the civil jurisdiction that recorded payment bonds. On 7 December he promised together with his associate in the edition, Friedrich Biel, to pay the sum of one pound less one shilling [i.e. 19 ß] to the carpenter Michel Schmid. Two days later he admitted another debt towards the same carpenter of 2 lb $5^{1/2}$ ß [i.e. $45^{1/2}$ ß]; both returns may have settled the carpenter's service in assembling the printing press.[40] Where this example refers to payments for services provided, other payment bonds clearly verify that Wenssler ran his workshop on a basis of debt capital. Before 1490 Jacob Steinacher advanced the amount of 200 fl. with which Wenssler bought 30 bales of paper. Shortly after Steinacher provided Wenssler with another 150 fl. in order to print "etlich Brevier".[41] In the case of Wenssler there is evidence that financiers decided to invest in the workshop from the mid-1470s at the latest and the printer's dependency on such investments is obvious. In fact, all of the abovementioned merchants were not only involved in the city's printing industry in general, but in one way or another specifically in the funding of Wenssler's workshop.

It must be taken into consideration, however, that the written evidence that demonstrates Wenssler's career as a debtor from the very beginning of his activity as a printer does not give us a complete picture of actual economic practices. Sources such as *Vergichtbücher* do not mark the beginning of a credit relation but the moment at which repayment was long overdue. Once recorded, the debtor promised to refund his creditor within one month. Thus, the processes that are documented in the *Vergichtbücher* reveal the magistrates' readiness to mediate between creditor and debtor in a low-threshold manner; as long as the settlements were agreed consensually, their services were free of charge. Beyond the *Vergichtbücher* the Basel civil jurisdiction provided other different procedures to regulate credit relations and to collect debts. In all this documentation, much attention is paid to provisions stating how active debts were to be

---

city's civil jurisdiction in which printers were involved. This collection is a unique hoard of information for a socio-economic analysis of early printing. Nevertheless, it never has been exploited systematically. See Karl Stehlin, *Regesten zur Geschichte des Buchdrucks bis zum Jahre 1500* (3 vols., Basel: B.G. Teubner, 1887–1888).

40   Late medieval Basel had basically a silver currency system similar to the existing English one including pound, shilling and pence [1 lb. = 20 ß; 1 ß = 12 p]. Additionally, a gold currency known as Rhenish guilders circulated or at least was used for calculation; towards the end of the fifteenth century 1 fl equalled to between 23 and 25 ß. From an entry in the *Vergichtbuch* involving Wenssler (January 1486) we know that 1 fl equalled to 25 ß. See StABS, Gerichtsarchiv C 13, 24 January 1486. On the currency system of late medieval Basel in all its details see Geering, *Handel und Industrie der Stadt Basel*, p. xxiii.

41   StABS, Gerichtsarchiv C 14, 6 February and 17 February 1490.

paid back.⁴² Nevertheless, all these sources document only a small fraction of the credit relations that had actually been established; more specifically, they only document that fraction that was in danger of failing as an economic practice. In other words, they are only the tip of the iceberg. Most credit agreements never made it to court because they worked smoothly and by consequence left no traces in juridical sources.⁴³ As a general rule, working credit relations were written down on informal slips of paper if at all, or found their way into private account books; as long as debts were paid there was no reason for the authorities to intervene. Research on cities like Marseille or Nuremberg has shown that no other issue kept late medieval civil jurisdiction busier than debt.⁴⁴ With all due respect towards quantitative analysis, there is strong evidence that debts shaped both the late medieval urban economy as well as everyday life.⁴⁵ In this sense, Michel Wenssler and his steady presence in court are representative of the late medieval urban economy and particularly telling for how the debt economy is essential in understanding how he ran his printing workshop.

Debts and loans have always been a part of any economy grounded in the exchange of goods.⁴⁶ Recent historical research has emphasized, however, that credit relations did not merely encompass economic exchange. In their pioneering studies Craig Muldrew, Laurence Fontaine, Jürgen Schlumbohm and others have highlighted the social and cultural aspects that distinguished debt economies in the pre-modern period.⁴⁷ In his work on Ulrich Meltinger and his account book, Matthias Steinbrink has shown convincingly that Basel was,

---

42   For civil jurisdiction in late medieval Basel see Hans-Rudolf Hagemann, *Basler Rechtsleben im Mittelalter* (2 vols., Basel and Frankfurt am Main: Helbing und Lichtenhahn, 1981–1987), II, Zivilrechtspflege.

43   Hans-Jörg Gilomen, 'Der Kleinkredit in spätmittelalterlichen Städten. Basel und Zürich im Vergleich', in Rudolf Hobach and Michel Pauly (eds.), *Städtische Wirtschaft im Mittelalter. Festschrift für Franz Irsigler zum 70. Geburtstag* (Cologne: Böhlau, 2011), pp. 109–148: 109.

44   Daniel Lord Smail, *The Consumption of Justice. Emotion, Publicity and Legal Culture in Marseille, 1264–1423* (Ithaca: Cornell University Press, 2003). Valentin Groebner, *Ökonomie ohne Haus. Zum Wirtschaften armer Leute in Nürnberg am Ende des 15. Jahrhunderts* (Göttingen: Vandenhoeck & Ruprecht, 1993).

45   Peter Schuster, 'The Age of Debt? Private Schulden in der spätmittelalterlichen Gesellschaft', in Gabriele B. Clemens (ed.), *Schuldenlast und Schuldenwert. Kreditnetzwerke in der europäischen Geschichte 1300–1900* [Trierer Historische Forschungen 65] (Trier: Kliomedia, 2008), pp. 37–52.

46   David Graeber, *Debt. The first 5000 years* (New York: Melville House, 2011).

47   Craig Muldrew, *The Economy of Obligation. The Culture of Credit and Social Relations in Early Modern England* (Basingstoke: Macmillan, 1998). Laurence Fontaine, 'Espaces, usages et dynamiques de la dette dans les hautes vallées dauphinoises (XVIIe–XVIIIe siècles)', *Annales: Histoires, Sciences Sociales*, 49 (1994), pp. 1375–1391. Jürgen Schlumbohm, *Soziale Praxis des Kredits: 16. bis 20. Jahrhundert* (Hannover: Hahn, 2007).

so to speak, a paradigmatic case. "Being indebted means to depend on people but at the same time to be included in a system of relations that was economically vital for both debtors and creditors".[48] This kind of research owes much to the analysis of juridical sources such as those studied in this chapter. It has been convincingly argued, however, that debts must be dissociated from a clear notion of poverty or of lower social rank. Debts were rather a way to cope with a lack of cash in an economic system that was structurally characterized by tight money. Thus, written sources suggest that all strata of society were involved in the debt economy.[49] Moreover, in an economic system based on debts there was no stable distinction of roles either: creditors were at the same time debtors themselves and the other way around.[50] In fact, against this backdrop Wenssler appears as a typical model of late medieval urban industry and its financial and economic practices. At least for a certain time he must be numbered among the wealthiest citizens of late medieval Basel even though he was constantly indebted and involved in a debt network of numerous "credit chains". At the same time, he was also a creditor. At the beginning of 1486 two couples, Frydlin Hirsinger and his wife Elsin together with Adam von Spir and his wife Margret, admitted to being in Michel Wenssler's debt for 200 fl. because the printer had bought paper for them. The debtors promised to pay the money back before the following Frankfurt book fair.[51]

In the printing industry, the debt economy was not limited to investments by wealthy merchants or the delay in paying for services, but provided the underlying financial structure for the industry as a whole. Indeed, those who took part in the industry recognized debt to be an integral part of it. Master Michel was repeatedly reported to the city's officials because he owed his workers their wages. This could be explained by a temporary shortage of cash, though it has been argued that debts were also very effective devices to retain expertise and know-how; as long as a master was indebted to his employees they would not leave the workshop. In April 1486, Jacob Lemplin from Strasbourg reported that he had not been paid his wages.[52] In November 1487, four assistant printers filed a lawsuit in which they accused Wenssler as their

---

48   Steinbrink, *Ulrich Meltinger*, p. 92.
49   For the nobility in particular see Joseph Morsel, 'Adel in Armut—Armut im Adel? Beobachtungen zur Situation des Adels im Spätmittelalter', in Otto Gerhard Oexle (ed.), *Armut im Mittelalter* (Ostfildern: Thorbecke, 2004), pp. 127–164.
50   For the changing roles of creditors and debtors in general see Elaine Clark, 'Debt litigation in late medieval English Vill', in James A. Raftis (ed.), *Pathways to English Medieval Peasants* (Toronto: Pontifical Institute of mediaeval studies, 1981), pp. 247–279: 268.
51   StABS, Gerichtsarchiv C 14, 12 January 1486.
52   StABS, Gerichtsarchiv A 35, 12 April 1486.

former master of having prevented them from working for other printers; in consequence they suffered a loss, which they now claimed from Wenssler.[53] From what we know of Wenssler's business performance, these claims were asserted when the workshop still operated successfully. Finally, when the workshop was already starting to decline, a group of at least 13 printers, typesetters and proof-readers of master Michel lodged a complaint with the court's officials demanding payment of outstanding wages in fairly small amounts such as 2 ß (Peter Narr) to 7 or 10 fl. (Master Ludwig von Elchingen, Ulrich Brobstlin).[54]

Handling debts, however, was not a mere competence of debtors but equally of creditors. Basel's wealthy merchants quite naturally calculated debts and distributed them like commodities. We learn from an entry of the city's *Urteilsbücher*, in which the civil court's sentences were recorded, that Wenssler sold to a certain Conrat Gylgenstein, called Hablützel, 600 divine offices according the Utrecht liturgical calendar (*breviaria*) for 400 fl. Half of the money was paid in cash, while for the other half Gylgenstein accepted a responsibility for a debt Wenssler owed Barbara Bischöffin, the widow of the merchant Andreas Bischoff.[55] The authorities not only acknowledged this commerce of credit but took part in it themselves. In June 1490 it has been decided that Jacob Steinacher, the workshop's main creditor, had to pay the wages of the workshop's employees because he held as a mortgage several editions printed by them. As was customary, they deserved to be paid immediately for their work and the court referring to the "Lidlon's Recht" assigned that obligation to the owner of the books. For his own claims (he held the books as a mortgage for outstanding debts), the court argued, he had to lodge a complaint against Wenssler.[56] Although the court was perfectly capable of using wages, commodities and credit as different sorts of capital, a higher juridical priority was attached, at least in this case, to work rather than to credit.

As much as credit—from small payday loans to capital investments—was widely diffused in the late medieval urban economy in general and in the printing industry in particular, and as much as we can only presume what fraction of that is documented in written evidence, we know that the debt economy was no guarantee for economic success. In what follows, Wenssler's debt econ-

---

53 StABS, Gerichtsarchiv A 36, 28 November 1487.
54 StABS, Gerichtsarchiv C 14, 5 June 1490.
55 StABS, Gerichtsarchiv A 35, 1 June 1486.
56 *Lidlon* means the wage of servants and day labourers. See *Schweizerisches Idiotikon. Wörterbuch der Schweizerischen Sprache* (17 vols., Basel: Schwabe, 1881–2015), III, col. 1288.

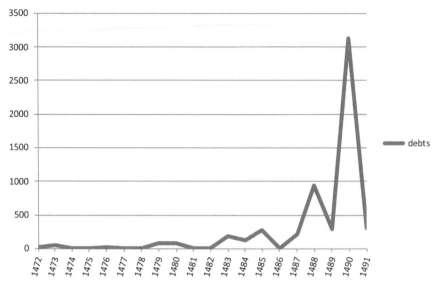

FIGURE 2.7 Progression of Michel Wenssler's debts from 1472 to 1491
BASED ON *VERGICHTBÜCHER*

omy will be analysed on the basis of the cases in which repayments were not made within due terms and therefore were documented in the *Vergichtbücher*. As mentioned above, debts were part of the workshop's economy from its very beginning in 1472. This system seems to have worked fine for more than fifteen years, since master Michel managed to keep debts fairly low and make necessary repayments.

By the mid-1480s Wenssler's debt had grown very significantly. In 1484 he owed money to two well-known merchant bankers, Ludwig Zschekabürlin (160 lb.) and Jacob Steinacher (64 fl.), who repeatedly operated as his creditors; additionally, Wenssler promised to refund 44 fl. to a certain Jacob Eichelberg.[57] The following year, debts recorded increased considerably adding up to almost 300 lb. from five different creditors, with the single loans ranging from 2.5 ß owed to a carpenter for services provided to 178 fl. By collecting debts due to him in 1486, Wenssler seems to have restored the balance in his personal debt economy. In that year, the printer was called upon only once to pay back a debt, a very small one of only 30 ß.[58] As a consequence, in 1487 accounting seems to have been pretty much under control. This was not to last: claims recorded in the *Vergichtbücher* in the following year climbed to a remarkable 1,000 lb. Although master

---

57 StABS, Gerichtsarchiv C 13, 6 May, 25 August and, 20 October 1484.
58 StABS, Gerichtsarchiv C 13, 31 July 1486.

Michel somehow managed to reduce debt the following year to around 300 lb., bankruptcy seems to have been inevitable in 1490. On 8 February Wenssler promised to pay back a credit of 460 fl. he had obtained from his main banker, Jacob Steinacher.[59] Two weeks later he arranged that the costs of a *breviarium* he was able to print only thanks to another down payment of 200 fl. would be set against the sum of 660 fl. he still owed Steinacher.[60] Under such financial pressure, and in order to keep his workshop running, Wenssler sold his printing tools for 253 fl. to his main creditor.[61] The very same day he and his wife liquidated another debt of 200 guilders by handing over several female garments.[62] Wenssler had to draw on his private wealth and his wife's personal adornments in order to keep his main creditor at bay. Deprived of his means of production, however, a happy ending for Wenssler became less and less probable.

From Wenssler's downfall we learn how much the debt economy was based on trust, and how quickly trust was lost. Whereas Wenssler's main creditor Steinacher tried to make the best of a bad job still hoping for things to turn out well, other creditors had already lost their faith in the city's most prolific printer.[63] Already in March Ulrich Meltinger and Hans Fünffinger from Laufenburg claimed Wenssler's house as a warrant for an unspecified loan.[64] From this point on Wenssler could no longer stop the downward spiral of debt, not even by using new loans to pay back older ones. Whereas Wenssler was still able to seek out new creditors in 1489 and 1490, the claim to confiscate parts of his estate became the starting signal for a general withdrawal of capital invested. In consequence, the surviving sources are now no longer from the

---

59   StABS, Gerichtsarchiv C 14, 8 February 1490.
60   StABS, Gerichtsarchiv C 14, 17 February 1490.
61   StABS, Gerichtsarchiv C 14, 18 March 1490. The original reads: "[…] allen und yegklichen werckzlig und truckgeschirr, es syent bressen, ramen, formen und sust, mit aller zugchörd, alle sin ußbereitt geschrifften, klein und groß, matrices und alle annder bereittschaft und Verckzüg so der druckereye gehört […]"; this translates as: "[…] all and any printing tools and devices, presses, frames, forms, and everything else belonging to the craft, including the fonts, small and big, matrix and all other tools and instruments that belonged to the workshop … […]".
62   StABS, Gerichtsarchiv C 14, fol. 48v. Several entries in the *Vergichtbücher* record debts Wenssler had towards tailors and dressmakers. The amount of these debts were considerable as for instance in 1485 when he owed 50 fl. to Hanss Stehelin, Gewantmann. See StABS, Gerichtsarchiv C 13, 26 December 1485.
63   For a discussion of how quickly people became credit unworthy or uncredit worthy see Evelyn Welch, *Shopping in the Renaissance. Consumer Cultures in Italy 1400–1600* (New Haven and London: Yale University Press, 2005), pp. 231–235.
64   StABS, Gerichtsarchiv C 14, 23 March 1490.

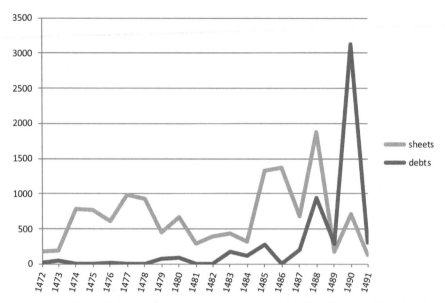

FIGURE 2.8   Aggregated view of progression of output and debts (lb) of Wenssler's Basel workshop between 1472 and 1491

Vergichtbücher but from the testimonies (*Kundschaften*), sentences (*Urteilsbücher*), executions (*Verbotsbuch*) and drafts of charters (*Liber diversorum*). This suggests that the most important part of Wenssler's ability to do business, the trust in his credit-worthiness, had disintegrated, and the printing activity in Basel that was based from its beginning on his credibility was designed to end. Against this backdrop, it is no surprise that Wenssler decided to flee the city along with anything that might be useful for him as a printer in the future.

Humanism, Printing and Historical Change

This concludes our story of the fortunes and misfortunes of a Basel printer and his workshop in the incunabula age. They follow his steep rise, his activity as the most prolific among all printers, but also his financial downfall around 1490. They are, however, of more far-reaching importance insofar that they illuminate not only an individual case but highlight the social, economic and cultural framework of early printing in one of the most important centres of this recently established industry.

The evidence analysed in this case sheds particular light on how printers of the first generation decided what to print. It has been argued that the works that Wenssler and his colleagues chose to print were generally rather conventional and satisfied demand in two conservative domains of book consumption: the Church and the education industry in both Latin schools and universities. As an industry, printing was highly capital intensive and a master printer was therefore in most cases dependent on financiers. As an important commercial centre, located at the crossroads of commerce routes in late medieval Europe, Basel offered wealthy merchants the opportunity to invest in an emerging new technology such as printing. Wenssler's case illustrates very well early printing's basic economic structure as an industry primarily financed by debt capital. From the very beginning, master Michel relied on borrowed capital to keep his workshop running in a debt economy. What has survived as written evidence of this economic practice, however, shows only the tip of the iceberg; in most cases, relationships between creditors and debtors worked well and therefore left no traces in the legal sources of civil jurisdiction. It is striking that Wenssler, the city's most productive printer, is continuously recorded in the *Vergichtbücher*. Regardless of the vicissitudes in running his workshop, he repeatedly appeared before the city's courts and offices to promise the imminent repayment of money owed. The evidence suggests strongly that printers in the age of incunabula had to test everybody's patience, customers, investors, and suppliers as well as employees, in order to have sufficient credit to carry on printing. In other words, printing was based on debt capital and a system of mutual trust that organized not only economic production but also social encounter. Michel Wenssler probably belonged to the most successful printers of his time because he mastered well this juggling act between making profit and hazarding ruin for almost twenty years.

The early printing industry was a gamble where losing one's fortune could always be a possibility, as was the case for master Michel: he went bankrupt in 1491. The cause of his downfall is significant though; taking out new loans to pay back old ones and thus accumulating more and more debts, his creditors lost faith in the workshop's economic solidity and capacity to earn money. Once the capital of trust was of doubtful value, the adverse dynamic could not be halted; most creditors tried to withdraw their investments and commenced legal proceedings to confiscate the tools of Wenssler's trade, accelerating the economic ruin of the workshop. Only Jacob Steinacher, the main creditor and therefore the person who bore the biggest risk, tried to act differently in order to save his capital. His conduct clearly documents how people in 1490 Basel thought one could make money with printing.

In March 1490, master Michel transferred his printing tools to Steinacher in order to liquidate a debt of 253 fl. to his creditor. As a matter of fact, from this moment on, the banker owned the means of production and the master printer had become his employee. This shift of property seems to find an immediate

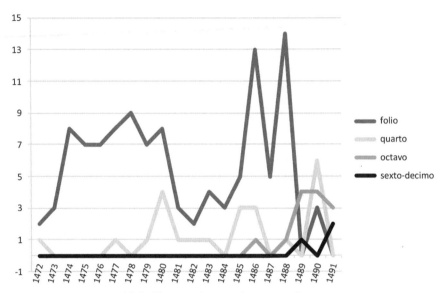

FIGURE 2.9 Imprints published by Wenssler according to page format

echo in what books the workshop printed and what they looked like. Whereas most of the publications that left Wenssler's workshop between 1472 and 1489 were in folio format, the books printed in 1490 and 1491 were in the smaller quarto, octavo and even sexto-decimo formats. From the 18 books that can be dated to these years, only three were still in folio. Size alone, however, was not decisive for the question whether printing was profitable or not. More important was the ability to sell the product—or at least these expectations were reflected in the decisions taken as to what should be printed. In fact, we observe a remarkable shift in Wenssler's output since his debts increased in 1487. From the 43 imprints dated 1487 or later, the vast majority (34) were liturgical books including *breviaria, missalia, gradualia* and *antiphonaria* for different dioceses and churches; a small number (4) were concerned with standard grammar education, legal studies (2) or recreational literature (3). This shift continued and even accentuated when Wenssler printed in Steinacher's service (*Gedinge*). From this, it is obvious that in moments of deep crisis the workshop shifted production to those books that promised to yield most profit while creating the smallest risk. These books were mostly small in size, largely liturgical texts intended for the most reliable customer for early printed books: the Church.

The promise and perhaps the hope that traditional historiography believed to recognize in early imprints such as the *Epistolae* by the renowned Italian humanist Gasparino Barzizza, was not confirmed by Wenssler's further career. In the twenty years he was active as a printer in Basel, he printed just a few

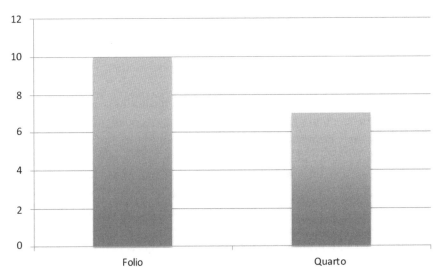

FIGURE 2.10   Non-datable imprints according to page format

other humanist texts, no more classical authors and never in *antiqua* script, the most suitable for humanism. At the head of the biggest workshop in town, Wenssler printed most of all conventional texts for religious and liturgical use and standard education following medieval rather than humanist traditions and agendas.

By examining the evidence concerning Wenssler, it has been argued that printing production and entrepreneurial organization in the age of incunabula was deeply embedded in the socio-economic and cultural context of late medieval urban life. Thus, continuities from the time before Gutenberg's invention strongly characterized the printing industry for at least one generation. Wenssler's example shows clearly that the connection between the technical invention of printing with movable types and the philological, educational, scientific and cultural innovation of humanism needs reconsideration. Printing and humanism, of course, did develop strong mutual inspiration but they did so as a result of cultural practices that emerged only slowly.

When in 1486 Johannes Amerbach published as the first printer in Basel a book that was entirely printed in *antiqua* fonts and started to orientate his editions towards a more humanist programme, Michel Wenssler's business was already declining.[65] Even if Amerbach stands for a new type of printer who

---

65 Pierre Louis van der Haegen, 'Sortimentspolitik der Basel Inkunabeldrucker. Amerbach als Drucker konservativer Standardwerke und als Promoter neuartiger humanistischer Literatur', *Basler Zeitschrift für Geschichte und Altertumskunde*, 110 (2010), pp. 127–142.

epitomised a blend of humanist learning and commercial expertise, change in print culture as well as in the consumption of books only happened slowly. Of the works published by Amerbach between 1486 and 1500, roughly a third were printed with (pure and mixed) *antiqua* fonts; in other words, he implemented the realignment of his workshop towards antiquity and humanism very carefully. At the same time he continued to run his business at least partially based on a debt economy. In the uniquely rich correspondence of the Amerbach family, there is much evidence for a wide range of sophisticated financial instruments, promises of repayment and requests for overdue payments. The letters sent, for instance, to his Nuremberg associate, Anton Koberger speak volumes; from what they report and negotiate these letters almost read as the entries of the Basel *Vergichtbücher* that document so impressively Wenssler's debt economy. In this sense, the parts of the Amerbach correspondence that are concerned with printing can be understood as the iceberg underneath the water surface; they represent the social encounter of a debt economy that worked quite effectively, and precisely because it worked, it did not leave any traces in legal documentation. They do however document relations between creditors and debtors that are hardly different from those that found their way into the files of the civil jurisdiction.

Taken all together, the case of Michel Wenssler is much more than the economic failure of a master printer in the second half of the fifteenth century. Despite his financial ruin, he served as a model to follow for the economic foundation of the emerging printing industry well into the sixteenth century. The written evidence this individual case produced can even be regarded as a benefit, in that it allows for a new approach to the study in how printing emerged: not primarily as a revolutionary industry introducing a humanist agenda from its inception, but rather remaining for the first decades deeply rooted in the traditions of late medieval urban society, economy and culture.

CHAPTER 3

Venetian Incunabula for Florentine Bookshops (ca. 1473–1483)

Lorenz Böninger

The history of reading in Modern Europe is firmly linked to that of the book trade, permitting fresh texts to reach ever growing numbers of new readers, preparing them for cultural change. Florence is a very interesting case in this respect. In the shadow of its cathedral, in what we now either call the Late Middle Ages or the Early Modern period, the historiography of reading, just like that of writing, of higher and lower education, of private and public libraries, has always found extremely fertile grounds. The city's public collections preserve innumerous manuscripts written by humanists and citizens from very different social backgrounds and the superbly rich archival sources document nearly every aspect of everyday life. This wealth of documents is a direct consequence of the widespread literacy among merchants and artisans alike which was, incidentally, rather due to commercial and professional reasons than to deeper intellectual interests.[1]

The changes brought to Florentine manuscript culture by the invention of the printing press were profound. Although the production of ever more luxurious manuscripts was not immediately abandoned as many works have shown (and schools for the *ars scribendi* as late as 1492 prove),[2] Florence soon found itself at the centre of a network with other printing hubs like Rome and Venice, with whom exchange and competition were utterly unequal.[3] Whereas up to

---

1   See Christian Bec, *Les livres des Florentins (1413–1608)* (Florence: Olschki, 1984); Armando F. Verde, 'Libri tra le pareti domestiche. Una necessaria appendice a 'Lo studio fiorentino 1473–1503'', *Memorie domenicane*, n. s., 18 (1987), pp. 1–225; Robert D. Black, *Education and Society in Florentine Tuscany. Teachers, Pupils and Schools c. 1250–1500*. Vol. 1 (Leiden: Brill, 2007); Richard A. Goldthwaite, *The Economy of Renaissance Florence* (Baltimore: The Johns Hopkins University Press, 2009), pp. 353–354.

2   Archivio di Stato, Firenze (henceforth: ASF), Notarile antecosimiano, 9604, fol. 164v: lease contract of a workshop for Niccolò di maestro Iacopo Brancaleoni da Forlì *scriptor* and *docens ars scribendi*.

3   For the history of Florentine printing in the fifteenth century, see Roberto Ridolfi, *La stampa in Firenze nel secolo XV* (Florence: Olschki, 1958); Dennis A. Rhodes, *Gli annali tipografici fiorentini del XV secolo* (Florence: Olschki, 1988); Mary A. and Richard H. Rouse, *Cartolai, Illumina-*

the early 1470s Florentine bibliophiles had either worked as scribes or had employed others for copying their texts, now they swiftly turned into buyers of the much cheaper printed books.[4] The introduction of printing in Florence roughly coincided with the transfer of its university to Pisa (1473), so it comes as no surprise that a number of important sources on the early Tuscan book trade have been edited by the historian of the Pisan university, Armando F. Verde, and then adapted by Angela Nuovo in her work *The Book Trade in the Italian Renaissance*.[5] Surprisingly, however, the fifteenth-century trade of incunabula in Florence itself has not received much attention.

Traditionally the Florentine book trade, including that of imported incunabula, was in the hands of the so-called *cartolai* who were members of the guild of the doctors, grocers and spice traders ('Arte dei medici e speziali').[6] Little is known about the mechanisms and the networks through which they acquired books on foreign markets but it must be assumed that the bulk of them arrived through merchants operating where these books were produced. Florentine merchants had particularly close relations to Venetian printers: in 1476, Girolamo di Carlo Strozzi and Giovanbattista Ridolfi had three Florentine works printed in Venice by Jacques Le Rouge and Nicholas Jenson.[7] There were, however, important exceptions: already with respect to the very first printed books

---

tors, *and Printers in Fifteenth Century Italy: the Evidence of the Ripoli Press*, UCLA University Research Library Occasional Papers (Los Angeles: UCLA University Research Library, 1988); Melissa Conway, *The Diario of the Printing Press of San Iacopo di Ripoli 1476–1484. Commentary and Transcription* (Florence: Olschki, 1999) (but see the review by Neil Harris in *The Book Collector*, 52 (2001), pp. 10–32, and the following discussion on pp. 33–50).

4   See for example the case of the humanist Lorenzo Guidetti whose memories have recently been published: Lorenzo di Francesco Guidetti, *Ricordanze*, ed. Lorenz Böninger (Rome: Edizioni di storia e letteratura, 2014).

5   Armando F. Verde, *Lo Studio fiorentino 1473–1503. Ricerche e documenti* (9 vols., Florence: Istituto nazionale di studi sul Rinascimento and Olschki, 1973–2010); Angela Nuovo, *The Book Trade in the Italian Renaissance* (Leiden: Brill, 2013).

6   Raffaele Ciasca, *L'Arte dei medici e speziali nella storia e nel commercio fiorentino dal secolo XII al XV* (Florence: Olschki, 1927), pp. 50–52; Alessandro Guidotti, 'Indagini su botteghe di cartolai e miniatori a Firenze nel XV secolo', in *La miniatura italiana tra gotico e Rinascimento. Atti del II Congresso di storia della miniatura italiana Cortona 24–26 settembre 1982* (2 vols., Florence: Olschki, 1985), II, pp. 473–507; Gustavo Bertoli, 'Librai, cartolai e ambulanti immatricolati nell'Arte dei medici e speziali di Firenze dal 1490 al 1600', *La Bibliofilía*, 94 (1992), I, pp. 125–164, and II, pp. 227–262.

7   Florence Edler de Roover, 'Per la storia dell'arte della stampa in Italia. Come furono stampati a Venezia tre dei primi libri in volgare', *La Bibliofilía*, 55 (1953), pp. 107–117; for the list of the Florentine *cartolai* chosen to sell the copies, see pp. 112–113. Other books were sent to London and Bruges; see also Martin Lowry, *Nicholas Jenson and the Rise of Venetian Publishing in Renaissance Venice* (Oxford: Blackwell, 1991), pp. 129–132.

arriving from Germany in the early 1460s it can be argued that a certain *librarius* from Strasburg, a cleric called Albertus Liebkind, may have brought them to Italy with the help of the Florentine Spinelli bank.[8]

The first Florentine *cartolaio* to have sold the products of the Venetian printing press of John of Cologne in 1473 seems to have been the rather famous Zanobi di Mariano, who initially either bought the books directly or took them on commission from the prior of the Badia Fiesolana, Don Arcangelo da Vicenza.[9] The Prior's origins may have helped him in maintaining his connection with the Venetian printers and by 1477, the Badia had sold books of "maestro Giovanni da Colonia stampatore di libri" worth the considerable sum of 145 gold florins; this money had then been spent for the needs of the Badia itself. In 1477 John of Cologne's outstanding credits with his Florentine customers were collected by a canon of the Badia, Don Gregorio di Matteo.

As far as we know, the first time John of Cologne ("dominus Iohannes olim Gherardi de Collonia de Allamania habitans ad presens Venetiis") presented himself in Florence was in August 1478, when he named his own procurator to collect these credits, a certain Giuliano di Giovanfrancesco da Modena.[10] It must be assumed that in these days John of Cologne also arrived at a first compromise with Zanobi di Mariano (30 September 1478), of which we hear only five years later (see below, p. 66). In the later accounts of the Badia Fiesolana, we then find the names of other procurators, for example that of the Florentine Antonio di Bartolomeo Nelli, and, in 1485, that of Giampiero (Bonomini) of Cremona.[11] John of Cologne maintained his personal account with the Canons

---

8 Lorenz Böninger, 'I primi passi della stampa a Firenze. Nuovi documenti d'archivio' in Adolfo Tura (ed.), *Edizioni fiorentine del Quattrocento e primo Cinquecento in Trivulziana. Biblioteca Trivulziana, 25 gennaio–10 marzo 2002* (Milan: Comune di Milano, 2001), pp. 67–75, p. 75; Böninger, *Die deutsche Einwanderung nach Florenz im Spätmittelalter* (Leiden: Brill, 2006), p. 298.

9 Florence, Archivio dell'Ospedale degli Innocenti, n. 11655 (Badia di Fiesole, Libro de' debitori e creditori, 1456–1484), fol. 140 (left). Albinia de la Mare first noted the importance of these account books and was planning a study on 'Vespasiano da Bisticci and the library of the Badia of Fiesole', to be published by the Warburg Institute, which was never completed (but see Alison Brown and Albinia de la Mare, 'Bartolomeo Scala's Dealings with booksellers, scribes and illuminators, 1459–62', *Journal of the Warburg and Courtauld Institutes*, 39 (1976), pp. 237–245: 240–241, especially nos. 18 and 23). Also see Angela Dressen, *The Library of the Badia Fiesolana. Intellectual History and Education Under the Medici (1462–1494)* (Florence: SISMEL—Edizioni del Galluzzo, 2013), p. 16.

10 ASF, Notarile antecosimiano, 19607, fol. 131r. Interestingly, the identity of John of Cologne was confirmed by the same Don Gregorio di Matteo and another friar "converso" of the Badia Fiesolana, Marco Corbali da Vicenza. Giuliano Raspondio da Modena is known to have been a collaborator or "familiaris" of John of Cologne.

11 Florence, Archivio dell'Ospedale degli Innocenti, n. 11655 (Badia di Fiesole, Libro de' deb-

of the Badia until the 1490s when he—that is, his Florentine representatives—
was repaid in natural goods like wood, grain, wine and beans (1486–1494). In
these years his Florentine procurators were the well known "Bartolo (di Fruosino) cartolaio" and a certain "Silvestro".[12]

John of Cologne was really not so much a printer as the most important
promoter of Venetian printing of his time who in nearly two decades "shaped
its relationship with the transnational market".[13] From 1474 he was in partnership with another German merchant, Johannes Manthen of Gerresheim, and
five years later he formed together with the brilliant French printer Nicholas
Jenson the so-called 'Compagnia' which soon dominated the Italian book market and continued to operate even after Jenson's premature death in 1480.[14]
Rather commonly in commercial matters but unfortunately for our goals, today
most of the surviving Florentine sources on the 'Company' are single notarial
acts regarding the nominations of legal representatives, the so-called *procurae*. The preponderance of these sources over other types of documents, like
for example account books, is the reason why only exceptionally one can find
bibliographic detail about imported books, or the value of a transaction.[15]

---

itori e creditori, 1456–1484), fol. 182 (left and right). On Don Gregorio di Matteo, cfr. Verde, *Lo studio*, II, 321, 761 (university bidel's payment to "domno Gregorio monacho Abatie de Fezuli" in 1481, almost certainly for books); Lorenzo de' Medici, *Lettere XVI (settembre 1489-febbraio 1490)*, ed. Lorenz Böninger (Florence: Giunti-Barbèra, 2011), pp. 192–194; on Bonomini: Nuovo, *The Book Trade*, pp. 33–37, 41, 44–45.

12 Florence, Archivio dell'Ospedale degli Innocenti, n. 11656 (Badia di Fiesole, Libro de' debitori e creditori, 1483–1500), fols. 33, 72 and 73 (left and right). On Bartolo di Fruosino, see Verde, *Lo studio*, ad indices; Caterina Chiarelli, *Le attività artistiche e il patrimonio librario della Certosa di Firenze (dalle origini alla metà del XVI secolo)* (2 vols., Salzburg: Analecta Cartusiana, 1984), I, pp. 78–79; Silvestro was probably one of the two sons of Zanobi di Mariano (Bec, *Les livres des Florentins*, pp. 113, 325–337; Verde, 'Libri tra le pareti', pp. 151–170; Giovanni Bonifati, *Dal libro manoscritto al libro stampato. Sistemi di mercato a Bologna e a Firenze agli albori del capitalismo* (Turin: Rosenberg & Sellier: 2008), p. 195).

13 Nuovo, *The Book Trade*, p. 21; Philippe Braunstein, *Les allemands à Venise (1380–1520)* (Rome: École Française de Rome, 2016), *ad indices*; on his identity, see Christian Coppens, 'Giovanni da Colonia, aka Johann Ewylre / Alwylre / Ahrweiler: the early printed book and its investors', *La Bibliofilía*, 116 (2014), pp. 113–119.

14 On Jenson see also Paolo Veneziani, 'Jenson, Nicolas', in *Dizionario Biografico degli Italiani* (Rome: Istituto della Enciclopedia italiana, 1960–) [henceforth: *DBI*], LXII (2004), pp. 205–208; his name was so well known that it was kept in the Company's official title even after his death, also in Florence.

15 Most but not all of these acts have been mentioned in Böninger, *Die deutsche Einwanderung*, pp. 300–304. I plan to analyse the Florentine sources regarding the Venetian printer Francesco della Fontana in a future publication.

One of the earliest relevant documents dates from April 1481, when the agent of Johannes Manthen and his Venetian business partners, a certain "ser Conradus de Usin de Openen prope Maguntiam", appointed two Florentine merchants as procurators, Niccolò di Antonio and Niccolò di Ugolino Martelli.[16] The two Martelli cousins were partners in an important trading company that had wide spread interests all over Europe. The firm's director (*negotiorum gestor*) in Florence was a certain Francesco Venturi,[17] and Antonio di Bartolomeo Nelli—named in the notarial act as one of the witnesses[18]—, was working as their apprentice (*giovane* or *discepolo*).[19] It would thus seem that behind Nelli's role in these and the Badia's book dealings, stood the direct interest of the Martelli company. Nelli's work was that of collecting the outstanding credits. As had been explained in a merchant's handbook some years earlier, for this task young men were preferred to their 'masters' because with respect to the debtors they were not so afraid of being 'importunate and fastidious'.[20]

Roughly a year later, on 15 April 1482, the cleric "Henricus quondam Gerardi franciosus venditor librorum in partibus Tuscie", claimed not only to be the authentic legal representative of John of Cologne ("egregii viri domini Iohannis de Colonia quondam domini Gerardi mercatoris habitatoris Venetiarum"), but also that of his business partner, the merchant Peter Ugelheimer.[21] In this role and particularly in that of a commissary of the firm 'Nicholò Ienson et compagni', he named a new procurator for the whole of Tuscany (*per omnes partes, civitates, castra et loca Tuscie*), the afore mentioned *cartolaio* Bartolo di Fruosino d'Angelo.[22] Very little is known about this Henricus or Arrigo, but it is possible that he had worked in Jenson's workshop, possibly as a type setter.[23]

---

16 ASF, Notarile antecosimiano, 13957, fol. 6r. Conrad's Venetian power of attorney had been drawn up on 8 June 1480 by the notary ser Iacopo d'Avanzo di ser Francesco da Venezia, known there as Giacomo del fù Francesco Avanzo.
17 ASF, Notarile antecosimiano, 17903, fols. 17v, 19r, 20v, 34v.
18 Another witness was a certain Cione di Damiano di Matteo *cartolaio* who is known to have had very early interests in the printing of books.
19 Sometimes, as in 1482, he was also acting as their representative in legal causes, cfr. ASF, Mercanzia, 4496, fols. 239v–240r. His testament from 1500 is in ASF, Notarile antecosimiano, 16825, fols. 235r–243v.
20 Benedetto Cotrugli Raguseo, *Il libro dell'arte di mercatura*, ed. Ugo Tucci (Venice: Arsenale Editrice, 1990), p. 156.
21 According to Arrigo, this nomination was in the testament of Nicholas Jenson himself, dated 7 September 1480, written by the Venetian notary ser Girolamo Bonichardi, and other acts of the same notary. In Jenson's testament, however, there is no mention of Arrigo (see Lowry, *Nicholas Jenson*, pp. 228–234).
22 ASF, Notarile antecosimiano, 5106, fols. 3v–4r.
23 Although most Florentine documents before 1490 describe Arrigo di Gherardo either as

The French priest, in any way, did not enjoy his Venetian masters' trust unconditionally, as the Florentines soon learnt.

Two months later still another agent of 'John of Cologne and Nicholas Jenson' arrived in Florence, the Milanese merchant Francesco di messer Cristoforo Gaffuri.[24] After a short dispute on 14 June he signed a settlement with "Arrigus Gherardi de Francia venditor librorum in stampa clericus Metensis diocesis" in the Florentine archbishop's court. The bitter conclusions were that Arrigo had to transfer to Gaffuri both the rented bookshop ("pro vendendo libros in stampa") and all the books and papers preserved there, especially those belonging to John of Cologne's and Nicholas Jenson's company. In turn, Gaffuri agreed to write up a detailed inventory of these items and to deliver Arrigo a legally valid receipt; the same rules had also to be extended to other towns with book deposits, especially Perugia, Siena, Pisa, Lucca, Pistoia and Prato. Finally, Arrigo renounced the validity of a certain protest drawn up by him two days earlier,[25] and the nomination of his legal representatives in the now settled dispute for the possession of the bookshop.[26]

After only two weeks, Gaffuri decided to leave Florence. For this reason on 28 June he first signed a working contract with Antonio di Bartolomeo Nelli for two years as his 'giovane',[27] and then commissioned, in a meeting in the private home of the patrician Filippo di Bartolomeo Valori, the shop and its merchandise to a certain 'Giovanni di Niccolò di Lorenzo cartholaio' (see Appendix I). According to this agreement Giovanni di Niccolò—also known by the nickname 'El Guazza'—promised to live in the shop and work exclusively for the Company, sell the books at the prices indicated in Gaffuri's price-list, and finally to deliver all his profits to the already well known "Antonio Nelli sta co' Martelli".

---

librarius or as *venditor librorum in stampa*, in 1483 he was actually called a *scriptor in forma* and in 1487 an *impressor librorum*. However, no printed books signed by him have survived. In 1492 Arrigo was described as living in Siena when he was involved in a court case with a lawyer regarding an edition of the decretals and a bible (I owe this reference to Philippa Jackson whom I would also like to thank very much for a critical reading of this text).

24   On 22 June, Gaffuri actually called himself the 'principal' procurator of only one of the new partners of the Company, the merchant Peter Ugelheimer from Frankfurt, but then also "Iohannis de Colonia et Nicholai Janson et sociorum de Venetiis" (ASF, Notarile antecosimiano, 16033, fol. 5v; Gaffurri's own Venetian appointment was drawn up by the same ser Girolamo Bonichardi on 17 May 1481). On Gaffuri and Ugelheimer, see Nuovo, *The Book Trade*, pp. 25, 31–33, 36 and n. 49.

25   The notary responsible for this document was "ser Iohannes Guiducci Bartholomei notarius florentinus", but it is not preserved (see ASF, Notarile antecosimiano, 9603–9604).

26   ASF, Notarile antecosimiano, 10086, fol. 234r–v.

27   ASF, Notarile antecosimiano, 20612, fasc. III, n. 171 (verso; unfortunately hardly legible).

A crucial condition required the *cartolaio* to sell the books only for cash; if the payment was promised for a later date ('fare (a) tempo'), then these contracts had to be written in Antonio Nelli's name and not that of Giovanni di Niccolò. If Nelli was to reach the conclusion that Giovanni was not working well, he was thus given full authority to dismiss him. Before paying Nelli, in any case, Giovanni's first profits up to 150 florins had to be consigned to Filippo Valori himself who had promised this sum on Francesco Spina's behalf to another merchant company, that of Francesco di Bartolomeo Martelli and Antonio Corsini (unfortunately no details are given on their specific roles in the book trade). The involvement of Valori in this case is extremely interesting. He was one of the leading politicians of his age and also a friend and pupil of Marsilio Ficino; in 1484 he sponsored the printing of the Latin edition of Plato's works with the Ripoli press, and it would come as no surprise if then he used the Venetian Company's trading network to commercialize it.[28] In one of several legal cases promoted in 1486 by the new procurator of the Company, Giampiero Bonomini da Cremona, Filippo Valori still acted as his legal guarantee ('mallevadore').[29]

Roughly two months after the contract drawn up in Valori's house, on 30 August 1482, Antonio Nelli presented the notary with a letter written on 24 July by John of Cologne, Nicholas Jenson and partners in Venice, which had arrived in Florence on 8 August. In this document, the Company officially declared their discontent with Giovanni di Niccolò's conduct and therefore obliged Nelli to send him away, after paying his stipend for the last two months (Appendix II).

Before considering the possible reasons for these continuous and rather abrupt changes in the Company's policy, one may first take a closer look at the bookshop itself. The shop owner and grain dealer Chimenti di Taddeo Gualzelli actually possessed two shops below his house in the 'Garbo' (also 'Canto' or 'Via del Garbo'). This house lay on the crossing between Via della

---

28 Paul Oskar Kristeller, 'The first printed edition of Plato's works and the date of its publication (1484)', in Kristeller, *Studies in Renaissance Thought and Letters* (4 vols., Rome: Edizioni di storia e letteratura, 1984–1996), III, pp. 135–146; see also Lorenzo Polizzotto and Catherine Kovesi, *Memorie di casa Valori* (Florence: Nerbini, 2007), pp. 78–88; Mark Jurdjevic, *Guardians of Republicanism. The Valori Family in the Florentine Renaissance* (Oxford: Oxford University Press, 2008), pp. 46–51.

29 ASF, Mercanzia, 4505, fol. 15v (15 May 1486, against 'Francesco d'Antonio Balducci fu cartolaio'); when in September 1488 the Frenchman Arrigo di Gherardo sued Balducci 'olim cartularius' for the restitution of nine florins and several books worth ten florins, he named another legal guarantee (ASF, Mercanzia, 327, fol. 234v). On the Company's commerce with Balducci, see also Verde, *Lo Studio*, II, pp. 254–255.

Condotta and Via del Proconsolo in the parish of Sant'Apollinare, in an area where the most important Florentine bookshops grouped around the Benedictine monastery of the Badia.[30] In the fiscal records, the 'Catasto' of 1480, Gualzelli declared that only one of these two very small shops ('botteghini') was rented out to a certain "Charlo di Ridolfo francioso da Lione", for the very modest sum of four florins a year.[31] This Frenchman was a rather well known printer and bookdealer to whom Florentine sources sometimes attributed a last name like 'Duple' or 'Dubbue', who came from Normandy (and not from Lyon) and who had previously worked in Padua, Pisa and Colle Valdelsa. In the summer of 1481 he married the owner of a public bath, Bella di Giovanni da Colonia 'stufaiuola', and is thereafter documented in Florence until 1496.[32] Almost certainly, Arrigo di Gherardo had taken over Carlo's shop in May 1481, when he professed his debt with him of sixteen gold florins and four lire, presumably the value of the books or the furniture left in the premises.[33] Arrigo then kept the shop for approximately six years, after the dismissal of Giovanni di Niccolò, together with a Florentine *cartolaio* as partner, Cione di Damiano di Matteo (on him, see above, n. 18).[34] Finally, in August 1487 Gualzelli rented both shops together anew to the medical doctor Raffaele Chellini who on his part agreed to sublease them only "ad usum cartolarii".[35]

One may now also have a brief look at Giovanni di Niccolò's professional career. Eleven years earlier, this *cartolaio et miniatore* had rented, together with his brother Antonio, a bookshop from the da Rabatta family which was adjacent to that of Arrigo di Gherardo. His brother Antonio was himself a well-known miniaturist.[36] In 1480 Antonio acquired considerable numbers of relatively cheap 'consumer' books from the Ripoli press.[37] Among the two brothers' specializations were probably the rubrication, flourishing and illumination of

---

30 On a rather famous print of Giuseppe Zocchi of around 1744 most of these shops are still to be seen (Anne Leader, *The Badia of Florence: Art and Observance in a Renaissance Monastery* (Bloomington-Indianapolis: Indiana University Press, 2012), p. 26).
31 ASF, Catasto, 1015, fols. 475r–476r (and see also Catasto, 923, fols. 386r–387r, from 1469). For an earlier use of these shops, see ASF, Notarile antecosimiano, 16944, fol. 41r–v.
32 See Böninger, *Die deutsche Einwanderung*, pp. 302–304.
33 ASF, Notarile antecosimiano, 5112, IV, ad diem 4 maii 1481.
34 ASF, Notarile antecosimiano, 13296, fols. 80r–81r (Cione had invested some of his fortune in the wooden furniture of the shop).
35 ASF, Notarile antecosimiano, 12025, fols. 14r–15r.
36 Guidotti, 'Indagini', pp. 481 (and n. 36); 492–493, 502–507 (doc. 12); Bertoli, 'Librai', p. 138, n. 14; see also ASF, Notarile antecosimiano, 14418, fol. 89r–v; 3032, ad diem 11 iunii 1473; 4839, fol. 10r (new lease in the Chiasso dello studio, 1487); 13296, fols. 106r–107v (sublease of the old bookshop, 1488); 2879, fol. 343v; 21180, fol. 12v.
37 Conway, *The Diario*, pp. 197–198.

initials in incunabula. In the late 1470s Giovanni di Niccolò had financially sustained a German copyist, Niccolò di Giovanni tedesco "scrittore", who in 1478 had travelled to Germany together with the Florentine citizen Leonardo di Giovanni Buonafé. One and a half year after their departure, Giovanni demanded the payment of his expenses.[38] From two official acts of sequestrations in Giovanni's bookshop dated 1486 and 1489 it appears that Antonio and Giovanni di Niccolò dealt both in manuscripts and in printed books, apparently mostly Florentine. In the 1489 inventory we find for example a book called *La storia di Santa Filicita* (a "libretto bechuto di charte pechore"), two copies of Marsilio Ficino's *De christiana religione*, one copy of Cicero's *De ufficiis* "in forma", one copy of Luigi Pulci's *Morgante* "in forma", one copy of *Vergilio chol chomento in forma*, two copies of Mesuè, one copy of Giovanni Boccaccio's *Decamerone* and one "vochabulista grecho" (that is, the *Lexicon Graeco-Latinum* by Johannes Cratonus, or the *Lexicon Latino-Graecum*).[39]

On 16 November 1482, the already complicated story of the Venetian Company's book trade in Florence arrived at a new turning point. According to a notarial document drawn up on that day by one of the Mercanzia's notaries, ser Antonio di messer Benedetto Ubaldini, the French cleric Arrigo di Gherardo was now back into the saddle. Antonio Nelli was forced to hand over to Arrigo all the Company's credits.[40] The list of the debtors' names contained in their notarial agreement allows us a brief glimpse into the shop's business under the direction first of Arrigo di Gherardo and then of Giovanni di Niccolò. In both cases their books had not only been sold for cash money but also on credit. From the first period there were in fact five debtors recorded, three of whom

---

38   ASF, Mercanzia, 1506, fols. 187r–188r (10 January 1480; the German town's name they had moved to is given as 'Necholono' or 'Nicholono'). Buonafé was born around 1457; on an incident in his early youth, see ASF, Signori e Collegi. Duplicati delle Deliberazioni in forza di ordinaria autorità, 17, fol. 17r; ASF, Notarile antecosimiano, 4886, fol. 30r; ASF, Catasto, 1022, fol. 277v: "Lionardo di Giovanni detto d'età d'anni 23, sanza aviamento alchuno" (1480). Buonafé after his return to Florence became a Carthusian monk, Prior of the Certosa of Galuzzo, head ('spedalingho') of the hospital of Santa Maria Nuova and an important patron of the arts (on his early career, see Chiarelli, *Le attività artistiche*; Verde, *Lo studio*).
39   ASF, Mercanzia, 11585, fols. 11v, 42r (no single prices are given, only the overall sum). The *Storia di Santa Filicita* was probably the *Rappresentazione di Santa Felicita* which was printed about a year later (USTC 995061); on the early Greek 'vocabolisti', see Cristina Dondi and Neil Harris, 'Exporting books from Milan to Venice in the fifteenth century: evidence from the 'Zornale' of Francesco de' Madiis', *La Bibliofilía*, 116 (2014), pp. 121–148: 136–137. The *Vergilio chol chomento in forma* is a likely match for the anonymous Florentine imprint described as USTC 989982.
40   ASF, Notarile antecosimiano, 20162, fasc. III, n. 195.

were private buyers: a certain messer Tommaso di Iacopo degli Agli (?), who owed four gold florins; the canon—and later prior—of San Lorenzo Francesco di Giovanni Campana, owing four florins; and a student of law at Pisa, messer Bartolomeo Rigogli, indebted for one florin. The two highest debts, on the other hand, were attributed to 'Zenobius chartolarius in Garbo' (19 lire), and to the heirs of a certain 'Benedictus chartolarius' with 56 gold florins, 9 lire and 18 soldi.[41] This Benedetto can be identified with Benedetto di Giovanni, partner of the *cartolaio* Matteo di Biagio Caccini from the 1460s, who was quite active in the trade with Venetian incunabula.[42] In the 1470s, for example, he had sold Malerbi's Italian bible translation to Guidetto Guidetti.[43]

More copious was the second part of the debtors' list, relating to Giovanni di Niccolò's management of the shop; in only two months Giovanni had in fact collected twice the number of Arrigo's debtors. Again, the highest sum was owed by a *cartolaio*, 'Bartolomeus Fruosini chartolarius in Pisa' with 43 gold florins (who possessed shops in both Florence and Pisa), while his colleague Zanobi di Mariano had a considerably lower debt (3 gold florins, one lira). Among the clerics one finds the *praepositus* of the baptistery of San Giovanni, messer Ricciardo di Marco d'Anghiari (10 gold florins, 10 soldi), a priest from Careggi with an astonishingly high debt ('ser Iohannes Dominichus presbiter in Sancto Pietro a Chareggi: fiorini 10, lire 3, soldi 15') and a canon from Prato, messer Bartolomeo (5 gold florins).[44] In this case we may actually advance a hypothesis on the books in question. To him—or another 'Bartholomeus canonicus'—belonged a Duns Scotus, *Quaestiones in quattuor libros sententiarum*.[45] He also had a Plutarch printed by Adolph Rusch (or the 'R-Printer') in

---

41   The identity of 'Zenobius chartolarius in Garbo' is not certain. Presumably he is to be identified with Zanobi di Mariano, and not the much lesser known Zanobi di Giovanni di Lapo *cartolaio*.
42   Guidotti, 'Indagini', p. 483; cfr. ASF, Notarile antecosimiano, 13280, fasc. I, fol. 143r–v. In October 1481, the heir of Benedetto di Giovanni, his son ser Francesco (a cleric), sued the ex-partner of his father Matteo Caccini in the Mercanzia court for 150 gold florins, regarding this partnership.
43   Guidetti, *Ricordanze*, p. XXIII, n. 74; on the large diffusion of this book, see Edoardo Barbieri, 'La fortuna della 'Biblia vulgarizata' di Nicolò Malerbi', *Aevum*, 63 (1989), pp. 419–500.
44   He is to be identified with messer Bartolomeo di Andrea di Lapo da Prato, member of the Spighi family. He was a canon in the church of Santo Stefano, and probably died before 1493.
45   Johannes Duns Scotus, *Quaestiones in quattuor libros sententiarum* (Venice: Giovanni da Colonia and Johann Manthen, 1474–1478), USTC 995162. See now Piero Scapecchi (ed.), *Catalogo degli incunaboli della Biblioteca Nazionale Centrale di Firenze* (Florence: Biblioteca Nazionale Centrale di Firenze-Nerbini, 2017), p. 203.

Strasburg in the early 1470s, now in the Biblioteca Marucelliana in Florence.[46] This could indicate that our shop sold titles printed not only in Venice, but also in Central Europe.

From an academic background came both the medical doctor Giovanni Gualberto di ser Paolo Paoli (2 gold florins, 3 lire) and a professor of law at Pisa, messer Antonio di Piero Malegonelle (2 gold florins). We do not know the background of a certain messer Tommaso Belcari (?), who owed one gold florin and three soldi. The two most intriguing names, however, are those of Braccio di messer Domenico Martelli, with the rather high debt of eighteen gold florins, and that of the humanist Cristoforo Landino ('d. Christoforus de Pratoveteri: fl. 8'). Martelli was a rather famous collector of manuscripts, many of which have been identified, but was clearly also a voracious buyer of printed books.[47] For him as for other members of the Florentine elite there was no contradiction. For Landino, of course, there could not be: having already seen his works in print in the 1470s, in these years he was heavily involved with the printing and commercializing of his *Comento* on Dante's 'Divine Comedy' (30 August 1481) and his commentary on Horace's 'Ars poetica' (5 August 1482).[48] The books bought from Giovanni di Niccolò might in his case have served not only as literary sources, but also as illustrative material, as examples to learn from.

The credits accrued by Giovanni di Niccolò in his two months' management of Gaffurri's bookshop thus amounted to more than one hundred gold florins, a considerably higher sum than the approximately seventy gold florins claimed by Arrigo di Gherardo for the preceding period. The different approaches to selling examined here might partly be explained by Giovanni's cultural background. Traditionally, commercial transactions in Florence were based either on barter, or 'a tempo', with a postponed payment.[49] If this, however, was unac-

---

46 Plutarchus, *Vitae illustrium virorum*; Sextus Rufus, *De regia, consulari imperialique dignitate ac de accessione romani imperii*, USTC 748217. See Piero Scapecchi (ed.), *Biblioteca Marucelliana Firenze. Catalogo incunaboli* (Rome: Istituto Poligrafico e Zecca dello Stato, 1989), p. 19, n. 15, inscribed: 'Bartholomei andree canonici pratensi liber iste est manu propria subscripsi'.

47 Albinia de la Mare (†) with Xavier van Binnebeke, 'A list of books from the Florentine Braccio Martelli', in Susan d'Engle and Gerald B. Guest (eds.), *Tributes to Jonathan J.G. Alexander. The Making and Meaning of Illuminated Medieval and Renaissance Manuscripts, Art and Architecture* (London-Turnhout: Harvey Miller Publishers, 2006), pp. 35–67.

48 Lorenz Böninger and Paolo Procaccioli (eds.), *Per Cristoforo Landino lettore di Dante. Il contesto civile e culturale, la storia tipografica, la fortuna del «Comento sopra la Comedia». Atti del Convegno internazionale, Firenze, 7–8 novembre 2014* (Florence: Le Lettere, 2017).

49 For the continuous practice of barter in the early modern Italian book trade, see the article by Domenico Ciccarello in this volume.

ceptable for the Venetian Company, then Arrigo di Gherardo would have easily been able to criticise Giovanni's management.

This seems to be exactly what happened after Gaffurri had taken over the shop in June 1482. In a later notarial act of July 1483, Arrigo named three new procurators of John of Cologne and Nicholas Jenson's Company, claiming that his own authorization in this case came from the German merchants Peter Ugelheimer and Gaspar von Dinslaken in the Company's name.[50] The Venetian record of this power of attorney was dated 29 July 1482 and was made even more authoritative by a letter of the Venetian Doge written two days later.[51] It is thus clear that after having been ousted from his shop in June, Arrigo di Gherardo had travelled back to Venice where he must have pressed his charges against Gaffurri and Giovanni di Niccolò's new directorship. In addition, one might finally mention that the Florentine power of attorney of July 1483 regarded an older—but unspecified—credit to be claimed with the *cartolaio* Zanobi di Mariano of which the original settlement on 30 September 1478 had been written up by another colleague, the *cartolaio* Matteo di Biagio Caccini.[52]

What conclusions can be drawn from this as yet confusing and fragmentary information on the early trade for Venetian printed books in Florence? Economically valid conclusions cannot be drawn on the basis of the few sources available so far. The very first impression is that even if the business in Florence may not always have been extremely profitable, many more merchants and middle-men were involved in it than has hitherto been known. The incoming flow of European, mostly German, incunabula was possibly regulated by the Venetian Company as well. Florentine citizens were as eager buyers of printed books at home as abroad but often preferred to postpone their payments. The commercial conflicts to be observed in Florence, however, do not seem to have been caused exclusively by different 'mentalities' but almost certainly also by the high number of actors involved in the Company's trade and the fluctuations in its policies and partnerships.

50　On Ugelheimer, see above n. 24; Tiziana Pesenti, 'Dinslaken, Gasparre' in *DBI*, XL (1991), pp. 167–169; Braunstein, *Les allemands*, pp. 254–255, 735, n. 428, *passim*.
51　ASF, Notarile antecosimiano, 14419, fols. 380v–381r. The Venetian notary was again ser Iacopo d'Avanzo di ser Francesco (about this notary, see above, n. 16).
52　See above, n. 42.

Appendix 1 (ASF, Notarile antecosimiano, 7619, Acts of ser Giovanni di Lazzaro Ferrini, 1482–1496, fol. 5r–v)

A dì XXVIII[53] di giugno 1482, in casa Filippo Valori in Firenze.

Sia noto a ciascuno come questo dì, in presentia degli infrascripti testimoni,[54] Francesco per l'adrieto di Cristofano Gaffuro mercatante da Milano, come procuratore et in nome di procuratore, come disse, di Giovanni di Colognia et di Niccolò Gianson mercatanti nella città di Vinetia et de' loro compagni et compagnia, et ancora come factore ed administrator di detta compagnia cantante soto detti nomi[55] et in qualunche di detti modi et nomi da una parte, et [fol. 5v] Giovanni di Niccolò di Lorenzo cartholaio et cittadino fiorentino dall'altra parte, convengono insieme et fanno la infrascritta conventione et pacto colle infrascritte condictioni, promesse et oblighi et altro che apresso si dirà, et prima:[56] Conciosia cosa che ditto Francescho per detta compagnia et in detti nomi habbi nella città di Firenze et in luogo che si dice Garbo una bottega a suo [sic!] pigione, et in essa bottega habbi più somma di libri di forma[57] appartenenti a essa compagnia per finirgli et darne ritracto a essa compagnia come ha in commessione, et conciosia cosa che esso Francescho sia costretto per giuste cagione per facti d'essa compagnia partirsi di Firenze et andare altrove, et che llui desideri che detti libri si finischino con buon modo et di quelli si venga al ritracto del danaio più facilmente et con più prestezza è possibile, però esso Francescho in detti nomi et per ogni miglior modo sa et può, tutti detti libri existenti in detta bottega et de quali esso Francescho n'à[58] inventario et copia, capo per capo li consegna et dà in accomandita al ditto Giovanni presente et ricevente, e quali[59] esso Giovanni confessa havere appresso di sè, per farne tanto et come apresso si dirà, et de' quali esso Giovanni dicie averne dato copia di sua mano di tutti quelli ha ricevuto a esso Francescho. Et debbe detto Giovanni tenere detti libri in detta bottega et quivi stare et habitare solo per finire et vendere detti libri in quel modo et per

---

53 '28' added in the interlinear.
54 Follows, cancelled: 'che'.
55 Follows, cancelled: 'per li quali et qualunche di loro esso Francescho promette di ratho et di fare et curare sì et in tal modo sotto la infrascritta pena ch'essi compagni et compagnia ratificheranno le infrascripte cose et observeranno le infrascritte cose et la presente conventione altrimenti di suo proprio observare sotto la infrascritta pena'.
56 'et prima' added in the interlinear; follows (cancelled): 'che'.
57 Follows, cancelled: 'per'.
58 Follows, cancelled: 'dato et facto'.
59 Follows, cancelled: 'et de' quali'.

quelli pregii che a esso Giovanni parrà conveniente et giusto,[60] et farne tanto quanto potrebbe detto Francescho se fussi presente, salvo le condictione dette et scritte,[61] et non possa ne debba esso Giovanni finire detti libri se nonne per contanti, et in caso faciessi altrimenti vadi sopra / [*fol. 5v*] di lui, et sia tenuto fargli buoni di suo, et volendone pure fare tempo alcuno,[62] ne debba contentare della detta o promessa Antonio Nelli sta co' Martelli, et non possi detto Giovanni in detta bottega dare opera né fare altro exercitio che vendere detti libri, et sia tenuto detto Giovanni[63] il prezzo che di tempo in tempo si ritrarrà di detti libri darlo et consegnarlo a esso Antonio Nelli, chon questo pacto[64] che innanzi cominci a consegnarne a esso Antonio alcuna cosa, detto Giovanni sia tenuto et obligato de' primi ritracti dare et pagare[65] sanza exeptione[66] ducati cento cinquanta larghi a Filippo Valori per dovergli pagare[67] a stanza di detto Francescho a Francescho Martelli e Antonio Corsini, per tanti promisse detto Filippo Valori a stanza d'esso Francescho, et detti fiorini 150 larghi sia tenuto detto Giovanni pagare a detto Filippo liberamente et non obstante qualunche altra commissione gli fussi facta[68] in contrario, et così sono d'achordo e convengono detto Giovanni et Francescho et fare et pagare[69] promette detto Giovanni a detto Filippo presente et ricevente di consentimento di detto Francescho,[70] et dipoi facto detto pagamento di fiorini 150 larghi sia tenuto ogni altro ritracto consegnare a esso Antonio, come è detto, tempo per tempo, et così fare promette detto Giovanni insino a tanto detto Giovanni non arà alcuna commessione da detta compagnia,[71] et sia tenuto detto Giovanni insino a tanto non harà da' detti compagni et compagnia altra commissione a esso Antonio Nelli rendere e asegnare conto di quello farà et finirà per detta compagnia ogni volta ne fussi da esso Antonio richiesto, et in caso non paressi a esso Antonio Nelli che esso Giovanni non faciessi circha le predette et infrascritte cose il bisogno per detta compagnia, allora sia lecito a esso Antonio privare ditto Giovanni di tale exercitio e della presente

---

60 Follows, cancelled: 'non uscendo però dal pregio che lui ha per inventario'.
61 'et farne—scritte' added in the interlinear.
62 Follows, cancelled: 'de'.
63 Follows, cancelled: 'tutto'.
64 'pacto' added in the interlinear.
65 Follows, cancelled: 'a Francescho Spina'.
66 'sanza exceptione' added in the interlinear.
67 Follows, cancelled: 'et'.
68 Follows, cancelled: 'et così sono d'achordo ditto Francescho et Giovanni'.
69 'et pagare' added in the interlinear.
70 'a Filippo Valori per dovergli pagare—di detto Francescho' added on the left margin.
71 'insino a tanto—compagnia' added in the interlinear.

conventione, sì et in caso che esso Giovanni non habbi alcuna commissione da detta compagnia o veramente che detto Antonio habbi da detta compagnia legittimo mandato et auctorità[72] di potere privare detto Giovanni da detto exercitio et presente commessione et non altrimenti. Et con conditione che detto Giovanni debba dare a detto Francescho in detti nomi uno mallevadore, el quale prometta et oblighisi a detta compagnia che esso Giovanni renderà buon conto et observerà le cose predette et infrascritte,[73] altrimenti rendere et observare di suo proprio, et da altra parte detto Francescho in detto nome si conviene col detto Giovanni et è contento[74] et promettegli di tutto quello che detto Giovanni vendessi per detta compagnia delle cose et libri consegnatogli per inventario, come è detto,[75] o che per l'avenire se gli consegneranno per sua faticha e premio dargli et pagarli a ragione di ducati undici per cento, et così è contento detto Francescho possa detto Giovanni trarre di detto ritracto. Et non sia tenuto detto Giovanni ad alcuna spesa né di pigione né d'altro che occorressi, ma tutto vada a conto di detti libri et comandita, et così convennono et promesso insieme l'uno all'altro detto Francescho et Giovanni in detto nome, le quali cose promossono dette parti in detti nomi l'una all'altro observare sotto la pena di fiorini 500 larghi et sotto l'obligo loro et de' loro heredi et beni presenti et futuri, r[ogantes] etc., r. etc., per guar[entigiam] etc.

Presentibus Marchionne Iohannis Torrigiani, Filippo Valori et Francescho Iohannis Spina.

Appendix II (ASF, Notarile antecosimiano, 7619, Acts of ser Giovanni di Lazzaro Ferrini, 1482-1496, fol. 11r)

1482.[76]

Item postea dictis, anno, indictione et die xxx.a augusti, actum Florentie nel Garbo, presentibus testibus ad infrascripta vocatis etc., videlicet ser[77] Laurentio Zenobii Ciati clerico florentino populi Sancte Felicitatis et Antonio Iacobi Boccaccini Alamanni de Florentia.

---

72 Corrected on: 'auctoritade'.
73 'et infrascritte' added in the interlinear.
74 'et è contento' added in the interlinear.
75 Follows, cancelled: 'et'.
76 On the left margin: 'Data fides ut hic. Protesto d'Antonio Nelli'.
77 Follows, cancelled: 'Zenob'.

Cum hoc sit quod iam sint pluries dies[78] Iohannes olim Niccolai vocatus El Guazza cartholarius de Florentia[79] ex una et Francischus Gaffurio de Mediolano[80] pro et vice et nomine Niccolai Gianson et Iohannis de Cologna et sociorum de Venetiis et dicte societatis[81] ex altera, fecerunt quasdam conventiones in qua[82] inter cetera continetur qualiter[83] prefatus Iohannes fuit relictus gubernator et administrator cuiusdam apothece site in civitate Florentie[84] nel Garbo ad hoc ut venderet libros formatos sive de forma pertinentes dicte sotietati et alia faceret in dicta conventione contenta, et cum condictione quod Antonius de Nellis civis florentinus possit in certis casibus de quibus in dicta conventione fit mentio[85] ipsum Iohannem privare tali exercitio et negocio, prout constat in dicta conventione et contractu rogato manu mei notarii infrascripti, idcirco constitutus dictus Antonius de Nellis coram testibus suprascriptis et dicto Iohanne et me notario infrascripto, habens in manibus quasdam litteras sibi directas a dictis Iohanne di Cologna et Niccolao Giansone et sotiis de Venetiis,[86] scriptas et factas die xxiiii Iulii et receptas die octava presentis[87] ⟨mensis⟩ augusti,[88] in quibus et per quas continetur qualiter dicti socii et societas non sint contenti[89] de servitio dicti Iohanni cartholarii et quod dictus Antonius Nelli eidem Iohanni det licentiam,[90] facto cum dicto Iohanni debita solutione de toto tempore sui servitii prout in ipsa conventione continetur,[91] qui Antonius omni meliore modo quo potuit, vigore omnium predictorum, dicto Iohanni presenti et audienti et intelligenti, protestatus fuit omnia predicta et qualiter amplius de cetero se non intromicteret vel aliquid faciat in dicta apotheca nec in aliquo negocio pertinenti dicte societati dicti Niccolai Gianson et Iohannis de Cologna, nec aliquid venderet vel faceret, alias protestatus fuit eidem Iohanni quod si ⟨non⟩ satisfecerit,[92] ipse Antonius et ipsi socii vel alius eorum nomine ageret contra ipsum ad omnia iurium et statutorum

---

78 Follows, cancelled: 'Nicc'.
79 'de Florentia' added in the interlinear.
80 Follows, cancelled: 'fac'.
81 'et dicte societatis' added in the interlinear.
82 Follows, cancelled: 'in effec'.
83 'qualiter' added in the interlinear.
84 Follows, cancelled: 'ad hoc ut vend'.
85 'de quibus in dicta conventione fit mentio' added on the left margin.
86 'de Venetiis' added on the left margin.
87 'presentis' added on the left margin.
88 Follows, cancelled: 'presentis'.
89 'contenti' corrected on: 'continentes' (?).
90 Follows, cancelled: 'fac'.
91 'prout in ipsa conventione continetur' added on the left margin.
92 Recte: 'satisdederit' (?); not totally clear.

remedia, et prout eisdem promissum erat vigore supra nominatorum iurium,[93] et qualiter ipse Antonius et seu dicti socii sunt et est paratus eidem solvere omne id totum quod sibi debent vigore supradicte conventionis.[94]

Presente decto Iohanne cartholario et predicta audiente et intelligente et dicente et protestante eidem Antonio dicto nomine, quod ipse intendit sibi satisfieri de eo quod sibi debetur antequam discedat a dicto exercitio etc., rog[ans] etc.

---

93   Not totally clear; follows, cancelled: 'rogans, etc.'.
94   'et qualiter ipse Antonius—conventionis' added on the left margin.

CHAPTER 4

Book Prices in Early Modern Europe: an Economic Perspective

Jeremiah Dittmar

> Este libro costó 8 negmit en Anvers a 29 de julio de 1531 y el ducado de oro vale 320 negmit.
> HERNANDO COLÓN

∴

Book Prices in History*

One of the remarkable features of early modern print culture is that activities in book production and the book trades were overwhelmingly organised to serve and shape markets and in pursuit of profit. Historical buyers and sellers in these markets left a trail of prices. These prices carry information—about how books were produced, about distance and transport, and about desire and purchasing power. This essay lays out some questions and approaches to the evidence on the prices of early modern books.

From an economic perspective, the diffusion of printing and print media delivered a supply shock to European book markets and, more broadly, the production and circulation of ideas. European society was—in historical terms rather suddenly—exposed to what contemporaries described as "artificial writing". This technology diffused across cities and was adopted by entrepreneurs producing a highly varied set of products. The range of books available and the set of places where one might purchase books expanded considerably. The conditions under which books came to be produced and circulated changed. Media markets and the economics of book production were transformed.

---

* This research has benefited from financial support from the Centre for Economic Performance at the London School of Economics and the European Research Council, through the European Union's Horizon 2020 research and innovation programme under grant number No. 638957.

It is widely acknowledged that the diffusion of printing had a profound impact on culture, politics and religion that was shaped by the reduction in the costs of transmitting and accessing books and other print media such as pamphlets. Contemporaries suggested that the decline in book prices was considerable. In 1468, Giovanni Andrea Bussi observed that prices had declined by 80 percent, enabling "even the pauper to acquire books".[1] In 1474, the Bolognese manuscript producer Lupoto began selling printed books and offered a printed breviary for 4 gold ducats, one fifth the price of hand-written breviaries he previously sold.[2] In 1481 Angiolo Martinozzi similarly wrote that "forms [movable type] has wrought that the book that was worth 10 florins is today worth 2".[3]

While the effects of changes in prices were arguably of first order importance for European society, the social history literature has generally focused on relatively small and local measures of book prices. As Angela Nuovo observes, "The price of books, which was paramount when it came to their diffusion and impact on various levels of society, still awaits overall investigation".[4]

This essay examines a relatively large body of evidence on book prices. The evidence comprises prices from almost three thousand purchases made between the 1460s and the early seventeenth century and is drawn from both the existing book history literature and an examination of historical evidence that has not yet been studied systematically. In particular, this paper studies the book purchases made by Hernando Colón, who was Christopher Columbus' son, a functionary of the Spanish Crown, and the initiator and organiser of what may have been the most ambitious book-buying and library assembly programme in early modern Europe.

The data on prices are used here to consider the questions: How did book prices compare to incomes in the fifteenth and sixteenth centuries? And what factors may explain the observed variation in prices? While this research examines a relatively large set of book prices, it does not attempt to provide a com-

---

1   Rudolf Hirsch, *Printing, Selling, and Reading, 1450–1550* (Wiesbaden: Harrassowitz, 1974), p. 1.
2   Anna Melograni, 'The illuminated manuscript as a commodity: production, consumption and the *cartolaio*'s role in fifteenth-century Italy', in Michelle O'Malley and Evelyn Welch (eds.), *The Material Renaissance* (Manchester: University of Manchester Press, 2007), p. 219.
3   Francesca Cenni, 'La penna e il torchio: una questione di soldi', in Outi Merisalo and Caterina Tristano (eds.), *Dal libro manoscritto al libro stampato* (Spoleto: Centro Italiano di Studi Sull'Alto Medioevo Spoleto, 2010), translation mine.
4   Angela Nuovo, *The Book Trade in the Italian Renaissance* (Leiden: Brill, 2013), p. 335. To be clear, this essay is one contribution to a larger body of work on book prices. For example, Angela Nuovo is investigating the European book market, including evidence on prices in the sixteenth and early seventeenth centuries. Cristina Dondi and Neil Harris also present rich evidence on book prices, discussed below.

prehensive overall investigation of prices. It also explicitly defers certain questions for a more properly quantitative and economic inquiry. In particular, the question of how variations in prices at any given time and in the dynamics of prices over time were driven by changes in the mix of formats, physical features of books including binding and illustration, and subject matter changes is one I address more formally in separate but complementary research.

From the perspective of the larger history of printing, this essay restricts itself to a small piece of the big picture, by focusing on patterns in price data. This focus should be seen as a complement to research that privileges the local and case studies. A rich body of literature shows us that the way the changes associated with print media unfolded at the local level was highly varied. These variations reflected the particularities of local cultures, city-level regulation and industrial organisation, and the talents, proclivities, and connections of individual entrepreneurs. Even the technology itself was dynamic, subject to further innovation and improvement, for example in the development of type, in the diffusion of ideas concerning formats and finding aids embedded in books themselves.

Economics and Historical Prices

Prices occupy a special place in economic thinking as carriers of information. On the one hand, prices carry information about the conditions of supply. In prices, we see the trace of technology, work organisation, the ways goods were moved across land and water, and the nature of competition among producers. Prices simultaneously carry information on the landscape of desire and demand.[5] The willingness to pay tells us about tastes and about the distribution of purchasing power. However, prices frequently provide limited, complicated, and cloudy signals. Many goods and experiences are hard to price, large swathes of historical activity including in the book trades have operated outside the immediate reach of markets, and untangling supply and demand is complicated. These facts are themselves central to the study of variation in prices within economics.

---

5 Research that examines prices and untangles or 'identifies' the impact of shifts in supply from shifts in demand is the subject of very extensive literatures within economics. That particular objective is not pursued in this paper. For a review, see for example, Josh Angrist and Alan Krueger, 'Instrumental variables and the search for identification: from supply and demand to natural experiments', *Journal of Economic Perspectives*, 15.4 (2001), pp. 69–85.

The research challenge has several inter-related components. The first is that price data are both rich and limited. In particular, the available evidence comes from multiple sources and reflects the heterogeneity and differences in market transactions. Books were themselves highly varied commodities, both in terms of subject matter and as physical objects. The same text could printed in different formats, and sold with or without rubrication, bound or unbound. The same text-object might be sold at different prices in different times and places—perhaps reflecting transport costs or differences in local demand. A book-seller might sell the very same text-object at different prices to different buyers at virtually the same time, for reasons that might reflect differences in what an economist would consider buyer characteristics, or indeed for hard to assess and potentially quasi-random reasons. For example, the accounts of the Venetian bookseller Francesco de Madiis reveal that copies of the same Bible were sold for £5 s10 and for £4 s4—a 25 percent difference—a mere six days apart in June 1484.[6] While key features of the observed variation in prices are specific to the early modern book trade, generically many markets reflect similar dynamics. In our current moment, markets exist for labour, homes, automobiles, and indeed incunabula—all of which exhibit interesting and sometimes profound forms of heterogeneity and differentiation. Economics is concerned with, among other things, prices in markets with these features.

Evidence on Prices

How expensive were books relative to historic incomes? This is a question about what economists would describe as the 'real price' of books, and one that is particularly relevant in our context given the quite dramatic price inflation of the sixteenth century. The records of book purchases made by Hernando Colón provide unusually rich evidence on prices in the 1500s and a starting point for this essay. Cristina Dondi observes that, "The great collection ... which the natural son of Christopher Columbus, Hernando arranged between 1509 and 1539 probably has no equal in this time".[7] Klaus Wagner records that Colón bought

---

[6] See Cristina Dondi and Neil Harris, 'Oil and green ginger. The Zornale of Francesco de Madiis, 1484–1488', in Malcolm Walsby and Natasha Constantinidou (eds.), *Documenting the Early Modern Book World: Inventories and Catalogues in Manuscript and Print* (Leiden: Brill, 2013).

[7] Cristina Dondi, 'The Venetian booktrade: a methodological approach to and first results of book-based historical research', in Bettina Wagner and Marcia Reed (eds.), *Early Printed Books as Material Objects: Proceeding of the Conference Organized by the IFLA Rare Books and Manuscripts Section* (Berlin: De Gruyter, 2010), pp. 219–228: 222.

all types of books, "without restrictions on ideological type or language"—including, for example, books by Protestant authors.[8]

Colón's collection was not only unusually large in sheer numbers, but was initiated with the express objective of constructing a universal library that would comprise *all* printed books. In a letter to the Spanish crown seeking financial support for his endeavours, Colón explained his intention to establish "a place in Your Majesty's kingdoms where will be collected all the books in all the languages and faculties [disciplines] that can be found in Christendom and even beyond".[9] The fact that Colón's purchases were motivated by a desire to accumulate all possible books makes this collection especially interesting and invites an examination of the actual scope of the collection.

Colón's purchases are in addition an unusually rich as a source of quantitative evidence on prices. Colón made purchases in over forty cities. For almost two thousand purchases, Colón recorded the price paid for specific volumes in the local currency as well as the prevailing exchange rate between the local currency and the gold ducat. A typical entry in the purchasing notebooks will record the price paid for a book in a local currency, the location of purchase, and the prevailing exchange rate as follows: "Este libro costó 8 negmit en Anvers a 29 de julio de 1531 y el ducado de oro vale 320 negmit". This structure in the purchasing records enables us calculate prices in a common metric—golden ducats and their silver equivalents—and thus to compare book prices to prevailing incomes, as discussed below.[10]

Even more broadly, the evidence from Colón's purchases provide a window onto the circuits of trade, wealth, power and knowledge that characterized early modern Europe. The financial underpinnings of Colón's book collecting efforts reflected the fact that Colón was Christopher Columbus' son. We observe Columbus himself writing from the Americas to the Spanish Crown in

---

8   Klaus Wagner, 'La Biblioteca Colombina en tiemps de Hernando Colón', *Historia, Instituciones, Documentos*, 19 (1992), pp. 485–495: 486 (translation mine).

9   Henry Harrisse, *Excerpta Colombiana: Bibliographie de quatre cents pièces gothiques françaises italiennes et latines du commencement du XVIe siècle* (Paris: Welter, 1887), p. 284 (translation mine).

10 Tomás Marín Martínez, José Manuel Ruiz Asencio and Klaus Wagner, *Catálogo concordado de la Biblioteca de Hernando Colón* (Madrid: Mapfre y Cabildo de la Catedral de Sevilla, 1993); Archer Huntington (ed.), *Catalogue of the Library of Ferdinand Columbus: Reproduced in Facsimile From the Unique Manuscript in the Colombine Library of Sevilla* (New York: E. Bierstadt, 1905). Tomás Marín Martínez, *Abecedarium B y Supplementum. Ed. facsímil de los manuscritos conservados en la Biblioteca Colombina de Sevilla* (Madrid: Fundación Mapfre y Cabildo de la Catedral de Sevilla, 1992). I exclude from consideration a limited number of purchases which are either illegible or incorrectly transcribed. For example, where putative exchange rates are erroneous.

the 1498 to explain: "In the name of the Holy Trinity, we can send from here all the slaves and brazil wood which could be sold. If my information is correct, one could sell 4,000 slaves that would bring at least 20 millions".[11] On Christopher Columbus' first return from the Americas, Hernando was appointed as a page to the Crown Prince. As a teenager, Colón travelled with Columbus to the Americas on a subsequent voyage. After Columbus' death, Colón again travelled to the Americas with his elder half-brother in 1509, a voyage the latter made to assume his position as Governor of Hispaniola. Colón returned to Spain in 1509, entered government service and immediately embarked on his efforts to build an unparalleled library, financed by revenues generated by, among other things, forced labour in the Indies. By the 1530s, Colón received an annuity from Spanish crown to support his library project,

> on account of Don Hernando's past and present services, and the services that Admiral don Cristóbal Colón, his father, did for us ... every year, and during all his life, 500 pesos in gold ... to support and sustain the library he is establishing in the city of Seville, and that these moneys be paid from the rents and profits that we may have in that land.[12]

Colón made purchases in over forty European cities. Figure 4.1 maps both the cities where Colón bought books and the cities where the books Colón purchased were produced. Cities with purchases are marked by darker blue markers. Production is indicated by lighter red markers. Markers are scaled to reflect the number of purchases (printed editions).

How much did books purchased in these cities cost in real terms? One way to answer this question is to calculate the price of books relative to prevailing incomes. Calculating the price of books relative to workers' wages is just one way to gauge the accessibility of books. Indexing prices to wages has the merit of controlling for wage inflation, but is a strategic simplification for the purposes of illustration. The ratio of prices to wages provides a transparent metric of how accessible books were even to people on relatively modest incomes.

---

11 Cited in Tsvetan Todorov, *The Conquest of the Americas: The Question of the Other* (Norman: University of Oklahoma Press, 1984), p. 47.
12 Juan Guillén, *Hernando Colón. Humanismo y bibliofilia* (Sevilla: Fundación José Manuel Lara, 2004), p. 205. In the original: "acatando lo que don Hernando Colón nos ha servido y sirve y lo que el almirante don Cristóbal Colón, su padre, nos hizo ... en cada un año, para en toda su vida, quinientos pesos de oro de a cuatrocientos y cincuenta maravedís cada peso, que suman doscientos y veinte y cinco mil maravedís para ayuda a su sustentación y de la librería que hace en la ciudad de Sevilla, y que se le paguen de las rentas y provechos que tuviésemos en esa tierra".

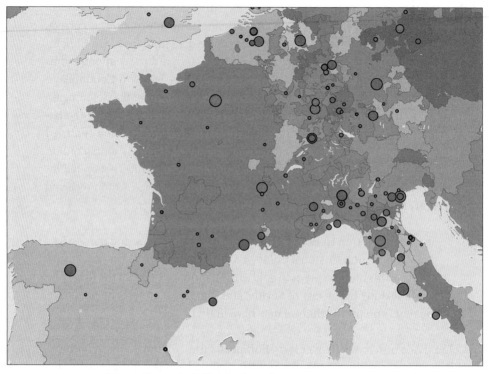

FIGURE 4.1 Cities in Hernando Colón's book purchases

Wage data are not readily available in all cities and times in which we observe book purchases. But we do have wage series for 15 European cities from research by Robert Allen, and these provide a pan-European benchmark.[13] I will refer to this as the 'European worker's wage' as a heuristic.[14] I consider the price of book relative to the incomes of salaried university professors and bureaucrats below.

Figure 4.2 presents the distribution of purchase prices relative to wages for unskilled labour and shows that more than half the books purchased cost

---

13   Robert Allen, 'The great divergence in European wages and prices from the Middle Ages to the First World War', *Explorations in Economic History*, 38 (2001), pp. 411–447. A broadly similar qualitative picture emerges if we disaggregate wages and prices by city and retain only prices in those cities for which wage data are available. An alternate approach would be to compute an overall consumer price index and compare the evolution of book prices to 'prices in general' or to prices of a basket of goods that represents the consumption bundle of book purchasers.

14   Further research may identify data on incomes across a wider range of cities. But the key magnitudes and findings reported here are unlikely to be driven by local variations in wages.

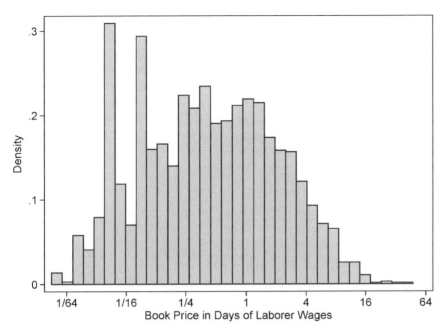

FIGURE 4.2 Distribution of book prices in Colón's purchases

less than one day's worth of wages. Colón's purchases were remarkable in including a large number of pamphlets, booklets, and other ephemera. In Figure 4.2, Colón's large-scale purchases of pamphlets show up in the two places in lower tail of the price distribution where there are spikes in the distribution—indicating that a large share of total purchases were made at these prices.[15]

Workers' wages clearly provide just one benchmark for understanding the level of prices. Wage data has the advantage of providing a relatively transparent benchmark, but the typical purchaser of books was highly educated, commanded a higher income, and thus faced prices that were substantially cheaper in relative terms. If surviving records on wages are fragmentary, information on incomes and purchasing power for highly educated professionals

---

15   Prices in Figure 4.2 are presented as prices in days of worker's wages on a *ratio scale* along the horizontal axis. The ratio scale has units that advance in constant multiples. In this case, the graph shows prices in multiples of 4: books that cost 1/4 of day's wages, 1 day's wages, 4 day's wage, etc. The ratio scale enables us to more easily visually inspect price variations at the lower end of the distribution. This scale shows us that prices were approximately log normally distributed, with the exception of the two concentrations of pamphlets. Equivalently, this tells us that the underlying raw prices were skewed, with a thick upper tail extending to include purchases of books that cost dozens of days' worth of wages for an unskilled labour.

is arguably more so and poses its own challenges. However, we have enough evidence to draw some provisional conclusions. For example, in Florence in the 1450s, skilled craftsmen typically earned 50 percent more than unskilled workers. Meanwhile an official at the Florentine chancery earned almost five times as much over a year as an unskilled labourer, and in the 1450s the most highly compensated university professors commanded salaries as much as 18 times the annual income of an unskilled labourer.[16] We can thus imagine scaling prices shown in Figure 4.2 down depending the relative income level we wish to consider.

A larger question concerns the representativeness of the books Colón purchased. One way to shed light on the distribution of types of books purchased by Colón is to classify these books by subject and compare the distribution of subject matter in Colón's purchases to the distribution in the Universal Short Title Catalogue (USTC). Given the potential for survival bias, and the fact that the size of print runs varied across literatures and individual publications, some caution may be in order when drawing inferences from data on the subject matter of *known* editions produced in early modern Europe. That said, the distribution of subject matter in books in the USTC provides a benchmark for considering the range of purchases made by Colón. Figure 4.3 presents a scatter plot that shows how the share of Colón's purchases in a given subject area compares to the share of titles in the USTC classified with that subject. For illustration, the 45-degree line is presented. Were the subjects of Colón's purchases to exactly match the distribution of editions in the USTC, all observations would follow this line. Instead we see that while Colón's purchase of religious books approximately matched their overall share in the USTC (top right observation), Colón purchased far more 'Philology' and far less basic 'Education' than we find in the USTC. More broadly, we see a strong correlation between Colón's purchases and overall output, but that Colón tended to invest more heavily in philosophy, dialectics, poetry, science and mathematics, and academic dissertations—and less heavily in law, classical authors, music, and books on politics and government.

---

16   Wages for skilled and unskilled labour are from Allen, 'The Great Divergence in European Wages and Prices'. See online 'Laborers' relative wages (Allen)', http://gpih.ucdavis.edu/, last accessed 28 May 2018. Compensation for chancery officials and university professors are from Albinia de la Mare, 'New research on humanistic scribes in Florence', in Annarosa Garzelli (ed.), *Miniatura fiorentina del Rinascimento (1440–1525). Un primo censimento* (Florence: Giunta Regionale Toscana, 1985).

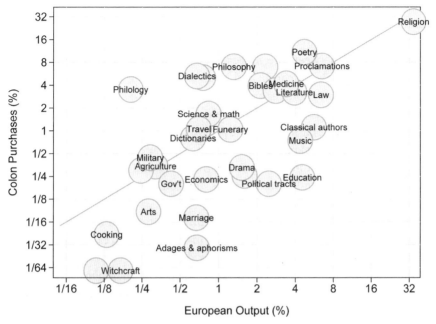

FIGURE 4.3 The subject matter of Colón's purchases compared to the USTC

Prices over Time: Comparisons across Sources

While the evidence we have from Colón's purchases is extremely rich, it is also characterized by the limited temporal scope of these purchases and by the fact that they were all made by a single and an unusual buyer. It is natural to wonder how these sales compare to book prices recorded in other times and places and made by other buyers. It thus useful to compare the evidence on books purchased by Colón to other evidence on purchases and prices.[17]

To illustrate and to begin to consider the wider sweep of early modern printing, this paper examines several other sources stretching from the 1460s

---

17 An interesting point of comparison is between the prices of Colón's purchases and the advertised prices of the same books in bookseller's catalogues. Klaus Wagner provides evidence on catalogue prices advertised by Aldus Manutius. See Wagner, 'Aldo Manuzio e i prezzi dei suoi libri', *La Bibliofilía*, 77 (1975), pp. 77–82. A direct comparison is complicated not only by the fact that catalogue prices are not transaction prices, but also by the fact that Colón bought these books several years after the catalogue was issued (making the books subject to subsequent price changes) and at foreign locations (implying transport costs). While typically books might depreciate, stable values and even appreciation were certainly possible, and the Aldine editions were distinguished.

through the early 1600s. I set the Colón evidence against evidence on book prices from: the 1484 sales records of Venetian bookseller Francesco de Madiis studied and brought to our attention by Cristina Dondi and Neil Harris; purchases made in between the mid-1500s and the early 1600s by the Tuscan bibliophile Bellisario Bulgarini; and a range of book prices recorded by Uwe Neddermeyer.[18] These sources are each transcribed into a database. In the case of Bulgarini's purchasing records this entails identifying and coding the transcriptions in which Bulgarini lists the price paid for each volume in his records. These sources are not exhaustive, and each raises interesting questions, which may be explored in future research. But they provide a large and revealing set of observations on market transactions. In total, there are over 2,500 prices observed.

Figure 4.4 plots the raw data on book prices in terms of days of labourer's wages and reveals dramatic price declines in the 1400s, with each marker representing an individual transaction.[19] This evidence suggests most of the decline in the prices of printed books occurred in the 1400s, when books are initially observed costing over 100 days' worth of wages, and suggests a subsequent levelling out of book prices over the 1500s. However, this pattern in the data reflects the fact that the unit of analysis is a price for a book—with as yet no accounting for differences in length or indeed other characteristics. To underscore the interesting nature of this underlying variation, Figure 4.4 labels one interesting highly priced book printed in Hebrew in the mid-1500s: a *Machzor* prayer-book used for devotional purposes on the Jewish High Holidays of Rosh Hashanah and Yom Kippur. The graphical evidence and this example immediately raise questions about the differences in book purchases recorded in different sources. Similarly, the evidence naturally invites questions about changes in the nature of books produced and purchased over time—as the mix of formats

---

18 Dondi and Harris, 'Oil and green ginger'. For Bellisario Bulgarini, see Daniele Danesi, *Cento anni di libri: la biblioteca di Bellisario Bulgarini e della sua famiglia, circa 1560–1660* (Pisa: Pacini Editore, 2014). Uwe Neddermeyer, *Von der Handschrift zum gedruckten Buch: Schriftlichkeit und Leseinteresse im Mittelalter und in der frühen Neuzeit; quantitative und qualitative Aspekte* (Wiesbaden: Otto Harrassowitz Verlag, 1998), provides evidence on book prices from a large and heterogeneous set of sources largely comprising purchases from Southern Germany, the upper Rhine, and Italy, including among many others Peter Drach's accounts, Johann Petz, *Geschichte der Bücherei des Nurnberger Rates* (Nuremberg: Mitteilungen des Vereins für Geschichte der Stadt Nürnberg, 1886), and Vera Sack, *Die Inkunabeln der Universitätsbibliothek und anderer öffentlicher Sammlungen in Freiburg im Breisgau und Umgebung* (Wiesbaden: Otto Harrassowitz Verlag, 1985).

19 Data from Neddermeyer, Colón, and Bulgarini are as cited above. The 'Zornale' series is from Dondi and Harris, 'Oil and green ginger'.

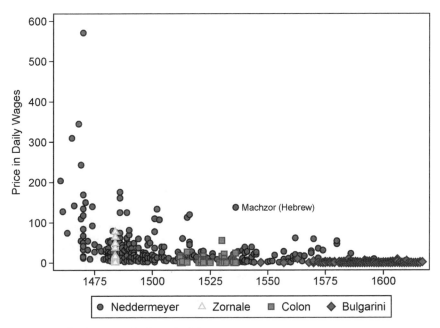

FIGURE 4.4 Book prices 1460 through 1618

changed, as decorative and physical characteristics evolved, and as new content hit the market. It should also be noted that because our evidence includes several very expensive books, the scale of the graph leaves us effectively unable to interrogate visually the variation in prices across the vast majority of books. The vast majority of books cost in the neighbourhood of one day's worth of wages, and frequently less.

When we account for variation in book characteristics a somewhat different picture emerges. Specifically, we observe marked, persistent, and relatively stable declines in relative prices across the sixteenth century. Figure 4.5 plots the price data accounting for differences in length and *on a ratio scale*.[20] The underlying data here are identical to those in Figure 4.4, with each marker representing one transaction. Here, however, the prices are calculated per-sheet and presented for a hypothetical 25 sheet book.[21] This calculation is straight

---

20 This figure excludes pamphlets and booklets of 32 pages or fewer. Several of these pamphlets were outliers—among most expensive items purchased by Colón on a per page basis.

21 This is simply illustrative. Self-evidently, books varied on multiple dimensions. This presentation of the data is merely a first-step towards a more developed and precise measure of real prices.

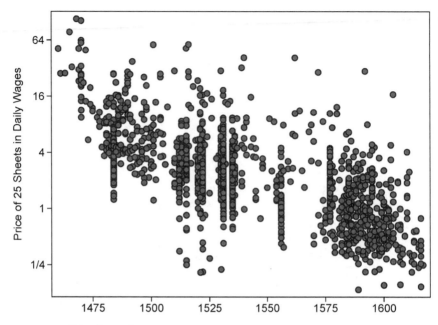

FIGURE 4.5 Prices for 25 sheets

forward: for a 25-sheet book, consider the price as is; for a 50 sheet book, divide the price by two. This adjustment is designed as a simple heuristic and a first step towards a more comprehensive assessment of prices. The *ratio scale* (along the vertical axis) presents prices going up multiplicatively and serves two illustrative functions. First, it enables us to assess visually variations in prices at the bottom of the distribution, including for books sold for the equivalent of one-half or one-eighth of a day's wages. Second, when data follow a linear trend on a ratio scale this implies an underlying constant *rate* of change. Visual inspection of the data suggest some preliminary conclusions. In particular, Figure 4.5 strongly suggests an approximately stable and certainly persistent decline in the per-sheet price of books spanning the entire period from the later 1400s through the early 1600s.

There are several possible explanations for the persistent price declines we observe. One possibility is that the characteristics of books examined changed. Perhaps the observed price declines were driven by changes in book characteristics? For example, we might wonder whether variations in prices principally reflected variations in the mix and type of books we observe in evidence on purchases and sales. The obvious question is whether our story is one of shifts over time away from folios and towards quartos, octavos, and other smaller formats—and the rise of more popular print. We might similarly wonder about the size of pages and fonts *within* formats, the presence of illustrations, printing in multiple colours, or indeed the subject matter of books. The hypothesis that changes along these dimensions drove price declines is very plausible, but interestingly does not appear to be the key underlying determinant of either price declines over time or the variation in prices across books at a point in time. For example, we observe price declines over time *within* the Bulgarini data despite limited shifts in the physical nature and content of the books in these purchasing records. We similarly see wide variation in book prices even for identical books sold by the same seller, raising the possibility of considerable idiosyncratic variation in demand and bargaining.[22] In our setting, we might be interested in how book prices change unconditionally—which is what Figure 4.4 illustrates. But we may be also interested in how prices evolve after controlling progressing for the sources of variation in book characteristics. I pursue precisely this analysis and formalise these questions and findings quantitatively in related but separate research.[23]

A second possible explanation for price declines concerns technology and the organization of production. Consideration of these questions returns us to classic observations in the book history literature. Several decades ago, in *L'Apparition du Livre*, Febvre and Martin observed that the basic equipment of the printing press hardly changed between the sixteenth and eighteenth centuries. Yet they simultaneously observed that over the sixteenth century composition shifted from being done seated to being done by workers standing on their feet. In addition, type with notches marking the orientation of letters was introduced so that letters could be picked from a container and type set without the compositor needing to look at his work "like a modern typist at a keyboard".[24] These observations strongly suggest that the organization of the composition and larger printing work environment mattered for productivity—and that technology broadly conceived was dynamic. Similarly, Jean-François Gilmont documents both the remarkably high output of press

---

22 See, for example in Dondi and Harris' evidence on Venetian prices from the 1480s, discussed above.
23 See, for example, Jeremiah Dittmar and Skipper Seabold, 'New media and competition: printing and Europe's transformation after Gutenberg' Centre for Economic Performance, working paper at www.jeremiahdittmar.com/research, last accessed 11 June 2018.
24 Lucien Febvre and Henri-Jean Martin, *The Coming of the Book* (London: Verso, 1976), p. 62. Febvre and Martin also observe technological changes within the 'basic' printing press framework—for example, the adoption of metal in place of wooden screw threads and the displacement of original North German type presses by a Lyonnais variant.

workers in the sixteenth century and the salience of labour disputes over the length of the work day, the pace of work, and the per-worker quantity of output demanded by employers each day.[25] These disputes signal that behind the product prices we observe there were struggles and bargains over labour inputs and worker compensation. As Gilmont observes: "Does the identical nature of the equipment necessarily entail identical working arrangements? Not necessarily. The historical facts suggest that there were at least partial reorganizations".[26]

A third and related explanation for the observed declines in book prices is competition amongst producers. In a world with more producers, and with closer substitutes in the market place, we would expect the monopoly power of individual producers to decline and for prices to fall. Indeed, given a particular compensation structure for workers, the ability of early modern capitalists in the printing industry to increase worker effort and output would be expected to show up in lower book prices—as opposed to in profits—in so far as the market for books was relatively competitive. A rich body of evidence suggests that printers developed creative and varied strategies to secure market power, but that competition was frequently fierce, quasi-monopoly positions frequently crumbled, and that the range of publications available to consumers broadly was increasing.[27]

Taken as a whole, the evidence on book prices presented here suggests that contemporary observers were not far off—there was great variation, but by the 1480s books had fallen in price by around 80 percent. Perhaps as remarkably, steady price declines persisted across the 1500s. By the late 1500s, books and not just pamphlets frequently cost less than a day's worth of wages. However, market prices remained extremely variable, including for closely comparable and even identical books. Research on the nature, determinants, and dynam-

---

25 Jean-François Gilmont, 'Printers by the rules', *The Library*, 6th s., 2.2 (1980), pp. 129–155.
26 Gilmont, 'Printers by the rules', p. 130.
27 For example, Ian MacLean studies the competitive conduct of Frankfurt printer André Wechel, in the textbook market in the later 1500s. When competitors printed school books, Wechel used a quantity competition response strategy and unleashed, "a massive and systematic onslaught ... aiming at little short of a monopoly ... by putting into practice the commercial principle: if a competitor produces an edition, do the same". This was almost textbook game-theoretic behaviour. See Ian MacLean, *Learning and the Marketplace: Essays in the History of the Early Modern Book* (Leiden: Brill, 2009), p. 177. Examples of partnerships and syndicates that operated to secure market power are documented in Nuovo, *The Book Trade in the Italian Renaissance* and Christoph Reske, *Die Buchdrucker des 16. und 17. Jahrhunderts im deutschen Sprachgebiet: auf der Grundlage des gleichnamigen Werkes von Josef Benzing* (Wiesbaden: Harrassowitz, 2007).

ics of early modern book prices provides one setting where perspectives from economics may offer insights to and should be in dialogue with the cultural history and history of the book literatures.

CHAPTER 5

Privileging the Common Good: the Moral Economy of Printing Privileges in the Seventeenth-Century Dutch Republic

Marius Buning

The Dutch Republic was one of the major printing hubs of the early modern period. Estimations vary, but according to a recent estimate as many as 350,000 separate works must have been printed in the seventeenth century alone.[1] These books were not just conveyors of information but also part of a broader trade in commodities. However, a problematic issue with books was that they were highly susceptible to imitation and counterfeiting. Illegal copying allowed printers to save on editing and translation costs, making it possible to bring reproductions onto the market at a lower cost. Following a practice that existed all over Europe,[2] therefore, the Dutch authorities decided to issue specific patents, so-called 'printing privileges', shortly after the de facto independence of the Republic in 1581.[3] These privileges provided printers with tem-

---

1 Andrew Pettegree and Arthur der Weduwen, 'What was published in the seventeenth-century Dutch Republic?', *Livre. Revue Historique* (2018), pp. 1–27.
2 As far as we know, the first privilege that prohibited copying a work without permission was issued in 1479 by the Bishop of Würzburg. The habit then spread fast and widely throughout early modern Europe, and by mid sixteenth century there was not a single sovereignty on the European continent where a system of printing privileges was not in place. For an overview, see Chris Schriks, *Het kopijrecht, 16de tot 19de eeuw: Aanleidingen tot en gevolgen van boekprivileges en boekhandelsusanties, kopijrecht, verordeningen, boekenwetten en rechtspraak in het privaat-, publiek- en staatsdomein in de Nederlanden, met globale analoge ontwikkelingen in Frankrijk, Groot-Brittannië en het Heilig Roomse Rijk* (Zutphen: Walburg, 2004), pp. 175–258; Christopher L.C.E. Witcombe, *Copyright in the Renaissance: Prints and the* Privilegio *in Sixteenth-Century Venice and Rome* (Leiden: Brill, 2004), pp. 59–73.
3 Privileges were just one of the possibilities to seek protection against piracy, and possibly not even the most effective. Printers frequently entered into collusions, and there were plenty of other trade customs (*usanties*) to seek protection against piracy. It is important here to make a distinction between 'printing privileges' and the 'right to copy'. The right to copy was a printer's right. Printers would buy off the manuscript from an author, thus obtaining the eternal 'right to copy' (*kopijrecht*). This right, which was transferable, implied that others could not print the same work; however, strictly speaking, it gave no legal protection against piracy. Printing privileges, on the other hand, gave a right to exclusive publication, even if this right was always limited in time.

porary exclusive rights for the commercial exploitation of their work, allowing them to reap the benefits of their investments.[4]

Although printing privileges have been identified as an important mechanism of trade regulation, we still know very little about their effect on the seventeenth-century Dutch book market.[5] In particular, it remains unclear why certain printers sought privileges for specific titles and not for others, and why some printers never applied for a privilege at all. Paul Hoftijzer argued that printers considered the process of obtaining a privilege worthwhile only when they expected resounding success from a work that was yet to appear in print, when a book had already proven to be a bestseller, or when the production process was very costly.[6] Arie Cornelis Kruseman, per contra, claimed that printers had little to fear from copyright infringers when production costs were very high, because the prospect of making large investments would deter potential

---

4   Printing privileges soon became tradable commodities that played a signal role in the development of our present-day system of copyrights. The history of copyrights is complicated and differs from country to country. For an overview, see for instance the commentaries that form part of the project *Primary Sources on Copyright (1450–1900)*, edited by Lionel Bently and Martin Kretschmer and accessible online at: www.copyrighthistory.org, last accessed on 23 January 2017.
5   Dutch printing privileges for the production of books have been the explicit topic of study of: Isabella H. van Eeghen, *De Amsterdamse boekhandel 1680–1725* (5 vols., Amsterdam: Scheltema & Holkema, 1960–1978), V, part I, pp. 193–236; Ellen M. Grabowsky, ''Op de goede beterschap van ons sieke privilegie': Over Amsterdamse schouwburgregenten, drukkers en censuur', *Jaarboek voor Nederlandse boekgeschiedenis*, 2 (1995), pp. 35–55, 213–214. Simon Groenveld and Jacobus B. den Hartog, 'Twee musici, twee stromingen. Een boekoctrooi voor Anthoni van Noordt en een advies van Constantijn Huygens, 1659', in Arie T. van Deursen, Eddy K. Grootes and P.E.L. Verkuyl (eds.), *Veelzijdigheid als levensvorm: Facetten van Constantijn Huygens' leven en werk* (Deventer: Sub Rosa, 1987), pp. 109–127. Simon Groenveld, 'The Dutch Republic, an island of liberty of the press in 17th-century Europe? The authorities and the book trade', in H. Bots and F. Waquet (eds.), *Commercium litterarium. La communication dans la République des Lettres [1600–1750]* (Amsterdam: APA-Holland University Press, 1994), pp. 281–300: 294; Paul Hoftijzer, 'Nederlandse boekverkopersprivileges in de zeventiende en achttiende eeuw', *Jaarboek Nederlands Genootschap van Bibliofielen*, 1 (1993), pp. 49–62: 49. Paul Hoftijzer, ''A sickle unto thy neighbour's corn': book piracy in the Dutch Republic', *Quaerendo*, 27 (1997), pp. 3–18; Paul Hoftijzer, 'Nederlandse boekverkopersprivileges in de achttiende eeuw. Kanttekeningen bij een inventarisatie', *Documentatieblad werkgroep 18e eeuw*, 22.2 (1990), pp. 159–180; Arie Cornelis Kruseman, *Aanteekeningen betreffende den boekhandel van Noord-Nederland* (Amsterdam: Van Kampen, 1893), pp. 340–354. Schriks, *Het kopijrecht*; Lajb Fuks, 'De twee gelijktijdig te Amsterdam in de 17ᵉ eeuw verschenen Jiddische Bijbelvertalingen', *Het boek: Tweede reeks van het tijdschrift voor boek- en bibliotheekwezen*, 32 (1955), pp. 146–165.
6   Hoftijzer, 'Nederlandse boekverkopersprivileges in de achttiende eeuw', pp. 159–180: 163–164.

pirates. Kruseman further stated that printers would not even take the trouble of obtaining a privilege were the production process to be inexpensive, if only because the procurement of a privilege would be more trouble than its worth. As a result, printers only petitioned for privileges on medium sized and moderately prized books, in which case the privilege functioned as a form of advertisement for forthcoming books rather than a legal protection.[7] Both Kruseman and Hoftijzer, in short, evidently put the emphasis on the interests of publishers, attributing only a subordinate and passive role to the authorities.

This essay will reassess the above arguments in the light of the available source material, demonstrating that privileges were in fact also issued for cheaper prints, and that the Dutch authorities were anything but a disinterested party when it came to privilege conferment.[8] In a sense, this argument is in line with earlier observations made by Nadine Orenstein, who suggested that privileges for artistic prints "added a certain faux prestige" to particular engravings through means of suggesting that they had been approved by the authorities.[9] The degree to which this argument is also applicable to the domain of book privileges will be explored. This essay will first offer a brief introduction to the political embedment of the Dutch privilege system, and then describe the nature of the privileged material. The narrative will subsequently move on to the relationship between privileges and reprints, before turning to the question of the legal validity versus the social scope of privileges. The conclusion circles back to the overarching query of which benefits a privilege might have had on the Dutch book market, and for whom.

---

7   Kruseman, *Aanteekeningen*, p. 345.
8   A lot of the source material can be found in the Dutch National Archives, Den Hague, States General, access number 1.02.02 (hereafter NL-HaNA, States General, 1.01.02). Primary source material has been presented using original spelling and grammar, except that the long 's' has been replaced by its modern equivalent. In the translations, interpunction has been added and capitalization has been modernized. Translations are by the author unless otherwise stated. For the States General, I have also used the entries to the resolutions as printed in the publication series *Rijks Geschiedkundige Publicatiën: Resolutiën Staten-Generaal 1576–1609* (14 vols., The Hague: Martinus Nijhoff, 1915–1970) [henceforth: RSG], and *Resolutiën Staten-Generaal 1610–1670* (7 vols., The Hague: Martinus Nijhoff, 1971–1984, and Instituut voor Nederlandse Geschiedenis, 1989–1994) [henceforth: RSG NR]. The new series, although intended to include sources up to 1670, halted at seven volumes, thus including sources up to 1625 only.
9   Nadine Orenstein, 'Sleeping caps, city views and state funerals: privileges for prints in the Dutch Republic 1580–1650', in Amy Golahny, Mia M. Mochizuki and Lisa Vergara (eds.), *In His Milieu: Essays on Netherlandish Art in Memory of John Michael Montias* (Amsterdam: Amsterdam University Press, 2006), pp. 313–346: 320. Groenveld made a similar suggestion for book privileges; however, the idea was never much elaborated upon. Groenveld, 'The Dutch Republic', pp. 281–300: 291. See also Kruseman, *Aanteekeningen*, pp. 345, 350.

Privileging Books in the Dutch Republic

Printing privileges were characterized by a number of specific facets.[10] One of those was that a privilege provided an exception to the common law, and another that privileges, as a general rule, had to be issued by the highest authority of a particular territory. This invariably proved complicated in the case of the Dutch Republic, as The Republic consisted of a loose amalgamation of semi-autonomous Provinces which joined forces in the federal Assembly of the States General only on a limited number of issues. As a natural consequence, the structure of the privilege regime remained somewhat fragmented. The States General initially took the lead within the privilege system. During the second half of the seventeenth century, however, the States of Holland proceeded to issued most of the privileges in the Republic in an attempt to demarcate its authority ever more clearly.[11] Accordingly, speaking of an 'administrative unity' from the perspective of the long seventeenth century is difficult. Nevertheless, one persistent characteristic was that the privilege regime was strongly regulated on a supra-urban level.

This did not mean that local authorities were, by definition, sidelined. Especially from the second half of the seventeenth century onwards, the Provincial States usually consulted with the governors of the booksellers' guilds first before deciding upon a privilege.[12] The advice of the local guild masters related

---

10   Printing privileges were nothing but a variation on the more widely spread phenomenon of legal privileges. The standard work on legal privileges is Barbara Dölemeyer and Heinz Mohnhaupt (eds.), *Das Privileg im europäischen Vergleich* (2 vols., Frankfurt am Main: Klostermann, 1997–1999).

11   Hoftijzer situates this change directly after the expiry of the privilege for printing the States Bible in 1652. Hoftijzer, 'Nederlandse boekverkopersprivileges in de achttiende eeuw', pp. 159–180: 164. See also Hoftijzer, 'Nederlandse boekverkopersprivileges in de zeventiende en achttiende eeuw', pp. 49–62: 55; Kruseman, *Aanteekeningen*, p. 347. From that point onwards, individual provinces ever more often claimed the right to issue privileges on their own behalf, and even privileges still issued by the States General had to be granted *attaché* (confirmation) by the Provinces in order to gain legal validity. This latter practice has not yet been studied in much detail, but see Schriks, *Het kopijrecht*, p. 66. There is currently no systematic information available about printing privileges granted by other Provinces except Holland.

12   The guild system was relatively weak in the Dutch Republic. But as the Golden Age advanced, the number of guilds as well as their importance increased. For an overview, see Jan Lucassen and Piet Lourens, 'Ambachtsgilden in Nederland: Een eerste inventarisatie', *Nederlandsch Economisch-Historisch Archief Jaarboek voor economische, bedrijfs- en techniekgeschiedenis* 57 (1994), pp. 34–62. For the most part of the seventeenth century, booksellers still subsided under the Guild of St Luke. Unlike the later bookseller guilds, these guilds were not directly involved in giving advice about upcoming privileges. Bookseller

to the question of whether there was any opposition among the other booksellers in town, for instance, because the project was under press somewhere else, or because the scope of the privilege was excessive. The guilds, in that way, evidently became part of the decision-making process. However, the higher authorities could always decide to issue a privilege without consultation on the basis of their sovereign powers. The fact that the States asked for advice from local guilds just proves that power was negotiated rather than imposed.

Applying for a privilege was voluntary in the Dutch Republic. According to estimates, only one percent of the total book production was eventually produced under privilege.[13] Even if it remains unclear to what extent a privilege really provided a commercial advantage, we may assume that the motivation for requesting a privilege was a matter of honor and profit. However, privileging literature did not guarantee market success, nor did the denial of privilege preclude publication. Plenty of examples exist of books that had been denied a privilege, yet nevertheless became successful. One example related to Johann Heidfeld's *Sphinx theologico-philosophia*, first published in Latin, at Herborn in 1600. Ten years later, the Amsterdam-based printer Dirk Pietersz Pers requested a privilege to compensate the costs that he would incur in the process of translating the work.[14] The printer's request was denied for unknown reasons; however, two years later Pietersz Pers put out a Dutch edition of the *Sphinx theologico-philosophia*, translated by Pieter Jacobsz van Suyderwoude.[15] This translation was printed on several occasions in the seventeenth century (Amsterdam: Dirck Pietersz Pers, 1627 and 1658).

---

guilds were erected in Middelburg (1590), Utrecht (1599), Haarlem (1616), Leiden (1651), Amsterdam (1662), Rotterdam (1699), and The Hague (1702).

13 Hoftijzer, 'Nederlandse boekverkopersprivileges in de zeventiende en achttiende eeuw', pp. 49–62: 49. There are numerous examples of high risk printing projects that were not privileged, such as the richly illustrated multilingual artist manual *The Light of Painting* by Crispijn van de Passe. Crispijn van de Passe, *La prima [-quinta] parte della lvce del dipingere et disegnare. = Eerste [-vijfde] deel van 't light. = La premiere [-cinquiesme] partie de la lumiere. = Der erste [-fünffte] Theil vom Liecht.* (Amsterdam: sold by J. Iansz. and the author, 1643), USTC 15515149.

14 The request can be found in NL-HaNA, States General, 1.01.02, inv. no. 7476. The denial of the privilege is recorded in J.J. Dodt van Flensburg, *Archief voor kerkelijke en wereldsche geschiedenissen, inzonderheid van Utrecht.* (7 vols., Utrecht: N. van der Monde, 1838–1848) [henceforth abbreviated as JDF], V, p. 250.

15 Johannes Heidfeld, *Sphinx Theologico-Philosophica, ofte de schriftuerlijcke ende philosophische tijt-korter.* Translated by Pieter Jacobsz (Amsterdam: Dirck Pietersz Pers, 1612), USTC 1012486.

Stamp of Approval

The authorities of the Republic issued no more than the modest number of about five to ten privileges per year. Privileged works included patriotic literature, religious propaganda, and schoolbooks (such as astronomical textbooks, catechisms, compendia, and grammar books).[16] The commercial value of these books varied wildly. However, a differentiation between two categories may be identified, with on the one hand a category consisting of cheap print directly related to governmental interests, and on the other hand books that were expensive to produce. Especially in the latter case, the privilege functioned as a means to compensate publishers for making large investments.

A recurring fear among privilege applicants was that pirate printers would be able to market their products cheaper by saving on translation and editing costs. As a result, the first printer would be stuck with copies that he had to sell for lower than the cost price.[17] Another concern was that copper engravings would be replaced by cheap imitation woodcuts. A case in point can be found in the justification of the privilege issued to Jan Lucasz Wagenaer for the publication of his famous *Mariner's Mirrour*. The States of Holland recorded that:

> [Wagenaer] intends to publish and have printed a remarkable Chartbook, called the Mirror of Navigation and containing many different charts which are very well and artistically executed. And that he, in addition to the greatest possible work having been done on this, will be obliged to bear his exceptionally high costs for having these charts engraved on copper plates. And therefore fears that someone else, to his complete ruin, should be able to copy or reprint or otherwise shall have more or less the same examples cut in wood with less cost or make a small change in them by enlarging or diminishing of their size or in another manner, so as to profit by the industry, work and difficulties of another, through his insatiable avarice to the complete ruin of his neighbour, which is contrary to all right and reason.[18]

---

16   For an overview, see Groenveld, 'The Dutch Republic', pp. 281–300: 295.
17   For an example, see M.M. Kleerkooper and Wilhelmus P. van Stockum Jr. (eds.), *De boekhandel te Amsterdam voornamelijk in de 17e eeuw: biographische en geschiedkundige aanteekeningen*. (2 vols., The Hague: Nijhoff, 1914–1916), II, p. 1276 (29 May 1680).
18   Cornelis Koeman, *The History of Lucas Janszoon Waghenaer: And His "Spieghel Der Zeevaerdt"* (Lausanne: Sequoia, 1964), p. 59. Translation by Koeman. The *Spieghel der zeevaerdt* appeared in 1584 and 1585, in folio, in Plantin's Leiden print shop.

Copper engravings seem to have held a greater appeal for the public.[19] However, in this case, the choice for engravings may have had a practical side as well. From the perspective of the mercantile government of the Dutch Republic, the use of woodcuts could have dangerous consequences since they did not indicate the navigation routes with enough precision. Similar arguments relating to the use of a privilege to guarantee a certain quality returned in other cases as well. In 1680, for example, a publishers' consortium obtained a privilege for a navigation manual, not only because pirate printers disturbed the market equilibrium, but also because the imitation copies contained calculation mistakes, and the publishers "would not like to see that navigators would be tempted by those books".[20] The example illustrates how a privilege functioned as a governmental hallmark to guarantee the quality of circulating information.

The underlying notion of governmental approval explains why privileges were repeatedly issued for cheap print as well. In these cases, it generally concerned material that had to be diffused because of governmental interests.[21] One example was the privilege issued by the States General for "printing, selling and distributing the Bills of Lading to the benefit of merchants and skippers with the coat of arms of the Generality".[22] Another example was the publication of the official proceedings against the Land's Advocate, Johan van Oldenbarnevelt, who was executed for treason on 13 May 1619. The States General decided almost instantly that the verdict had to be circulated, stating:

> [The verdict] has to be printed in Latin, Dutch and French. Therefore, consent and privilege has been granted to Aert Meurs, bookseller in The Hague, to exclusively print and publish the before-mentioned verdict in Latin. Item to Hillebrants Jacobss., sworn-in printer of the High and Mighty States General and of the States of Holland to print and publish

---

19   For the rise of public interest in the last quarter of seventeenth century for publications with intaglio illustrations, see Karen L. Bowen and Dirk Imhof, *Christopher Plantin and Engraved Book Illustrations in Sixteenth-Century Europe* (Cambridge: Cambridge University Press, 2008), pp. 7–9.
20   "... niet gaerne souden sien, dat de zeevaerende luijden door soadanige boeeken souden werden verleijt". Kleerkooper and Van Stockum Jr., *De boekhandel te Amsterdam*, II, p. 1276.
21   I am talking here about individual publications and not about the routine work of the state printer, who operated under a general privilege without having to petition for a separate privilege on each publication.
22   "... te mogen drucken, vercoopen ende distribueren vande cognoscenten tot dienste vande Coopluyden ende Schippers ende daerop te drucken de Wapenen vande generaliteit ..." NL-HaNA, States General, 1.01.02, inv. no. 12300, fol. 141v (12 December 1609).

the ubi supra ruling in Dutch, and to Loys Elsevier to exclusively print the ubi supra ruling in French, for two years.[23]

The fact that the verdict was printed in three different languages shows that the States General wanted to reach an international audience. This multilingual aspect returned in particular when it revolved around political propaganda. Yet, occasionally, the States General interfered with international debates conducted in Latin as well. In 1608, for example, the Carmelite theologian Anastasius Cochelet published a pamphlet with the title *Calvini infernus adversus Joannem Polyandrum ministrum calvinisticum*, which was marketed in Antwerp under a privilege of the Archdukes Albert and Isabella.[24] Less than a year later, the States General granted a Dordrecht-based printer a five-year privilege to diffuse the written reply by Polyander.[25] The printing costs of this octavo booklet, consisting of four gatherings, and without engravings or woodcuts, could not have been expensive. Again, the privilege suggested that it concerned a sanctioned version.

The real value of a privilege, then, lay in the fact that it enabled a printer to market his work by distinguishing it from similar publications. Thus, on April 13, 1619, the directors of the *Austraalse Compagnie* petitioned for a privilege to print the "original, sincere and authentic Journal of the deceased Jacob LeMaire ... who discovered a new passage [round Cape Horn], the more so because a impertinent and fabricated Journal regarding the voyage has been printed under the name and title of Willem Cornelis".[26] The States General

---

23 "... sal doen drucken ende vuytgeven in de Latynsche, Nederlantsche ende Francoische spraecke. Is dienvolgende geaccordeert consent ende octroy aen Aert Meurs, bouckverkooper in den Hage, omme voor den tyt van twee jaeren naestcommende de voors. sententie alleene te mogen drucken ende vujtgeven in de Latynsche spraecke. Item aen Hillebrants Jacobss., gesswooren drucker van de Ho. ende Mo. heeren Staten-Generael ende van de Ed. Mo. heeren Staten van Hollant int particulier, omme voor gelycken tyd de voors. sententie alleene te mogen drucken ende vuytgeven in de Nederlantsche spraecke, ende aen Loys Elsevier, om de voors. sententie alleene te mogen drucken ende vuytgeven voor gelycken tyt van twee jaeren, in de Francoische spraecke". JDF, VII, p. 64 (15 May 1619).

24 Anastase Cochelet, *Calvini infernus adversus Joannem Polyandrum ministrum Calvinistam* (Antwerp: Ex officina Plantiniana, apud Joannem Moretum, 1608), USTC 1004453. The privilege was issued on 16 June 1608.

25 NL-HaNA, States General, 12300, folio 141v (12 December 1609). The resulting book was: Johannes Polyander, *Responsio Johannis Polyandri ad interpolata Anastasii Cocheletii* (Dordrecht: Françoys Bosselaer, 1610), USTC 1010555.

26 "... het originael oprecht ende auctentijcq Journael van wijlen Jacob Le Maire, die ... uijtgevonden heeft de nieuwe gevonden vaert ende passage, nu ter tijt Fretum Le Maire genaempt;" [sic!] te meer daar men reeds gedrukt heeft: seecker impertinent ende gefab-

decided to grant the privilege for LeMaire's *Mirror of Australian Navigation* to Michiel Colijn, who eventually printed the book in 1622.[27] The book had not yet proven to be a bestseller, nor did the printer have to make any exceptional investments in this case. Rather, the objective was to receive a kind of testimonial that could be employed to gain a foothold on the economically unstable seventeenth-century book market.

Conversely, the authorities made explicit mention of the fact in cases where they did not fully endorse the content of particular writings. In 1684, for example, the directors of the municipal theater of Amsterdam obtained a privilege from the States of Holland:

> In the understanding that we only gratify the Suppliants this privilege to prevent any damages by reprinting of the mentioned Works, not in any manner in the understanding that we would authorize or advocate the content thereof, or give that work any more credit, authority or repute under Our protection ...[28]

An additional condition was that the privilege was not to be published in abbreviated form, as usual, but had to be printed in full at the beginning of the book. These two clauses were increasingly used from the latter part of the seventeenth century onwards.

The transition of the privilege as a badge of honor to a purely economic legal remedy against illegal reprinting was directly related to changing political cir-

---

riqueert Journael dese voijagie aengaende, onder den naem ende titule van schipper Willem Cornelis uijtgegeven." Kleerkooper and Van Stockum Jr., *De boekhandel te Amsterdam*, II, pp. 1231–1232. The RSG let it be recorded that the decision on the privilege was delayed in the first instance because several delegates raised objections. RSG NR, IV, p. 97.

27 Jacob Le Maire, *Spieghel der Avstralische navigatie* (Amsterdam: Michiel Colijn, 1622), USTC 1033076. Colijn marketed the book bound together with the P. Ordoñez de Ceballos, *Eyghentlijcke beschryvinghe van VVest-Indien*, 1621 and the *Nievvve vverelt, anders ghenaempt VVest-Indien* by Antonio de Herrera y Tordesillas. For that latter title, the printer had obtained a privilege on 31 March 1620; the same day that the concept privilege for the erection of the Dutch West Indies Company was approved. RSG NR, IV, p. 420.

28 "Alles in dien verstande, dat wy de Supplianten met dezen Octroie alleen willende gratificeren tot verhoedinge van hare schade door nadrukken van voorsz. Werken, daar door in geenige deelen verstaan, den inhoude van dien te authorizeren ofte advoueren, ende veel min de zelve onde Onze protectie ende bescherminge eenig meerder credit, aenzien ofte reputatie te geven ...". The regents of the municipal theatre functioned as an intermediary, attributing the privilege for individual playto subsidiary printers. The general privilege was printed in the front matter; the example above is taken from Lingelbach, David. *De Ontdekte Schyndeugd, Bly-Spel* (Amsterdam: J. Leskailje, 1687). On the privilege for the directors of the Amsterdam theatre, see Grabowsky, 'Op de goede beterschap'.

cumstances, and to one case in particular. On 10 December 1668, the famous cloth manufacturer Pieter de la Court (1618–1685) had obtained a fifteen-year privilege from the Grand Pensionary of Holland Johan de Witt (1625–1675) for the publication of his *Aanwysing der heilsame politike gronden en maximen van de republike van Holland en West-Vriesland*, a text composed under the direct influence of De Witt.[29] Soon thereafter, however, the delegates of the Synod of South Holland filed a complaint at the States of Holland that the book contained both political and religious fallacies, propagating the objectionable view that state and religion should be separated.[30] The delegates wished to report the text as libel, but were unable to do so because it had been granted a privilege. Accordingly, they maintained that the privilege made it "seem that Your Noble High Mighty Lords would be the patrons and advocates of such huge, exorbitant, and filthy blasphemy", as in their view the separation of church and state would be contradictory to the Gospel, and undermine the government as the rightful keepers of true religion.[31] Therefore, so the delegates argued, it could not be otherwise than that the privilege had been falsely obtained.

The Delegates of the States of Holland reacted on 28 May 1669, with a ruling in which they deplored the idea of religious freedom, but also expressed their concern that De La Court might offend "friends, confederates and allies" by proclaiming that "tracts, pacts, and alliances" did not necessarily have to

---

29   Pieter de la Court de jonge, *Aanwysing der heilsame politike gronden en maximen van de republike van Holland en West-Vriesland* (Leiden and Rotterdam: Hakkens, 1669).

30   The petition by the Synod, as well as the resolution of the States of Holland have been reproduced in B.W. Wttewaall, *Proeve uit een onuitgegeven staathuishoudkundig geschrift* (Leiden: Luchtmans, 1845), pp. 185–191. The resolution is also available online in English translation in Lionel Bently and Martin Kretschmer (eds.), *Primary Sources on Copyright (1450–1900)*, 'Revocation of the privilege granted to Pieter Hackens, The Hague (1669)', www.copyrighthistory.org, last accessed on 23 January 2017. Further information about this case can be found in Guillaume Groen van Prinsterer, *Handboek der geschiedenis van het vaderland. Derde aflevering—Van den vrede van Munster tot den vrede van Utrecht* (Leiden: Luchtmans, 1843), p. 467; W.P.C. Knuttel (ed.), *Acta der Particuliere Synoden van Zuid-Holland 1621–1700* (6 vols., The Hague: Nijhoff, 1908–1917), IV: *Acta der Particuliere Synoden van Zuid-Holland 1657–1672*, p. 494; Johannes H. Kernkamp, 'De 'Aanwysing' op de lijst van verboden boeken', *Bijdragen voor Vaderlandsche geschiedenis en oudheidkunde*, 7.6 (1935), pp. 102–110.

31   "In alle schijn, of Uw E. Groot Moog. Patroonen en Voorstanders souden syn van sulcke groove, Exorbitante, Vuyle lasteringe". I follow here the handwritten transcription in the preliminary matter of the 1669 edition that was part of the auction of De La Court's papers on 5 April 1906. The book is available at the University Library Amsterdam (OTM: O 60-820) Netherlands. Citation at p. 2. This transcription seems more accurate than the one provided by Wttewaall, *Proeve*, p. 186.

be respected.[32] They rebuked the author for creating the impression that one "was allowed to think and write anything" in Holland, misusing the privilege "to make his private opinions appear [to have been published] under public consent and approbation".[33] The delegates unanimously decided to repeal the privilege, and to announce that:

> The intention of the Noble High Mighty Lords in issuing the above-mentioned Privilege [of De La Court] and similar privileges had never been anything other than to protect the claimants of such privileges against illegal reprinting, and by no means to authorize the content of any books either in part or as a whole, and even less so to provide [these books] with any more credit, prestige, or reputation than others books not equipped with such a privilege.[34]

The States ordained that, to avoid further misunderstandings, from then on, a clause had to be included in all privileges to discharge the authorities of any responsibility.[35] The "Act of Indemnity" (sic!) for De La Court had been allotted for the wrong reasons, and the *Aanwysing* was censored on punishment of 600 florins.[36]

The tumult surrounding the privilege for the De La Court's *Aanwysing* erupted in a political context where Grand Pensionary De Witt was losing his

---

32 The two expressions read in the original: "vrienden, Bondgenooten en Geallieerden" and "Verbonden ende Alliantien". Wttewaall, *Proeve*, p. 187 and p. 189 respectively.

33 "... alles Denken en oock schrijven Moogen ten dienste des welgemelten Vaderlandts. Misbruykendede ... brieven van Octrooij, omde voorschreve syne particliere opinien ... quasi onder desselver publyke adveu en approbatie te doen Voorkomen". Wttewaall, *Proeve*, p. 187.

34 "... de intentie van Haar Ed. Gr. Mog. uyt verleen van't Voorschreeve en andere Diergelijcke privilegien, nooyt anders is geweest, als alleen om de Impretranten van deselve privilegien teegen het naadrucken van Boeken ... te verseekeren, en geensins om daar Meede de Inhoude van al sulke Boeken int geheel of ten deele te Authoriseeren, veel min om de selve onder de publike protectie bescherminge van staat eenig meer Credijt, aansien, of Reputatie dan alle andere particuliere Boeken met soodanige privilegien niet gemunieert sijnde te geeven". Wttewaall, *Proeve*, p. 188.

35 Chris Schriks speaks of a "Missive" of the Court of Holland, dated on the same date (28 May 1668). Schriks, *Het kopijrecht*, p. 117. Schriks, however, fails to mention a source, so it is unclear whether the Court of Holland was indeed involved in this case, or where the expression "no value or credibility" (*geen waerdigheyt ofte meer geloof en credit*) comes from. As a matter of fact, it is incorrect to state, as Schriks does, that such noises were heard even 100 years earlier.

36 "acte van Indemniteijt". Wttewaall, *Proeve*, p. 188.

control over the States General.³⁷ The *Aanwysing* had been a signal to France—an "old and constant friend" in the wordings of De Witt—that it was still possible to break away from the obligations of the Triple Alliance (1668).³⁸ Although De Witt appeared to be the mastermind behind the Alliance, it was already clear to contemporary insiders that the Pensionary "would find some means to elude the conclusion or effect of it [i.e. the Alliance], without appearing himself in any such design".³⁹ The privilege for De La Court was probably part of this design. However, De Witt's opponents in the States General, proponents of the House of Orange and the restoration to power of the Stadtholder, appreciated the benefits of an alliance with England, which would assist in driving De Witt and France further apart.⁴⁰ Most likely, it was on their authority that the privilege for the *Aanwysing* had to be revoked as to make sure that the Alliance would be upheld, which would eventually mark the end of the First Stadtholderless Period (1650–1672). It was only at that point that privileges would no longer be perceived as a sign of governmental approval, but instead as a pure legal-economic means of protection against piracy.⁴¹

Reprint and Privilege

A printing privilege gave the exclusive right to "print, have printed, publish and sell" certain books for a limited period of time (mostly 6 to 15 years).⁴²

---

37 On this point, I disagree with the opinion of Kernkamp, who attributed the conflict to a tiff between De La Court and De Witt, the latter of whom would have left the former in a lurch. Kernkamp, 'De 'Aanwysing'', pp. 102–110: 107. It is the chapters on maintaining alliances, still omitted in the earlier version of *Het Interest*, that fit well in the strategy of De Witt's in these years. That the decision of the States of Holland had no further effect is incidentally also incorrect. In the later octavo edition of the *Aanwysing* (Leiden/Rotterdam: Hakkens, 1671), the indication *"met privilegie"* was removed from the title page and replaced with the *"na de Copie."* Other than that, the actual privilege was removed from the front matter.
38 Craig E. Harline, 'John De Witt and the Triple Alliance', in Craig E. Harline (ed.), *The Rhyme and Reason of Politics in Early Modern Europe: Collected Essays of Herbert H. Rowen* (Dordrecht: Springer, 1992), pp. 121–138: 126. De Witt just wanted to negotiate with France to getter better terms on the division of the 10 provinces.
39 Temple to Bridgman, 27 January 1668, Temple I, 336, as cited in Harline, 'John De Witt', pp. 121–138: 127.
40 The Orangists, as De Witt's opponents were also called, hoped that Charles II could contribute to the installation of his cousin William III of Orange as the legitimate Stadtholder of the United Provinces.
41 *Pace* Kruseman, *Aanteekeningen*, p. 343.
42 "... drucken, doen drucken, uijt geven ende vercopen ...". From the privilege issued to Johan

After this initial period, the work entered into the public domain unless the privilege owner could adduce weighty reasons for why the privilege should be prolonged.[43] In general, the authorities were only inclined to prolong privileges that had recently exchanged ownership, so that the new owner could fully enjoy his or her rights. Nonetheless, the authorities could also decide to prolong a privilege in case the printing project had been delayed by *cause majeure*, or should it preserve employment. On December 13, 1649, for example, the Amsterdam-based printer Johannes van Ravesteyn approached the States of Holland because he had "bought the entire stock of the late Hendrik Laurensz, consisting of round and about 3,000 copies of the *Cathechism* by Ursinus, translated by Festus Hommius, as well as the *Belydenis-predicatie* of the late Jacobus Laurentius" which had been privileged on 22 March 1647.[44] Both books were re-issues of older editions. Van Ravesteyn had invested his entire capital in the acquisition, and requested a prolongation of the privilege because he feared:

> that after the expiration of the privilege on 22 March 1654, the above-mentioned booklet would not be sold out, and that then, such being the case, undoubtedly it would happen that the booklet would be reprinted by somebody, which, in either case, would ruin the suppliant completely.[45]

The Mayors of the City of Amsterdam supplied Van Ravensteijn with a letter of a recommendation to further his case. Based on this recommendation, the States of Holland decided to prolong the printing rights for seven years.

Bleau on 30 November 1676, reproduced in Kleerkooper and Van Stockum Jr., *De boekhandel te Amsterdam*, II, p. 1164.

43   The notion of a 'public domain' was not yet developed in the modern legal sense of the word; however, one does encounter the idea that exclusive rights would not be prolonged in the interest of the common good (*respublica*).

44   "... hoe dat hij suppliant gecocht hadde van de erffgenamen van wijlen Henrick Laurensz den gantschen druck, bestaende in noch omtrent de drij duijsent Exemplaren vanden Catechismus Ursiny, met de tafelen Feste Hommy, mitsgaders de Belijdenis-predicatie van wijlen Jacobus Laurentius ...", Kleerkooper and Stockum Jr., *De boekhandel te Amsterdam*, I, p. 580.

45   "... dat na d'expiratie van 't voorss. Octroy, welcke wesen soude den 22en Marty 1654, op verre na de voorss. boecken noch niet vercocht en soude wesen, ende dattet alsdan, noch niet gedaen zijnde, ongetwijffelt sonde geschieden dat deselve boucken bij d'een off d'ander herdruckt ofte nagedruckt souden werden, het welcke een van beijden gebeurende, hem suppliant totaliter zoude ruineeren", Kleerkooper and Stockum Jr., *De boekhandel te Amsterdam*, I, p. 580.

The example of Van Ravensteijn shows that privileges for reprints were not issued merely because of the commercial success of certain works. Indeed, they were a means used by the government to manipulate the market. Also, in a broader sense, the authority of the States could be felt repeatedly at all stages of the privileging process. When, for example, Jan Janssoon obtained a ten-year privilege for his plans to reprint the work of the minister Johannes Drusius, the States General

> agreed to write to Abelius Curiandrus, the son-in law of the late famous and most learned Johannes Drusius, that he is to hand over the original of the above-mentioned book to his brother-in-law Jan Janssoon, bookseller in Arnhem, in order for it to be printed.[46]

Yet another example of direct state involvement related to a new translation of the *Paraphrases* of Erasmus by Ellert de Veer. On 19 December 1592, De Veer obtained a privilege for his enterprise even if at that point his work was still very much at a project stage.[47] When a year later a second printer applied for a privilege to translate the work of Erasmus as well, the States decided to summon De Veer to the Assembly in order to verify the status of his work and what could be expected of it.[48] De Veer must have taken this decision as a fair warning, and promptly put his translation on the market in the following year.[49] It was this translation by De Veer that would indeed become the standard translation of Erasmus' work, going through numerous reprints throughout the seventeenth century.

---

46 "Is voorts geaccordeert te schryven aen Abelium Curiandrum, schoonsoone van wylen den wytberoemden hoochgeleerden Johannis Drusii, dat hy Jan Janss. boeckvercooper tot Aernhem, zyns swaegers, in handen stelle het origineel vant voors. bouck, om dat te drucken". JDF, VII, p. 57 (7 March 1619).
47 RSG, VII, p. 745.
48 RSG, VIII, p. 151 (14 October 1593).
49 Desiderius Erasmus, *Het eerste(-tweede) deel, der Paraphrasis. Dat is, verclaringhe op het Nieuwe Testament*. Translated by Ellert De Veer (Amsterdam: E. de Veer, 1594), USTC 429529. In his dedication letter, De Veer explained that a delay in the printing process had led him to publish the work in two parts, at the urgent request of several "pious men" (*vroomhertighen*). Erasmus, *Paraphrasis*, fol. A-III.

Scope and Effect

The legal validity of a privilege was determined by the jurisdiction of the authorities that first issued the privilege.[50] Hence, a privilege granted by the States of Holland was valid in the province of Holland, but not in the Province of Utrecht.[51] A privilege granted by the States General was binding in all seven provinces of the Generality, but not in the Kingdom of France. Because of this limited legal validity of privileges, authors and publishers frequently travelled from place to place in order to amass as many privileges as possible. One example in this context relates to the enlarged edition of the *Theologia gentilii* written by Gerard Vossius, which first appeared in Amsterdam at the printing house of Joan Bleau in 1668. The first edition was printed with a privilege from both the States of Holland (27 July 1668) and the Holy Roman Emperor (27 August 1668. See Figure 5.1).[52] On 6 November 1668, Bleau empowered a member of the Council of the elector of Saxony to obtain a fifteen-year privilege for the territory of Saxony as well.[53] Bleau's representative apparently managed to conclude his business quickly, and a later impression indeed included the privilege issued by the Elector of Saxony (18 January 1669, see Figure 5.2).

Although the legal validity of the privilege was limited to a specific territory, privileges had a social scope that went well beyond that. One way of illustrating this would be by drawing attention to the five-year privilege issued for the publication of William Baudartius' *De Nassavsche oorloghen*.[54] The Amsterdam-based printer Michiel Colijn first published the book in 1615, in Dutch.[55] One year later, he decided to bring a French version of the book onto the market

---

50   There were no international agreements about the enforcement of privileges in early modern Europe; the internationalization of copyright law started only with the Berne Convention, adopted in 1886.
51   Hoftijzer argued that privileges issued by the States of Holland were *de facto* respected elsewhere in Republic as well. Hoftijzer, 'Nederlandse boekverkopersprivileges in de zeventiende en achtiende eeuw', pp. 49–62: 55.
52   Gerardus Joannes Vossius, *De theologia gentili, et physiologia christiana; sive De origine ac progressv idololatriæ* [...] *libri IX* (Amsterdam: J. Blaeu, 1668). The book was dedicated to Jean-Baptiste Colbert.
53   Kleerkooper and Van Stockum Jr. (eds.), *De boekhandel te Amsterdam*, II, p. 1163.
54   JDF, VI, p. 363 (27 February 1615). The States General later decided to buy off 13 exemplars for about 25 guilders per copy.
55   Willem Baudartius, *Afbeeldinghe, ende beschrijvinghe van alle de Veld-slagen, Belegeringen, en and're notable geschiedenissen, ghevallen in de Nederlanden, Geduerende d'oorloghe teghens den Coningh van Spaengien* (Amsterdam: M. Colijn, 1615), USTC 1033122.

PRIVILEGING THE COMMON GOOD   103

as well.⁵⁶ The title page of the French version (see Figure 5.3) indicated that the work was sold in Paris at the shop of the famous engraver and notorious Huguenot Melchior Tavernier (1594–1665). This implies the existence of a French market, yet Colijn did not request a privilege from the French authorities. Instead, he included a French translation of the Dutch privilege on the front pages of the book even if that privilege had no legal validity in France. One could argue that Colijn simply wanted to issue a warning to his French colleagues not to reprint the book and export it to the Dutch Republic. Perhaps this was indeed an underlying thought, yet Colijn also reprinted the privilege in a 1621 edition of Baudartius' book in Latin, that is after the expiration of the privilege, in which case the idea of a 'warning' made little sense.⁵⁷ Rather, it appears that Colijn used the privilege to give the work a certain allure within clearly defined Reformed circles: within that context, Dutch privileges functioned as a form of advertisement.

A similar logic underpins other cases as well, such as the 1614 edition of the *Tumultuum anabaptisticarum liber unus* written by the historian Lambertus Hortensius (1500–1574). Hortensius' work on the revolt of the Anabaptist was originally written in Latin, and first published in 1548. In 1614, a Dutch translation (see Figure 5.4) appeared on the market under the elaborate title:

> The Book of Dr. Lambertus Hortensius, who was a rector of the school in Naarden during his life. On the revolt of the Anabaptists. First written in Latin, and printed in Basel, with Privileges of the Emperor. And now translated into Dutch.⁵⁸

The original privilege had long since expired by the time the Dutch translation entered onto the market. It would have had no legal validity in the Dutch Republic anyhow. The publisher, however, took the trouble to explain in his Preface to the Reader that the work was:

---

56   Willem Baudartius, *Les gverres de Nassav* (Amsterdam: M. Colin, 1616), USTC 1514875.
57   Willem Baudartius, *Viva Delineatio, ac descriptio omnium prœliorum quæ adversus Hispaniarum Regem in Belgij provincijs gestæ sunt* (Amsterdam: M. Colinium, 1622), USTC 1008378.
58   Lambertus Hortensius, *Het Boeck D. Lamberts Hortensii van Montfoort, in syn Leven Rector van de Schole tot Naerden. Van den oproer der Weder-Dooperen. Eerst Int Latyn beschreven, ende ghedruckt tot Basel, met Privilegien van de Keyserlycke Majesteyt. Ende Nu in Nederlandts overgheset.* (Enchuysen: J.L. Meyn, 1614), USTC 1026231. The privilege issued by the Holy Roman Emperor was not reproduced in the book, nor was another privilege requested for the translation. The translation nevertheless became highly successful, going to several reprints up until the very end of the seventeenth century.

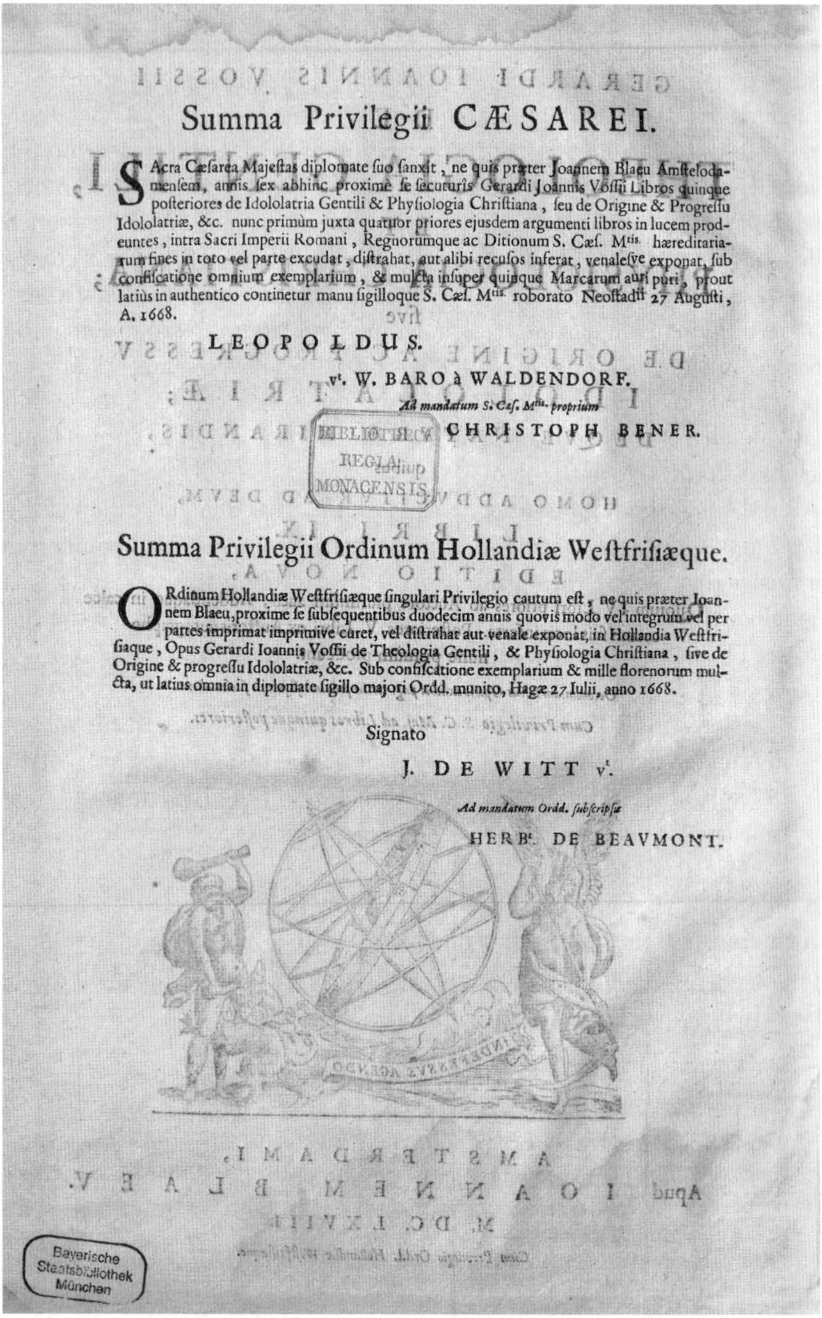

FIGURE 5.1 Gerardus Ioannes Vossius, *De theologia gentili et physiologia christiana* (Amsterdam: Blaeu, 1668)
BAYERISCHE STAATSBIBLIOTHEK MÜNCHEN, 2 DOGM. 354-1/2

Summa Privilegii CÆSAREI.

Acra Cæsarea Majestas diplomate suo sanxit, Ne quis præter Joannem Blaeu Amsteloda-mensem, annis sex abhinc proximè se secuturis Gerardi Joannis Vossii Libros quinque posteriores de Idololatria Gentili & Physiologia Christiana, seu de Origine & Progressu Idololatriæ, &c. nunc primùm juxta quatuor priores ejusdem argumenti libros in lucem prodeuntes, intra Sacri Imperii Romani, Regnorumque ac Ditionum S. Cæs. M^{tis} hæreditariarum fines in toto vel parte excudat, distrahat, aut alibi recusos inserat, venalesve exponat, sub confiscatione omnium exemplarium, & mulcta insuper quinque Marcarum auri puri, prout latiùs in authentico continetur manu sigilloque S. Cæs. M^{tis} roborato Neostadii 27 Augusti, A. 1668.

LEOPOLDUS.

v^t. W. BARO à WALDENDORF.

Ad mandatum S. Cæs. M^{tis} proprium

CHRISTOPH. BENER.

Summa Privilegii ELECTORIS SAXONIÆ.

Serenissimus Elector manu sigilloque cavit, Ne quis præter Joannem Blaeu Amstelodamensem, annis dehinc decem proximis Gerardi Joannis Vossii Libros quinque posteriores de Idololatria Gentili & Physiologia Christiana, seu de Origine & Progressu Idololatriæ, &c. nunc primùm suis sumptibus unà cum quatuor prioribus, ejusdem materiæ ac auctoris libris in lucem editos, intra Electoratus, & Ducatuum Saxoniæ, hisque annexarum terrarum, ac Episcopatuum terminos, conjunctim aut divisim recudat recudive curet, distrahat, aut alibi impressos inserat, venumve exponat, sub amissione omnium exemplarium & mulcta pariter quingentorum aureorum Rhenanorum, ut latiùs hæc in authenticis datis Dresdæ 18 Ianuarii, A. 1669.

JOANNES GEORGIVS ELECTOR.

CAROLVS à FRIESEN.

JOANNES CHRISTIANVS WILHELMI S.

Summa Privilegii Ordinum Hollandiæ Westfrisiæque.

Ordinum Hollandiæ Westfrisiæque singulari Privilegio cautum est, Ne quis præter Joannem Blaeu, proximè se subsequentibus duodecim annis quovis modo vel integrum vel per partes imprimat imprimive curet, vel distrahat aut venale exponat, in Hollandia Westfrisiaque, Opus Gerardi Joannis Vossii de Theologia Gentili, & Physiologia Christiana, sive de Origine & progressu Idololatriæ, &c. Sub confiscatione exemplarium & mille florenorum mulcta, ut latiùs omnia in diplomate sigillo majori Ordd. munito, Hagæ 27 Iulii, anno 1668.

Signato

J. DE WITT v^t.

Ad mandatum Ordd. subscripsit

HERB. DE BEAVMONT.

FIGURE 5.2 Gerardus Ioannes Vossius, *De theologia gentili et physiologia christiana* (Amsterdam: Blaeu, 1668)
AUSTRIAN NATIONAL LIBRARY, SCANNED BY GOOGLE

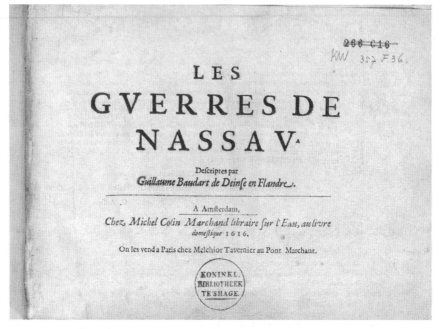

FIGURE 5.3 Willem Baudartius, *Les gverres de Nassav* (Amsterdam: M. Colin, 1616)
NATIONAL LIBRARY OF THE NETHERLANDS, 357F36

to be considered all the more authentic and believable, because he [i.e., Hortensius] had dedicated his book to the honorably Magistrate of Amsterdam, which undoubtedly was well informed on these matters, and [because he] had published it in print with a Privilege from his Royal Majesty.[59]

Mentioning the existence of a privilege added to the credibility of the work. It seems safe to assume that it was displayed on the title page to increase the sales.

---

59 "… welckes schrijven oock so veel te autentijcker ende gheloofwaerdigher is te achten, om dat hy t'selve sijn boeck heeft ghededuceert ende toegheschreven den Eer. Magistraet der voorsz stadt Amsterdam, onghetwijfelt van alles wel onderricht ende gheinstrueert zijnde, ende in druck uytghegheven met Octroy vande K.Mt.". Hortensius, *Het Boeck*, f. A4r.

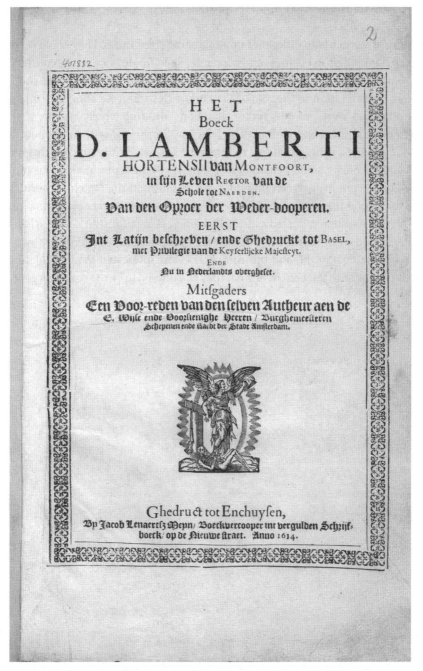

FIGURE 5.4 Lambertus Hortensius, *Het Boeck D. Lamberts Hortensii* [...] *Van den oproer der Weder-Dooperen* (Enchuysen: J.L. Meyn, 1614)
NATIONAL LIBRARY OF THE NETHERLANDS, 942A14:2

Conclusion

Printing privileges held different functions at different times. They could serve to keep booksellers in business and to counter specific ideas, or on the contrary, to promote them. What this study demonstrates is that we should give more serious consideration to the role of the authorities when we come to explain why privileges were granted, rather than concentrating wholly on the motivation of publishers and authors. The Dutch authorities gave their support to specific projects, using privileges to intervene actively in the market. Despite the fact that only a small percentage of the overall book production was produced under privilege, it can therefore not be said that the Dutch authorities tried to counter the monopolistic structures on the book market by any means. The privilege system reflected a mutually beneficial relationship between local printers and governmental interest, where printers and booksellers were interested in making a profit, and the authorities were interested in manipulating public discourse to the benefit of what they considered to be the common good.

PART 2

*Day to Day Practices
of Book Buying and Selling*

∴

CHAPTER 6

The Business of Browsing in Early Modern English Bookshops

Philip Tromans

The question of whether books could be thumbed through in early modern English bookshops before being bought is a contentious one. Two prominent scholars of the book have recently averred in high-profile publications that books were displayed in such a way which meant that only their title-pages could be viewed. Adrian Weiss' analysis of sixteenth- and seventeenth-century English print publications in *Thomas Middleton and Early Modern Textual Culture* states that:

> At the bookseller's shop … the sheets [that made up the books were] … dissembled, re-folded as per format, and re-collated for offering to the public unbound as a packet of folded sheets tied crosswise with cord (and sometimes loosely stitched together at the gutter). The title-page functioned as the modern dust jacket in advertising the book because it was well-nigh impossible to examine the contents of the packet of folded sheets (unless it was a folio). The sheets had not been opened at the top to produce free-swinging leaves, nor had the rough deckle edges of the sheet been trimmed (cut) to permit 'thumbing through' the book.[1]

Eugene Giddens' bibliographical handbook also declares the title-page to be the only straightforwardly perusable part of a book on display in a shop, although Giddens envisages a different arrangement of stock to Weiss:

> because sheets of a book were stacked together and then simply folded in half, the book could not be 'read' as part of the browsing process … Therefore, the title page … was … the only part of the book that might be easily consulted.[2]

---

1 Adrian Weiss, 'Casting compositors, foul cases, and skeletons: printing in Middleton's age', Gary Taylor and John Lavagnino (eds.), *Thomas Middleton and Early Modern Textual Culture: A Companion to the Collected Works* (Oxford: Clarendon Press, 2007), pp. 195–225, p. 224.
2 Eugene Giddens, *How to Read a Shakespearean Play Text* (Cambridge: Cambridge University Press, 2011), p. 53.

Neither Weiss nor Giddens provide supporting evidence or citations for their claims.

Books were browseable though, and there are scholars who present some of the evidence as part of essays on wider thematic concerns. These proofs of in-shop, pre-purchase browsing lie scattered however in a few contributory essays to collected editions, and are less visible as a result. This is perhaps one of the reasons why distinguished bibliographers such as Weiss and Giddens err in their depiction of early modern English bookshops' merchandising of stock. Another reason is that the literary studies which state or imply that books could be browsed eloquently elucidate the metaphorical configurations by which a book's paratext attempted to establish an intimate, emotive relationship between itself and readers but fail to present cast-iron evidence that the figurations are pre- rather than post-purchase.[3]

This article will first join together the most important fragments of evidence presented by scholars who have addressed these issues. It will then highlight the largest, most persuasive and largely untapped evidential base for in-shop browsing: books themselves. Lastly, a limited but necessary commentary on how prospective purchasers' ability to browse display copies should impact on our understanding of the design and make-up of extant editions will hopefully leave readers with a desire to reappraise the structure, appearance and form of the early modern printed texts they work with.

The Evidence for Bookshop Browsing

One of the outstanding overviews on bookselling during the mid to late seventeenth century, written by Giles Mandelbrote, takes the insides of early modern bookshops as one of its subjects, describing along the way six seventeenth-century images of bookstalls and bookshops.[4] The six include Abraham Bosse's well-known *La Galerie du Palais* (c. 1640) where, on the right-hand side, a seller opens a book for her customer's perusal (the image features on the dust jacket of this volume). Just as interesting though is the book seen to the north-west of the figure furthermost to the right, the leaves of which are wedged ajar between

---

3 Paul J. Voss, 'Books for sale: advertising and patronage in late Elizabethan England', *Sixteenth Century Journal*, 29.3 (1998), pp. 733–756; Michael Saenger, *The Commodification of Textual Engagements in the English Renaissance* (Aldershot: Ashgate, 2006).
4 Giles Mandelbrote, 'From the warehouse to the counting-house: booksellers and bookshops in late 17th-century London', in Robin Myers and Michael Harris (eds.), *A Genius for Letters: Booksellers and Bookselling from the 16th to the 20th Century* (Winchester: St Paul's Bibliographies, 1995), pp. 49–84, pp. 55–61.

the books it lies on and the shelf above. Another of the illustrations Mandelbrote presents is that of the bookseller found in the English translation of Johann Amos Comenius' *Orbis Sensualium Pictus*. Two of the keyed captions that accompany the illustration state that "The Bookes are placed on shelves, 4. and are laid open for use upon a desk, 5".[5] These captions verbalise what the other images show: that bookshop browsers could take books down from the open-access shelves and browse through the books' free-swinging leaves, with neither a cord-tied copy nor a half-folded stack of sheets in sight.

To the pictorial evidence laid out by Mandelbrote can be added known textual portraits of bookshop browsers reading one of the bookseller's wares. Many of these are the satirical descriptions of pretentious and often foolish readers found in the drama and the witty, scurrilous pamphlets of the late sixteenth and early seventeenth centuries. Four examples of this kind are presented by an essay by Gary Taylor, dedicated to the marketing of Shakespeare's First Folio (1623).[6] One of Taylor's examples comes from Thomas Lodge's *Wits Misery*:

> In the Stationers shop he sits dailie, Jibing and flearing over every pamphlet with Ironicall jeasts; yet heare him but talke ten lines, and you may score up twentie absurdities.[7]

One description of a foolish book browser Taylor does not include—though it is a wonderfully descriptive example—is from an unattributed play, *The Return from Parnassus*. At the end of act 3 scene 3 Amoretto's servant, Page, mocks Amoretto's affectatious (and surely ineffectual) attempts to gull bystanders into thinking that Amoretto understands the foreign language books the shopkeepers fetch off their shelves for him:

> Why presently this great linguist my Maister [Amoretto], will march through Paules Churchyard, Come to a booke binders shops, and with a

---

5 Johann Amos Comenius, *Orbis Sensualium Pictus* (London: for Joshua Kirton, 1659), N8v–O1r.
6 Gary Taylor, 'Making meaning marketing Shakespeare 1623', in Peter Holland and Stephen Orgel (eds.), *From Performance to Print in Early Modern England* (Basingstoke: Palgrave Macmillan, 2006), pp. 55–72, pp. 55–60.
7 Thomas Lodge, *Wits Misery* (London: Adam Islip, to be sold by Cuthbert Burby, 1596), USTC 513182, C1r. The others Taylor lists are: Thomas Dekker, *Patient Grisill* (London: [Edward Alde] for Henry Rocket, 1603), USTC 3001093, C1r; Ben Jonson, *Every Man out of His Humour* (London: [Adam Islip] for William Holme, 1600), USTC 514819, H3r; and Thomas Dekker, *The Gulls Horne-Book* (London: [Nicholas Oakes] for Richard Sergier, 1609), USTC 3003976, F3v.

big Italian looke and Spanish face aske for these books in Spanish and Italian; then turning through his ignorance, the wrong ende of the booke upward, use action, on this unknowne tongue after this sort; first looke on the title and wrinckle his brow, next make as though he read the first page and bites a lip, then with his naile score the margent as though there were some notable conceit, and lastly when he thinkes hee hath gulld the standers by sufficiently, throwes the booke away in a rage, swearing he could never finde bookes of a true printe since he was last in Joadna.[8]

Amoretto not only pretends to understand the books' content but criticises their aesthetics. Amoretto declares that the publications lack the "true printe" of well-inked books printed using elegant typefounts. This apparent desire for "true printe[d]" books is perhaps part of the satire. While Amoretto hopes his performance will fool onlookers his outburst over the apparently poor appearance of the texts—rather than the quality of the books' content, which, of course, he has not the language skills to discern—hints at Amoretto's shallowness. For readers of the printed version of *The Return to Parnassus*, Amoretto's stupidity is emphasised by his citing of the fictional, ridiculously-named "Joadna" as the marketplace for the typographically-sophisticated publications he pretends to yearn for. (The surviving manuscript version of the play reads "Padua" however.[9]) Yet Amoretto's outburst also hints at a general truth: printers, publishers, some authors and some browsers *were* interested in the layout of texts, and the importance of mise-en-page as a presentational tool will be discussed below.

Gary Taylor and Giles Mandelbrote present one mid-seventeenth-century representation each of shop stock being promoted in-store by being read aloud, in one by the shopkeeper, and in the other by a shopkeeper's apprentice. Mandelbrote's example comes from Richard Head's *The English Rogue Continued* (1668):

If a Customer comes into our Shop to buy a book, he [the bookseller] hath such ways of preferring and recommending of it that they seldom go and not buy, for he will open the book, and if it be Divinity, shew them one

---

8 Anonymous, *The Return from Parnassus* (London: George Eld for John Wright, 1606), USTC 3002502, E4r.
9 J.B. Leichmann, 'Introduction', in *The Three Parnassus Plays*, ed. J.B. Leichmann (London: Nicholson and Watson, 1949), p. 13.

place or another, out of which he will preach to them and tell them, that very saying or discourse is worth all the money in the word.[10]

Taylor quotes from Robert Heath's epigram 'To my Booke-seller', in which Heath pleads with the seller to not "bid thy 'prentice read it [Heath's book] and admire,| That all i' th' shop may what he reads enquire".[11]

Instances of direct requests to browsers to buy the book in hand, found mainly in preliminary gatherings, constitute, however, the largest and most persuasive evidential base. Forty-four titles, represented by 134 extant editions published between 1567 and 1695, are known to contain such pleas. These are gathered in the appendix to this article. In each case I note the page on which the address to the browser is to be found. These appeals, whether a clause, a line or two, or a significant portion of an often much lengthier stretch of prose or verse, are obviously pre-purchase petitions. Two of the shorter pleas are found in Clement Robinson's *A Handful of Pleasant Delights* (1584) and Robert Lewes *The Merchants Map* (1638): "Doubt not to buy this pretie Booke,| the price is not so deare";[12] "If thou would'st be a Merchant, buy this Booke:| For 'tis a prize worth gold".[13] More follow below. Many of the pleas were largely redundant once the item had been bought. Three titles apart, these commercial appeals were located using a proximity keyword search of the open-access, transcribed texts hosted by Early English Books Online's Text Creation Partnership.[14] The results however must represent the tip of the iceberg: the 53,834 texts transcribed by the Text Creation Partnership that are currently searchable represent roughly 43% of Early English Books Online's, which counts over 125,000 records. That leaves nearly 75,000 untranscribed, non-searchable printed texts. It is also the case that that some of the Text Creation Partnership's transcripts are imper-

---

10   Richard Head, *The English Rogue Continued* (London: For Francis Kirkham, to be sold by him and Thomas Dring the Younger, 1668), p. 206, quoted in Mandelbrote, 'From the warehouse to the counting-house', p. 61.
11   Robert Heath, *Clarastella* (London: For Humphrey Moseley, 1650), USTC 3040311, pp. 36–37, quoted in Taylor, 'Making Meaning Marketing Shakespeare 1623', p. 58.
12   Clement Robinson, *A Handful of Pleasant Delights* (London: Richard Jones, 1584), USTC 510101, A1v.
13   Robert Lewes, *The Merchants Map* (London: by Richard Oulton, Eliot's Court Press, Thomas Harper and Felix Kingston for Ralph Mabb, 1638), USTC 3019654, a6r.
14   Three of my examples—The Appendix's BB14, 19 and 22—were found reading Randall Ingram's 'Lego Ego': reading seventeenth-century books of epigrams', in Jennifer Andersen and Elizabeth Sauer (eds.), *Books and Readers in Early Modern England: Material Studies* (Philadelphia: University of Pennsylvania Press, 2002), pp. 160–176, pp. 163–165.

fectly done, are sometimes made from incomplete copies, and are transcriptions of text only. Many publications are lost, and the method of proximity keyword searches is only as good as the search engine and the individual using it. Bearing all this in mind there must be more books with pre-purchase pleas. Even so, the 134 known editions containing pre-purchase appeals are known to have been published over a span of 128 years, representing a mean average of just above one self-promoting edition every year. Put another way, the 134 known editions represent hundreds of exemplars with point-of-sale pleas and, if the relative regularity of the dates of the books' publication is factored in, the Appendix's examples alone suggest there was probably no time between 1550 and 1695 when a browser could not have found a pre-purchase plea in at least one item of a London seller's book stock.

134 editions of forty-four titles is a large enough sample to prove the importance of this phenomenon but not large enough to detect widespread presentational trends. Some observations are possible however. The forty-four titles are spread over an array of genres. Fourteen of the forty-four are religious treatises. Fiction is represented by three titles of satirical prose, two play-texts and six poetry books. There are four medical publications, two travel texts, two philosophy books and a history of Britain. Lastly, there are ten conduct books, and their content ranges from the practical pursuits of horsemanship and hunting to books on the social precepts underpinning a cohesive body politic and political governance.

In most cases it is also possible to identify the author of the exhortation to purchase. The two most active types of contributor are the authors of the books' main texts, and those that supply commendatory prose or verse for the books. Publishers are also responsible for a significant minority of the pre-purchase petitions. Another interesting case is where the books themselves seem to be pleading for purchase. The book personified figured in numerous reader-book relationships, some of which are commercially driven.[15] In *Wits ABC* a proem appeals to the implicitly good-hearted browser to pay the sixpence ransom to release the copy the browser holds in his hand from a sadistic bookseller-torturer:

> I hardly did escape the Printers Presse,
> It did so rudely crush my tendernesse:
> And now I feare more harme will me befall,
> If I long lye upon the Stationers stall.

---

15   Saenger, *The Commodification of Textual Engagements*, pp. 95–99; 105–106; 110–115.

> Sometime I shall be nayld vnto a post,
> And somtime rashly torne, pincht, scratcht, & crost:
> Reader therefore, in kindnesse let me wooe thee:
> To free me hence, sixepence will not undoe thee.[16]

One of the proems to John Davies' *Wits Bedlam* initially seeks to define its readership as both witty and moral only to immediately abandon the criteria:

> Art good; and bad thy wit? then, touch me not:
> For, I doe often jerke the honest Sot.
> Art bad, and thy wit good? Forbeare, much more,
> To touch mee: for, I lash such till they roare.
> Or, art thou good, and great thy Wits extent?
> Th'wilt love me, tho thou loathe mine Excrement.
> But be thou good or bad: for Sixpence, I
> Will glad and grieve thee, make thee laugh & cry
> O! take my money,
> For this Sowre-Honey.[17]

It is unlikely however that many of the book's original browsers would have imagined themselves as dim or dissolute.

Many of the pre-purchase appeals listed in the appendix are enlivened by the use of common but effective rhetorical schemes and tropes. They are evident in publications as apparently diverse and utilitarian as a medical self-help publication, a book of moral philosophy and practical guides to horsemanship and hunting. The prose pre-purchase pleas of these respective publications flow rhythmically through the use of alliterative and assonantal anaphora, parison, and personal pronouns, and the deployment in one or two of the below quotations of rhetorical questions (erotema), hendiadys, antithesis and tricolon:

> much have I saide by waie of advertisement, uppon occasion of this present booke, whose benifits as they are diverse, so are they singuler: and in them all is Gods goodnesse highly commended. Note my wordes, and then judge of the value and worthinesse of the booke. Art thou diseased in thy heade? Art thou greeved in thy heart? Arte thou pained with ache?

---

16 Anonymous, *Wits A. B. C.* (London: [George Eld] for Thomas Thorpe, to be sold [by Lawrence Lisle], 1608), USTC 3003340, A4r.
17 John Davies, *Wits Bedlam* (London: George Eld, to be sold by James Davies, 1617), USTC 3007550, A6v.

Art thou tormented with a fever? Art thou wounded? Arte thou troubled with any yrkesome sore? Doeth thy sight faile? Doeth thy hearing waxe weake? Doeth thy youth weare away? Doth age creepe on apace? Finally, doest thou feele thy selfe infected with the poyson of the Plague & Pestilence? Then delay no time, but with a small price, buy a gemme worth golde, (this booke I meane) whiche though it bee little in quantitie, yet it is great in qualitie and vertue.[18]

heere you may buy obedience to God, performed in the carefull mayntenaunce of his true religion, here you shal see curiously sette out reverence to Magistrates, fayth to freendes, love to our neyghbours, and charitie to the poore: who covets to know the duety of a Christian, the offyce of a Ruler, the calling of a Cittizen: to be breefe, the effects Tullie pende down in his Officies eyther for the embracing of vertue, or shunning of vice, let him repayre to this Royall Exchange, and there he will find himself generally furnished.[19]

If you take pleasure either in an Horse to Hunt, or for the Warre, or for the Race, or for to Draw, or a Hackney, come hither, buy, see, and welcome.[20]

Who list to learne, the properties of hounds,
To breede them first, and then to make them good,
To teach them know, both voice and horne, by sounds,
To cure them eke, from all that hurts their blood:
Let him but buye this booke: So shall he finde,
As much as may, (for hounds) content his minde.[21]

These lines are hardly Shakespearean. One's intuition is that the writers would deny the charge of rhetoric brought against them. The schemes and tropes are present in their hawking, however. Other writers promoted books by claiming to be artlessly sincere in their appeal. John Taylor's preface, four verse lines notwithstanding, begins thus:

---

18   Thomas Cartwright, *Hospital for the Diseased* (London: [Richard Tottell? for] Thomas Man and William Hoskins, 1578), USTC 508482, A2r–v.
19   Orazio Rinaldi, *The Royal Exchange* (London: John Charlewood for William Wright, 1590), USTC 511613, ¶4r.
20   Gervase Markham, *Faithful Farrier* (London: Thomas Cotes for Michael Sparke, to be sold by Richard Royston, 1630), USTC 3014558, A3r–4r.
21   George Gascoigne, *The Noble Art of Venery or Hunting* (London: Henry Bynneman for Christopher Barker, 1575), USTC 508033, A4v.

> And because I would not have you either guld of your mony, or deceived in expectation, I pray you take notice of my plaine dealing; for I have not given my booke a swelling bumbasted title, of a promising inside of newes; therefore if you looke for any such matter from hence, take this warning, hold fast your mony, and lay the booke downe: yet if you do buy it (I dare presume) you shall find somewhat in it worth part of your mony.[22]

Fifty-four years later Robert Godfrey declared that

> Reader, don't ever the more under value this Discourse, because thou findest it neither dedicated to some Great Man, nor yet set off with flattering Verses in commendation of me and my Work. The last I disesteem, because though some ingenious Physical Tracts at a chance comes forth with some, and deserve them, yet almost every Mass of Collections, or Bundle of Insignificancies, have them to perswade the Reader to buy it. I am therefore resolv'd to have mine come simple and naked, that if thou likest it so, thou mayest buy it; if otherwise, let it alone.[23]

These two last examples are further testimony to widespread book browsing. Taylor pledges that his book does not feign "a promising inside of newes", as others did. Such deception was, at least according to Taylor, one of the two staples of pre-purchase advertising, the other being the "bumbasted titles" found on books' title-pages. Equally, while Godfrey's contention that "almost every Mass of Collections, or Bundle of Insignificancies, have them to perswade the Reader to buy it" is an exaggeration, it demonstrates that pre-purchase appeals were familiar enough to make the hyperbole persuasive, rather than preposterous.

Illustrations of bookshops, references to individuals who sit and read copies of sellers' stock in shops and the pre-purchase pleas constitute a formidable body of evidence. To that body can be added the location of the unquestionably commercial petitions in many of the publications listed in the Appendix. The publications' leaves had to be free-swinging for the adverts to be of any use. If the books' bolts remained unopened, as Weiss suggested, the adverts would be obscured. First, consider quartos: Figure 6.1 shows that the only eas-

---

22   John Taylor, *Taylor His Travels* (London: Nicholas Oakes for Henry Gosson, to be sold by Edward Wright, 1620), USTC 3009184, A2r.
23   Robert Godfrey, *Various Injuries & Abuses in Chemical and Galenical Physic* (London: John Darby for Richard Jones, 1673), A7r.

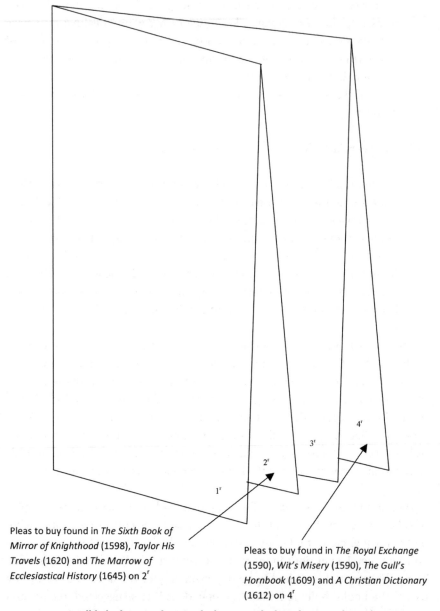

Pleas to buy found in *The Sixth Book of Mirror of Knighthood* (1598), *Taylor His Travels* (1620) and *The Marrow of Ecclesiastical History* (1645) on 2^r

Pleas to buy found in *The Royal Exchange* (1590), *Wit's Misery* (1590), *The Gull's Hornbook* (1609) and *A Christian Dictionary* (1612) on 4^r

FIGURE 6.1 A still-bolted quarto showing the location of selected pre-purchase pleas

ily perusable leaves in a folded quarto gathering where the bolts remain are the title-page (or one recto), two verso, three recto and four verso.

Yet Figure 6.1 also shows that the pleas to buy found in *The Sixth Book of Mirror of Knighthood*, *Taylor His Travels* and *The Marrow of Ecclesiastical History* on two recto, *The Royal Exchange*, *Wits Misery*, *The Gull's Hornbook* and *A Christian Dictionary* on four recto (to name just some) would have been difficult to read if not impossible if they were placed on a shop or stall shelf with still-bolted leaves. Likewise, unopened octavo gatherings allowed easy access to the title-page, four verso, five recto and eight verso only.

Figure 6.2 demonstrates where the bolts are on unopened leaves, and shows that the pre-purchase appeals in *A Letter by a Young Gentlewoman to her Inconstant Lover*, *A Handful of Pleasant Delights* and *Some Opinions of Mr Hobbs* would have been obscured if the leaves of books on bookshops' shelves had remained unopened. *A Letter by a Young Gentlewoman to her Inconstant Lover*, *A Handful of Pleasant Delights* and *Some Opinions of Mr Hobbs* have been chosen as examples because the adverts in the first two were written by the printer-publisher-seller Richard Jones, and the one in the last by the bookseller, Walter Kettilby. Neither Jones nor Kettilby would have penned their own advertisements only for them to be concealed. Jones would not have allowed his compositors and pressmen to print his promotional proems on a page which could not be read. We can only conclude that the leaves of display copies of books were free-swinging, and that customers' propensity to browse before they either bought or put back the copy of the book they were perusing on the shelf led a number of contributors to place pleas to buy within books' front matter.

Free-swinging leaves meant that pre-purchase engagements were not limited to preliminaries. John Andrews' verse is a significant example because the same point-of-sale proem found at the beginning of *Andrew's Resolution* (1624; 1630) was placed at the back of *Sovereign Salve* (1621; 1636), suggesting that, at least by the end of the first quarter of the seventeenth century, the back of the book was a suitable locale for pre-sale promotional petitions.[24] Moreover, publishers' placed promotional yet selective booklists "virtually anywhere in a volume" from the 1640s, and lengthier, fuller catalogues of their stock at the back of books in the latter half of the seventeenth century.[25] Some browsers indeed may have gone straight to the back of the book only to ascertain whether a catalogue was present, and to see what else the publisher had to offer, being wholly uninterested in the main text of the copy they held in their hands. But browsers could skim through the preliminaries, where most of the pre-purchase appeals

---

24 John Andrews, *Andrews Resolution* (London: Nicholas Oakes, 1621), USTC 3009903, C6r; John Andrews, *A Sovereign Salve* (London: Nicholas Oakes, to be sold by Francis Grove, 1624), USTC 3011442, A2v.
25 Peter Lindenbaum, 'Publishers' booklists in late seventeenth-century London', *The Library*, 11.4 (2010), pp. 381–404.

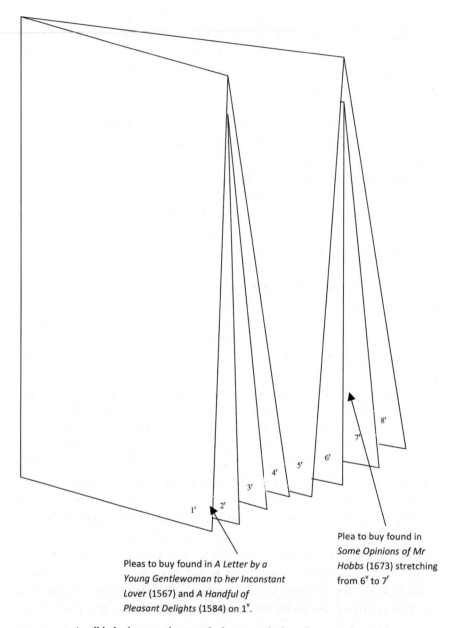

FIGURE 6.2 A still-bolted octavo showing the location of selected pre-purchase pleas

are, or skip to the end, so they could thumb through, scan or read what lay in between, as the locales of the shorter booklists show.

Once we accept that books could be browsed, it is imperative we consider the browsing of books in bookshops as part of the history of reading. And one of the goals we should set ourselves is to better understand how customers engaged with books in bookshops. Closets, bedchambers, the court, coffee houses and the Inns of Court are, after all, not only recognised as places where reading took place but have been seen as sites whose environment helps to shape the character of that reading.[26] As Robert Darnton points out:

> the 'where' of reading is more important than one might think, because placing the reader in his setting can provide hints about the nature of his experience.[27]

This is true at least in one respect for readers in bookshops. William H. Sherman explains that some readers of books were taught to annotate their books and that forms of intensive reading which led to annotation were the proper use of books. The educated understood that they should signpost the knowledge or aphorisms they found in their books for immediate or future practical or academic reuse.[28] The presentation of a study in Comenius' *Orbis Sensualium Pictus* contains a caption which describes the book-buried student either picking

> the best things out of them into his own Manual, 5. or marketh [marking] in them with a dash, 6. or a little star, 7. in the [books'] Margent.[29]

For Sherman, this mid-seventeenth-century depiction of the student is indicative of the period's gradual shift away from the extensive annotating of margins in favour of the use of separate blank notebooks.[30] Yet Comenius' student does in the study what he cannot (or perhaps should not) in the shop: annotate the book. *Orbis Sensualium Pictus'* depiction of the shop, remember, presents a book "laid open for use upon a desk, 5" but this "use" precludes annotation. Likewise, Amoretto in *The Return From Parnassus* "score[s] the margent" of a new unsold book with his fingernail but does not write or draw in it. Neither of course were browsers permitted to turn down page corners nor remove or

---

26 Harold Love, *Scribal Publication in the Seventeenth Century* (Oxford: Clarendon Press, 1993), pp. 195–230; Heidi Brayman Hackel, *Reading Material in Early Modern England: Print, Gender, and Literacy* (Cambridge: Cambridge University Press, 2005), pp. 34–43.
27 Robert Darnton, *The Kiss of Lamourette: Reflections in Cultural History* (New York: Norton, 1990), p. 167.
28 William H. Sherman, *Used Books: Marking Readers in Renaissance England* (Philadelphia: University of Pennsylvania Press, 2008), pp. 3–5.
29 Comenius, *Orbis Sensualium Pictus*, O4v–5r.
30 Sherman, *Used Books: Marking Readers in Renaissance England*, p. 7.

cut leaves away from the items on display, although the latter activities having been recently shown to be more widespread among early modern readers than the scholarly community had previously imagined.[31] Scholarly reconstructions of browsers' pre-purchase engagements with books cannot then rely for their data on the modification of, and marginalia in, certain exemplars. Rather, it is physical forms of print publications that must influence our investigations.

Browsing the Book: the Location and Appearance of Promotional Paratexts

Formulating schemes of browserly behaviour will prove difficult. If organising the "indistinguishable plurality of individual acts" that constitutes early modern post-sale reading habits "according to shared regularities" remains problematical, pre-purchase browsing appears to be even more difficult to codify, even if its study is limited to analyses of publications' material features.[32] For a start, browsing is not limited to fleeting textual engagements, as Cordatus' remark about Clove in Ben Jonson's *Every Man Out Of His Humour* demonstrates:

> Monsieur Clove ... will sit you a whole afternoon sometimes, in a booksellers shop, reading the Greeke, Italian and Spanish; when he understands not a word of either.[33]

Devising taxonomies of browserly behaviour is not impossible. Fundamentally, attention must first be focused on the possibilities presented by relationships between narrative and paratext, and those between one paratext and another, that pertain at the level of the composite main text page or opening, before comparing pages.[34] Sidenotes and running-titles are particularly important. These common paratexts occupied fixed, known positions on the page. Running-titles (and sidenotes to a lesser extent) are concise and imme-

---

31 Hackel, *Reading Material in Early Modern England*, pp. 21–22; Adam Smyth, "'Shreds of Holinesse': George Herbert, Little Gidding, and cutting up texts in early modern England', *English Literary Renaissance*, 42.3 (2012), pp. 452–481.
32 Roger Chartier, 'Texts, printing, readings', in Lynn Hunt (ed.), *The New Cultural History* (Berkeley: University of California Press, 1989), pp. 154–175: 156.
33 Jonson, *Every Man out of His Humour*, H3r.
34 This sentence is an adaptation of a statement by James A. Knapp. See his *Illustrating the Past in Early Modern England: The Representation of History in Printed Books* (Aldershot: Ashgate, 2003), p. 24.

diately comprehensible segments of text, foregrounded by surrounding white space. Subtitles are also normally quickly digestible, certainly when compared to main texts, though their visibility varies from publication to publication. More obviously visible to browsers thumbing through books, and frequently more striking, were illustrations. Ruth Samson Luborksy and Elizabeth Morley Ingram's catalogue of illustrated books published between 1536 and 1603 records that around only around 1,800 items of the roughly 13,500 extant print publication feature illustrations, making them irregular companions of sixteenth-century printed text.[35] Examinations of pre-purchase engagements of illustrated books must obviously integrate significant work on localised word-image relationships. Equally important is an appreciation of the deployment of various typefounts to structure either the main text or set off the paratexts from the main text. Sigla, tables, fleurons, other ornamental borders or initials are less often studied presentational devices, but potentially no less powerful as structural or formal signposts for readers, or browsers.

Running-titles are arguably the most important paratext to any future history of browsing. They are often visually distinguishable from the main texts by the use of a larger typefount and a different typeface, as well as being spatially divorced from the main texts below by the white space between the two. Where a shorter title repeated at the head of every page runs throughout the effect is mnemonic: browsers need only the most cursory of glances to ascertain its continuing presence. One such powerful running-title heads the pages of Bartolome de las Casas' *The Spanish Colony* (1583). *The Spanish Colony*'s full title is:

> The Spanish colonie, or briefe chronicle of the acts and gestes of the Spaniardes in the West Indies, called the newe World, for the space of xl. yeeres: written in the Castilian tongue by the reverend Bishop Bartholomew de las Casas or Casaus, a Friar of the order of S. Domincke.[36]

Yet *The Spanish Colony*'s known readers did not refer to the book by this title or a shorter form of the title. Walter Raleigh, for instance, confidently wrote that *The Spanish Colony* was "intituled The Spanish Cruelties".[37] Robert Payne admitted

---

35   Ruth Samson Luborsky and Elizabeth Morley Ingram, *A Guide to English Illustrated Books, 1536–1603* (2 vols., Tempe: Arizona: Medieval and Renaissance Texts & Studies, 1998).
36   Bartolome de las Casas, *The Spanish Colony* (London: [Thomas Dawson] for William Broome, 1583), USTC 509693, title-page.
37   Walter Raleigh, *Last Fight of the Revenge* (London: [John Windet] for William Ponsonby, 1591), USTC 511938, D1V.

that he had forgotten *Spanish Colony*'s title, but nevertheless echoed Raleigh's phrase in his attempt to make known which book he was referring to: "If you have not the sayd booke of the Spanishe cruelties, I pray you buy it".[38] It was *The Spanish Colony*'s running-title which Raleigh and Payne were invoking. It reads "The Spanish cruelties". The preface was similarly if more verbosely subtitled "Spanish cruelties and tyrannies perpetrated in the West Indies, commonly termed The newe found worlde".[39] Yet the punchier, repetitive, prominently-placed running-title is almost certainly what stuck, its "The Spanish cruelties" fitting Raleigh and Payne's label exactly. For some then, Raleigh and Payne included, it is not the title-page title but the running-title that was *The Spanish Colony*'s pre-purchase identifier, at least for those seeking to follow the exhortation to find this book and buy it. Interested browsers might admittedly have been confident enough to buy the book on the basis of the author's name alone, regardless of the disjunction between the actual title and the title the book was known by. (Raleigh and Payne had after all named las Casas as the author). Only by thumbing through *The Spanish Colony* might others have established that *The Spanish Colony* was the publication Raleigh and Payne had advocated. The running-title was seemingly *The Spanish Colony*'s most effective marketing device and shaped its reception; it did presentational work pre- and post-purchase.

Another important feature to attend to when formulating hypothetical forms of browserly behaviour based on printed pages is sidenotes. Pithy sidenotes were, as William E. Slights colloquially put it, encouragements to "read in the fast lane, often passing up the author, leaving his ponderous discourse well behind".[40] Browsers could have scoured the margins for summaries of the pages' content, thereby arriving at an understanding of the book's structure, or found there clues as to the opinions of the author(s) and their stylistic approach, whether dry, measured, defensive, confrontational, comic or scurrilous. A good example of sidenotes which reveal the narrative structure of a publication to browsers while staying true to the publication's caustic tone is the anti-Marprelate *Martin's Month's Mind* (1589). The structural sidenotes to the main text announce "Sundrie reports of Martins death" (E1v), followed by "The true manner of [or reason for] old Martins death" (E3v), "Martins [dying] oration at his death to his two sonnes" (E4v) and the "Three causes of Mar-

---

38 Robert Payne, *Brief Description of Ireland* (London: Thomas Dawson, 1589), USTC 511286, A4r.
39 las Casas, *The Spanish Colony*, ¶2r.
40 William E. Slights, *Managing Readers: Printed Marginalia in English Renaissance Books* (Ann Arbor: University of Michigan Press, 2001), p. 41.

tins death" (F1v), being "1 Foolerie" (F1v), "2 Ribaudrie" (F2r) and "3 Blasphemie" (F3r). They then reveal the points at which "Martins Will" is fetched (F4v) and "Martins death" (G3r), "Martins Anatomie" (G3v), or autopsy, and "His Buriall" (G4r) occurs.

Some sidenotes are straightforwardly critical of the Martin Marprelate persona's tactics. Two criticise what they see as Martin's attribution of a blasphemous adaptation of Christ's words on the cross to John Aylmer, Bishop of London, in Martin's *Epistle*. Apparently out of the running for the bishopric of Ely, Aylmer supposedly uttered the words "Eli, Eli lamma sabachthani. Eli/ Eli why hast thou forsaken me".[41] *Martin's Month's Mind's* retorting sidenotes read: "In his Pistle tacking on a blind jest of a Benefice, to a text of S. Peter"; he "Jesteth with the scriptures".[42] Some caustic sidenote comments are unsophisticated: "Martin answereth nothing but with whoopes and haloes"; "His workes of Machivell".[43] Others are sharper, as one would expect from a publication involved in the Marprelate controversy. One sidenote temporarily requests the Martin whose fictive death the narrative describes to bear with the adjacent lengthy main text sentence: "This Period Martin is long, but it containneth great store of neccessarie matter, and therefore you must beare with it".[44] One of the first Marprelate tract's great jests, of course, was the prolixity of John Bridges' attack on Presbyterianism.[45] (The "necessarie matter" is, for the record, the variety of people, "frends and foes, both good and bad" who condemn Martin.) Another uses one of Martin's own syllogisms against him: "Martins wardrop, a woodden dagger & [ab]surd night cap" alerted knowledgeable browsers to the main text's retort of Martin's two slightly different syllogisms dubbing Bridges a fool.[46]

Such inventive use of the margins was indeed characteristic of some of the pamphlets involved in the Marprelate controversy, and it is plausible that browsers checked the Martinist and anti-Martinist margins for salacious, scurrilous barbs. In the Martinist *Epistle*, for instance, Martin ventriloquises the

---

41   Martin Marprelate, *Oh Read over D. John Bridges. Epistle* (East Moseley, Surrey: [Robert Waldegrave], 1588), USTC 511029, G2r.
42   Anonymous, *Martin's Month's Mind* (London: [Thomas Orwin], 1589), USTC 511292, B3r and F3v.
43   Anonymous, *Martin's Month's Mind*, D2v and G2r.
44   Anonymous, *Martin's Month's Mind*, E4r.
45   John Bridges, *Defence of the Church of England* (London: John Windet [and Thomas Orwin] for Thomas Chard, 1587), USTC 510694.
46   Anonymous, *Martin's Month's Mind*, F2r; Marprelate, *Oh Read over D. John Bridges. Epistle*, G1v–2r; Martin Marprelate, *The Just Censure and Reproof of Martin Junior* (Wolston, Warwickshire? John Hodgkins, 1589), USTC 511303, C2r–v.

bishops in his main text, and ridicules them from the edges of the page, before reversing the roles, and rebuffing the now sidelined bishops speaking in the sidenotes from the central main text.[47] The placing of scathing put-downs in the margins was of course nothing new. Browsers au fait, for example, with the often lengthy refutation publications that English Protestant and Catholic divines regularly unleashed on one another regarding contested matters of doctrine, liturgy and episcopacy would be used to seeing choleric invective sharing the margins of the page with patristic reference points. As the Catholic and Protestant texts either summarised the other side's standpoint or reproduced it verbatim, the sidenotes aided the separate typefounts in separating for readers (or browsers) the antagonists' arguments.[48]

Not all publications contained sidenotes. Heidi Brayman Hackel's truism is apposite:

> a reader [or browser] may anticipate a very different experience when turning to a page blackened with [printed] marginalia than when opening a book with blank margins.[49]

To parrot part of the title of Mark Bland's landmark article, the appearance of the text matters.[50] In that article Bland charts the English book trade's decisive shift away from black-letter to roman as the principal typeface for works of literature during the 1590s. The shift was in part due to the desire of certain authors and printer-publishers to emulate the elegant, neo-classical modes of textual presentation found on the continent. Added to the deployment of roman typefounts during the latter part of the sixteenth century were the wider use of fleuron borders to structure the text and page, and reglets, which opened up the page by creating thick white rows between lines of verse. Understanding these typographical practices and their effects is as important to the history of reading as it is to the history of design, as Bland points out:

---

47   Evelyn B. Tribble, *Margins and Marginality: The Printed Page in Early Modern England* (Charlottesville: University Press of Virginia, 1993), pp. 109–112.
48   Alexandra Walsham, 'The spider and the bee: the perils of printing for refutation in Tudor England', in John N. King (ed.), *Tudor Books and Readers: Materiality and the Construction of Meaning* (Cambridge: Cambridge University Press, 2010), pp. 163–190, pp. 167–169.
49   Hackel, *Reading Material in Early Modern England*, p. 92.
50   Mark Bland, 'The appearance of the text in early modern England', *Text: Transactions of the Society for Textual Scholarship*, 11 (1998), pp. 91–154.

The effect of these changes, which enhanced saccadic eye movement and the parafoveal recognition of adjacent material, was at least as important for the history of reading as the technical transition from black-letter to roman.[51]

The effects that the changes in the layout of the printed page had in encouraging jerky, discontinuous reading is arguably though more relevant to pre-purchase browsing than it is to reading, as browsers could move from page to page, opening to opening, as well as from one textual segment to an adjacent one. Browsers in bookshops could, for example, recognise the intimacy of the 1594 decimo-sexto *Delia*, which was set using a smaller long primer typefount with arabesques beneath the verse, imitating the mise-en-page of pocketbook religious meditations, as they thumbed through the volume.[52] This history of the appearance of the early modern English printed page is not just part of the history of reading but part of that history's commercial subdivision, the yet to be written history of bookshop browsing. The mise-en-page of trail-blazing editions such as Philip Sidney's *Arcadia*, Edmund Spenser's *Faerie Queen* and the various editions of Samuel Daniel's *Delia* undoubtedly communicated to many bookshop browsers, at every turn of a leaf, the ostentation and fashionable design of the book they held in their hands, just as the typefounts which structured and surrounded the text in animadversive publications expressed either their broadly scholarly or vituperative character, or both.

It is perhaps then not unsurprising that the most effective of the advertisements listed in the appendix is in Gabriel Harvey's *The Trimming of Thomas Nashe*, given Harvey's humanism, wide-ranging scholarly interests, substantial library replete with continental publications, and friendship with Edmund Spenser, whose *Faerie Queen* was designed along the lines of the new, neo-classical typographical model.[53]

Technically, the single-page advert immediately connotes a keenness of wit through its brevity, Latin and the pointedness of the strikingly isolated black lines against the paler background, the sharpness of which in turn conveys something of the cantankerous nature of the Harvey-Nashe quarrel, of which *The Trimming of Thomas Nashe* was a part. Its anaphora, alliterative personal pronouns and tricolon give it a mnemonic cadence, infusing the brief prose

---

51   Bland, 'The Appearance of the Text', p. 94.
52   Bland, 'The Appearance of the Text', pp. 121–122.
53   Bland, 'The Appearance of the Text', pp. 110–113.

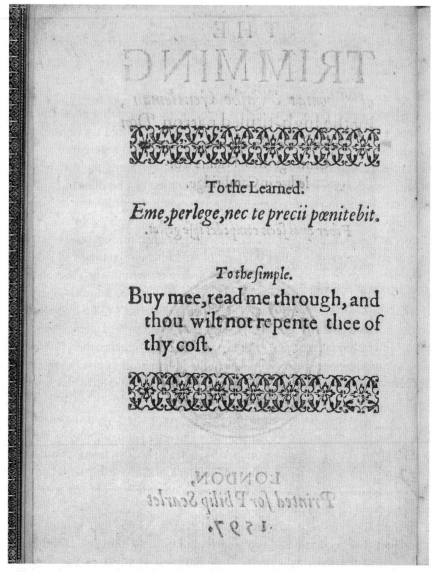

FIGURE 6.3 The pre-purchase plea in Gabriel Harvey's *The Trimming of Thomas Nashe*, A1ᵛ, from RB 61318
THE HUNTINGTON LIBRARY, SAN MARINO, CALIFORNIA

puff with a rhetorical richness. The textual subtlety of the advert is furthermore enhanced by its neo-classical design. The rhythmic, repetitive language of the text, the corresponding syllabic beat of "To the Learned" and "To the Simple", and the near-symmetry of the typographical elements of the page, not least the two enclosing fleuron borders, create a neo-classical feel. The fleuron borders also visually separate this preliminary from the preceding title-page and following preface, and sharpens the focus, even if momentarily, on the pre-purchase plea. Its centralised position and surrounding white space adds to the effect. Further, the typefounts used to set the twenty-six-word advert reveal it to be humanist in conception. Roman and italic founts are juxtaposed, in a manner increasingly fashionable in England. Italic was understood to be expressive of orality, or direct speech, and here the second line, set with a double pica italic, is used by the Latinate Harvey, a notable humanist scholar, to create the illusion that Harvey is speaking directly to the readers he identifies with, university-educated, Latinate humanists.[54] There is indeed, an intimacy to the italic Latin, given italic typefounts' other association: handwriting.[55] Conversely, the paragon roman typefount used to set the address to "the Simple" lacks the personal affect of the italic address to "the Learned". Despite the roman "Buy mee" being the same size (paragon) as the italic "Eme, perlege", the roman looks larger and, in this instance, louder and impersonal. And even the space between the addresses is meaningful: the textual distance and attendant pause in a browser's reading distances the two polar readerships, and grants Harvey's preferred readers, "the Learned", greater importance through syntactical and spatial priority. (The "Learned" are elevated above "the Simple", spatially and figuratively.) Remarkably, this sophisticated arrangement also manages to usher readers towards the preface with the key message: buy this book. The use of four separate typefounts and two ornaments, as well as the text's rhetorical intricacies, represents a far greater degree of care and attention than most preliminaries receive, let alone one so brief. The textual and physical subtleties and humanist, neo-classical character of the page suggest strongly that it is Harvey's work. Most of the other pre-purchase requests listed in The Appendix are expressed in short prose or verse texts. But, technically and typographically, Harvey's easily surpasses the rest.

It is well known that Ben Jonson deplored the "vile arts" by which title-pages were displayed "on posts, or walls,| Or in cleft-sticks, advanced to make calls" to buyers.[56] Similarly, Thomas Churchyard lamented that "Stationers stall[s]" saw the kind of browser who

---

54   Bland, 'The appearance of the text', pp. 99–100.
55   Philip Gaskell, *A New Introduction to Bibliography* (New Castle, DE: Oak Knoll Press, 1972), p. 24.
56   Ben Jonson, *Works* (London: William Stansby, to be sold by Richard Meighen, 1616), USTC 3007070, 3T1v.

> ... reades awhile, but nothing buyes at all,
> For in two lines, they give a pretty gesse,
> What doth the booke, contayne ...[57]

Churchyard's observation of the browser who "reades awhile" shows, alongside the rest of the evidence presented in this essay, that the title-page was not the only element of the "vile arts" publishers and booksellers used to attract custom, a state of affairs of which Jonson was surely cognisant. While the extensive Latin glosses he added to his controversial *Sejanus* (1605) were designed to quash any sense that the realpolitik in the play was topical, they were also clearly intended to help define the play's target readership as university-educated, Latinate classicists, and ward off browsers uncomfortable with the side-notes' unusually considerable scholarly encroachment upon the printed version of the play.[58] Harvey's advert in *The Trimming of Thomas Nashe*, conversely, demonstrates how sophisticated the pre-purchase pleas found inside the book could be. It is time therefore for us to stop placing the burden of pre-purchase engagements solely on the title-page, in effect falsely deeming browsing as a largely tactile and oral experience, with only the most limited of textual-visual engagement. Admittedly, this essay does not consider the continuing life and effectiveness of these pleas, which could be browsed by the friends of the books' owners. Browsing in shops must nonetheless be fully incorporated into the history of reading. And that aspect of the history of reading will have to take greater account than it has done so far of the interrelated history of buying and selling.

Appendix

Below are the forty-four titles which are known to me to have requests to shop browsers to buy the book in question. They are in chronological sequence, ordered by the date of first extant editions. The pages cited refer to the locations of adverts in first editions. The advertisements are reproduced almost verbatim in subsequent editions, give or take the accidentals of spelling and punctuation. They are normally but not always found in the same place in subsequent editions. The advertisement which witnesses the most significant change in form is the famous "But, what ever you do, Buy" line in the preface

---

57 Thomas Churchyard, *The Mirror of Man* (London: Arnold Hatfield for William Holme, 1594), USTC 517337, A2v.
58 Ben Jonson, *Sejanus* (London: George Eld for Thomas Thorpe, 1605), USTC 3002127.

"To the great Variety of Readers" fronting William Shakespeare's *Comedies, Histories and Tragedies* (1623),[59] and even here the variation is typographical, not textual. In the second edition of *Comedies, Histories and Tragedies* (1632) the capital 'B' of the first edition's "Buy" is dropped: "But, whatever you do, buy".[60] In the third edition (1664) the word "Buy" is given greater emphasis through italicisation and reinstating the capital 'B': "But, whatever you do, *Buy*".[61] And when, in the fourth edition (1685), the preface is set mainly in an italic typefount, the word "Buy" is visually set off by the roman fount it appears in: *"But, whatever you do,* Buy".[62]

Only those editions which feature the advertisements are cited. Hence, the second known edition of Margaret Cavendish's *World's Olio* (1671) is omitted, as the promotional proem lacks the 1655's edition's key final couplet: "And this Imaginary Feast pray try,| Censure your worst, so you the Book will buy". Similarly, there is no way of knowing if the plea to buy was included in the other two editions of *A Handful of Pleasant Delights*, extant only in small fragments and tentatively dated 1575 and 1595 by the revised *Short-Title Catalogue* (STC). The STC, USTC and Wing numbers refer to a title's first known printing. Where titles are reprinted, the number of subsequent editions and date spans are noted only up to 1700. (There are post-1700 editions of *Sincere Convert*, for instance). 'BB' is a shortening of the first part of this essay's title, "The Business of Browsing".

- BB1: 1567, Isabella Whitney, *A Letter by a Young Gentlewoman to her Inconstant Lover*, A1v, STC 25439, USTC 506724
- BB2: 1572, Amadís de Gaula, *Amadis of France*, ²¶¶1v, STC 545, USTC 507531
- BB3: 1573, Thomas Tusser, *Five Hundred Points of Good Husbandry*, B2v, STC 24375, USTC 507680 (19 more extant editions between 1573 and 1672)
- BB4: 1575, George Gascoigne, *The Noble Art of Venery or Hunting*, A4v, STC 24328, USTC 508033 (1 more extant edition in 1611)
- BB5: 1578, Thomas Cartwright, *Hospital for the Diseased* A2r–v, STC 4303.5, USTC 508482 (11 more extant editions between 1579 and 1638)

---

59 William Shakespeare, *William Shakespeare's Comedies, Histories, & Tragedies* (London: Isaac Jaggard and Edward Blount, at the charges of William Jaggard, Edward Blount, John Smethwick, and William Aspley, 1623), USTC 3010710, A3r.
60 William Shakespeare, *William Shakespeare's Comedies, Histories, & Tragedies* (London: Thomas Coates for Richard Hawkins, John Smethwick, Robert Allot, William Aspley and Richard Meighen, 1632), USTC 3015912, A4r.
61 William Shakespeare, *Mr. William Shakespeare's Comedies, Histories, & Tragedies* (London: Roger Daniel, Alice Warren, [and another] for Philip Chetwind, 1664), A4r.
62 William Shakespeare, *William Shakespeare's Comedies, Histories, & Tragedies* (London: for printed for Henry Herringman, Edward Brewster, Richard Chiswell, and Richard Bentley, 1685), A2r.

- BB6: 1579, Henry Chettle, *Forest of Fancy*, A2r–v, STC 4271, USTC 508775
- BB7: 1584, Clement Robinson, *A Handful of Pleasant Delights*, A1v, STC 21105, USTC 510101
- BB8: 1585, Johann Jacob Wecker, *Compendious Surgery*, *12r, STC 25185, USTC 510410 (1 more extant edition in 1633)
- BB9: 1590, Orazio Rinaldi, *The Royal Exchange*, ¶4r, STC 12307, USTC 511613
- BB10: 1591, Joseph du Chesne, *A Brief Answer*, A3v, STC 7275, USTC 511815
- BB11: 1596, Thomas Lodge, *Wits Misery*, A4r–v, STC 16677, USTC 513182
- BB12: 1597, Gabriel Harvey, *The Trimming of Thomas Nashe*, A1v, STC 12906, USTC 513416
- BB13: 1606, Barnabe Barnes, *Four Books of Offices*, a1r, STC 1468, USTC 3002652
- BB14: 1608, Anonymous, *Wits A. B. C.*, A4r, STC 25262, USTC 3003340
- BB15: 1609, Thomas Dekker, *The Gulls Hornbook*, A4r, STC 6500, USTC 3003976
- BB16: 1612, Francis Davis, *A Catechism*, A2v, STC 6368, USTC 3005193
- BB17: 1612, Thomas Wilson, *A Christian Dictionary*, A7v, STC 25786, USTC 3005182 (4 more extant editions in 1616, 1622, 1635 and 1647)
- BB18: 1614, Michael Scot, *Philosopher's Banquet*, A4r, STC 22062, USTC 3005902 (1 more extant edition in 1633)
- BB19: 1617, John Davies, *Wits Bedlam*, A6v, STC 6343, USTC 3007550
- BB20: 1620, John Taylor, *Taylor His Travels*, A2r, STC 23802, USTC 3009184
- BB21: 1621, John Andrews, *Andrew's Resolution*, C6r, STC 590, USTC 3009903 (1 more extant edition in 1630)
- BB22: 1621, William Slatyer, *The History of Great Britain*, ¶¶2r, STC 22634, USTC 3009696
- BB23: 1623, William Shakespeare, *Comedies, Histories and Tragedies*, A3r, STC 22273, USTC 3010710 (3 more extant editions in 1632, 1663 and 1685)
- BB24: 1624, John Andrews, *Sovereign Salve*, A2v, STC 595.4, USTC 3011442 (1 more edition in 1636)
- BB25: 1630, Gervase Markham, *Faithful Farrier*, A3r–4r, STC 17367, USTC 3014558 (5 more extant editions in 1631, 1635, 1638, 1640 and 1647)
- BB26: 1638, Robert Lewes, *The Merchants Map*, a6r, STC 21094, USTC 3019654
- BB27: 1639, M. de La Serre, *The Mirror that Flatters Not*, B4r, STC 20490, USTC 3020350 (3 more extant editions in 1658, 1664 and 1673)
- BB28: 1640, Thomas Shepard, *Sincere Convert*, A5v, STC 22404.7, USTC 3021228 (22 more extant editions between 1641 and 1695)
- BB29: 1640, Richard Ward, *Theological Questions*, Zz6v, STC 25024, USTC 3020959 (1 more extant edition in 1646)
- BB30: 1645, George Gillespie, *Wholesome Severity Reconciled with Christian Liberty*, A4v, Wing G765, USTC 3031882

- BB31: 1646, Humphrey Mill, *The Second Part of The Nights Search*, A8r, Wing M2058, USTC 3033069 (1 more extant edition in 1652)
- BB32: 1648, Jeremiah Burroughs, *Rare Jewell of Christian Contentment*, A4r, Wing B6102, USTC 3038302 (10 more extant editions between 1649 and 1685)
- BB33: 1650, Samuel Clarke, *The Marrow of Ecclesiastical History*, ²b3r, Wing C4543, USTC 3041470 (2 more extant editions in 1654 and 1675)
- BB34: 1655, John Davis, *Seismos Megas*, A5v, Wing D422
- BB35: 1655, Margaret Cavendish, *World's Olio*, A6v, Wing N873
- BB36: 1656, Athanasius Davies, *The Protestant's Practice*, A9r, Wing D385
- BB37: 1657, Laurence Price, *Fortune's Lottery*, A2r, Wing P3365A
- BB38: 1662, T.W., M.W. and I.T., *Gratiae Theatrales*, *4r, Wing G1580
- BB39: 1667, Oliver Heywood, *Heart-Treasure*, A2r, Wing H1767
- BB40: 1669, E.C., *The Poor Doubting Christian Drawn to Christ*, B4v, Wing C26
- BB41: 1669, Samuel Malbon, *Death and Life, or, Sin's Life*, A3r, Wing M312
- BB42: 1673, John Eachard, *Some Opinions of Mr Hobbs*, A6v–7r, Wing E64
- BB43: 1674, Robert Godfrey, *Various Injuries & Abuses in Chemical and Galenical Physic*, A7r, Wing G927
- BB44: 1675, William Okeley, *Ebenezer*, π4r, Wing O191 (2 more extant editions in 1676 and 1684)

CHAPTER 7

Printing for the Pilgrims: Krakow Seventeenth-Century Guidebooks

Justyna Kiliańczyk-Zięba

The history of the early printed book is one of imitation as well as innovation.[1] Choosing a title for publication meant finding the right balance between making conservative choices and bringing to the market new texts that could attract readers and sell in large numbers. For printers like those of the Commonwealth of Poland-Lithuania, whose market was relatively small and mostly peripheral, one of the strategies to tackle this problem was to imitate the earlier success of books published in large centres of production. This was a very good policy if 'imitation' did not involve the direct copying of texts that could otherwise be easily imported, but rather meant the adaptation of tested bestsellers produced elsewhere. For example, such inspiration was commonplace in areas of recreational literature. Translating into Polish a popular text that first circulated in Latin, German or Italian was normal practice. It generated a number of abiding bestsellers for the Polish sixteenth and seventeenth-century market: books reprinted in many editions and published over a very long time span.[2] Another, more refined strategy was to appropriate bestselling foreign works to produce books designed for the local market.

Such was the case of a pocket-size book in the vernacular that appeared in Krakow in 1603 under the title *Przewodnik abo Kościołów krakowskich i rzeczy w nich widzenia i wiedzenia godnych krotkie opisanie* ("The guidebook or a short

---

1 These features of early printing are often discussed with regard to the appearance of fifteenth-century books. Early printing was "inescapably imitative … in that it involved the adaptation of new technology to old models", see David McKitterick, *Print, Manuscript and the Search for Order, 1450–1830* (Cambridge: Cambridge University Press, 2003), p. 35.
2 Attesting to this are, for instance, the publishing histories of the Polish Aesop, Marcolf and Eulenspiegel. See, respectively: Stanisław Grzeszczuk, 'Wstęp', in Janusz S. Gruchała (ed.), *Biernat z Lublina, Ezop*, wstęp Stanisław Grzeszczuk (Krakow: Universitas, 1997), pp. 23–25; Kazimierz Piekarski, 'Fragmenty czterech nieznanych wydań "Marchołta"', *Pamiętnik Literacki*, 32 (1935), pp. 481–520; Radosław Grześkowiak, Edmund Kizik, 'Wstęp', in Radosław Grześkowiak and Edmund Kizik (eds.), *Sowiźrzał krotochwilny i śmieszny. Krytyczna edycja staropolskiego przekładu "Ulenspiegla"* (Gdańsk: Wydawnictwo Uniwersytetu Gdańskiego, 2005), pp. XLIII–LXI.

description of Krakow's churches and things in them that are noteworthy and interesting to see"). *Przewodnik* was not a guidebook to the artistic or intellectual life of the city, but an introduction to its mirabilia: Krakow's churches, relics, and miracle-working images (see Figure 7.1).

In this article I will first discuss the circumstances leading to the publication of *Przewodnik*. I will then describe the book's content and form, and suggest its inspiration in bestselling Roman guidebooks. I will speculate on the market for such a publication and examine the evidence in the surviving copies to demonstrate that the guide attracted a popular audience and that the 1603 editions remained in use for many decades. In the final part of my article I will briefly reconstruct the process in which *Przewodnik* evolved and mutated in later editions of seventeenth- and eighteenth-century guidebooks to Krakow's sacred sites.

The Circumstances Leading to the Publication of *Przewodnik*

In mediaeval Poland, Krakow attracted travellers as the country's principal metropolis: a seat of secular and religious authority, a university town, and an economic hub situated on a junction of trade routes important for the region. As early as the twelfth century, however, Krakow also started to draw visitors as a centre of pilgrimage, where a growing number of churches housed relics and miracle-working images, and convents provided shelter to holy men and women. In early modern times the political and economic importance of Krakow in the Polish-Lithuanian Commonwealth declined.[3] At the same time the city's significance as a centre of religious life grew: "between 1450 and 1650 Krakow, the state's political capital, evolved into its spiritual, ecclesiastical heart".[4]

The earliest *loca sacra* (sacred sites) in Krakow were associated with the relics of the patrons of the Kingdom of Poland: the 'imported' saint, saint Flo-

---

3 For the evolution of Krakow's role in Poland and then the Polish-Lithuanian Commonwealth see for instance Janina Bieniarzówna and Jan M. Małecki, *Kraków w wiekach XVI–XVIII* (Krakow: Wydawnictwo Literackie, 1984), pp. 167–180; Maria Bogucka and Henryk Samsonowicz, *Dzieje miast i mieszczaństwa w Polsce przedrozbiorowej* (Wrocław: Ossolineum, 1986), pp. 329–392; 489–508; Jan M. Małecki, 'La dégradation de la capitale. Cracovie aux XVIe, XVIIe et XVIIIe siècles', *Studia Historiae Oeconomicae*, 19 (1988), pp. 85–99.
4 Maria Bogucka, 'Krakau-Warschau-Danzig. Funktionen und Wandel von Metropolen 1450–1650', in Evamaria Engel, Karen Lambrecht and Hanna Nogossek (eds.), *Metropolen im Wandel. Zentralität in Ostmitteleuropa an der Wende vom Mittelalter zur Neuzeit* (Berlin: Akademie Verlag, 1995), pp. 71–91: 91.

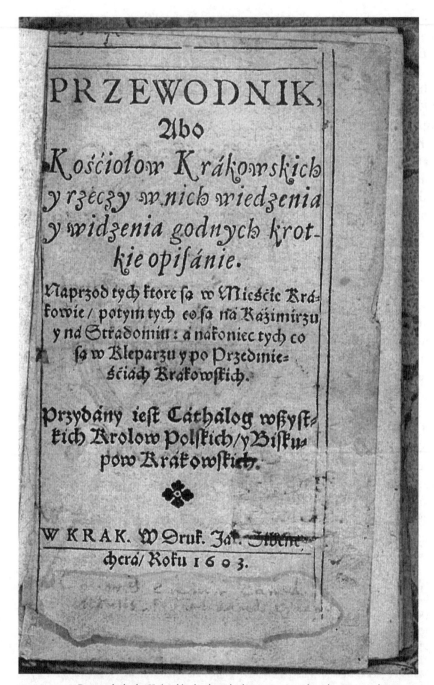

FIGURE 7.1   *Przewodnik abo Kościołów krakowskich i rzeczy w nich widzenia i wiedzenia godnych krotkie opisanie* (Krakow: Jakub Siebeneicher, 1603)
WARSAW, BIBLIOTEKA NARODOWA, SD XVII.1.1154

rian, and the twelfth-century Krakow bishop Stanislaus, whose cult as a martyr was promoted by Polish church authorities long before his official canonisation in 1253. In the fourteenth and fifteenth centuries local patronates and cults gradually grew further in importance. Relics and graves of people who, like the queen Jadwiga Andegaweńska (Jadwiga of Poland, 1374–1399), had once lived in Krakow or died in the city *in fama sanctitatis* were especially venerated, along with miracle-working statues and paintings (principally those of the Virgin Mary) in the capital's churches. The religious life of Krakow, very often developing in association with its sacred sites, added to the pilgrimage attraction of the city, where both residents and visitors could take part in pious processions, join in the charitable work of local confraternities, and obtain indulgences in the privileged churches that were usually to be visited on prescribed festive days.[5] What further intensified the religious atmosphere of the capital was the number of places of worship in Krakow, its satellite towns Kazimierz and Kleparz, and the suburban areas closely connected to them.[6] At the beginning of the seventeenth century, at the time when the 1603 guidebook was first published, there were thirty-two churches and twenty-one convents, sixteen of which had their own churches clustered within the relatively small area of 500 hectares.[7]

In these circumstances the production of a traditional guidebook for Christian pilgrims—both those rushing to Krakow from afar, and the city's residents themselves—would not appear an unusual undertaking. But what actually

---

5 The literature on the Krakow cults of saints, relics and miracle working images, as well as on devotional practices in the city is extensive. See for instance Aleksandra Witkowska, *Kulty pątnicze piętnastowiecznego Krakowa. Z badań nad miejską kulturą religijną* (Lublin: Wydawnictwo Towarzystwa Naukowego KUL, 1994); Grażyna Jurkowlaniec, 'Cracovia altera Roma. Medieval images, medieval saints, and the shaping of urban piety in Krakow of the seventeenth century', in Luise Schorn-Schütte (ed.), *Gelehrte Geistlichkeit—geistliche Gelehrte. Beiträge zur Geschichte des Bürgertums in der Frühneuzeit* (Berlin: Duncker & Humblot, 2012), pp. 155–184. Bieniarzówna and Małecki, *Kraków w wiekach*, pp. 262–296; Hanna Zaremska, *Bractwa w średniowiecznym Krakowie. Studium form społecznych życia religijnego* (Wrocław: Ossolineum, 1977); Aleksandra Witkowska, 'Przestrzeń sakralna późnośredniowiecznego Krakowa', in Halina Manikowska and Hanna Zaremska (eds.), *Ecclesia et civitas. Kościół i życie religijne w mieście średniowiecznym* (Warsaw: Instytut Historii PAN, 2002), pp. 37–48.
6 Mediaeval and early modern Krakow was the principal city in a larger urban area comprised of two other towns (Kazimierz and Kleparz) circuited by suburbs (the biggest were Garbary and Stradom). Formally separate entities, they were closely connected economically, socially and culturally. See Leszek Belzyt, *Kraków i Praga około 1600 roku. Porównanie topograficznych i demograficznych aspektów struktury społecznej i etnicznej dwóch metropolii Europy Środkowo-Wschodniej* (Toruń: Wydawnictwo Adam Marszałek, 1999), pp. 26–34, 42 and *passim*.
7 Henryk Gapski, *Klasztory krakowskie w końcu wieku XVI i w pierwszej połowie XVII w. Analiza przestrzenna środowisk zakonnych* (Lublin: Katolicki Uniwersytet Lubelski. Redakcja Wydawnictw, 1993), pp. 14–15: 48. Belzyt, *Kraków i Praga*, pp. 49–50.

prompted the publication of *Przewodnik* was a new factor: the Jubilee Year of 1600, celebrated in Krakow in 1603.

The Jubilee Year was first established by pope Boniface VIII in 1300 and accompanied by a special indulgence: a complete remission of sins for pilgrims coming to Rome and fulfilling certain conditions.[8] Initially the indulgence of *Anno Sancto* was only granted to those travelling to Rome, but already by the end of the fourteenth century it was possible to obtain it in other privileged locations, Krakow included. Church politics changed by the middle of the sixteenth century. In 1550 and in 1575 (the first post-Tridentine *Anno Santo*) it was again necessary to make the effort of travelling to Rome to obtain the Holy Year indulgence, and the Roman celebrations were to manifest the glory and power of regenerating Catholicism. Consequently, no special indulgence for Krakow could be issued. Clement VIII however, even if he proclaimed the Jubilee Year of 1600 with similar intentions in mind, again agreed to extend the spiritual effects of the Holy Year to all those who would celebrate it by pilgrimage to the Polish capital city. The papal bull offered a plenary indulgence to those who would (between 2 March and 2 July 1603) pray for 15 consecutive days in Krakow's cathedral and make a sacramental confession to one of the priests designated by the pope. The participation of pilgrims in the Krakow celebrations was so massive that the cathedral could not accommodate all the visitors and Clement VIII agreed to give Jubilee privileges to seven more churches in the city, while the bishop of Krakow Bernard Maciejowski increased the number of confessors to 140.

There can be no doubt that many of those who wanted to be granted the indulgence, would be interested in a guide providing an account of Krakow's churches as well as the relics and indulgences associated with each sanctuary. The preparations to publish *Przewodnik* might have begun before the opening of the Krakow Jubilee celebrations at the beginning of March—in anticipation of the demand for the pilgrims' guide. Or, more probably, they might have started at the time when the religious fervour of the Holy Year was already felt in Krakow and it had been realised that there was a ready market for such a publication. At any rate, the book was issued a little late: in mid-April, six weeks after the inauguration of the Krakow Jubilee Year, at a time when hundreds of pil-

---

8 Henryk Damian Wojtyska, 'Lata święte w XV i XVI wieku', *Roczniki Teologiczno-Kanoniczne*, 23.4 (1976), pp. 11–24; Henryk Damian Wojtyska, *Miłościwe lata. Dzieje Wielkich Jubileuszów Chrześcijaństwa (z udziałem Polaków)* (Olsztyn: Hosianum, 2000), pp. 6–53; Herbert L. Kessler, Johanna Zacharias, *Rome, 1300. On the Path of the Pilgrim* (New Haven and London: Yale University Press, 2000); Olaf Kwapis, *Do Rzymu! Sztuka i wielkie jubileusze (1300–1575)* (Warsaw: Stowarzyszenie Pro Cultura Litteraria, Instytut Badań Literackich PAN, 2014), pp. 39–131.

grims were arriving in the capital every day, piety and penance were declared publicly, and flagellants beat themselves through the streets.[9] The printer of the guidebook, Jakub Siebeneicher, signed his dedication letter on 12 April. Offering the book to the bishop of Krakow Bernard Maciejowski, he described his publication as "the little book" for both the pilgrims rushing to Krakow on the occasion of the Holy Year, and those who were to visit the city in the years to come. *Przewodnik* was designed as an edifying read, it was intended "to ignite greater zeal" ("pobudzić do większego nabożeństwa") as, thanks to it, the pilgrims were to learn about Krakow's places of worship, hear miraculous tales associated with particular churches, and be informed about the indulgences and spiritual graces that could be obtained by pilgrimage to the sacred sites of Krakow.

Content

But *Przewodnik* was not only devout, it was also practical. The book was composed as a useful tool, helping the pilgrims find their way around the capital's churches. To the pilgrims to Krakow (many of them first time visitors who had little or no knowledge of the city) it proposed a logical method of visiting the sacred sites of the city, by organising a sequential list of 45 churches that comprised a route through Krakow for the pilgrim to follow. The itinerary begins at

---

9 One printed report of the Jubilee Year celebrations in Krakow is the diary by Jan Januszowski published first as *Jubileusz Wielki od Ojca Świętego papieża Klemensa VIII na żądanie króla J. M. polskiego i szwedzkiego Zygmunta III królestwu wszytkiemu do kościoła katedralnego krakowskiego pozwolony* (Krakow: Jakub Siebeneicher, 1603), then as *Krótkie opisanie blisko przeszłego Jubileuszu i rzeczy widzenia godnych, które się na nim w Krakowie Roku Pańskiego 1603 z pociechą wielką katolików toczyły* (Krakow: Jakub Siebeneicher, 1603), and in Latin translation by Stanisław Nigritius as *Compendium Iubilei et rerum cognitu dignarum* (Krakow: Oficyna Łazarzowa, 1603). It has been suggested that Januszowski could have also been the author of the anonymously published *Przewodnik*; see Karol Estreicher, 'Emanuela Murraya "Opisanie Krakowa" a literatura o Krakowie i Plan Kołłątajowski', *Rocznik Krakowski*, 48 (1977), pp. 57–68, and Michał Rożek, 'Mirabilia urbis Cracoviae', *Krzysztofory*, 11 (1986), pp. 49–53. This hypothesis, even if not totally convincing; see Justyna Kiliańczyk-Zięba, *Czcionką i piórem. Jan Januszowski w roli pisarza i tłumacza* (Krakow: Universitas, 2007, p. 289), still remains better founded than a suggestion put forward by Almut Bues, who proposed to identify Martin Gruneweg as *Przewodnik*'s author (Almut Bues, 'Mirabilia Cracoviensia. Kto był autorem przewodnika po Krakowie z roku 1603?', *Rocznik Krakowski*, 80 (2014), pp. 19–37). About the authorship of *Przewodnik* see also: Witkowska, *Kulty pątnicze*, pp. 60–61; Janina Bieniarzówna, *Mieszczaństwo krakowskie XVII wieku. Z badań nad strukturą społeczną miasta* (Krakow: Wydawnictwo Literackie, 1969), p. 88.

Wawel castle hill with Krakow cathedral, the centre of the Holy Year celebrations, and two other Wawel temples (St George, St Michael), which were also privileged churches of the Jubilee. Then the guidebook turns to descriptions of the churches in the south-western part of the town (St Mary Magdalene, All Saints, St Francis), leads the pilgrims to the university quarter (St Anne), and directs them to the churches of the north-eastern quarter of Krakow (St Stephen, St Mark, St John, Holy Spirit and Holy Cross). Having covered the main square churches (St Mary, St Barbara, St Wojciech) the route heads back southwards to the churches on Grodzka street (Holy Trinity, St Peter and Paul, St Andrew, St Martin, St Giles) leading to the city gate into the neighbouring suburb Stradom and the Krakow satellite town—Kazimierz. In the second part of the guidebook the Bernardine church at the foot of the castle hill marks the beginning of a circuit that covered the churches of Stradom and Kazimierz. Later on shrines and chapels outside Kazimierz city walls (St Leonard, St Benedict) are also mentioned. The third part of *Przewodnik* provides descriptions of churches and chapels in the northern part of Kazimierz and Stradom (Corpus Christi, St Hedwig) and the horticultural suburbs of Krakow east of the city (St Sebastian, St Gertrud, St Nicholas). The itinerary then heads north towards Kleparz (with the town's principal church—St Florian), the churches and shrines in Garbary (St Peter, St Mary), and on Smoleńsk (Divine Mercy) to end at Zwierzyniec (St Augustine, St Margaret, St Saviour).

A short passage is devoted to each sanctuary named on the circuit, the longest being those about the cathedral at the Wawel castle hill and the St Mary's Church (Mariacki) on the main square. The narrative combines the historical background of the temple's foundation, renovations and artistic commissions, with an account of its relics and indulgences, miracle stories and local worship traditions.[10] Naturally the latter are the author's main focus since

---

10   The content of the entries was certainly based on the author's own devotional experience accumulated over the years. But for the history of the churches, *Przewodnik* often repeated the accounts of fifteenth-century historian Jan Długosz and his *Liber beneficiorum*. See Jan Długosz, *Opera omnia*, ed. A. Przezdziecki (Krakow: Drukarnia "Czasu" Kirchmajera, 1863); Stanisław Kuraś, *Regestrum Ecclesiae Cracoviensis. Studium nad powstaniem tzw. Liber beneficiorum Jana Długosza* (Warsaw: Państwowe Wydawnictwo Naukowe, 1966); Justyna Kiliańczyk-Zięba, 'Wstęp', in J. Kiliańczyk-Zięba (ed.), *Przewodnik abo kościołów krakowskich krótkie opisanie* (Krakow: Universitas, 2002), pp. 43–52. The text also made use of a German diary by a Dominican friar Martin Gruneweg; see Almut Bues (ed.), *Die Aufzeichnungen des Dominikaners Martin Gruneweg (1562–ca. 1618) über seine Familie in Danzig, seine Handelsreisen in Osteuropa und sein Klosterleben in Polen* (4 vols., Wiesbaden: Harrassowitz Verlag, 2008). He also quoted other written sources, for instance Maciej z Miechowa, *Chronica Polonorum* (Krakow: Hieronim Wietor, 1521), and explicitly recalled local oral traditions. It has also been proposed that among *Przewodnik*'s sources were the

Przewodnik was directed to a reader who, in wandering the Krakow streets, was motivated by the desire to venerate relics and obtain spiritual graces by visiting the sacred sites. *Przewodnik* centres on Krakow's *mirabilia*, but at the same time it frequently draws the readers' attention towards the riches of the churches, splendid religious ceremonies, confraternities and charity works that all attest to the social popularity of Catholicism. *Przewodnik* thus fits into the mainstream of Catholic policy as decided at the Council of Trent: it endorses the veneration of relics and memorials to saints as a significant part of the religious ritual, perpetuates traditional practices, and consequently promotes the Church's secular authority, by confirming the notion of its power and wealth.

The 1603 edition ends by listing the sovereigns of Poland and the Krakow bishops, giving information about the date their rule started, commenting on their personality traits and noting important events in their lives. These genealogies must have provided the reader with a system of reference to historical developments, which added to the popularising character of the guide.

Models

The *Przewodnik* of 1603 had no predecessors in the existing print literature on Krakow.[11] Its anonymous author modelled his work on the guidebooks to Christian Rome—both in terms of the organization of the text and the design of the edition. This was only appropriate since, even in mediaeval times Krakow was locally famed as 'a second Rome', *minor Roma*. A few years before *Przewodnik* was printed, in 1596, Giovanni Paolo Mucante, a secretary for cardinal Enrico Caetani, the papal legate to Poland, wrote in his diary that Krakow was rightly seen as a Polish *compendium mundi*: "the old saying repeated here is right: 'Kiedyby Rzym nie był Rzymem, tedyby Kraków był Rzymem', if Rome was not Rome, Krakow would be Rome".[12] In 1620, Hungarian traveller Márton Csombor noted a Latin version of the same saying, ridiculing Krakow's citizens,

---

acts of the visitation of the Krakow diocese, compiled at the end of the sixteenth century (Rożek, 'Mirabilia', p. 50).

11 Estreicher, 'Emanuela Murraya', pp. 57–58; Jerzy Duda, 'Przewodniki po Krakowie (do 1914 roku). Książki, ich autorzy i wydawcy', *Rocznik Krakowski*, 62 (1996), pp. 54–56; Elwira Buszewicz, *Cracovia in litteris. Obraz Krakowa w piśmiennictwie doby Odrodzenia* (Krakow: Universitas, 1998).

12 Jan Władysław Woś (ed.), *Itinerario in Polonia del 1596 di Giovanni Paolo Mucante Cerimoniere Pontificio* (Rome: Il Centro di Ricerca, 1981), p. 39. The original reads: "onde per proverbio sogliono dire 'Kiedyby Rzym nie był Rzymem, tedyby Krakow był Rzymem', cioè se Roma non fusse Roma, Cracovia saria Roma. È ben vero ...".

who boasted: "If Rome were not Rome, our Krakow would be Rome ... If Peter had not been the first bishop, our Stanislaus would have been".[13] Even if the capital of the Polish kingdom could not justifiably be considered equal to Rome by any means, the saying noted by the papal legate and the Hungarian Calvinist distinctly echoed the local well-established belief that Krakow could be compared to the Eternal City.[14] At a time when the post-Tridentine Church encouraged the revival of interests in traditional devout practices, the association of Krakow and Rome was especially relevant with regards to the Polish city's religious life (sacred sites, relics, privileges associated with its churches, popular public events, ceremonies, public piety, festivities). In 1602 Martin Gruneweg, who was born in a Lutheran family in Gdansk, but came to live in Krakow as a Dominican friar, wrote in his diary: "Understand, how rich is Krakow in churches, in bodies of the saints, innumerable places of worship, and non-stop religious services, as if the city was another Rome".[15]

For Rome, a tradition of producing descriptions of the city as well as guides for visitors and local inhabitants had developed over the centuries. The body of texts formed as a result is often referred to as "mirabilia urbis Romae", and consists of four different works that circulated in Europe in numerous editions, both in Latin and in the vernaculars.[16] The *Mirabilia* proper (as Nine Robijntje

---

13 Jan Ślaski (ed.), *Martona Csombora podróż po Polsce* (Warsaw: Czytelnik, 1961), pp. 101–102: "Si Roma non esset Roma, nostra Cracovia esset Roma ... Si Petrus non fuisset primus episcopus, noster Stanislaus fuisset primus episcopus".

14 The motive was described by Tadeusz Ulewicz, 'Krakow—polski Rzym (jak, kiedy, dlaczego)', in Róża Godula (ed.), *Klejnoty i sekrety Krakowa. Teksty z antropologii miasta* (Krakow: Wydawnictwo Wawelskie, 1994), pp. 63–73 (published previously in Giovanna Brogi Berghoff (ed.), *Filologia e letteratura nei paesi slavi. Studi in onore di Sante Graciotti* (Rome: Carucci, 1990), pp. 785–791). See also Buszewicz, *Cracovia in litteris*, pp. 211–219; Jurkowlaniec, *Cracovia altera Roma*.

15 Bues, *Die Aufziechnungen*, p. 831: "Hie verstehe, wie reich ist Krakaw an kirchen, an Heiligen leichen, an untzeilichem heyligthueme, ann unaufhörigem Gottes dienste, gleich were sie ein anderes Roem".

16 The following paragraph summarises information provided by Nine Robijntje Miedema, *Die "Mirabilia Romae": Untersuchungen zu ihrer Überlieferung; mit Edition der deutschen und niederländischen Texte* (Tübingen: Niemeyer, 1996), pp. 1, 11–16, and by introductory parts in Nine Robijntje Miedema, *Rompilgerführer in Spätmittelalter und Früher Neuzeit. Die "Indulgentiae ecclesiarum Urbis Romae" deutsch/niederländisch. Edition und Kommentar* (Tübingen: Niemeyer, 2003). Miedema also provides a bibliography of "mirabilia urbis Romae", both in manuscript copies and in early printed editions, and in *Rompilgerführer* gives an overview of contemporary research on the subject of pilgrim guides. For the history of the Roman guides see also Ludwig Schudt, *Le guide di Roma: Materialien zu einer Geschichte der römischen Topographie* (Wien: Benno Filser Verlag, 1930); Alberto Caldana, *Le guide di Roma. Ludwig Schudt e la sua biografia. Lettura critica e catalogo ragionato*

Miedema has it), is a description of Rome that focuses first on the city's antiquities, then records the legends associated with the famous sites, and finally provides an almost continuous route through Rome (which begins at the Vatican and ends in Trastevere). In the form in which contemporary scholars know it, the text was composed by the middle of the twelfth century. In mediaeval times *Mirabilia* were one of the most popular texts about Rome, as is attested to by the number of recorded manuscript copies, editions and translations. The *Mirabilia* proper was not conceived as a guidebook, in contrast to the so-called *Mirabilia urbis Romae vel potius Historia et descriptio urbis Romae* that consisted of a historical introduction (Rome's foundation myth etc.) followed by *Indulgentiae ecclesiarum urbis Romae* (listing the churches of Rome with their relics and indulgences) and *Stationes ecclesiarum urbis Romae* (listing station days and the proscribed churches to be visited on those days). Those three texts were first put together in fifteenth-century editions. Because the copies of *Mirabilia urbis Romae vel potius Historia et descriptio* were often bound together with the *Mirabilia* proper, which usually had no colophon, the older text started to be erroneously regarded as *Historia et descriptio*'s first part. To add to the confusion both *Indulgentiae* and *Stationes* circulated separately first as hand-written copies (*Stationes* as early as the eighth century, *Indulgentiae* in the twelfth century) and later as printed booklets.

Even in the fifteenth century printed "mirabilia urbis Romae" were a steady bestseller, books to be consulted by travellers to the Eternal City as well as virtual pilgrims.[17] Similar pilgrimage guides were also composed and reproduced in numerous editions for other religious centres in Europe: cities like Cologne or Milan, the destination of *peregrinatio maior*, Santiago de Compostela, as well as smaller, usually locally popular sites collecting relics and indulgences or those famous for miracle-working images.[18] The anonymous author of *Przewodnik* was certainly familiar with the genre, if for no other reason than that numerous copies of the Roman guides were in circulation in contemporary Poland, both owned by individuals and in the book collections of secular and church institutions, such as monastic libraries.[19] More specif-

---

(Rome: Palombi Editori, 2003); Massimo Pazienti, *Le guide di Roma tra Medioevo e Novecento. Dai Mirabilia urbis ai Baedecker* (Rome: Gangemi Editore, 2013).

17 Sergio Rossetti, *Rome. A Bibliography from the Invention of Printing through 1899, vol. I: The Guide Books* (Florence: Olschki, 2000).

18 Halina Manikowska, *Jerozolima—Rzym—Compostela. Wielkie pielgrzymowanie u schyłku średniowiecza* (Wrocław: Wydawnictwo Uniwersytetu Wrocławskiego, 2008), pp. 249–252.

19 For examples of the availability of Roman guidebooks in Poland see for instance Alojzy Sajkowski, *Włoskie przygody Polaków, wiek XVI–XVIII* (Warsaw: Państwowy Instytut Wydawniczy, 1973), p. 194; Manikowska, *Jerozolima*, pp. 215–216. For Polish early modern

ically, the Krakow author might have found inspiration in Andrea Palladio's *Descritione de Chiese, Stationi, Indulgenze & Reliquie de Corpi Sancti, che sonno in la Città de Roma*—a sixteenth-century guidebook, that was a modern alternative to the "mirabilia urbis Romae" of early mediaeval origin. Palladio's work was first published in 1554.[20] All subsequent versions of the text, which came to be known as *Le cose maravigliose dell'alma città di Roma*, were issued as the work of an anonymous author. It became a bestseller and "the source for one of the most enduring descriptions of Christian Rome".[21] It might have been in this popular book—"modest in length and devout in nature"[22]—that the unknown Polish writer found the idea of proposing an attractive method of visiting Krakow's churches, listing facts about their foundation, relics, indulgences and stations, and closing the book by the chronology of the kings of Poland (instead of the sovereigns of Europe) and local bishops (in place of the popes).

The Market

In much the same way as with Palladio's work in its repeated editions, in *Przewodnik* a similar combination of material was squeezed into an unembellished, portable volume. The duodecimo format was chosen for *Przewodnik*, and the book contained 82 small pages. Some of the Roman guidebooks were already illustrated in the fifteenth century, but in *Przewodnik* no woodcuts accompanied the text and no plan or map of Krakow has been preserved in any of the known copies. The 1603 guidebook must have been designed as a practical reference work, unpretentious in appearance, inexpensive to produce and, as a result, sold at a modest price.

It seems that *Przewodnik* found eager buyers among pilgrims to Krakow, since the three extant copies dated 1603 document two different editions identical in content, page design and the spatial composition of type and woodcut

---

descriptions of Rome and translations of guidebooks to Rome and Italy see: Andrzej Litwornia, *W Rzymie zwyciężonym Rzym niezwyciężony. Spory o Wieczne Miasto (1575–1630)* (Warsaw: Wydawnictwo Instytut Badań Literackich PAN, 2003).

20 USTC 846288.

21 Eunice D. Howe, 'Introduction', in Andrea Palladio, *The Churches of Rome*, ed. E.D. Howe (Binghamton, New York: Center for Medieval and Early Renaissance Studies, 1991), pp. xi–xii. About the advent of 'modern guidebooks' to Rome also see Pazienti, *Le guide di Roma*, pp. 47–74 (chapters *Giubilei ed evoluzione delle guide* and *Roma diventa "meravigliosa"*).

22 Howe, *Introduction*, p. xii.

material.²³ However, rather against expectations, we do not know of any other edition of the guidebook printed in the first decades of the seventeenth century. We could speculate about lost editions, remembering that *Przewodnik* was precisely the kind of book whose copies must have perished soon after the book's initial circulation; or we can assume that the guidebook to Krakow's sacred sites was not in high demand after the fervour of the Holy Year had faded away. Perhaps the market for the guidebook was not lively enough to encourage Jakub Siebeneicher or the printers of the following generation to publish further editions of *Przewodnik*.

Evidence in Surviving Copies

At the same time, surviving copies of the Krakow guide give some indication of the book's enduring appeal. For example, the copy now in Biblioteka Narodowa in Warsaw is inscribed with marginalia in two different hands correcting the text, adding information about newly built churches, and updating the chronology of the Polish kings and Krakow bishops (see Figure 7.2).²⁴ The reader who first owned the guide updated the list to the 1640s. The one into whose hands *Przewodnik* passed afterwards annotated it as late as 1700, since Stanisław Dąmbski—the last name added to the chronology of the Krakow bishops—was nominated for his office in 1700 and died in the same year. Thus the copy must have been in continuous use well into the seventeenth century and perhaps beyond. Even almost a hundred years after its publication, the guide could still be consulted for advice on the sacred sites of Krakow, the history of the local churches or simply as edifying reading.

Perhaps more interesting is the evidence in another copy of *Przewodnik*, preserved in Warsaw.²⁵ Notes of ownership in this book demonstrate that in the late seventeenth century it belonged to the tailors' guild in Krakow and used to be borrowed by the craftsmen. In 1673 a senior member of the guild, Andrzej Koczowicz, recovered the guide for the guild's collection when its reader, one Gabriel Eliasz Ciepielik, died (see Figure 7.3). In 1684 the tailors had the book rebound. That means that 70 years after the guide was printed it was still valued, and the book, remaining in the ownership of the institution, was taken

---

23   Edition A: Warsaw, Biblioteka Narodowa, SD XVII.1.1154; Warsaw, Biblioteka Publiczna miasta stołecznego Warszawy, XVII.1.85; edition B: Katowice, Biblioteka Śląska, 221072 I. Typographical errors of edition A are absent from edition B.
24   Warsaw, Biblioteka Narodowa, SD XVII.1.1154.
25   Warsaw, Biblioteka Publiczna, XVII.1.85.

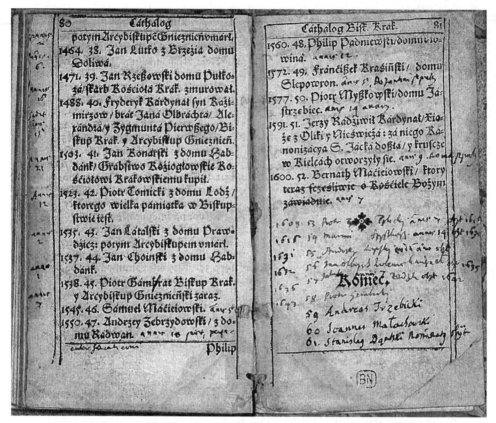

FIGURE 7.2 *Przewodnik abo Kościołów krakowskich i rzeczy w nich widzenia i wiedzenia godnych krotkie opisanie* (Krakow: Jakub Siebeneicher, 1603)
WARSAW, BIBLIOTEKA NARODOWA, SD XVII.1.1154

good care of. Eighty years after the guide first found its way to the reading public, the tailors did not think its text outdated and were ready to pay for a new binding to preserve the plain, unadorned book for further usage. Thus the evidence in those two Warsaw copies suggests that the volumes printed in 1603 remained in circulation for decades. It also indicates that a book designed as a companion guide for a pilgrim, could also be read and inscribed at home and enjoyed by people less familiar with Krakow geography as well as by the city's residents.

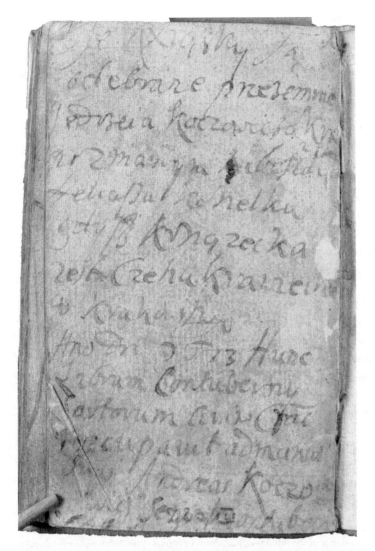

FIGURE 7.3 *Przewodnik abo Kościołów krakowskich i rzeczy w nich widzenia i wiedzenia godnych krotkie opisanie* (Krakow: Jakub Siebeneicher, 1603)
WARSAW, BIBLIOTEKA PUBLICZNA MIASTA STOŁECZNEGO WARSZAWY, XVII.1.85

Re-editions

That said, the 1603 guide was not forgotten by the printers. In the mid to late 1640s, the Krakow printer Franciszek Cezary resuscitated the old text and in 1647 brought it to the market under a changed title: *Stołecznego miasta Krakowa kościoły i klejnoty* (The churches and jewels of the capital city of Krakow, further referred to as *Klejnoty*; see Figure 7.4). Cezary issued three editions of the revised guide over a short period of three years: the first and second editions are dated 1647, and in 1650, a Jubilee Year, a re-edition followed.[26]

In the dedication letter that opens all the mid-seventeenth century editions of the guide, Franciszek Cezary did not mention *Przewodnik* as the source text for the *Klejnoty*. Instead, he presented the text as his own work ("having prepared a description of all the churches of the capital ... I decided to offer it to pious readers) and revealed its inspiration in Italian guides".[27] Addressing his readers in the preface *Do czytelnika gościa* he recalled the idea of Krakow as another Rome: "There are reasons for you to be proud, venerable Krakow, of being a second Rome, as the proverb has it".[28]

The juxtaposition of the editions of *Przewodnik* and *Klejnoty* shows that Cezary—not only the printer of the guide, but also the author of the revisions to the original text—brought the 1603 work back to life in much the same way as the editors of the Roman guides, as in the case of Palladio, did with their constantly revised versions. Thus the heart of the 1647 guidebook consisted of the account of 1603, and the sequence of churches established in the original edition still formed the framework. However, the text was updated and amplified. Firstly, Cezary added a short historical introduction. Next, he expanded and updated the church descriptions that had appeared in the 1603 guide, mostly by appending short passages to the end of many paragraphs. These contained information about church renovations, new chapels, altars

---

26 The Union Catalogue of the Biblioteka Narodowa in Warsaw (the Polish National Library) records 15 copies of the 1647 edition of *Klejnoty*, and 38 copies of the 1650 edition.

27 The original text of the dedication reads: "miasta tego stołecznego kościoły wszytkie porządnie opisawszy ... ludziom nabożnym do czytania podać umyśliłem". Franciszek Cezary, *Stołecznego miasta Krakowa kościoły i klejnoty* (Krakow: Franciszek Cezary, 1647), f. A2v–A3r. At the same time Cezary presented the guidebook to the reading public as an anonymous work or added to the information on the title page the name of Piotr Hiacynt Pruszcz, an official of the Krakow University, hence the bibliographical confusion regarding *Klejnoty*. See Marian Malicki, *Repertuar wydawniczy drukarni Franciszka Cezarego starszego, 1616–1651. Część 1: Bibliografia druków Franciszka Cezarego starszego 1616–1645* (Krakow: Księgarnia Akademicka, 2010), nos. 618, 619, 718.

28 In the original: "Możesz się godnie z tego szczycić cny Krakowie, Żeś jest drugim Rzymem, jako masz przysłowie". Cezary, *Stołecznego*, f. A4v.

> Stołecznego Miáftá
> # KRAKOWA
> # KOŚCIOŁY
> ʆ
> ## KLEYNOTY,
> Co w nich ieft widzenia godnego
> y zacn go.
>
> *Do tego przydáne ieft Opifánie*
> ### SWIETYCH BOZYCH
> W Krákowie leżących,
> Krolow Polfkich, y Bifkupow Krákowfkich.
> *Teraz, nowo zebráne y do druku podáne.*
>
>
>
> Cum licentia Superiorum.
>
> W KRAKOWIE,
> W Drukárni Fránćiszká Cezárego / Roku P. 1647.

FIGURE 7.4 *Stołecznego miasta Krakowa kościoły i klejnoty* (Krakow: Franciszek Cezary, 1647)
WARSAW, BIBLIOTEKA NARODOWA, SD XVII.3.2521

and other monuments, but more frequently told miracle stories absent from the 1603 text or reported on cults that had only gained in popularity in recent decades. Secondly, the revised text included descriptions of eleven churches constructed during the intervening years, incorporated into the itinerary proposed in 1603. Finally, Cezary widened the guide's geographical range. In a fourth part, appended to the revised text of 1603, the printer presented information about monastic foundations—both old and new—in the vicinity of

Krakow (Tyniec, Bielany, Mogiła, Staniątki). Naturally the chronology of the kings and bishops at the end of the volume was also updated. The book was closed with a list of station churches in Krakow and instructions on how best to benefit from making a pilgrimage to them. The result was a book which offered current, and occasionally more detailed, information to the reading public. Obviously the editorial interventions in the *Klejnoty* of 1650 were slight compared to those introduced in 1647. The Krakow religious scene could not change that much over three years. But even in the 1650 book the editor's desire to keep his publication alive by bringing its text up to date is very clear—here and there he altered the guide's descriptions further, added information about church renovations or emerging cults and amended the lists of kings and bishops. The innovations of the 1647 and 1650 editions gave the early seventeenth-century publication new life, making it once again a useful and comprehensive reference work to be consulted for decades to come.

That the 1603 guide in its mid-seventeenth-century incarnation persisted throughout the eighteenth century is not only confirmed by the annotations in surviving copies.[29] In about 1712, Franciszek Cezary's son, Franciszek Cezary młodszy, issued a pamphlet which provided information about the churches constructed in Krakow in the second half of the seventeenth century (*Klejnotów duchownych stołecznego miasta Krakowa aukcyja znamienita*; see Figure 7.5). The only two known copies of this edition survived bound together with the 1650 *Klejnoty*, which is a clear indication that the volumes printed in the mid-seventeenth century remained in circulation at the beginning of the eighteenth century. Even though outdated, readers still consulted these editions for advice on visiting the sacred sites of Krakow. The pamphlet's content was subsequently incorporated into another edition of the guide that was printed by Drukarnia Akademicka in Krakow in 1745 as *Klejnoty stołecznego miasta Krakowa albo Kościoły*. The text of the 1603 guide was further expanded, and this time finally accompanied by a city plan.

The plain book of 1603 that imitated the guidebooks published to accompany the international crowd on their Roman pilgrimage or to be taken home for those unable to travel to the Eternal City could not possibly have become as successful as its inspiration. Nevertheless, the Krakow *Przewodnik* enjoyed considerable popularity. The volumes issued in 1603 remained in use for generations. Then the descendants of the initial edition circulated well into the eighteenth century, reaching the hands of pilgrims born two centuries after the Krakow guide was first composed and printed.

---

29 For example, as implied by evidence in a copy from 1650 now in the Biblioteka Kórnicka Polskiej Akademii Nauk (call no. 11706).

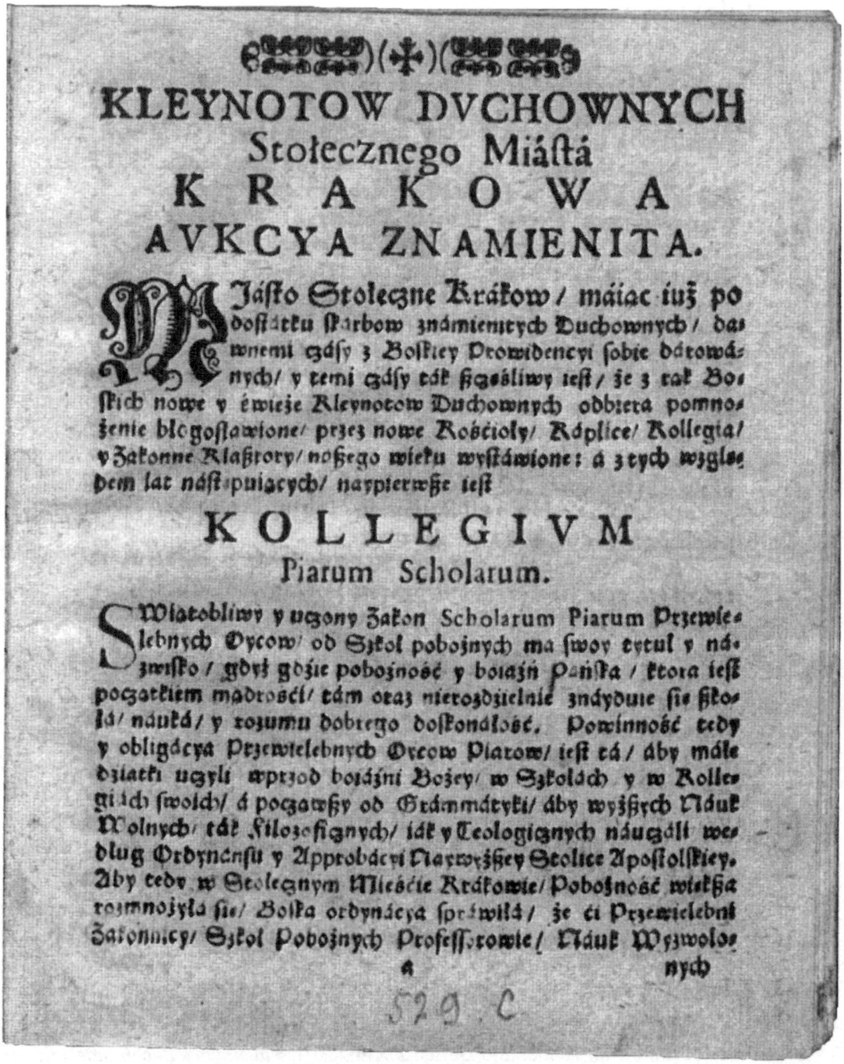

KLEYNOTOW DVCHOWNYCH
Stołecznego Miáſtá
KRAKOWA
AVKCYA ZNAMIENITA.

Iáſto Stołeczne Krákow / máiąc iuż po doſtátku ſkárbow známienitych Duchownych / dánemi ądſy z Boſkiey Prowidencyi ſobie dárowánych/ y temi ądſy ták ſąśliwy ieſt / że z ták Boſkich nowe y świeże Kleynotow Duchownych obbiera pomnożenie błogoſławione/ przez nowe Kośćioły/ Káplice/ Kollegia/ y Zakonne Klaſztory/ noßego wieku wyſtáwione: á ztych wzglądem lat náſtępuiących/ naypierwße ieſt

KOLLEGIVM
Piarum Scholarum.

Wiatobliwy y uczony Zakon Scholarum Piarum Przewielebnych Oycow/ od Stkoł pobożnych ma ſwoy tytuł y námieſzto / gdyż gdźie pobożność y boiáźń Páńſka / ktora ieſt początkiem mądrości/ tám oraz nierozdźielnie znáyduie ſię ſkłoná naucá/ y rozumu dobrego doſkonáłość. Powinność tedy y obligácya Przewielebnych Oycow Piarow/ ieſt tá/ áby máłe dźiatki ucżyli wprzod boiáźni Bożey/ w Szkołách y w Kollegiách ſwoich/ á począwſzy od Grámmátyki/ áby wyżßych Náuk Wolnych/ ták Filozofignych/ iák y Teologicznych náuczáli wedlug Ordynánſu y Approbácyi Naywyßßey Stolice Apoſtolſkiey. Aby tedy w Stołecznym Mieśćie Krákowie/ Pobożność więkßa rozmnożyła ſię/ Boſka ordynácya ſprawiła/ że ci Przewielebni Zakonnicy/ Szkoł Pobożnych Profeſſorowie/ Náuk Wyzwolonych

FIGURE 7.5 *Klejnotów duchownych stołecznego miasta Krakowa aukcyja znamienita* (Krakow: Franciszek Cezary młodszy, post 1711)
KRAKOW, BIBLIOTEKA NAUKOWA PAU I PAN, PAU ST. DR. 529 ADL.

CHAPTER 8

Book Lotteries as Sale Events for Slow-Sellers: the Case of Amsterdam in the Late Eighteenth Century

Daniel Bellingradt

In early modern Europe, selling books by lottery was a practiced but uncommon selling technique. The practice of offering books as prizes in a lottery can be traced back to as early as the mid-seventeenth century. The oldest known book lotteries were probably organized in England and the Holy Roman Empire, followed by many more locations elsewhere in Europe, including the Dutch Republic, Scotland, and within the Slovene and Hungarian territories of the Habsburg monarchy.[1] However, due to scant research on the topic, a truly

---

1 Following Michael Harris, book lotteries were regularly held in England by the mid-seventeenth century, although evidence of British book lotteries is found from the late 1690s. See Michael Harris, 'Newspaper advertising for book auctions before 1700', in Robin Myers, Michael Harris and Giles Mandelbrote (eds.), *Under the Hammer* (London: Oak Knoll Press, 2001), pp. 1–14, esp. p. 11. For two broadside advertisements for book lotteries in England of 1698 and 1699, see the anonymous editor's note on two broadside advertisements for book lotteries in England of 1698 and 1699, published in: *Factotum*, 35 (1992), p. 4. Further on English and Scottish contemporary book lotteries: David Pearson, 'The distribution of books by lottery', *Factotum*, 30 (1989), pp. 19–20; Ian Beavan, 'Book lotteries in Aberdeen', *Factotum*, 34 (1991), pp. 11–13; Murray C.T. Simpson, 'Every one is sure to get something for his money: a 1712 book lottery and auction in Edinburgh', *Journal of the Edinburgh Bibliographical Society*, 5 (2010), pp. 45–64. See the evidence of book lotteries taking place in eighteenth century South-Eastern Europe, within the Habsburg monarchy and the Holy Roman Empire, and the book markets near the Slovene and Hungarian territories, in the city of Linz 1768, 1774 and 1776: Rudolf M. Henke and Gerhard Winkler, *Geschichte des Buchhandels in Linz* (Linz: Archiv der Stadt Linz, 2002), pp. 177–178; Norbert Bachleitner, Franz M. Eybl and Ernst Fischer, *Geschichte des Buchhandels in Österreich* (Wiesbaden: Harrassowitz, 2000), pp. 127–128. Also see for the Holy Roman Empire: Gerd Quedenbaum, *Glücksspiel und Buchhandel: die Bücherlotterien des 18. Jahrhunderts* (Düsseldorf: Selbstverlag, 1997); Franz S. Pelgen (ed.), *Bücherlotterien des 18. Jahrhunderts* (Roßdorf: Fröhlich, 2008); and the short glimpse in Johann Goldfriedrich, *Geschichte des Deutschen Buchhandels vom Westfälischen Frieden bis zum Beginn der klassischen Litteraturperiode (1648–1740)* (Leipzig: Verlag des Börsenvereins der Deutschen Buchhändler, 1908), chapter 6 ("Der Buchhandel. Weitere Vertriebsmittel: Aushang, Vordatierung, Titelauflage, Schlußbogen, Freiexemplar, Prospekt, Titeländerung, Preisherabsetzung; Bücherauktion, Bücherlotterie"). For book lotteries held in Slovenia in 1776: Anja Dular, 'Johann Thomas Edler von Trattner (1719–1798) and the Slovene book market of the 18th century', in Johannes Frimmel and Michael Wögerbauer (eds.), *Kommunikation*

European picture of early modern book lotteries cannot yet be drawn satisfactorily.[2] Despite a general lack of knowledge about the contexts and characteristics of book lotteries within the early modern book trade industry, the roots of

---

und Information im 18. Jahrhundert. Das Beispiel der Habsburgermonarchie (Wiesbaden: Harrassowitz, 2009), pp. 45–54. For the situation in the Netherlands: Isabella H. van Eeghen, De Amsterdamse boekhandel 1680–1725 (Amsterdam: Scheltema & Holkema NV, 1965), III, pp. 212–221 and IV (1967), pp. 195–272; Isabella H. van Eeghen, 'De boekhandel van de Republiek 1572–1795', in van Eeghen (ed.), De Amsterdamse Boekhandel 1680–1725 (Amsterdam: N. Israel, 1978), V, pp. 11–128, here: p. 51, footnote 127; Hannie van Goinga, 'Lotteries for Books in the Dutch Republic in the late 18th Century. A new method of marketing', in Marieke van Delft, Frank de Glas and Jeroen Salman (eds.), New Perspectives in Book History (Zutphen: Walburg Pers, 2006), pp. 101–116.

2 Strikingly, there are no entries in the relevant handbooks, dictionaries, encyclopaedias, and introductions to the interdisciplinary field of book studies. See for example: Simon Eliot and Jonathan Rose (eds.), A Companion to the History of the Book (New York: Wiley-Blackwell, 2009); John Barnard, Donald F. McKenzie and Maureen Bell (eds.), The Cambridge History of the Book in Britain, vol. IV, 1557–1695 (Cambridge: Cambridge University Press, 2002); Michael F. Suarez and Michael L. Turner (eds.), The Cambridge History of the Book in Britain, vol. V, 1695–1830 (Cambridge: Cambridge University Press, 2009); Stephen W. Brown and Warren McDougall (eds.), The Edinburgh History of the Book in Scotland, vol. II, Enlightenment and Expansion 1707–1800 (Edinburgh: Edinburgh University Press, 2012); Bill Bell (ed.), The Edinburgh History of the Book in Scotland, vol. III, Ambition and Industry 1800–1880 (Edinburgh: Edinburgh University Press, 2007); Michael F. Suarez and H.R. Woudhuysen (eds.), The Oxford Companion to the Book, vol. I, Essays, A–C (Oxford: Oxford University Press, 2010); Raymond Gillespie and Andrew Hadfield (eds.), The Oxford History of the Irish Book, vol. III, The Irish Book in English 1550–1800 (Oxford: Oxford University Press, 2006); John Feather (ed.), A Dictionary of Book History (London: Routledge, 1988); Frederick H. Collins (ed.), Authors' and Printers' Dictionary (Oxford: Oxford University Press, 1973); Willem E. Clason (ed.), Elsevier's Dictionary of Library Science, Information and Documentation (Amsterdam: Elsevier, 1973); Geoffrey A. Glaister (ed.), Encyclopedia of the Book (New Castle, DE: Oak Knoll Press, 2001); Geoffrey A. Glaister (ed.), Glossary of the Book. Terms Uses in Papermaking, Printing, Bookbinding and Publishing (London: Allen & Unwin, 1960); Leonard M. Harrod (ed.), Harrod's Librarians' Glossary of Terms Used in Librarianship, Documentation and the Book Crafts and Reference Book (Aldershot: Gower, 1987); Mary C. Turner (ed.), The Bookman's Glossary (New York: Bowker, 1961); Horst Machill (ed.), Handbuch des Buchhandels, vol. I Allgemeines (Hamburg: Verlag für Buchmarktforschung, 1974); Joachim-Felix Leonhard and Herbert Ernst Wiegand (eds.), Medienwissenschaft. Ein Handbuch zur Entwicklung der Medien und Kommunikationsformen, 15.1. (Berlin: de Gruyter, 1999); Birgit Althaus, Das Buch-Wörterbuch. Nachschlagewerk für Büchermacher und Buchliebhaber (Erftstadt: Area-Verlag, 2004); Marion Janzin and Joachim Güntner (eds.), Das Buch vom Buch. 500 Jahre Buchgeschichte (Hanover: Schlüter, 2007); Dietmar Strauch and Margarete Rehm (eds.), Lexikon Buch, Bibliothek, Neue Medien (Munich: Saur, 2007); Konrad Umlauf, Stefan Gradmann and Peter Lohnert (eds.), Lexikon der Bibliotheks- und Informationswissenschaft, vol. I, A–J (Stuttgart: Hiersemann, 2011); Severin Corsten, Günther Pflug and Friedrich A. Schmidt-Künsemüller (eds.), LGB², vol. I (Stuttgart: Hiersemann, 1987); Ursula Rautenberg (ed.), Sachlexikon des Buches (Stuttgart: Reclam, 2015); Wilhelm Hellwig (ed.), Wörterbuch der Fachausdrücke des Buch- und Papiergewerbes (Frank-

such activities are clearer. They are rooted in the lottery culture of early modern Europe that developed during the sixteenth century in both theory and practice. The first lotteries of the early sixteenth century took place in German- and Dutch-speaking Europe (for example in 1521 in the German city of Osnabrück, and in 1549 in the Dutch city of Amsterdam) and were public, state-sponsored charitable events. By the time the first public lottery in Britain was held (1567), lotteries were already established as a continental practice in the sixteenth century—and could occasionally take weeks, as a nocturnal public lottery in Amsterdam in 1592 demonstrated.[3] The main attraction of lotteries lay in the ritualized procedure of drawing lots publicly and manufacturing unforeseen outcomes.[4] In early modern times, this spectacular production of an unforeseen outcome—the lottery effect—was connected to contemporary popular religious-wisdom practices and rooted in human attraction to a present div-

---

furt am Main: Klimsch, 1926); Stephan Füssel and Helmut Hiller (eds.), *Wörterbuch des Buches* (Frankfurt am Main: Klostermann, 2006); Roger Chartier and Henri-Jean Martin (eds.), *Histoire de l'édition française. Le livre conquérant. Du Moyen Age au milieu du XVII siècle* (Paris: Fayard and Promodis, 1990); Roger Chartier and Henri-Jean Martin (eds.), *Histoire de l'édition française. Le livre triomphant 1660–1830* (Paris: Fayard and Promodis, 1990); Roger Chartier and Henri-Jean Martin (eds.), *Histoire de l'édition française. Le temps des éditeurs Du romantisme à la Belle Époque* (Paris: Fayard, 1985); Congrès international des Éditeurs (ed.), *Vocabulaire technique de l'editeur, Congrès international des Éditeurs* (London: Ballantyne Press, 1913); Marieke van Delft and Clemens de Wolf, *Bibliopolis: History of the Printed Book in the Netherlands* (Zwolle: Waanders, 2003); Marco Santoro, *Storia del libro italiana. Libro e società in Italia dal Quattrocento al nuovo millennio* (Milan: Editrice Bibliografica, 2008); Palle Birkelund, Esli Dansten and Lauritz Nielsen (eds.) *Nordisk Leksikon for Bogvæsen*, vol. I (Copenhagen: Nyt Nordisk Forlag Arnold Busck, 1951).

3   See on the Amsterdam lottery of 1592: Norbert Middelkoop, 'Gillis Coignet and the Amsterdam lottery of 1592: locating an extraordinary night scene', *Journal of Historians of Netherlandish Art*, 2 (2010). See on early modern lotteries in general: C. L'Estrange Ewen, *Lotteries and Sweepstakes* (London: Heath Cranton, 1932); John Pick and Malcolm Anderton, *Building Jerusalem. Art, Industry, and the British Millennium* (Amsterdam: Routledge, 1999), Chapter "Industriousness and the lottery", pp. 55–72. On early modern lotteries in the Netherlands: Anneke Huisman and Johann Koppenol, *Daer compt de Lotery met trommels en trompetten! Lotterijen in de Nederlande tot 1726* (Hilversum: Uitgeverije Verloren, 1991); Marie-Laure Legay, *Les loteries royales dans l'Europe des Lumières, 1680–1815* (Villeneuve-d' Ascq: Presses universitaires du Septentrion); G.A. Fokker, *Geschiedenis der loterijen in de Nederlanden. Eene bijdrage tot de kennis van de zeden en gewoonten der Nederlanden in de XV, XVI, en XVIIe eeuwen* (Amsterdam: Frederik Muller, 1862); Kitty Kilian, 'De Haarlemse loterij van 1606–1607: Loterijen en loterijrijmpjes', *Haerlem Jaarboek*, (1989), pp. 8–37; Ilse Eggers L. de Mecheleer and M. Wynants (eds.), *Geschiedenis van de loterijen in de Zuidelijke Nederlanden (15de eeuw–1934)* (Brussels: Algemeen Rijksarchief, 1994); Claude Bruneel, 'Les loteries de l' Europe méridionale', in Loterie Nationale (ed.), *Loteries en Europe. Cinq siècles d'histoire* (Brussels: Loterie Nationale, 1994).

4   See L'Estrange Ewen, *Lotteries and sweepstakes*.

inatory dimension.⁵ Producing decisions by lotteries of all sorts—from tossing a coin, rolling a die, drawing straws or picking a name out of a hat—were attractive because decisions were made partly on a supernatural basis, without reliance on reason.⁶ Peter Stone, a leading lottery theorist, coined the term 'the lottery principle', to describe this, stating that, "lotteries sanitize decisions by keeping reason out".⁷

Book lotteries, built on the assumed attraction of such publicly held events, were set up to sell books as prizes in a lottery draw. As private commercial enterprises, book lotteries were not set up to offer charity—as most of the state lotteries in early modern Europe usually were—but to move stock and make money. However, like all contemporary lotteries, book lotteries too were events licensed by the territorial governments, meaning that the organizers still had to pay a fixed fee (of about 15–20% of the proceedings) to the relevant authorities. Although book lotteries in early modern Europe did not follow a standard procedure, they did have common features of procedure, practice, and setting. While it was a characteristic feature of a book lottery to offer written media of all sorts—ranging from bound scholarly books, to journals and periodicals, copperplate prints, almanacs, pamphlets, broadsides, etc.—there seems to have been no regular offer of relevant additional book trade items such as ink or paper. Book lottery prizes ranged from costly single books to "win-packages" of many books, or even to packages of books coupled with other items of value (like porcelain, household goods, and so on). These prizes had to be announced by the organizers of the lottery in detail months before the event. As a potential buyer of a lottery ticket, you were informed about the prizes, the

---

5   Michael Witmore, *Culture of Accidents: Unexpected Knowledge in Early Modern England* (Stanford: Stanford University Press, 2001); John Considine, 'Wisdom-literature in early modern England', *Renaissance Studies*, 13.3 (1999), pp. 325–342. See for example on the producing of wisdom and religious meaning in ritualistic processes such as the "Bibelorakel" lotteries in German Pietism where excerpts from the bible were drawn from a "Lotterie-Schätzkästchen" (often a wooden box/later on books containing cards with written media) and read aloud and collectively debated about: S. Brückner, 'Von biblischen Chartenspielen, geistlichen Lotterien und erbaulichen Stammbüchern. Einblicke in pietistische Geselligkeitspraktiken', in S. Görtz, Ute Pott and Cornelia Zimmermann (eds.), *Geselligkeiten im 18. Jahrhundert* (Halle: Mitteldeutscher Verlag, 2012), pp. 108–114.
6   Since the earliest times, humans have employed "chance devices" (V. Aubert) in order to receive divinatory instructions or supernatural guidance. See on this point in lottery theory: Vilhelm Aubert, 'Chance in Social Affairs', *Inquiry*, 2 (1959), pp. 1–24, esp. p. 4. On the ever-growing literature devoted to the subject of lotteries see the literature mentioned in: Peter Stone (ed.), *Lotteries in Public Life. A Reader* (Exeter: Imprint Academic, 2011).
7   Peter Stone, *The Luck of the Draw. The Role of Lotteries in Decision-Making* (Oxford: Oxford University Press, 2011), p. viii.

exact number of tickets, the quantity of blanks, tickets with no prize attached, and about the date and place in which the draw was to take place. The selling and buying of tickets started a process that has been termed the "payoff condition" of a lottery.[8] As a buyer, the purchase of a ticket made you a member of the group of potential beneficiaries of the lottery: it gave you a chance at the prizes, that is, the books. The chance of winning a prize was determined by the conditions of the particular book lottery.

Participating in a book lottery "without blanks" (and this was the normal case, at least in continental Europe) meant that you were always a lucky winner and so would always get some books out of the event. When every ticket wins, your luck is determined by what book package you win. Winning participants were the norm in continental book lotteries. However, when you were participating in book lotteries with blanks—as seems to have been the case mostly in England and Scotland—there was the chance for loss. In 1786, a book lottery in Aberdeen had 200 tickets and only 3 prizes (a 66 to 1 chance), and another book lottery of the same year had 442 tickets and 109 of them would win prizes (a 1 in 4 chance).[9] A book lottery of London (1699) had 400 tickets of which 350 were blanks—so only 50 tickets would win, (a 1 in 7 chance).[10] Whatever the details of the lottery, they all offered packages of books for ready sale. And this practice of selling a number of books in certain packages as "prizes" to lucky winners makes one point clear: book lotteries were designed as quick-selling events. In order to attract enough ticket-buyers or "winners" the lotteries had to have sufficiently attractive prizes in order to ensure that all the tickets sold, and that the books offered as prizes were disposed of. The first-place prize had to be spectacular, extraordinary items that the ticket buyers would never under normal circumstances be able to afford. It was this attractive mixture of chance, covetable prizes, and the ritualized performances of drawing lots publicly that made book lotteries sensational events.

This article focuses on the extraordinary sale events of book lotteries in early modern Europe by highlighting the aspect of rapidly selling books in high quantities. By analysing 15 book lotteries in Amsterdam from the late eighteenth century, it will be shown that this selling technique, resulting from the

---

8 Lewis A. Kornhauser and Lawrence G. Sager, 'Just lotteries', *Social Science Information*, 27 (1988), pp. 483–516.

9 Another lottery by the same bookseller, William Mortimer, had 972 tickets and 233 prizes (1794). In fact, often only about one third of the tickets won book packages of certain value in Aberdeen. See Beavan, 'Book lotteries in Aberdeen', pp. 11–13.

10 See on this an anonymous editor's note on two broadside advertisements for book lotteries in England of 1698 and 1699; published in: *Factotum*, 35 (1992), p. 4.

most common network activities of the contemporary book trade, was more than just another way to foster sales. As will be demonstrated in the following section on the communicative setting of book lotteries in Amsterdam, these strategic co-operations and alliances of book people were contextualized in an economic climate of crisis and driven by the motivation to boost book sales quickly and liquidate stagnant stock rapidly. The subsequent section will analyse the book lotteries themselves and their organisational background. It will be shown that above all it was the economic goal of book lotteries to free up storage, to empty overstocked warehouses of slow-selling items, and to make money quickly.[11] In this respect, and as the title puts it, book lotteries were sale events for slow-sellers.

Stagnant Stock in Amsterdam

Amsterdam was a true book city, full of bestselling, slow-selling and non-selling books. As one of the most important centres of publishing and print distribution in Northern Europe during the seventeenth and eighteenth centuries, the city was contemporarily known as "the bookshop of the world".[12] In this respect Amsterdam was a book city full of successful, steadily-selling varieties of contemporary written media. On the flip side (and connected to the on-going stream of new publications) this book city was full of stagnant

---

11 This interpretation of the general aim of organizing a book lottery to unload a complete stock of books in one event is in line with argumentation put forward for the German and Dutch book lotteries of the seventeenth and eighteenth centuries in Pelgen (ed.), *Bücherlotterien des 18. Jahrhunderts* and van Goinga, 'Lotteries for Books in the Dutch Republic in the late 18th Century'.

12 Lotte Hellinga, Alastair Duke, Jacob Harskamp and Theo Hermans (eds.), *The Bookshop of the World. The Role of the Low Countries in the Book-Trade 1473–1941* ('t Goy-Houten: Hes & De Graaf, 2001). See further O. Lankhorst, 'Le transfert des livres entre la Hollande et l'Europe centrale (XVIIe–XVIIIe siécle)', in F. Barbier (ed.), *Est-Ouest. Transferts et réceptions dans le monde du livre en Europe (XVIIe–XXe siécles)* (Leipzig: Leipziger Universitäts-Verlag, 2005), pp. 151–163; Christiane Berkvens-Stevelinck, Hans Bots, Paul G. Hoftijzer and Otto S. Lankhorst (eds.), *Le magasin de l'univers. The Dutch Republic as the Centre of the European Book Trade* (Leiden: Brill, 1992). However, a printing and publishing history of early modern Amsterdam is yet unwritten. See on the contemporary strategic position of Amsterdam within the Dutch book distribution system: J.D. Popkin, 'Print culture in the Netherlands on the eve of Revolution', in Margaret Jacob and Wijnand W. Mijnhardt (eds.), *The Dutch Republic in the Eighteenth Century. Decline, Enlightenment, and Revolution* (Ithaca: Cornell University Press, 1992), pp. 273–291; Hannie van Goinga and Jeroen Salman, 'Expansie en begrenzing van de interne markt. De achtiende eeuw', *Jaarboek voor Nederlandse boekgeschiedenis*, 17 (2010), pp. 171–219.

booksellers' stock—warehouses full of slow-sellers and non-sellers. Taken as a whole, this urban 'bookshop of the world' constantly produced a great variety of printed works in many European languages that ranged from novels and romances, to newspapers, journals, and a non-stop stream of 'cheap print' such as almanacs, chapbooks, and pamphlets. However, not all of these press products sold quickly (or at all). In fact, the only material of the early modern book trade that was quickly and constantly in Amsterdam was paper.[13] While the Dutch and Amsterdam book trade in general was in an economic crisis in the late eighteenth century (as will be addressed in the following pages), the paper-trade of Amsterdam continued to flourish and expand, and its agents—mainly paper-traders and sellers—eagerly looked for more warehouse spaces in the city to organize the export of paper varieties in the millions of sheets, mainly to other European destinations.[14]

This situation of jammed warehouses became a regular problem in times of increased economic crisis. Like many other contemporary Dutch publishing centres, Amsterdam's book trade found itself in one of these increasingly tense economic situations beginning in the 1730s and becoming worse from the 1760s onwards.[15] During these decades the book industry of the Dutch Republic (and many more European territories) witnesses a change in the distribution system. Sale on commission started to replace the older barter trade and this caused not only a new division between large publishing houses and smaller entrepreneurs (such as booksellers and publishers) in terms of market influence, but led to jammed warehouses full of slow-selling or non-selling stock.

---

13   In the words of Isabella Henrietta van Eeghen, Amsterdam was the main European export city of Dutch paper in general (van Eeghen, 'De boekhandel van de Republiek', vol. 5 (1978), p. 35). See on Amsterdam as a city literally full of paper and being an important hub of the continental paper trade in the eighteenth century: D. Bellingradt, 'Paper networks and the book industry. The business activities of an eighteenth-century paper dealer in Amsterdam', in Daniel Bellingradt, Jeroen Salman and Paul Nelles (eds.), *Books in Motion in Early Modern Europe. Beyond Production, Circulation and Consumption* (Houndsmills: Palgrave Macmillan 2017), pp. 67–85; Daniel Bellingradt, 'Trading paper in early modern Europe. On distribution logistics, traders, and trade volumes between Amsterdam and Hamburg in the mid-late-eighteenth century', *Jaarboek voor Nederlandse Boekgeschiedenis*, 21 (2014), pp. 117–131.
14   See on the roughly 100 million sheets of annually exported paper from Amsterdam to Hamburg in the 1770s and 1780s: Bellingradt, 'Trading paper in early modern Europe', p. 128.
15   See on the general economic crisis in 1760 in the Republic that enforced the tensions of the book business sector: Elisabeth E. de Jong-Keesing, *De economische crisis van 1763 te Amsterdam* (Amsterdam: Intern. Uitgevers en Handelsmatschappij, 1939). See on the crisis of the book industry: Hannie van Goinga, *Alom te bekomen. Veranderingen in de boekdistributie in de Republiek 1720–1800* (Amsterdam: De Buitenkant, 1999).

This stagnant stock was not only jamming storing spaces but severely slowing down the cash flows of the contemporary book business in the Dutch Republic.[16] This general situation of both a shortage of cash and credit and overstocked warehouses could be found during the eighteenth century all over the European book trade. Throughout continental Europe, the two common practices of bartering books for books and selling books on commission produced too many slow-selling or unsaleable books, tying up capital. Publishers and booksellers needed liquidity to keep their businesses running and to invest into new publishing projects, advertisement campaigns and distribution organization. These systems either produced too much unusable, slow and unselling stockage (barter trade), or ran on low-cash transactions (commission trade). In both instances, the systems of exchange (barter trade) and commission were blockading future economic activities. The first symptoms of this economic stress can be seen all over Europe in the many extraordinary selling activities which occurred at this time, including the selling of remaindered books, i.e. offering books at greatly reduced prices, in order to clear space in the warehouses and to improve cashflow.[17]

Among the extraordinary contemporary selling activities, the option of organizing a book auction was, in the Dutch Republic, one of the most popular. However, in Amsterdam, this option to sell off stock and quickly gain money was forbidden by the Amsterdam booksellers' guild until 1769.[18] The local *Boek-Kunstverkopers en Boekdrukkersgilde* was, like many other craft guilds of early modern Europe, a powerful interest group that regulated local market competition (that is, the book market in Amsterdam), in favour of its members. Among other relevant aspects of book production and distribution, the guild especially oversaw and regulated the sale of books within the city's jurisdiction.[19] It is no coincidence that the ban on selling stock by auctions locally

---

16 See for the Dutch Republic: van Goinga, *Alom te bekomen*, esp. pp. 121–182. On the situation of Amsterdam actors in this tense economic situation: van Eeghen, 'De boekhandel van de Republiek', 5 (1978), pp. 305–334.

17 For the Dutch Republic: van Goinga, *Alom the bekomen*, esp. pp. 174–178; for Germany: Reinhard Wittmann, *Geschichte des deutschen Buchhandels* (Munich: C.H. Beck, 1991), pp. 131–133; Goldfriedrich, *Geschichte des deutschen Buchhandels*, pp. 209–210. For England: James Raven, *The Business of Books: Booksellers and the English Book Trade* (New Haven: Yale University Press, 2007).

18 Following these regulations, it was strictly forbidden until 1769 to organize and perform the selling of any bookseller's stock in the city. The only exception made was in the case of a local bookseller's bankruptcy. Then the guild organized a stock selling by the way of auctioning. Further information on the complex struggles of book auctioning in eighteenth-century Amsterdam will be provided in a forthcoming monograph on the topic.

19 See the guild regulations on selling books ("Verkopingen", paragraphs 15–21): *Ordonnantie*

was revoked in the climate of economic crisis in the late eighteenth century. Although the ban was initially designed to protect and guarantee the prices of books within the city—a form of guild behaviour that may be interpreted as aimed at securing rents for guild members—this regulation caused turmoil within the guild, finally resulting in local booksellers receiving authorisation to offer the stock of their jammed warehoused once a year in an extraordinary auction sale.[20] The option to sell off stock without special permit from the guild was highly welcomed by local book people struggling under stagnant stock and shortages of money during a general climate of crisis.[21] A lottery was another opportunity to dispose of surplus stock. The increased numbers of Dutch book auctions were one symptom of the contemporary moneyless trading systems of the book trade in a situation of economic crisis; book lotteries were another. Both extraordinary ways of selling books functioned as pressure release valves to gain cash, to clear warehouse stocks, and to get rid of unselling or slow-selling stock.

Organising Amsterdam's Book Lotteries

There were 46 Dutch book lotteries during the eighteenth century (starting in 1758), and one third of these occurred in and around Amsterdam from 1787 onwards.[22] By this time lotteries in general had been part of everyday life in the

---

voor het boek- en konst-verkopers, nevens boek-kaart-plaatdrukkers, en boekbinders gilde deser Stede Amstelredamme (Amsterdam 1769, printed by Pieter Mortier). See further on the bookseller's guild regulation in Amsterdam: Isabella H. van Eeghen, *De gilden theorie en praktijk* (Bussum: Van Dishoeck, 1965), esp. pp. 115–120.

20 See Sheilagh Ogilvie, 'The economics of guilds', *Journal of Economic Perspectives*, 28.4 (2014), pp. 169–192.

21 As more and more non-selling and slow-selling books started to pile in the warehouses of the booksellers, and as booksellers in most other Dutch cities did not have these limitations on auctioning off old stock, a local initiative of 60 big Amsterdam booksellers—led by Stephanus Jacobus Baalde—finally managed to change the guild regulation in 1769. See my forthcoming monograph for more details and in-depth analysis on these deregulating ideas within the Amsterdam booksellers' guild. The data provided in this chapter derives from my ongoing research project on markets, spaces and networks of the early modern book trade ('Publizistik als Handelsware. Transregionale Märkte, Räume und Netzwerke im frühneuzeitlichen Europa') which is funded by the German Research Association. As a section of this project—in which I am mainly reconstructing the network activities of the book trade—I have compiled an "Amsterdam database" of the book trade between 1750–1799 that includes for example data on many book trade cooperations of Amsterdam actors.

22 Although Isabella van Eeghen found hints for a possible book lottery (of bibles) taking

Dutch Republic since the end of the sixteenth century, and were—after a short national ban after 1725—part of a developing lottery craze.[23] In fact, lotteries for all kinds of valuables regularly took place on a national, regional and local level, organized either privately or officially (by the various levels of authority in the Dutch Republic).[24] The fifteen book lotteries of interest analysed here (for the years 1787–1799) had both common and strikingly different features. Beginning with the differences: not all of these fifteen book lotteries took place in the city, that is, within the city walls and within the city's jurisdiction. From 1787–1798 no book lotteries were actually held in Amsterdam but often right in front of the city.

Because book lotteries were not permitted by the magistrate to be held within the city's jurisdiction prior to 1798, these events took place in small towns, as near as possible to the city boundaries. As the city's jurisdiction applied to a fringe zone of 720 meters out of city walls—in contemporary terms: "Buiten de Stad", 200 Roeden outside of the city—inns and taverns used to conduct the lotteries were often immediately outside this perimeter. So, eleven out of the fifteen Amsterdam book lotteries discussed in this article were actually lotteries held just outside the city boundaries.

Next, they were not all public events open to everyone. A book lottery held in September 1791 (3 September 1791) in the Bramenburg inn, just outside Amsterdam, was an exclusive event for professional booksellers, a trade sale by

---

place in Groningen in 1704 and 1714, the first real book lottery of the Dutch Republic seems to have happened 1758 in Harderwijk. See on the bible lotteries: van Eeghen, *De Amsterdamse boekhandel*, III (1965), pp. 212–221, and V (1978), p. 51, footnote 127. See on the 1758 book lottery: van Goinga, 'Lotteries for books', esp. pp. 103–104; Bert Stamkot, *Het Gorcumse boek. Vijf eeuwen drukken, uitgeven, verzamelen, lezen en leren te Gorinchem* (Gorinchem: Gorcums Museum, 2004), esp. p. 15. For the period from 1787 see the private data base on the Dutch book trade from the late Hannie van Goinga, dated December 2012, of which she made a copy for me to work with. Following this data, lotteries took place in Amsterdam, Harderwijk, Zaandam, Buiksloot, Alkmaar, Sneek, Haarlem, Nieuweramstel (Amstelveen), Leiden, 's-Hertogenbosch, Den Haag, Delft, Franeker, Breda, Harlingen, Hasselt, Oostzaan, Westzaan, Rotterdam.

23   See for the temporal lottery craze in late seventeenth and early eighteenth-century Low Countries and on the ban after 1725: Huisman and Koppenol 1991; Fokker 1862. As a result of the ban, *Lotery-Verkoping* or *Verkoping by manier van Verlotinge* seems to have vanished from public life for some decades. Due to missing research, the history of lotteries in the Republic of the Netherlands after 1726 remains to be written. Following Hannie van Goinga (van Goinga, 'Lotteries for Books', p. 102) regional and local magistrates began eventually to allow private lotteries on occasion again. The result was that despite being nationally forbidden publicly held lotteries for, for example, jewellery, silverware and furniture, took place from the 1770s onwards.

24   See van Goinga, 'Lotteries for books', esp. pp. 101–102.

way of lottery. On offer in this exclusive event with only 200 tickets for sale at 30 guilders each (with no blanks) were unbound Dutch language books and copyrights worth an estimated value of 19,000 guilders. This lottery was surely an exception among the other book lotteries because of its specialisation, but nevertheless was organized by the same kind of book trade alliances that were responsible for all the other book lotteries: in this case a cooperative between the local bookbinder Jan Roos, the bookseller Gerbrand Roos, and the bookseller-publisher Frans Christiaan Hermanus Nathanael König.[25] Another difference were the prizes: some lotteries offered books (or other forms of written media) only, and others offered books next to prizes such as musical longcase clocks, gold watches, or porcelain cups.

The last main difference was whether the organizers of the lottery produced a catalogue or not. If a catalogue were published, the prices of the tickets, the total estimated value of the offered books, and details on the valuable prizes would be given in detail. A common feature amongst the fifteen Amsterdam book lotteries was that they were all set up without blanks ("zonder Nieten"), as the many advertisements for the events continued to stress every ticket—available for sale all over the Republic—won. In other words, every participant in an eighteenth-century Amsterdam book lottery was a winner. Another common feature was the variety of books offered in prize-packages. Besides the spectacular grand prizes, the other prize-packages were filled with all imaginable varieties of written media circulating in the channels of the book trade: from cheap periodicals on agriculture, to almanacs for the next year, to copies of French, Dutch, German or English romances, and so on. Often the prizes comprised about 100–400 copies of each edition or title.

All but one of the fifteen book lotteries discussed were private commercial enterprises. The exception was a forced sale of an (unknown) book stock after a bankruptcy that was executed via lottery within the city walls of Amsterdam on 14 September 1797.[26] Moreover, it was also a common feature amongst all the book lotteries that advertisements in Dutch newspapers announced these events for weeks and sometime even months prior to the event. But the most striking common feature was the organization of these lotteries in partnerships. In all cases, these lotteries were organized by local agents of the book trade (booksellers, paper dealers, printer-publishers) who were already experi-

---

25   See the details given in the newspaper advertisement announcing the auction, published in *Oprechte Haarlemse Courant* 1791 on 4 August.
26   The Amsterdam bookseller and auctioneer Jan Frederik Nieman organized the selling. 800 tickets were offered for 30 stuivers each. See Bibliotheek Koninklijke Vereniging van het Boekenvak, Cahais 1791–1797, p. 186.

enced book auctioneers and could count on a well-established network. In fact, most often these local book people were industrious networkers who cooperated in groups of two to five members to ensure that these public events ran smoothly and offered enough enticing books and high-value items to make the lottery a success. And a lottery became a success story as soon as an overstocked warehouse was emptied of surplus stock.

The first Amsterdam book lottery took place on 4 June 1787 right in front of the city—the location was announced in many newspaper advertisements as "Hof van Ouderkerk aan de Amstel", "overstaan van het Gerecht te Ouderkerk-aan-den Amstel, in het Rechthuis".[27] The organizers of this big event joined forces in order to offer no fewer than 12,000 copies of about 150 different titles that were packaged together with other items of value (like a musical longcase clock, a gold watch with 400 diamonds, etc.) into 4,500 prizes and 312 awards.[28] Tickets were on sale months before the event in the Dutch Republic (for 14 guilders each), and the range of different books was impressive: among the 150 different titles were rare illustrated travel books (all bound, and in four instances, in folio) as well as relatively cheap periodicals on agriculture, or a very valuable complete encyclopaedia in 68 volumes.[29] Those who organized this large event had to be, and were, experienced networkers in the contemporary book and paper trades of Amsterdam and the Dutch Republic. In this case, the local bookseller, Johannes van Emenes, and the Amsterdam-based paper dealer, Cornelis de Vries, joined forces to manage the selling of the complete stock of the Amsterdam bookseller, Willem Holtrop, and of more than 6,000 additional copies of unknown ownership.[30] This cooperation included the publication and announcement of a lottery catalogue and of several advertisements in different Dutch newspapers.[31]

Both organizers anticipated that this event was going to be a success, because the stocks they were offering were not "old books", in fact, most of the 150 titles of the lottery were relatively new books, mostly printed in the decade

---

27 See the details given in the newspaper advertisements announcing the auction, published in *Oprechte Haarlemse Courant* on 10 and 24 April, and 31 May 1787.
28 All details are taken from the newspaper advertisements.
29 See van Goinga, 'Lotteries for books', p. 109 for a detailed analysis of the prices of this very event.
30 Van Goinga, 'Lotteries for books', p. 109 found out that the stock came from Willem Holtrop. Holtrop's share of the offered books was slightly under 50% of the total number of copies offered.
31 *Catalogus van eene zeer aanzienlyke verzameling van kostbaarheden en boeken* (Book Sales Catalogues, IDC-CAT. 496; MF. 834–835); see for example the advertisements in the *Oprechte Haarlemse Courant* from 10 and 24 April 1787, and 31 May 1787.

preceding the book lottery.[32] It was probably not by chance that Johannes van Emenes and Cornelis de Vries were the first organisers of such an event. Emenes was an experienced auctioneer, and as a bookseller had contacts to other colleagues with stagnant stock. Cornelis de Vries, of the influential and rich de Vries Dynasty, was in these years engaged mainly in paper trading and partially in bookselling. In 1787, he and Emenes were already cooperating in an economic partnership that may have developed out of an auction cooperation of the de Vries dynasty with Emenens of the year 1786.[33]

The second book lottery followed the same pattern of organisation. A group of three local booksellers and bookselling publishers—this time Wijnand Wijnands, Johannes Weege, and Hendrik Brongers Jr.—who were all contemporarily managing (book) auctions, frequently worked with industry colleagues, not least in managing the stock liquidations of retired booksellers. Brongers was active in book auctions during the 1780s, and cooperated several times with Wijnand in different publishing projects of the late 1780s. From 1789 these two cooperated within groups of 1 or 2 more additional participants—regularly in organizing and managing book auctions in Amsterdam.[34] Wijnand Wijnands

---

32   See the analysis in van Goinga, 'Lotteries for books', p. 111.

33   Following some of the contemporary advertisements, the book lottery organizers referred to themselves in 1787 as "EMENES en DE VRIES, Boekverkoopers op het Rockin". See *Oprechte Haarlemse Courant* 1787, 10 April and *Leeuwarder Courant* 1787, 21 April. Before and after 1787 we only find Emenes and de Vries as individual actors—and not as a company. See on the cooperation of the de Vries dynasty with Emenens for example: Emenens acted as an auctioneer (together with [Hendrik] de Vries) for Ferdinand Sundorff on 03 March 1786 (Bibl. Kon. Ver. v.h. Boekenvak, Archief Boekverkopersgilde Amsterdam B 161).

34   See for example the auctions (not for books) organized and managed by Brongers—in his working location: "op het Rokin, oostzijde tegenover de Beurs"; i.e. in the middle of the relevant book district of Amsterdam—together with w.w. from May to November 1789 only: 26 May 1789; 9 September 1789; 30 November 1789 (on the auction for J.C. Keijser on 26 May 1789 see the remark in: Bibl. Kon. Ver. v.h. Boekenvak, Archief Boekverkopersgilde Amsterdam B 164; for the auction for Willem Smit and P. Kok on 9 September 1789 see the advertisement in *Oprechte Haarlemse Courant* 1789, 29 August; on the auction on behalf of Mouw, Jan und Tolling, (juffrouw de) weduwe—in cooperation with w.w.—on 30 November 1789 see the advertisement in *Oprechte Haarlemse Courant* 1789, 21 November). As an example of his book auctions of the time see the auction for his own stock on 29 October 1792, located in his working space, where he offered (advertised in the *Leidse Courant* 1792, 24 October): "A fine Collection of Dutch Books, amongst which are a lot of Works of good taste, a couple of Prints, Portraits and Curiosities, amongst which a fine Illumination box, Magic Lantern, Phials &c, everything is on display this Saturday, and the Catalogue can be obtained at the above mentioned". ("een fraaije Verzameling van Nederduitsche Boeken, waar onder zeer veel Werken van smaak, eenige Prenten, Pourtraiten en Rariteiten, waar onder een fraaije Illumineer Kast, Toverlantaarn, Fioolen

started his book auctioning career in 1789, and became a very busy auctioneer mainly of stock liquidations of retired booksellers in late 1790s.[35] The third partner of the organisation team behind the second Amsterdam book lottery, Johannes Weege, was by far the most experienced and active person in Amsterdam book auctioning at the time. Although his first organized book auction occurred in the year 1791—in which he was offering his own stock: books and printing papers, and copperplate prints etc.—he was active as an auctioneer from as early as 1780.[36] Among his many organized book auctions, mostly in

&c., alles Zaturdag voor de Verkooping te zien, en de Catalogus by bovengemelde te bekomen").

[35] For example in 1797 and 1798 he cooperated with several other local booksellers to manage and organize stock liquidations of retired booksellers or simply expendable stock and equipment (on offer were books, copperplates, printing papers, copyrights, sometimes even printing types). See for example the auctions organized and managed by w.w. and Fredericus Johannes van Tetroode and Johannes Weege on 5 September 1798—located in Amsterdam at the residence of the Citizen J.C. Kölle, bearing the Old Coat of Arms of Embden on the New Dike, amongst the Booksellers ("te Amsterdam ten Huyze van den Burger J.C. Kölle, in het Oude Wapen van Embden op de Nieuwen Dyk, onder de Boekverkoopers")—where they are offering: "a fine Collection of Latin, French, English and Dutch unbound Books, amongst which a few exquisite Copies and Neat Selections, as well as a few copper plates, Paper, Quils, Playing Cards &c" ("een fraaye Verzameling Latynsche, Fransche, Engelsche en Nederduitsche ongebonden Boeken, waar onder eenige beste Copyen en keurige Assortimenten, benevens eenige kopere Plaaten, Papieren, Schryfpennen, Speelkaarten &c.") [advertisement in the *Leidse Courant*, 23 May 1798].

[36] See his auction on 18 January 1791 (advertised in *Oprechte Haarlemse Courant*, 8 January 1791 and *Leidse Courant*, 12 January 1791): "On Tuesday the 18th of January 1791 and the following days there will be an auction, in Amsterdam at the Residence of J. Weege, Bookseller in the Kalverstraat, where he will sell a fine Collection of Latin, French and Dutch Books, amongst which many neat and beautifully bound Works, like: in Folio, Bibles with Engravings, Flav. Josephus, Patrik Polus and Wells, Charters of Amsterdam, J. Cats, Hoogstraten, Ferwerda, in Quarto: Curtenius, de Moor, Vondel, Gesscher, Cochin, Westerbaan, Hartzink; in Octavo: Niemeyer, Hamelsveld, Schubert, Nollet, Lavater, Martinet, Gellert, National History, Kok Dictionary, Sophia's Travels, and many others, as well as a Neat Collection of German Books, amongst which de Works of Bahrdt, Hess, Jerusalem, Michaëlis, Seiler, Tiede, Spalding, Zollicofer, Sturm, Hermes, Klopstock, Salsman, Richters, Rass, Busching, Hume, Zimmerman, Pope, Rabener, Siegwart, Shakespear, Sophiens, Zucharia, Young, Milton, Lessing, Kotzebue, Campe, Dusch, Gellert, Hagedorn, Jacobi, Wieland, Meisner, Miller, Mendelsohn, Stilling, &c. a few Prints and Portraits, Wallpaper, Book cases &c.; can be seen on the Auction days Saturday and Monday. The Catalogue can be attained at the above mentioned" ("Op Dingsdag den 18 January 1791 en volgende dagen, zal men te Amsterdam te Huize van J. Weege, Boekverkooper in de Kalver Straat, verkoopen een fraaije Verzameling van Latynsche, Fransche en Nederduitsche Boeken, waar onder veele keurige Werken en fraay gebonden, als: in Folio, Bybel met Plaaten, Flav. Josephus, Patrik Polus en Wells, Handvesten van Amsterdam, J. Cats, Hoogstraten, Ferwerda; in Quarto: Curtenius, de Moor, Vondel, Gesscher, Cochin, West-

his own working location in Amsterdam ("te Amsterdam ten Huize van den Boekverkooper J. Weege in de Kalver Straat") were those for colleagues and for other private collectors.[37] It seems that Weede was auctioning regularly, and he was one of Amsterdam's busiest book auctioneers between 1780 and 1799; on various occasions he even organized the auction of complete printing houses, including all of their equipment.[38] It is hardly a surprise that a book lottery organized by these three local experts was quickly set up. On 4 September 1790

---

erbaan, Hartzink; in Octavo: Niemeyer, Hamelsveld, Schubert, Nollet, Lavater, Martinet, Gellert, Vaderl. Historie, Kok Woorden-Boek, Sophia's Reize, en meer andere, als mede een keurige Collectie Hoogduitsche Boeken, waar onder de Werken van Bahrdt, Hess, Jerusalem, Michaëlis, Seiler, Tiede, Spalding, Zollicofer, Sturm, Hermes, Klopstock, Salsman, Richters, Rass, Busching, Hume, Zimmerman, Pope, Rabener, Siegwart, Shakespear, Sophiens, Zucharia, Young, Milton, Lessing, Kotzebue, Campe, Dusch, Gellert, Hagedorn, Jacobi, Wieland, Meisner, Miller, Mendelsohn, Stilling, &c., eenige Prenten en Portraiten, Behangzel-Papieren, Boekenkasten &c.; Zaturdag en Maandag voor de Verkoopdag te Zien. De Catalogus is by bovengemelde te bekomen").

37 An example of such a private auction is the sale of the stock of the medical doctor Paulus Snijderhans on 11 November 1791, announced in catalogues and advertisements in the *Oprechte Haarlemse Courant* of 8 November 1791 and the *Leidse Courant* of 4 November 1791], "[...] for sale is a fine collection of French, German and Dutch books, amongst which many outstanding Works, like Dutch Bibles, Josephus, Basnage, Wagenaar, Commelin, Hoogstraaten, Lutherus, de Marre, Feitama, Pater, Pocock, Keysler, Ives, Martinet, Niemeyer, Lavater, National History, Kok, Wolff, Gellert compl., Voltaire, Crevier, Corneille, Cerisier; as well as outstanding German Works, Prints and Portraits, Music Instruments and Works of music, in good condition: can be viewed on the day before the Auction. The Catalogue can be obtained at the above mentioned". ("verkog worden een fraaije Verzameling van Fransche, Hoog- en Nederduitsche Boeken, waar onder veele beste Werken, als Nederd. Bybels, Josephus, Basnage, Wagenaar, Commelin, Hoogstraaten, Lutherus, de Marre, Feitama, Pater, Pocock, Keysler, Ives, Martinet, Niemeyer, Lavater, Vaderl. Historie, Kok, Wolff, Gellert compl., Voltaire, Crevier, Corneille, Cerisier; als mede de beste Hoogduitsche Werken, Prenten en Poutraiten, Muzyk-Instrumenten en Muzyk-Werken, fraai geconditioneert: daags voor den Verkoopdag te zien. De Catalogus is by bovengem. te bekomen") [quoted from the advertisement in the *Leidse Courant* of 4 November 1791].

38 See his auction on 11 December 1799, advertised in the *Leidse Courant* of 4 December 1799: "On Wednesday the 11th of December 1799, in Amsterdam, at the residency of H. van Munster on the Nieuwezyds Agterburgwal, behind the former Brewery de Zwaan, at 10 o'clock in the morning, one will sell a complete and well-ordered Printing Shop, composed of fine Letters and Flowers, in addition to an excellent Printing Press, and additional Tools; details in the Catalogue, which can be obtained at the above mentioned and at J. Weege; it can be viewed the day before the Auction" ("Op Woensdag den 11 December 1799, zal men te Amsterdam, ten Huize van H. van Munster, op de Nieuwezyds Agterburgwal, agter de geweezene Brouwery de Zwaan, 's morgens ten 10 uuren, verkoopen een compleete en welgeschikte Boekdrukkery, bestaande in fraaije Letteren en Bloemen, benevens een kapitaale Boekdrukpers, en verdere Gereedschappen; breeder volgens Catalogus, die by de bovengem. en by J. Weege te bekomen is; daags voor de Verkooping te zien").

their first book lottery took place north of Amsterdam, in a town called Buiksloot, about 7 km out of the city.[39] The organizers had produced a catalogue and rented the local Inn (Red Hart, *Roode Hart*) for their event; the catalogue has not survived but is mentioned in the accompanying newspaper advertisements. Although we do not know how many tickets were on sale, each ticket cost 1 guilder 10 stuivers. On offer at this lottery were only books in the Dutch language (bound and unbound books, prints, portraits, etc., including new and antiquarian books) in different win packages—of which we do not have more details—mixed with the usual other items of value: here for example a hunting rifle inlaid with silver.

The next public book lottery followed directly after a sale limited to professional booksellers; a common industry procedure though this one also employed a lottery. Using the same location, the Bramenburg inn just outside Amsterdam, two of the four organizers of the trade sale managed their own public book lottery that was scheduled for 1 October 1791. The Amsterdam booksellers, Dirk Schuurmann and Johannes van Emenes, both with their own bookshops situated in the nearby quarter "op Het Rokkin", functioned as organizers of this lottery where books were only part of the offer. In fact, a complete house and household, including a private library full of books, were on offer in October 1791. According to an advertisement of that event, the house was to the north of Amsterdam (in Purmerend).[40] Next to tea-sets and silver spoons, books were on offer as well: "en laatstelyk eene Verzameling van Nederduitsche Boeken en Prenten, waaronder veelen van de voornaamste en kostbaarste voorkomen".[41] Tickets cost 10 guilders and 10 Stuivers, and were available at a dozen Amsterdam booksellers. Next to Emenes, who has already been highlighted as a trade networker and as an organizer of book auctions,

---

39   Advertisements were published in several Dutch newspapers such as the *Oprechte Haarlemse Courant* (3, 17, 21 and 31 August, and 2 September 1790). More details on this book lottery can be found in van Goinga, 'Lotteries for Books', p. 104 and pp. 111–112.

40   Advertisement published in the *Oprechte Haarlemse Courant*, 10 September 1791; and the *Leydse Courant*, 9 September 1791. Selling a complete house by auction was not too uncommon in eighteenth century Europe. As Astrid Blome recently investigated, about 20 percent of the announcements in German local periodicals of German bigger cities ("Intelligenzblätter") of late eighteenth century were offers on renting and selling complete households and houses. Most of these announcements for selling were done by auctions. See Astrid Blome: "'Zum Wohlstande der Nahrung und des gemeinen Wesens'. Aspekte der ökonomischen Aufklärung im lokalen Wochenblatt', in Rudolf Stöber, Michael Nagel, Astrid Blome and Arnulf Kutsch (eds.), *Aufklärung der Öffentlichkeit—Medien der Aufklärung* (Stuttgart: Franz Steiner Verlag, 2015), pp. 69–91, esp. pp. 81–82.

41   Advertisement published in the *Oprechte Haarlemse Courant*, 10 September 1791; and the *Leydse Courant*, 9 September 1791.

the bookseller, Dirk Schuurman, only acted as an organizer of book lotteries or book auctions on two occasions.

There were four more book lotteries in 1791 and 1792, and then the activity seems to stop for 5 years. Between early 1792 and late 1798 there were no book lotteries in Amsterdam or near the city boundaries.[42] There were two main reasons for this. The first was a prohibition by the Council of State (of the Dutch Republic), issued 19 September 1792, aimed at protecting local traders in general, prohibiting all sales of wares and moveables by way of so called-shares.[43] The second reason is to be found in contemporary high politics: France declared war on and invaded the Dutch Republic (1793–1794), helping to form the Batavian Republic (1795), France's first satellite state within the European state system. During these troubled months, book lotteries seemed not to have been very high on the agenda.

The four book lotteries of 1791/92 were the last "buiten de stad", held outside of the city of Amsterdam. These followed the same patterns as previous lotteries: they were organized by local book trade alliances of experienced auctioneers and networkers or by single influential book auctioneers like Mathijs Schalekamp.[44] Schalekamp managed to organize a book lottery on the 7

---

42 Lotteries, book lotteries or even trader's requests for holding a book lottery are not mentioned in the archives of the Amsterdam booksellers' guild for these years. Due to the practice of the magistrate of Amsterdam asking the booksellers' guild for advice in case of incoming requests (to hold a book lottery), we can be almost sure that no book lotteries happened or were planned to happen in Amsterdam or by Amsterdam actors in these years.

43 Fokker, *Geschiedenes der loterijen*, p. 150.

44 He was managing and organizing auctions, and book auctions in Amsterdam from 1774 onwards, and was very busy doing so in Amsterdam and in small towns nearby—such as the Inn in Buiksloot—in the 1790s. In doing so, Schalekamp, cooperated with many colleagues (booksellers, bookbinders and publishers) in Amsterdam. We have proof from the advertisements on his auctions that he seems to have cooperated with more than 30 other actors during his career. See for example his book auction organised in December 1774—in cooperation with the Amsterdam bookseller Jacob van Woensel jr.—that seems to have taken place in Amsterdam ("t'Amsterdam ten Huize van den Boekverkooper Jacob van Woenzel Junior") and was for the stock owner "A. van Eldik". On 13 December 1774 a catalogue offered: "Een fraaije Verzameling van welgeconditioneerde Latynsche en Nederduitsche Boeken, bestaande in Godgeleerde, Rechtsgeleerde, Medicynsche, Poëtische, Historische, Romans en anderen, waaronder verscheide voornaame Werken; waarvan de Catalogus by bovengemelde en M. Schalekamp, te bekomen is" (Advertisement of 1 December 1774 in the *Oprechte Haarlemse Courant*). As an example of the many auctions of 1791 see the one of 21 April 1796 of an unknown stock, advertised in the *Haarlemse Courant*, 16 April 1796: "Op aanstaande Donderdag, den 21 April, 1796, zal men te Amsterdam ten Huize van M. Schalekamp, Boekverkooper in de Warmoesstraat, verkoopen: Een fraaije Verzameling Latynsche, Fransche, Engelsche en Nederduitsche Boeken, bestaande

and 8 October 1791 in Buiksloot (in the local inn "Hof van Noordholland"), in which 775 tickets were offered for sale at 5 guilders each, and in which a range of valuable books (such as the multi-volume luxury edition of "Historie der Hedendaagsche Volken ..." in 28 volumes) and various gold and silver items were among the first prizes.[45] The three remaining book lotteries of 1791 and 1792 were organized however by larger co-operations of between two to eight partners. All three of these lotteries took place in the Bramenburg inn. On 19 November 1791 the most experienced group of local book lottery organizers joined together to hold such a lottery.[46] Among this group—booksellers Wijnand, Johannes Davidz Weege, Gerbrand Roos, Jan Gerritsz ten Brink and Hendrik Vermandel; printer-publisher-booksellers Hendrik Brongers Jr. and Frans Christiaan Hermanus Nathanael König; and bookbinder Jan Roos; only two, Hendrik Vermandel, and Jan Gerritsz ten Brink, had no experienced in organizing an Amsterdam book lottery. The others had not only organized book lotteries, but some had already done so in partnership: Brongers, Wijnand and Weege were book-lottery-partners in 1790, and Jan and Gerbrand Roos co-operated together with König in the exclusive trade sale lottery of 1791.

Announced in many newspaper advertisements, this book lottery offered "moderne boeken"—and not old books—and a great variety of cheap prints like almanacs ("Nieuwen Almanachen, voor 1792"). 600 tickets were offered for sale at 1 guilders 1 stuiver each, competing over 400 prizes; the first prize was a package of valuable books worth 42 guilders.[47] Six out of the eight partners (namely J. Roos, G. Roos, J. ten Brink, J. Weege, W. Wynands and H. Vermandel) were also a shadow network for a book lottery that was officially run under the name of experienced book auctioneer and Amsterdam based bookseller, Pieter Jansz, on 21 January 1792.[48] Compared to these big networks for book lottery

---

in Godgeleerde, Rechtsgeleerde, Genees-, Heel-, Natuur-, Dichtkundige, Historische, Reisbeschryvingen, benevens een aantal Werken van Vernuft en Smaak. Alles daags te vooren te zien". Also advertised in the *Leidse Courant*, 15 April 1796.

45 Advertisement published in the *Oprechte Haarlemse Courant*, 20 September 1791. There is no information on how many prizes were offered. See on the details of first prizes the advertisement published in the *Leydse Courant*, 3 October 1791.

46 *Oprechte Haarlemse Courant*, 3 November 1791; 10 November; *Leydse Courant*, 11 November 1791, p. 4.

47 *Oprechte Haarlemse Courant*, 3 November 1791; 10 November.

48 See for example the auctions of unknown stock on the 25th of October 1798 via the shadow network, officially run by Pieter Jansz, which were advertised in the *Leidse Courant* of 17 October 1798]: "On Thursday the 25th and Friday the 26th of October 1798, in Amsterdam at the residency of the Bookseller Pieter Jansz, on the Leydsche Straat, a fine Collection will be sold, of Dutch, Latin and French Books, in all Faculties, amongst which are many exceptional Work of good Taste, usually in good condition. The Catalogue can be obtained

organization, the last book lottery that took place outside of the city's jurisdiction was a rather small event. On 7 January 1792 the two Amsterdam booksellers, Albrecht and Johannes Borchers ("De Boekhandelaars A. BORCHERS en ZOON, in de Stilsteeg te Amsterdam"), father and son, organized a book lot-

---

at the above mentioned: can be viewed the day before the Auction" ("Op Donderdag en Vrydag den 25 en 26 October 1798, zal te Amsterdam ten Huyze van den Boekverkooper Pieter Jansz, op de Leydsche Straat, verkogt worden een fraaije Verzameling van Nederduitsche, Latynsche en Fransche Boeken, in alle Faculteiten, waar onder veele beste Werken van Smaak, meestal goed geconditioneerd. De Catalogus is by bovengem. te bekomen: daags voor de Verkooping te zien") and also the auction together with Johannes Weege & Tetroode, Fredericus Johannes van on the 20 December 1798, advertised in the *Leidse Courant* of 10 December 1798]: "On Thursday the 20th December 1798 and following days, in Amsterdam at the Residency of F.J. van Tetroode in the Kalver Straat, a fine collection will be sold, consisting of Dutch, Latin and French Books, in all Faculties, amongst which are many outstanding Works that are in good condition, a couple of unbound Book; as well as a Collection of large and small Paper Theatres, a fine Collection of coloured and blank English and French Prints, in gilded and black Frames with Glass; bequeathed by a prominent Devotee; can be viewed the day before the Auction. The Catalogue can be obtained in Amsterdam at F.J. van Tetrood, J. Weeg and P. Jansz. for 2 Stivers". ("Op Donderdag den 20 December 1798 en volgende dagen, zal te Amsterdam ten Huyze van F.J. van Tetroode in de Kalver Straat, verkogt worden een fraaije Verzameling Nederduitsche, Latynsche en Fransche Boeken, in alle Faculteiten, waar onder veele keurige Werken en wel geconditioneerd, eenige ongebonden Boeken; als mede een Collectie groot en klein Papieren Toneelspeelen, een fraaije Verzameling gecouleurde en ongecouleurde Engelsche en Fransche Prenten; als mede een keurige Collectie gecouleurde en ongecouleurde Prenten, in vergulde en zwarte Lysten met Glaazen; Nagelaaten door een voornaam Liefhebber; daags voor de Verkooping te zien. De Catalogus is voor 2 Stuivers te bekomen te Amsterdam by F.J. van Tetroode, J. Weege en P. Jansz"). See about the auction of 21 January 1792 the advertisements published in the *Leidse Courant* of 1792 on: 4 January, p. 2; 6 January, p. 2; 13 January, p. 2; 16 January, p. 4; 18 January, p. 1; 20 January, p. 4. For this lottery we do not have information about how many tickets were offered and how many prizes there were. We only know that each ticket was offered for sale at 1 guilder 1 stuiver, and that the organizer was the Amsterdam bookseller Pieter Jansz. The shadow network can easily by observed in the journal advertisements preceding the events. Here, the only shops where tickets for this lottery could be bought were the bookshops of the aforementioned booksellers. See for example the *Leidse Courant*, 4 January 1792: "The Lottery-shares and Tickets are successfully distributed: at f. 1:10 and can be obtained in Amsterdam from P. Jansz, J. Roos, G. Roos, J. ten Brink, J. Weege, W. Wynands and H. Vermandel, as well as from A. Segenboogen, Castelein in Bramenburg; Haarlem C.B. van Brussel; Leiden de Does and J. Meerburg; Utrecht H. van Emenes; Zaandam J. Kool; Deventer Brouwer; 's Hage at d'Agé" ("De Aandeelen en Biljetten worden met succes uitgegeeven: à f. 1:10 en zyn te bekomen te Amsterdam by P. Jansz, J. Roos, G. Roos, J. ten Brink, J. Weege, W. Wynands en H. Vermandel, als mede by A. Segenboogen, Castelein in Bramenburg; Haarlem C.B. van Brussel; Leyden de Does en J. Meerburg; Utrecht H. van Emenes; Zaandam J. Kool; Deventer Brouwer; 's Hage by d'Agé").

tery in the Bramenburg inn, offering 800 tickets for 1 guilder 1 stuiver each.[49] As announced in the advertisements, the books offered were exclusively in the Dutch language ("Eene fraaije Verzameling van Nederduitsche BOEKEN"), and had a total value of 1,500 guilders. The tickets were only sold in Amsterdam by the organizers, and by selected partners in other Dutch cities.[50]

Following the gap of 1792 to 1798, six more Amsterdam book lotteries followed in the eighteenth century—this time within the city's jurisdiction, mostly in the booksellers' hotspots in the centre of Amsterdam. Organizers of these six book lotteries were a familiar crew: Gerbrand Roos[51] and Fredericus Johannes van Tertroode[52] in cooperation with Johannes Weege or Pieter Jansz and sometimes both. Only one newcomer can be found in the business of selling books via lottery: the distinguished networker of the Amsterdam book trade of those years, printer-publisher-bookseller Jan Barend Elwe. Three out of these six book lotteries were organized by Gerbrand Roos and at all times located at "ten Huyze van de Castelein J. Muerman, in de Toren van Cordaan", as the

---

49 Advertisements published in the *Oprechte Haarlemse Courant*, 17 December 1791, and the *Leydse Courant*, 16 December 1791, p. 4; 26 December, p. 4.
50 "[...] everything more in detail in a brochure, that can be obtained, and is further to be obtained, and in the following cities for free, as well as the Lottery-shares at f. 1–10, in Alkmaar Hand and Hartemink, Haarlem C.B. van Brussel and Tetmans, Leiden Herding and Pluygers, Delft J. de Groot, Rotterdam D. Vis, C. van den Dries and Cornel, Schiedam Poolman, Gouda Verblauw, The Hague Leeuwenstyn and L. Gautier, Dordp[recht] Krap and J. de Leeuw, Utrecht J. Visch and H. van Emenes, Hoorn Brebaart, Enkhuizen Franx, Zaandam Kool, Deventer Brouwer, Leeuwaarden Cahais, Zutphen van Eldik, Campen Brok, Zwol Clement, Groningen Oomkes and Huyzing, 's Hertogenbosch J. and H. Palier, Bergen op den Zoom van Riemsdyk and van Bronkhorst, &c." ("... alles breeder by Notitie, die by bovengemelde, en verder alom, alsmede in de navolgende Steden gratis, en de Aandeelen à f. 1–10, te bekomen zyn, als te Alkmaar Hand en Hartemink, Haarlem C.B. van Brussel en Tetmans, Leyden Herding en Pluygers, Delft J. de Groot, Rotterdam D. Vis, C. van den Dries en Cornel, Schiedam Poolman, Gouda Verblauw, 's Hage Leeuwenstyn en L. Gautier, Dord Krap en J. de Leeuw, Utrecht J. Visch en H. van Emenes, Hoorn Brebaart, Enkhuizen Franx, Zaandam Kool, Deventer Brouwer, Leeuwaarden Cahais, Zutphen van Eldik, Campen Brok, Zwol Clement, Groningen Oomkes en Huyzing, 's Hertogenbosch J. en H. Palier, Bergen op den Zoom van Riemsdyk en van Bronkhorst, &c.") [*Oprechte Haarlemse Courant*, 17 December 1791].
51 Roos was a busy (book) auctioneer from 1779 onwards, usually cooperating for these auctions with up to 2 additional partners. Moreover, as my database shows by comparing Roos' advertisements from the same time, he regularly sold other booksellers' stock by auction in his own shop.
52 Van Tertroode was a busy (book) auctioneer from 1779 onwards, usually selling stock of other booksellers like on 9 February 1779, when he sold the stock of C.H. Elshof, J.J. Bertina and Jan Bent in his own shop in the Kalverstraat (see the advertisement for this auction in: *Oprechte Haarlemse Courant* 1779, 28 January).

many newspaper advertisements announced. It was typical of Roos' management that no catalogues were produced for the book lotteries on 22 September 1798, 16 March 1799, and 26 October 1799, and that all events were allowed by the city administration: "met Consent van de Municipaliteit".[53] As an example of the advertisements for such events, see the advertisement for the book lottery of October 1799 published in the newspaper *Leydse Courant* on 9 October:

> The bookseller G. Roos from Amsterdam will hold a lottery, with consent of the municipality, on the 26th of October 1799, in the house of the Innkeeper J. Muerman, in the Tower of Cordaan, of an exceptional beautiful and neat Collection of Books, which consists mainly of exquisite historical Travelogues and Novels of the latest fashion, amongst which there are a few precious Works, including very rare ones, as well as four Pendulum Clocks and finally excellent Prints in Frames with Glass: everything more in detail in the Catalogue, which can be obtained with the Lottery-share, at f. 2: 6, at above-mentioned G. Roos, by whom they are signed, as well as from J. Muerman, and furthermore in Amsterdam and at most booksellers in the rest of the whole Republic. NB. These lotteries, which are extra beneficial for participants, consist of 1550 Lottery-shares, where there is a prize with every draw, and which are drawn for 1550 Prizes and 4 Bonuses, in all Ranges of prices of the total sum of f. 8500.—and even the smallest Prize has more value than the original stake—he who takes 12 lottery-shares simultaneously, or reserves them at his Bookseller, receives the 13th share as a Bonus.[54]

---

53 See the newspaper advertisements for the events: *Leydse Courant*, 7 September 1798; 19 September; 24 September; 5 October; 31 October; *Leydse Courant*, 22 February 1799; 11 March; *Leydse Courant* 1799, 30 September; 9 October; 16 October. On 20 July 1798 Roos had asked for consent by the city administration to hold his lotteries in the city (Bibl. Kon. Ver. v.h. Boekenvak, Archief Boekverkopersgilde Amsterdam B 86, 75; entry of 20 July 1798). The book lottery of 22 September 1798 had 1,200 tickets for sale at 2 guilders each, valuing 5,000 guilders in total. The book lottery of 16 March 1799 had 1,400 tickets were offered for sale at 2 guilders and 4 stuivers, valuing 7,000 guilders in total. The book lottery of 26 October 1799 had 1,550 tickets for sale at 2 guilders 60 stuivers each.

54 The original reads: "De Boekverkooper G. Roos te Amsterdam, zal op den 26 October 1799, ten Huyze van de Castelein J. Muerman, in de Toren van Cordaan, met Consent van de Municipaliteit laaten Verlooten, een ongemeen schoone en keurige Verzameling van Boeken, bestaande meerendeels in fraaije Historische Reisbeschryvingen en Romans van de nieuwste smaak, en daar onder eenige kostbaare Werken, neven eenige Superbe Rariteiten, waar onder Vier Keurige Pendules, en laatstelyk Capitaale Prenten in Lysten met Glazen: alles breeder by Catalogus, welken met de Aandeelen te bekomen zyn: à f 2: 6, by bovengem. G. Roos, door wie dezelve getekend zyn, als ook by J. Muerman, en

BOOK LOTTERIES AS SALE EVENTS FOR SLOW-SELLERS 175

The consent granted by the city administration ("met Consent van de Municipaliteit") was a new feature of Amsterdam's book lotteries in 1798 and the years to follow. After Roos received consent, the same was granted upon request to the booksellers Johannes Fredericus van Tertroode and Johannes Weege on 29 September 1798. Both had asked for consent to hold a lottery for books within the city: in a tavern on the Kalverstraat ("by J.R. Kuhn in het Hollandsche Huys in de Kalver Straat te Amsterdam").[55] Their book lottery took place on 9 November 1798—"met consent van de Municipaliteit" and with consent of the supervisors of the booksellers' guild.[56] Why the booksellers' guild decided for the first time to give consent—having denied all earlier requests—cannot be answered conclusively.[57] Regardless, the book lottery held with the guild's consent offered 1,250 tickets for sale at 2 guilders and 4 stuivers, valuing 5,500 guilders in total. Again, no catalogue was produced, perhaps due to the short preparation time. On 3 August 1799 a new actor in the lottery business, Jan B. Elwe, held his first book lottery in Amsterdam—again at the location "Ten huize van Jacob Muerman, kastelein in de Toren van Cordaan op de Kadyk".[58] Elwe had applied successfully for consent[59] and managed a lottery (without a catalogue) of Dutch language books and other prints mixed with some more items of value ("een extra fraaije Verzameling van Nederduitsche Boeken, eenige Prenten en kostbaare Rariteiten") with 2,000 tickets for sale at 2 guilders and 10 stuivers each, amounting to 11,000 guilders in total.[60] This book

---

verder zoo in Amsterdam als door de geheele Republiek by de meest Boekverkoopers. NB. Deze voor den Deelnemer extra voordeelige Verlootinge, bestaat in 1550 Aandeelen, Geheel Zonder Nieten, waar tegen getrokken worden 1550 Pryzen en 4 Premien, in alle Pryscours waarden de Somma van f 8500.—en hebbende de minsttrekkende Prys meerder Prys-Courants waarde dan de Inleg.—Die 12 Aandeelen tegelyk neemt, of by zyn Boekverkooper bespreekt bekomt het 13de tot een Premie".

55   See the protocol of the guild on 8 October 1798 (Bibl. Kon. Ver. v.h. Boekenvak, Archief Boekverkopersgilde Amsterdam B 86, 76; fiat 8 October 1798). The organizers had to pay 50 guilders for this consent after the event.
56   Advertisements published in the *Leydse Courant*, 17 October 1798, p. 4; 22 October, p. 3; 12 November, p. 3; 16 November.
57   This very 'sale by lottery' was allowed by the supervisors of the booksellers' guild, who were always asked by the magistrate in such cases, because they pointed out that the guild's statutes provided no explicit power to ban such lotteries. See van Goinga, 'Lotteries for books', p. 106.
58   At first Elwe announced the lottery to take place on 20 July 1799 (*Leydse Courant*, 17 June), while he later delayed the lottery to take place on 3 August 1799 (*Leydse Courant*, 19 July 1799).
59   See the request by Elwe dated 12 May 1799 (Bibl. Kon. Ver. v.h. Boekenvak, Archief Boekverkopersgilde Amsterdam B 86, 83; fiat 20 May 1799).
60   *Leydse Courant*, 17 June 1799.

lottery took place on 26 October 1799 in a location that had been used previously for the lottery of 29 September 1798—the location on the Kalverstraat ("ten Huyze van den Burger J.R. Kuhn in de Kalver Straat"). It was organized by the three busiest contemporary auctioneers and book lottery managers: Amsterdam booksellers Pieter Jansz, Fredrik Johannes van Tertroode and Johannes Weege.[61] On the same date, Roos' book lottery mentioned above, was also held. This day in October 1799 was both the last date of eighteenth-century book lotteries in Amsterdam, and the only day two book lotteries were held in the city at the same time.[62]

Slow-Sellers, Book Lotteries, and Book History

Focusing on eighteenth century book lotteries in Amsterdam reveals that these extraordinary events were strongly connected to the economic needs of the local book trade. In the cases presented, the lotteries aimed to sell high quantities of books quickly through procedures rooted in the popular lottery culture of the time. Amsterdam's book lotteries functioned as pressure-release valves to recoup cash, to clear warehouse space, and to get rid of stock during a tense economic situation. This stagnant stock however, was mainly composed of slow-sellers rather than of old books or second-hand books waiting for buyers in the corners of a bookseller's warehouse.[63] In fact, Amsterdam's book

---

61 Advertisements published in: *Leydse Courant*, 30 September 1799.
62 For this event we are lacking information on the total value of offered books and on the exact number of tickets, however we do know that each ticket was for sale for 2 guilders and 4 stuivers (*Leydse Courant*, 30 September 1799).
63 This argumentation of book lotteries as jumble sales ('Ramsch') can be found in many studies on these selling events (for example in: Goldfriedrich, *Geschichte des Deutschen Buchhandels*, esp. p. 403; Quedenbaum, *Glücksspiel und Buchhandel*), but could recently be more accentuated by Pelgen, *Bücherlotterien*, and van Goinga, 'Lotteries for books'. It seems very likely that these old positions have their origins in the contemporarily brought forward, hostile arguments of booksellers who looked with envy on these 'immoral' sales but did not engage in lotteries themselves. Criticism against book lotteries came mainly from two sides: from other booksellers who did not engage in this business, and from moral theorists who condemned lotteries as part of a gambling culture. See for example on the last aspect: Johann C. May, *Lottologie und Perspectivische Aussicht in das Reich der Lotterien und besonders des Lotto* (2 vols., Altona, 1770/71). See on the harsh (and often anonymous) criticism by contemporary booksellers and publishers who did not engage with the practices of auctioning and lottery sale in Germany: Anonymous, *Charlatanerie Der Buchhandlung, welche den Verfall derselben Durch Pfuscheryen, Praenumerationes, Auctiones, Nachdrucken, Trödeleyen u.a.m. befördert. Von zwey der Handlung Beflissenen unpartheyisch untersuchet. Zweyte Auflage* (Sachsenhausen: Claus Peter Misstütze, 1732),

lotteries were sale events for slow-sellers as they aimed to empty overstocked warehouses from slow-selling items—most of the stock offered was relatively new, less than ten years old, and often comprised of recently published media (such as almanacs, periodicals, etc.).

By coining the term "slow-sellers", this article sets out to rethink and reinterpret the imprecise terms used for the time-displaced selling of written media including old and second-hand books.[64] What defines an old or second-hand book for a book-trader in early modern Europe, or for book-trade history? Was it these slow-selling items which caused problems within the book trade rather than old or second-hand books? In this respect, the focus on book lotteries, book auctions, and even the raffling of books—all extraordinary ways of selling—opens up relevant perspectives on book industry dynamics in early modern Europe by highlighting one fundamental aspect: what to do with slow-moving items? The economic problems caused by slow-sellers could lead to anything from temporal inactivity (of publishing, printing, advertising, distributing etc.) to bankruptcy. When shifting our views from the bestselling and success stories of the book trade to books that sold slowly or proved quite unsaleable, we may better understand the contemporary book industry by discovering the hidden rhythms and rules of debt economies. As this article has explored, selling slow-moving stock in fast-moving events such as lotteries was the result of previous periods of weak sales and stagnation in the book trade.

---

p. 73 ("Bücher=Lotterien, Bücher=Verloosungen, Glücks=Töpffen seien eine Art der Charlatanerie im Buchhandel"); [Johann Abraham Birnbaum], *Eines Aufrichtigen patrioten Unpartheyische Gedancken über einige Quellen und Wirckungen des Verfalls der ietzigen Buch=Handlung, Worinnen insonderheit Die Betrügereyen der Bücher=Pränumerationen entdeckt, Und zugleich erwiesen wird, Daß der unbefugte Nachdruck unprivilegirter Bücher ein allen Rechten zuwiederlauffender Diebstahl sey* (Schweinfurth: Tobias Wilhelm Fischer, 1733), pp. 15–16.

64 See for example the entry on "book auctions" in Suarez and Woudhuysen, *The Oxford Companion to the Book*, vol. 1 (2010), pp. 543–544.

PART 3
Selling Strategies

CHAPTER 9

Neither Scholar nor Printer: Luxembourg de Gabiano and the Financial Structure of Merchant Publishing in Sixteenth-Century Lyon

Jamie Cumby

Scholarly book production in the sixteenth century was a messy, mercenary and occasionally cutthroat world.[1] As many of the essays in this volume can confirm, printers and publishers were less interested in a noble Eisensteinian revolution in knowledge than in taking advantage of the academic market.[2] Indeed, even an intellectual scholar-printer like Aldus Manutius held the profit motive as his bottom line.[3] Early modern printing and publishing was, as it is today, a business, and the trappings of scholarship were marketing tools in the hands of bookmen. In Lyon, the subject of this article and a city where merchant-publishers dominated the printing business, some printers and publishers went so far as to falsify the scholarly introductions to their Latin books.[4] One of the offenders with the highest profile, merchant-publisher Jean Huguetan, funded several unauthorized reprints of classical works that had been edited by Josse Badius.[5] In the prefatory epistles, written by Badius with praise for the original printers and publishers, Huguetan transposed his own name, and altered the date to fit with his editions. In the most extreme

---

1   It was quite literally cutthroat for Symphorien Beraud, a later member of the same merchant-publishing company that the subject of this article helped found. Ian Maclean, *Learning and the Market Place: Essays in the History of the Early Modern Book* (Leiden: Brill, 2009), pp. 227–272.

2   Elizabeth L. Eisenstein, *The Printing Press as an Agent of Change: Communications and Cultural Transformations in Early-Modern Europe* (Cambridge: Cambridge University Press, 2009).

3   Martin Lowry does an excellent job of establishing the economic world of early Venetian printing in *The World of Aldus Manutius: Business and Scholarship in Renaissance Venice* (Oxford: Blackwell, 1979).

4   Henri-Louis Baudrier, *Bibliographie lyonnaise: recherches sur les imprimeurs, libraires, relieurs et fondeurs de lettres de Lyon au XVIe siècle, publiées et continuées par J. Baudrier* (13 vols., Lyon: A. Brun, 1895–1921), XI, pp. 296–297 and 464.

5   Micheline Lecocq, 'Simon Vincent, libraire-éditeur à Lyon de 1499 à 1532' (Unpublished PhD Dissertation, Université Jean Monnet, 1988), pp. 90–93; Baudrier XI pp. 296–297, 303–306; Notable examples: USTC 123553, USTC 143473.

case, Balthazar de Gabiano and Barthelemy Trot pirated Aldus' octavo classics from 1502 to 1525.[6]

This article will focus on a specific producer of scholarly books who provides an excellent example of a true businessman in the world of learned books. Luxembourg de Gabiano, who took charge of the Lyon branch of his family's firm from his brother in 1512, made a tidy fortune in the publishing industry. However, he published the vast majority of his editions anonymously. Gabiano was a principal actor in Lyonnais publishing, but, by Sybille von Gültlingen's count, his name appears on only 14 editions.[7] Rather than promoting a personal brand, Gabiano worked exclusively under the auspices of his two publishing companies: the Gabiano family firm, the *Compagnie d'Ivry*, and the Lyonnais merchant-publishing association, the *Compagnie des Libraires*. Not only did Gabiano apparently lack interest in leaving a personal mark on the book world, but he himself appeared to have owned only six printed books at the time of his death in 1558.[8]

During Luxembourg's period of activity, the book trade in Lyon entered a golden age. From 1520 to the 1550s, the number of merchants and craftsmen working in printing and related trades had grown from 80 to between 500 and 600.[9] The city's print output more than tripled during that same period, when measured in terms of editions.[10] Given Lyon's initial, more modest status in the geography of European print, its prodigious expansion in the mid-sixteenth century appears remarkable, particularly when compared with the overall European output. Figure 9.1 compares the compounded annual growth

---

6   Studies of these editions have been done by David J. Shaw, 'The Lyons counterfeit of Aldus's italic type: a new chronology', in Denis V. Reidy (ed.), *The Italian Book 1465–1800: Studies Presented to Dennis E. Rhodes on his 70th Birthday* (London: British Library, 1993), pp. 117–133, by Dennis E. Rhodes, *Studies in Early European Printing and Book Collecting* (London: Pindar Press, 1983), and by William Kemp, 'Counterfeit Aldines and italic-letter editions printed in Lyons 1502–1510: early diffusion in Italy and France', *Papers of the Bibliographical Society of Canada*, 4 (1997), pp. 75–100. Kemp also discusses them in William Kemp, 'Printing Erasmus in italic in Lyons: Jacques Moderne to Sebastian Gryphius', *The Yale University Library Gazette*, 75 (2000), pp. 22–36.

7   Sybille von Gültlingen, *Bibliographie des livres imprimés à Lyon au seizième siècle* (14 vols., Baden-Baden: V. Koerner, 1992–), VI.

8   Natalie Zemon Davis, 'Le monde de l'imprimerie humaniste: Lyon', in Henri-Jean Martin, Roger Chartier and Jean-Pierre Vivet (eds.), *Histoire de l'édition française* (4 vols., Paris: Promodis, 1982–1986), I, p. 260.

9   Figures from Davis, 'Le monde de l'imprimerie humaniste', p. 255.

10 Based on figures calculated from USTC data and my unpublished doctoral thesis. Both datasets will be integrated in the USTC's online database upon completion of my PhD. Jamie Cumby, 'A Publishing Monopoly in Learned Europe: The *Compagnie des libraires* of Lyon, 1509–1562' (Unpublished PhD Dissertation, University of St Andrews, 2018).

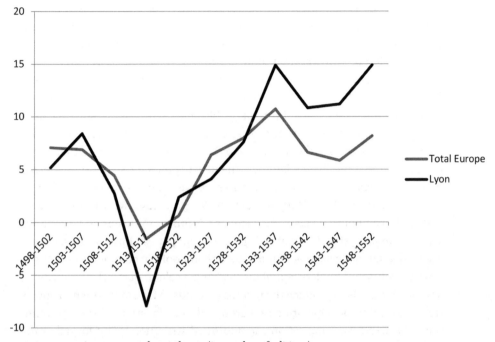

FIGURE 9.1 Average annual growth rate (in number of editions)

rate of Lyon's print output with all of the USTC's edition data for Europe. The 1530s were especially strong years of expansion for Lyon, with the city's print output nearly doubling that of the prior decade.[11] Here, we see Lyon's expansion exceeding the average growth of the book industry in Europe as a whole, a feat that it maintained through the early 1550s.

Using editions as a measure of print output does not generate a perfect representation of productivity. Most notably, it ignores the key indicators of the amount of labour and resources involved in producing a book: its length and the size of its print run. The great merit of focusing on editions is the substantial available bibliographic data, which allows for Figure 9.1's broad comparisons.[12]

---

11   Cumby, 'Publishing Monopoly'.
12   Data represented in this graph is also from figures based on the USTC and my PhD thesis. "Editions" here excludes broadsheets for reasons of their poor and uneven documentation and survival. Jonathan Green and Frank McIntyre, 'Lost incunable editions: closing in on an estimate', in Flavia Bruni and Andrew Pettegree (eds.), *Lost Books: Reconstructing the Print World of Pre-Industrial Europe* (Leiden: Brill, 2016), p. 61; Goran Proot, 'Survival factors of seventeenth-century hand-press published in the southern Netherlands: the importance of sheet counts, *Sammelbände* and the role of institutional collections', in Bruni and Pettegree, *Lost Books*, p. 183.

The growth statistics represented in Figure 9.1 are especially impressive considering that so many Lyonnais editions were folio volumes of civil and canon law, which could require upwards of 1,400 sheets for a single multivolume set.[13]

This period of growth might more accurately be described as a golden age of merchant publishing, for it was during this period that the *Compagnie des libraires* consolidated its power. The organization first appeared in 1509 as a loose conglomerate of local Lyonnais publishers: Aymon de la Porte, Jacques and Jean Huguetan, Simon Vincent and Martin Boillon.[14] In 1520, it formed anew, this time with a core of Venetians who came from some of their city's most prominent publishing families. The new *Compagnie*, sometimes referred to as the *Grande Compagnie des libraires*, consisted of its wealthiest original members, Aymon de la Porte and Simon Vincent, along with Venetian newcomers Luxembourg de Gabiano, Jacques Giunta and Vincent de Portonariis. The *Compagnie* existed to control legal publishing by establishing a monopoly. They selected the texts to be printed, held their books in common warehouses, shared profits and pooled capital for this large-scale project, which relied just as much on funds to produce the texts as on funds to distribute them to buyers throughout Europe. Operating as a group allowed Lyon's publishers to minimize risk, decrease competition and improve distribution.[15] This formal agreement reified the power of the company, effectively creating a proto-capitalist monopoly that was able to regulate the trade in legal books.[16]

While this was technically a scholarly project, legal books demonstrate the mercenary character of early modern printing perhaps better than any other. The genre's dispersed market and high initial cost leant itself particularly well to the strict internal regulation set out by the company. The development of scholastic legal education from the eleventh century onwards created, by the mid fifteenth century, a dense agglomeration of important supplements to the key civil and canon law texts.[17] This created an attractively broad but standard-

---

13   For a longer discussion of sheet counts for legal editions, see Cumby, 'Publishing Monopoly', Chapter 2.
14   For a discussion of the first iteration of the *Compagnie* and determining its members in the absence of clear documentary evidence: Cumby, 'Publishing Monopoly', Chapter 2.
15   Jeanne-Marie Dureau, 'Recherches sur les grandes compagnies de libraires lyonnais au XVIe siècle', in Henri-Jean Martin (ed.), *Nouvelles études lyonnaises* (Geneva: Droz, 1969), pp. 5–64: 11.
16   William Pettas, 'The Giunti and the book trade in Lyon', in Istituto di Biblioteconomia e Paleografia dell'Università degli Studi, Parma (ed.), *Libri, Tipografi, Biblioteche: Ricerche storiche dedicate a Luigi Balsamo* (2 vols., Florence: Olschki, 1997), I, pp. 169–192: 176.
17   Ian Maclean, *Interpretation and Meaning in the Renaissance: The Case of Law* (Cambridge: Cambridge University Press, 1992), pp. 13–14.

ized group of required works that students and some practitioners needed to buy.[18] Not only were these texts essential, but their forms were fixed, saving a savvy publisher the trouble and cost of acquiring new manuscripts and editors. However, like other purchasers of scholarly books, the consumers of legal texts were spread throughout Europe, requiring costly, time-consuming and hazardous transportation for sale.[19]

Producing full editions of any one of these works required tremendous resources. Full sets of the major canon and civil law commentaries, produced in folio, demanded large quantities of paper with little variation. Niccolò Tedeschi's commentaries on canon law, for example, needed 831 sheets for a single set of the editions of 1524, and 819 for the editions of 1562.[20] The complete *Corpus Iuris Civilis* could require between 1,000 and 1,500 sheets for a single multivolume set. The 1530 editions had a sheet count of 986 sheets per full set, while a set from the 1547 edition used 1,442 sheets, and the 1562 edition a more moderate 1,119 sheets.[21] Printing any one of these editions also required full founts of types of at least two different point sizes for the gloss and the text, along with an appropriately skilled compositor. A printer or publisher wanting to produce such a work independently would not only need sufficient capital to purchase materials, but would incur a substantial time cost. Depending on the size and efficiency of the workshop, a printer's presses might be tied up in production of a single *Corpus Juris Civilis* or set of *postglossator* commentaries for a year or more. Taking these factors into account, the *Compagnie*'s cartel model makes sense as an approach to creating legal editions.

From the turn of the sixteenth century, the number of legal texts and commentaries published in Lyon grew consistently. The average annual rate of increase in jurisprudential editions printed was about ten percent through 1552, preceded by an impressive 128 percent between 1493 and 1502.[22] As represented in Figure 9.2, this growth translated into a spike in legal book production, with

---

18   Michael H. Hoeflich, 'Bibliographical perspectives on Roman and Civil Law', *Law Library Journal*, 89 (1997), pp. 41–54: 44; Steven Rowan, 'Jurists and the printing press in Germany: the first century', in Gerald P. Tyson and Sylvia S. Wagonheim (eds.), *Print and Culture in the Renaissance: Essays on the Advent of Printing in Europe* (Newark: University of Delaware Press, 1986), pp. 74–89: 75–77.

19   Ian Maclean, *Scholarship, Commerce, Religion: The Learned Book in the Age of Confessions, 1560–1630* (Cambridge: Harvard University Press, 2012), pp. 97–100.

20   Sheet counts estimated from the bibliographic survey of *Compagnie* editions I have conducted for my doctoral thesis. Some of these editions will not be available on the USTC's online database until my data has been fully integrated.

21   Cumby, 'Publishing Monopoly'.

22   Figures based on my unpublished doctoral thesis: Cumby, 'Publishing Monopoly'.

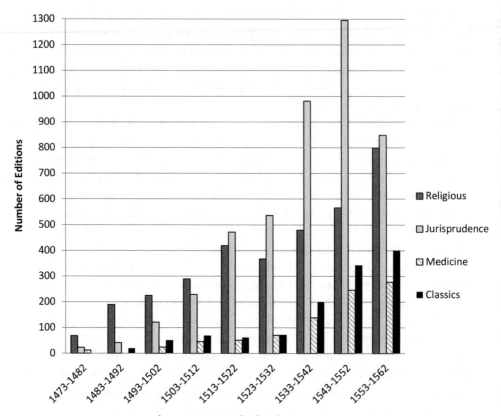

FIGURE 9.2 Most popular genres in Lyon by decade

law books occupying the largest share of Lyon's print output from the mid-1520s through the early 1550s. The most dramatic increase took place in the 1530s, when legal editions outnumbered religious works more than two to one.[23] Recalling Figure 9.1, the comparatively high overall growth rate in Lyonnais printing in the 1530s and 1540s maps to the increase in legal texts printed. During the Lyonnais book industry's most productive years, law books were its primary output, constituting just over a third of all books printed in the city, and probably, since these works were so substantial, about half the workload of the city's presses.[24] Given their status as kingpins of law book printing in Lyon, Lyon's international success in the first half of the sixteenth-century was tied to the activity of the *Compagnie*.

---

23   Cumby, 'Publishing Monopoly'.
24   Cumby, 'Publishing Monopoly'.

The Gabiano Inventory: a Financial Snapshot

As a longstanding director of the cartel, Luxembourg de Gabiano was at the centre of this powerful group. Despite not participating in its first iteration, it was under Gabiano's direction that the organization took on a defined shape and function. The 1520 contract divided the conglomerate's administrative duties into two parts: the *Compagnie des Textes* for the corpora of civil and canon law, and the *Compagnie des Lectures* for legal commentaries.[25] Gabiano acted as sole director of the *textes* until 1535, at which point the role rotated among the shareholders, and then again from 1541 to 1555.[26] Though Luxembourg began his career with his uncle's Venetian company, he immersed himself fully in his Lyonnais publishing conglomerate in the first half of the sixteenth century. Under his direction, the Gabiano firm ceased to be just a Venetian organization benefitting from Lyon's legal freedoms and became a principal actor in a distinctly Lyonnais cartel. The mechanics of Luxembourg's personal financial success can provide an instructive example of how the business of publishing functioned in the early modern book world.

To explore Gabiano's finances, I will draw on a particular document: the inventory of his assets taken after his death in 1558.[27] For Luxembourg's children by his first wife, the inventory was to provide a complete survey of everything he owned, tangible and intangible, so that they could settle his estate between themselves.[28] As a tool for the use of his heirs, the inventory prioritized unpaid over paid contracts, annual rents over closed sales and subsequently ignored several documents that did not have pressing relevance to their purpose. The documents logged are therefore not fully representative of Luxembourg's career, but can provide the basis for a partial reconstruction of his finances.

The aggregate set of contracts in the inventory reveal broad patterns in Luxembourg's activity. Of the total group, about 45% record specific monetary values.[29] As Figure 9.3 demonstrates, printing comprised a substantial portion of his income—at least 35% of the total. This percentage is less certain because, although the *Compagnie d'Ivry* was primarily a publishing company, several of Luxembourg's contracts relating to the company cannot immediately

---

25   Cumby, 'Publishing Monopoly'. Chapter 2.
26   Cumby, 'Publishing Monopoly'.
27   Archives Départementales du Rhône (henceforth: ADR), 3 E 3962; Baudrier, *Bibliographie lyonnaise*, VII, pp. 39–133.
28   Baudrier, *Bibliographie lyonnaise*, VII, pp. 40–42.
29   Baudrier, *Bibliographie lyonnaise*, VII, pp. 39–133.

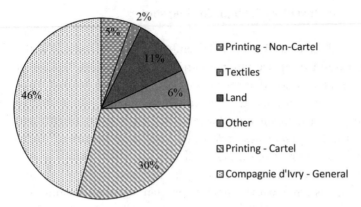

FIGURE 9.3 Cash flow by industry

be traced to printing. Indeed some explicitly related to the company's investments outside of printing. Bearing this in mind, the actual percentage of funds from non-publishing activities was likely more than the 19% recorded in the inventory.

Even so, those contracts that cannot be attributed to printing make up a comparatively small fraction of his total financial activity. Luxembourg and, indeed, the entire Gabiano family drew their income from other trades, but most of their funds came from publishing.[30] Although the Gabiano's primary business was publishing, they were not so much publishers as merchants who invested heavily in publishing.

Textiles

As the secondary literature on Lyonnais merchant publishers frequently notes, the Gabiano family was also involved in the textile industry.[31] This is certainly true of Luxembourg, judging from the inventory, but his involvement appears slight in comparison with his apparent printing activity (Figure 9.3). Unlike land and printing contracts, which are distributed relatively evenly over the

---

30   Angela Nuovo, *The Book Trade in the Italian Renaissance*, trans. Linda G. Cochrane (Leiden: Brill, 2013), p. 167.
31   Davis, 'Le monde de l'imprimerie humaniste', p. 261; Richard Gascon, *Grand commerce et vie urbaine au XVIe siècle: Lyon et ses marchands (environs de 1520—environs de 1580)* (2 vols., Paris: Mouton, 1971), p. 395, Guy Parguez, 'L'imprimerie à Lyon au temps de Dolet', in Centre V.L. Saulnier (ed.), *Etienne Dolet, 1509–1546* (Paris: Ecole normale supérieure de jeunes filles, 1986), pp. 63–77: 66.

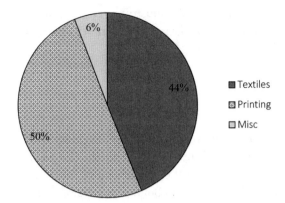

FIGURE 9.4 *Livre de Raison*: total funds by industry

course of the inventory, the textile records come almost exclusively from the 1550s. All of these records appear between 1546 and 1558, but only appear in significant numbers after 1555. The contracts from 1555 and beyond, constituting six of the eleven total textile contracts, come from Luxembourg's *Livre de Raison*, a notebook created to aid his heirs in the settling of estates.[32]

This document, left for his sons so that they could settle his ongoing affairs, can be taken as a snapshot of Luxembourg's primary activities at the end of his career.[33] Because six of the fifteen total contracts recorded therein dealt with textiles, it is interesting that this ratio is unique to the *Livre de Raison*. In the rest of the inventory, there are only five other contracts with members of the textile industry. It should be noted that one of these is for rent paid by a fabric dyer to Gabiano on one of the properties he owned within the city.[34] It is possible that the textile merchants Luxembourg dealt with were faster in paying off debts than some publishers and printers, and therefore it would have been less useful to preserve old, paid contracts.

The sums of money changing hands between Gabiano and textile merchants, mostly dyers of fabric, were larger on average than contracts with printers. In the *Livre de Raison*, for example, the average value of the textile contracts is about 148 livres, with a lowest recorded value of 66 livres and a highest of 379 livres and 7 sous. The printing contracts, by contrast, were significantly smaller. With the exception of an especially large debt owed by the booksellers Gaspard Molina and Alessis Derrere, the average contract value was a modest 39 livres. Overall, the projected income in the *Livre de Raison* was weighted

---

32 Baudrier, *Bibliographie lyonnaise*, VII, p. 69.
33 Baudrier, *Bibliographie lyonnaise*, VII, p. 69.
34 Baudrier, *Bibliographie lyonnaise*, VII, p. 45.

towards printing, but the funds from the textile industry suggest that it was more important to the Gabiano business model than the inventory otherwise suggests (Figure 9.4).

Publishing

In addition to omitting many textile industry contracts, the inventory artificially deflates Gabiano's publishing income. The records of both the *Compagnie d'Ivry* and the *Compagnie des libraires* preserved in the inventory come from the journals of each organization, held in Luxembourg's possession. These largely undocumented journals recorded transactions with smaller booksellers, merchants and printers as well as compounded credit. The inventory excludes almost all of the documents relating to Luxembourg's activity with the *Compagnie des libraires*. Unlike the *Compagnie d'Ivry* account books, which are all partially transcribed, the inventory merely mentions the *Compagnie des libraires* documents. No further treatment was necessary, because all ongoing company business had been in the hands of Luxembourg's heirs, Henri, Balthazar and Barthélemy de Gabiano, as of 1555. As such, the account books were no longer relevant either to the ongoing business of the company or to the settling of Luxembourg's estate.

The contracts relating to Lyon's critically important four annual fairs are another unfortunate gap in the inventory. As with the books of the *Compagnie*, Luxembourg's transactions from the fairs were deemed 'not able to serve for any purpose' by Henri de Gabiano and his brothers, the primary agents in charge of the inventory.[35] Unlike the *Ivry* books, the books of the *Compagnie* were neither numbered nor inventoried. This sweeping omission comprised 60 notebooks, and spanned a period from 1538 to 1552. Those from 1553 and 1554 are also mentioned, but these appear to have been of immediate service to the three adult Gabiano sons. The text describes them as already open by Luxembourg to his heirs, though their contents remain unknown.[36] A glance at the contracts recorded from 1553 and 1554 turns up only land purchases and rental income, with the exception of Luxembourg's previous inventory of goods taken in 1553.[37]

The chronological distribution of contracts recorded in the inventory highlights just how much information is missing. The surviving documents were

---

35 Baudrier, *Bibliographie lyonnaise*, VII, p. 77: "ne pouvant server d' aulcune chose".
36 Baudrier, *Bibliographie lyonnaise*, VII.
37 Baudrier, *Bibliographie lyonnaise*, VII, pp. 39–133.

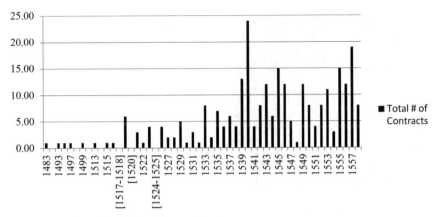

FIGURE 9.5 Chronological distribution of the inventory

weighted towards the last twenty years of Luxembourg's career (Figure 9.5). This is unsurprising, given that more recent contracts were both more likely to be ongoing, and therefore relevant, and also more likely to survive. The high point in 1557 relates directly to Luxembourg's *livre de raison*.[38] Additionally, the significant spike in 1540 relates to the many rental contracts that came along with his major land acquisition, the estate at Vourles, purchased at the beginning of the previous year. The small uptick in contracts in 1519 relates to the founding of the *Grande Compagnie des libraires*.

The presence of these lacunae indicate that Gabiano was an even larger player in Lyon's merchant world than can be concretely established by surviving documents. But, even bearing these gaps in mind, the inventory's representation of Luxembourg's work as a publisher is still significant. Small transactions between Luxembourg and a network of master-printers and booksellers predominate in terms of sheer numbers (Figure 9.6). The single largest individual sums come from the compounded income derived from publishing cartels, with the two companies comprising 85% of the recorded printing-related funds (Figure 9.7).

There are only two documents relating to the *Compagnie* that receive any detailed treatment in the inventory. The contracts both reimburse Luxembourg for investments he had in the company's ongoing projects after his retirement.[39] They are both from 1557, one from the *Compagnie des Textes* and the other from the *Compagnie des Lectures*. Interestingly, though Luxembourg was

---

38 Baudrier, *Bibliographie lyonnaise*, VII, p. 69.
39 Baudrier, *Bibliographie lyonnaise*, VII, p. 76.

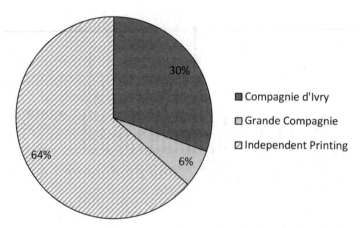

FIGURE 9.6 Number of printing contracts with recorded funds

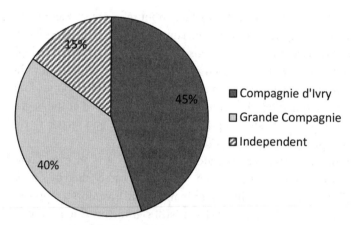

FIGURE 9.7 Total funds recorded from printing contracts

formerly the director of the *Compagnie des Lectures,* Hugues de la Porte's *Compagnie des Textes* contributed a far greater sum. In total, the *Compagnie* paid Gabiano 11,000 livres that year.[40] He appears to have established a financial base in the *Compagnie,* intended to provide him with income during his retirement as director.

Fortunately, some documentation on the *Compagnie*'s distribution of finances exists outside of the inventory. It is impossible to say for which years Luxembourg was directly in charge of the two branches of the company. But, during his period of activity, the director of the *Compagnie,* a role that rotated

---

40 Baudrier, *Bibliographie lyonnaise,* VII, pp. 33–35.

among the *compagnons*, would draw a salary from the other members. From 1535 to 1559, this was a modest 200 livres annually, and was intended to compensate for the added trouble the administrator took on.[41] In addition to this undocumented salary, the books of the company would have contained information pertaining to shared profits. The *compagnons* were required to share profits from any books taken from the communal warehouse.[42] A surviving contract provides an example of one such settlement: the five principal members split a total profit of more than 50,000 livres between them in 1541.[43]

Although the *Compagnie d'Ivry* had been dissolved more than ten years prior to Luxembourg's death, its associated network figured prominently in the inventory. Several of the company's books contained outstanding contracts, meriting individual documentation. By contrast, the books of the Lyon fairs and of the *Compagnie*, both balanced, paid, and closed at the time the inventory was taken, were only inventoried as volumes, without detailing their contents. The inventory's compilers enumerated the *Compagnie d'Ivry* contracts after listing the company's books, to highlight debts unpaid. For each journal, the inventory records the total number of leaves of the book, the number of leaves that had been written on, and the final entry. In some cases, this entry appears to be a recording of current profits, as in the book of the company from 5 July 1519 to 24 April 1523.[44] Whereas the final entry of that journal records 2003 livres 15 sous and 11 deniers credited to the company, other final journal entries record individual transactions.

All of the records preserved from the *Compagnie d'Ivry*, in contrast to the *Compagnie des libraires*, include specific financial values. This points to a unique and critical facet of the Gabiano firm's business model. It was the policy of Jean-Barthélemy de Gabiano, Luxembourg's uncle and the company's director, to only accept cash payments, rather than books or exchanges of debt, and this practice apparently extended throughout the firm.[45] This is especially interesting, as, in the trade as a whole, payments between bookmen were often done in exchanges of stock.[46] Booksellers affiliated with the *Compagnie d'Ivry*, because they were required to pay for books in cash, would have had to bear

---

41   Dureau, 'Recherches sur les grandes compagnies de libraires', pp. 7, 23–27; ADR, Fonds Charton, 23 J 22.
42   Dureau, 'Recherches sur les grandes compagnies de libraires', pp. 7, 20 (warehouse) and 8, 23–27 (profit sharing). See also Cumby, 'Publishing Monopoly', Chapter 2.
43   Dureau, *Recherches*, p. 8, Baudrier, *Bibliographie lyonnaise*, VII, pp. 33–34.
44   Baudrier, *Bibliographie lyonnaise*, VII, p. 72.
45   Nuovo, *The Book Trade*, p. 76.
46   Maclean, *Scholarship, Commerce, Religion*, pp. 101, 184.

the brunt of the risk under this business model. Until stock sold, the bookseller would be operating at a loss.

However, as the records in the inventory show, these exchanges seem to have been effectively done on credit. The enumerated contracts all relate to outstanding payments, one of which was 37 years old.[47] The merchants dealing with the company all appear to have had a wide window to repay the company, even if they could not send stock to repay the Gabianos.

Surviving *Compagnie* records also provide the sum of money distributed to the *compagnons* to settle its contract of 1529–1535.[48] Jean-Barthélemy de Gabiano, as director of the company, split a sum of 62,618 ducats between his son-in-law Laurent Aliprandi, and his nephew, Luxembourg de Gabiano, with 22,322 going to Aliprandi.[49] Though Luxembourg's share remains unspecified, it stands to reason that he would receive a similar amount to Aliprandi, as both occupied similar roles as branch directors.[50] Interestingly, for the Italian book firms operating before the seventeenth century, this is the only document known to record accumulated capital.[51]

Translating this sum into livres to compare it against the income from the inventory presents some difficulty. The value of various currencies was a source of dispute for international enterprises in the sixteenth century, even within family firms like the Giunti.[52] However, I have generated an estimate by drawing on extant mid-sixteenth-century exchange rate information between the Medina del Campo fairs and the Lyon fairs. If the écu au soleil was valued at roughly 440 Spanish maravedis, and the Venetian ducat at 375 maravedis, 22,322 ducats would be approximately 26,191 écus soleil.[53] With an écu au soleil defined as 45 sous tournois, the total value of Luxembourg's 1535 share in the *Compagnie d'Ivry* would have been close to 58,929 livres and 15 sous tournois.[54]

---

47 Baudrier, *Bibliographie lyonnaise*, VII, p. 79.
48 Nuovo, *The Book Trade*, 77–79.
49 Nuovo, *The Book Trade*, p. 79.
50 Nuovo, *The Book Trade*, p. 78.
51 Nuovo, *The Book Trade*, p. 78.
52 William Pettas lays out a series of credit disputes between Giovanni (Juan) Giunti in Salamanca and Giacomo (Jacques) Giunti in Lyon, but these give sums of Venetian ducats and of Spanish maravedis, William Pettas, *The Giunti of Florence: Merchant Publishers in the Sixteenth Century* (San Francisco: B.M. Rosenthal, 1980), pp. 110–112.
53 Marie-Thérèse Boyer-Xambeau, Ghislain Deleplace, and Lucien Gillard, *Private Money & Public Currencies: The Sixteenth-Century Challenge*, trans. Azizeh Azodi (Armonk: M.E. Sharpe, 1994), pp. 76–87 for écus to maravedis; Pettas, *The Giunti of Florence*, pp. 110–112 for ducats to maravedis.
54 Boyer-Xambeau, Deleplace, and Gillard, *Private Money*, p. 76.

TABLE 9.1 Movable goods

Location	Value—livres
Comptoir [office]	53
Rue Mercière	1,589
Warehouse	86
Shop	46
Vourles	1,094
Place de Millerie	107
Cash, Rings, Precious Stones, etc.	2,000
Total	4,977

Material Assets

These enormous influxes of cash in the 1530s and 1540s beg the question: where had this money gone by the end of Gabiano's life? The first place to look for answer might logically be in the part of the inventory that enumerates the monetary value of all furnishings and other items in his possession.

Luxembourg de Gabiano reportedly kept a lavish household.[55] The inventory confirms this from its opening pages, which describes the contents of four boxes containing jewelry, luxury fabric, precious stones and 18 gold écus.[56] However, the inventory clearly shows that this is not where his real wealth lay. Even factoring in valuable paintings, tapestries, precious stones and specie, the total value of his movable goods is still less than half his trade income from the *Compagnie* alone.

Furthermore, few traces of Luxembourg's printing activity appear among the practical items he kept. As a merchant publisher, he was not in the practice of owning presses. However, between his warehouse and shop, and the office in his home in the city, no mention is made of items like sets of type or even amounts of paper that a merchant publisher might be expected to provide.[57] The surviving contracts between Lyon's publishers and printers preserve some

---

55   Richard Gascon is extremely familiar with the finances and consumption patterns of the Lyonnais, and refers to Luxembourg's home, especially the chateau at Vourles as a space of luxury and rest. Gascon, *Grand commerce*, p. 845.
56   Baudrier, *Bibliographie lyonnaise*, VII, pp. 43–44.
57   Warehouse and shop: Baudrier, *Bibliographie lyonnaise*, VII, pp. 103–104; Rue Mercière office: Idem, pp. 84–86.

notable examples to suggest that this absence is peculiar. Antoine Vincent paid for two different Lyonnais typefounders, Pierre Bozon and Jean Montcher, to strike new matrices and cast new types for Vincent's Genevan operations in 1561.[58] The *Compagnie* had an ongoing relationship with the Juste family's typefoundry to produce the rotunda types in use across their editions.[59] In a 1504 contract between printer Jacques Sacon, publisher Louis Martin and early member of the *Compagnie* Aymon de la Porte, de la Porte and Martin were entirely responsible for supplying the paper for a print run of 1,250 copies.[60] Paper was so fundamental a commodity for publishers that both Guillaume Rouillé and the Senneton brothers vertically integrated paper mills into their publishing empires.[61]

Given that supplying paper and, depending on the project, supplying types, were both core duties of a publisher, and given that Gabiano was actively contracting printing work as late as May 1558, it is curious that there should be no mention of printing materials among his possessions.[62] Instead, these appear in an addendum to the initial inventory, which records an unspecified quantity of matrices for gothic types.[63]

Rather than containing paper and types, Luxembourg's workspaces contained goods relating to his other business activities. The warehouse on the river Saône held relatively little, aside from materials relating to the wine trade. Inside were barrels and stillings for wine vessels. Among shelves, benches and a box of candles, the cellar contained tools for working with leather and 17 barrels of "good claret".[64] Adjoining the warehouse, the shop held scales, a series of other devices for weighing goods and a black mule on hand in the stable.[65] Though there were no trade goods in the shop, it had recently been rented out to the merchants François and Huguet Durret for the fairs, according to the first

---

58   The contracts appear in the notebooks of Genevan notary J. Rageau, who migrated from Lyon in the 1500s. Archives d'État Genève notaire Ragueau tom. 4 pp. 125–127, 296–298. A third contract describes a series of six fonts that Vincent bought from Bozon—pp. 515–516; Eugenie Droz, 'Antoine Vincent. La propagande protestant par le psautier', in Gabrielle Berthoud (ed.), *Aspects de la propagande religieuse* (Geneva: Droz, 1957), pp. 276–293: 279; discussed at length in Cumby, 'Publishing Monopoly', Chapter 3.

59   Cumby, 'Publishing Monopoly', Chapter 3.

60   Dureau, 'Recherches sur les grandes compagnies de libraires', p. 5; ADR, Fonds Charton, 22 J 23.

61   Rouillé: Baudrier, *Bibliographie lyonnaise*, V, p. 393; IX, p. 20; Senneton: Baudrier, *Bibliographie lyonnaise*, VII, p. 363, 368–385; Davis, 'Le monde de l'imprimerie humaniste', p. 256.

62   Contracts from May 1558: Baudrier, *Bibliographie lyonnaise*, VII, pp. 70–71.

63   Baudrier, *Bibliographie lyonnaise*, VII, p. 126.

64   Baudrier, *Bibliographie lyonnaise*, VII, p. 103.

65   Baudrier, *Bibliographie lyonnaise*, VII, p. 104.

contract recorded in the inventory.[66] Additionally, a portion of the total value of his home within the city, which contained several boxes of tapestries and textiles, may be counted towards the value of his trade goods. Indeed, the reason that the goods in his home within the city were valued at 500 livres more than those at Vourles is because of these items, which were likely intended for sale.[67]

According to the inventory, Gabiano's trade wealth was not tied up in tangible, unsold goods at the time of his death. However, this is a somewhat misleading conclusion to draw. While the books that he published under the *Compagnie* umbrella fell to his *compagnons* and sons in 1555, Luxembourg was still contracting printing work up until his death.[68] None of these books counted towards the inventory because they were, by 1558, the property of his heirs.

Luxembourg de Gabiano's will, drawn up on 28 January 1555, may not have survived, but other documents hint at the value of the books he transferred.[69] Eleven years after his father's death, Hugues de Gabiano commissioned his nephew Ange de Gabiano to settle the accounts of a company between Catherine de la Tour and the late Luxembourg's former manservant turned bookseller Fleury Bolard.[70] This same company originally included the late Gabiano, and appears in the inventory in passing as a textile concern.[71] According to Baudrier, settling the company accounts included completing the liquidation of unsold stock that de la Tour inherited for herself and her children.[72] Archival documents uncovered to date can neither confirm nor deny the amount of books in the company accounts, but the final sale in 1581 yielded 687 gold écus.[73] There is

---

66 Baudrier, *Bibliographie lyonnaise*, VII, p. 44.
67 Baudrier, *Bibliographie lyonnaise*, VII, pp. 86–103.
68 Gabiano brothers entering the *Grande Compagnie*: Baudrier, *Bibliographie lyonnaise*, VII, p. 137.
69 The date of the will appears in a reference at the beginning of the inventory. Baudrier, *Bibliographie lyonnaise*, VII, p. 40.
70 Baudrier, *Bibliographie lyonnaise*, VII, p. 159. Bolard's transformation from "serviteur" to "libraire" and even "marchand-libraire" can be seen in Baudrier, *Bibliographie lyonnaise*, I, p. 54; VII, pp. 159, 160, 207, 290, also, as "marchand tainturier" in two 1579 documents in ADR, 3 E 3692.
71 Baudrier, *Bibliographie lyonnaise*, VII, p. 126. The word used to describe the company's main purpose is "fillaterye". Definitions for this spelling variant are elusive, but it appears to refer to thread and its use, possibly silk thread. Randle Cotgrave, *A Dictionarie of the French and English Tongves* (London: Adam Islip, 1611); Robert Grandsaignes d'Hauterive (ed.), *Dictionnaire d'Ancient Français: Moyen Age et Renaissanceçe* (Paris: Larousse, 1947); Alan Hindley, Frederick W. Langley, and Brian J. Levy (eds.), *Old French-English Dictionary* (Cambridge: Cambridge University Press, 2006).
72 Baudrier, *Bibliographie lyonnaise*, VII, p. 157.
73 Baudrier, *Bibliographie lyonnaise*, VII, p. 160.

even some indication that the three eldest sons reimbursed Bolard for assuming their father's role in the *Compagnie*. A year after Henry, Balthazar II and Barthélemy de Gabiano formally entered the cartel, they paid back a total of 8,500 livres for a series of debts connected to this transfer of power.[74]

Investments and Land

Judging from his 'sumptuous' material effects, Luxembourg clearly had ready funds for domestic use.[75] However, his personal financial reserves were either not preserved in the inventory or existed within his complex network of trade investments. To trace Luxembourg de Gabiano's wealth, and to understand him as a merchant and as a publisher, we have to turn to his investments. Considering the inventory as a whole, these investments were predominantly in land.

As Figure 9.3 shows, only about 11% of Gabiano's income came directly from rental payments. There are 52 instances where exact pensions or rents have been enumerated, out of 181 contracts relating to land ownership.[76] With only 29% of the total documents bearing exact values, the precise value of Luxembourg's real estate investments is difficult to gauge. This is especially significant when compared with the overall figure for land contracts in the inventory, 45%. Some of these documented legal proceedings, and some were left over from the previous owners of his properties. For the most part, the recorded rental payments were from small tenant farmers, who paid in wine, chickens and grain.

As modest income and incomplete record keeping indicates, considering rural properties as an index of wealth does not so much concern rental income, as it concerns of the total value of the land. Interesting evidence of this shows up in Lyon's tax records. Before 1538, Luxembourg was taxed at 400 livres. In 1538, the same year he acquired two rural estates, his taxes jumped by 200 livres.[77] Despite an active and, ostensibly, successful commercial life, the 600 livre taxation rate remained steady for the rest of his career.

These estates, at Vourles and Côte-sur-Brignais, were both located in popular wine-growing territory to the south of Lyon. As an investment for merchant publishers, these land purchases served as a relatively stable cushion against

---

74 ADR, BP 3894, partially transcribed in Baudrier, *Bibliographie lyonnaise*, VII, p. 359.
75 Gascon, *Grand commerce*, p. 845.
76 Baudrier, *Bibliographie lyonnaise*, VII, pp. 39–133.
77 Baudrier, *Bibliographie lyonnaise*, VII, p. 28.

the fluctuations of the book market in periods of economic inactivity.[78] Purchasing both estates made Luxembourg a *seigneur* of both regions, a title that solidified his entry into the city's elite and entitled him to draw income from his lands. A *seigneurie* could cost anywhere between 14,000 and 52,000 livres, and would only have been available to the wealthiest of the Lyonnais.[79] Recalling his massive cash inflow from the *Compagnie d'Ivry*, in 1535, perhaps it should not be surprising that he was able to buy not one but two *seigneuries* in the late 1530s. In total, Luxembourg bought about 45 parcels of land in addition to his two country estates.

Luxembourg's land ownership patterns were characteristic of Lyonnais merchants expanding into the countryside. Though his acquisition of a *seigneurie* put him among a rarefied minority, he used his lands in the same manner as many other urban merchants. Merchants expanded into the land surrounding Lyon to capitalize on rural goods, drawing wealth from the countryside into the city.[80] For the many smaller urban merchants, of which there were an estimated 1,500 to 2,000 by 1518, rents formed a desirable, but small supplemental income.[81] Three documents relating to rents due to Luxembourg from the Côte-sur-Brignais region are from one such merchant: a Didier Besançon, described as a money engraver from Lyon.[82] Besançon paid rent to Luxembourg in wine until he eventually bought a farm from the *seigneur* in 1556.[83]

Interestingly, several of Gabiano's *compagnons* also invested in land and amassed prestigious estates. Though their estates were in the Dauphiné and Champagne, respectively Hugues de la Porte and the three Senneton brothers, Jean, Jacques and Claude, were all *seigneurs*.[84] Antoine Vincent was practically Gabiano's neighbour both in Lyon and in the countryside. He, too was in the wine trade, and owned vineyard land bordering his country estate at Millery.[85]

Figure 9.8 illustrates the percentage of land owned by bourgeois Lyonnais in the parishes to the West of the city, and the most common crops produced those parishes. In that these territories were increasingly controlled by merchants from Lyon as the city's commercial wealth expanded during the golden age, they contributed to a further expansion of urban commercial capital.[86]

---

78   Davis, 'Le monde de l'imprimerie humaniste', p. 259.
79   Gascon, *Grand commerce*, p. 829.
80   Gascon, *Grand commerce*, p. 813.
81   Gascon, *Grand commerce*, pp. 819–820.
82   Baudrier, *Bibliographie lyonnaise*, VII, pp. 44, 53, 55.
83   Baudrier, *Bibliographie lyonnaise*, VII.
84   Baudrier, *Bibliographie lyonnaise*, VII, pp. 262, 368.
85   Gascon, *Grand commerce*, pp. 822–823.
86   Gascon, *Grand commerce*, pp. 818–822.

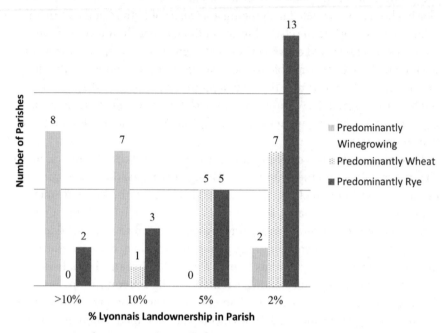

FIGURE 9.8 Land use patterns for rural holdings of Lyon residents, ca. 1518

Parishes with the highest concentrations of Lyonnais landholders were, for the most part, wine-growing regions. In four of the eight predominantly vineyard parishes with a rate of urban ownership of greater than 10%, over 50% of the total vines belonged to Lyonnais. These four were Vourles, Millery, Charly and Sainte Foy, in descending order, where almost 75% of Vourles vines belonged to urban merchants.[87] Owning vineyard estates in particular raised the social standing of merchant-publishers. As a result, in Vourles, Millery and Charly especially—all parishes where Lyon merchants owned more than 10% of the land—wine became almost a monoculture, with emphasis on production for upmarket sale.[88] In Luxembourg's case, wine from Charly, which dominated his rental income, was sought-after for the bourgeois table, and owning territory there was a sign of true respectability.[89]

87 Gascon, *Grand commerce*, p. 815.
88 Gascon, *Grand commerce*, pp. 822–823.
89 Gascon, *Grand commerce*, p. 822; Mentions of Luxembourg's properties in Charly are scattered throughout the inventory. Baudrier, *Bibliographie lyonnaise*, VII, pp. 59, 61–63, 65, 68, 83.

It also bears mentioning that Luxembourg owned at least twelve separate properties within the city of Lyon, though almost none of the rents per annum were recorded in the inventory. In one case, the purchase price of an urban property survives. Luxembourg appears to have sold a house to Pierre and Nicolas Noir in 1539. The receipt of payment set the value of the property at 1,575 livres. There were two other contracts that recorded urban annual rent. Luxembourg collected 50 livres in overdue pension from the widow Marguerite Didier, but the property she rented was not named.[90] A more precise figure came from one Antoine de Cotton, who paid Luxembourg 11 livres and 19 sous for a house.[91]

Although the record is incomplete, Luxembourg appears to have earned more income from his fewer urban properties than from his many rural holdings. This would have been characteristic of the difference between urban and rural rents for Lyonnais merchants in the sixteenth century. Antoine de Vinols, a textile merchant who built a network of urban and rural rents to support himself in his retirement, drew four times as much revenue from his urban as his rural properties.[92]

As Luxembourg's career progressed and he became more integrated into the city's politics and economy, he invested in and around Lyon. 1539 and 1540 were critical years, when he not only purchased his *seigneurie* at Vourles, but also acquired a number of properties within the city.[93] As the chronological distribution of rental contracts shows, this trend in high numbers of rural, supplemented by much smaller but not substantially less frequent urban rents and purchases, continued until his death.

The supplemental income from rents would not have been Luxembourg's primary purpose in purchasing land. High-cost investments, like the estate at Vourles, were ways of holding his trade income in stable deposits. Like opening a bank account, Luxembourg placed his publishing and other trade income into the acquisition of land. This was a popular practice among Lyon's bourgeois, as demonstrated by the rural *nommées* of 1518, which records an estimated 1,500 to 2,000 urban merchants who owned land in the Lyonnais countryside (Figure 9.8).[94] As noted above, Gabiano's *compagnons* in the Vincent, de la Porte, and Senneton families all maintained country estates like Luxem-

---

90   Baudrier, *Bibliographie lyonnaise*, VII, p. 51.
91   Baudrier, *Bibliographie lyonnaise*, VII, p. 67.
92   Gascon, *Grand commerce*, p. 823.
93   See Figure 9.9.
94   Archives Municipales de Lyon (henceforth: AML), CC 58; Gascon, *Grand commerce*, pp. 819–823.

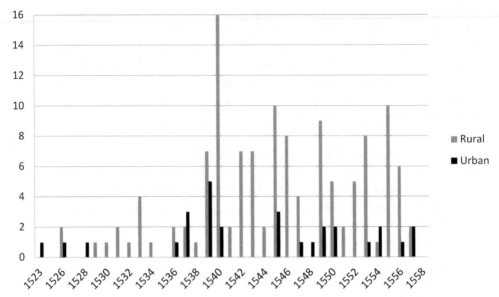

FIGURE 9.9 Urban vs. rural land-related documents

bourg's.[95] Their land appreciated in value over the course of their lives, functioning similarly to collecting interest on a bank account.

Closing the Inventory

The preface to the inventory makes frequent reference to the late Luxembourg's 1555 will, which stipulated that not only would an inventory be taken, but that his principal business contacts were to be present to assist his sons in conducting the inventory.[96] The initial meeting concerning the inventory took place at the home of Hugues de la Porte, the *compagnon* whose name most frequently appeared alongside Luxembourg's on his few non-anonymous editions.[97] However, although Luxembourg specifically requested that the then-active *Compagnie* members, de la Porte, along with Guillaume Regnault, Antoine Vincent and Claude Senneton be present to take the inventory, each refused in his turn.[98] All members of this core group of publishers cited press-

---

95 Baudrier, *Bibliographie lyonnaise*, VII, pp. 262, 368; Gascon, *Grand commerce*, pp. 822–823.
96 Baudrier, *Bibliographie lyonnaise*, VII, p. 40.
97 Baudrier, *Bibliographie lyonnaise*, VII, p. 40; Gültlingen, *Bibliographie des livres imprimés à Lyon*, VI, pp. 171–172.
98 Baudrier, *Bibliographie lyonnaise*, VII, pp. 40, 117–118.

ing business, and indicated that they preferred not to be involved at all with the Gabiano business.[99]

Luxembourg's decision to ask them to participate in the closing of his affairs indicates that, from among his associates, he felt they best constituted his peers. He had an expectation that they would supervise and verify the appropriate settling of his estate, based ostensibly on their familiarity with him as former associates in the *Compagnie*. It is interesting that he should have misjudged their readiness to come to his aid. Though no clear explanation for their reticence presents itself, it is possible they felt that their professional relationship with Luxembourg had already been dissolved. This seems particularly likely, as Luxembourg officially resigned from the company in 1555 and had been compensated for his existing investments in 1557.[100] It may also be that Gabiano's former colleagues, knowing how complicated his affairs were, simply wanted to avoid the headache.

The parties actually present for the conducting and closure of the inventory represent a more diverse cross-section of trades than the merchant publishers initially contacted. In addition to the *Compagnie* affiliates Louis Pesnot and Philippe Tinghi, the original group designated by Luxembourg's will sent representatives.[101] Fortunately, the inventory clearly supplies the professions of all of those present. Regnault sent his son Antoine, Senneton sent a manservant and the merchant draper Jean Dodo, de la Porte sent the haberdasher Antoine Grandon and noted punchcutter Pierre Haultin. Luxembourg's widow, Catherine de la Tour, brought Fleury Bolard and Francois Durret, a merchant haberdasher who frequented Lyon's fairs.[102]

As a gathering, they speak to the diversity of trades that the other members of the *Grand Compagnie* invested and participated in, as well as suggesting trade connections with Luxembourg outside of publishing. Both de la Porte and Luxembourg's widow brought haberdashers, which suggests the possibility of overlap in both publishers' investments in that trade. That Gabiano and de la Porte could be partners outside of publishing seems plausible, particularly given the intermarriage between their children.[103] It is also worth noting that François Durret rented Luxembourg's shop space during the fairs.[104] He appeared not only at the initial signing of the inventory, but as a witness to the

---

99   Baudrier, *Bibliographie lyonnaise*, VII, p. 40: "ne voulloient riend scavoir de leurs affaires".
100 Baudrier, *Bibliographie lyonnaise*, VII, pp. 27, 76.
101 Baudrier, *Bibliographie lyonnaise*, VII, pp. 41, 118.
102 Baudrier, *Bibliographie lyonnaise*, VII, p. 118.
103 Baudrier, *Bibliographie lyonnaise*, VII, p. 118; ADR BP 3890.
104 Baudrier, *Bibliographie lyonnaise*, VII, p. 44.

settling of subsequent disputes between Catherine de la Tour and her stepsons, suggesting that Luxembourg may have been more involved in his trade than the inventory bears out.[105] However, these records may have been omitted along with the other notebooks of the fairs.

This final picture of Luxembourg de Gabiano, as provided by the parties willing to play a role in the closing of the inventory, recalls the diverse set of trades hinted at in the *livre de raison*. Although each of the present witnesses listed in the will were principally law book publishers, the actual assortment of representatives was more varied. It is doubly interesting that the other *compagnons* should have sent representatives outside of the publishing trade, indicating that they too were deeply invested in more than just the book industry. In order to maintain their financial dominance in the Lyonnais book world, both Luxembourg and the *compagnons* took it upon themselves to create varied business profiles.

Concluding Thoughts—Status, Investment and Risk

It is interesting that the security of Gabiano's estate should have relied so closely on distance from the material he made his fortune marketing. Indeed, in the municipal tax records of 1545, and in other official documentation Luxembourg was identified as a "marchand-libraire", but also, particularly later in his life, as "seigneur".[106] Just as he was not interested in labeling his editions, he was not deeply committed to maintaining an identity as a publisher. Instead, he modeled himself on other wealthy Lyonnais merchants who purchased estates and sat on Lyon's *consulat*.[107]

Luxembourg de Gabiano continued work in the book trade until his death, but his land purchases ensured that several of his children did not. A *seigneurie* was prohibitively expensive for all but the richest merchants, but it could also serve as an alternative career path for those leaving their trades. Maintaining both a country seat and an urban business was costly, but some could and did sell off their assets in order to transfer fully to rural landowning.[108]

---

105 Baudrier, *Bibliographie lyonnaise*, VII, p. 123.
106 Gascon, *Grand commerce*, p. 372, Baudrier, *Bibliographie lyonnaise*, VII, pp. 39–133.
107 Natalie Zemon Davis, 'Publisher Guillaume Rouille, businessman and humanist', in R.J. Schoeck (ed.), *Editing Sixteenth-Century Texts: Papers given at the Editorial Conference University of Toronto October, 1965* (Toronto: University of Toronto Press, 1966), p. 75; Baudrier, *Bibliographie lyonnaise*, VII, pp. 49–50.
108 Gascon, *Grand commerce*, p. 813.

More importantly, the shift from trade to land ownership entailed social advancement. The purchase of rural seats by urban merchants was part of a greater trend; across France merchants with sufficient capital were using land purchases as a gateway to the nobility, enabling them to abandon their trades for offices and titles.[109] Lyon's *consulat* in the sixteenth century is a superb example of this trend. As of 1495, thanks to Charles VIII, bourgeois *conseilleurs* were granted the title and privileges of nobility upon election to the *consulat*.[110] Over the course of the sixteenth century, the *consulat* came to be controlled by its 15 most heavily taxed families, such that Lyon's merchants displaced the city's old, patrician families as the city's primary political and aristocratic figures.[111] At a tax rate of 600 livres, the Gabiano family was solidly among the six dominant houses of merchant publishers operating during Lyon's 'golden age'.[112] Alongside de la Porte, Giunta, Senneton, Vincent and Rouillé, the Gabiano firm controlled the largest and, by appearances, most lucrative share of the book trade in Lyon.[113] Luxembourg de Gabiano, like many of his peers, rose from being a foreign merchant to a citizen, *seigneur* and city administrator, whose children were of sufficient social standing to either marry nobles or become members of the nobility in their own right.

In addition to Hugues de Gabiano, who inherited the *seigneurie* at Vourles, Catherine de Gabiano, also the child of Catherine de la Tour, entered the nobility. Her second husband, Nicolas de Chaponay, though not a primary inheritor, was part of a very large and important Lyonnais family.[114] Their son, Humbert de Chaponay, drew up a genealogy, which provides a telling demonstration of the Gabianos' social ascent. Luxembourg's grandson Humbert invented a more exalted pedigree for his Italian ancestry. He erroneously recorded that Luxembourg de Gabiano was a lieutenant in charge of 60 armed men, and that

---

109 Robert J. Knecht, *The Rise and Fall of Renaissance France, 1483–1610* (Blackwell: Oxford, 1996), p. 262; Fernand Braudel, *The Mediterranean and the Mediterranean World in the Age of Philip II*, trans. Sian Reynolds (2 vols., Berkeley; Los Angeles; London: University of California Press, 1995), II, pp. 725–734.
110 Claude-Emmanuel de Pastoret, *Ordonnances des rois de France de la troisième race* (Paris: Imprimerie Royale, 1840), XX, pp. 490–492.
111 Jacques Rossiaud, 'Lyon, 1500–1562: la soie, le sang, les haillons et les raves', in Yves Krumenacker (ed.), *Lyon 1562, capital protestante: une histoire religieuse de Lyon à la Renaissance* (Lyon: Olivétan, 2009), pp. 15–55: 42; Gascon, *Grand commerce*, pp. 407–413.
112 Baudrier, *Bibliographie lyonnaise*, VII, p. 28.
113 Gascon, *Grand commerce*, pp. 369–373, 395; Davis, 'Le monde de l'imprimerie humaniste', p. 255.
114 See ADR, Fonds Chaponay, 44 J. For Nicolas II and Catherine de la Tour: Ibid., 44 J 88–94.

Catherine de la Tour was part of the de la Tour Gouvernet family.[115] In reality, the only military position Gabiano ever held was as leader of the town militia for his district in 1523.[116]

The almost total absence of publishing materials from among his goods, as well as the lack of a personal warehouse of unsold books, was not just a function of his focus on the *seigneuries*. Rather, it signals the key feature of Gabiano's commercial success: risk-sharing. It is no accident that he held little illiquid stock at his death. The value of an unsold book could depreciate rapidly over time, due as much to texts going out of date as to material conditions of flood, decay, or simple disorder. While holding stock for extended periods was a necessary part of the book trade, Gabiano ensured that at no point did he bear the full risk of owning such volatile assets. Instead, his publishing ventures involved joint ownership, such that he was never solely responsible for potential losses. Even the work he contracted outside of major firms was apparently jointly owned by himself, his wife and his assistant.[117]

In fact, some unsold stock from Gabiano's ventures remained, but, as it was not technically in his possession in 1558, it did not appear in the inventory. This includes the 687 gold écus worth of books that Catherine de la Tour inherited, as well as any *Compagnie* stock dating from the period between 1520 and 1555.[118] Some of these editions, like a 1553 printing of Giovanni de Anania's commentary on the *Decretales*, were still in the warehouses of the *Compagnie*'s shareholders as late as 1591.[119] However, Gabiano's business practices allowed him to consider these slow-selling, potentially deteriorating books principally as investments. He was a shareholder in joint ventures, which were built to continue after his death. So, when Luxembourg de Gabiano retired, his partners paid him for his share of the total value of their assets, rather than leaving him with the assets themselves. Responsibility for liquidating collectively produced books fell to his companies, a feature that protected the *compagnons* individually from the risks of a failed or unsaleable edition.

Similar to Lyon's Florentine bankers, the Medici, Capponi and Salviati, Luxembourg de Gabiano was primarily a holder of capital.[120] Merchant publish-

---

115 Excerpted in Claude le Laboureur, *Les masures de l'Ille-Barbe. Supplement* (Lyon: Emmanuel Vite, 1895), p. 540.
116 Baudrier, *Bibliographie lyonnaise*, VII, p. 29.
117 Baudrier, *Bibliographie lyonnaise*, VII, pp. 126, 157, 159–160.
118 Baudrier, *Bibliographie lyonnaise*, VII, p. 160.
119 Maclean, *Learning and the Market Place*, pp. 238–246, 253 6A; USTC 204113.
120 Jacqueline Boucher, 'Les Italiens à Lyon' in Jean Balsamo (ed.), *Passer les Monts: Français en Italie—l'Italie en France (1494–1525)* (Paris: Honoré Champion, 1998), pp. 39–46: 39, 42–46; Roger Doucet, *La Banque Capponi à Lyon en 1556* (Lyon: Imprimerie nouvelle lyonnaise,

ers in Lyon dealt in funding; their associations existed to protect the finances invested in large-scale projects. Luxembourg and the other members of the *Compagnie*, who typified publishing in Lyon in the 'golden age', were more concerned with holding and directing funds than with making books. The surplus from publishing within risk-insulated companies with multiple shareholders was not used for new printing projects, as often as it was held in safe land purchases and reinvested into other trades. To be a successful publisher in Lyon was to be a merchant first and a publisher second, relying on multiple sources of income and multiple avenues to invest that income.

> 1939); Nadia Matringe, *La Banque en Renaissance: Les Salviati et la place de Lyon au milieu du XVIe siècle* (Rennes: Presses Universitaires de Rennes, 2016); Gascon, *Grand commerce*, pp. 214–216.

CHAPTER 10

Editing the *Thesaurus Linguae Latinae*: Robert Estienne's Dream and Nightmare

Martine Furno

The *Thesaurus Linguae Latinae* published by Robert Estienne in Paris in 1543 was entitled 'secunda editio', probably because Estienne considered that it was only with this edition, and not with that of 1536, that he had actually improved, changed and augmented his work.[1] However, for us, this 'second edition' can be seen as the third one, since Estienne printed his very first *Thesaurus* in 1531, followed by a second version in 1536, which had already been augmented and corrected.[2]

However, Estienne was not mistaken, nor was he deceptively modest: the 1543 edition really was the culmination of a patient fifteen-years' worth of work, reading classics, listing words and examples to draw up indexes and definitions. It is a masterpiece of lexicographical construction, whose main components are the three editions of the monolingual *Thesaurus*. From this work also derive the smaller bilingual Latin-French and French-Latin dictionaries (*Dictionarium Latino Gallicum*, 1538 and *Dictionnaire Français Latin*, 1539), and the even smaller dictionaries for children, *Dictionarolum puerorum* (Latin-French, 1542) and *Les mots français selon l'ordre des lettres* (French-Latin, 1544).[3]

After the 1543 edition, no monolingual Latin dictionary appeared, either from Robert Estienne's workshop, or anywhere else in Europe, that could actually be considered 'new'. All later editions, in France (particularly in Lyon), in the German-speaking lands, or in Venice, derived from Estienne's master-

---

1   The two editions are identified with USTC 140870 and 187082 respectively. It is my duty and pleasure to thank, for their helpful support for my research, all the staff at the Blickling Estate, and especially John Gandy, Librarian, and Helen Bailey, General Manager; so many thanks also to Susan Baddeley, for her remarks on my essay and for her assistance in improving my written English.
2   The 1531 edition is to be identified with USTC 146288.
3   For a complete list and analysis of these publications, see Martine Furno, 'Les dictionnaires de Robert Estienne, sens et finalités d'une œuvre lexicographique', *Voces*, 10–11 (1999–2000), pp. 11–27; Benedicte Boudou and Judith Kecskeméti (eds.), *Robert et Charles Estienne. Des imprimeurs pédagogues* (Turnhout: Brepols, 2009). The editions are to be identified as: USTC 49529 and 78081 (1538); USTC 23431 (1539); and USTC 55928.

piece.⁴ Many of these later editions assembled parts of Estienne's *Thesaurus* together with parts of other dictionaries. Others were mere plagiarisms, concealed by a change in the order of the *lemmata*, from a rational and etymological order in Estienne's dictionary to an alphabetical order in the 'new' one. Estienne always showed a particular interest in the organization of his dictionaries: he was a great defender of the rational and etymological order connecting word-families by derivation, considered to be the only method that could really organise the lexicon in a well-constructed conception of language. Alphabetical order was widely used in other dictionaries competing with the *Thesaurus*, for obvious reasons of convenience. Estienne did not consider it to be a valid option, as it was not sufficiently explicative, and it did not shed light on the structure of language.

The rational order earned praise for the author of a dictionary. Making an alphabetical dictionary simply meant collecting words or phrases, and it did not entail any added intellectual work. In the early modern age, only a few learned and rich printers could sustain such an ambitious project, both intellectually and financially. Robert Estienne was one of them. It is easy to understand his distress at finding, during his time in Venice in 1550, alphabetical dictionaries made up with pieces of his former work.

These same dictionaries and their new organisation, however, are eloquent witnesses to why Estienne's *Thesaurus* was, in the mid-sixteenth century, the last monolingual Latin dictionary. Students' needs were changing. They no longer learned Latin as a mother tongue, or only from Latin-speaking teachers. By this time, Latin was being taught much as it still is, contrasted with students' own native language. Pupils required bilingual tools that were easy to use.⁵ An etymological dictionary was much less immediately serviceable, as well as being an expensive purchase to any customer. Printers could no longer afford the costs and risks associated with such a project. All of them preferred

---

4 In Lyon, several dictionaries with the title *Calepini dictionarium* were published by Sebastian Gryphius between 1546 and 1550, which were plagiarised versions and reconstructions of Estienne's *Thesaurus*; in Germany, it was the same with the *Latinae linguae universae promptuarium* of Theodosius Trebellius printed in Basel by Oporinus in 1545, and so in Venice for the *Calepinus* printed in 1550 by Paolo Manuzio and Johannes Gryphius.

5 We have an example (among numerous others) of these practises in the *Rudimenta Grammatices* translated by George Buchanan from the *Rudimenta* of Linacre, published by Robert Estienne in Paris in 1533. Buchanan not only translated the grammar, but he also adapted it to French pupils, describing some grammatical facts in a Latin which is strangely French-sounding. See Martine Furno, 'La tentation du vernaculaire: George Buchanan traducteur des *Rudimenta Grammatices* de Thomas Linacre', *Etudes Epistèmè*, 23 (2013), online publication: http://episteme.revues.org/260, last accessed on 19 August 2017.

to produce smaller books, sometimes monolingual but with more explanations and fewer examples, and otherwise with vernacular translations. Using extracts taken out of Estienne's *Thesaurus*, and also out of his Latin-French dictionary, they composed another dictionary, more cost- and time-effective, as well as more profitable.

Estienne himself never printed a new edition of his *Thesaurus*, for the same practical and economic reasons, but also for personal and intellectual ones. He was engaged in other projects, especially editions of Greek classics based on manuscripts from the Royal Library.[6] He was busy with his own defence against the attacks of the Sorbonne theologians, who had censored several passages of his bibles.[7] In 1543 and 1544 he brought out two issues of the *Dictionarium Latino gallicum* that were simple reprints of the first edition from 1538. A revised edition of this Latin-French dictionary appeared in 1546.[8] This was the last version to include textual revisions: later editions are all based on this text. Estienne's activity as a lexicographer and printer culminated with a second edition of the *Dictionaire Français Latin* in 1549, which is generally considered the cornerstone of French lexicography, and several later editions of his small vocabularies for children.[9] Even though the new edition of the *Thesaurus* was never completed, we can be sure that it was discussed in the Parisian workshop, and then again in Geneva where Estienne sought refuge in his later years.

---

6 For Estienne's activity as royal printer, see Elizabeth Armstrong, *Robert Estienne Royal Printer* (Appleford: Sutton Courtenay Press, 1986^2), and Martine Furno, 'Robert Estienne et les Pères de l'Eglise: quelques remarques sur l'édition d'Eusèbe de Césarée (1544)', in Aline Canellis (ed.), *L'Antiquité en ses confins. Mélanges offerts à Benoit Gain* (Grenoble: Ellug, 2008), pp. 85–94; also see Martine Furno, 'Robert I Estienne, imprimeur', in Boudou and Kecskeméti (eds.), *Robert et Charles Estienne*, pp. 21–26.

7 The long and painful procedure initiated against Estienne by the Sorbonne ended with the printer's exile to Geneva, where he wrote, in 1552, first in Latin then in French, his *Ad censuras theologorum parisiensium … responsio*, or *Les censures des théologiens de Paris … avec la réponse d'iceluy Robert Estienne*. See Hélène Cazes, 'L' intellectuel en procès: le cas Robert Estienne', *Renaissance et Réforme*, 24.4 (2000), pp. 95–114; Cazes, 'Robert Estienne et le «paradoxe de l'éditeur» dans Les Censures des Théologiens de Paris (Genève, 1552)', in M. Furno (ed.), *Qui ecrit?* (Lyon: ENS Editions, Institut d'Histoire du Livre, 2009), pp. 207–222; Cazes, 'Commenting on the hatred for Commentaries: Les Censures des Théologiens revised by Robert Estienne, 1552', in Judith Rice Henderson (ed.), *The Commentary in the XVIth century* (Toronto: University of Toronto Press, 2012), pp. 205–236, and M. Furno, '*L'Ad censuras theologorum parisiensium responsio* de Robert Estienne: un «dossier de textes» pour l'honneur d'une vie', in Christiane Deloince-Louette and Martine Furno (eds.), *Apta compositio, Formes du texte latin au Moyen Age et à la Renaissance* (Geneva: Droz, 2017), pp. 257–278.

8 USTC 41139.

9 The 1549 edition is to be identified with USTC 29527.

We are now in a position to document this complex history, and to take a glimpse into Estienne's workshop during the spring of 1543, while he was printing the *Thesaurus*, and again later, when he was still hoping to produce a revised edition. This is possible thanks an exceptional extant copy of Estienne's *Thesaurus*. Blickling Hall, a National Trust property in Norfolk, UK, holds, by inheritance, the book collection of Sir Richard Ellys (1682–1742). Ellys was an erudite scholar and collector who gathered many precious books, often with beautiful bindings, on a wide range of subjects.[10] This library is still in the process of being catalogued, which prevents us from making definitive statements on its character. However, browsing the records uploaded in the COPAC catalogue to-date, as well as the physical shelves in the library, we can suspect that Sir Richard Ellys, probably for personal religious reasons, had a particular interest in the printing of the sixteenth century, and for the production of Estienne's press. The collection contains several editions from the Estienne's catalogue, printed by both father and son.

The close friendship between Ellys and Michel Maittaire may have also led to the purchase of a substantial number of editions by the Estienne press.[11] Maittaire was a French Protestant who fled from France a few years before the Revocation of the Edict of Nantes in 1685, and then lived mostly in London until his death.[12] Recognized for his scholarship and his knowledge of the early handpress period, Maittaire was a collector of books as well as an author in his own right. Among his works were the extensive *Annales typographici*, an overview of the history of print from Gutenberg to the seventeenth century, and a most detailed *Stephanorum historia*, or history of the Estienne's press from Henri the first to Henri the third.[13] Maittaire probably helped and guided Ellys in buying

---

10 On Ellys's collection, see Giles Mandelbrote and Yvonne Lewis, *Learning to Collect: The Library of Sir Richard Ellys at Blickling Hall* (London: The National Trust, 2004).

11 It is not at this stage possible to provide a specific figure, as the cataloguing of the collection is in progress.

12 There has not yet been any comprehensive study on Michel Maittaire. Apart from an entry in the *Oxford Biographical Dictionary*, there is very little to be read about his scholarly activity. See Alice Stayert Brandenburg, 'English Education and the Neo-Classic Taste in the Eighteenth Century', *Modern Language Quarterly*, 8 (1947), pp. 174–193; F.J. Lelièvre, 'Maittaire and the Classics in eighteenth-century Britain', *Phoenix*, 10.3 (1956), pp. 103–115; Bettye Chambers, 'The first French New Testament printed in England?', *Bibliothèque d'Humanisme et Renaissance*, 39.1 (1977), pp. 143–148; G.B. Smith, 'An unknown translated panegyric poem of 1737: Michael Maittaire and Prince Antiokh Kantemir', *Slavonic and East European Review*, 45.2 (1977), pp. 161–171.

13 Michel Maittaire, *Annales typographici* (5 vols.; The Hague, Amsterdam and London, 1719–1741); *Stephanorum historia vitas ac libros complectens* (London: Bateman, 1709).

Estienne's imprints, and perhaps in providing him with a very important copy of the *Thesaurus Linguae Latinae*.

Ellys owned the working copy of the *Thesaurus*, which remained a work in progress for many years. Both Robert and Henri annotated the margins of almost every sheet in the Blickling Hall *Thesaurus Linguae Latinae*. This mass of almost 3,000 pages stands witness to the fact that the printer's job was always a rushed one. Reading the marginalia preserved here it is possible to trace the evolution of this volume in the intentions of the printer, from a set of proofs for a forthcoming edition, to a sort of note book, as the dream of re-editing the *Thesaurus* receded.

Form and Transmission of the Book

The Blickling copy of the *Thesaurus* is bound in four volumes, in a sixteenth or seventeenth century common binding, and printed on extra-large sheets. All volumes are thoroughly annotated, although the annotations are more frequent in the first and second volumes.[14] This copy, and arguably the first volume only, had been seen by Elisabeth Armstrong, who mentioned it in the second issue of her book *Robert Estienne Royal Printer*, and she easily identified Robert's neat handwriting.[15] I was also able to compare this hand with some notes in various documents still preserved today in Geneva and elsewhere.[16]

---

14 The four volumes are divided as follows: first volume, title page, forewords, and lemmas *A* to *Continenter* f. 394v; second volume: f. 395r (*Contentus*) to f. 816v (*K littera*); third volume: f. 817r (*Labasco*) to f. 1200v (*Pyxidâtus*); fourth volume: f. 1201r (Q) to f. 1544v (*Zythum*). Sheet dimensions: 460 mm × 375 mm.

15 It would seem that Armstrong only saw the first volume and not the entire copy. She gives account of having examined the volume (not "volumes") in Oxford, having this kindly been provided by Blickling Hall. It is also suspicious that she should neglect to mention the addition of three sheets, containing drafts in Estienne's own hand, which are found in the fourth volume.

16 See Armstrong, *Robert Estienne royal printer*, p. 290. According to this study, p. 341, only one autograph letter by Robert Estienne had survived until now, held in the Zürich Staatsarchiv. Other handwritten notes were documented by Armstrong: (1) in Geneva, found on Seneca, *Tragoediae* (Paris: Badius, 1514), USTC 144361; (2) in Paris, on a copy of Budaeus, *Commentarii linguae graecae* (Paris: Badius, [1529]), USTC 146015 (also see Luigi Alberto Sanchi, *Les* Commentaires de la langue Grecque *de Guillaume Budé* (Geneva: Droz, 2006), pp. 46–48); (3) in Oxford, on a copy of Lucian, *Dialogi* (Venice: Manuzio, 1503), USTC 762915. See Armstrong, *Robert Estienne royal printer*, pp. 272–273. To these items can be added a copy of *Scriptores rei rusticae* (Bologna: [Benedetto Faelli], 1504), USTC 801694, and of Columella, *Les douze livres des choses rusticques* (Paris: Kerver, 1551), USTC 29686, which I recently found at the Bibliothèque municipale in Lyon; and possibly a copy in

Armstrong noted it was probably a copy made in preparation for a new edition, and that it had remained in the family for a long time.

Obviously, the book was taken to Geneva, because it is marked on the first page with Henri's bookplate. This bookplate was pasted on the books he inherited from his father only after Robert's death in Geneva in 1559. Furthermore, notes in Henri's very recognizable hand can be read throughout the four volumes. How, when, why, and by whom the book was brought from Geneva to London, I cannot say precisely at the moment. It is possible that the book transited via Lyon, where Henri stayed many times before his death there in 1598. Perhaps he travelled with some books, or with precious material which could be sold. Although the travels of the volume are not altogether clear, it is possible to say that Philippe Tinghi, who printed a new, reduced and reworked version of the *Thesaurus Linguae Latinae* in Lyon in 1573, had seen the Blickling copy, as some precise details show us. Some instructions for the reordering of *lemmata*, handwritten in the Blickling copy, have actually been carried out in the 1573 version. One also finds a number of additions in the body of an article.[17]

Material evidence indicates that this copy remained for years in the family workshop. There is a first series of the handwritten notes by Robert, which can be dated from successive periods from before July 1543 to 1548 (possibly later), and a second strata of notes by both father and son. It is not yet possible to suggest a date for Henri's annotations, or to ascertain why he continued to use the book after his father's death. The 1740 edition of the *Thesaurus* curated by Anton Birr made use of autograph annotations by Henri, however these are not the ones found in the Blickling copy.[18] A second *Thesaurus*—a copy of the 1573 edition printed by Tinghi—was annotated by Henri. For a long time I had thought this copy lost, but I have recently succeeded in locating it at the Public Library in Geneva.[19] In this essay I shall concentrate my efforts on describing

---

Geneva of Robert's own Cicero's *Epistolae ad Atticum* (Paris: Estienne, 1543), USTC 140884, annotated to prepare the 1547 edition (USTC 195914).

17   For instance, in the *Thesaurus* printed by Tinghi in 1573 (USTC 141122), p. 216, lemma *appetitio*, the sentence *Hoc est ex triplici conatu apprehendendi Solem* and the whole paragraph *Appetitio et declinatio contraria* appear only in the margins of the Blickling copy (f. 148r), and are printed nowhere else: not in *addenda*, nor in other dictionaries such as the *Thesaurus* printed by Froben in 1561, nor in other versions of Estienne's bilingual dictionaries.

18   Robert Estienne, *Thesaurus Linguae Latinae in IV tomos divisus*, [...] *suasque passim animadversiones adjecit Antonius Birrius Philiater Basil.* (Basel: Thurnisios brothers, 1740). The introduction by Birr, ff. ****2r-*****v, indicates how the annotations in the copy used were identified as Estienne's, and the objective difficulty encountered in deciphering the marginalia.

19   The copy of Tinghi's *Thesaurus* is now held in Geneva, Bibliothèque de Genève, BGE Hb 392 Rés.

the Blickling copy, and how such an extraordinary book can help us to explain what the life of a printer, bookseller and scholar was like in a workshop like Robert's.

Scholar and/or Bookseller, a Never-Ending Dilemma

At the end of the 'regular' copies of the *Thesaurus*, Estienne put a list of addenda in a separate quire, and he introduced this list by a short text addressed 'to the reader' (*lectori*). Here he wrote that friends had brought him numerous suggestions and new quotations at the very time when the *Thesaurus* was already being printed, by which point he could not change anything in the typesetting.[20] So he had gathered some of the remarks and additions offered to him in these *addenda*, pending a future new edition in which he could insert them at their place.

These *addenda* show how Estienne was torn between his desire to provide precise and full documentation in his dictionary, and material necessity of the publisher and bookseller to place the book on the market as soon as possible. In the margins of Blickling copy, Estienne initially transcribed numerous notes we find printed in the *Addenda*. His neat humanist handwriting, reproducing for example the different sizes of the characters, could be defined as 'typographical'. But at one point, probably pressed for time, he abandoned the plan originally announced in his foreword to transcribe all the notes provided by friends and acquaintances to the margins of his working copy. Instead, he seems to have printed, perhaps directly from these *codices*, a first proof containing a selection of these *addenda*, on a single side, leaving the verso blank. He then cut this printed sheet in thin slices of paper, lemma by lemma, and pasted each of them at their places, in the margins of the book, just like post-it notes.

The next step was using a double-sided printed 'post-it note', and we can identify overall four strata among all the slips pasted in the four volumes. The stratification of these slips cannot, at the present, be assigned definite dates. After the single-sided printed proof of the *Addenda*, Estienne used others with both sides printed. However, the text has been composed again, as demonstrated by a difference of two lines between the two versions.[21] He also pasted

---

20   The distinct quire is signed KKKk8–OOOo8, without folio numbers. The text *Lectori* preceeds the list of *addenda*, on f. KKKk1r.
21   For example, on f. 859v in the Blickling copy, there is pasted a slice of paper cut in the text of the addenda to the lemma *Lumen*. The verso of this 'post-it note' is composed with a

in the margins of the Blickling copy a version with some *lemmata* in Roman characters and not in Gothic as in the final state, and of course he also used the final version as sold in his shop.[22]

All these elements are very suggestive: we can see the rush in the workshop, and difficulties that authors must regularly encounter in convincing printers and publishers to make textual changes. In the case of Estienne, being himself at the same time the scholar, the printer and the bookseller, the situation was probably even more painful.

After Printing: from the Working Copy to the Notebook

Initially, probably during a period of three or four years after the first edition of his dictionary, Estienne thought he could produce a new edition. Indeed he prepared one. We can see that special attention was paid in the marginal notes to the order of the *lemmata*. Estienne gave very precise typographical instructions, with signs repeated from a column or page to another, to move a whole article or part of one to another place (see Figures 10.1 and 10.2).[23] All these typographical instructions are in French, a detail that suggests caution in accepting Henri Estienne's own later recollection of the linguistic proficiency of his workshop. For example, in the foreword of his edition of Aulus Gellius in 1585, Henri stated that the entire family, in the sense of the Latin word *familia*, and even the entire workshop, spoke Latin during his childhood.[24] We may be inclined to accept the claim that he and his brother spoke in Latin to their father, and in French to their mother as he told us. It is reasonable to believe that, in certain circumstances, scholars with different native languages meet-

---

two lines gap between this version and the 'regular' one: in the Blickling copy version, the lemma *Maiestas* on verso is directly opposite to the third line of the *Lumen* text on recto, although in the final version (fol. MMMm3r) it is opposite to the first line of the same text.

[22] These 'post it notes' with *lemmata* in roman character appear in the fourth volume for *lemmata* beginning with T. They are found from f. 1432r, for the *addendum Thymion*, to f. 1456r, *addendum Triumphus*. Estienne used Gothic characters for the *lemmata* in the *Thesaurus* from f. 817r (letter L) to the end of the dictionary, probably because he didn't have enough Roman characters in his case to end the whole list of *lemmata* as he began it.

[23] Estienne generally used phrases such as 'Mettez ceci en la page/colonne sequente / suyvante / precedente' ou 'Prenez ceci a la page suyvante / precedente a tel signe'. See figures 10.1 and 10.2, f. 621r and 622r.

[24] Aulus Gellius, *Noctes Atticae* (Paris: Henri Estienne, 1585), USTC 172277. See the foreword in Judith Kecskeméti, Benedicte Boudou, Hélène Cazes and Jean Céard (eds.), *Henri II Estienne éditeur et écrivain* (Turnhout: Brepols, 2003), pp. 533–534.

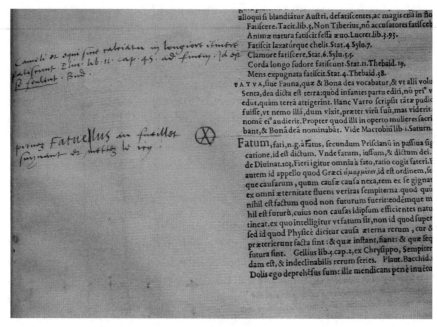

FIGURE 10.1   Robert Estienne, *Thesaurus Linguae Latinae* (Paris: Robert Estienne, 1543), Blickling Hall, f. 621r
REPRODUCED WITH THE AUTHORIZATION OF THE NATIONAL TRUST OF ENGLAND, BLICKLING ESTATE

ing in the workshop could engage in exchanges on erudite matters in Latin. However, the idea that the printer might have communicated in Latin with his workers on the press is less credible, and more likely to be an ideal reconstruction of Henri's boyhood, compiled many years later.

Estienne wanted even the smallest details to be rectified, and we can see in the Blickling copy how much care he took for the scientific and typographical correctness of his work. At times, he wished to modify the order of the examples proposed in the dictionary entries, for example following the alphabetical order by the first letter of a phrase or sentence. He enforced the correction by apposing letters of the Latin alphabet (a, b, c …) in the margins, according to the order he now wished to adopt. For instance, on f. 177r (Figure 10.3), the phrases containing the adjective *assiduus*, which did not seem to be in any particular order, are reorganised alphabetically. This is to be done following the first letters of the noun accompanying *assiduus*, and this new order is shown by the letters a (for *cantu*), b (for *febricula*), c (*fletu*), d (*frigore*), e (*fructibus*), f (*igne*), g (*labor*), h (*motu*), n (*noctes*), o (*operam*), p (*recordatione*), q (*venatu*), r (*ver*), s (*vertigine*). Estienne also rectified typographical errors, sometimes insignificant ones, such as adding or deleting commas, changing upper case letters into

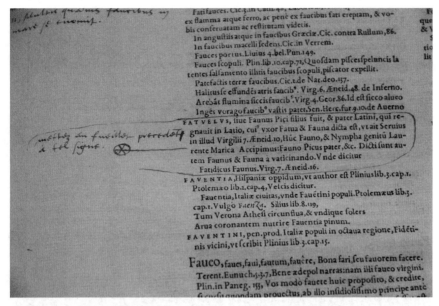

FIGURE 10.2   Robert Estienne, *Thesaurus Linguae Latinae* (Paris: Robert Estienne, 1543), Blickling Hall, f. 622r
REPRODUCED WITH THE AUTHORIZATION OF THE NATIONAL TRUST OF ENGLAND, BLICKLING ESTATE

lower case, adding accents, specifying the length of the vowels by expression such *pen. corr* (*penultima correpta*), or *pen. prod.* (*penultima producta*), or specifying the gender of certain words, as *f. g.*, (*feminino genere*) for *Palus* (f. 1031v), *m. g.* (*masculino genere*) for *Penis* (f. 1062r) or *n. g.* (*neutro genere*) for *Oxymeli* (f. 1026r).

It would appear that Estienne aspired to provide a comprehensive and serviceable work of reference for classical studies, from the linguistic tools to the original texts. Various classical quotations inserted in the margins, often with reference to the page number in his own editions, corroborate this hypothesis. For example, on f. 192v in the Blickling copy, in the margin next to the entry *Augustus*, Estienne added a quotation from the *Romanarum historiarum libri* of Dion, with the reference 'p. 344', which is the precise location for the quoted passage in his own edition, printed in 1548. This is therefore also a valuable way for us to date some of these handwritten notes following the *terminus post quem* of the editions in question.

But as the years went by, the project for a new edition of the *Thesaurus* appeared more and more difficult. The reasons for this are to be found both in changes of scholarly practices, and the difficulties Estienne experienced due to the censorship by the Sorbonne, which compelled him to absent himself from

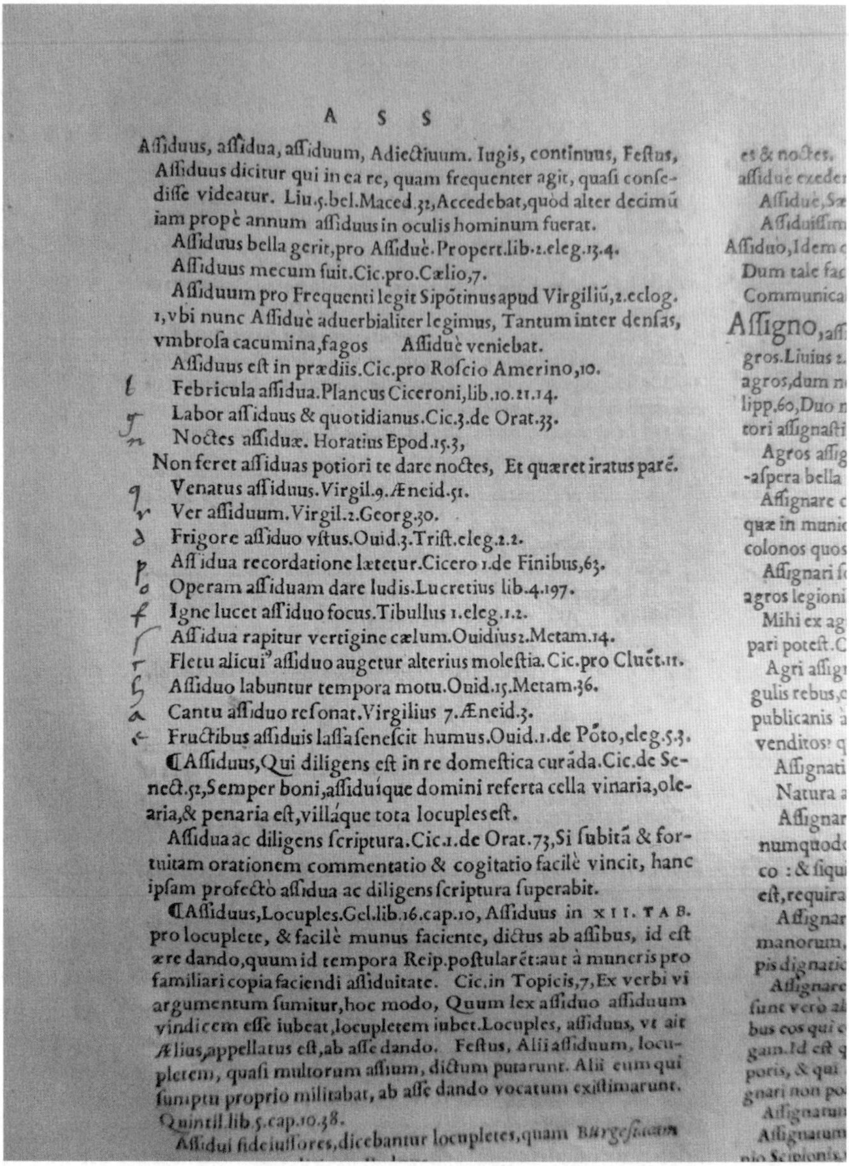

A S S

Aſſiduus, aſſidua, aſſiduum, Adiectiuum. Iugis, continuus, Feſtus, Aſſiduus dicitur qui in ea re, quam frequenter agit, quaſi conſediſſe videatur. Liu.5.bel.Maced.32,Accedebat,quòd alter decimú iam propè annum aſſiduus in oculis hominum fuerat.

Aſſiduus bella gerit,pro Aſſiduè.Propert.lib.2.eleg.13.4.

Aſſiduus mecum fuit.Cic.pro.Cælio,7.

Aſſiduum pro Frequenti legit Sipótinus apud Virgiliú,1.eclog. 1,vbi nunc Aſſiduè aduerbialiter legimus, Tantum inter denſas, vmbroſa cacumina,fagos   Aſſiduè veniebat.

Aſſiduus eſt in prædiis.Cic.pro Roſcio Amerino,10.

Febricula aſſidua.Plancus Ciceroni,lib.10.11.14.

Labor aſſiduus & quotidianus.Cic.3.de Orat.33.

Noctes aſſiduæ. Horatius Epod.15.3,

Non feret aſſiduas potiori te dare noctes, Et quæret iratus paré.

Venatus aſſiduus.Virgil.9.Æneid.51.

Ver aſſiduum.Virgil.2.Georg.30.

Frigore aſſiduo vſtus.Ouid.3.Triſt.eleg.2.2.

Aſſidua recordatione lætetur.Cicero 1.de Finibus,63.

Operam aſſiduam dare ludis.Lucretius lib.4.197.

Igne lucet aſſiduo focus.Tibullus 1.eleg.1.2.

Aſſidua rapitur vertigine cælum.Ouidius 2.Metam.14.

Fletu alicui' aſſiduo augetur alterius moleſtia.Cic.pro Cluét.11.

Aſſiduo labuntur tempora motu.Ouid.15.Metam.36.

Cantu aſſiduo reſonat.Virgilius 7.Æneid.3.

Fructibus aſſiduis laſſa ſeneſcit humus.Ouid.1.de Póto,eleg.5.3.

¶ Aſſiduus,Qui diligens eſt in re domeſtica curada.Cic.de Senect.52,Semper boni,aſſiduíque domini referta cella vinaria,olearia,& penaria eſt,villaque tota locuples eſt.

Aſſidua ac diligens ſcriptura.Cic.1.de Orat.73,Si ſubita & fortuitam orationem commentatio & cogitatio facilè vincit, hanc ipſam profectò aſſidua ac diligens ſcriptura ſuperabit.

¶ Aſſiduus,Locuples.Gel.lib.16.cap.10, Aſſiduus in x i i. t a b. pro locuplete, & facilè munus faciente, dictus ab aſſibus, id eſt ære dando,quum id tempora Reip.poſtularet:aut à muneris pro familiari copia faciendi aſſiduitate. Cic.in Topicis,7,Ex verbi vi argumentum ſumitur,hoc modo, Quum lex aſſiduo aſſiduum vindicem eſſe iubeat,locupletem iubet.Locuples, aſſiduus, vt ait Ælius,appellatus eſt,ab aſſe dando. Feſtus, Alii aſſiduum, locupletem, quaſi multorum aſſium, dictum putarunt. Alii eum qui ſumptu proprio militabat, ab aſſe dando vocatum exiſtimarunt.

Quintil.lib.5.cap.10.38.

Aſſidui fideiuſſores,dicebantur locupletes,quam *Burgeſiuum*

FIGURE 10.3   Robert Estienne, *Thesaurus Linguae Latinae* (Paris: Robert Estienne, 1543), Blickling Hall, f. 177r
REPRODUCED WITH THE AUTHORIZATION OF THE NATIONAL TRUST OF ENGLAND, BLICKLING ESTATE

his house and workshop for weeks, following the court and the King.[25] Eventually, the project for a new edition of his *Thesaurus* became impossible. It was a high risk for the press: current owners of the previous version would find it difficult to justify the purchase of a new and augmented edition when it was such an expensive book. The book was not suitable for prospective new purchasers, either, as study practices were by now requiring bilingual tools in teaching and learning Latin. That explains why, as time went by, the Blickling copy was no longer a real proof copy for Estienne, but rather something he kept on his desk and used for other projects.

One of these, soon after 1543, was a new edition of the Latin-French dictionary, which was printed in 1546. In this issue, we can find new entries, more translations into French, and more quotations, even though these are reduced to a simple phrase with the name of the author, rather than the whole text and reference as we find in the *Thesaurus*. These additions were prepared in the Blickling copy, often on the 'post-it notes' cut from the addenda which Estienne pasted in the margins. For example, on f. 482r in the Blickling copy, we find a 'post-it note' that served to expand the entry *differentia* between the 1544 and the 1546 versions of the Latin-French dictionary. The note contains a quotation from Pliny the Elder (21, 23: *odor colorque duplex, alius calicis, alius staminis, differentia angusta*) where the phrase *differentia angusta* is underlined, and a French translation, *Petite difference*, is handwritten at the end of the note (Figure 10.4). The entry *differentia* in the 1544 edition was a very short one: *Differentia, huius differentiae, difference.*[26] But the 1546 edition reads:

Differentia, huius differentiae, Cic. Difference
Differentia angusta, Plin. Petite Difference
Magna differentia. Plin.
Differentia and dissimilitudo Cic.

We can see that the first example from Pliny, with the translation *Petite difference*, is exactly what Estienne underlined and added in the note. The method is always the same, and everywhere we can find on a 'post it note' an underlined lemma and, at the end of the text, a handwritten French translation, it

---

25 See Robert Estienne, *Ad censuras theologorum parisiensium responsio* ([Geneva]: Robert Estienne, 1552), USTC 450398, p. 10, or *Les censures des Theologiens de Paris … traduictes de latin en français* ([Geneva]: Robert Estienne, 1552), USTC 85, f. 6v.
26 Robert Estienne, *Dictionarium Latino Gallicum* (Paris: Robert Estienne, 1543), USTC 65713, p. 212.

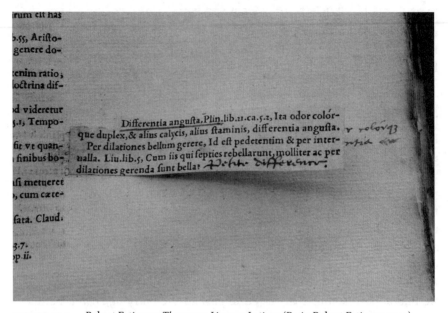

FIGURE 10.4   Robert Estienne, *Thesaurus Linguae Latinae* (Paris: Robert Estienne, 1543), Blickling Hall, f. 482r
REPRODUCED WITH THE AUTHORIZATION OF THE NATIONAL TRUST OF ENGLAND, BLICKLING ESTATE

makes us certain this note has been prepared between 1544 and 1546 for the Latin-French dictionary.

After this date, there were no new editions of this dictionary, nor of the smaller school dictionaries Estienne had printed by further reducing again the bilingual tools he had already drawn from the *Thesaurus*. But the life of the Blickling copy continued, probably on the desk of the printer, in Paris and in Geneva. Although Estienne was at this time unable to further his projects as a lexicographer, this did not prevent him from continuing to read and print the classics himself, looking out for new texts on Classical Antiquity or on encyclopaedic matters in Latin. His personal copy of the *Thesaurus* was by then used to store remarks, quotations, phrases, as a reminder to himself, for all sorts of erudite work.

From Dream to Nightmare: the *Calepinus* Printed in Geneva, 1553

Although we are unable to pin down a specific point in time, we know that Robert Estienne travelled to Italy around 1553. This is revealed by Robert's signature, detailing his location "Ex Vrbe", which ends the foreword of the Calepinus dictionary he printed in Geneva that year.²⁷ A passage of Henri Estienne's *Epistola de suae typographiae statu* (1569) tells us that during his Italian journey Robert saw in Venice plagiarised versions of his work, organised in alphabetical order and entitled *Calepini Dictionarium*.²⁸ As a reply to this larceny, Estienne decided to print his own *Calepini Dictionarium*, a name which had become a sort of trademark at that time, in which he organized the material by alphabetical order. In this new dictionary he developed explanations and definitions, but also drastically reduced the number of entries, quotations and references. Curiously, he states on the title page that this dictionary was 'augmented from the fourth and last *Thesaurus* of Robert Estienne', a phrase I could not clearly comprehend until I saw the Blickling copy.²⁹

Indeed, if we consider all the lexicographical works of Estienne, we can identify three *Thesauri*, in 1531, 1536 and 1543, but not a fourth one, unless we consider the Blickling copy as the fourth, unborn one, of which we can find slight traces in the *Calepinus* of 1553. Very few of the accumulated notes in the Blickling copy can be found in this last and bitter lexicographical work of Estienne: bitter because it is amounted to a defeat in the organization of the material, and because it was very far from the dream of a new edition of the erudite *Thesaurus* of 1543. The marginal notes Estienne had accumulated over ten years in the Blickling copy for a possible fourth *Thesaurus* are not widely used in the *Calepinus*, probably because they are too precise or erudite. This is a cruel turn of fate: the entries of the last *Calepinus* mainly contain the material of the 'old' *Thesaurus*, and only a few elements of the unpublished version. For example, some Greek words in a margin of the Blickling copy were introduced into their corresponding place in the *Calepinus*, as were some personal comments or opinions on a particular word or form.³⁰ This new dictionary is not only an answer to plagiarism. It is also considering and planning a strategy for buying and selling,

---

27 On the Calepinus printed in 1553 in Geneva, see Martine Furno, 'Le mariage de Calepin et du *Thesaurus Linguae Latinae*, sous l'Olivier de Robert Estienne, à Genève, en 1553', *Bibliothèque d'Humanisme et Renaissance*, 63.3 (2001), pp. 511–532.

28 Henri Estienne, *Epistola de suae typographiae statu* ([Geneva]: Robert Estienne, 1569), USTC 450587, p. 15; also see *Henri II Estienne éditeur et écrivain*, p. 247. The same story is told again by Henri in the foreword of the *Thesaurus Linguae Graecae* in 1573; see *Henri II Estienne éditeur et écrivain*, p. 308.

29 The transcription of the title page reads as follows: AMBROSII CALEPINI || Dictionarium, quarto & postremo ex || R. Stephani Latinae linguae Thesauro || auctum. || [printer's device] || OLIVA ROB. STEPHANI. || M. D. LIII.

30 For Greek words introduced in the *Calepinus*, see f. 9r, lemma *Acceptus*, phrase *acceptum ferre*: the three Greek verbs which are a translation of the phrase are in a handwritten note in the Blickling copy, f. 21v. And also *Calepinus* f. 236v, lemma *friuiculus*: the disposition of the entry reflects the advice in the margin of f. 657r in the Blickling copy, and intro-

through which Estienne tried to maintain a balance between economic constraints (the new product must be marketable) and scientific requirements, at least so as not to betray the erudite reputation of the press. The *Calepinus* was a different book and a different project entirely; though something of the Blickling copy remained in it, we can suppose it was not as Estienne had dreamt of it ten years earlier.

The Blickling copy of the *Thesaurus* allows us to enter both the library of the erudite scholar, and the workshop of the printer. However, the dreams of the scholar can be counteracted by the harsh realities of buying and selling, when the press business can no longer afford an expensive or hazardous edition, and the nightmare of plagiarism compels the scholar and printer to design a new product which is not entirely compliant with his wishes. We have here a very precious source to study, and which will allow us to understand more precisely the mechanisms of production of erudite books, not only in their intellectual aspects, but also in their commercial ones: two sides of the same activity, which could not find a perfect accomplishment one without the other.

---

duces into the text the personal comment "Quo tamen in loco malim legere frigusculum ..." handwritten in the margin.

CHAPTER 11

'Large Volumes Bought by the Few': Printing and Selling Postils in Early Modern Poland

Magdalena Komorowska

The postil, a collection of sermons for Sundays and feast days throughout the year, was not invented during the Reformation. Nor was preaching in German, or, more generally, in the vernacular languages. However, the publication of Luther's postils in print in the 1520s, first in Latin and then in German translation, marked a milestone in the history of the genre, not only in the German-speaking region. Luther's sermons were swiftly followed by printed collections in both German and Latin written by various authors. By 1620, Luther's postils alone were printed in a hundred and thirty editions in the Holy Roman Empire. The overall number of postils published in the German-speaking lands in the same period exceeded four hundred editions. In his book on early modern postils published in the Holy Roman Empire, John Frymire admits that he was surprised to realise that almost half of these editions were of Catholic postils. In his detailed study, he rectified the hitherto prevailing belief that preaching the gospel, both from pulpits and in print, was cultivated mainly in Lutheran churches, with Catholics lingering far behind. The proportion appeared to be far more balanced than previously believed. It is precisely this shared use of the postil as a pastoral and polemical tool by both Protestants and Catholics that justifies Frymire's conviction of the 'primacy of postils' in the first century of the Reformation.[1]

The discussion of postils published in the Polish-Lithuanian Commonwealth, to this point very much understudied, benefits from understanding this historical context. Needless to say, postils published in Poland-Lithuania, both in Latin and in Polish, were not nearly as numerous as their counterparts printed in the German-speaking region. However, general assumptions regarding Polish postils and, more generally, preaching in the early modern era have been similarly one-sided. Available studies mostly investigate Protestant publications, neglecting Catholic authors almost entirely. This results in distorting the role played by postils in inter-confessional exchanges and also in

---

1 See John M. Frymire, *Primacy of the Postils* (Leiden: Brill, 2009), pp. 2–4; 546–560 (App. 4.a.10, 4.b).

Counter-Reformation cultural change in Poland-Lithuania. These studies also foster the misleading conviction that Polish postils as a genre should be associated mainly with Protestant churches, which is as misleading as the beliefs refuted by Frymire.[2]

Little is known about the printing of postils in Poland in the first half of the sixteenth century. There are just two surviving editions of a relatively short Catholic postil in Latin.[3] A third is documented, but did not survive.[4] None of them were written by Polish authors. The genre became more popular only after the first postils in Polish were published in the mid-1550s in Królewiec in Prussia and in Krakow. The editions of postils published in the following twenty years were written by members of Protestant churches, either Lutherans or Calvinists. Catholics were initially more reluctant to write about matters of faith in the vernacular. The pattern changed completely from the early 1570s, as a number of Catholic postils were composed. Research in specialist bibliographies and rare book holdings has yielded 43 editions of 26 Polish postils printed between the mid-1550s and the end of the following century (Table 11.1).[5] By the end of the sixteenth century, ten titles (six Protestant and four Catholic) had been published in 21 editions (twelve Protestant and nine Catholic). However, this quantitative balance is misleading. Protestant authors were far more active up until 1572; after 1573, when the first Catholic postil by the Jesuit Jakub Wujek

---

2   The only available synthesis by Kazimierz Kolbuszewski, *Postyllografia polska XVI i XVII wieku* (Krakow: Polska Akademia Umiejętności, 1921) is incomplete. The author included only works that had the word 'postil' in the title and thus neglected a number of important Catholic collections. Protestant postils were excellently written about by Janusz T. Maciuszko, *Ewangelicka postyllografia polska XVI–XVIII wieku. Charakterystyka—analiza porównawcza—recepcja* (Warsaw: Akademia Teologii Katolickiej, 1987).

3   Guillermo de Paris, *Postilla super Epistolas et Evangelia* (Krakow: Mikołaj Scharffenberg, 1532), USTC 240942, and (Krakow: Mikołaj Scharffenberg, 1541), USTC 241246.

4   There is a record of a lost edition of a postil by Georg Witzel (1501–1573) in an inventory compiled after the death of Helena Unglerowa in 1551. See Artur Benis (ed.), *Materiały do historii drukarstwa i księgarstwa w Polsce* (Krakow: Polska Akademia Umiejętności, 1890), part I, no. 1343. Unfortunately, it is impossible to say which one of Witzel's postils was published in Poland. It was most probably an illustrated Latin edition. See Benis, *Materiały do historii drukarstwa*, no. 1358 and Frymire, *Primacy*, pp. 107–125.

5   By 'editions' I mean a complete set of parts for the whole liturgical year. Postils were usually divided into three parts. The first, called the 'winter' part ('pars hyemalis'), contained sermons for Sundays and feasts from Advent to the Pentecost; the second or 'summer' part ('pars aestivalis'), for Sundays and feasts from Holy Trinity Sunday to the end of the liturgical year. The third part, sometimes further divided, was devoted to the saints ('de sanctis'). Depending on the number of sermons (at least ninety-six, but a single Sunday or feast could have more than one sermon) and their length, parts of one postil might be bound together in one volume or separately in multiple volumes.

TABLE 11.1 Polish vernacular postils published in the years 1556–1700

	1551–1560	1561–1570	1571–1580	1581–1590	1591–1600
Protestant	4	1	3	1	3
Catholic			2	4	3
New titles P	4		1	1	1
New titles C			2	1	1

	1601–1610	1611–1620	1621–1630	1631–1640	1641–1650
Protestant		2			1
Catholic	3	3	2		1
New titles P		2			1
New titles C		1	1		1

	1651–1660	1661–1670	1671–1680	1681–1690	1691–1700
Protestant		1			
Catholic	3	1	2	3	1
New titles P					
New titles C	3	1	2	3	1

(1541–1597) was published, the Catholics became the more prolific. The number and frequency of Protestant postils published fell steadily. From the beginning of the seventeenth century until 1628, six titles were published in ten editions. Two of these were new Protestant postils in single editions. The remaining eight were Catholic postils—two new collections and six new editions of earlier titles. After a fifteen-year break between 1629 and 1644, a single Catholic edition was printed in the late 1640s. Four new Protestant postils appeared between 1650 and 1655, at the time of the Swedish invasion. Six Catholic editions appeared in the second half of the seventeenth century; five of these were new titles. In the same period only one Protestant edition appeared, a translation of Luther's *Hauspostille*.

Aside from their theological and cultural importance, Polish postils from the sixteenth and seventeenth centuries also provide interesting material for the history of the book in Poland. Firstly, they constitute one of the largest groups of surviving Old Polish publications, irrespective of genre. Secondly, the similarities in the structure (a usual postil for Sundays and feast days is a set of at least a hundred sermons, usually preceded by evangelical lections) and target audience of these publications offers the rare chance to compare the solutions (in terms of format, layout, illustrations, title-page composition, etc.) chosen by different printers. Thirdly, publication of postils involved religious groups—for example, the Jesuits or Protestant communities—and therefore left some trace in archives, which is extremely rare in the history of Polish printing. For these reasons, printed Polish postils offer a precious opportunity to look at the development and evolution of their physical form as printed books.

This essay focuses on selected vernacular postils published in the Polish-Lithuanian Commonwealth in the sixteenth and seventeenth centuries as physical objects, commodities intended for sale. Only four editions of the postils published in Poland-Lithuania were published in Latin. Two of these, mentioned above, were based on a medieval postil by Guillelmus Parisiensis; the third was compiled by Stanisław Grodzicki (started in Krakow in 1607, later completed in Ingolstadt); the last was a translation of sermons by Piotr Skarga (1536–1612) published in 1690s.[6] They do not constitute a coherent group and their influence was much more limited than that of vernacular postils. Therefore they will be mentioned only briefly for contrast.[7]

The Form of the Book and Its Commercial Function

One aspect of the postils in particular is worth closer attention: the commercial function of publishers' peritexts. Gérard Genette's theory of paratexts, that is elements that do not belong to the main text of the book but constitute a frame which at the same time helps the text become a book, can be useful not only for literary interpretations or for the reconstruction of how the meaning was made. A group of paratexts called publisher's or printer's peritexts—format, paper, title page, some elements of front- and back-matter material and, last but not least, typography—defines the form of a book as a physical

---

[6] Stanisław Grodzicki, *Quadripartitae conciones ... Quarum primae, Timorem sanctum incutiunt: secundae Fidem Catholicam confirmant: tertiae Spem erigunt: postremae divinam in nobis Charitatem excitant*, eight tomes (tome 1: Krakow, Mikołaj Lob, 1607; tomes 2–8: Ingolstadt, Andread Angermarius, 1609–1614); Piotr Skarga, *Conciones pro diebus dominicis et festis totius anni ... nunc vero in latinum idioma translatae ... a Joanne Odrowąż Pieniążek ...* (Krakow: Typographia Academica, 1691).

[7] The article draws from the research conducted in the years 2013–2014 in Polish libraries and that has been the basis for a more comprehensive study of Polish printed postils: Magdalena Komorowska, 'Kształt edytorski postylli polskich XVI i XVII wieku—w poszukiwaniu staropolskich konwencji wydawniczych', *Terminus*, 2 (2015), pp. 317–367.

object.⁸ From the author's and the reader's point of view, the form of a book serves mainly as a medium, a means of communication, and publisher's peritexts help shape this communication. For the publisher (or, in the context of early modern Poland, printer) peritexts also have a commercial aspect. This applies not only to title-pages, prefatory materials or indices, but also typography, for it is also the physical form itself that sells the book.

Certain formal solutions regarding paper, format or type-face are applied to certain types of publications.⁹ This also pertains to early modern postils. In the German-speaking area, vernacular postils, both Protestant and Catholic, appeared in a variety of formats and layouts. There were folio editions illustrated with woodcuts, as well as quartos and octavos, both with illustrations and without. The form of the book usually depended on the character of the published work: popular postils by Anton Corvin, Johann Spangenberg or Georg Nass, for instance, were printed *in octavo* with simple illustrations.¹⁰ The more learned postils by Johannes Eck were often printed in folio, and Luther's bestselling collections, which could be considered a class of their own, were initially available in a variety of formats and layouts.¹¹ This diversity was not repeated on the Polish market.

The Polish postil was from the start a deluxe item, despite the fact that for small Polish workshops (most print shops in this period had just one or two small presses) a lengthy work such as a folio volume of an illustrated postil could pose a considerable challenge. On the one hand, money had to be invested. On the other hand, the whole printing process was time-consuming, and from surviving sources it is clear that it took Polish printers about a year to a year and a half to prepare the average postil for distribution.¹² In the second

---

8   See Gérard Genette, *Paratexts: Thresholds of Interpretation*, trans. Jane E. Lewin (Cambridge: Cambridge University Press, 1997), pp. 1–2, 16–36. On a commercial and many other functions of Renaissance paratexts see for instance Helen Smith and Louise Wilson (eds.), *Renaissance Paratexts* (Cambridge: Cambridge University Press, 2011), *passim*.

9   See Arthur F. Marotti, *Manuscript, Print, and the English Renaissance Lyric* (Ithaca and London: Cornell University Press, 1995), pp. 288–290, with further references.

10 See for instance the postil by Johann Spangenberg, which in 1571 was printed in Erfurt as a set of volumes in octavo, in 1582 in Nuremberg as a single folio volume: J. Spangenberg, *Postilla, Das ist Außlegung der Episteln und Evangelien* (Nuremberg: Leonhard Heußler, 1582), USTC 685261; J. Spangenberg, *Postilla vom Advent bis Ostern* (Erfurt: Konrad Dreher, 1571), USTC 685321 [accessed digitally via BSB Munich].

11 See Frymire, *Primacy*, pp. 202–203.

12 See the documentation of the printing of a folio volume in the university press in Zamość in the 1590s in Alodia Kawecka-Gryczowa, *Z dziejów polskiej książki w okresie renesansu. Studia i materiały* (Wrocław: Ossolineum, 1975), pp. 305–309. See also Jakub Wujek's letters to Francisco Borgia, 17 September 1571, and to Jerome Nadal, 6 October 1572, in Jan Sygań-

half of the century, when the first Polish postils appeared, they introduced the genre to a new language and the new multi-confessional reality, thus giving it new, not only pastoral but also polemical, functions. Printers had to learn how such a work should be published.

Out of the many different formats and layouts, the publishers and printers of the first Polish postils chose probably the most attractive model: designs found in some of Martin Luther's postils printed in the Holy Roman Empire.[13] This choice is not surprising, given the Protestant provenance of the first Polish collections. Common features of designs based on Luther's *Hauspostille* are: (1) folio format, (2) Gothic type; (3) text typeset in one column; (4) evangelical lections typeset in larger type than sermons (the different size of type was used to visually differentiate the Word of God from the words of man); (5) woodcut illustrations, one for each Sunday and each feast day, filling the full width of the column. Taken together, the illustrations formed a consistent series of scenes from the New Testament and they appeared according to the order of pericopes, or daily readings from the gospel, in the liturgical year; the order of pericopes was the same for the Catholic and Protestant churches at this time. The design itself is important, because it determined the way Polish postils were published for almost fifty years.

According to John Frymire, the folio format of most of German postils published in the Holy Roman Empire implies that they were intended for pulpit reading. This, however, cannot be said about Polish collections of the kind. Of course, some Protestant postils as well as sermons by Piotr Skarga and Wujek's 'smaller postil' were intended for such usage. Indeed, each of Skarga's sermons could be read out loud in about an hour and Catholic priests were encouraged to do so.[14] But more learned works—for example 'bigger postil' by Wujek, *Postilla orthodoxa* by Marcin Białobrzeski or works by Grzegorz of Żarnowiec and Krzysztof Kraiński[15]—contained sermons too long and too complicated to be

---

ski (ed.), 'Korespondencja ks. Jakuba Wujka z Wągrowca z lat 1569–1596', part 1, *Roczniki Towarzystwa Przyjaciół Nauk Poznańskiego* 1919:44, pp. 195–359, 317, 334.

13   See for instance Martin Luther, *Haußpostil D. Martin Luthers* (Nuremberg: Johannes vom Berg and Ulrich Nueber, 1549), USTC 661770.

14   See the instructions for preachers issued for the first time in 1603 by the bishop of Krakow Bernard Maciejowski and reedited many times in the seventeenth century, for example in *Epistola pastoralis bonae memoriae illustrissimi cardinalis Maciejowski* (Posnan: Wojciech Regulus, 1640), ff. C1v–C3r. In the foreword to his collection of topical sermons Piotr Skarga named "clergymen and provosts" ("duchownych i plebanów") as the target audience of the book. Piotr Skarga, *Kazania o siedmi sakramentach*, f.)(5r. It is also known that Skarga usually spoke for one hour and timed his sermons; see for instance Piotr Skarga, *Areopagus* (Krakow: Andrzej Piotrkowczyk, 1612), ending of the third sermon.

15   Marcin Białobrzeski, *Postilla orthodoxa* (Krakow: Jan Januszowski, 1581), USTC 242378;

read out loud during a mass or a service. They were probably printed as folios because of the length of the text itself. The conventional character of the Polish postils' typography is also confirmed by the size of typefaces adopted through different formats. Folio editions use type of exactly the same size as many contemporary quartos and octavos. This indicates that the larger format of a postil did not necessarily guarantee the improved legibility of a text.[16]

Rej and Wujek: Content-Related Conflict and Form-Related Consent

The most influential of the early Polish postils was written by a nobleman, Mikołaj Rej (1505–1569), and printed for the first time in Krakow by Maciej Wirzbięta in 1557.[17] It was re-edited three times over the next sixteen years. The work, which in subsequent editions evolved from a mildly Protestant text to one of the first Calvinist postils, was very popular not only among Polish Calvinists and Lutherans, but also with the Catholic clergy. The book combined interesting content with an attractive design that brings to mind editions of Luther's *Hauspostille* printed in Nuremberg in the 1540s and 1550s (Figure 11.1).[18] Of course, the translation of *Hauspostille* by Hieronim Malecki published in Królewiec in 1573 was also based on a German design (Figure 11.2).[19]

The first Catholic postil in Polish, by the Jesuit Jakub Wujek, who is otherwise known for his translation of the Bible, was written and published in 1573 with the purpose of supplanting Rej's postil. Both author and printer failed to meet this objective, however. First of all, the text was too learned and too long; secondly, the book itself, presumably planned as an attractive publication, is far from typographically perfect. The printer did not copy any of the earlier designs in detail, though he did use larger type for the pericopes and a smaller one for the sermons. He also included illustrations for each pericope, but instead of

---

Grzegorz of Żarnowiec, *Postylla* (Krakow: Maciej Wirzbięta, 1557), USTC 240302; Krzysztof Kraiński, *Postylla Kościoła Powszechnego Apostolskiego słowem Bożym ugruntowanego* (Łaszczów–Raków: Sebastian Sternacki, 1611–1617).

16 The most popular *schwabacher* typeface used for typesetting of the main text in most of the books printed in Krakow in the sixteenth and seventeenth century, regardless of their format, measures ca. 89 mm for 20 lines.

17 Mikołaj Rej, *Świętych słów a spraw Pańskich, które tu sprawował Pan a Zbawiciel nasz (...) kronika albo Postylla* (Krakow: Maciej Wirzbięta, 1557), USTC 241661.

18 See note 11 above.

19 Martin Luther, *Postylla domowa*, trans. Hieronim Malecki (Królewiec: Dziedzice Jana Daubmanna, 1573).

FIGURE 11.1A–B Title pages of Martin Luther, *Haußpostil*, Nürnberg 1549 and Mikołaj Rej, *Świętych słów a spraw Pańskich, które tu sprawował Pan a Zbawiciel nasz (…) kronika albo Postylla*, Krakow 1557
BAYERISCHE STAATSBIBLIOTHEK MÜNCHEN, 889210 2 HOM. 283, URN=URN:NBN:DE:BVB:12-BSB10144042-5 (LEFT); BIBLIOTEKA JAGIELLOŃSKA, KRAKOW, CIM.F.8295 (RIGHT)

purchasing a full series of woodcuts, he recycled existing woodblocks, of different style and size, and taken from different series. These were often not fit for purpose (Figure 11.3).

One mitigating circumstance for Wujek's printer is the fact that he did not receive the whole postil at once. Wujek had the winter part (from Advent to Pentecost) ready and was keen to see it published as soon as possible, because of the eagerness of 'many pious people'.[20] The summer part (from Holy Trinity to the end of the year) was only submitted to the print shop a few months later. After another six months, when the printing of the second part was almost finished, the printer received parts three and four, for feast days. When the first

---

20 See the printer's note in Jakub Wujek, *Postylla katolicka większa*, part 2 (Krakow: Mateusz

FIGURE 11.2A–B   Title pages of Martin Luther, Hauspostil, Wittenberg 1552 and the Polish translation of this work by Hieronim Malecki, *Postylla domowa*, Królewiec 1556
BAYERISCHE STAATSBIBLIOTHEK MÜNCHEN, SIGN. 889211 2 HOM. 284, URN=URN:NBN:DE:BVB:12-BSB10144043-1 (LEFT); ZAKŁAD NARODOWY IM. OSSOLIŃSKICH, WROCŁAW, XVI.F.4177 (RIGHT)

two parts were completed in 1573, he decided to distribute them without the later parts, which was probably a sensible decision, as these only appeared in 1575.[21]

Siebeneicher, 1573), USTC 242157, f. CccciV; see also the printer's note in Grzegorz of Żarnowiec, *Postylla*, f. Aaa4r. In both cases distributing of an incomplete postil was justified with the target audience's anticipation. This could have been true, but certainly was convenient for the printer, who was able to start selling the book.

21 The publishing of Wujek's postil is documented in his correspondence; see Wujek's letters to Lorenzo Maggio, 18 March 1571; to Francisco Borgia, 17 September 1571; and to Jerome Nadal, 6 October 1572, in Sygański (ed.), 'Korespondencja ks. Jakuba Wujka z Wągrowca z lat 1569–1596', pp. 314, 317 and 334 respectively. In the letter to Maggio, Wujek mentions that printers were impatiently waiting for his text.

FIGURE 11.3 A page from the first edition of Jakub Wujek's 'bigger postil' or *Postylla katoliczna większa*, Krakow 1573. The printer used a woodblock originally designed for a prayer book.

ZAKŁAD NARODOWY IM. OSSOLIŃSKICH, WROCŁAW, XVI.F.4120

Despite its obvious failures, its impressive size, and therefore considerable price, Wujek's work quickly sold out.[22] Still, the printer did not wish to publish a second edition. The postil was only re-edited in 1584, shortly before the printer's privilege was due to expire, and once again in response to another Calvinist work, the *Postylla* by Grzegorz of Żarnowiec, which was as learned and lengthy as Wujek's postil. This time, however, a set of illustrations by Jost Amman was purchased especially for Wujek's postil and the book was printed in a uniform and familiar layout (Figure 11.4).[23]

In the meantime, because of the printer's refusal to republish the work, Wujek decided to write a shorter version, suitable to a wider, less specialised audience. His *Postylla katolicka mniejsza* ('smaller postil') was published in 1579 in Poznań, in the print shop of Jan Wolrab, who cooperated closely with the local Jesuit college. This is the only sixteenth-century edition of a Polish postil printed in quarto, a format that was better suited to the less learned status of the text.[24] The 'smaller postil' was an immediate success—it was shorter and easier to grasp for less educated clergymen; most probably it was also cheaper. Wolrab printed another edition in 1582, this time in folio, with illustrations filling the width of the column.[25]

In 1590, Wujek's smaller postil was edited again, this time in Krakow by Andrzej Piotrkowczyk. Visually, the edition was almost identical to Rej's postil printed twenty years earlier, because Piotrkowczyk used the same woodcut illustrations. They were used also in the *Postylla* by Grzegorz of Żarnowiec, published just eight years earlier. There is no known information as to how

---

22   In 1633 one of Wujek's postils cost 6 Polish zlotys, that is about 1.2 ducats. See R. Żurkowa, *Księgarstwo krakowskie w pierwszej połowie XVII wieku* (Krakow: Secesja, 1992), p. 43.

23   The Amman woodblocks had been used before in *Icones Novi Testamenti* (Frankfurt am Main: Martin Lechler and Sigmund Feyerabend, 1571), USTC 664941; see Ewa Chojecka, *Deutsche Bibelserien in der Holzstocksammlung der Jagellonische Universitat in Krakau* (Baden-Baden–Strasbourg: [Valentin Koerner], 1961), pp. 15–21. The Krakow editions of Wujek's 'smaller postil' were all entitled *Postylla katolicka mniejsza*.

24   See Wujek's preface in J. Wujek, *Postylla katolicka mniejsza*, pt. 1 (Poznań: Jan Wolrab, 1579), USTC 242320, f.)(2v: "Lastly, for two years there has been no copies left and the printer for reasons of his own has postponed the second edition, and people have been complaining that it [i.e. the 'bigger postil'] was nowhere to be found". The original reads: "Na koniec już ode dwu lat nie stało egzemplarzów, a drukarz dla swych przyczyn odkłada wtórą edycyją, a ludzie się skarżą, że jej nie mogą dostać".

25   The woodblocks used by Wolrab were described by Alina Chyczewska, 'Zasób drzeworytów ilustracyjnych i herbowych w XVI-wiecznych oficynach poznańskich', in Bohdan Horodyski (ed.), *Z zagadnień teorii i praktyki bibliotekarskiej. Studia poświęcone pamięci Józefa Grycza* (Wrocław: Ossolineum, 1961), pp. 354–382: 355–358, 378–382.

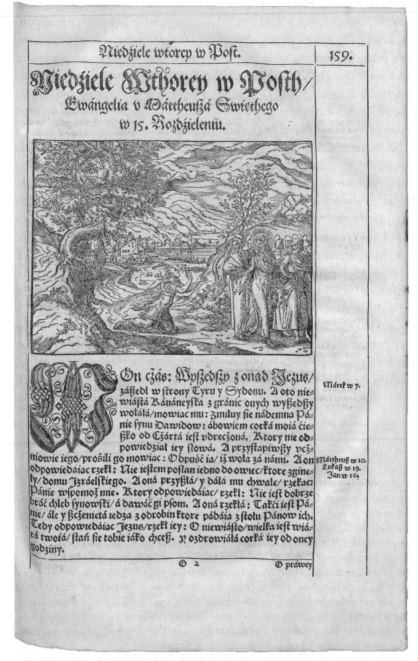

FIGURE 11.4　A woodcut by Jost Amman from the second edition of Jakub Wujek's 'bigger postil' or *Postylla katoliczna większa*, Krakow 1584
ZAKŁAD NARODOWY IM. OSSOLIŃSKICH, XVI.F.4156

FIGURE 11.5A–B   Pages from the Calvinist postil by Mikołaj Rej printed in Krakow in 1571 (*left*) and Jakub Wujek's counter-reformational *Postylla katoliczna mniejsza* or the 'smaller postil' printed in the same city but by a different printer in 1590 (*right*)
BIBLIOTEKA JAGIELLOŃSKA, KRAKOW, CIM.F.8295 AND MUZEUM NARODOWE, KRAKOW, VIII–XVI.93

the reading public reacted to the graphic similarities between the two works.[26] In 1596, when the 'smaller postil' was re-edited again, it was illustrated with the woodblocks by Amman used in the second edition of Wujek's larger postil. The only difference was that the text of the sermons was typeset in two columns (Figures 11.5 and 11.6). The same design was repeated in 1605, and the last edition of Wujek's postil, published in 1617, was again in quarto, but without illustrations.

---

26   Wujek certainly was aware that his postil was illustrated with these woodblocks. In the Czartoryski Library in Krakow there is a copy of the work by Grzegorz with Wujek's notes (shelfmark: 1242 III). See Magdalena Kuran, *Retoryka jako narzędzie perswazji w postyllografii polskiej XVI wieku* (Łódź: Wydawnictwo Uniwersytetu Łódzkiego, 2007), p. 266.

 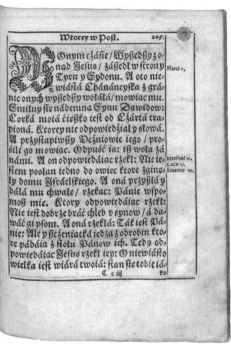

FIGURE 11.6A–B The first edition of *Postylla katoliczna mniejsza* or the 'smaller postil' by Jakub Wujek, in quarto
ZAKŁAD NARODOWY IM. OSSOLIŃSKICH, WROCŁAW, XVI.QU.1735

To make production easier and faster, re-edited texts were usually line-by-line reproductions, following the same layout as the earlier edition used as a model. The fortunes of Wujek's postil, when compared with Protestant works, can be considered a testimony to the search for the perfect form for the Catholic Polish postil. The difference between the attitudes of Protestant and Catholic printers can be seen clearly. The former group—and this applies to printers of all sixteenth-century Protestant postils—followed a distinctly 'German' design and were well prepared for the task from the start. The books they printed, both translations and original works, fitted well into the decades long tradition of similar German publications. The printers of Wujek's Catholic postils faced a more difficult task. They had to print a book that was starkly different in content from the earlier Protestant postils, whilst sharing characteristics typical to this genre, as well as structure and function of the text. It was therefore extremely hard for the printers of these Catholic postils to depart from the design already adopted in their Protestant forerunners, and the two groups of editions look remarkably similar.

New Postil, New Design

The situation changed in the 1590s, as the Counter-Reformation (and related publishing trends) gained some momentum. In 1595 the first edition of sermons for Sundays and feast days by another renowned Polish Jesuit, Piotr Skarga appeared in Krakow. Skarga was invested of an important role within the Catholic communities of northern Europe, as a court preacher to Sigismund III Vasa in the years 1588–1612. The design of his book was simple: the format was a folio, with the pericopes typeset in a single column in larger type, and the sermons in two columns in smaller type. There were no illustrations. Although Skarga's sermons were not the first Polish postil printed without illustrations, it was certainly this edition that most profoundly influenced the typography of later ones. The work, a true masterpiece of the genre, was published another three times before Skarga's death in 1612, and then again in 1618.[27] In 1621, a postil by Fabian Birkowski from the Dominican order was the first of many works to mimic the design of Skarga's sermons. This was copied at times down to the smallest details, or followed more loosely.[28] Skarga's sermons initiated a standard typographical form for Catholic postils. This standard would be retained for the next hundred years, especially in works printed in Krakow (Figure 11.7). However, its influence reached even further.

In the 1650s, the Czech Brethren from Leszno in Greater Poland signed a contract with a printer named Daniel Vetter. Vetter was commissioned to print a thousand copies of a postil by their minister Jan Bytner. In the contract, Vetter promised to typeset the book in the way Skarga's sermons had been typeset in Krakow. Although the final result of Vetter's printing differs significantly from Skarga's book, the contract is an important testimony. First of all, Skarga's sermons were still remembered and available to read over 30 years after their fifth edition in 1618, the last before a century-long break. Secondly, the members of what was quite a radical Protestant community must have found the design attractive and functional enough that it did not matter that

---

27 Piotr Skarga, *Kazania na niedziele i święta* (Krakow: Andrzej Piotrkowczyk, 1595), USTC 243071; subsequent editions in 1597, 1604, 1609 and 1618.
28 For examples, see Fabian Birkowski, *Kazania niedzielne i świąteczne* (Krakow: Andrzej Piotrkowczyk, 1620); Szymon Starowolski, *Arka Testamentu* (Krakow: Krzysztof Schedel, 1645); Franciszek Rychłowski, *Kazania na święta całego roku* (Krakow: Stanisław Piotrkowczyk, 1665). In Starowolski's *Arka Testamentu*, the typographical design of Skarga's sermons was imitated to the smallest details, including ornaments.

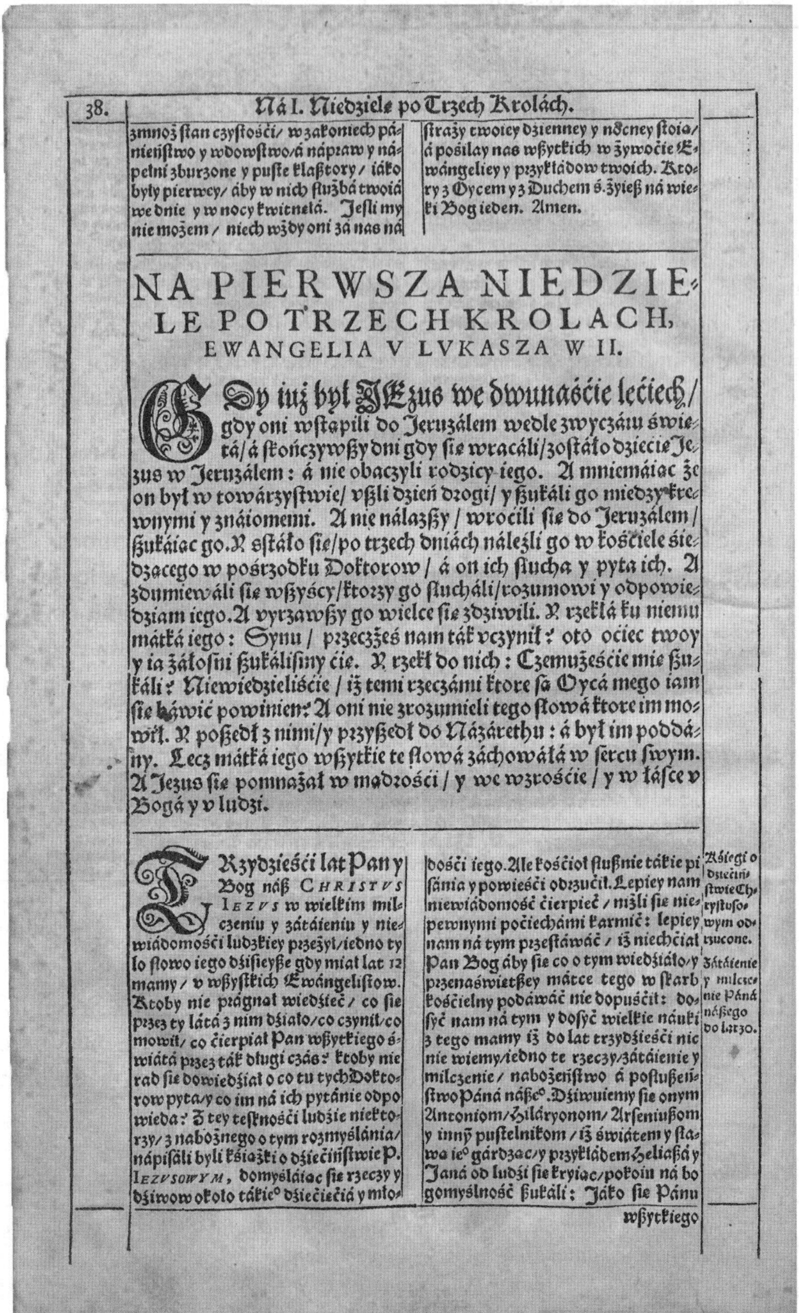

38. Ná I. Niedziele po Trzech Krolách.

zmnoż stan czystośći/ w zakoniech pánienstwo y wdowstwo/á nápraw y nápelni zburzone y puste klaßtory/ iáko były pierwey/ áby w nich służbá twoiá we dnie y w nocy kwitnelá. Jesli my nie możem/ niech wżdy oni zá nas ná straży twoiey dzienney y nocney stoią/ á posilay nas wßytkich w żywoćie Ewángeliey y przykłádow twoich. Ktory z Oycem y z Duchem ś. żyieß ná wieki Bog ieden. Amen.

NA PIERWSZA NIEDZIE-LE PO TRZECH KROLACH, EWANGELIA V LVKASZA W II.

Gdy iuż był JEzus we dwunaśćie lećiech/ gdy oni wstąpili do Jeruzálem wedle zwyczáiu świętá/ á skończywßy dni gdy się wracáli/ zostáło dziecię Jezus w Jeruzálem: á nie obaczyli rodzicy iego. A mniemáiąc że on był w towárzystwie/ vßli dzień drogi/ y ßukáli go miedzy krewnymi y znáiomemi. A nie nálazßy/ wroćili się do Jeruzálem/ ßukáiąc go. Y ستáło się/ po trzech dniách nálezli go w kośćiele siedzącego w pośrzodku Doktorow/ á on ich słucha y pyta ich. A zdumiewáli się wßyscy/ ktorzy go słucháli/ rozumowi y odpowiedziam iego. A vyrzawßy go wielce się zdziwili. Y rzekłá ku niemu mátká iego: Synu/ przecześ nam ták vczynił? oto oćiec twoy y ia żáłosni ßukáliśmy ćie. Y rzekł do nich: Czemużeśćie mię ßukáli? Niewiedzieliśćie/ iż temi rzeczámi ktore są Oycá mego iam się bawić powinien? A oni nie zrozumieli tego słowá ktore im mowił. Y poßedł z nimi/ y przyßedł do Názárethu: á był im poddány. Lecz mátká iego wßytkie te słowá záchowáłá w sercu swym. A Jezus się pomnażał w mądrośći/ y we wzrośćie/ y w łásce v Bogá y v ludzi.

TRzydzieśći lat Pan y Bog náß CHRISTVS IEZVS w wielkim milczeniu y zátáieniu y niewiádomośći ludzkiey przeżył/ iedno tylo słowo iego dźisieyße gdy miał lat 12 mamy/ v wßystkich Ewángelistow. Ktoby nie prágnął wiedźieć/ co się przez ty látá z nim dźiało/ co czynił/ co mowił/ co ćierpiał Pan wßytkiego świátá przez ták długi czás? ktoby nie rad się dowiedźiał o co tu tych Doktorow pyta/ y co im ná ich pytánie odpowieda? Z tey tesknośći ludźie niektorzy/ z nabożnego o tym rozmyślánia/ nápisáli byli kśiążki o dźiećiństwie P. IEZVSOWYM, domyśláiąc się rzeczy y dźiwow około tákie° dźiećięćiá y młodośći iego. Ale kośćioł słußnie tákie pisánia y powieśći odrzućił. Lepiey nam niewiádomość ćierpieć/ niżli się niepewnymi poćiecháni kármić: lepiey nam ná tym przestáwáć/ iż niechćiał Pan Bog áby się co o tym wiedźiáło/ y przenaświętßey mátce tego w skarb kośćielny podáwáć nie dopuśćił: dosyć nam ná tym y dosyć wielkie náuki z tego mamy iż do lat trzydźieśći nic nie wiemy/ iedno te rzeczy/ zátáienie y milczenie/ nabożeństwo á posłußeństwo Páná náße°. Dźiwuiemy się onym Antoniom/ Hiláryonom/ Arseniußom y innẏ pustelnikom/ iż świátem y sławą ie° gárdząc/ y przykłádem Heliaßá y Janá od ludźi się kryiąc/ pokoiu ná bogomyślność ßukáli: Jáko się Pánu wßytkiego

Kśięgi o dźiećiństwie Chrystusowym odrzucone.

Zátáienie y milczenie Páná náßego do lat 30.

FIGURE 11.7 Piotr Skarga, *Kazania na niedziele i święta*, Krakow 1595
ZAKŁAD NARODOWY IM. OSSOLIŃSKICH, WROCŁAW, XVI.F.4286

the book's content was written by a Jesuit priest known for his fiercely anti-Protestant stance.[29]

In the second half of the seventeenth century, in centres such as Poznan, Lublin and Kalisz, Roman types were used from the 1670s.[30] In Krakow the old design continued to determine the appearance of postils even into the late 1690s, although by that point most printers introduced different typesetting. Sometimes the layout of the peritexts—forewords, dedicatory letters etc.—was modernised, but the sermons were still printed in a traditional style.[31] Possibly, printers chose the older design in order to satisfy the taste of the reading public. This might have been the case with the title page attached to sermons for Sundays and feast days of the year written by Franciszek Rychłowski. This book had been printed in 1672 by Krzysztof Schedel, with an entirely typeset title page graced by a single, modest ornament. Over twenty years later, wanting to get rid of unsold copies still in his stock, the printer decided to re-issue the old sheets under a new title page (now dated 1695). The page was typeset more traditionally, with an ornamental frame reminiscent of title pages of the previous parts of the postil, and it was simply pasted over the original title (Figure 11.8).[32]

Selling the Less Successful Postils

Rej's, Wujek's and Skarga's are stories of success. Their works ran into multiple editions, and the postils of Wujek and Skarga were officially recommended by the Catholic Church authorities; they were also set as examples in instructions for preachers.[33] From the 1580s, every parish was supposed to have a library with a postil in Polish. At first, Wujek was the obvious choice, while later on

---

29 The contract between the Czech brethren and the printer is available in the National Archives in Poznań (Archiwum Państwowe w Poznaniu), Akta Braci Czeskich (1507) 1557–1817 (1961), sign. 1757: 'Kontrakt o druk *Postylli polskiej* między starszymi zborów wielkopolskich a Danielem Wetterusem'. See also Jolanta Dworzaczkowa, 'Geneza i losy Postylli na ewangelie Jana Bytnera', *Biblioteka*, 18.9 (2005), pp. 149–154.

30 See for example Paweł Kaczyński, *Kazania na niedziele całego roku* (Kalisz: Drukarnia Kolegium SJ, 1675); Tomasz Młodzianowski, *Kazania i homilije* (Poznań: Drukarnia Kolegium SJ, 1681); Jan Krosnowski, *Pochodnia Słowa Bożego* (Lublin: Drukarnia Kolegium SJ, 1689). All three were printed by the Jesuit college presses and typeset in a Roman typeface.

31 See Bazyli Rychlewicz, *Kazania począwszy od adwentu aż do Wielkiej Nocy* (Krakow: Schedel, 1698).

32 I have come across two copies of this 'title edition', one in Krakow Jagiellonian Library, Aug. 6112; the other in Wrocław, Zakład Narodowy im. Ossolińskich, XVII.6.6299.

33 See Maciejowski, *Epistola pastoralis*, ff. C1v–C3r; Stanisław Sokołowski, *Partitiones ecclesiasticae*, in idem, *Opera*, vol. 1 (Krakow: Jan Januszowski, 1591), USTC 242866, p. 755.

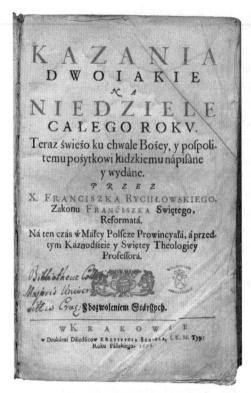 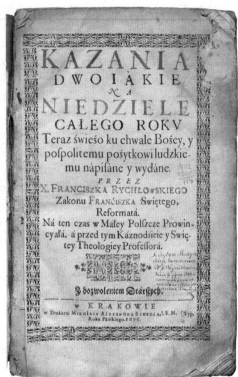

FIGURE 11.8A–B Title pages of *Kazania dwojakie* by Franciszek Rychłowski published in Krakow in 1672. The title page dated in 1695 is pasted over the original title
BIBLIOTEKA JAGIELLOŃSKA, KRAKOW, AUG. 6112 AND CAM.E.XV.6

Skarga was preferred. However, despite this obvious success, by the time the fourth edition was circulating Skarga was referring to his sermons as 'large volumes bought by the few' ('wielkie księgi, które rzadki kupi'). Unfortunately, little is known about the print runs in which Polish postils were printed. We know only that Bytner's postil was printed in about a thousand copies, as was Wujek's 'larger postil'. However, it is worth mentioning that Skarga was comparing his 'large volumes bought by the few' with pamphlets printed in several thousand copies and distributed for free.[34] He was, therefore, aware that the size of the book and its price could affect its distribution, although it is not clear

---

34   See Piotr Skarga, *Wzywanie do pokuty obywatelów Korony Polskiej i Wielkiego Księstwa Litewskiego* (Krakow: Andrzej Piotrkowczyk, 1610), f. A2r–v. See also Benis (ed.), *Materiały do historii drukarstwa i księgarstwa w Polsce*, no. 1343; Jan Ptaśnik (ed.), *Monumenta Poloniae typographica* (Lwów: Zakład Narodowy im. Ossolińskich, 1922), pp. 72–73 and nos. 705–708, 733–735.

exactly how postils were distributed. Some were certainly sold on the market, which is confirmed by booksellers' inventories and episcopal letters encouraging the clergy to purchase the books.[35] However, as the Counter Reformation gained strength in the last decades of the sixteenth century, Protestant postils could not be printed or sold as freely as before, especially not in Krakow. Since the 1590s, they were published instead outside the capital, in provincial centres such as Vilnius in Lithuania, Toruń in Prussia, Leszno in Greater Poland or Łaszczów in Lesser Poland. At least a part of those postils printed in the provinces were intended for a wider market—for communities all over Poland-Lithuania and also in Silesia. As early as 1556, when the first Lutheran postil was printed in Królewiec, it was supplied with two sets of forewords—one for readers in Prussia and the other for readers in Poland.[36] Censorship could also be one of the reasons why Protestant communities, such as the Czech Brethren, decided to distribute postils funded with their money themselves.[37]

Obviously, not every Polish postil was equally popular and not every one was a bestseller. The re-issue of Rychłowski's edition hints at the difficulties of selling a whole print run. It seems likely that Jan Januszowski, the printer of Marcin Białobrzeski's *Postilla orthodoxa*, also experienced difficulties selling the bulky work.

Białobrzeski's postil, although beautifully printed and furnished with a detailed system of marginal notes and divisions (but lacking an index), was complicated to follow and use. It was published in 1581, but eighteen months later Januszowski must still have had a substantial number of copies in stock. Some of the surviving copies have a reprinted first sheet, with a newly typeset title page and the verso slightly modified.[38] Januszowski probably can-

---

35   See Żurkowa, *Księgarstwo*, pp. 199–200.
36   See Orszak, *Postylla polska domowa*. The forewords are described by Maciuszko, *Ewangelicka postyllografia polska*, pp. 35–37.
37   Only fifty copies of Bytner's postil were distributed by the printer: he gave six copies to the author, sent fifteen to a bookseller in Toruń, left seven to be sold by himself and distributed twenty-two among ministers of the congregation. The remaining 950 copies were given to the elders of the Czech brethren community in Greater Poland who signed the contract and paid for the publication (see Dworzaczkowa, 'Geneza i losy Postylli na ewangelie Jana Bytnera', p. 151). The practice of distributing commissioned books not by the printer but by the person or community that had commissioned them was, however, not unusual. See for example Angela Nuovo, *The Book Trade in the Italian Renaissance* (Leiden: Brill, 2013), pp. 61–62 and Magdalena Komorowska, 'In the eye of the storm: books in the conflict between the Jesuits and the University of Krakow (1622–1634)', in T. Bela, C. Calma and J. Rzegocka (eds.), *Publishing Subversive Texts in Elizabethan England and the Polish-Lithuanian Commonwealth* (Leiden: Brill, 2016), pp. 56–71: 70.
38   Copies with the cancelled title page and the additional sheet can be found, among other

celled the sheet owing to an epigram addressed to King Stefan Batory, that had been placed on the verso of the title page. The author of the verse was Andrzej Trzecieski, a humanist and prominent Protestant, whose name obviously should not have appeared in the peritext of a Catholic postil. In the second version of the first sheet, Trzecieski's name was removed. The revised copies were supplemented by an extra sheet, containing letters of gratitude from King Stefan Batory and Queen Anna Jagiellon to the author, as well as two official recommendations for Białobrzeski's postil written by the primate of the Polish Church, Stanisław Karnkowski, and the bishop of the Krakow diocese, Piotr Myszkowski. The function of the additional sheet is clearly commercial, though it is impossible to say whether it actually influenced sales. However, Karnkowski's note contains an interesting detail that further confirms the popularity of Wujek's postil. The archbishop recommended the purchase of Białobrzeski's postil to those clergymen who had not been able to purchase Wujek's smaller postil, printed only two years earlier, due to the scarcity of copies.

In the late sixteenth century and in the course of the seventeenth, printers of Polish postils learned how to use other peritexts. One of these were indices. Fourteen editions of Polish postils, mostly from the seventeenth century, incorporated these devices for textual navigation, which were very useful from the point of view of any less eager preacher. The presence of an index allowed a reader (or, rather, user) of a postil to easily access teachings and arguments on chosen issues and incorporate them into his own orations without having to read the whole volume.[39] In 1584, for example, the printer of Wujek's postil used the title page to inform the reader that the book was furnished with two indices. These were typical for the majority of postils: one was an index of biblical *loci* (*index locorum Sacrae Scripturae*) and the other an *index rerum*. Eleven years later, when Skarga's sermons were printed, the reader was informed not

---

collections, in the Warsaw, National Library, XVI.F.126, and Katowice, Silesian Library, 235228 III.

39 This was common practice, sometimes disapproved of, but usually quietly accepted. For example, Adam Gdacjusz wrote in the foreword to his postil: "Even if I had copied some things from this author or the other, no wise man would have resented me. Why? Because it is no novelty that theologians imitate one another and take what they need for their own sermons". The original reads: "Chociażby też temu tak było, żebym z tego abo owego autora to i owo wypisał, wszakoż by mi nikt mądry tego za złe nie miał. Czemu? Bo to nie nowina, że teolog teologa imituje i z niego to, co mu do dyspozycyjej jego służy, wypisuje". Adam Gdacjusz, *Postilla popularis* (Leszno: Daniel Vetter, 1650), f. b3r. Indeed, bishop Maciejowski in his *Espistola pastoralis* praised postils by Wujek and Skarga as a useful source of sermonic matter—"abunde suppeditabunt ... non solum materiam, sed et tranctandae eius modum". See Maciejowski, *Epistola pastoralis*, f. c2.

only about the presence of indices, but also about their very specific and clearly Counter-Reformational purpose: one was of texts for the strengthening of the Catholic faith ('na zmocnienie katolickiej wiary') and the other for the correction of morals ('ku naprawie obyczajów').[40] However, indices could also play other, rather unexpected roles. In 1681, Tomasz Młodzianowski furnished his Polish postil with a Latin index. His wish, expressed at the beginning of the index, was to encourage educated clergymen to reach for his postil. He apologised to his readers for publishing his sermons in the vernacular and hoped that a Latin index would make the collection look more polished.[41]

After censorship regulations were tightened in the 1620s and 1630s, censorial approbations could also be used as a means of promotion.[42] Some form of censorial approbation was printed on most of the postils, both Catholic and Protestant. In the sixteenth century, the approval was usually briefly stated on the title page. Later on, the full text of approbations was added on a separate page or multiple pages in the peritext, usually after dedicatory letters and forewords. Approbations found in early modern Polish postils might play a role similar to the 'blurb' on the covers of modern books. They contained not only brief statements of the text's conformity with the faith of the given church, but also more general remarks in favour of the author and his work. According to the approbations, most of the postils were pious, learned, wise, useful for strengthening the faith, well-written and in a clear style. Moreover, some of the censors were renowned preachers themselves. A favourable approbation written by such a person served not only as proof of doctrinal orthodoxy but also as a powerful argument in the book's favour. Some of the postils contained three or four printed approbations given by various censors. One of them was usually printed in Polish. The episcopal authorities responsible for matters of censorship did not always insist on these approbations.[43]

---

40   Skarga, *Kazania na niedziele* ... (Krakow: Andrzej Piotrkowczyk, 1595), f. [ ](1)r (title page).
41   See Tomasz Młodzianowski, *Kazania i homilije* (Posnan: Drukarnia Kolegium SJ, 1681), vol. 1, f. Nnn3r.
42   On censorship in early modern Poland, see Paulina Buchwald-Pelcowa, *Cenzura w dawnej Polsce. Między prasą drukarską a stosem* (Warsaw: Stowarzyszenie Bibliotekarzy Polskich, 1997).
43   Postils with multiple approbations include Rychłowski, *Kazania na święta*; Kaczyński, *Kazania na niedziele*; Młodzianowski, *Kazania i homilije*, and Rychlewicz, *Kazania począwszy od adwentu*.

Conclusion

This brief overview of Polish postils from the sixteenth and seventeenth centuries shows that in the early modern age the shape of a book depended, as it does today, on its content and function, with financial concerns and aesthetic tastes following close behind. In the case of Polish postils printed in the sixteenth century, inter-confessional competition should probably also be taken into consideration. The wish not to be left behind and the drive to outshine one's confessional opponent might be among the main factors that shaped the Polish postil as a luxury item rather than as a book for everyday use. In contrast, it should perhaps be mentioned here that in 1607, when the first part of Stanisław Grodzicki's Latin postil was published in Krakow, it was designed as an unillustrated octavo volume, which was handy but much less impressive than a folio. The edition was continued in the following years in a similar design in Ingolstadt.[44] Młodzianowski's wish to elevate the status of his Polish postil by means of a Latin index suggests that even the most learned works published in Polish were considered inferior to their Latin counterparts. Yet this apparent inferiority did not preclude complex and elaborate typography.

The printing craft was above religious division. Printers took no notice of confessional differences between texts, when they chose to imitate design strategies. Very similar, and at times the very same illustrations, were used in both Protestant and Catholic texts. One is almost tempted to frame the striking graphic similarities within a general strategy of deceit.[45] The two designs that were most often adopted and adapted, associated with the postils by Rej and Skarga, also show how a combination of well-written content and well-designed and functional typography influenced the general form of the book in the long run. Last but not least, this survey has drawn attention to the use of peritexts as instruments of commercial promotion.

The golden age of the Polish postil ended around 1628 when the victory of the Counter Reformation became clear and indisputable. The greatest popularity of the genre should be framed within the Protestant-Catholic controversy. In Poland-Lithuania the inter-confessional battle was most of all a war of words, and the printed book played an important role. Polish postils were an important factor in this debate. They were not only a means of preaching the gospel, but also served to define doctrine and to refute the teachings of others. When

---

44   See note 7 above.
45   This idea was argued in I. Voisé-Maćkiewicz, 'Materiał graficzny pierwszego wydania "Postylli" Samuela Dambrowskiego z roku 1620', *Zeszyty Naukowe Uniwersytetu Mikołaja Kopernika w Toruniu. Nauki Humanistyczno-Społeczne*, 11 (1964), pp. 3–59: 15–16.

the controversy was over, postils lost some of their importance. From books dedicated to rulers, that defined beliefs and served as weapons in the fight for the purity of the faith, they became sources of devotional readings. Their typography evolved accordingly. Although decisions that shaped the form of the Polish postil were mostly taken by printers, who were mindful of profitability, it is hard not to draw a parallel between the history of the Reformation and Counter-Reformation movements in Poland-Lithuania and the history of the Polish postil as a printed book.

CHAPTER 12

Buying and Selling in One Trip: Book Barter in Times of Trouble for Francesco Ciotti's Printing and Bookselling House

Domenico Ciccarello

The Ciotti family of Italian booksellers, printers and publishers are well known on the international stage. After the extraordinary generation of the Manuzio, Giunti, Sessa, Varisco, Ziletti, Zoppino and other prominent Venetian branches of the printing industry, the Ciotti were among the few who were still showing remarkable skills as cultural entrepreneurs, in a city that had once been the most renowned across Europe for the production and distribution of books. Bibliographic and documentary evidence have yielded details about at least four members of the Ciotti family who were active in book trade at the end of the sixteenth century and in the first half of the seventeenth century: Giovanni Battista, Francesco, Simone, and Sebastiano.[1] This article is concerned with the relatively minor figure of Francesco Ciotti, drawing upon a set of documents held at the Municipal Library of Treviso.[2] This remarkable documentary evidence allows us to identify book bartering as a key expedient to the survival of the Ciotti business at a critical time.

---

1 For a short overview of the printing and bookselling business run by the Ciotti family, with some details about each individual member, see Domenico Ciccarello, 'Ciotti', in *Dizionario degli editori, tipografi, librai itineranti in Italia tra Quattrocento e Seicento* (3 vols., Pisa-Rome: Fabrizio Serra, 2013), I, pp. 268–276.
2 Treviso. Biblioteca comunale. Ms. 1492, *Scritture circa il Ciotti librajo in Palermo*. I am extremely thankful to Giuseppe Lipari, head of a research unit in the University of Messina, for covering the reproduction costs of the original manuscript within an Italian academic research project (PRIN 2008): *Mobilità dei mestieri del libro tra Quattrocento e Seicento: bilanci e linee di sviluppo*. I am also grateful to the head of the Municipal Library in Treviso, Emilio Lippi, for the permission to reproduce the illustrative materials for this publication. Finally, I must acknowledge a paper presented during a conference in Venice, where I first heard a discussion of the Ms. 1492: Agostino Contò, '"L'industria di comprar libri et vendergli ancora": i Ciotti da Venezia a Palermo', in Davide Canfora and Angela Caracciolo Aricò (eds.), *La Serenissima e il Regno. Nel V Centenario dell'Arcadia di Iacopo Sannazaro* (Bari: Cacucci, 2006), pp. 97–108.

The Ciotti Family of Printer / Publishers

The Ciotti family is perhaps best known through Giovanni Battista or Giambattista Ciotti, for whom we have a wide array of evidence.[3] He was a native of Siena, antecendents he continued to proclaim for many years, attaching the adjective 'senese' to his name on his imprints, and ran a prolific printing house and bookshop in Venice between the Rialto and Saint Mark's from 1583. His output represents a great proportion of all documented Ciotti imprints, counting over 700 individual editions. To put this in perspective, Francesco and Simone only produced around 30–35 editions each, and Sebastiano's name is found on just two surviving editions.

Giovanni Battista's workshop and bookshop were located between the churches of St Julian and St Bartholomew, from 1591 to 1597 "All'insegna della Minerva", and from 1597 onward "All'Insegna dell'Aurora". He was acquainted with Giordano Bruno, whom he met repeatedly in Frankfurt on the occasion of the book fairs. Due to this friendship, Ciotti was called to testify at Bruno's trial by the Inquisition in 1592.[4] Thanks to the rich documentation still preserved about his career, Giovanni Battista has been studied quite intensively, especially by Dennis Rhodes, who shed light on Ciotti's joint ventures with printers in the Italian peninsula, as well as abroad.[5] His foreign connections included publishers in Frankfurt, Cologne, and Basel, as well as several contacts with Spain.[6] Ciotti's connections extended as far as the British Isles, thanks to his friendship with Giacomo Castelvetro, who was a member of the Stationers' Company in the last decade of the sixteenth century. A note by Ciotti, dated 21 July 1593, regarding half a bale of books he had just received from William Fowler, the secretary to Queen Anne (wife of King James VI), has been preserved in Edinburgh.[7] The note contained a promise that Ciotti would deliver

---

3 For his biographical profile, together with a concise account of his professional activity, see: Agostino Contò, 'Ciotti, Giovanni Battista', in Marco Menato, Ennio Sandal and Giuseppina Zappella (eds.), *Dizionario dei tipografi e degli editori italiani. Il Cinquecento* (Milan: Editrice Bibliografica, 1997), I, pp. 293–295; and Massimo Firpo, 'Ciotti (Ciotto), Giovanni Battista', in *Dizionario Biografico degli Italiani* (Rome: Istituto della Enciclopedia italiana, 1960–) [henceforth: DBI], XXV (1981), pp. 692–696.

4 See Firpo, 'Ciotti (Ciotto), Giovanni Battista', in DBI, also for additional bibliography and published primary sources on Bruno's process.

5 Dennis Rhodes, *Giovanni Battista Ciotti (1562–1627?): Publisher Extraordinary at Venice* (Venice: Marcianum Press, 2013).

6 Dennis Rhodes, 'Some neglected aspects of the career of Giovanni Battista Ciotti', *The Library*, 6th s., 9.3 (1987), pp. 225–239; Rhodes, 'Spanish books on sale in the Venetian bookshop of G.B. Ciotti, 1602', *The Library*, 7th s., 12.1 (2011), pp. 50–55.

7 Edinburgh, National Library of Scotland, MS. Hawthornden 2065, fol. 84r.

those items to Fowler (or his agent) for the next Frankfurt Book Fair, to be held in September. Apart from Ciotti's national and international connections, Rhodes also investigated his involvement in the joint production of books. These include his association with Bernardo Giunta the Younger (1607–1615), as well as his long-lasting agreements with prominent authors of his time, such as Battista Guarini, Tommaso Stigliani and Giambattista Marino, for the printing of their literary works.[8]

From 1620 onwards, the generic expressions "appresso il Ciotti", "dal Ciotti" and "nella stamperia del Ciotti" were increasingly associated with the Venetian editions, rather than the full name of Giovanni Battista. This was most likely in preparation of Giovanni Battista's move to join Francesco Ciotti in his new business. It would seem that a fifth member of the Ciotti family, called Giovanni, replaced him in his printing and publishing business around 1622–1624. At this time, Giovanni Battista left Venice for Sicily—a journey from which he would never return. An account of the final months in the life of Giovanni Battista is given in a 1630 letter by Tommaso Stigliani, a contemporary of Giambattista Marino. Ciotti, Stigliani reported, "transported his shop to Sicily, and there in the short space of six months went bankrupt, went mad, went blind and died".[9] Giovanni was a son of Giovanni Battista, as we know from a dedication letter addressed to the Venetian Senate member Domenico Molino, dated 6 July 1624, in the work *Il Tebro festante*.[10]

---

8   Dennis Rhodes, *Giovanni Battista Ciotti*. See chapter IX, *Ciotti's relations with contemporary authors*, pp. 53–57. This printing society (in which the Venetian printed Pietro Dusinelli was also involved in a minor capacity), after a promising beginning in 1607, had already sent to the press around one hundred titles within the first three years of activity. In 1608, a printed sale catalogue (114 leaves long) of the Giunta-Ciotti bookshop was offered to the international public, see: *Catalogus librorum qui prostant in bibliotheca Bernardi Iuntæ, Io. Bapt. Ciotti, et sociorum* (Venice: [Bernardo Giunta & Giovanni Battista Ciotti & C.], 1608), USTC 4034258. However, from 1610 on, surviving editions show that the rhythm of their joint production seems to have decreased significantly (with about sixty editions printed in the 1610–1612 period), until the raising of some controversy must have caused the final separation of the society, approximately between 1614 and 1615.

9   Translation by Dennis Rhodes. The original reads: "trasportò la bottega in Sicilia, e là nello stretto spazio di sei mesi fallì, impazzì, accecò e morì". Rhodes, *Giovanni Battista Ciotti*, p. 72.

10 Giovanni Battista Marino, *Il Tebro festante* (Venice: appresso il Ciotti, 1624), USTC 4001653. This is an anthology of Marino's works, bearing the title of the first work in the list (a *panegirico*). Marino died the following year. Another impression, without changes in the text, was issued in 1628.

Between Venice and Palermo: Francesco Ciotti

Francesco Ciotti is documented as a publisher in Venice in the early seventeenth century, before he moved to Palermo to set up his own printing press around 1620.[11] He may have been the eldest son of Giovanni Battista, although we lack explicit documentary evidence. Despite being a highly interesting figure himself, he has received significantly less attention than Giovanni Battista Ciotti.

The beginnings of Francesco Ciotti's career as a printer in Venice in 1606–1607 should be examined in close connection with one of the many occasions Giovanni Battista became embroiled with the Holy Inquisition. Giovanni Battista completed the publication of the last volume of Francisco Suarez, *Disputationum de censuris in communi, excommunicatione, suspensione, et interdicto... Tomus quintus* (1606) in partnership with Giacomo and Giovanni Antonio De Franceschi.[12] These two were the sons of Francesco De Franceschi, also a native of Siena who had moved to Venice to become a successful printer.[13] The text by Suarez was a commentary on the work of Thomas Aquinas, of which the first two volumes had already been published in 1593 by the Minima Societas in Venice. Ciotti and the De Franceschi had neglected some passages of the original text; all three were accused of *crimen falsi* by the Roman Congregation of the Index, and forbidden ever to sell that edition. The punishment was later converted into an obligation to restore the omitted passages before it was put back into circulation. During those months, being at risk of excommunication *latae sententiae*, Giovanni Battista was unable to sell or print any books under his own name. His temporary inactivity may therefore explain the first appearance of the name of Francesco on the title page of works issued from Ciotti's printing house. Such a ready-made solution to guarantee continuity in the daily running of the family business may suggest that Francesco was already one of Giovanni Battista's employees at the time. The material ties between the two are clear; all the editions documented for the years 1606–1607, seven in total, would appear to be reissues of older Ciotti imprints, with the exception

---

11 For a short account of his professional life, see Ciccarello, 'Ciotti Francesco', in *Dizionario degli editori, tipografi, librai itineranti*, I, pp. 274–276.
12 USTC 4030631.
13 Alessandra Basso, 'Uno stampatore 'senese' a Venezia: Francesco de' Franceschi (1561–1599)', *Bullettino senese di storia patria*, 112 (2005), pp. 328–339 (short essay) and 113 (2006), pp. 130–252 (annals); Lorenzo Baldacchini, 'De Franceschi, Francesco', in *DBI*, XXXVI (1988), pp. 30–35; Marcello Brusegan, 'De Franceschi, Francesco', in *Dizionario dei tipografi e degli editori italiani. Il Cinquecento*, I, pp. 450–453.

of a medical work of Aurelio Anselmo, *Gerocomica sive de senum regimine*.[14] It should also be noted that, after Giovanni Battista had returned to business as usual, Francesco's name disappeared again from all imprints until 1615.

Financial Difficulties

The years between 1607 and 1615 saw the Ciotti family engaged in a shared venture with Bernardo Giunti the Younger and other associates. However, contemporary sources demonstrate that Giovanni Battista Ciotti's own contribution to the joint business was at best half-hearted. Paolo Sarpi's correspondence sheds light on several business trips Ciotti undertook within a short period of time, with a focus on business dealt in Sicily. Although the Giunti family had agents in Messina, the destination for Ciotti seems rather to have been Palermo. Not only were these travels obviously more of a priority to Ciotti than his business with the Giunti, but the circumstances proved overall rather unfortunate. At the end of October 1609 Ciotti returned from the Frankfurt Fair; on 11 November he was already departing again, this time for business in Ferrara.[15] On 22 December Sarpi wrote that Ciotti was going to Naples, planning to proceed to Sicily afterwards; but this was just the beginning of a new cycle of misfortune.[16] A letter dated 20 January 1610 reported Ciotti's unfortunate shipwrecking near Lanciano.[17] In March, Sarpi supplied further details of the difficulties Ciotti encountered in Sicily: his stock had been confiscated by the Sicilian Inquisition offices due to the presence of a work by Pietro Aretino.[18] On 25 May Sarpi reported that Ciotti was still in Palermo; on 17 August he indicated that the publisher had not yet left Sicily, and the date of his return was unknown.[19] Yet it appears that the quarterly book fairs in Frankfurt were a good enough reason to venture back north, and during the Lent of 1611 Ciotti attended the event.

---

14   USTC 4030590. The other editions printed by Francesco are: *La falsa riputatione della fortuna* (USTC 4036790) and *Florinda* (USTC 4035975) by Giovanni Battista Leoni, two different impressions of poems by Antonio Ongano, with a slight change in the title (*Opere poetiche* and *Alceo*, USTC 4035255 and 4031254 respectively), a comedy by Giovanni Battista Della Porta, *Gli duoi fratelli rivali*, (USTC 4036780), and *La prova amorosa* by Gaspare Cesana (USTC 4038452).
15   Paolo Sarpi, *Lettere ai protestanti*, ed. Manlio Duilio Businelli (2 vols., Bari: Laterza, 1931), II: *Lettere a Francesco Castrino, Christoph e Achatius von Dohna, Philippe Duplessis-Mornay, Isaac Casaubon, Daniel Heinsius*, pp. 58 and 60 respectively.
16   Sarpi, *Lettere ai protestanti*, II, p. 70.
17   Sarpi, *Lettere ai protestanti*, II, p. 74.
18   Sarpi, *Lettere ai protestanti*, II, p. 81.
19   Sarpi, *Lettere ai protestanti*, II, pp. 86 and 99 respectively.

A second journey to Sicily took place from the end of 1611 to the summer of 1612, as is documented by Camaldolese monk Benedetto Pucci in his letter-writing manual.[20] One of the texts included in the manual as examples was a letter to Giovanni Battista Ciotti himself, and it provides useful insights:

> As your departure from Venice to Palermo, shortly after my own departure to Fabriano on grave and important business, not uncommon in my misfortune, grieved me greatly; and was sorely regretted by your family, and many illustrious gentlemen in this great city [Venice] who love you dearly, all the more so as they saw how your beloved wife, your children, your home, and the whole family were deprived of your steering hand and care. Thus upon my return, hearing that you were soon expected to be back, and with good outcomes from your business, I was all the more delighted in virtue of our old friendship, and I gave thanks to God, who allowed that your goodness (despite your rivals) shines around the world, and justice has taken its place, thanks to the protection that his Majesty grants to good and honorable men such as yourself ... In the meanwhile, I wished to send you greetings, and beg you to return as soon as possible, for the rejoicing of your home. With you will return that happy crowd of old to your bookshop in Venice that used to gather around your presence, much desired and anticipated by all who love you dearly, as I do. Our Lord God grant you a safe and happy journey back home.[21]

---

20   Benedetto Pucci, *Aggionta all'idea di varie lettere usate nella Segretaria d'ogni principe, e signore* (Venice: Giunti & Ciotti, 1612), USTC 4028101. This edition is an addendum to the first part of this text, *L'Idea di varie lettere usate nella segretaria d'ogni principe e signore* (Venice: Giunti & Ciotti, 1612), USTC 4025895.
21   Pucci, *Aggionta all'idea di varie lettere*, pp. 48–49. My translation. The original reads: "Sì come la partita vostra da Venezia per Palermo, successiva alla mia per Fabriano, per interessi molto gravi, & importanti, non difficili alla mia disgratia, augumentò assai il mio affanno, & anco molto dispiacque ai vostri parenti, e a tanti illustrissimi signori, che vi amano di cuore in questa inclita patria del mondo, e tanto più, quanto consideravono, come restava la vostra amata consorte, i figliuoli, la casa, e la famiglia tutta priva del governo, e della vostra vigilanza, s'io dico che me ne rammaricai assai, così tornando qua, & intendendo, che voi ancora dovevi esserci presto, con felice successo delle cose vostre, ne presi quel contento maggiore, che a bastanza potè corrispondere all'antica nostra benevolenza, e ne resi gratie a Dio, c'havesse permesso, che la vostra bontà (mal grado de gl'emuli vostri) riluca per tutto il mondo, e la giustitia habbi il suo luogo, mediante la protettione, che Sua Maestà tiene de gli huomini honorati, e da bene pari vostri ... In tanto ho voluto salutarvi con questa mia, e pregarvi a tornare quanto prima, acciò rallegriate la casa vostra, e ritorni insieme con voi quel fausto, e quel antico concorso, che prima havea la vostra libraria qui in Venetia mediante la vostra amabilissima presenza, desiderata, &

Dennis Rhodes has pieced together the dates of various letters by Pucci, concluding that Ciotti must have left Venice as early as September 1611.[22] One may add that by September 1612 Ciotti was surely in Venice again, as together with Bernardino Giunta he printed the fourth volume of *Commentariorum in concordiam, & historiam quattuor Euangelistarum* by Sebastião Barradas, where he signed the dedication letter to cardinal Metello Bichi "Venetijs tertio Idus Septemb.".[23] The printing license is dated 16 July 1612. These contemporary sources strongly indicate that the personal commitment of Giambattista Ciotti to the joint venture with Bernardo Giunti was very limited, which may well have damaged the projected income of the business. It is only natural that such a weak performance should cause Giunti dissatisfaction and, in the long term, his withdrawal from their former agreement. The situation quickly deteriorated. On 4 September 1614 the poet Alessandro Tassoni wrote to one of his correspondents: "Your Lordship will send me the second part of the Boccalino that you have received from Ciotti.[24] I have not received any letters from him in a long time, but I heard that the Giunta [Bernardo] his partner torments him and has seized all of his goods".[25] The same year, Giovanni Battista Ciotti was imprisoned and fined 25 ducates for his failure to request the printing license for the third part of the *Lira* by Giambattista Marino.[26]

All the information we have reported so far shows that by 1615, despite the large output produced by Giovanni Battista and his partners in Venice, he seemed to have had more troubles than benefits from his professional work. In particular, the heavy consequences of the company's closure in Venice and the repeated difficulties with the Inquisition must have proved a heavy burden. In those years the Giunti were still the most powerful and influential family of printers and publishers in Venice. For the future of Ciotti's enterprise in Venice, alienating the Giunti was risky. After 1615 the Ciotti Venetian output dwindled,

---

aspettata da tutti quelli, che vi amano di cuore, come fo io. N. Sig. Dio vi conceda lieto, e felice viaggio".

22   Dennis Rhodes, *Giovanni Battista Ciotti*, p. 65, footnote n. 2.
23   USTC 4039983.
24   The edition in question is to be identified with Traiano Boccalini, *De' ragguagli di Parnaso* (Venice: Guerigli, 1614), USTC 4029501.
25   My translation. The original text reads: "v.s. mi manderà la seconda parte del Boccalino che ebbe dal Ciotti, dal quale non ho lettere un pezzo fa, ma intendo che il Giunta suo compagno il travaglia e gli ha sequestrato ogni cosa". Alessandro Tassoni, *Le lettere*, ed. Giorgio Rossi (2 vols., Bologna: Romagnoli Dall'Acqua, 1901), I, p. 54.
26   The edition in question is USTC 4040345. The documentation on this episode is kept in Venice State Archives. Santo Uffizio. Esecutori contro la bestemmia, Busta n. 63. For more information on the topic, see Giuliano Pesenti, 'Libri censurati a Venezia nei secoli XVI–XVII', *La Bibliofilía*, 68–69 (1956–1957), pp. 15–30.

being largely confined to reprints of earlier editions. Taking all these factors into account, it would seem likely that any financial help granted to the new family business in Palermo may have been rather limited.

The Ciotti Business in Palermo

During the early years (1615–1620) of his activity in Palermo, Francesco Ciotti acted exclusively as a publisher, making contracts and agreements with other printers who were already well-established in town. Among these were Giovanni Battista Maringo, Angelo Orlandi, Decio Cirillo and Giovanni Antonio De Franceschi. This led him to contribute substantial investments for the production of expensive legal editions.[27] Between 1620 and 1629 Francesco continued to publish legal treatises, but he also tried to differentiate his publishing plans through a number of new titles in the fields of theology, devotion and history.[28] From 1620, Francesco began to be named on his Palermo publications as printer, while previously he had only ever appeared as a publisher. A very good example of this professional shift can be observed in a four-volume legal treatise entitled *Decisiones Consistorij Sacrae Regiae Conscientiae Regni Siciliae*, published in Palermo between 1619 and 1624. Here the imprint of the first volume reads "Panormi, sumptibus Francisci Ciotti Veneti, apud Ioannem

---

27 Just a few examples: Garsia Mastrillo, *Ad indultum generale* (Palermo: Francesco Ciotti and Giovanni Battista Maringo, 1616), USTC 4037306; Mastrillo, *De magistratibus* (Palermo: Francesco Ciotti and Giovanni Battista Maringo, 1616), USTC 4023546; Manuel Rodriguez, *Aggiunte, et additioni alla somma di casi di conscienza, sopra l'esplicatione della Bolla della S. Crociata* (Palermo: Francesco Ciotti, Angelo Orlandi and Decio Cirillo, 1617), USTC 4022355; *Decisiones Consistorii Sacrae Regiae Conscientiae regni Siciliae* (Palermo: Francesco Ciotti and Giovanni Antonio De Franceschi, 1619), USTC 4003859 (subsequent volumes of the latter were published in later years).

28 We can ascribe to this period, among others, the editions of Fernando del Castillo, *Dell'historia generale di S. Domenico* (2 vols., Palermo: Francesco Ciotti, 1626), I: USTC 4004518; II: USTC 4005181; Tommaso Fazello, *Le due deche dell'historia di Sicilia* (Palermo: Francesco Ciotti and Decio Cirillo, 1628), USTC 4005398. A list of 14 editions (including the 1606–1607 Venetian titles) printed by Francesco Ciotti is provided in Dennis Rhodes, *Giovanni Battista Ciotti*, pp. 317–321. A more comprehensive catalogue, including 30 Sicilian editions by Ciotti, has been compiled in Domenico Ciccarello, 'Le edizioni siciliane del XVII secolo' (Unpublished PhD dissertation, Università degli Studi di Siena, 2012). This work, including the full description with copy locations for more than 4,000 printed editions, is currently under revision for publication. Most recently, see also Carlo Pastena, Angela Anselmo and Maria Carmela Zimmardi (eds.), *Bibliografia delle edizioni palermitane antiche (BEPA)*, II, *Edizioni del XVII secolo* (Palermo: Regione Siciliana, 2014), listing and describing around 30 editions as well.

Antonium de Franciscis, 1619", while the other three volumes (dated 1620, 1621 and 1624 respectively) read "ex officina typographica Francisci Ciotti".[29]

Substantial information on the Sicilian business can be drawn from documents held in the Municipal Library in Treviso, exceeding by far any details that can be inferred through output or paratext analysis. The Treviso ms. 1492 was donated by the librarian Luigi Sorelli to the Municipal Library in 1942, and was first described by the librarian Roberto Zamprogna in a manuscript inventory, compiled during the years 1948–1949 and kept in the same library. This small folder contains various documents (notarial acts, letters, commercial notes), all of which were used by the Venetian bookseller Leonardo Paulini in order to provide evidence in a legal controversy against Francesco Ciotti, who had been his employer at least for the years 1623–1629. It is worth mentioning that Paulini's name never appears in printed works. Paulini took legal action as one of Ciotti's creditors, although the collected documents do not tell us whether he succeeded.

The notarial acts clarify the terms of working agreements between the two, and the problems that soon arose. In 1623, and then again in 1628 (see Figure 12.1) Francesco Ciotti fully acknowledged his debt of 78 *onze* to Leonardo Paulini, incurred in the course of a number of bookselling trips undertaken by Paulini to different parts of Italy before 1627.

Book Barter as a Business Strategy

The Treviso documents show that by the late 1620s, Leonardo Paulini had not received his wages for several years spent in Ciotti's service. Other sources disclose an unpaid debt contracted by Francesco Ciotti in 1624 with the Lyonnaise society of publishers and booksellers and printers formed by Jacques Cardon and Pierre Cavellat the Younger. This amounted to the large sum of 2,907 *scudi*. Francesco Brogiotti, a bookseller and publisher from Rome, had been tasked with the recovery of this debt on their behalf.[30] As the employer was short of cash, he proposed that Paulini should undertake another journey to Naples and other Italian towns with the aim of disposing by sale or barter books from Ciotti's stock. According to the agreement, signed on 12 October 1628 before the notary Mariano Zapparrata, the net income could be deducted from the employer's debt with Paulini.

---

29 USTC 4003859.
30 Valentino Romani, 'Notizie su Andrea Brogiotti libraio, editore e stampatore camerale', *Accademie e biblioteche d'Italia*, 46 (1973), pp. 72–87.

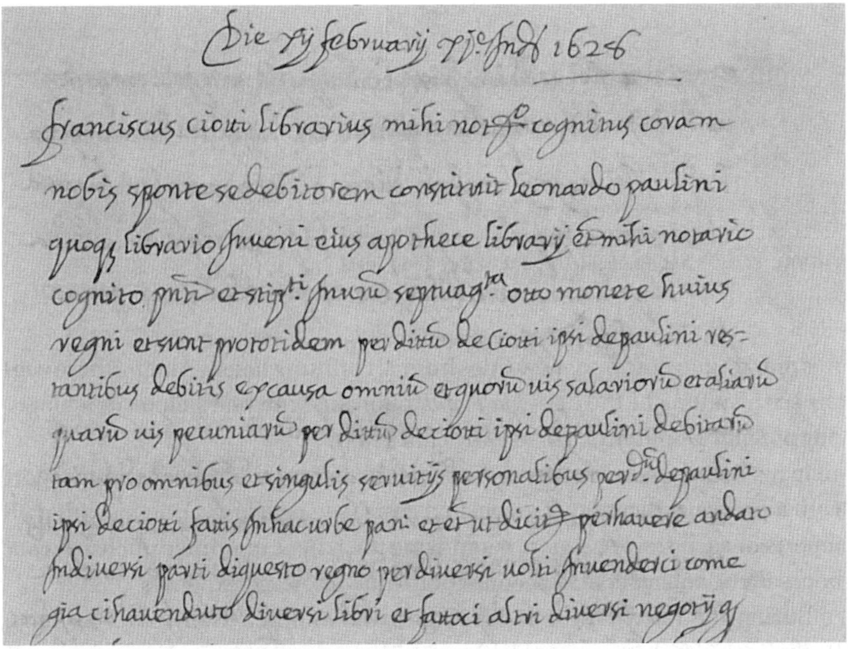
Die xij februarij xij Ind. 1628
Franciscus Ciotti librarius mihi not[ari]o cognitus coram
nobis sponte se debitorem constituit Leonardo paulini
quoque librario juveni eius apothece librarij et mihi notario
cognito pnti et stip[ulan]ti in uncias septuaginta otto monete huius
regni et sunt pro totidem per dictum de Ciotti ipsi de paulini res-
tantibus debitis ex causa omnium et quorumcumque salariorum et aliarum
quarumcumque pecuniarum per dictum de Ciotti ipsi de paulini debitarum
tam pro omnibus et singulis servitijs personalibus per d[ic]tum de paulini
ipsi de Ciotti factis in hac urbe pan[ormi] et et ut dicitur per havere andato
in diversi parti di questo regno per diversi nostri servendoci come
gia ci havendo diversi libri et fattoci altri diversi negotij q[ue]

FIGURE 12.1 Partial reproduction of the act signed before notary Mariano Zapparrata of Palermo on 12 October 1628, concerning a contract between Francesco Ciotti and Leonardo Paulini for sale and bartering of books in Naples and elsewhere in Italy.
BIBLIOTECA MUNICIPALE, TREVISO, MS. 1492, S. 2

The commercial notes written by Paulini during the course of the book bartering mission, taken alone, form almost half the overall content of the manuscript. They consist of a gathering of small sheets of paper with accounting notes (sheets 5 to 16), bearing the title "Barati e di contanti di libri fatti in Napoli pel M.co S.re Franc.co Ciotti" ("Bartering and sale of books made in Naples on behalf of the Magnifico Signore Francesco Ciotti"). The information contained is of remarkable interest.

After travelling from Palermo to Naples in 1628, Paulini did not come back but proceeded to Rome, and Venice, where he remained in the early months of 1629. Francesco Ciotti may have thought the bartering trip to be a timely opportunity, shortly after the publication of Tommaso Fazello's *Le due deche dell'historia di Sicilia*.[31] The booklists contained in Ms. 1492 show that Francesco

31 Tommaso Fazello, *Le due deche dell'historia di Sicilia* (Palermo: Francesco Ciotti, 1628), USTC 4005398.

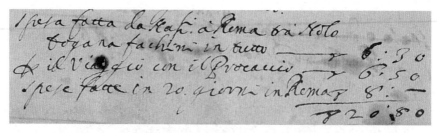

FIGURE 12.2   Naples, 1628. Account of travelling costs.
BIBLIOTECA MUNICIPALE, TREVISO, MS. 1492, S. 7

was marketing an array of new titles from his printing house. Among these were the sixth volume of the *Capitula Regni*, published the year before, or a biography of Saint Domenico, issued two years before.[32]

In his notes, Paulini reported the routes he followed, his means of transport, with a precise indication of associated costs (see Figure 12.2), along with daily reports of each single bargain, comprising the names of printer-publishers and booksellers, and a detailed account of the incomes and expenses.

During the forty days spent in Naples and another twenty days in Rome, Paulini sold books to private clients, such as the Jesuits in Naples. In addition, he made bargains with other booksellers. Some of these names are otherwise undocumented, which shows once again the documentary value of Ms 1492. Among these were Pietro Paolo Gallo, Giambattista Cimino, Gian Giacomo Angrisano, Francesco Montora, Giovanni Antonio Farina, Giovan Domenico Montanari and Paolo Peloso.[33] As for the items on sale, among Ciotti's bestsellers we notice the *Historia di S. Domenico*, with 61 copies disposed of to the following clients: Jesuits (1), Delfino (1), Montanari (6), Gallo (26), Cimino (5), Angrisano (2), Farina (10), Peloso (10). Twenty-four copies of *Le due deche dell'Istoria di Sicilia* were also successfully dispersed to: Delfino (1), Montanari (2), Gallo (11), Cimino (2), Angrisano (2), Farina (2) and Peloso (4).

A number of letters sent by Francesco Ciotti to Leonardo Paulini during the trade mission to Naples and Rome offer important additional information. Ciotti was following Paulini's mission closely, and provided almost in real time, according to necessity, more than one shipment of book bales both for selling

---

32   Mario Muta, *Capitulorum Regni Siciliae incliti regis Ioannis commentariorum tomus sextus* (Palermo: Decio Cirillo for Francesco Ciotti, 1627), USTC 4005364. Ferdinando del Castillo, *Dell'historia generale di S. Domenico, et dell'ordine suo de' Predicatori* (Palermo: Francesco Ciotti, 1626), USTC 4005181.

33   Agostino Contò, 'L'industria di comprar libri', p. 105.

and for barter. He continued to give directions on how the book trade transactions had to be conducted: "and above all, try to barter with all booksellers and get a good variety [of books]; and if you need other books, just write to me and I will send you more ...".[34]

From a sample examination of one of the booklists included in Paulini's commercial documents, we can see how a concise but very clear description accompanied each individual bargain. The list (see Figure 12.3) has four columns. These are, from left to right: (1) the number of copies that were sold; (2) a short-title description of the edition, with the title and author; (3) the total number of sheets for each copy; (4) the total number of sheets that were sold (that is, the multiplied value of the first and the third column).

A sample entry has been used to confirm that the data provided was absolutely correct (see Figure 12.4). The entry reads: "3 Pietro d[i] Gregorio, d[e] Censib[us]. F. 61—183". The edition is to be identified with Pietro De Gregorio, *Ad bullam apostolicam Nicolai Quinti, et regiam pragmaticam Alphonsi regis, de censibus. Commentaria.* Panhormi, ex officina typographica Francisci Ciotti, 1622 (colophon date: 1621).[35] This was a folio edition, with the following physical description: pp. [8] 207 [29]. 244 pages in folio corresponds to 61 sheets, which amounts to 183 sheets for three copies.

These lists and numbers show that the price of the item proposed for book bartering was not influenced at all by any criteria regarding the author's prestige, the type of content, the composition style, the paper quality, etc. The calculation of value was based exclusively on a numeric comparison of the number of total sheet that were exchanged. Occasionally, this raw but practical parameter for selling and buying books at the same time could also make it necessary for the booksellers to find ways of adjusting the value, when the respective total value offered by the number of sheets was not exactly the same from both parts. This was the case for a bargain with Giovanni Giacomo Angrisani in Naples, where Angrisani was required to add money (4 ducats) to match the value agreed with Paulini after the bookstock exchange was completed.

A final account of overall incomes and expenses (see Figure 12.5) is given at the end of the folder containing the bargain notes. The figures show that Ciotti could only partially repay his debt towards his assistant at the end of the prolonged bookselling trip made by Paulini on his behalf.

---

34   Letter from Palermo by Francesco Ciotti, dated 28 October 1628, just a few days after Paulini's arrival to Naples. The original reads: "... e sopra il tutto procurate de barattare con tutti librari et fare un buon asortimento [di libri]; et se vi fa bisogno di altri libri, scrivete che ve ne manderò delli altri". Treviso, Municipal Library, Ms. 1492, fol. 30.
35   USTC 4005365.

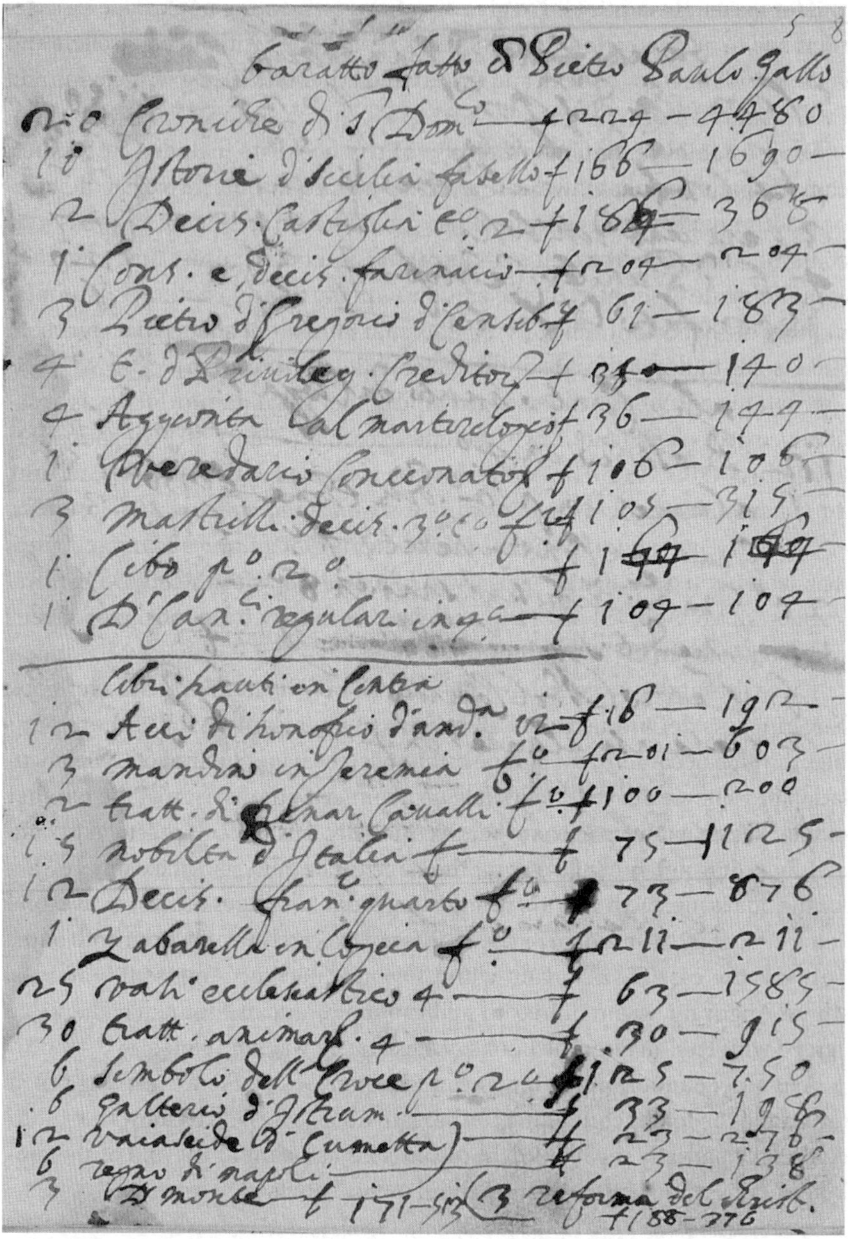

FIGURE 12.3 Naples, 1628: "Book bartering with Pietro Paulo Gallo"—"Books received in exchange"

BIBLIOTECA MUNICIPALE, TREVISO, MS. 1492, S. 8

FIGURE 12.4　Naples, 1628: Value measurement for book bartering by printed sheets. A sample entry
BIBLIOTECA MUNICIPALE, TREVISO, MS. 1492, S. 8

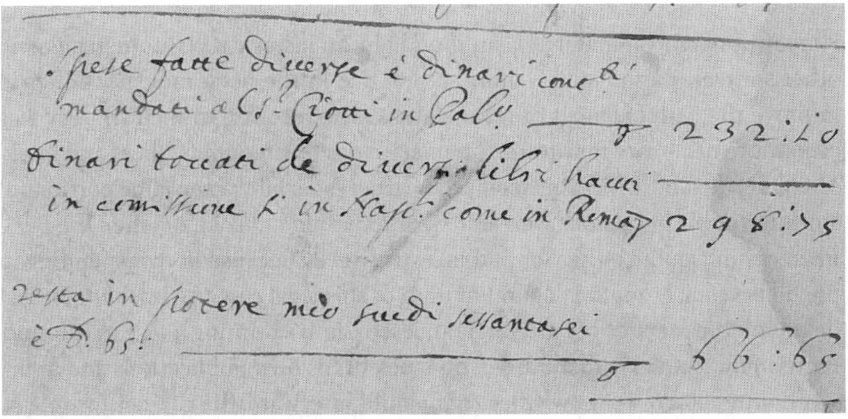

FIGURE 12.5　Rome, 1628: Final account of the bookselling trip to central Italy, including various expenses and money sent to Ciotti in Palermo; profit of book sales in Naples and Rome; unsold books.
BIBLIOTECA MUNICIPALE, TREVISO, MS. 1492, S. 15

This extraordinarily rich archive leaves many questions still to be resolved, not least whether the 1628 trip was really cost-effective for Ciotti, as Leonardo Paulini persisted in claims for his wages for some years after 1628. A second closely-related question is whether Francesco Ciotti might have gone bankrupt, as he disappeared from Palermo and possibly started a new activity as a printer-bookseller in Gubbio (1631–1637), in association with Carlo Triangoli (but we know only of 4 editions by Ciotti up to 1637, and then nothing more).[36] A slight

---

36　Paulini sought him in vain, writing from Venice to Francesco Ciotti's family (we have replies from Girolamo and Giovanni Battista the Younger) who were still residing in Palermo in 1631. For the participation of Francesco Maria Ciotti in the activity of the printing house owned in Gubbio by Marco Antonio Triangoli, see Fernando Costantini, 'Sconosciute o poco note tipografie eugubine nei secoli XVII–XX', *Bollettino della Deputazione di storia patria per l'Umbria*, 60 (1963), pp. 147–155; Andrea Capaccioni, 'Alcuni aspetti dell'attività editoriale di un comune del ducato di Urbino: Gubbio nel XVII secolo', in Patrizia Castelli and Giancarlo Pellegrini (eds.), *Storici, filosofi e cultura umanistica a Gubbio tra Cinque e Seicento* (Spoleto: Centro italiano di studi sull'alto medioevo, 1998), pp. 289–306.

difference in the name—Francesco Maria Ciotti, as opposed to Francesco Ciotti—might lead to uncertainty whether the Palermo and the Gubbio printers were the same person.

Conclusions

Sometimes archival materials can shed light on historical phenomena like no other sources. Barter was a common practice in the book industry, either to improve the cash balances or refresh stock. The recourse to such strategy was even more necessary for businessmen acting as printers/publishers and booksellers at the same time. This seems to be true, especially when large portions of a printer-publisher's stock were at risk of remaining unsold, or when the business was in trouble either for bad investments or because of overspending in previous years. From the documentation of this legal case, we learn important details on the practice of barter in Francesco Ciotti's printing house in Palermo. Bartering was an expedient to sell off stock of his own publications and at the same time to acquire new titles that would afterwards be offered for sale in Palermo from his bookshop, and help resolve the increasingly acute crisis of liquidity facing the family firm.

CHAPTER 13

The State of Scottish Bookselling circa 1800

Vivienne Dunstan

The late eighteenth and early nineteenth centuries in Scotland saw a dramatic growth in venues for reading as well as bookshops to support a growing enthusiasm for the written word.[1] Yet most attention for this period has focused on library history, and surprisingly little has been published about the Scottish book trade, at least at a national level.[2] Even the relevant volumes of *The Edinburgh History of the Book in Scotland* series are of limited use. The eighteenth-century volume has a number of chapters about bookselling, but none provide a nationwide overview.[3] The nineteenth-century volume is better in this respect, including a Scotland-wide survey by Iain Beavan, but even this is somewhat limited, relying mainly on examples from Edinburgh and northeast Scotland, which are not always representative of Scotland as a whole.[4] In addition, Beavan's ambitious chapter aims to cover nearly a whole century, so is limited in how much depth it can probe the subject.

Booksellers were vital for supporting readers, and are worth studying for that reason alone. Investigating the quantity of bookshops in a given locality, as well as the variety of their stock when such information is present, gives us a far

---

1 For a fuller discussion of change in Scottish reading habits during this time see Vivienne S. Dunstan, 'Reading habits in Scotland circa 1750–1820' (Unpublished PhD dissertation, University of Dundee, 2010).
2 For examples of individual library studies see David Allan, 'Provincial readers and book culture in the Scottish Enlightenment: the Perth library, 1784–c1800', *The Library*, 3.4 (2002), pp. 367–389; and Mark Towsey, 'First steps in associational reading: book use and sociability at the Wigtown Subscription Library, 1795–9', *Papers of the Bibliographical Society of America*, 103 (2009), pp. 455–495. There are also pieces about the Scottish book trade in the *Print Networks* series of books about British book trade history. But generally these are case studies of individual booksellers or local areas, rather than larger studies.
3 Stephen W. Brown and Warren McDougall (eds.), *The Edinburgh History of the Book in Scotland*, Vol. II, *Enlightenment and Expansion 1707–1800* (Edinburgh: Edinburgh University Press, 2011). Bookselling topics covered by individual chapters include local case studies of Edinburgh, Glasgow and Aberdeen; as well as studies of Gaelic books and the market for French books in Scotland.
4 Iain Beavan, 'Bookselling', in Bill Bell (ed.), *The Edinburgh History of the Book in Scotland*, Vol. III, *Ambition and Industry 1800–80* (Edinburgh: Edinburgh University Press, 2007), pp. 123–140.

more detailed image of what and how many books readers could, and did, purchase. This kind of information cannot be deduced simply by looking at the printed output, because that is often lacking any further characterisation of quantity and quality. Estimating how many editions were printed of certain texts can only give an impression as to the consumption of these texts; but establishing how many were sold, where, and when, offers a far better insight, which takes into account the presence of imported and second-hand books, as well as new ones. By undertaking such a study at a national level we can better understand a country's reading habits, including the opportunities readers had to purchase books. It also provides a basis from which to compare findings with other countries. Studying this particular time period can also help to facilitate comparisons with scholars studying the book trade in earlier periods.

This chapter examines the state of the Scottish bookselling trade at the crucial transition point between the eighteenth and nineteenth centuries, assessing its size, considering how bookselling fitted into the urban hierarchy, and looking at the type of books sold. This chapter is developed from a wider doctoral study into Scottish reading habits during this period, but expands on that earlier study considerably, involving both new research and new analysis.[5]

Size of Scottish Bookselling

There is no easy way to estimate the size of the Scottish booktrade at this time. Booksellers' records are remarkably scarce for the period around 1800—to the extent that useful analogies can be drawn between researching lost books and 'lost' booksellers.[6] This was before the era of widespread trade directories: generally only the largest Scottish cities like Edinburgh and Glasgow had any local directories before 1820.[7] Nor are there comprehensive lists of booksellers at this time. There was no central register of bookselling in Scotland, and no need, for example, to have a license to trade as a bookseller. As a result, we have only sporadic references to booksellers, and estimating their numbers is somewhat fraught.

---

5 Dunstan, 'Reading habits in Scotland circa 1750–1820', in particular pp. 29–30.
6 The subject of lost books has been discussed at length in Flavia Bruni and Andrew Pettegree (eds.), *Lost Books. Reconstructing the Print World of Pre-Industrial Europe* (Leiden: Brill, 2016).
7 Edinburgh had directories from 1773 onwards, and Glasgow from 1783. Many early Scottish directories are available online as part of the National Library of Scotland's digitised collection.

An obvious source to check is the Scottish Book Trade Index (SBTI), hosted at the National Library of Scotland website.[8] This provides a listing, with sources, of booksellers, printers, publishers and other people involved with the book trade, known to have been active in Scotland before 1850. This resource, despite being the most advanced currently available for the scope of this study, is based on information which is necessarily incomplete. References to booksellers before 1800 are drawn from various primary sources, such as probate inventories, business records and court cases. Of course, this leaves out an unknown number of individuals who may well have been active in the period of this investigation, but have not yet been found in any extant document, and therefore do not appear in SBTI. Nevertheless the SBTI is a valuable resource, which continues to improve with new finds, and is a vital reference work for researchers studying the Scottish book trade and print history at this time.

Entries in the SBTI for booksellers vary in terms of their detail, depending on how much information has been found in documentary sources for each bookseller. Typically, though, each entry gives the name of the bookseller, their place of activity (down to street address if known), and the dates they are known to have been active. In addition, if further information about their trading is known, such as a bankruptcy or probate inventory of their stock after death, then this will be detailed in the SBTI too.

Looking through the SBTI for booksellers known to be active between 1790 and 1810—a time range hopefully long enough to maximise references to traders active in 1800, but not too long to catch others active at other dates— identifies 411 relevant entries. There is some overlap in these entries, between booksellers trading under different partnerships and combinations. This figure probably underestimates the number of booksellers active in the 20-year period, missing those unrecorded anywhere in surviving records. Likewise, it probably slightly overestimates those active in 1800. But it is an approximate guide. Helpfully we can compare this estimate of booksellers active in 1800 with the number of booksellers recorded two decades later in the 1825 Pigot's directory, one of the earliest nationwide trade directories for Scotland.[9] Pigot's 1825 lists 369 booksellers trading throughout Scotland, again possibly an approximate number, but reassuringly close enough to the 1800 SBTI estimate to give confidence about the earlier number. It is worth pausing to reflect how this number of booksellers relates to the overall population. Scotland's population

---

8   Scottish Book Trade Index: http://www.nls.uk/catalogues/scottish-book-trade-index, last accessed 4 June 2018.
9   *Pigot & Co's New Commercial Directory of Scotland for 1825–6* (London: J. Pigot and Co, 1825).

in 1801 was 1,608,420, suggesting that with about 400 booksellers trading there was a bookseller for approximately every 4,000 people in the country.[10]

The estimates above are based on traders identified explicitly in historical records as booksellers. Bookselling would have been their primary occupation, and in many cases their only one. SBTI only collects references to this type of bookseller. However dedicated booksellers were not the only sellers of reading material during this period, and we underestimate the scale and quality of the Scottish book trade if we rely upon them alone.

Other Scottish sellers of print at this time were merchants or general dealers, and chapmen. These sellers were not too different from newsagents or other small shops selling a limited range of books today. Such dealers would not have carried the same range of reading material as a more dedicated bookseller, but could have filled a gap in the retail network, selling print in places in both town and countryside where conventional booksellers were not found, or were limited in number.

The importance of this hitherto little considered aspect of bookselling becomes apparent when the inventories made of the stock of relevant traders after their death are examined. Consider, for example, the case of John Brown merchant in Thornhill. After he died in 1784 an inventory of his goods, including his shop stock, was drawn up as part of the process of assessing the value of his estate.[11] This reveals that in addition to carrying goods such as cloth, various food stuffs and other miscellaneous household goods, he stocked reading material to sell, in particular the following items:

> Item three Common Bibles worth Four shillings & nine pence. Item three small gilt Bibles worth seven shillings. Item a pair gilt Bibles worth Four shillings. Item a New Testament & Willis's Directory worth One shilling & two pence. Item a Bible with Margins worth Three shillings.

Although 'merchant' as a term was used at this time in Scotland for major importers and exporters, especially in port towns and cities, it was also used, and much more frequently, for the more numerous small shopkeepers, usually found in towns.[12] Such traders, who are also referred to in historical records as

---

10   James Gray Kyd (ed.), *Scottish Population Statistics including Webster's Analysis of Population 1755* (Edinburgh: Scottish Academic Press, 1952), p. xvii.
11   Edinburgh, National Records of Scotland (NRS), Dumfries Commissary Court testaments, CC5/6/16, 15 March 1784.
12   The *Dictionary of the Scots Language* is useful in this context. Its entry for 'merchant' is available online at http://www.dsl.ac.uk/entry/snd/merchant, last accessed 4 June 2018.

grocers, general dealers or shopkeepers, sold a mixture of food stuffs and other everyday items. Note that such 'merchants' in Scotland are different from more specific shopkeepers, like fishmongers, ironmongers etc. Rather they are closer to the concept of a modern small corner shop keeper, selling a general mix typically of food stuffs, household goods, and, sometimes, also a modest range of reading material.

There are no reliable lists of merchants in Scotland before the 1820s, when national trade directories began. Pigot's 1825 national directory is one of the earliest comprehensive listings, recording local tradesmen for each town and village across the country. A search for merchants (recorded under different terms in different parts of the directory) finds nearly 5,000 such traders in Scotland in 1825, over ten times the number of dedicated booksellers known to exist at the same time. Not all of these merchants would have sold reading material, but it is likely that many of them did, and they should not be overlooked in the wider picture of the book trade.

Merchants were not the only less visible sellers of print. In particular we should consider the role of chapmen, sellers of cheap goods, often including print, and often taking their goods far into the countryside to sell to householders.[13] Again post mortem inventories provide useful clues, indicating the type of goods such dealers sold. Consider, for example, James McTurk chapman in Chanlockfoot (d. 1780).[14] He seems to have specialised in selling print, as his inventory reveals:

> Item Catechisms & Ballads worth Threepence. Item A Margin'd Bible worth Four shillings. Item a new paper book worth Three shillings. Item Rochester's Poems worth Six pence. Item a French Spelling book worth Five pence. Item Introductor of Grammar worth Fourpence. Item a Memorandum book worth Two pence. Item The Gentle Shepherd worth a penny. Item Court against Whigs worth Six pence. Item Confession of Faith worth a Shilling. Item Isaac Ambrose Looking to Jesus worth one shilling and sixpence. Item an English psalm book worth two pence. Item a pair of Half Bibles worth Two shillings & sixpence. Item a pocket Bible with a Slip worth Two shillings.

---

13 For more on Scottish chapmen see John Morris, 'The Scottish Chapman', in Robin Myers, Michael Harris and Giles Mandelbrote (eds.), *Fairs, Markets & the Itinerant Book Trade* (New Castle, DE, and London: Oak Knoll Press, 2007), pp. 159–186.
14 NRS, Dumfries Commissary Court testaments, CC5/6/16, 19 September 1780.

Not all chapmen would have carried such a high concentration of reading material. Some would have carried none at all, favouring other more traditional chapman goods such as handkerchiefs, buttons and ribbons, all low-cost everyday items that would always find buyers. Other chapman would have carried a few pamphlets or a cheap psalm book or bible to sell alongside other goods. It is impossible to quantify what percentage of Scottish chapmen carried print to sell, but any of them could have done, so it is worthwhile considering how many traders this may have involved.

Counting chapmen is much harder than counting merchants, because chapmen do not appear in trade directories. Indeed, they are only mentioned rarely in historical records at all. Chapmen are rarely recorded in surviving probate inventories, unlike other tradesmen such as shopkeepers, including booksellers. Fortunately, there are rare exceptions to this lack of historical evidence, which we can use to estimate the size of the trade. The Fife Chapman Society seems to have been a communal trade organisation, registering chapmen in Fife as members ('brothers') of the society, and possibly offering assistance to chapmen in difficulty. The society's manuscript records in the late eighteenth century give a useful indication of the distribution and concentration of chapmen in this area, revealing them active in numerous communities, from towns, through villages to large numbers of smaller hamlets and isolated rural settlements. Many of these chapmen would have travelled around their local areas, carrying goods to sell to people in their homes. Such a distribution, both in number and types of communities represented, was probably mirrored throughout much of Scotland, certainly in Lowland areas.[15] From the number of known Fife chapmen in the late eighteenth century, and comparing the Fife population and geographic area to the Scotland-wide figures, we can cautiously suggest that there were probably over a thousand chapmen active throughout Scotland at this time, and possibly significantly more than this.[16] Any of these chapmen could have sold print.

Booksellers and the Urban Hierarchy

The previous sections considered the numbers of booksellers active throughout Scotland at this time, both specialist booksellers, and more general traders such as merchants and chapmen, who often sold reading material alongside

---

15   Edinburgh, National Library of Scotland, Fife Chapman Society records, MS 200.
16   For a fuller discussion of how this estimate is computed see Vivienne Dunstan, 'Chapmen in Eighteenth-Century Scotland', *Scottish Literary Review*, 9 (2017), pp. 41–57: 50.

other goods. This section develops that idea further by examining the way in which these different aspects of the book trade interacted with the Scottish urban hierarchy. As we shall see different types of bookseller were found in different types of town and village, collectively catering for a diverse range of customers.

Dedicated booksellers tended to be found in towns rather than villages. By 1800 it would have been unusual for a Scottish town not to have had at least one bookseller. By contrast general merchants were found in all sizes of community, including the smallest villages. Chapmen extended the reach of the book trade still further, carrying goods to customers dwelling in country areas, often far from more populous towns, though some chapmen were based in towns rather than the countryside.

This retail pattern can be demonstrated by considering a local case study of a single Scottish county and a number of communities inside it. Consider the example of Fife. By 1801 Fife had a population of 93,743, and included approximately twenty towns, as well as a large number of smaller villages.[17] For this case study we will consider three of these communities in more detail: Kirkcaldy, St Andrews and Kingsbarns.

Kirkcaldy on the south coast was one of the largest towns in Fife, with a probable town population in 1801 of approximately 9,000 inhabitants.[18] Yet it was not the official county town, which was Cupar, so had no concentration of professionals associated with county towns such as lawyers. Nor was it an elite centre, attracting gentry and associated services. Rather it was a fishing and manufacturing town, albeit very populous. From Pigot's directory of 1825 we find that there were three bookshops in Kirkcaldy, and about fifty merchants or general dealers. Similarly from the Fife Chapman Society we know that there were at least three chapmen in Kirkcaldy in the closing decades of the eighteenth century. The number of bookshops is a reflection of Kirk-

---

17   House of Commons Parliamentary Papers 1801–1802 (09), *Abstract of Answers and Returns under Act for taking Account of Population of Great Britain (Enumeration Abstract), 1801*, p. 531. Pigot's 1825 directory is a good guide to Scottish towns in this era, though many were very small, often little more than villages. Some were royal burghs, others burghs of barony, both giving them trading rights.

18   *The New Statistical Account of Scotland* (Edinburgh and London: William Blackwood and Sons, 1845), vol. 9, pp. 741 and 750. The parish accounts for the *New Statistical Account* were compiled by the relevant Church of Scotland parish ministers, and often include useful qualitative local information in addition to the bare statistics available elsewhere. For example the Kirkcaldy account reveals that the town then included inhabitants from a number of separate parishes, all counted separately in the census. So the 1801 Kirkcaldy parish population is only part of the likely population total for the town then.

FIGURE 13.1　Herman Moll's *The Shires of Fife and Kinros* (1732)
REPRODUCED BY PERMISSION OF THE NATIONAL LIBRARY OF SCOTLAND

caldy's population, as is the large number of general dealers. Scotland at this time seems to have had relatively high literacy levels, and it is likely that many inhabitants in towns such as Kirkcaldy would have been able to read.[19] Even those who could not read could listen to other people reading to them.

By contrast St Andrews, in the north-east of the county, was a much smaller town, with only about 3,000 inhabitants in 1801.[20] Yet it was an intellectual hotspot, a university town, and a major centre for learning. This is probably why it had as many as two dedicated bookshops in 1825, more than might have

---

19　For a fuller discussion of the debates about Scottish literacy at this time and its implications for reading habits see Dunstan, 'Reading habits in Scotland circa 1750–1820', pp. 26–27.

20　*New Statistical Account*, vol. 9, p. 471. This estimated town population for 1801 is based on a St Andrews parish population in 1801 of 4,203, and suggestions from later census returns that probably over 1200 of these people lived in the rural parts of the parish, outside the main town area.

been expected given its population alone. The location of one of the bookshops, George Scott's, is not recorded in the directory, but the other bookshop, Joseph Cook's, was in the town centre, in Market Street. The SBTI records a great deal of detail about the history of this shop, which Joseph Cook took over in 1824, and which stayed in his family until 1900. Yet again these dedicated bookshops were greatly outnumbered by small general shopkeepers, with fourteen in 1825. There was only one known chapman in the town in the late eighteenth century, George Hutton, which also offers insights into the typology of printed items that would have been purchased in town.[21] St Andrews had an unusual status as a university town. Most towns of its size around 1800 would have had one bookseller at the very most, and a number of more general dealers providing important access to print too.

The third community considered here, Kingsbarns, lies about nine miles south-east of St Andrews. This was, and still is, a tiny village, with only about 600 inhabitants in the village in 1801.[22] Kingsbarns exemplifies a community too small to support a dedicated bookshop, but it had one grocer or merchant in 1825, who may have sold print alongside everyday essential items. Likewise there was a chapman in Kingsbarns in the late eighteenth century, who could have sold cheap print to the village's inhabitants. Some of the Kingsbarns residents would have travelled occasionally to larger towns, such as St Andrews, giving them the opportunity to visit dedicated bookshops. But it seems likely that for many this would have been an occasional event at best. As a consequence less visible sellers of print—the grocer and the chapman—may have played a vital role in the provision of reading material to this small rural community.

Studying a Fife Bookseller in More Detail: George Scott in St Andrews

The Pigot's 1825 directory lists two booksellers active in St Andrews in 1825. One of these, George Scott, left a detailed record of his bookshop stock after death, which is well worth analysing further, giving a vivid glimpse of a bookshop at this time.[23] The inventory was drawn up after George Scott died on 24th Jan-

---

21   George Hutton was admitted as a member ('Brother') of the Fife Chapman Society on 13 April 1774.
22   *New Statistical Account*, vol. 9, p. 93. Again this is an estimated figure, based on the village/rural split recorded in the statistical account for the census of 1811.
23   NRS, Cupar Sheriff Court testaments, SC20/50/3, 20 August 1828.

uary 1828. Four pages of the inventory list debts owing to him when he died. Many of the names listed would be bookshop customers, such as university Principal Nicoll, Professor Alexander, and various university students, including Mr Leslie who owed Scott 17 shillings 3 pence. Even the University of St Andrews appears in the list as a debtor, owing Scott 6 shillings 6 pence. Teachers also appear, such as Samuel Messieux, teacher of French at the town's school, Madras College. Outside academia a number of local gentry are named, both those within the town, such as Alexander Binny Esquire who lived in South Street, and those further afield, such as Thomas Horsbrugh Esquire at Cupar, probably the Sheriff Clerk at the time of that name. Local ministers are also included in the list of debtors, as well as other less identifiable people, often owing smaller amounts. Whether all were customers buying on account is not clear, but it seems likely that George Scott catered for a wide range of customers.

Even more informative is the 14-page detailed inventory of the bookshop's stock. As well as recording specific titles and how many copies were held it indicates how the shop was physically arranged. It was not possible to locate the shop precisely, nor to restrict its location to a specific street, but it is likely that it was in the town centre, most probably in Market Street or South Street. From the inventory we learn that the books placed in the shop window leaned heavily towards an academic readership. Mathematical texts were on display, as well as a French grammar and a Greek-Latin dictionary. Books appealing to more general readers were also promoted, such as *Tours thro Scotland* and Lempriere's *Dictionary* of myths and legends, although the latter could also appeal to classics scholars. Finally, beside the books in the window was a case of instruments, probably mathematical, again targeting the academic community, and ink stands, reflecting the shop's other function as a stationer's.

The front room of the bookshop held the main stock for sale. Here were about 250 different titles, probably upwards of a thousand books in total.[24] There were novels, particularly those by Maria Edgeworth and Sir Walter Scott. But these were greatly outnumbered by educational books, especially religious texts, classical works and language primers. Such educational books probably targeted both university students and school pupils. Many of the university-level texts can be found on surviving class reading lists from this time.[25] Ref-

---

24   This figure does not treat multi-volume works separately. So, for example, a three-volume novel counts as one book in the same way that a single-volume dictionary would.

25   Fortunately details of typical expenses for St Andrews students in 1827, including on books by subject, are recorded in a Royal Commission report compiled between 1826 and 1837: *Evidence, oral and documentary, taken and received by the commissioners, appointed by His Majesty George IV, July 23rd 1826, and re-appointed by His Majesty William IV, October 12th,*

erence works were also stocked, for example dictionaries and books useful for business men, as well as a number of pamphlets and magazines. The shop also sold rarer and sometimes more obscure texts, such as the recently published *Account of the ferry across the Tay at Dundee*. Books for sale were arranged around the room, some in cupboards (presses); other items were displayed in glass cases. Alongside the books were stationery items for sale, including numerous types of paper, as well as quills, ink stands, and games like backgammon and chess.

Behind the main public area of the shop was a back room. Here more stationery items were stocked, as well as '700 odd vols of old novels &c in circulg. libry'. Running a circulating library from a bookshop was common practice in Scotland, but this particular library has not been noted in the literature before.[26] Circulating libraries were strongly associated with novels, but also stocked other texts to borrow, and could provide low-cost access to reading material for the local community. Also detailed in Scott's inventory are the contents of the 'Binding Shop', revealing that Scott bound books for customers, so essential in an age when books were often sold unbound. Indeed the shop's binding tools were some of the most valuable items that George Scott possessed when he died, valued at £5 5 shillings.

George Scott was just one bookseller, but he exemplifies many common features of booksellers at this time in Scotland, giving a rich insight into how such a shop could be managed and physically arranged. From the books displayed in the window through to those in the front room and beyond, the stock seems to have been largely typical, albeit with a leaning towards educational texts, reflecting his location in a university town. The additional presence in the bookshop of a circulating library, here stored in the back room, was also typical for this time, providing another valuable income stream for a bookseller, meaning that he did not have to rely purely on sales alone. Finally, the bindery was also a typical element of a Scottish bookshop around 1800, though rarely recorded in such detail as in this example.

1830, for visiting the universities of Scotland (London: HMSO, 1837), volume III ('University of St Andrews'), pp. 292–293.

26 For example it is not included in the SBTI entry for George Scott, which is unaware of his inventory.

Types of Books Sold

Having considered the size and distribution of the bookselling trade it is worth considering more fully what types of books were sold. Here we are on firmer ground, with a good body of evidence, from varied sources such as newspaper advertisements, bookseller catalogues, and personal inventories of book owners, similar to the example of George Scott cited above, but drawing on a broader survey of surviving documentary records.[27]

Dedicated booksellers sold the widest range of reading material, in contrast to merchants or general dealers, who may have only carried a few pamphlets or cheap bibles alongside other goods. Likewise chapmen were particularly associated with cheap print, and again religious books such as bibles or psalms, which could always find a market. The discussion that follows focuses primarily on dedicated booksellers, and the wider range of reading material that they sold.

Although we might assume that dedicated bookshops sold more expensive books, evidence from their stock lists indicates that they sold books ranging across a broad range of prices, from a few pennies to many shillings.[28] Many titles were available in the same bookshop in multiple editions, making the books affordable to poorer customers, as well as wealthier customers who may have bought more expensive editions. Books were often sold unbound, providing another opportunity for variation in quality, with some customers choosing to buy more expensive bindings.[29] Many booksellers, like George Scott, offered binding services in-house as part of their services; in other cases customers could take their books to external binders to be bound, at least in larger towns, where there were bookbinders trading separately from booksellers.

Mail order was also an important factor in Scottish bookselling, both in terms of sourcing books for bookshops to sell, and customers buying from the bookshops. Contemporary newspaper advertisements from booksellers show

---

27 This was a large-scale survey, and the numerous examples found are not referenced individually here. For fuller information about the methodology and range of sources used see throughout Dunstan, 'Reading habits in Scotland circa 1750–1820'.

28 See for example Vivienne S. Dunstan, 'Two booksellers in south-west Scotland in the late eighteenth and early nineteenth centuries: the records of Ebenezer Wilson and James Meuros', *Journal of the Edinburgh Bibliographical Society*, 11 (2016), pp. 43–63.

29 Provincial bookselling in eighteenth-century England is described in John Feather, *The Provincial Book Trade in Eighteenth-Century England* (Cambridge: Cambridge University Press, 1985), pp. 69–97 (Chapter 5, 'The Bookselling Business'), including the widespread practice of selling books unbound. It is likely that a Scottish provincial bookseller from the same period would have followed a largely similar pattern.

the prestige associated with books sourced from Edinburgh or London, with provincial booksellers often advertising that they could get these in for their local customers.[30] Equally, though, customers at a distance from their preferred bookshop could buy books by mail order if need be, though at the extra cost of paying for carriage, which would make it an option only for the wealthier members of society.

In terms of subject matter, the eighteenth century saw dramatic changes in the books Scots were reading, something that was reflected to a large extent by the books available to buy. Whereas in 1700 Scots were likely to read only religious works, by 1800 they were reading a wider range of books. Religious reading continued, particularly of the Bible, but increasingly took its place alongside other subjects and genres, such as history and biography, voyages and travels, books about new scientific discoveries and ways of thinking, and the increasingly popular and numerous novels.[31] Though as the example of George Scott illustrates, there could be a difference between the subjects customers would buy compared with what they might be more likely to borrow, even within the same bookshop.

This was also the era following the copyright trials of the 1770s which led to a relaxation of copyright controls, and a flood of low-cost reprints of so-called 'Old Canon' works by writers such as Shakespeare, Pope and Dryden.[32] Even near contemporary authors like Fielding were being reprinted cheaply, opening up an increasing range of affordable texts to the wider population. It is less clear what impact a flood of cheap books would have had in terms of the viability of bookselling as a business.[33] There is certainly evidence that bookselling could be a vulnerable trade in Scotland, with a relatively high number of bankruptcies among booksellers. Figure 13.2 shows one of these, reported in an advertisement in *The Scotsman* newspaper.[34]

The bookseller in this case, Andrew Orr, had been trading since at least 1820, with the earliest reference found to him in Cupar in Pigot's directory of 1820. It is likely that he was in business in the town for some years before then. After

---

30   There are countless examples of this practice recorded in Scottish newspaper advertisements, easily found by looking in provincial newspapers from this period.
31   For more discussion of this change over time see Dunstan, 'Reading habits in Scotland circa 1750–1820', pp. 76–151.
32   For perhaps the most detailed account of this phenomenon see William St Clair, *The Reading Nation in the Romantic Period* (Cambridge: Cambridge University Press, 2004), pp. 122–139.
33   I am grateful to one of the attendees at the original conference on 'Buying and Selling' for stimulating some thought on this issue.
34   *The Scotsman*, 8 January 1825, p. 5.

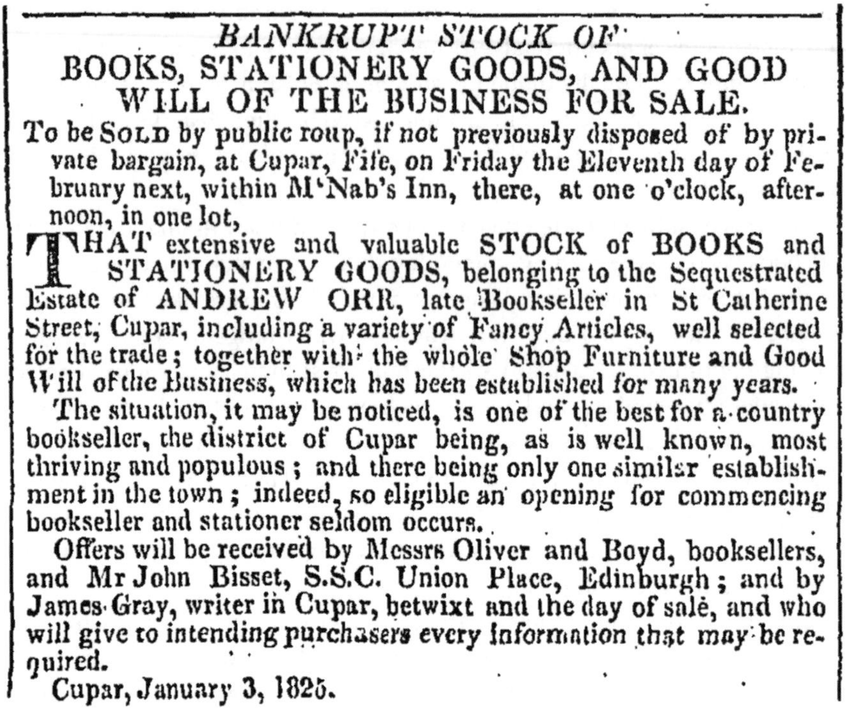

> **BANKRUPT STOCK OF**
> **BOOKS, STATIONERY GOODS, AND GOOD**
> **WILL OF THE BUSINESS FOR SALE.**
>
> To be SOLD by public roup, if not previously disposed of by private bargain, at Cupar, Fife, on Friday the Eleventh day of February next, within M'Nab's Inn, there, at one o'clock, afternoon, in one lot,
>
> THAT extensive and valuable STOCK of BOOKS and STATIONERY GOODS, belonging to the Sequestrated Estate of ANDREW ORR, late Bookseller in St Catherine Street, Cupar, including a variety of Fancy Articles, well selected for the trade; together with the whole Shop Furniture and Good Will of the Business, which has been established for many years.
>
> The situation, it may be noticed, is one of the best for a country bookseller, the district of Cupar being, as is well known, most thriving and populous; and there being only one similar establishment in the town; indeed, so eligible an opening for commencing bookseller and stationer seldom occurs.
>
> Offers will be received by Messrs Oliver and Boyd, booksellers, and Mr John Bisset, S.S.C. Union Place, Edinburgh; and by James Gray, writer in Cupar, betwixt and the day of sale, and who will give to intending purchasers every information that may be required.
>
> Cupar, January 3, 1825.

FIGURE 13.2   Newspaper advertisement for sale of goods of bankrupt bookseller. *The Scotsman*, 8 January 1825

his business failed his entire stock and the goodwill of the business and its customers was up for sale: although whether this would have been as good a prospect for someone else to invest in as the advert suggests is questionable.

Andrew Orr was just one of many booksellers who the SBTI reveals went bankrupt. In addition we find many booksellers appearing in the records of sequestrated estates in the National Records of Scotland.[35] These were records seized as part of Court of Session cases, often, although not always, involving bankruptcy. Finding a bookseller among these papers means that there is often a detailed paper trail recording the bookseller's stock and their customers, allowing their business and wider business networks to be probed more fully. We must bear in mind that many of the booksellers in these records were book-

---

35   These records are held in the CS96 category at the National Records of Scotland in Edinburgh. These records can be searched using the National Records of Scotland catalogue, including online. In addition there are a number of published indexes for these records, including the List and Index Society's Special Series Volume 23 *Scottish Record Office Court of Session Productions c1760–1840* (Richmond: List and Index Society, 1987).

sellers whose businesses had failed, and that they may not be representative of wider bookselling business practices at this time.

Conclusion

This paper can only provide a brief overview of a large and varied bookselling trade in Scotland circa 1800. Yet in doing so it provides new perspectives, in particular about the size of the trade, and the ways in which it interacted with the urban hierarchy. Perhaps the most surprising finding is how many traders could be selling books in Scotland at this time. It is relatively easy to calculate the number of dedicated bookshops, but these were dwarfed by a larger number of more general retail shops, run by small-scale merchants, many of which sold print as well as other goods. In addition, many chapmen, low-cost sellers of cheap goods, carried and sold print into urban and rural Scotland, and again in larger potential numbers than dedicated bookshops alone.

Studying options for book buying in terms of the urban hierarchy illustrates how complex the picture was across Scotland. The case of Fife demonstrates the variety of bookselling options found in a range of communities, from larger commercial centres, through to smaller towns, and then to the level of villages and the countryside beyond that. It is too easy in book history to focus on the larger and better-known population centres, and in the process overlook the experiences of people living in smaller and more isolated communities. It is remarkable how affordable books were for many people. Even dedicated bookshops sold books at a range of prices, often the exact same title available in a variety of editions, costs and quality, catering for different customers. This was also the era of low-cost 'copyright free' reprints, which brought more cheap books onto the market. This could also have had consequences for the viability of a bookseller's business.

From the perspective of a historian of reading, perhaps the most positive point to take from such a large and widespread bookselling trade is how this must reflect a national enthusiasm in Scotland circa 1800 for reading. Such a large and vibrant bookselling trade, albeit one with some bankruptcies, could only be sustained by a population with a considerable appetite for reading, an activity they were willing to invest money in. Likewise, the range of prices of books available, and the spread of bookselling far through the urban hierarchy, reaching the smallest and most remote villages, and even rural country areas, reflects an eagerness for reading by this time that spread throughout Scottish society, and was not restricted to the wealthy elite.

CHAPTER 14

Cashing in on Counterfeits: Fraud in the Reformation Print Industry

Drew B. Thomas

Martin Luther was interrupted one evening in 1525 with some disturbing news. His manuscript for a new collection of sermons had been stolen by an assistant and taken to a printer in a neighbouring town.[1] Luther's works were in high demand and printers knew they would sell quickly; a first edition was a prized possession. This troubled Luther, as he knew there were many unauthorized copies of his works, but feared their inaccuracies corrupted his Reformation message. Yet even at the height of his fame, there was little he could do.

That same year during the German Peasants' War, Luther published *An Admonition to Peace: A Reply to the Twelve Articles of the Peasants in Swabia*. It was an extremely popular work with thirteen editions that year alone, ten of which were printed in Luther's hometown of Wittenberg. At least that is what printers wanted you to think. In reality only three editions were printed in Wittenberg.[2] The rest were counterfeits.

Luther's Protestant Reformation caused a surge in printing activity across early modern Europe. By 1521, only four years after he posted his *Ninety-Five Theses*, more books had been published by Luther than any other author since the invention of the printing press in the mid-fifteenth century.[3] Due to the growth of the industry many new printers entered the trade, hoping to make their fortune. Many participated in a widespread practice of re-printing unauthorized copies of popular editions. This was a common and accepted practice within the industry at this time. However, many printers took it a step further. In addition to unauthorized reprints, several printers intentionally printed false publication information on the title page. This was particularly true when it came to Wittenberg. During Luther's lifetime, hundreds of editions were printed that were falsely attributed to Wittenberg. The practice was prevalent

---

1 Luther recalls this in the preface of *Auslegunge der Episteln und Evangelien von der heyligen drey Koenige fest bis auff Ostern gebessert* (Wittenberg: Melchior II Lotter for Lucas Cranach & Christian Döring, 1525). USTC 613951.
2 The three Wittenberg editions, all by Joseph Klug, are USTC 653523, 653524, and 653525.
3 Figures from the USTC.

across Europe, encompassing the Holy Roman Empire, the Swiss Confederation, the Low Countries, and even reaching all the way to London and Paris.

While there have been documented cases of piracy of other printers or authors, this is the first case in which a single printing city was the focus of such widespread fraud. Wittenberg was the fulcrum of the Reformation movement and its presence on the title page brought authority and authenticity to a document. Printers recognized this and used it to their advantage. They knew that works from Wittenberg sold well and that their works were more likely to sell well too if thought to be from Wittenberg. They accomplished this by printing 'Wittenberg' on their title pages and omitting the truthful city of publication.

In 1895, the bibliographer George Frederick Barwick noted a wide variety of typefaces used in the large number of Wittenberg pamphlets in circulation. He concluded that Wittenberg imprints could not be trusted.[4] He was correct. The reason there was such a large variety of typefaces was because they belonged to around seventy different printers who published counterfeit Wittenberg editions. Hans-Jörg Künast also remarked upon this practice in his analysis of the Augsburg printing industry.[5] Although this phenomenon has been remarked upon before now, it has never been the subject of systematic investigation. In this essay I attempt the first systematized examination of these counterfeits by dividing them under four categories: works that were false by association, false by implication, simple counterfeit, and advanced counterfeit. This essay offers a methodological discussion of each category, with practical examples. It then presents different ways in which Luther and the printers of Wittenberg attempted to fight the counterfeits, which was made more difficult by wider geographical distribution. The concluding section offers some broader considerations about the role played by misleading or fraudulent imprints in the buying and selling of early modern books.

False by Association

Numerous Reformation pamphlets were printed that provide no publication information. Sometimes the year was listed, but the printer and place of publication were absent. Even Wittenberg editions often excluded the place of publication. At this point there was no standard practice in the German print

---

4 George Frederick Barwick, 'The Lutheran press at Wittenberg', *Transactions of the Bibliographical Society*, 3 (1896), pp. 9–25: 10.
5 Hans-Jörg Künast, *Getruckt zu Augsburg: Buchdruck und Buchhandel in Augsburg zwischen 1468 und 1555* (Tübingen: Niemeyer, 1997) pp. 167–168.

industry. However, even if the place of publication was omitted in Reformation pamphlets, printers were still sure to include 'Wittenberg' on the title page, but not necessarily in the imprint. Rather, they listed 'Wittenberg' at the end of the title, using phrases such as *'Doctor Martini Luthers Augustiner zu Wittenberg'* or *'Predig zu Wittenberg'*. This was especially common at the beginning of the movement, when Luther's name was not as well known, but people were aware of a movement by an Augustinian monk in Wittenberg. These works were published sometimes with or sometimes without a colophon. Regardless, Wittenberg was often the only city mentioned on the title page.[6] While there was no intent to deceive, as there was no untruthful information printed, printers were clearly keen to associate their works with Wittenberg.

In 1520 the Augsburg printer Silvan Otmar printed a controversial sermon by Luther on excommunication.[7] The title page is in a large typeface surrounded by a four-piece, floriated woodcut title page border. Only the year is listed in the imprint. However, the title ends with '*zu Wittenberg*' broken over two lines of text. It is the only city mentioned on the title page (Figure 14.1).[8]

Another edition of that sermon was printed in Nuremberg.[9] This title page is much simpler with no woodcut border or imprint. There is only a three-line title with the first line in a larger typeface. In this example, 'Wittenberg' is also listed at the end of the title: *'Augustiner zu wittenbergk.'* Although the typeface is smaller, 'Wittenberg' is not split over two lines, as in the previous example. This improves the visibility of the word, thus making it more recognisable.

We may also cite the example of a work published by Hans Froschauer in Augsburg in 1519.[10] It also has a title page border and a title with the first line in a larger typeface. There is no imprint. In this example 'Wittenberg' is the last word of the title and the only city mentioned on the title page. Unlike the previous examples, 'Wittenberg' is on a line by itself. The decreasing centre

---

6   However, while outside the scope of this research, even works with an imprint stating another city, but also using Wittenberg in the title, are still trying to associate the work with Wittenberg.
7   Martin Luther, *Ain sermon von dem bann* (Augsburg: Silvan Otmar, 1520), USTC 610282. Bibliothèque de la société de l'histoire du protestantisme français, 4° 1317 Rés.
8   All images from the Bayerische Staatsbibliothek are used under the CC BY-NC-SA 4.0 license.
9   Martin Luther, *Ein sermon von dem bann* (Nuremberg: Jobst Gutknecht, 1520), USTC 647046. Bibliothèque de la société de l'histoire du protestantisme français, 4° 1318 Rés.
10 Martin Luther, *Ain sermon von dem gebett unnd procession. In der Creütgwochen. Mit einer kurtzen Außlegung des vatter unnsers für sich und hinter sich oratio dominica dicitur et oratur duplici via recta et versa* (Augsburg: Hans Froschauer, 1519), USTC 610357. Bayerische Staatsbibliothek, 4 Hom. 1185 http://www.mdz-nbn-resolving.de/urn/resolver.pl?urn=urn:nbn:de:bvb:12-bsb10161421-5, last accessed: 4 January 2019.

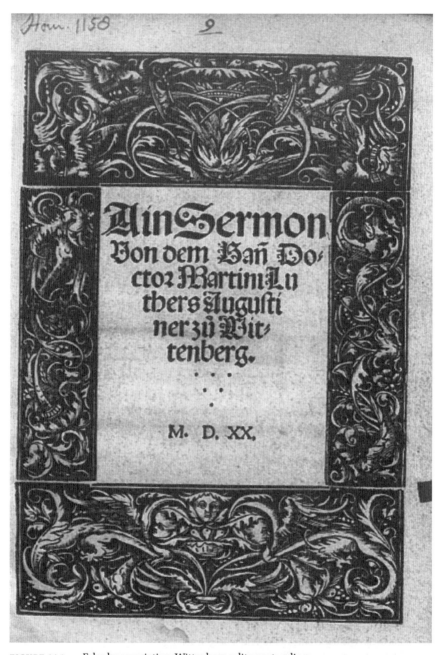

FIGURE 14.1 False by association. Wittenberg split over two lines.
BAYERISCHE STAATSBIBLIOTHEK, MUNICH (BSB), 4 HOM. 1158. USTC 610282

alignment of the title, giving an upside-down triangle appearance, guides the eye to 'Wittenberg' (Figure 14.2).

These printers were not deceiving the reader with false information, as they are only stating Luther was from Wittenberg. But by omitting publication information, Wittenberg becomes the focus of attention, and a selling point.

False by Implication

Unlike the previous category, this group of Wittenberg counterfeits represent a deliberate attempt to deceive the reader. These editions have a false imprint, but list the real print city in the colophon. Printers highlighted Wittenberg on the title page instead of the place where it was actually printed to imply the work was from Wittenberg. 'Wittenberg' is separated from the title, often in larger type, sure to grab the attention of the buyer. Barwick states that he never discovered any editions with a false Wittenberg imprint that listed the actual printer.[11] However, I have identified numerous examples with false imprints that have a truthful colophon.

A perfect example is a 1536 edition by the Strasbourg printer Wendelin Rihel.[12] The text is a sermon originally printed in Wittenberg by Joseph Klug.[13] It has a simple title page with the title arranged in a half diamond, with decreasing centre alignment and the first line in a larger typeface (Figure 14.3). Luther, separated from the title, is identified as the author. 'Wittenberg' is listed below, followed by the date. The 'W' in 'Wittenberg' is from the large typeface used on the first line of the title. It is the largest typeface used on the page, larger than the type used to identify Luther. 'Wittenberg' is inserted on the lower part of the page, and combined with the large initial letter, stands out on the page. In fact, the spacing between the title, author and city follows the layout of the original Wittenberg edition. While the printer was clearly implying this work was from Wittenberg, there is a full colophon with the real city, printer and year. (Figure 14.3).

---

11   Barwick, 'The Lutheran press at Wittenberg', p. 10.
12   Martin Luther, *Ein trostliche predigt von der zukunfft Christi und den vorgehenden zeichen des juengsten tags* (Strasbourg: Wendelin I Rihel, 1536), USTC 647263. Bibliothèque de la société de l'histoire du protestantisme français, 4° 1391 Rés.
13   The original Wittenberg edition by Klug is USTC 647219. Universitäts- und Landesbibliothek Sachsen-Anhalt, Pon Vg 2425, QK.

FIGURE 14.2   False by association. Wittenberg on its own line
BSB, 4 HOM. 1185. USTC 610357

In 1535 Peter Braubach of Haguenau printed a copy of the Augsburg Confession, which was first presented to Emperor Charles V at the imperial Diet in 1530.[14]

---

14   *Confessio fidei exhibita invictiß. Imp. Carolo V. Caesari aug. In comiciis augustae. Anno M.d xxx. Addita est apologia confeßionis* (Haguenau: Peter Braubach, 1535), USTC 624444.

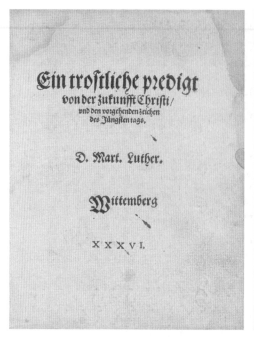

FIGURE 14.3 False by implication. A false Wittenberg imprint from Strasbourg with a truthful colophon
BSB, HOM. 2098 Z. USTC 647263

Braubach used a single piece title page border and lists 'Wittenberg' in capital letters at the bottom of the title page, above a verse from Psalm 119 (Figure 14.4). However, Haguenau is listed in the colophon as the real city of publication: 'IMPRESSVM HAGANOAE || ANNO D. M.D.XXXV. || Mense Martio.'

In the first example Rihel used a false Wittenberg imprint, but identified himself as a Strasbourg printer in the colophon. It is odd that he identifies himself while knowingly using a false imprint. Perhaps he would argue that it does not say 'printed in Wittenberg' and that he simply meant the sermon was preached in Wittenberg. Regardless, in both examples, Wittenberg is the only city on the title page. A broader examination of Rihel's and Braubach's output reveal that both printers often adopted full, accurate imprints on the title pages of their editions. The fact that they varied their usual practice in these examples indicates a clear intention to deceive prospective buyers.

Bayerische Staatsbibliothek, H.ref. 92 http://www.mdz-nbn-resolving.de/urn/resolver.pl?urn=urn:nbn:de:bvb:12-bsb10179007-8, last accessed: 4 January 2019.

FIGURE 14.4   False by implication. A false Wittenberg imprint from Haguenau with a truthful colophon
BSB, H.REF. 92. USTC 624444

Simple Counterfeits

This category encompasses works that are fully counterfeit. There is no ambiguity as in the previous categories. These are works that have a false Wittenberg imprint and no city listed in the colophon. They are by far the most numerous, with hundreds of examples, and were clearly meant to deceive. They often followed the line breaks of the title on the original Wittenberg edition. In one case, they even preserved an error in the Roman numeral date of the Wittenberg edition. This suggests that the compositor was copying the Wittenberg edition without noticing the mistake, possibly under explicit instruction to follow the model exactly.

An early example is a short pamphlet by Luther against Johann Eck, printed in 1520 in Basel by Adam Petri.[15] It is a very simple title page with only one typeface. The wide spacing and decreasing centre alignment of the title, which

---

15   Martin Luther, *Von den niüwen Eckischen bullen und lügen* (Wittenberg [=Basel]: Adam

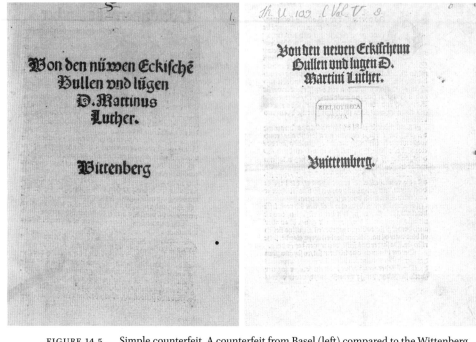

FIGURE 14.5   Simple counterfeit. A counterfeit from Basel (left) compared to the Wittenberg original
BSB, RES/4 POLEM. 1885#BEIBD.1 AND RES/4 TH.U. 103,V,8. USTC 703267 AND 703265

directs the eye, puts all the focus on 'Wittenberg'. The layout is like the original Wittenberg edition by Melchior Lotter, but has different line breaks (Figure 14.5).[16] The two editions also have the same paragraph breaks and only list the year in the colophon.

In 1524, the Augsburg printer Silvan Otmar printed a copy of Luther's work on Psalm 127 (Figure 14.6).[17] Following the title is Luther's name and an imprint with the city and year. There is very good spacing between each item and Luther's name is on a separate line. Both Luther's name and the imprint are in the larger typeface. There is also a four-piece, floriated, woodcut title page

Petri, 1520), USTC 703267. Bibliothèque de la société de l'histoire du protestantisme français, 4° 1324 Rés.

16 The Wittenberg edition by Lotter is USTC 703265. National Library of Scotland, Crawford. R. 203.

17 Martin Luther, *Der hundert und siben und zwaintzigest psalm* (Wittenberg [=Augsburg]: Silvan Otmar, 1524), USTC 633613. Bayerische Staatsbibliothek, 4 Exeg. 484 http://www.mdz-nbn-resolving.de/urn/resolver.pl?urn=urn:nbn:de:bvb:12-bsb10159313-8, last accessed: 4 January 2019.

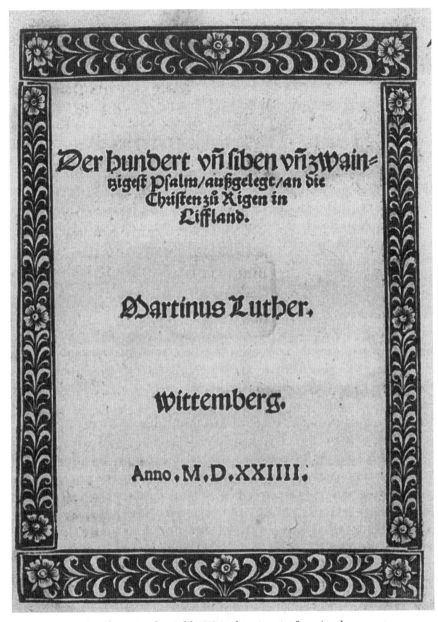

FIGURE 14.6　Simple counterfeit. A false Wittenberg imprint from Augsburg
BSB, 4 EXEG. 484. USTC 633613

border. Otmar actually produced two different editions of this counterfeit in 1524. There was also another counterfeit edition produced in Constance.[18]

A further example of a simple counterfeit is an Augsburg edition of Luther's *That Jesus Christ Was Born a Jew*, printed in 1523 by Melchior Ramminger (Figure 14.7).[19] It also has a four-piece woodcut title page border. Like the previous example, Luther's name is separated from the title. However, this time 'Wittenberg' is located directly above the year. Here there is no doubt 'Wittenberg' is part of the imprint. The work must have been popular, as Ramminger produced three counterfeit editions in 1523.

Wittenberg counterfeits such as these were produced quickly and on a wide scale. As the examples show, unlike the previous categories, they were deliberately produced to deceive. Readers thought they were buying works from Wittenberg, the source for Reformation news and Luther's writings. While many of these works were easy to reproduce, the final category focuses on works that required more time and a more advanced design.

Advanced Counterfeits

In addition to copying the title page design, advanced counterfeits also copied the woodcut title page borders from Wittenberg editions. The famed Renaissance artist Lucas Cranach the Elder was the court painter to the Elector of Saxony, Frederick the Wise. His workshop in Wittenberg supplied many woodcuts to local printers, most notably his woodcut illustrations in the 1522 edition of Luther's New Testament translation.[20] His title page borders featured prominently on many Reformation pamphlets and helped elevate the quality and status of Wittenberg print.[21] Many printers in other cities copied his borders, although these copies were often of inferior quality. These counterfeits required more skill and a greater investment by the printer, and consequently, more time. Thus, they were rarer. Nonetheless, over fifty counterfeits have been so far identified where printers copied Wittenberg title page borders.

---

18   The other Augsburg edition is USTC 633614. The Constance edition is USTC 633626.
19   Martin Luther, *Das Jhesus Christus ain geborner Jude sey* (Wittenberg [=Augsburg]: Melchior Ramminger, 1523), USTC 627551. Paris, Bibliothèque de la société de l'histoire du protestantisme français, 4° 1360 Rés.
20   Martin Luther, trans. *Das Newe Testament* (Wittenberg: Melchior II Lotter for Lukas Cranach & Christian Döring, 1522), USTC 627911. Forschungsbibliothek Gotha, Theol 2° 00035/01.
21   See Andrew Pettegree, *Brand Luther: 1517, Printing and the Making of the Reformation* (New York: Penguin Press, 2015), pp. 158–163.

FIGURE 14.7   Simple counterfeit. A false Wittenberg imprint from Augsburg
BSB, 4 POLEM. 1871. USTC 627551

FIGURE 14.8   Advanced counterfeit. A counterfeit from Augsburg (left) next to the Wittenberg original
BSB, RES/4 TH.U. 103,XIV,10 AND UNIVERSITÄTS- UND LANDESBIBLIOTHEK SACHSEN-ANHALT, URN:NBN:DE:GBV:3:1-108767. USTC 700033 AND 700034

An early example is a 1522 edition of Luther's *The Misuse of the Mass*, printed by Heinrich Steiner in Augsburg (Figure 14.8). Steiner printed two editions that year, which have identical title pages.[22] Luther's name is in the middle of the page and the imprint is at the bottom. The line breaks in the title are identical to the original Wittenberg edition (Figure 14.8).[23] Both also include imprints with the city and year. The Wittenberg edition has an error in the dating, which is corrected in the Augsburg edition. Also, the Wittenberg edition abbreviates 'Luther' as 'Lu.' The Augsburg edition spells Luther's name out in full.

22   Martin Luther, *Vom mißbrauch der Messen* (Wittenberg [=Augsburg]: Heinrich Steiner, 1522), USTC 641123 and 700033. Bibliothèque de la société de l'histoire du protestantisme français, 4° 1361 Rés. and Bayerische Staatsbibliothek, Res/4 Th.u. 103,XIV,10 http://daten.digitale-sammlungen.de/bsb00028966/image_1, last accessed: 4 January 2019.

23   Martin Luther, *Vom miszbrauch der Messen* (Wittenberg: Johann Rhau-Grunenberg, 1522), USTC 700034. Universitäts- und Landesbibliothek Sachsen-Anhalt, Ib 3676 a (4) http://digitale.bibliothek.uni-halle.de/vd16/content/titleinfo/999670, last accessed: 4 January 2019.

The most interesting aspect is that Steiner copied the Cranach woodcut title page border from the Wittenberg edition. The two borders are nearly identical; however, there are differences in the shading in the man's clothing on the right and the man's moneybag on the left. Another interesting aspect of this counterfeit is the ornate initial used at the beginning of the title. This is unusual as ornate initials were generally reserved for the text, not the title page. Steiner even copied this initial, though there are slight differences.

Intricate title page borders were not cheap. They added to the production costs and the amount of time needed to reproduce a Wittenberg edition. In order to recuperate the cost, printers would reuse the title page borders in multiple editions. One such example was a Luther pamphlet on the sacraments. It was printed in 1524 by Hieronymus Höltzel in Nuremberg (Figure 14.9).[24] Höltzel printed a false Wittenberg imprint and used a copy of a Cranach title-page border. The border has a small area for text and features two lions prominently in the bottom corners. This is a border used in many Wittenberg editions.

This example also reveals copying practices within the print shop. In the Nuremberg copy, the lions are in the opposite corners from the Wittenberg border. The artist copied the woodcut as it appeared in the printed Wittenberg edition. Thus, since woodcuts are carved in relief, the copy was reversed when inked and pressed against a new sheet of paper. Given more time, an artist could produce a correctly oriented copy, such as in the previous example, but the method used in this example was a quicker process. Printers also used copies of Cranach's borders in non-counterfeit editions. This allowed printers to recuperate their investment over multiple editions. It is also a testament to the effectiveness of Wittenberg design and its ability to influence other printers. However, the counterfeits did not go unnoticed in Wittenberg. The solution was to develop methods to combat the competition.

Combatting Counterfeits

In 1524, the Saxon Elector granted Luther a coat of arms decorated with a cross in the middle of a white rose, flanked by Luther's initials on either side.[25] This symbol became a seal used on Luther's works printed in Wittenberg to prove

---

24 Martin Luther, *Von der frucht und nutzparkayt des heyligen Sacraments* (Wittenberg [=Nürnberg]: Hieronymus Höltzel, 1524), USTC 700131. Bayerische Staatsbibliothek, Res/4 Th.u. 103,XXVI,23 a http://reader.digitale-sammlungen.de/resolve/display/bsb10204485 .html, last accessed: 4 January 2019.

25 Steven Ozment, *The Serpent & the Lamb: Cranach, Luther, and the Making of the Reformation* (New Haven: Yale University Press, 2011), p. 112.

FIGURE 14.9   Advanced counterfeit. A false imprint and copied border from Nuremberg (left) next to the original border from Wittenberg
BSB, RES/4 TH.U. 103,XXVI,23 A AND RES/4 TH.U. 104,VII,37. USTC 700131 AND 655628

their authenticity (Figure 14.10). In one edition, Luther notified readers and warned other printers to "Let this symbol be proof that these books have passed through my hands, for many are today engaged in falsifying publications and ruining books."[26]

But this emblem was not a guarantee of authenticity. It too was soon copied. That same year the border was copied by Philip Ulhart in Augsburg. But there was one major difference. Ulhart copied the Cranach title page border, including Luther's initials, but did not reproduce the white rose (Figure 14.11). Instead, he inserted a blank shield.[27] It is odd that he went to the trouble of reproducing the entire border, but not the rose, especially given the fact that he also used another title page border that did include the rose (Figure 14.11). Although the architectural border is slightly different and Luther's initials are missing, the resemblance to Luther's white rose is indisputable.

26   Ozment, *The Serpent & the Lamb*, p. 113.
27   Martin Luther, *Wider den neuwen Abgott und allten Teuffel der zu Meyssen soll erhaben werden* (Wittenberg [=Augsburg]: Philipp I Ulhart, 1524), USTC 706627. Bibliothèque de la société de l'histoire du protestantisme français, 4° 1378 Rés.

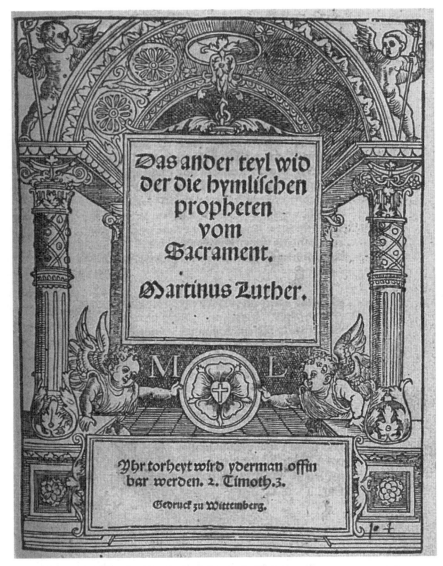

FIGURE 14.10   A Wittenberg border featuring the Luther rose
BSB, 4 POLEM. 1893#BEIBD.1. USTC 626862

The Nuremberg printer Jobst Gutknecht also copied Luther's white rose. However, he also incorporated the Saxon Electoral shield—the sign of Luther's protector—into his border (Figure 14.12).[28] Thus, while Wittenberg printers

---

28   Martin Luther, *Eyn kurtze unterrichtug warauff Christus seine Kirchen oder gemain gebawet*

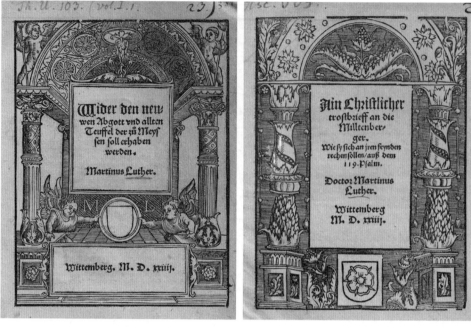

FIGURE 14.11   Copied borders by Ulhart in Augsburg
BSB, RES/4 TH.U. 103,I,1 AND 4 ASC. 605. USTC 706627 AND 609762

attempted to combat the unusual competition they faced from counterfeiters, the counterfeiters quickly adapted. There was little Wittenberg printers could do, as counterfeits were produced all over Europe.

Geographic Distribution of Counterfeits

Every major printing centre in the Holy Roman Empire produced counterfeit Wittenberg editions. A vast majority—nearly 70%—were produced between 1520 and 1525. This coincided with Luther's most active years.[29] But counterfeiting was not limited to the imperial realm. They were also produced in England,

---

hab (Wittenberg [=Nürnberg]: Jobst Gutknecht, 1524), USTC 656115. Bayerische Staatsbibliothek, Res/4 Polem. 3365,17 http://www.mdz-nbn-resolving.de/urn/resolver.pl?urn=urn:nbn:de:bvb:12-bsb10204013-0, last accessed on: 4 January 2019.

29   The figures in this section only include editions that have a false Wittenberg imprint. Only items from the last three categories discussed (False by Implication, Simple Counterfeits, and Advanced Counterfeits) are included, as the items in the first category are not truly fraudulent.

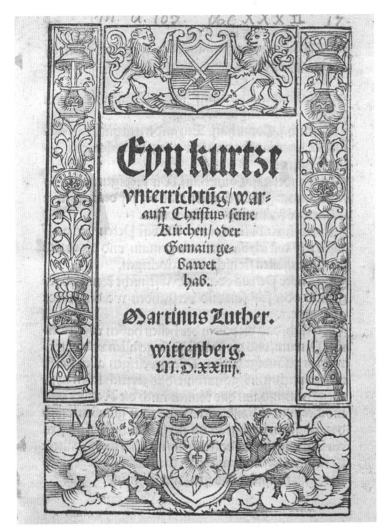

FIGURE 14.12   A border by Gutknecht in Nuremberg featuring the Luther rose
BSB, RES/4 TH.U. 103,XXXII,17. USTC 656115

France, the Low Countries, Poland and the Swiss Confederation, 33 cities in all. The bulk of the false Wittenbergs, however, came from three cities: Augsburg, Erfurt, and Nuremberg. Together they account for nearly 60% of all Wittenberg counterfeits (Figure 14.13).

Augsburg produced more counterfeit editions than any other city, approximately 150 editions. A Free Imperial City located in Bavaria, Augsburg was home to the important Fugger and Welser banking families, and one of the centres of international trade. Due to the concentration of such wealth in the city,

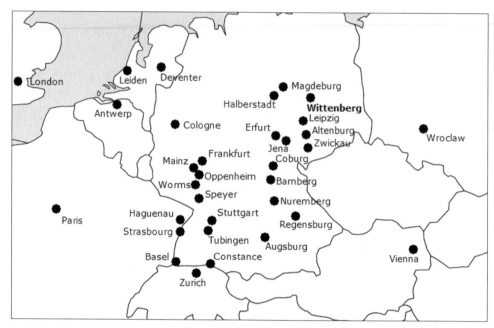

FIGURE 14.13 The geographic distribution of Wittenberg counterfeits

there was plenty of capital to support a vibrant print industry.[30] Ten different printers manufactured counterfeit editions. Augsburg's three largest printers, Heinrich Steiner, Melchior Ramminger and Jörg Nadler, were among the top Wittenberg counterfeiters in all of Europe.

Erfurt, located southwest of Leipzig, was where Luther went to university and joined the Augustinian order in 1505. During his lifetime, Erfurt printers produced over one hundred Wittenberg counterfeits. Erfurt's counterfeits were more evenly split among four printers: Johann Loersfeld, Matthes Maler, Wolfgang Stürmer, and Melchior Sachse. Nearly two-thirds of Luther's works printed by Loersfeld were counterfeits. For Maler, one in every three Luther works was a counterfeit. Surprisingly, there are only two instances of copied title page borders in Erfurt. Copying a Cranach border would have taken more time to execute. Since Erfurt was the closest city to Wittenberg among the top counterfeiting centres, they needed to reproduce Luther's works quickly before the Wittenberg editions flooded their own regional market.

---

30   For a detailed analysis of the Augsburg industry, consult Künast's *Getruckt zu Augsburg*. See note 5.

Nuremberg publishers were responsible for approximately one hundred Wittenberg counterfeits. Although the Nuremberg printer Jobst Gutknecht was the largest counterfeiter in the city and one of the top in Europe, counterfeit editions in Nuremberg were much more evenly divided among thirteen printers. Hieronymus Höltzel was one of four printers in the city that produced advanced Wittenberg counterfeits. He copied the Cranach title page border with the two lions and made frequent use of it.[31] It was not uncommon for printers to use copies of Cranach's title page borders even if the original Wittenberg edition did not.

In the thirty-three places where Wittenberg editions were counterfeited, over seventy printers produced counterfeit Wittenberg editions. Clearly it was not a niche market confined to a single printer within a locality; rather, it was a widespread practice. And for a few printers, counterfeiting was extremely lucrative, making up a large percentage of the Reformation works they printed. The Imperial cities had a particular advantage, in that not being part of an ecclesial or princely territory, they were outside the jurisdiction of other printers' privileges or bans instituted by anti-Lutheran princes or bishops. Nuremberg did pass a ban against Luther's works, but the city council turned a blind eye to their publication.[32]

In any case, the items printers counterfeited were unlikely to have a privilege because of their short length. A significant number of the counterfeits required only four sheets of paper or less per copy, meaning it was not a large investment. Printers mostly sought privileges to minimise risk for larger works that had higher production costs. For example the Saxon Elector John the Steadfast issued a privilege to the Wittenberg publishers Lucas Cranach and Christian Döring for the Old and New Testaments.[33] Those works required a far larger investment and a privilege protected their profits.

Most of the items counterfeited were short works such as Luther's sermons, commentaries, and polemical tracts. Luther excelled at this genre. They were cheap to produce and easy to counterfeit for these same reasons. Many counterfeiters specifically focused on these shorter works. This practice may indeed have been more widespread than is evidenced in this essay. Short pamphlets were ephemeral by nature, often distributed unbound. Thus, their survival rates are much lower.

---

31 For an example of Höltzel's copy of Cranach's title page border see USTC 627386. Bayerische Staatsbibliothek, Res/4 Th.u. 103,IX,1.
32 Pettegree, *Brand Luther*, 220.
33 John L. Flood, 'Lucas Cranach as publisher', *Life & Letters*, 48 (1995), pp. 241–262: 243.

Many counterfeits might also be 'hiding' behind catalogue descriptions. Differences between true and false Wittenberg imprints are, as demonstrated here, often almost imperceptible. In many cases, even a diplomatic title page transcription would not be able to highlight them. For the present work, I systematically investigated all of Luther's works printed before 1550 in the leading German print centres. I intend to continue my investigation by examining multiple copies of the same edition, which is likely to turn up even more counterfeits yet undiscovered.

Counterfeiting Wittenberg books was not confined to the Empire. More than two dozen editions were produced abroad in England, France, the Low Countries, Poland, and the Swiss Confederation. Most interesting are the editions printed in Paris and London. The Paris editions were printed in 1521 at a period when scholars were still curious about Luther and his ideas. They were all printed in Latin, which is expected, as Paris would not have been the market for Luther's vernacular pamphlets. Scholars at the University of Paris were curious about Luther's ideas and were selected to provide an official response to the Leipzig Debate between Luther and Johannes Eck in 1519. In the end, they refrained from issuing a public response. The London editions, however, were not printed in Latin; they were printed in English and much later in 1547. While the Paris editions were likely counterfeit to avoid local bans on printing such documents, the London imprints must have been intended satirically, as there was no English printing in Wittenberg. Regardless, both instances raise interesting questions about the ability of Luther's works to travel across international borders. When compared to other contemporary, high profile authors, such as Erasmus of Rotterdam, Luther's works were generally confined to German speaking lands due to his practice of writing in the vernacular.[34] Erasmus wrote mostly in Latin, facilitating international exchange. The large amount and vast reach of Wittenberg counterfeits provide a unique insight into the geographical distribution of works printed in Wittenberg. While surviving bookseller catalogues or estate inventories offer individual instances of an edition's distribution patterns, mapping counterfeit production exposes larger distribution networks. The counterfeiter had to have a Wittenberg copy in his possession to produce an accurate counterfeit, for example with identical title page line breaks. Cheap counterfeits thus also demonstrate the reach of authentic Wittenberg editions.

---

34 According to the USTC, for the sixteenth century there were 3,770 Luther editions printed in German. There were only 705 printed in Latin.

Cashing in on Counterfeits: Incorporating Wittenberg into Marketing Strategies

The counterfeiting of Wittenberg editions was not the first instance of false information on title pages. False imprints were not a new phenomenon. They were as old as the innovation of the title page in the third quarter of the fifteenth century. Publication information, usually reserved for the colophon at the end of the book, slowly made its way to the title page in the form of an imprint.[35] Early sixteenth-century books often had both an imprint and a colophon. A book might list the city and year of publication in the imprint on the title page and list the printer in the colophon. These three important pieces of information—city, printer, and year—were arranged in a number of combinations, often inconsistently in works by the same printer.

Colophons appeared regularly in books from 1457 onwards.[36] Even though they were developed to identify the details of publication, a large number contained incorrect information. While in many instances the incorrect information was deliberate, the majority of cases were accidental.[37] Most were simply errors in dating, such as MCDLXIX (1469) instead of MCDLXXI (1471). Curt Bühler documents many such instances and claims printers were indifferent to the accuracy of the date.[38] This discussion however is not concerned with false imprints that were accidental. Rather, it concentrates on places of publication—in this case, Wittenberg—that have been deliberately falsified in the imprint.

There were many reasons why a printer would lie about the place of publication. Printers often sought privileges for their works from local authorities, which legally guaranteed a monopoly for a particular title. Another printer might print an unauthorized copy, but change the imprint so that the work appeared to originate from outside the jurisdiction of the privilege. For example, in 1499 the Italian printer Bernardinus de Misintis printed a copy of Politian's *Opera* in Brescia, but listed Florence in the colophon.[39] As Brescia was

---

35 See Margaret M. Smith, *The Title-Page: Its Early Development, 1450–1510* (London: The British Library & Oak Knoll Press, 2000).

36 Curt F. Bühler, 'False information in the colophons of incunabula', *Proceedings of the American Philosophical Society*, 114.5 (1970), pp. 398–406: 398.

37 Bühler, 'False Information', pp. 398–399.

38 Bühler, 'False Information'.

39 The colophon of the edition reads: "Impressum Florentiae: & accuratissime castigatum op[er]a & impensa Leonardi de Arigis de Gesoriaco Die decimo augusti .M.ID." (USTC 991841, copy at Munich, Bayerische Staatsbibliothek (2 Inc.c.a. 3798 n), consulted digitally via the Münchener DigitalisierungsZentrum).

within the jurisdiction of Venice, Bernardinus was attempting to conceal his violation of a privilege granted to the famed printer Aldus Manutius. Aldus was not fooled and complained to the Venetian senate.[40]

A similar example is that of the Italian printer Lorenzo de' Rossi who listed Venice as the place of publication on some of his works even though they were printed in Ferrara. He was not copying other editions, but thought placing Venice on the title page would make it more attractive in a local Venetian market.[41] In Lyon, Jacobinus Suigus and Nicholas de Benedictis also falsified Bolognese and Venetian imprints. But none of these were on the scale of the false Wittenberg editions.

Another reason printers would dissemble about the place of publication was to circumvent local prohibitions on printing certain books. The more restrictions and interference imposed by authorities, the more likely printers would resort to deception.[42] If a work was on a list of banned books, a printer would use a false imprint to disguise his involvement in the project.[43] Such was the case in Leipzig, the largest printing centre in the Holy Roman Empire at the beginning of the Reformation. Leipzig was a centre of trade in ducal Saxony, which remained Catholic until the death of the Saxon Duke George in 1539. Leipzig printers were forbidden from printing Luther's works, much to their dissatisfaction and to the detriment of their industry.[44] They felt disadvantaged that they were prohibited from printing items that would sell quickly and

---

40   Bühler, 'False Information', p. 401. The document has been digitized by the Archivio di Stato in Venice on the occasion of the 500th anniversary celebrations of Aldus's death in 2015, and is freely accessible online at http://www.archiviodistatovenezia.it, last accessed: 4 January 2019. The original text reads: "Et p[er]che li vengono tolte le sue fatiche, et guasto quello che lui conza, come e stato facto in bressa, che hano stampato una de sue opere, et falsato: dicendo Impressum Florentiae": "and as his efforts are taken away from him, and what he creates is ruined, as it was done in Brescia, that they printed one of his works falsely, saying Printed in Florence". Venice, Archivio di Stato, Senato, Deliberazioni, Terra, reg. 14, c. 112r. 17 October 1502, *Conferma decennale dal Senato dei privilegi concessi ad Aldo Manuzio per i caratteri greci e corsivi e contro le contraffazioni delle sue edizioni*. Thank you to Dr Shanti Graheli for the translation.

41   Bühler, 'False information in the colophons of incunabula,' p. 401.

42   Lotte Hellinga, 'Less than the whole truth: false statements in 15th-century colophons', in Robin Myers and Michael Harris (eds.), *Fakes and Frauds: Varieties of Deception in Print & Manuscript* (New Castle, DE, and Winchester: Oak Knoll Press and St. Paul's Bibliographies, 1989), pp. 1–27: 5.

43   Michael Treadwell, 'On False and Misleading Imprints in the London Book Trade, 1660–1750', in Myers and Harris (eds.), *Fakes and Frauds*, pp. 29–46: 32.

44   For more on the collapse of the Leipzig industry, see Drew Thomas, 'Circumventing censorship: the rise and fall of Reformation print cities', in Alexander Wilkinson and Graeme Kemp (eds.), *Conflict and Controversy* (Leiden: Brill, forthcoming).

guarantee a profit. This did not stop them however. Michael Bloom was an active printer in Leipzig during the Reformation and he printed multiple works with 'Wittenberg' listed in the imprint. One such edition was the *Admonition to Peace* described at the beginning of this essay.

While circumventing privileges and local bans were good reasons to lie about the place of publication, by far the most popular reason to print a fake Wittenberg imprint was to increase its marketability. People wanted news from Wittenberg. And Luther satisfied this demand, writing tract after tract. Readers were assured of a text's authenticity and accuracy if it was from Wittenberg.

Luther was well aware of unauthorised editions of his works. In the preface of the *Exposition of the Epistles and the Gospels from the Nativity to Easter* in 1525, he chastised printers who made unauthorised copies of his works.[45] He complained about the inferior quality of counterfeit editions, claiming they were so full of errors that he was forced to renounce them as his own work. While Luther was of course concerned about the accuracy of his texts, he was also looking out for the interests of Wittenberg printers, many of whom were his friends.

The case of Wittenberg is unique because it is the first instance of a place of publication being the target of such widespread fraud. Usually printers and authors, not cities, were the subjects of fraud. Aldus Manutius is probably the best-known example of a printer being the target of counterfeits. Printers in Lyon went to such extraordinary lengths to produce counterfeit Aldus editions that they even copied his italic type.[46] In terms of authors, Erasmus was probably the most prolific author, along with Luther, to be the subject of counterfeiting. In fact, it was Johann Froben's unauthorized edition of an Erasmus work printed by Aldus that attracted Erasmus to Basel.[47]

In the case of false Wittenberg imprints, printers were using the imprint as a marketing tool to promote their editions. Instead of the imprint simply providing the details of publication, it was incorporated into printers' larger marketing strategies. In this sense, Wittenberg was becoming a brand to be copied. In addition to the Wittenberg imprint, the layout and title page borders

---

45   Martin Luther, *Auslegunge der Episteln und Evangelien von der heyligen drey Koenige fest bis auff Ostern gebessert* (Wittenberg: Melchior II Lotter for Lucas I Cranach & Christian Döring, 1525), USTC 613951.

46   David J. Shaw, 'The Lyons counterfeit of Aldus's italic type: a new chronology', in Denis V. Reidy (ed.), *The Italian Book 1465–1800: Studies Presented to Dennis E. Rhodes on his 70th Birthday* (London: The British Library, 1993), pp. 117–133.

47   Eileen Bloch, 'Erasmus and the Froben press: the making of an editor', *The Library Quarterly* 35.2 (April 1965), pp. 109–120: 109. Also see Percy Stafford Allen, 'Erasmus' relations with his printers', *The Library*, 13.1 (1913), pp. 297–322.

were also copied. Over fifty of the counterfeit editions were by authors other than Luther. When another author did not possess the same name recognition as Luther, a false Wittenberg imprint helped the reader to associate the work immediately with the Reformation movement.

"They have also learnt the trick of printing Wittenberg upon some books which never appeared at Wittenberg at all!"[48] Luther was very aware that false Wittenberg imprints were in use during the Reformation. Over seventy printers in numerous cities produced more than five hundred counterfeits of Wittenberg editions. They incorporated the imprint, usually reserved for publication information, into their marketing strategies, knowing it would increase their market appeal. This was not reserved for Luther's texts alone, but used with the works of other reformers as well. Furthermore, it was not the work of lone printers, as multiple, prominent printers in the same cities produced Wittenberg counterfeits at the same time. If anything, this essay has shown that producing Wittenberg counterfeits was not an anomaly within the industry, but rather a common occurrence and widely practiced. The print industry played a large role in the success of the Protestant Reformation. It is now clear, fraud was an important tool in that success.

---

48   Luther, in the preface of *Auslegunge der Episteln und Evangelien von der heyligen drey Koenige fest bis auff Ostern gebessert* (Wittenberg: Lucas Cranach & Christian Döring, 1525), USTC 613951.

PART 4

List and Inventories

CHAPTER 15

'Men and Books under Watch': the Brussels' Book Market in the Mid-Sixteenth Century through the Inquisitorial Archives

Renaud Adam

Scholars working on the book trade during the Ancien Régime face two major obstacles.* The first one is of a heuristic nature: there is no reference work either listing all archives still preserved or providing a list of all those who have already been the subject of a critical edition. The second difficulty is related to the number of documents available; few lists related to the book trade have been preserved.[1] The city of Brussels is no exception.[2] However, for the mid-sixteenth century, a source of an exceptional nature counterbalances that statement: the booklists established by the Council of Troubles in 1569. This article

---

* The author would like to thank Dr Emmanuel Joly (Royal Institute for Cultural Heritage, Brussels) for the rereading of this article; Prof. Annick Delfosse (University of Liège—*Transitions*, Research Department on Middle Ages and Early Modern Period), Prof. Andrew Pettegree (University of St Andrews) and Dr Shanti Graheli (University of Glasgow) for their remarks and comments.
1 Considerations on book trade lists: Graham Pollard and Albert Ehrman, *The Distribution of Books by Catalogue from the Invention of Printing to A.D. 1800, Based on Material in the Broxbourne Library* (Cambridge: Roxburghe Club, 1965); Annie Charon and Elisabeth Parinet (eds.), *Les ventes de livres et leurs catalogues XVIIe–XXe siècle* (Paris: École des Chartes, 2000); Annie Charon, Claire Lesage and Eve Netchine (eds.), *Le livre entre le commerce et l'histoire des idées. Les catalogues de libraires (XVe–XIXe siècles)* (Paris: École des Chartes, 2011); Malcolm Walsby, 'Book lists and their meaning', in Malcolm Walsby and Natasha Constantinidou (eds.), *Documenting the Early Modern Book World. Inventories and Catalogues in Manuscript and Print* (Leiden and Boston: Brill, 2013), pp. 1–24: 7–8; Angela Nuovo, *The Book Trade in the Italian Renaissance* (Leiden and Boston: Brill, 2015), pp. 347–387.
2 Regarding the early eighteenth century in Brussels, there is an outstanding source for the study of the book trade: the account book of the bookseller Guillaume Fricx covering the period from the 23 October 1705 to 2 January 1708 (Brussels, Archives of the City, Old Archives, 3438). See: Claude Sorgeloos, 'Les réseaux commerciaux de Guillaume Fricx, imprimeur et libraire à Bruxelles (1705–08)', in Renaud Adam, Ann Kelders, Claude Sorgeloos and David Shaw (eds.), *Urban Networks and the Printing Trade in Early Modern Europe (15th–18th Century)*. Papers presented on 6 November 2009, at the CERL Seminar hosted by the Royal Library of Belgium (London: CERL, 2010), pp. 1–37; Claude Sorgeloos, 'Travaux et clients de Guillaume Fricx, imprimeur et libraire à Bruxelles (1705–1708)', *In Monte Artium. Journal of the Royal Library of Belgium*, 6 (2013), pp. 141–166.

provides an overview of the context in which the Council of Troubles was established, as well as describing the documentary evidence it produced. It then examines the lists produced in Brussels, and proceeds to an in-depth analysis of an individual bookshop and its stock.

The Booklists of the Council of Troubles as Historical Evidence

In the years 1565–1566, the Low Countries were shaken by a vast political and religious revolt directed against Philip II. In response to the uprising, the king established the so-called Council of Troubles, a special court active from 1567 to 1576. This institution was led in its early years by Fernando Álvarez de Toledo, Duke of Alba and Governor General of the Low Countries. The repression that followed claimed 10,000 victims; the most famous were the Counts of Hornes and Egmont, beheaded the 5 June 1568, in the main square of Brussels. The population renamed this court "the Bloody Council".[3] The Council of Troubles also turned its attention to the book trade, that is, the production, the distribution as well as at the ownership of books. This investigation generated a considerable archive, which, in spite of their incomparable precision, have barely been used by scholars concerned with the study of the socio-professional milieu of the artisans of the book, or the dissemination of books, either as commodities, or as a cultural substrate of the Low Countries. The documents are mostly made of minutes of investigations of people working in the milieu of printing offices, as well as of inventories of thousands of books found in bookshops located in the southern provinces, and in libraries belonging to people suspected of sedition.[4] All the books documented by these investigations were listed, whether

---

3   Alphonse Verheyden, *Le Conseil des Troubles* (Flavion-Florennes: Le Phare, 1981); Solange Deyon and Alain Lottin, *Les casseurs de l'été 1566. L'iconoclasme dans le Nord* (Villeneuve d'Ascq: Presses universitaires de Lille—Westhoek: Éditions des Beffrois, 1986); Gustaaf Marnef and Hugo de Schepper, 'Conseil des Troubles (1567–1576)', in Erik Aerts, Michel Baelde and Herman Coppens (eds.), *Les institutions du gouvernement central des Pays-Bas habsbourgeois (1482–1795)* (2 vols., Brussels: Archives générales du Royaume, 1995), I, pp. 470–478; Aline Goosens, *Les Inquisitions modernes dans les Pays-Bas méridionaux (1520–1633)* (2 vols., Brussels: Presses de l'Université libre de Bruxelles, 1998), I, 114–121; Henry Kamen, *The Duke of Alba* (New Haven: Yale University Press, 2004), pp. 75–105; Caroline Payen, *Aux confins du Hainaut, de la Flandre et du Brabant: le bailliage d'Enghien dans la tourmente iconoclaste (1566–1576). Étude de la répression des troubles religieux à la lumière des archives du Conseil des troubles et des Comptes de confiscation* (Courtrai: UGA, 2013).
4   Some documents were edited: Philippe Rombouts, *Certificats délivrés aux imprimeurs des Pays-Bas par Christophe Plantin et autres documents se rapportant à la charge du Prototypographe* (Antwerp: Buschmann—Ghent: Hoste, 1881); Hendrik A. Enno Van Gelder, *Gege-*

they were forbidden or not. With the survival of these documents, the repressive measures taken by the Duke of Alba could be the entry point of a large multidisciplinary study on the state of book culture, its industry and its players in the different cities of the Low Countries during the last third of the sixteenth century.

One of the most famous measures taken by the Council of Troubles was the realisation and the publication of three indexes of prohibited books (1569, 1570, 1571). These reproduced and completed the Tridentine Index (1564), which itself reproduced and completed the Index of the University of Louvain (1546, 1550, 1558).[5] According to the rules of application of the Roman Index, local inquisitors and bishops were invited to augment it as they saw fit. For this reason, the Duke of Alba tasked Benito Arias Montano with a catalogue of prohibited books specific to the Netherlands. The Spanish Orientalist was present in the Low Countries to help Christopher Plantin with the production of his famous Polyglot Bible. In the early months of 1569, Christopher Plantin, having been granted a privilege, published the first Index of Antwerp. The text of this was effectively the Tridentine Index, with further additions made by Montano.[6] After its publication, the Duke ordered the Councils of Justice to search for prohibited books in all bookstores and printing offices of the Low Countries. The Duke of Alba wished, as he said, to "faire casser, abolir et anéantir tous livres deffendus et réprouvez" (to break, remove and destroy all books that were prohibited and frowned-upon) in order to "extirper les sectes hérésies et mauvaises doctrines régnans ès pays de par dacha" (to eradicate heretical sects and bad doctrines in the Low Countries).[7]

On 14 March 1569, the local judicial authorities passed on the Duke of Alba's instructions.[8] Two days later, inquisitors, theologians and police officers paid

---

vens betreffende roerend en onroerend bezit in de Nederlanden in de 16ᵉ eeuw (2 vols., The Hague: Martinus Nijhoff, 1973–1975).

5 On this, see: Fernand Willocx, *Introduction des décrets du Concile de Trente dans les Pays-Bas et dans la Principauté de Liège* (Louvain: Librairie universitaire, 1929), pp. 140–148; Jesus Martinez De Bujanda (ed.), *Index d'Anvers 1569, 1570, 1571* (Sherbrooke: Centre d'Études de la Renaissance—Geneva: Droz, 1988); Kamen, *The Duke of Alba*, p. 118.

6 *Librorum prohibitorum index ex mandato regiae catholicae majestatis, & illustrissimi ducis Albani, consiliique regii decreto confectus, & editus* (Antwerp, Christopher Plantin, 1569), USTC 411461.

7 The quotations come from: Louis-Prosper Gachard and Joseph Lefèvre (ed.), *Correspondance de Philippe II sur les affaires des Pays-Bas* (6 vols., Brussels: Librairie ancienne et moderne, 1848 [vol. I]; Brussels-Ghent-Leipzig: C. Muquardt, [1851–1879] [vols. II–V]; Tongres, Imprimerie Michiels-Broeders, 1936 [vol. VI]), II, pp. 674–675.

8 For the example of Ypres, see: Isidore Lucien and Antoine Diegerick, *Documents du XVIᵉ siècle faisant suite à l'inventaire des chartes* (4 vols., Bruges: De Zuttere, 1874–1877), IV, 250–251.

unexpected visits to various bookshops; suspicious books were seized and submitted to the examination of local authorities. In Tournai, Nicolas Soldoyer, a member of the Catholic bourgeoisie of the city, was sufficiently struck by this raid to mention it in his memoirs: "le 16 dudit mois [i.e. mars], on prit tous les livres chez les libraires, et on les mena dans des tonneaux à la cour spirituelle pour y estre examinez" (on the 16th of this month [i.e. March], all books found in bookshops were seized and taken in barrels to the spiritual court for examination).[9] Two months later, on 16 June, Soldoyer mentioned that "on brusla sur le Marché deux tonneaux pleins de livres erroniques qu'on avait trouvés dans les boutiques des libraires" (they burned on the Market two barrels full of erroneous books found in the bookstores).[10] These barrels contained nearly 550 works, mostly French bibles, New Testaments and psalters printed in Geneva.[11]

The lists of authorised and prohibited books found in the bookstores visited were sent to Brussels. In September, Alba instituted a commission of censors under the authority of Montano. Their work was completed on 3 October 1569. They established a catalogue, which was added as an appendix to the Tridentine Index published at the beginning of 1570 by Christopher Plantin.[12] The State Archives of Belgium, located in Brussels, still preserve some inventories established in Hainaut, Flanders, Picardy and Brabant (i.e. Ath, Avesnes, Bavai, Mons, Binche, Enghien, Maubeuge, Arras, Tournai, Kortrijk, Mechelen, St Omer and Brussels). These archives are exceptional. They offer a sort of radioscopy of the book market in the Low-Countries on the eve of the Counter-Reformation.[13]

---

9   Alexandre Pinchart (ed.), *Mémoires de Pasquier de La Barre et de Nicolas Soldoyer pour servir à l'histoire de Tournai 1565–1570* (2 vols., Brussels: Société de l'histoire de Belgique, 1865), II, p. 330.
10 *Mémoires de Pasquier de La Barre et de Nicolas Soldoyer*, II, p. 339.
11 The list is edited in: Gérard Moreau, 'Catalogue des livres brûlés à Tournai par ordre du duc d'Albe', in Léon-Ernest Halkin, Henri Piatelle and Nicolas N. Huyghebaert (eds.), *Horae tornacenses. Recueil d'études d'histoire publiées à l'occasion du VIIIe centenaire de la consecration de la cathédrale de Tournai* (Tournai: Archives de la Cathédrale, 1971), pp. 194–213.
12 *Index librorum prohibitorum: cum regulis confectis per patres a Tridentina synodo delectos, auctoritate sanctissimi domini nostri Pii IIII pontificis maximi comprobatus, cum appendice in Belgio ex mandato regiae catholicae majestatis confecta* (Antwerp, Christopher Plantin, 1570), USTC 401447.
13 On these archives and their contribution to the book history, see: Moreau, 'Catalogue des livres brûlés à Tournai par ordre du duc d'Albe', pp. 194–213; Henri Vanhulst, 'Les éditions de musique polyphonique et les traités musicaux mentionnés dans les inventaires dressés en 1569 dans les Pays-Bas espagnols sur ordre du duc d'Albe', *Revue belge de musicologie*, 31 (1977), pp. 60–71; Gustaaf Janssens, 'Plantijndrukken in de Henegouwse boekhandel in 1569', in Marcus de Schepper and Francine de Nave (eds.), *Ex officina Plantiniana. Studia in memoriam Christophori Plantini (ca. 1520–1589)* (Antwerp: Vereeniging der Antwerpsche

Brussels Lists and the Bookshop of Michiel van Hamont

Three representatives of the civil and religious authorities visited the eleven booksellers working in Brussels in the second half of March 1569. This committee was composed of Laurentius Metsius, dean of Saint Gudula and the official censor of the Council of Brabant; Gislenus de Vroede, pastor of the parish church of Our Lady of the Chapel; and a member the Municipal Council, Guiliemus Busleyden.[14] Among the book-merchants who were paid a visit, only seven are known from other sources, either as a result of their relationship with Christopher Plantin or for their role in the production of books (they are identified in the table below with an asterisk).[15] The remaining four are known only through this document. The register contains 75 folios, where all the books

---

Bibliophielen, 1989), pp. 349–379; Renaud Adam and Nicole Bingen, *Lectures italiennes dans les pays wallons à la première Modernité (1500–1630), avec des appendices des livres en langue italienne et des traductions de l'italien en français* (Turnhout: Brepols, 2015), pp. 61–63, 65–71; Renaud Adam and Nicole Bingen, 'La réception du livre italien dans les anciens Pays-Bas à la première Modernité: regards sur le Hainaut et le Tournaisis', in Lorenzo Baldacchini (ed.), *Il libro e le sue reti* (Bologna: Bononia University Press, 2015), pp. 31–42.

14 On these men, see: 'Variété historiques', *Analectes pour servir à l'histoire ecclésiastique de Belgique*, 5 (1868), pp. 220–226: 226; Edward Reusens, 'Documents relatifs à l'histoire de l'Université de Louvain (1425–1797). III. Collèges et pédagogies. 34. Pédagogie du Lis', in *Analectes pour servir à l'histoire ecclésiastique de Belgique*, 20 (1886), pp. 284–438: 366; Arthur C. de Schrevel, *Histoire du Séminaire de Bruges* (Bruges: Imprimerie de Louis de Plancke, 1895), pp. 371–372; Arthur-C. De Schrevel, 'Metsius (Laurent)', in *Biographie nationale [de Belgique]* (43 vols., Brussels: Bruylant, 1866–1986), XIV, pp. 622–629; Olivier de Patoul, '(Généalogie de la famille) de Busleyden', in *La noblesse belge. Annuaire de 1892* (2 vols., Brussels: Imprimerie Veuve Monnom, 1892), I, p. 83; Henri de Vocht, *History of the Foundation and the Rise of the Collegium Trilingue Lovaniense 1517–1550* (4 vols., Louvain: Bibliothèque de l'Université. Bureaux du Recueil Publications universitaires, 1951–1955), III, pp. 221–222; Guy Van Calster, 'La censure louvaniste du Nouveau Testament et la rédaction de l'Index érasmien expurgatoire de 1571', in Joseph Coppens (ed.), *Scrinium erasmianum* (2 vols., Leiden: E.J. Brill, 1969), II, pp. 387–388; Milo Hendrik Koyen and Leo Cyriel Van Dyck, 'Abbaye de Tongerlo', in *Monasticon belge* (8 vols., Liège: Centre national de recherches d'histoire religieuse, 1890–1993), VIII, pp. 327–328; *Index d'Anvers 1569, 1570, 1571*, p. 38.

15 Anne Rouzet, *Dictionnaire des imprimeurs, libraires et éditeurs belges des XVe et XVIe siècles dans les limites géographiques de la Belgique actuelle* (Nieuwkoop: De Graaf, 1975), pp. 30, 75, 87–88, 119, 187, 223, 226. Since the publication of this dictionary in 1975, Edmond Roobaert's researches have refined our knowledge of the environment of Brussels' booksellers: 'De zestiende-eeuwse Brusselse boekhandelaars en hun klanten bij de Brusselse clerus', in André Tourneux (ed.), *Liber amicorum Raphaël De Smedt* (4 vols., Louvain: Peeters, 2001), IV, pp. 47–70.

TABLE 15.1 Brussels bookshops inspected by the Council of Troubles, 1569

Bookseller	Approx. number of titles	Completion of the inventory
Joachim de Reulx*	300	17/03/1569
Johannes vander Hagen	400	19/03/1569
Franciscus Trots*	800	21/03/1569
Nicolaus Torcy*	200	21/03/1569
Laurentius vander Broeck*	320	23/03/1569
Michiel van Hamont*	800	24/03/1569
Theodoricus Hermans	400	26/03/1569
Ferdinand Liesvelt	400	26/03/1569
Peter Goÿ*	500	31/03/1569
Jasperus Eyens	80	31/03/1569
Petrus Van Tombe*	1,000	01/04/1569
Total	**5,200**	

present on the stalls of these merchants are listed; the lists include all their stock, whether these books are forbidden or perfectly orthodox.[16]

It is very difficult to give the exact number of books described in these registers. Some bibliographical descriptions are much too laconic. For this reason the figures given below are rounded totals.

These figures already give us a fascinating picture of a diverse and varied marketplace, in a city large enough to sustain a wide variety of book-selling businesses. For a more detailed analysis we have chosen to focus on the inventory of Michiel van Hamont, sworn printer to the King. Hamont makes an excellent case study, as his life is better documented than any of the other booksellers listed.[17] He settled in Brussels around 1557 and his presses were running until his death in 1585. His production of books was negligible, comprising less than 15 titles, mainly in Dutch. These included texts by the abbot Louis

---

16   Brussels, State Archives of Belgium, *Council of Troubles*, reg. 28.
17   Léopold Le Clercq, 'Michel van Hamont, 'figuersnijder' te Brussel (1556–1585)', *De Gulden Passer*, 21 (1945), pp. 113–118; Rouzet, *Dictionnaire des imprimeurs*, pp. 87–88; Edmond Roobaert, 'Michiel van Hamont. Hellebaardier van de keizer, rederijker en drukker van de koninklijke ordonnanties en plakkaten', in Frank Daelemans and Ann Kelders (eds.), *Miscellanea in memoriam Pierre Cockshaw (1938–2008)* (2 vols., Brussels: Archives et Bibliothèques de Belgique, 2009), II, pp. 465–485.

de Blois and his Dutch translator Josse Schellinck, the schoolmaster Noël de Berlaimont, the historian Nicolaus Mameranus and the Franciscan Frans Vervoort. In addition, Hamont printed almost two hundred edicts and ordinances on behalf of the central government, in both Dutch and French. The privilege given to Hamont to allow him to print books specifies that he was also authorised to publish woodcuts and engravings (3 February 1557). Christopher Plantin confirmed this, twenty years later, in the certificate renewing Hamont's licence to exercise his profession (15 July 1570). He described him with these words:

> [...] expert [...] in the art of printing [...] is able to speak Latin, Spanish, German and Flemish well but no French, is able to carve wood engravings, and knows how to correct in formes and printed proofs, and is able to design images and other things.[18]

thus informing us that Hamont was also able to speak Latin, Spanish, German and Dutch, but not French.

The inventory of Hamont's store contains over 800 items, representing about 850 titles including around sixty books considered as suspicious or prohibited.[19] The descriptions are basic: a short title and the name of the author. Sometimes, we can find additional information, such as the place of printing, the name of the printer or the presence of illustrations. For example, we can find this description of a four-language dictionary printed in Louvain: "Colloquia Ende vocabulaer In vier spraken Lovanii".[20] Elsewhere, we can read "Die Nieuwe werelt gedruckt by Jan van Loo", which is the Dutch translation of the book of Simon Grynaeus dedicated to the New World printed in Antwerp by Jan van der Loe in 1563.[21] The Universal Short-Title Catalogue (USTC) was a very helpful tool in identifying the books. Some titles were easy to identify, others

---

18   The original reads: "[...] expert [...] audit estat d'imprimerie [...] entendant for bien latin, espagnol, haut alleman et flameng et aucunnement François et taille aussi figures en bois, et sçait corriger sur le plomb et espreuves, et patronner figures et autres choses [...]", Rombouts, *Certificats*, p. 5.
19   Brussels, State Archives of Belgium, *Council of Troubles*, reg. 28, ff. 27r–37v.
20   Brussels, State Archives of Belgium, *Council of Troubles*, reg. 28, fol. 31r. This edition is: *Vocabulaer in vier spraken duytsch, francois, latin, ende spaensch* (Louvain: Bartholomaus Gravius, 1551), USTC 347890.
21   Brussels, State Archives of Belgium, *Council of Troubles*, reg. 28, fol. 34r. This edition is: Simon Grynaeus, *Die nieuwe weerelt der landtschappen ende eylanden, die tot hier toe allen ouden weerelt bescrijveren onbekent geweest sijn maer nu onlancx van den Poortugaloiseren en Hispanieren, inder nedergankelijcke zee ghevonden* (Antwerp: Jan van der Loe, 1563), USTC 411135.

less. Sometimes there is a big gap between the spelling of the title mentioned in the inventory and that of the title page recorded in USTC. Despite our efforts, about 7 per cent of the books remain unidentified. We could not find them in the USTC or in other bibliographical tools. One such example is the entry: "Crancheyt des Ooghen", apparently a treatise about eyes diseases, presumably lost.[22] Identification was at times prevented by too laconic a bibliographical description. It was not possible to indicate with certainty which edicts or ordinances were described as "multa edicta Regis", though one might reasonably infer that they were among those printed by Hamont.[23] It can also be the case that only the author's name is cited without further details. Which text by the Venerable Bede was simply described as "Beda"?[24] Or "Een devoet boecxken" ("one devotion book") of John Chrysostom?[25] Nevertheless, even when full identification was not possible, the name of the author or the title still allowed us to allocate the book a subject classification. So the "Crancheyt des Ooghen" fits into the category medicine and the "multa edicta" in law. Consequently, only 2 per cent of the entries remain unclassified.

Figures 15.1 and 15.2 present a break-down of Hamont's stock by literary category and language.

From this, we can infer that Hamont's bookshop was not specialized in any particular discipline. His stock mainly concerned itself with religious matters (342 books or about 40 per cent) and literary subjects (267 books or about 32 per cent). Medicine is in third place (64 books or about 7.5 per cent). History, philosophy, legal works and scientific disciplines are present in similar proportions, around 30–40 books (around 4 per cent). The other categories ('varia', 'music' and 'almanac and calendar') each contain fewer than ten titles. Almost 44 per cent (369 titles) of the works present in Hamont's stock were in Latin. Dutch books accounted for 36 per cent (307 titles). There are a far more modest 95 French-language titles (11 per cent). The number of works printed in other languages was minor, though not entirely negligible: 34 books were printed in a combination of languages (i.e. French-Dutch, Latin-Dutch, Latin-Greek, French-Spanish, four-language dictionary, etc.), 15 in Spanish, 9 in Italian, 6 in German, 4 in Greek; English and Hebrew are represented by only one each.

Almost a third of the religious books stocked by Hamont were small devotional texts printed in the vernacular, mainly in Dutch and often anonymous,

---

22 Brussels, State Archives of Belgium, *Council of Troubles*, reg. 28, fol. 31r.
23 Brussels, State Archives of Belgium, *Council of Troubles*, reg. 28, fol. 28r.
24 Brussels, State Archives of Belgium, *Council of Troubles*, reg. 28, fol. 33r.
25 Brussels, State Archives of Belgium, *Council of Troubles*, reg. 28, fol. 31v.

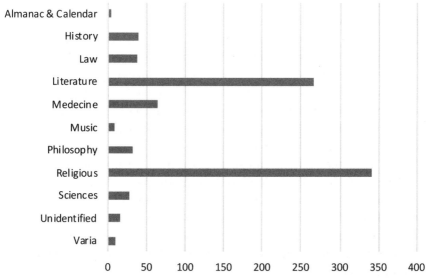

FIGURE 15.1   Michiel van Hamont's bookshop by literary category

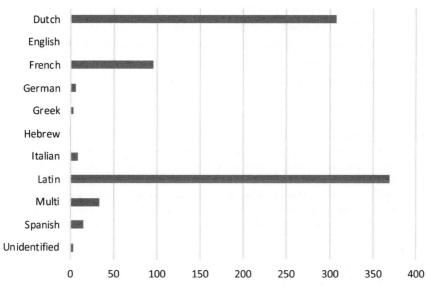

FIGURE 15.2   Michiel van Hamont's bookshop by language

encouraging the reader to meditate on the life and the passion of Christ, the Virgin Mary and her Seven Sorrows or the Holy Sacraments.[26] The inventory lists works such as the anonymous *Devoet gebet om smorgens ende tsavons*, Cornelis Donthers' *Een zeer devote oeffeninge ende contemplatie op de seven principale bloetstortingen in der passien Jesu Christi* in three copies or the anonymous *Dit sijn die seven ween van onser liever vrouwen int lange*.[27] Among these books, some were printed by Hamont, such as Josse Schellinck's *Devote ghebeden op d'evangelien van sondaghen, heylich daghen ende sommighe andere vanden jare* (1567).[28] The presence of theological treatises should also be noted, including texts by both medieval and contemporary authors, such as Bernard of Clairvaux, Heinrich Suso, Louis de Blois, Juan de Dueñas or Franciscus Sonnius, bishop of 's-Hertogenbosch and Antwerp.[29] Treatises of spirituality are also present in numbers, such as the evergreen *Imitatio Christi* by Thomas a Kempis, held in several copies, both in Latin and Dutch.[30] The Church Fathers are also represented in the inventory, including St Augustine, Cyprian of Carthage or John Chrysostom.[31]

In addition to these long-established bestsellers, Hamont's list also reflected the recent impact of the Counter-Reformation. These included the decrees of the Council of Trent, the catechism of Petrus Canisius (in Latin and in Dutch), the Index of prohibited books, and anti-Protestant texts by Martinus Cromerus, Richard Smith or Antoine Du Val.[32] One could also find bibles, either the whole text or individual sections, as well as several commentaries written by theologians such as Desiderius Erasmus, Peter Titelmann or Jacques Lefèvre

---

26   On the devotion to the Seven Sorrows of the Virgin and the Holy Sacraments in Brussels, see: Susie Speakman Sutch and Anne-Laure Van Bruaene, 'The Seven Sorrows of the Virgin Mary: devotional communication and politics in the Burgundian-Habsburg Low Countries (c. 1490–1520)', *Journal of Ecclesiastical History*, 61 (2010), pp. 252–278; Luc Dequeker, *Het Sacrament van Mirakel. Jodenhaat in de Middeleeuwen* (Louvain: Davidsfond, 2000); Renaud Adam, 'L'*Histoire de Saint sacrement de Miracle* d' Étienne Ydens (1605), œuvre de dévotion ou œuvre polémique?', *Revue Belge de Philologie et d'Histoire*, 92 (2014), pp. 413–433; Emily S. Thelen (ed.), *The Seven Sorrows Confraternity of Brussels. Drama, Ceremony, and Art Patronage (16th–17th Centuries)* (Turnhout: Brepols, 2015).
27   Brussels, State Archives of Belgium, *Council of Troubles*, reg. 28, ff. 27v, 30r, 34v, 35v.
28   USTC 409886. Two copies are mentioned in the register (Brussels, State Archives of Belgium, *Council of Troubles*, reg. 28, ff. 28r, 32v).
29   Brussels, State Archives of Belgium, *Council of Troubles*, reg. 28, ff. 28r, 30r–31v, 32v, 34r, 35r.
30   Brussels, State Archives of Belgium, *Council of Troubles*, reg. 28, ff. 30r–30v, 32r–32v, 35r–36r.
31   Brussels, State Archives of Belgium, *Council of Troubles*, reg. 28, ff. 28r, 31r–32v, 33v, 35r–36r.
32   Brussels, State Archives of Belgium, *Council of Troubles*, reg. 28, ff. 27v, 28v–31v, 32v, 34r, 35r–36r.

d'Étaples.[33] Hamont also contributed to the satisfaction of spiritual needs of both priests and laymen by maintaining the provision of liturgical and paraliturgical texts. These included books of hours, psalters or breviaries according to the local or Roman Uses.[34] There are few hagiographic books listed (4), all in Dutch, such as a relation of miracles that occurred in 1433 in the land of Cleves written by Arent Bosman and an anonymous life of Saint Anna.[35] To conclude this inventory of religious books, it is worth mentioning the famous *Malleus maleficarum*, one of the most important treatises dedicated to the prosecution of witchcraft.[36]

In quantitative terms, secular literature was the second most important part of Hamont's stock. His fund can be divided into four main categories: books to learn or improve command of a language (classical or vernacular), novels, poetry and theatre. The most frequent authors from all disciplines are, in order of popularity, Erasmus (12 titles), Gabriel Meurier (9 titles), Johannes Despauterius (6 titles), Ovid (8 titles), Terence (8 titles), Johannes Murmellius (7 titles), Georg Fabricius (5 titles), Johannes Sartorius (5 titles), Cornelis Lauerman (4 titles), Ravisius Textor (4 titles), Juan Luis Vivès (4 titles) and Noël van Berlaimont (3 titles).[37] Medieval romances translated from French into Dutch and adapted to suit urban bourgeois values were particularly successful.[38] Hamont was offering for sale such titles as *Histoire amoureuse de Flores et Blanchefleur*, *Die Historie van Peeter van Provencen*, *Historie van Hughe van Bourdeus*, or the *Historie van Karel ende Elegast*.[39] There were also great names of Italian literature, including Pietro Aretino, Ludovico Ariosto, Baldassare Castiglione, Niccolò Machiavelli and Petrarch.[40] These authors were present either in their original language or in translation in French, Dutch and even in Spanish such as Antonio Beccadelli's *Libro de los dichos y hechos del rey don Alonso* translated

---

33   Brussels, State Archives of Belgium, *Council of Troubles*, reg. 28, ff. 27v–30r, 32r, 34v, 36v–37r.
34   Brussels, State Archives of Belgium, *Council of Troubles*, reg. 28, ff. 27r–30v, 31r, 32r, 33r, 34r, 35r.
35   Brussels, State Archives of Belgium, *Council of Troubles*, reg. 28, ff. 33r, 34v.
36   Brussels, State Archives of Belgium, *Council of Troubles*, reg. 28, fol. 29v.
37   Brussels, State Archives of Belgium, *Council of Troubles*, reg. 28, ff. 27r–29v, 30v–35v, 36r–37r.
38   On this topic, see: Herman Pleij, 'La littérature dans les villes aux XVe et XVIe siècles', in Jan Van der Stock (ed.), *La ville en Flandre. Culture et Société 1477–1787* (Brussels: Crédit communal de Belgique, 1991), pp. 171–182; Herman Pleij, 'Le bas Moyen Âge et le temps de la rhétorique', in Hanna Stouten, Jaap Goedegebuure and Frits van Oostrom (eds.), *Histoire de la littérature néerlandaise (Pays-Bas et Flandre)* (Paris: Fayard, 1999), pp. 71–155.
39   Brussels, State Archives of Belgium, *Council of Troubles*, reg. 28, ff. 29v, 31v, 33r.
40   Brussels, State Archives of Belgium, *Council of Troubles*, reg. 28, ff. 29r–29v, 33r–34r, 36r.

by Antonio Rodríguez Dávalos.[41] Alongside these titles, the customer could also find local imprints, especially the works of local playwrights, Cornelius Crocus, Gregorius Holonius or Cornelis Lauerman, and rhetoricians (*rederijkers*) from Brussels, Jan van den Dale and Jan Baptist Houwaert.[42] Hamont himself was a member of the local chamber of rhetoric.[43] Indeed, on their behalf, he printed in 1563 several poems that had been declaimed at a rhetoricians' competition held in Brussels in 1562.[44] The poems were still available in his shop in 1569.[45]

Compared to the body of religious and literary texts, the other categories were significantly smaller. Among these fields, the best-represented discipline is medicine (just over 7 per cent).[46] At that time, the dominant model of medical practice was the humoral theory of Galen and the ancients.[47] For

---

41   Brussels, State Archives of Belgium, *Council of Troubles*, reg. 28, fol. 30r. We have further investigated the dissemination of Italian literature in Brussels from 1500 to 1650 in 'Le livre italien à Bruxelles (1500–1650)', in Renaud Adam and Chiara Lastraioli (eds.), *Itinéraires du livre italien à la Renaissance: regards sur la Suisse romande, les anciens Pays-Bas et la Principauté de Liège* (Paris: Garnier, 2019; forthcoming).

42   Brussels, State Archives of Belgium, *Council of Troubles*, reg. 28, ff. 27v–28v, 31v–32v, 35r–35v, 36v.

43   On the rhetorical chamber of Brussels, see: Susie Speakman Sutch, 'Dichters van de stad. De Brusselse rederijkers en hun verhouding tot de Franstalige hofliteratuur en het geleerde humanisme', in Jozef Janssens and Remco Sleiderink (eds.), *De macht van het schone woord. Literatuur in Brussel van de 14de tot de 18de eeuw* (Leuven: Davidsfond, 2003), pp. 141–159; Speakman Sutch, 'Jan Pertcheval and the Brussels Leliebroeders (1490–1500). The Model of a Conformist Rhetoricians Chamber?', in Bart Ramakers (ed.), *Conformisten en rebellen. Rederijkerscultuur in de Nederlanden (1400–1650)* (Amsterdam: Amsterdam University Press, 2003), pp. 95–106; Remco Sleiderink, 'De schandaleuze spelen van 1559 en de leden van De Corenbloem. Het socioprofessionele, literaire en religieuze profiel van de Brusselse rederijkerskamer', *Revue Belge de Philologie et d'Histoire*, 92 (2014), pp. 847–875; Remco Sleiderink, 'The Brussels Plays of the Seven Sorrows', in *The Seven Sorrows Confraternity*, pp. 51–66.

44   *Refereynen ende liedekens van diversche rhetoricienen uut Brabant, Vlaenderen, Hollant, ende Zeelant: ghelesen en ghesonghen op de Corenbloeme Camere binnen Bruessele, 26.07.1562, op de vraghe, wat dat de landen can houden in rusten?* (Brussels: Michiel van Hamont, 1563), USTC 402949.

45   Brussels, State Archives of Belgium, *Council of Troubles*, reg. 28, fol. 27v.

46   This percentage is higher than the one generally seen in other shops at that time, close to 4%. See: Renaud Adam, 'La circulation du livre médical dans les anciens Pays-Bas au second tiers du XVIe siècle', *Histoire des Sciences Médicales*, 51 (2017), pp. 47–59; Pierre Delsaerdt, '*Suam quisque bibliothecam*'. *Boekhandel en particulier boekenbezit aan de oude Leuvense universiteit 16de–18de eeuw* (Louvain: Leuven University Press, 2001), p. 129.

47   On this, see: Vivian Nutton, 'The fortune of Galen', in Robert James Hankinson (ed.), *The Cambridge Companion to Galen* (Cambridge: Cambridge University Press, 2008), pp. 355–390.

the sixteenth century alone, nearly 600 editions of Galen are documented.[48] The Hamont stock echoes this influence with four titles of his works, all in Latin.[49] The other prominent name from classical antiquity is Hippocrates, with two titles, one in Latin, the other one in Dutch.[50] From the Middle Ages, there is the French translation of Albertus Magnus' *Secretum*. Hamont's bookshop also offered treatises written by Renaissance physicians who denounced the limitations and errors of these authorities, questioning the prominent place still occupied by an erudition now considered sterile.[51] For example, Hamont had five titles of Paracelsus in stock, in German, Dutch and French, and Ambroise Paré's text on the healing of wounds inflicted by harquebuses and arrows, in the original French and in Dutch translation.[52] No title is listed for Andreas Vesalius. Different branches of medicine were also represented in the shop: treaties on diseases, pharmacology, herbal medicine, nutrition or surgery. One notes the name of Dioscorides with his *De herbis*, Girolamo Ruscelli to whom has been attributed the authorship of *De secreti del reverendo donno Alessio Piemontese* (in Dutch translation), and Jacques Guérin's *Traicté très excellent contenant la vraye manière d'estre preservé de la peste en temps dangereux*, the only known edition of which was published by Christopher Plantin 1567.[53]

Other scientific disciplines listed in the 1569 inventory include mathematics, geography, economy and agriculture. Geography seems to be of greater interest than other disciplines. Even if we still find books of Ptolemy, there is a growing audience for books describing exploration of the New World, with for example Levinus Apollonius, *De Peruviae, regionis*, mentioned twice, and Simon Grynaeus, *Die nieuwe weerelt der landtschappen ende eylanden*.[54] Various legal texts were also available. Customers could buy practical books intended for daily use as well as theoretical treatises. One finds books by contemporary jurists from the Low Countries, France, Italy or Germany, such as François Baudoin, François Hotman, Emilio Ferretti or Johann Aurpach.[55] There are also anonymous

---

48 Data from USTC. See also: Richard J. Durling, 'A chronological census of Renaissance editions and translations of Galen', *Journal of the Warburg and Courtauld Institutes*, 24 (1961), pp. 230–305.
49 Brussels, State Archives of Belgium, *Council of Troubles*, reg. 28, ff. 29v, 31r, 35v.
50 Brussels, State Archives of Belgium, *Council of Troubles*, reg. 28, ff. 33r, 35v.
51 Andrew Wear, Roger K. French, Iain M. Lonie, *The Medical Renaissance of the Sixteenth Century* (Cambridge: Cambridge University Press, 1985).
52 Brussels, State Archives of Belgium, *Council of Troubles*, reg. 28, ff. 29r–v, 30v, 31r, 33v.
53 Brussels, State Archives of Belgium, *Council of Troubles*, reg. 28, ff. 28v, 31r, 32v.
54 Brussels, State Archives of Belgium, *Council of Troubles*, reg. 28, ff. 27v, 32r, 35r.
55 Brussels, State Archives of Belgium, *Council of Troubles*, reg. 28, ff. 34r, 35v, 37r–v.

treatises, such as *Les exceptions de droit, les defenses contre le demandeur* and *La maniere pour demener un proces*, dedicated to criminal procedure.[56]

Hamont's own role as sworn printer to the King ensured the presence in his store of many royal edicts or ordinances. Some are related to the regulation of the book market and the ban of heterodox books, such as his *Placcaet ende ordinancie tegens de ghene die eenige fameuse, schandaleuse oft seditieuse boecxkens, artickelen oft scriften maken, versieren, saeyen, divulgeren, drucken, ten voirschijne bringen, oft onder hen houden* (1568).[57] The enduring authority of Aristotelian philosophy is reflected by Hamont's stock. Almost a third of the category 'philosophy' is represented by Aristotelian works or commentaries.[58] In terms of historical works, Hamont's stock contains books spanning ancient to recent history. The history of the Low Countries is represented by works such as the *Chronike of Historie van Hollant, van Zeelant ende Vriesland ende van den sticht van Utrecht* or the memoirs of Olivier de La Marche. There are also texts devoted to German, Italy, Spain and even Peru, written by Herman Bote, Niccolò Machiavelli, Lorenzo de Sepúlveda and Pedro de Cieza De Leon.[59]

The bookshop also sold musical texts and books that can be classified in a wide variety of fields such as military treatises, cookbooks, heraldic works, games books, and alchemy treatises, among other minor categories. Hamont stocked works by Jacobus Clemens non Papa, a master of Renaissance polyphony; the *Instructions de toutes manieres de guerroier tant par mer que par terre* by the jurist Georges Vivien, from Antwerp; the collection of culinary recipes composed by the physician Gheeraert Vorselman and entitled *Een nyeuwen Coock Boeck*; the famous book of fortune-telling by Lorenzo Spirito in his French translation, *Le passetemps de la fortune des dez*; or a heraldic compilation on families from the Low Countries by Jean Lautte, *Le jardin d'armoires, contenant les armes de plusieurs nobles royaumes et maisons de Germanie inferieure*.[60]

The inventory of Michiel van Hamont's shop also provides valuable information on how books were brought from other parts of the European book

---

56   Brussels, State Archives of Belgium, *Council of Troubles*, reg. 28, fol. 36r.
57   USTC 402960. Brussels, State Archives of Belgium, *Council of Troubles*, reg. 28, fol. 27r.
58   Brussels, State Archives of Belgium, *Council of Troubles*, reg. 28, ff. 29r–29v, 31v, 33v, 34r. Only the Cartesian revolution put an end to Aristotle's influence, although it was not until the end of the 17th and beginning of the 18th century that the last Aristotle treatises were removed from the curriculum in Louvain. See Michel Reulos, 'L'enseignement d'Aristote dans les collèges au XVIe siècle', in Jean-Claude Margolin (ed.), *Platon et Aristote à la Renaissance. XVIe colloque international de Tours* (Paris: Vrin, 1976), pp. 147–154.
59   Brussels, State Archives of Belgium, *Council of Troubles*, reg. 28, ff. 28r, 30r, 33r, 34r, 36r, 37r.
60   Brussels, State Archives of Belgium, *Council of Troubles*, reg. 28, fol. 30v, 32v, 33r, 34r.

market for customers in Brussels. For some entries, we have a more detailed bibliographic description, including the place of publication or the printer's name. In other cases, although the description in itself is rather limited, it is possible to identify the edition with a fair degree of certainty. This process overall has allowed us to identify a wide variety of places of publication, including Antwerp, Louvain, Paris, Deventer, Lyon, Ghent, Cologne and Leipzig. It is possible that Hamont relied on his personal network, and had direct connections in some of these cities; one can reasonably believe so in the case of editions from Antwerp and Leuven. We do not know if he had personal trade links with printers located in Paris or Cologne, or if he acquired these books through intermediaries.

Closer to home, Christopher Plantin in Antwerp recorded various direct transactions with Hamont, spanning the period between 1564 and 1580.[61] It is interesting to note that, a few weeks after receiving a visit from Alba's emissaries, Hamont asked Plantin to send him numerous copies of the "Catalogus prohibitorum" and "Index librorum prohibitorum". Plantin's business archives give details of the shipment to Hamont, between the end of March and June 1569, of 250 copies of these texts.[62] In other cases, whether acquired through direct contacts or intermediaries, the geographical distribution of the editions stocked by Hamont testifies to a bustling business. It also seems likely that Hamont dealt in second-hand books as well as new titles. Various entries in the inventory seem indeed to refer to books printed well before Hamont's years of activity. For example, the only surviving edition that can be satisfactorily identified with the entry "Logices adminicula aut. Themst" was printed by Henri Estienne in 1511.[63] Second-hand books may also be detected in early modern inventories through the presence of a binding—as most new books were likely to be sold unbound, stitched, or in temporary covers. However, as the concern of those compiling this list was to produce a list of titles, and not an appraisal of the stock, the bibliographical descriptions analysed here do not extend to the materiality of individual copies.

---

61 Marc Lefèvre, 'Libraires belges et relations commerciales avec Christophe Plantin et Jean Moretus', *Gulden Passer*, 41 (1963), pp. 1–47: 18.
62 Antwerp, Museum Moretus Plantin, Archives, 17, fol. 141.
63 Brussels, State Archives of Belgium, *Council of Troubles*, reg. 28, fol. 31v. The edition is: Aristotle, *Logices adminicula hic contenta: Ammonius in predicabilia Porphyrii, Pompon. praedicamenta Aristotelis editio una, In Peri hermenias editio prima. In praedicamenta Aristotelis editio una, In Peri hermenias editiones due ... Themestii in posteriora* (Paris: Henri Estienne, 1511), USTC 180624.

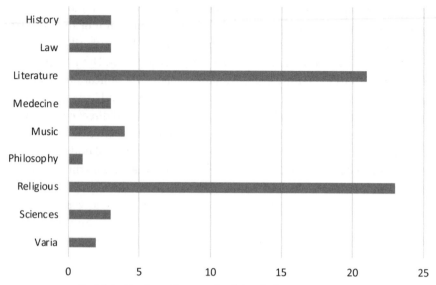

FIGURE 15.3   Prohibited books in Hamont's bookshop by literary category

Prohibited and Suspicious Texts in the Bookshop of Michiel van Hamont

As mentioned above, Hamont's bookshop also stocked a number of prohibited books. In all, 63 books (or just over 7 per cent of the whole stock) were regarded as suspicious or prohibited.[64] These are both religious and lay books, mainly printed in Latin and Dutch. Figures 15.3 and 15.4 detail their distribution according to discipline and language.

Religious literature accounts for 23 titles (36.5 per cent), closely followed by lay literature with 21 titles (33.5 per cent). The emissaries of Alba did not find forbidden Vernacular bibles or Genevan psalters similar to those seized in Tournai by their colleagues. They mainly discovered books written by humanists and books dedicated to Bible studies and in the fields of devotion and spirituality. A handful of titles were found for the disciplines of music (four songbooks), history, law, medicine, and science (three titles each). The most represented author is Erasmus, with 18 books (28.5 per cent). There are three different editions of the *Colloquiorum*, which were banned by the Roman Indexes, and other religious books, as the *Novum Instrumentum* or *Paraphrases* of the Gospel of St John and of St Paul's epistles. The fact that Hamont still stocked so many titles

---

64   Brussels, State Archives of Belgium, *Council of Troubles*, reg. 28, ff. 36v–37r.

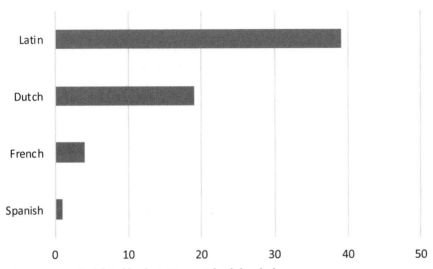

FIGURE 15.4   Prohibited books in Hamont's bookshop by language

by Erasmus is a clear indication of the high-esteem in which the author was still held in mid-sixteenth-century Brussels, notwithstanding the condemnation of Rome and some other theologians. The University of Louvain had been reluctant to join in the official condemnation of Erasmus.[65] Alba's emissaries did find books written by banned authors, including Georg Fabricius, Sebastian Münster and Poggio Bracciolini. The only name of a prominent reformer mentioned in the document sent to Alba is Sébastien Castellion, listed for his *Dialogorum sacrorum ad linguam simul et mores puerorum formandos libri quatuor*. Most of the forbidden books were in Latin, with 39 titles, followed by Dutch books (19 titles). The French (three titles) and Spanish books (one title) are in the minority.

One of the most interesting revelations of this list, is that only half of the books seized in Hamont's shop had to this point been formally condemned, either by the Faculty of Theology of Louvain or in the Roman Indexes. Eight titles were listed in the indexes of Louvain promulgated in 1546 and 1550. There are nearly all Dutch books, mainly songbooks, such as *Een suyverlyck leysen boecxken*. The songs in this volume, better known as the "Antwerps liedboek", contained open mockery of monks, nuns, beguines and beghards.[66] One also finds, amongst these small prohibited Dutch books, *Een ghyestelick en seer*

---

65   Guy Van Calster, 'La censure louvaniste du Nouveau Testament', pp. 381–436.
66   Brussels, State Archives of Belgium, *Council of Troubles*, reg. 28, fol. 36v.

troestelick A.B.C., a volume of religious poetry written by the Antwerp rhetorician Cornelis Crul, who was also one of the Dutch translators of Erasmus.[67] The presence of such titles in Hamont's stock may seem surprising, considering that he also had in his shop a copy of the Index of Louvain printed by Merten Verhasselt in 1558; but as ever, having access to a text does not necessarily mean that the text has been read.[68] The 1569 inventory did not contain copies of the Roman Indexes promulgated by Paul IV (1559) or the Tridentine Index promulgated by Pius IV in 1564.

The remaining titles in Hamont's stock that were identified as suspicious by the emissaries of Alba had never been listed as prohibited books. Of these, fourteen were added to the Index printed by Plantin in 1570, while another would be inserted in the subsequent Index he printed the year after. The remaining twelve titles were never prohibited. Titles may have been flagged up by association with the author's name, if other works by the same individual had been prohibited. This was the case with François Baudouin, whose *Constantinus magnus* was listed in the Roman Index. His *Disputationes duae de jure civili*, found in Hamont's stock, were not themselves listed, and yet considered as suspicious.[69] The emissaries of the Duke of Alba were perhaps following the spirit of the Pauline Index in its overwhelming assumption that the religious convictions of an author contaminated all of his or her writings.[70] The 1569 inventory also shows that the struggle against the prominent Reformed texts was yielding results. A mid-sixteenth-century Brussels bookseller would not dare to offer titles by Luther or Calvin on open sale.

Conclusions

The inventory of the Hamont's bookshop offers a snapshot of its customers and their taste. The typology of titles in stock suggests that a variety of readers would be frequenting the shop, from local clerks to students from Latin schools, merchant-readers or members of the local chambers of rhetoric. A bookshop was not simply a place of business, but also a place of encounter. It is also interesting to see that suspicious or forbidden books discovered in Hamont's

---

67 Brussels, State Archives of Belgium, *Council of Troubles*, reg. 28, fol. 37r.
68 Brussels, State Archives of Belgium, *Council of Troubles*, reg. 28, fol. 35v.
69 Brussels, State Archives of Belgium, *Council of Troubles*, reg. 28, fol. 37r.
70 Paul F. Grendler, 'Printing and Censorship', in Charles B. Schmitt (ed.), *The Cambridge History of Renaissance Philosophy* (Cambridge: Cambridge University Press, 1990), pp. 25–54: 45–46.

bookstore were mainly books written by humanists, as for example Erasmus, Sebastian Münster or Poggio Bracciolini. Erasmus was still highly appreciated in Brussels forty years later, pleas from theologians that his works be prohibited. His influence was such that the University of Louvain itself hesitated to place all his work under a blanket ban.

The inventories compiled at the request of the Duke of Alba, although they stand witnesses to a time of cruel repression and deep fear, today contribute to offering a portrait of Brussels as a bustling hub of the book trade in the mid-sixteenth century, showcasing the variety of titles available even in a relatively small bookshop.

CHAPTER 16

'Beautiful Intellects Should Not Hide': the Bookshop of Luciano Pasini, Bookseller and Publisher between Perugia and Venice in the Late Sixteenth Century

Natale Vacalebre

The Cultural Context: Perugia after the "Salt War"*

In the sixteenth century, Perugia passed through many important institutional and cultural changes. The main event of this period was certainly the so-called "Salt War". In March 1540 Perugia openly defied the will of Pope Paul III, who had ordered a sharp increase in the price of salt within the Papal States. The conflict between Rome and the independent city continued for three months and, after a fierce resistance, the army of Pier Luigi Farnese, son of Paul III, finally defeated the Perugian forces. Consequently, Perugia lost its freedom as an independent city for the second time in its history and was once again placed under the direct control of the Holy See.[1] However, the definitive integration of Perugia within the Ecclesiastical State did not cause it to regress to a state of intellectual subordination, even when compared to its new capital Rome.[2]

---

* A part of this chapter was made possible by the award of a Research Fellowship from the Bibliographical Society of America.
1 Girolamo Di Frolliere, 'La guerra del sale. Ossia racconto della guerra sostenuta dai perugini contro Paolo III nel 1540', *Archivio storico italiano*, 16, Special Issue: 'Cronache e storie inedite della città di Perugia', ed. F. Bonaini, A. Fabretti e F. Polidori (1851), pp. 405–476; Rita Chiacchella, 'Per una reinterpretazione della «guerra del sale» e della costruzione della Rocca Paolina in Perugia', *Archivio Storico Italiano*, 145 (1987), pp. 3–60.
2 Arturo Gabrijelcic, 'Alle origini del Seminario di Perugia (1559–1600)', *Bollettino della Deputazione di storia patria per l'Umbria*, 68 (1971), pp. 1–200: 1–5; Renzo Paci, 'La ricomposizione sotto la Santa Sede: offuscamento e marginalità della funzione storica dell'Umbria pontificia', in *Orientamenti di una regione attraverso i secoli: scambi, rapporti, influssi storici nella struttura dell'Umbra. Atti del X Convegno di studi umbri, Gubbio 23–26 maggio 1976* (Gubbio-Perugia: Centro di studi umbri Casa di Sant'Ubaldo—Università degli Studi di Perugia, 1978), pp. 207–225; Christopher F. Black, 'Perugia and Papal Absolutism in the Sixteenth Century', *The English Historical Review*, 96 (1981), pp. 509–539; Erminia Irace, 'Una voce poco fa. Note

Before the war, the cultural life of the city was dominated by its famous University, with an ancient and prestigious law school that boasted jurists such as Bartolo da Sassoferrato and Baldo degli Ubaldi. After 1540, the situation changed significantly.[3] Political and cultural connections with Rome became very intense, mainly due to ane improvement in career opportunities for many members of the Perugian aristocracy.[4]

The influence of the Roman cultural world within the Umbrian environment manifested itself also in other ways; for example, through the establishment of several educational institutions directly linked to the new religious orders, created as a consequence of the so-called Counter-Reformation. In 1552, the fathers of the Society of Jesus made their entry into Perugia, sponsored by the bishop of the city Fulvio Della Cornia, nephew of Pope Julius III, and future cardinal of Porto-Santa Rufina.[5] Because of their excellent humanistic and scientific training, the Jesuits became the leading educators of the city. In 1554 the representatives of the city *Studium* proposed to the Society the chair of Greek and Latin, which had remained vacant for that academic year.[6] The task of 'Lettore Straordinario' was granted, after the authoriza-

---

sulle difficili pratiche della comunicazione tra il centro e le periferie dello Stato Ecclesiastico (Perugia, metà XVI—metà XVII secolo)', in Armand Jamme and Olivier Poncet (eds.), *Offices, écrit et papauté (XIIIe–XVIIe siècle)* (Rome: École Française de Rome, 2007), pp. 273–299.

3 On the relationship between Perugia and its University from Middle Age to Renaissance, see Giuseppe Ermini, *Storia della Università di Perugia* (Florence: Olschki, 1971); Carla Frova, Ferdinando Treggiari and Maria Alessandra Panzanelli Fratoni (eds.), *Maestri, insegnamenti e libri a Perugia. Contributi per la storia dell'Università 1308–2008* (Milan: Skira, 2009).

4 Erminia Irace, *La nobiltà bifronte. Identità e coscienza aristocratica a Perugia tra XVI e XVII secolo* (Milan: Edizioni Unicopli, 1995).

5 The story of the Jesuits' arrival and of their gradual accommodation in Perugia is minutely described in an unpublished diary of the Perugian College, held in the General Archive of the Society in Rome. The original reads: 'A 9 di maggio 1552 entrorno in Peruggia [sic] li nostri primi Padri mandati dal Beato Padre Ignatio, sotto la guida del P. Everardo Mercuriano che fu poi Generale, per satesfare a Mons. Ill.mo il quale li ricevette in certe stanze a tetto del vescovato molto esposte al freddo l'inverno, et al caldo l'estate, e senza alcuna commodità, et ivi per molti mesi esercitorno la patienza, non tralasciando i loro esercitii'. Translation: 'On 9 May 1552, under the guidance of Father Everard Mercurian, who was then General [of the Order], our first Fathers entered in Perugia. They were sent by the Blessed Father Ignatius, in order to satisfy the desire of Monsignor [Della Cornia] who hosted them in several very uncomfortable rooms under the roof of the episcopal palace, very cold in winter time, and hot in summer. There, for many months, they demonstrated their patience without forgetting their spiritual exercises'. ARSI (Archivum Romanum Societatis Iesu) Fondo Gesuitico. Series "Collegia", n° 1516, *Perugia*, fol. 1rv.

6 Ermini, *Storia della Università di Perugia*, p. 227.

tion of Ignatius of Loyola, to the refined Sicilian humanist Giovanni Antonio Viperano,[7] at that time not yet twenty, whose lectures were attended by the scions of the most important Perugian families.[8] In a short time Jesuits were able to establish a college that could accommodate more than two hundred students and in which young people received a full humanistic education based on the study of Latin, Greek and rhetoric. In 1556 the Jesuits recorded the presence of 200 students within their school. This extraordinary success suggests that the Jesuit college was now the most important institution in the Perugian education system.[9] The Jesuit college was therefore the place where most of the local youth was trained through a tried and tested canon (the *Ratio Studiorum*), which followed a strict reading program.[10]

---

7   On Giovanni Antonio Viperano's life and work see: Emilio Springhetti, 'Un grande umanista messinese: Giovanni Antonio Viperano (Cenni biografici)', *Helikon*, 1 (1961), pp. 94–117.
8   Pietro Tacchi Venturi, *Storia della Compagnia di Gesù in Italia*, 11/2, *Dalla solenne approvazione dell'Ordine alla morte del fondatore (1540–1556)* (Rome: Civiltà cattolica, 1951), p. 454.
9   On the Jesuit book culture in Perugia in the early modern age, see: Enrico Pio Ardolino, 'La Biblioteca del Collegio dei Gesuiti di Perugia: prospettive di ricerca', *Diomede*, 16 (2010), pp. 103–108; Natale Vacalebre, 'Organizzazione della cultura gesuitica a Perugia in età Moderna', *Diomede*, 19 (2012), pp. 75–81; Vacalebre, 'The Library of the Jesuit College of Perugia: New Research Tools', in K. Földváry (ed.) *International Research Universities Network and Catholic Universities Partnership Graduate Students' Conference, Conference Proceedings* (Piliscsaba: Pázmány Péter Catholic University, 2013), pp. 11–15.
10 In the dense literature on the relationship between the Society of Jesus and book culture, see at least: Brendan Connolly, 'Jesuit library beginnings', *The Library Quarterly*, 30 (1960), pp. 243–252; Bernabé Bartolomé Martinez, 'Las librerias e imprentas de los jesuitas (1540–1767): una aportación notable a la cultura española', *Hispania Sacra*, 40 (1988), pp. 315–388; Dominique Julia, 'La constitution des bibliothèques des collèges. Remarque méthodique', *Revue d'histoire de l'Église de France*, 83 (1997), pp. 145–161; Paul F. Gehl, 'Religion and politics in the market for books: the Jesuits and their rivals', *Papers of the Bibliographical Society of America*, 97 (2003), pp. 435–460; Paolo Tinti, 'Gesuiti sotto il torchio: stampa, collegi e Università nell'Italia del Settecento', in Gian Paolo Brizzi and Maria Grazia Tavoni (eds.) *Dalla pecia all'e-book. Libri per l'università: stampa, editoria, circolazione e lettura. Atti del convegno internazionale di studi, Bologna, 21–25 ottobre 2008*, (Bologna: CLUEB, 2009), pp. 261–274; Natale Vacalebre, '«Como un hospital bien ordenado». Alle origini del modello bibliotecario della Compagnia di Gesù', *Histoire et civilisation du livre*, 10 (2014), pp. 51–68; Paul Begheyn, *Jesuit Books in the Dutch Republic and its Generality Lands 1567–1773. A Bibliography* (Leiden: Brill, 2014); Natale Vacalebre, 'Produzione e distribuzione libraria gesuitica nel Cinquecento: il caso delle *Adnotationes et meditationes in Evangelia* di Jerónimo Nadal (Anversa, Martin Nuyts, 1594–1595)', *Titivillus. Revista Internacional sobre Libro Antiguo*, 1 (2015), pp. 305–323; Noël Golvers, *Libraries of Western Learning for China. Circulation of Western Books between Europe and China in the Jesuit Mission (ca. 1650–ca. 1750)* (3 vols., Leuven: Ferdinand Verbiest Institute KUL, 2012–2015); Natale

Cultural relationships between Rome and Perugia were not confined to the religious and academic environment. Contacts between the intellectuals of both cities increased significantly and many Roman and Perugian men of letters took part in cultural circles and shared publishing ventures. In addition to the local University, this dense network of cultural exchange was also developed within the many academies established in Perugia from the mid-sixteenth century.[11] Among these, the academies of the Atomi, Eccentrici, Scossi and, above all, the Insensati were structured according to the model of humanistic literary academies.[12] The academies of Disegno, Insipidi and Unisoni focussed principally of the fine arts, law and music.[13] These different cultural environ-

   Vacalebre, *Come le armadure e l'armi. Per una storia delle antiche biblioteche della Compagnia di Gesù. Con il caso di Perugia* (Florence: Olschki, 2016).
11 The phenomenon of Italian Academies has been the subject of many studies in recent years. Among these, see at least: Claudia Di Filippo Bareggi, 'Cultura e società tra Cinque e Seicento: le Accademie', *Società e storia*, 6 (1983), pp. 641–665; Di Filippo Bareggi, 'L'Accademia: una struttura ambigua fra integrazione, opposizione e retorica', *Nuova rivista storica*, 71.3–4 (1987), pp. 339–356; Cesare Mozzarelli, 'Dell'Accademie: onore, lettere e virtù', in Adriano Prosperi (ed.), *Il piacere del testo. Saggi e studi per Albano Biondi*, 11 (Rome: Bulzoni, 2001), pp. 645–663; Girolamo De Miranda, 'Tra storia politica e ragioni sociologiche. Rassegna di studi per una definizione delle accademie italiane sei-settecentesche', *Esperienze letterarie*, 28 (2003), no. 4, pp. 103–109; Massimo Rinaldi, 'Le accademie del Cinquecento', in Gino Belloni and Riccardo Drusi (eds.), *Il Rinascimento italiano e l'Europa*, 11, (Treviso-Vicenza: Fondazione Cassamarca, 2007), pp. 337–359; Erminia Irace and Maria Alessandra Panzanelli Fratoni, 'Le accademie in Italia dal Cinquecento al Settecento', in Erminia Irace (ed.) *Atlante della letteratura italiana*, 11, (Torino: Einaudi, 2011), pp. 314–322; Simone Testa, *Italian Academies and their Networks, 1525–1700. From Local to Global* (Basingstoke: Palgrave Macmillan, 2015).
12 The Accademia degli Insensati was established in 1561 by Giovanni Tinnoli, Rubino Salvucci, Tommaso Perigli and Ottaviano Colombano. Over and above its local members, the Academy's high reputation attracted many important figures of the Sixteenth century's Italian cultural environment. Poets like Giovan Battista Marino and Battista Guarini, artists and influential cardinals such as Federico Zuccari, Bonifacio Bevilacqua and Maffeo Barberini (the future pope Urban VIII), were all elected members. The Accademia degli Insensati, like many other important Italian academic institutions (Academies of Cimento, Intronati and so on), demonstrated to be both rooted in the city culture and open to contacts with other centers. A detailed analysis of the history of this academy is that of Lorenzo Sacchini, 'Verso le virtù celesti. La letterata conversazione dell'Accademia degli Insensati di Perugia: 1561–1608' (Unpublished dissertation, Durham University, 2013) http://etheses.dur.ac.uk/7723/, last accessed: 4 January 2019.
13 On the academies in Perugia in the late sixteenth century, see: Erminia Irace, 'Le Accademie letterarie nella società perugina tra Cinquecento e Seicento', *Bollettino della Deputazione di storia patria per l'Umbria*, 87 (1990), pp. 155–178; Irace, 'Le Accademie e la vita culturale', in Raffaele Rossi (ed.), *Storia illustrata delle città dell'Umbria. Perugia*, 11 (Milan: Sellino, 1993), pp. 481–496; Irace, 'Accademie e cultura ecclesiastica in antico regime', in Rita Chiacchella (ed.), *Una Chiesa attraverso i secoli. Conversazioni sulla storia della diocesi di Perugia*, 11 (Perugia: Quattroemme, 1996), pp. 59–73; Galliano Ciliberti,

ments created the context in which print culture developed in Perugia in the second half of Sixteenth century.

Luciano Pasini, Bookseller, Publisher and Literary Man

One of the most interesting figures within the Accademia degli Insensati was the bookseller and publisher Luciano Pasini.[14] Born in Perugia probably around the 1520s, Pasini came from a wealthy family of booksellers. He was the son of Antonio Pasini, originally from Verona, established as a bookseller in Perugia since the 1520s. Antonio was one of the most important book dealers in the city.[15] As well as owning a well-stocked bookshop, he had many contacts with Venetian book trade. The first evidence of the presence of Antonio Pasini in Perugia dates back to 1522. According to a document quoted by Adamo Rossi, on 1 December 1522 Costanzo of Gisberto returned to "Maestro Antonio Pasino da Verona", some incomplete books that Antonio sold to him a few years earlier.[16] It is likely, therefore, that Antonio started working in Perugia in the mid-

---

Musica e società in Umbria tra Medioevo e Rinascimento (Turnhout: Brepols, 1998), pp. 200–235.

14   Some informations on Luciano Pasini's life are provided in: Giovanni Battista Vermiglioli, *Biografia degli scrittori perugini* (2 vols., Perugia: Bertelli and Costantini, 1829), II, pp. 148–149; Domenico Tordi, 'La stampa in Orvieto nei secoli XVI e XVII', *Bollettino della regia Deputazione di storia patria per l'Umbria*, 7 (1901), pp. 247–252; Andrea Capaccioni, *Lineamenti di storia dell'editoria umbra. Il Quattrocento ed il Cinquecento* (Perugia: Volumnia, 1996), *ad indicem*; Elena Scrima, 'Pasini, Luciano', in Rosa Marisa Borraccini, Giuseppe Lipari, Carmela Reale, Marco Santoro and Giancarlo Volpato (eds.), *Dizionario degli editori, tipografi, librai itineranti in Italia tra Quattrocento e Seicento* (3 vols., Pisa: Serra, 2013), II, pp. 783–784.

15   On the book trade in Perugia in the early modern age, see: Giocondo Ricciarelli, 'Mercanti di incunaboli a Perugia', *Bollettino della Deputazione di storia patria per l'Umbria*, 70.1 (1973), pp. 1–20; Jeremy M. Potter, 'Nicolò Zoppino and the book-trade network of Perugia', in Denis V. Reidy (ed.), *The Italian Book 1465–1800. Studies presented to Dennis E. Rhodes on his 70th birthday* (London: British Library, 1993), pp. 135–160; Alberto M. Sartore, 'Il commercio del libro a Perugia nei primi anni del Cinquecento: la società dei Giunta', in Vittoria Garibaldi and Francesco Federico Mancini (eds.), *Perugino il divin pittore* (Milano: Silvana, 2004), pp. 583–588; Rita Liurni, 'Nuovi documenti su Francesco Cartolari e sulla stampa a Perugia nei primi anni del Cinquecento', *Bollettino della Deputazione di storia patria per l'Umbria*, 102, no. 2 (2005), pp. 305–324; Nuovo, *The Book Trade*, *ad indicem*.

16   'Maestro Antonio Pasino da Verona che sta a vender libri nella bottega sotto le case del fu Baldo de' Perigli, riprende da maestro Costanzo di maestro Gisberto da Perugia, perché mancanti di alcuni quaderni, i volumi di maestro Ugo vendutigli parecchi anni innanzi' [*Ex act. Herculani Francisci in prot. ab an. 1521 ad 25, c. 143ᵗ*] (Master Antonio Pasino from Verona, who sells books in the shop under the house of the late Baldo de' Perigli, takes

1510s. Perugia was well suited to book retailing, given that it was one of the most important Italian university cities; as Angela Nuovo noted, "Padua, Pavia, Perugia, Bologna, Naples, and the lesser university towns, with all their students and professors, could not but provide excellent markets for books".[17] This was also a moment of opportunity, since the most important bookseller in the city, Leonardo di Bartolomeo Giunti, director of the Giunti's branch in Perugia, had died in 1517.[18] Antonio bought a house from the printer Baldassarre Cartolari, son of Francesco Cartolari and nephew of Baldassarre *senior*, heir of one of the most important printers' families of Perugia. On 12 December 1528, Baldassarre *junior* sold to Antonio a house at the price of 200 Perugian florins.[19] This witness tells us that the bookseller, active in Perugia now for about ten years, had decided to move permanently in the Umbrian city.

Antonio remained active in Perugia until at least the mid-1540s.[20] We know that in the 1530s he devoted himself to publishing, funding the printing of Bartolomeo da Castello's *De unione anime cum supereminenti lumine*, published by Girolamo Cartolari in 1538.[21] On 17 October 1538, Antonio was involved in a legal case at the book fair of Recanati. Pasini had a debt of 43 *carlini* with the Venetian publisher and bookseller Giovanni Tacuino, who requested that a box of books belonging to Pasini and entrusted to the bookseller Zaccaria Zenaro be impounded. The dispute was resolved on the same day by the Fair's Officer with the restitution of the books as a result of Pasini's formal promise to honour the debt.[22]

---

from master Costanzo, son of master Gisberto from Perugia, because lacking some files, master Ugo's volumes sold to him several years before). Adamo Rossi, *L'arte tipografica in Perugia durante il secolo XV e la prima metà del XVI* (Perugia: Boncompagni, 1868), p. 63.

17 Nuovo, *The Book Trade*, p. 173.
18 Sartore, 'Il commercio del libro'.
19 Archivio di Stato di Perugia (ASPg) Notarile, register 907, fol. 96.
20 Léon Dorez, 'Le Cardinal Marcello Cervini et l'imprimerie à Rome (1539–1550)', *Mélanges d'Archéologie et d'Histoire*, 12 (1892), pp. 303–304.
21 Bartolomeo da Castello, *De unione anime cum supereminenti lumine* (Perugia: Girolamo Cartolari for Antonio Pasini, September 1538), Edit16 CNCE 4476; USTC 812620.
22 Archivio Storico Comunale di Recanati (ASCRe), vol. 1144. '*Consulum nundinarum Rechaneti liber 1538*, 17 ottobre: Jo. Nocentius Perludovici [...] vnus ex socijs militibus nundinarum retulit mihi notario Innocentio se ivisse et ad instantiam Iohannis Tacuini librarj, ut creditoris Antonij Paginj librarij in Perusia in carlenis quadraginta tribus, sequestrasse vnam cassam librorum spectantem et pertinentem ad dictum Antonium penes Zacchariam librarium in nundinis Recaneti, sub pena arbitrij M.D. Consulum' (*Book of the Recanati's Fair Officier 1538*, 17 October: One of the soldiers of the fair told me, Notarius Innocentius [Perludovici], that he went and confiscated, upon request of Giovanni Tacuino, a box of books deposited at the workshop of the bookseller Zaccaria, that is

Luciano Pasini inherited his father's strong instinct for business; he also developed a refined literary sensibility. His erudition and literary patronage led him to be accepted into the Accademia degli Insensati, where he was known as "L'Immobile" ("The Static one"). This academic affiliation influenced part of his publishing production. In 1572, Pasini commissioned the Perugian typographer Valente Panizza to print the *Erofilomachia*, the first play by the lawyer and academic Sforza degli Oddi (called "Il Forsennato", "The Frenetic").[23] Four years later, Baldo Salviani printed in Perugia "ad istanza di M. Luciano Pasini" another of Oddi's work, *I morti vivi*.[24]

As well as with his hometown, Pasini entertained business relationships with Venetian printers to pursue his publishing activities. In this regard, it is useful to remember that in 1572, while printing the *Erofilomachia* in Perugia, he commissioned the printing of Giovanni Antonio Campano's *L'Historie et vite di Braccio Fortebracci* from the Venetian printer Francesco Ziletti, in the Italian translation made by the Perugian historian Pompeo Pellini.[25] Relationships between Pasini and the Serenissima continued for many years. In 1573 he financed the publication of Tobia Nonio's *Consilia* printed by Girolamo Scoto.[26] Eleven years later, Pasini created in Venice a company with the publisher Marco Amadori from Brescia, with whom he published Vincenzo Carocci's *Tractatus locati et*

---

property of Antonio Pasini, bookseller in Perugia, who has a debt [with Giovanni] of forty three *carlini*). This document is quoted and transcribed in Rosa Maria Borraccini, 'Un sequestro librario alla fiera di Recanati del 1600', in Borraccini and Roberto Rusconi (eds.), *Libri, biblioteche e cultura degli ordini regolari nell'Italia moderna attraverso la documentazione della Congregazione dell'Indice: atti del Convegno internazionale, Macerata, 30 maggio–1° giugno 2006* (Vatican City: Biblioteca Apostolica Vaticana, 2006), pp. 416–417.

23 Sforza degli Oddi, *L'Erofilomachia, ouero il duello d'amore, et d'amicitia, comedia nuoua, de l'eccellentiss. dottor di leggi m. Sforza d'Oddo gentil'huomo perugino. Ad instantia de Luciano Pasini* (Perugia: Valente Panizza, 1572), Edit16 CNCE 28366; USTC 845242.

24 Sforza degli Oddi, *I morti vivi comedia del molto eccell. signore Sforza d'Oddi, nell'Academia degli Insensati detto il Forsennato* (Perugia: Baldo Salviani at the request of Luciano Pasini, 1576), Edit16 CNCE 28392; USTC 845243.

25 Giovanni Antonio Campano, *L'historie et vite di Braccio Fortebracci detto da Montone, et di Nicolo Piccinino perugini. Scritte in latino, quella da Gio. Antonio Campano, & questa da Giouambattista Poggio fiorentino, & tradotte in uolgare da m. Pompeo Pellini perugino. Doue non solo s'ha cognitione delle guerre fatte da essi nel perugino, ma etiandio nella Lombardia, Romagna, Marcha, et Regno di Napoli. Mandate pur'hora in luce da Luciano Pasino* (Venice: Francesco Ziletti, 1571–1572), Edit16 CNCE 8813; USTC 818225.

26 Tobia Nonio, *Consilia, seu responsa clarissimi, et acutissimi iurisconsulti Thobiae Nonii Perusini. Nunc recens in studiosorum gratiam edita, cum rerum summis, ac indice locupletissimo* (Venice: Luciano Pasini [printed by Girolamo Scoto], 1573), Edit16 CNCE 28393; USTC 844891.

conducti[27] and the first edition of Sforza Oddi's *De restitutione in integrum*.[28] After the death of Amadori (1590) the company continued between Pasini and the heir of Amadori, the son Pellegrino, through the publication of the second edition of Oddi's *De restitutione*.[29]

The Address to the Reader in *L'Historie et vite di Braccio* offers an insight into the two sides of Pasini's activity as a bookseller and as a publisher. Pasini himself, addressing the reader, said:

> And since I believe that beautiful intellects should not hide, I will endeavor to publish soon the first volume of Perugian academics' lessons, together with the first volume of their poems; because, since I am engaged in the book trade, I think that this task falls upon me rather than others.[30]

This testimony indicates that the activity of Pasini as a bookseller began well before the 1570s and that probably he joined the Accademia degli Insensati in the first years of its existence. In 1573 Pasini, after marrying the daughter of the publisher and bookseller Pier Matteo Tesori from Orvieto, obtained permission to take over the workshop of his father in law, creating a branch of its main activity in another Papal city.[31] It is probable that the branch-office in Orvieto represented a secondary business and that its day-to-day management was entrusted to his wife's relatives. In fact, contrary to what was previously thought, it is now clear that Pasini lived in Perugia throughout the 1570s, as evi-

---

27 Vincenzo Carocci, *Tractatus locati et conducti: in quo de pensionibus, fructibus, caducitatibus, remissionibus, salarijs & similibus pertractatur. d. Vincentio Carocio Tudertino auctore* (Venice: Luciano Pasini and Marco Amadori, 1584), Edit16 CNCE 9665; USTC 819064.

28 Sforza degli Oddi, *De restitutione in integrum tractatus d. Sfortii Oddi i.u.c. Perusini acutissimi, atque praeclarissimi, cum duplici indice quaestionum, et materiarum omnium locupletissimo* (Venice: Luciano Pasini and Marco Amadori, 1584), Edit16 CNCE 28396; USTC 845248.

29 Sforza degli Oddi, *De restitutione in integrum tractatus d. Sfortiae Oddi i.v.c. Perusini acutissimi atque praeclarissimi, cum duplici indice quaestionum, & materiarum omnium locupletissimo, insertis quoque in hac secunda editione additionibus aliquot ex tomo auctoris manuscriptis desumptis* (Venice: Luciano Pasini and the heir of Marco Amadori, 1591), Edit16 CNCE 28398; USTC 845251.

30 'Et perché mi pare, che non debbono stare occolti i parti de' belli ingegni, m'ingegnerò di farui leggere in brieue il primo volume delle lettioni di diuersi Academici Perugini, col primo volume delle rime de' medesimi. Parendomi, ch'essendo io occupato nel negotio de' libri, à me perauentura più che ad altri ciò fare conuenga'. G.A. Campano, *L'historie et vite di Braccio Fortebracci*, fol. B1r–v.

31 Tordi, 'La stampa in Orvieto', pp. 249–250.

denced by some legal documents, drawn up by the notary Ottaviano Aureli and now held in the State Archive of the city, where the bookseller figure both as a witness and protagonist in legal proceedings.[32] In 1580 he sold the Orvieto bookshop to Rosato Tintinassi, deciding to focus his energies on his Perugian business only. Domenico Tordi reports, without citing an archival source, that in 1584 Pasini obtained from the governors of the city permission to open a new bookshop in Orvieto; but there are no traces of this second Orvietan adventure.[33] Pasini died in his hometown on June 1591, one year after his Venetian partner Marco Amadori. In his last testament he left a considerable inheritance to his nephew and collaborator Giovanni Battista Costantini, who continued his uncle's activity as "the Heir of Luciano Pasini".[34]

The Inventory

The inventory of Luciano Pasini's bookshop was drawn up a few months after the bookseller's death. Probably this delay was due to some bureaucratic difficulties encountered by his nephew in receiving the inheritance.[35] On 19 September 1591, the notary Fulvio Fustini went to Pasini's bookshop and drew up a list of the surviving stock. The document is now preserved at the State Archive of Perugia and consists of 80 unpaginated leaves.[36] The inventory's text is distributed in two parts (fols. 1r–22v and 54r–80r), making a total of 95 pages. It lists about 2,600 books, together with a number of other possessions. The inventory records the number of copies of each items, and an assessment of their monetary value. The list ends with the indication of the working tools held in the shop, and of Pasini's properties held outside Perugia. The document, written in legible, humanist hand, was created initially as a simple list of the books held in the shop, but clearly it was later converted into a general inventory of Pasini's properties. This hypothesis is supported by the fact that the document was titled "Inventory of books of the shop of the heirs of Luciano Pasini"; later

---

32   ASPg Notarile. Notary Ottaviano Aureli, register 2009, fols. 170v–173v. '1571, Luciani Magistri Antonii Pasini a domino Antonio Gallo, debito confessio—Idem cum Antonio Joannis refutatio'; '1575, Luciani Magistri Antonii de Pasinis ab Antonio Joannis Soana promissio'; '1579 Idem a Cola Justino renuncia'; '1583, Luciani Pasini bibliopolae cum Francisco Iudici inventio'; '1588, Luciani Antonii de Pasinis a Jacobo Parelutio emptio'.
33   Tordi, 'La stampa in Orvieto', p. 251.
34   ASPg Notarile. Notary Ottaviano Aureli, register 1987, fols. 104v–109r. See *Appendix*, doc. 1.
35   ASPg Notarile. Notary Fulvio Fustini, register 2198, doc. 2–3.
36   ASPg Notarile. Notary Fulvio Fustini, register 2198, doc. 1.

this title was crossed out and corrected to "Inventory of the properties left and found in the inheritance of Luciano Pasini".[37]

The inventory was probably drawn up in one or two days. Pasini's books are classified by discipline and format. The only deviation from this common practice is with the vernacular books, left as a mixed category that includes texts of various disciplines. The list describes in the first place the unbound books in the shop, then the bound ones. The second part of the inventory contains a description of the books kept in the warehouse, both bound and unbound. The final part of the list includes parchment and tools to engrave leather.[38] This clearly indicates that Luciano also ran a bindery, in order to provide a finished product for those customers who wished to buy books in this way.

Within each section the inventory follows an alphabetical order, applied to various degrees of precision. Descriptions are extremely concise, often only consisting of the author's name. The poor bibliographical descriptions make it difficult to identify the individual editions recorded in the document. Nevertheless, for several items the inventory gives the place of publication: it features editions printed in Lyon, Paris, Cologne, Basel, Salamanca as well as Venice, Florence, Bologna and Rome, but, among these few cases, only Lyon (92 editions) and Paris (36 editions) appear to have been systematically recorded.[39]

The list starts with the unbound books of theology and philosophy, which amounted respectively to 271 titles in 671 copies and 160 titles in 427 copies. The following section lists the ecclesiastical books (here called 'Rossi e Neri', because of the common practice of printing these items in red and black) and contains 109 titles in 313 volumes. The third section includes the legal books and is organised into three categories: legal texts (276 titles in 522 volumes); second-hand legal texts, which were therefore already bound (76 titles in 81 volumes); lectures and commentaries (67 titles in 101 volumes). Overall, this

---

37 ASPg Notarile. Notary Fulvio Fustini, register 2198, doc. 1, fol. 1r. 'Inventario delli libri della Botega degli Eredi delli beni lassati e ritrovati nella eredità di Luciano Pasini'.

38 ASPg Notarile. Notary Fulvio Fustini, register 2198, doc. 1, fol. 90v. 'Cento carte pecore diverse, sc. 42 [...] Sei torcoli da incollare, sc. 12; Due torcoli da tagliare con castelletti, sc. 8 [...]; Una pietra da battere, sc. 6; Tre martelli da battere piccoli e grandi, sc. 12 [...]; Venti pezzi di ferri da stampare diversi, sc. 12; Quattro marche da stampare piccoli di legno, sc. 6; Due para di forbice piccole, sc. 1.4; Due martelli piccoli, sc. 1; Otto pezzi di ferri da lavorare per bottega diversi, sc. 6' (One hundred different parchments, sc. 42 [...] Six presses for gluing, sc. 12; Two presses for cutting with their locks, sc. 8; One stone for beating, sc. 6; Three small and large hammers for beating, sc. 12 [...] Twenty different printing tools, sc. 20; Four small printing wood-marks, sc. 6; Two pairs of small scissors, sc. 1.4; Two small hammers, sc. 1; Eight different shop tools, sc. 6).

39 See Appendix B.

section therefore consists of 512 items in 704 copies. The following section lists the vernacular books, a general category which served as a container for texts in various disciplines. It includes 374 items in a total of 1053 volumes. After this the shop inventory lists the medical texts (176 items in 403 volumes) and books in the humanities (277 items in 791 volumes), and it concludes with five groups of bound books that mirror the subject matter and proportions of the sections previously described.

The second part of the document lists the warehouse volumes, mirroring the subject division already used for the volumes held in the bookshop: law, theology and philosophy, medicine, grammar, ecclesiastical and vernacular books. In addition to these categories, we find the indication of 250 unspecified "old and ancient bound books" and of 4 "bales of ancient books in different bundles", for a total of almost 265 items in 1095 volumes. The bibliographical descriptions of the volumes held in the warehouse are as detailed as the shop inventory. The warehouse contained duplicate copies of items available in the shop as well as works that were not displayed in the bookshop. The sum of the titles held within the shop with those stored in the warehouse amounts to about 2,600 items for a total of almost 7,000 volumes.

An analysis of the inventory's contents brings home the great variety of what the shop had to offer. Legal books make up the largest proportion of the stock, which clearly responded to a professional demand in the university's law school. Here we find the works of medieval legal authors as well as texts related to the modern legal writers. For this reason, it is not surprising to find alongside Baldo degli Ubaldi's *Super feudis* and Bartolo da Sassoferrato's *Consilia*, the works of Silvestro Aldobrandini and Andrea Alciati, as well as the legal works by Sforza Oddi (3 copies, 36 scudi) and Tobia Nonio (2 copies, 8 scudi) published by Pasini himself. In addition to many cheap books such as the pocket editions of Justinian's *Institutes* (1 scudo), the books of legal procedure by Ubertus de Bonacurso (1.5 scudi), Baldus and Giacomo Belvisi (2 scudi), available in more than 3 copies for the university students, the law section also contains the most expensive books of Pasini's shop. The *Lecturae* subsection lists titles with very high evaluations. Fustini valued the books by Giasone Maino, Bartolo da Sassoferrato and Alberico da Rosate at respectively 43, 54 and 60 scudi, while the works by Giovanni da Imola, Battista Fulgosi and Gilles de Bellemère received an evaluation of 30, 42 and 48 scudi. This means of course that these books were destined mostly for professionals such as lawyers or law professors rather than university students.

Another substantial portion of the shop's stock was made up of vernacular books, which includes literary texts as the works of Petrarch, Cecco d'Ascoli, Bembo, Boccaccio, Dante, Ariosto and Tasso. Pasini also stocked works of his-

TABLE 16.1 Structure of Pasini's bookshop inventory

Topic	Editions	Copies	Folios
Bookshop (Unbound)			
Theology	271	671	1v–4v
Philosophy	160	427	5r–7v
'Rossi e Neri'	109	313	8r–9r
Law			(9v–16v)
Unbound	276	522	9v–13v
(Used and Bound)	76	81	14r–15r
Lectures	67	101	15v–16v
Vernacular	374	1053	17r–22v
Bookshop (Bound)			
Vernacular	97	111	64v–67v
Law (Used)	93	95	68r–69v
Theology and philosophy	24	25	69v
'Rossi e Neri'	23	88 + 200	70r
Bound in 16°	50	52	74r–74v
Bound in 8°	50	52	74v–75v
Bound in 4°	16	18	75v
Humanities in 8°	61	69	76r–76v
Humanities in 4°	14	15	77r
Medicine	176	403	77v–80r
Humanities	277	791	80v–85v
Warehouse			
Old and ancient Bound books	?	250	86r
Bales of ancient books in different bundles	?	4 bales	86r
Law	113	237	86r–87v
Theology and philosophy	47	106	88r–88v
Medicine	10	19	89r
Grammar	18	80	89r
'Rossi e Neri'	28	246	89v
Vernacular	39	157	90

tory such as the *History of Italy* by Guicciardini or the *History of Skanderbeg* by Marin Barleti; books of arithmetic such as the works of Euclid edited by the Jesuit Christoph Clavius and translations of the Latin classics into Italian, such as the works of Livy, Ovid, Vergil, Caesar and Sallust. Religious bestsellers, such as the *Directory* by the Jesuit Juan de Polanco or the *Manual for confessors* by Manuel de Azpilcueta, were also included in the stock.[40] Very interesting is the presence within this section of seven titles in the Spanish language, all held in a single copy: Lucianus' *Historia*, Alonso de Ulloa's *Comentarios*, Miguel Sabucos' *Nueva filosofia*, the chivalric novel *Primaleon*, translations of Sallust and Caesar's *Commentaries* and the works of Juan Boscan.[41] Most of the titles listed in this section were available in more than 2 copies, sometimes up to 12 or 15 copies per title.[42] Unlike the legal books, this section mostly lists books with prices in the middle of the range, as well as very cheap books. A series of printed

---

40 These are to be identified, respectively, with: (1) Francesco Guicciardini, *La historia d'Italia*. Uncertain identification; USTC records three different editions between 1561 and 1580. (2) Marin Barleti, *Historia de vita et gestis Scanderbegi Epirotarum principis*. Uncertain identification; USTC records thirteen different editions between 1508 and 1580. (3) Euclides, *Elementorum libri XV* (Köln [i.e. Venice]: Giovanni Battista Ciotti, 1591), USTC 654843. (4) Juan de Polanco, *Breve directorium*. Uncertain identification; USTC records thirty-five different editions between 1554 and 1591. (5) Manuel de Azpilcueta, *Manual de confessors y penitents*. Uncertain identification; USTC records one-hundred-nineteen different editions between 1561 and 1591.

41 These are to be identified, respectively, with: (1) Lucianus, *Historia verdadera de Luciano traduzida de griego en lengua castellana* (Strasbourg: Augustin Friess, 1551), USTC 348269. (2) Alonso de Ulloa, *Comentarios del S. Alonso de Ulloa* (Venice: Domenico Farri, 1569), Edit16 CNCE 49699; USTC 340645. (3) Miguel Sabuco y Alvarez, *Nueva filosofia de la naturaleza del hombre, no conocida ni alcançada de los grandes filosofos antiguos la qual mejora la vida y salud humana. Compuesta por doña Oliva Sabuco* (Madrid: Pedro Madrigal, 1588), USTC 341474. (4) *Primaleon. Los tres libros del muy esforçado cauallero Primaleon et Polendos su hermano hijos del emperador palmerin de Oliua* (Venice: Giovanni Antonio Nicolini da Sabbio and Giovanni Battista Pederzano, 1534), Edit16 CNCE 32003; USTC 337939. (5) Gaius Sallustius Crispus, *Cathilinario & Jugurthino de Salustio historiador romano* (Logroño: Miguel de Eguia, 1529), USTC 341518. (6) Caius Iulius Caesar, *Libro de los comentarios de Gayo Iulio Cesar delas guerras dela Gallia, Africa, y Espana tambien dela ciuil traduzido en espanol, nuevamente imprimido, y emendado en muchas partes* (Paris: Jacques De Puys, 1549), USTC 440070. (7) Juan Boscan Almogaver, *Las obras de Boscan y algunas de Garcilasso de la Vega repartidas en quatro libros* (Venice: Gabriele Giolito de Ferrari, 1553), USTC 347072 and 816465; Edit16 CNCE 7191.

42 Such are the cases for Juan de Godoy, *Comentari della guerra fatta nella Germania da Carlo Quinto Imperadore* (Venice: Comin da Trino, 1548), Edit16 CNCE 21406; USTC 833619 (12 copies in stock) and Andrea Cambini, *Libro d'Andrea Cambini fiorentino della origine de Turchi, et imperio delli Ottomanni* (Florence: Benedetto Giunti, 1537), Edit16 CNCE 8665; USTC 818040 (15 copies in stock).

madrigals, listed in the order of one hundred copies per title, were valued at less than one scudo per volume.[43]

The third largest portion of the stock is made up by books in the humanities, including texts of grammar, rhetoric, Greek and Latin literature. The works of theology, philosophy and medicine, although not present in comparable quantities, show a substantial demand from a wide range of customers: professionals, students, professors and clergymen represented the public for these types of book.

Conclusions

It seems clear that the stock of Pasini's bookshop was structured to satisfy the needs of the wide Perugian clientele. As was the case before the Salt War, the largest part of the client base was emerged from the university and the legal professions. In addition, a cultural institution such as the *Studium* must have provided an important portion of the reading public. The broad range of customer demand is also confirmed by the large quantity of texts of theology, medicine and philosophy, all disciplines represented in the university courses available in Perugia. Nevertheless, the conspicuous presence of vernacular literary texts, musical texts, handbooks of rhetoric and other humanistic texts is an obvious symptom of the cultural change that Perugia underwent after its integration with the Papal State. A cultured and shrewd bookseller like Pasini was able to gauge demand from the various new audiences in order to meet the cultural needs of *literati*, new teachers, university professors, as well as those of professionals, students and clergymen. In this way, he became a point of reference for the cultural environment of the city, and the inventory of his rich bookshop not only provides an in-depth insight into the book culture of Perugia, but also it represents a perfect image of the evolution of the bookseller's work in Italy in the late sixteenth century.

---

43 ASPg Notarile. Notary Fulvio Fustini, register 2198, doc. 1, fol. 56r. '120 Mute di Madrigali diversi a cinque, sc. 120; 80 Mute di Madrigali diversi a quattro, sc. 60; 100 Mute di Messe, Mottetti, e Vesperi diversi, sc. 100; 40 Mute di Canzone Napolitane diversi a tre, sc. 24'.

Appendix 1. The Will of Luciano Pasini[44]

Summary of the document (followed by a full transcription):

After having entrusted his soul to God, Luciano Pasini disposed that his body be buried in the church of San Domenico in Perugia. Later, he arranged to leave different amounts of money to some religious institutions in the city. Pasini appointed as heir his nephew Giovanni Battista Costantini, who was to continue the bookselling business under the denomination: "The heir of Luciano Pasini". To his wife Livia, he left his house, to be bequeathed to his heir after her death. He also disposed that the Accademia degli Insensati be allowed to continue holding its meetings in his house in the country.

In nomine Domini amen. Anno Domini millesimo quingentesimo nonagesimo primo, indictione quarta, tempore pontificatus S.D.N. Domini Gregorij XIIII divina providentia Pontificis Maximi, die vero decima septima mensis Junij. Actum Perusiae in domo infrascripti testatoris sita in platea maiori de civitatis in angulo stratae novae seu Crispae. Presentibus ibidem domino Ioannes Andrea quondam Pauli de Bontempis de Perusia Portae Sanctae Susannae, domino Antonio quondam Gentilis de Barisianis de Perusia Portae Eburneae, Francisco quondam Andreae de Gregoriis de Perusia Portae Solis, Andrea quondam Gregorij de Surcijs de Perusia Portae Sancti Petri, Philippo quondam Andreae de Anastasijs de Perusia Portae Sanctae Susannae, Angelo quondam Federici Antonij de Perusia Portae Eburneae et Bartolo quondam Petrini de Anigis de Perusia Portae Sancti Angeli testibus ad infrascripta vocatis habitis, et ab infrascripto testatore ore proprio rogatis.

LUCIANUS quondam Antonij de Pasinis de Perusia sanus, Deo optimo maximo favente; visu, mente, et intellectu, et in bono ac rectu sensu christianus, licet corpore infirmus et in lecto iacens, si mens casum mortis, et nolens intestatus decedere, hoc suum ultimum testamentum nuncupatorium, quod etiam sine scriptis de iure dicitur, condere procuravit et condidit in hunc qui sequitur modum et formam.

Imprima raccomanda l'anima sua all'Onnipotente Iddio, alla sua santissima Madre sempre Vergine Maria, alla gloriosa Vergine et martire santa Lucia sua avvocata, et a tutti i santi del Cielo.

Item giudica et lassa, che il suo corpo sia sepelito nella Chiesa di San Domenico, nella sepoltura di esso testatore, et che sia portato alla sepoltura scalzo, vestito solo con la veste della Fraternità della Giustizia.

---

44   ASPg Notarile. Notary Ottaviano Aureli, register 1987, fols. 104v–109r.

Item giudica et lassa per amor di Dio allo Spedale di Santa Maria della Misericordia di Perugia diece fiorini di moneta Perugina.

Item giudica et lassa alla Fraternità della Giustizia, nella quale esso testatore è descritto, ogni anno in perpetuo il giorno di Santa Lucia, tanto pane, et vino, quanto basti per governar quel giorno annualmente i prigioni soliti governarsi da detta fraternità talmente che ogni anno in quel giorno detti prigioni siano governati a spese della heredità di esso testatore.

Item giudica et lassa alla Compagnia di San Martino per amor di Dio, diece fiorini, per sovvenire i poveri infermi miserabili.

Item giudica et lassa per amor di Dio alla Compagnia del Santissimo Rosario nella Chiesa di San Domenico di Perugia un par di guanciali, che esso testatore ha lavorati et recamati di seta et perle.

Item giudica et lassa per ragion di legato, et per recognitione della sua servitù, alla Girolama sua serva, fiorini cento di moneta Perugina; con questo che essa non possa domandare né conseguire altro per il suo salario per il tempo che è stata, et starà con detto testatore e sua famiglia et anco per il tempo che starà con l'infrascritta sua moglie.

Item giudica et lassa per ragion di legato et in ogni altro miglior modo a donna Agata sua sorella carnale monaca professa nel monasterio di Santa Margarita di Perugia, dodici fiorini ogni anno, mentre ella viverà, per li bisogni della sua persona, volendo che né essa, né il monasterio per la sua persona né altri in nome suo possa domandar altro; et domandandolo altro, stiano privati della presente lassita, et di ogni altra successione.

Item giudica et lassa all'Accademia de gli Insensati di Perugia, nella quale esso testatore è sotto nome dell'Immobile, et suoi Academici, che possano et sia loro lecito ad ogni lor libito et volontà, raddunarsi, et legger lettioni, et fare qual si voglia essercitij Academici in casa di esso testatore nella sala solita, dove al presente è la catedra di detta Academia et alcune imprese. Et vuole che gli heredi di esso testatore, o chi sarà possessore di detta casa, non possano in modo alcun prohibire tali raddunanze; ma debbiano con ogni patientia permettere che si facciano le Academie et raddunanze di essa in detta sala.

Item giudica et lassa che se messer Giacomo Paolucci ricomprerà due stanze, che esso ha venduto ad detto testatore con patto di poterle ricomprare, per scudi ducento, con detti denari si debba estinguere un censo che esso ha col monasterio di Santa Margherita di Perugia.

Item giudica et lassa che se avverrà, che l'infrascritto Giovanni Battista suo herede si partisse mai per alcun tempo di Perugia, et che la sua absentia fosse per più tempo d'un mese, la bottega di detto testatore si debbia amministrare intanto da Pietropaolo di Giuliano, che ora sta con detto testatore in detta bottega; et che per ciò egli sia pagato convenientemente secondo che sarà giudicato da i periti.

Item che detto Giovanni Battista suo herede sia obligato pagare sempre la pigione della bottega à i ministri dello Spedale della Misericordia à i tempi debiti anticipatamente. Et che la ragione di detta bottega si debbia sempre chiamare "de gli heredi di Luciano Pasini" et non altramente.

Item giudica et lassa a madonna Livia sua diletta consorte, per restitutione della sua dote, che se le restituiscano tutti li beni stabili che esso testatore ha compro con la dote di lei, ò che altramente ha hauto per sua dote, con tutte le bonificationi che esso testatore ha fatto in detti beni; le quali bonificationi glie le lassa per ragion di legato; et anco se le restituiscano fiorini cento settanta sette et soldi novantasei che esso testatore ha hauto da Pietrogiapeco Nettoli per prezzo di certa parte di detti beni dotali à lui venduta, come ne appare instrumento per mia mano. Et anco se le restituisca tutto il suo arriedo, che è in essere. Et di più le lassa tutte le vesti et gioie che esso testatore ha fatto per detta sua moglie, che saranno in essere.

Item giudica et lassa alla detta madonna Livia sua moglie in vita sua tanto l'appartamento di sopra della casa di esso testatore; ciò è tutte le stanze al piano della cucina, et il resto di sopra sino al tetto con la metà della cantina, la quale si debbia dividere et consegnare a lei l'entrata di detta cantina dentro in casa, et all'infrascritto suo herede l'entrata di fuori, con la metà di tutto il mobile che ora si truova in detta casa. Il quale appartamento di casa, et mobile dopo la morte di detta madonna Livia tornino à gli heredi di detto testatore.

Item giudica et lassa a Fabrizio Pasini suo nipote al presente prete giesuita, che possa et gli sia lecito sempre tornare a casa di esso testatore, et quivi da i suoi heredi debba essere alimentato.

Et in tutti gli altri suoi beni, ragioni, attioni, et nomi di debitori, instituisce herede universale Giovambattista di Costantino suo nipote figliuolo di madonna Anna sorella carnale di esso testatore. Con questo che detto Giovambattista non possa mai per alcun tempo alienare alcun de i beni di esso testatore tanto stabili, quanto mobili, né il fare della bottega di libri, né cedere il sito di essa a nessuno, se non per pagare i debiti di esso testatore. Et contra facendo, i beni alienati ipso facto devengano a i sustituti fidecommissarij come di sotto. Et morendo detto Giovanni Battista con figliuoli legitimi et naturali, et nati di legitimo matrimonio, quelli pleno iure, et senza detrattione di trebellianica sustituisca al detto Giovanni Battista. Et in evento che morisse detto Giovanni Battista senza figliuoli legitimi et naturali et di legitimo matrimonio nati maschi o femine; sustituisce nella vigna fuor della porta di Porta San Pietro con tutto il mobile che in essa si trova al presente, il sopra detto Fabrizio suo nipote in vita sua, et dopo morte sua, tanto se egli morisse vivente detto Giovanni Battista, quanto se sopravvivesse, sustituisce il Collegio dei Padri della Compagnia di Giesù di Perugia; et nel resto dell'heredità per la metà messer Pietro Pasini da Brescia, e suoi figliuoli et descendenti; et per l'altra metà i figliuoli et descendenti di messer Nicolò Pasini suoi parenti, in stirpe et non in capi, con piena ragione et senza alcuna diminutione di trebellianica. Con questo peròche se avvenisse che se avvenisse che, morendo detto Giovanni Battista senza figliuoli legitimi et naturali, come di sopra, sopravivesse detta madonna Livia, ella debbia havere in vita sua tutta la casa di esso testatore; et dopo morte sua ritorni a gli heredi di esso testatore sopradetti.

Et hoc est suum ultimum testamentum, sua ultima voluntas, et suorum bonorum ultima dispositio. Quod et quam valere voluit iure testamenti. Et si iure testamenti non valeret, vel non valebit, valere voluit iure codicillorum, aut donationis circa mortis, vel eiuscunque alterius ultimae voluntatis, prout melius de iure valere et tenere poterit. Cassans, irritans et anullans omne aliud testamentum, codicillos, donationem causa mortis et quandus aliam ultimam voluntatem per cum hactenus forsan factum, factos vel factam; volens presens testamentum et ultimam voluntatem caeteris omnibus prevalere.

Appendix 11. Some Identifications: the French Books

Pasini's bookshop was a thriving environment, and among the volumes available to the clientele were many foreign imprints. French editions stand out for quantity and quality. This appendix offers the transcription of all books explicitly identified in Pasini's inventory as French. The bibliographic information given by the document has been compared to descriptions in the Universal Short Title Catalogue and the SBN Opac to identify the editions cited.[45] It has been possible to identify 73 of the 92 Lyonnese editions, and as many as 30 out of the 36 Parisian editions.

---

45   USTC: http://ustc.ac.uk/index.php/search; SBN: http://www.sbn.it/opacsbn/opac/iccu/antico.jsp.

No.	Quantity in warehouse	Transcription of the entry
Section: Libri di Teologia et Filosofia		
[Fol. 1r]		
1.	2	[Augustini] sopra salmi in folio Parise, 18 sc.[46]
2.	9	Anton Florambelli de Autoritate Ecclesie in 4° Lione, 9 sc.[47]
3.	2	Augustini Steuchi de perenni filosofia folio Paris, 24 sc.[48]
4.	1	Ambrosi Catterini in Epistolas Pauli folio Paris, 8 sc.[49]
5.	4	Idem opuscula in 4° Lione, 8 sc.[50]
6.	2	Anton Broich super Evangelia 8° Paris, 8 sc.[51]
7.	1	Bollario in 8° Par Lione, 3 sc.[52]
8.	1	Alfonso de Castro contra Ereses folio Paris, 5 sc.[53]
9.	2	Idem [Basili Magni] de spiritu santo 4° Lione, 2 sc.[54]
[Fol. 1v]		
10.	1	Canisi Dotrina Cristiana folio Paris, 18 sc.[55]
11.	1	Canisio de Verbi Dei Corruptelis folio Paris, 12 sc.[56]

46   Aurelius Augustinus, *Enarrationes, sive Commentarii in Psalmos mysticos* (Paris). Uncertain identification; USTC records eight different editions between 1542 and 1571.
47   Antonio Fiordibello, *Liber de autoritate Ecclesiae* (Lyon: Sébastien Gryphius, 1546), USTC 122858.
48   Agostino Steuco, *De perenni philosophia* (Paris: Michel Sonnius the Elder, 1578), USTC 171473.
49   Ambrosio Catarino Politi, *In omnes divi Pauli apostoli epistolas commentaria* (Paris: Nicolas Chesneau, 1566), USTC 154908.
50   Ambrosio Catarino Politi, *Opuscula* (Lyon: Macé Bonhomme, 1542), USTC 140709.
51   Antonius Broickwy von Konigstein, *Eruditissimarum in quatuor Euangelia enarrationum* (Paris). Uncertain identification; USTC records twelve different editions between 1545 and 1555.
52   *Ecloge bullarum, et motupropriorum* (Lyon: Charles Pesnot, 1582), USTC 141926.
53   Alfonso de Castro, *Adversus omnes hereses* (Paris: Josse Bade & Jean Roigny, 1534), USTC 187349.
54   Basilius Magnus, *De Spiritu Sancto* (Lyon). No Lyonnese edition of this work is recorded in USTC. However, there were two editions in 1532, one printed in Paris (USTC 185205), and one printed in Basel (USTC 640556). Unless this is a lost Lyonnese edition, format identification would indicate that it could be the Basel edition instead.
55   Petrus Canisius, *Opus catechisticum* (Paris: Thomas Brumen, 1585), USTC 170790.
56   Petrus Canisius, *Commentariorum de verbi Dei corruptelis* (Paris: Nicolas Nivelle, 1584), USTC 172309.

(cont.)

No.	Quantity in warehouse	Transcription of the entry
12.	7	Catechismi Catolici in 8° Lione, 6 sc.[57]
13.	1	Concili in 4° Lione, 2.10 sc.[58]
14.	1	Claudi Guillandi super Job 8° Paris, 3 sc.[59]
[Fol. 2r]		
15.	6	Corneli Janseni 8° Lion, 12 sc.[60]
16.	1	Caviniane confusiones 8 Paris, 4 sc.[61]
17.	1	Demonstratio Religionis Cristiane in 8° Lione, 3 sc.[62]
18.	2	Francisci romei in 4° Lione, 3 sc.[63]
19.	1	Defensio per Canonibus 8° Lutetia, 4 sc.[64]
20.	1	Cartusiano sopra salmi in folio Paris, 7 sc.[65]
[Fol. 2v]		
21.	2	Eutimi in salmos in 8° Lione, 6 sc.[66]
22.	3	Cartusian super Evangelia in folio Lione, 27 sc.[67]
23.	2	Economia Pauperum Cura 8° Paris, 2 sc.[68]

---

57 *Catechismus ex decreto sacrosancti Concilij Tridentini* (Lyon: Guillaume Rouillé, 1588), USTC 156673.

58 *Canones et decreta sacrosancti Concilii Tridentini* (Lyon: Guillaume Rouillé, 1566), USTC 158069.

59 Claude Guillaud, *Homiliae quadragesimales* (Paris: Michel de Roigny, 1568), USTC 198992.

60 Cornelius Jansenius, *Commentariorum in suam concordiam* (Lyon). Uncertain identification; USTC records twelve different editions between 1577 and 1591.

61 Archibald Hamilton, *De confusione Calvinianae sectae apud Scotos Ecclesiae* (Paris: Thomas Brumen, 1577), USTC 170364.

62 Franciscus Sonnius, *Demonstrationum religionis christianae* (Lyon: Guillaume Rouillé, 1564), USTC 125262.

63 Francesco Romeo, *De libertate operum* (Lyon: Sébastien Gryphius, 1538), USTC 157219.

64 Francisco Torres, *Pro canonibus apostolorum defensio* (Paris: Nicolas Chesneau and Sébastien Nivelle, 1573), USTC 170176.

65 Godefroy Tilmann, *Ioannis Chrysostomi Homiliae in partem multò meliorem Davidici Psalterij* (Paris: Sébastien Nivelle, 1554), USTC 151546.

66 Euthymius Zigabenus, *Commentarii in omnes psalmos* (Lyon: Jean Carré, 1573), USTC 156118.

67 Denis le Chartreux, *In quatuor evangelistas enarrationes* (Lyon: Barthélemy Honorat, 1579), USTC 156302.

68 Lorenzo Villavicencio, *De oeconomia sacra circa pauperum curam* (Paris: Michel Sonnius the Elder, 1564), USTC 153506.

(cont.)

No.	Quantity in warehouse	Transcription of the entry
24.	1	Eusebij Opera in folio Paris, 18 sc.[69]
25.	2	Flores Bibblie in 16 Lion, 3 sc.[70]
[Fol. 3r]		
26.	9	Guglielmi Parisiensi de 7 sacramentis in 16 Paris, 4 sc.[71]
27.	2	Ocularia Fratrum Minorum in 8° Paris, 8 sc.[72]
28.	1	Istoria Ecclesiastica Calisti 8° Paris, 8 sc.[73]
29.	2	Janseni sopra salmi Folio Lione, 28 sc.[74]
30.	7	Giovanni Gerson latt in 16 Lion, 10.10 sc.[75]
31.	1	In Cantica Canticorum 8° Paris, 3 sc.[76]
32.	1	Joannis Chrisostomi sopra san Paolo 8° Paris, 4 sc.[77]
33.	2	Omiliarus Doctorum in Lione (e Venezia) Folio, 15 sc.[78]
34.	1	Jeronnimi sopra salmi in folio Lione, 6 sc.[79]
35.	1	Istoria Veterum Patrum folio Paris, 18 sc.[80]
36.	4	Opera divi Cipriani 8° Lione (e Venezia), 12 sc.[81]

---

69 Eusebius Caesariensis, *Opera omnia* (Paris: Michel Sonnius the Elder, 1581), USTC 172329.
70 *Flores Bibliae sive Loci communes* (Lyon: Guillaume Rouillé, 1572), USTC 140965.
71 Guillaume d'Auvergne, *De septem sacramentis libellus* (Paris: Sébastien Nivelle, 1560), USTC 152862.
72 Yves Magistri, *Ocularia et Manipulus fratrum Minorum* (Paris: Michel Sonnius the Elder, 1582), USTC 170632.
73 Callistus Xanthopulus Nicephorus, *Ecclesiasticae historiae libri* (Paris). Uncertain identification: USTC records twenty four different editions between 1562 and 1587.
74 Cornelius Jansenius, *Paraphrasis in psalmos omnes* (Lyon: Charles Pesnot, 1580), USTC 113322.
75 Jean Gerson, *De Imitatione Christi* (Lyon). Uncertain identification: USTC records fourteen different editions between 1529 and 1587.
76 Franz Titelmans, *Commentarii doctissimi in Cantica Canticorum Salomonis* (Paris). Uncertain identification: USTC records fourteen different editions between 1529 and 1587.
77 Ioannes Chrysostomus, *In omnes divi Pauli epistolas commentarii* (Paris). Uncertain identification: USTC records thirteen different editions between 1543 and 1548.
78 *Homiliarius doctorum* (Lyon: Jean Clein, 1516), USTC 144586.
79 *Commentarios in Psalterium* (Lyon: Sébastien Gryphius, 1530), USTC 122063.
80 *Historia Christiana veterum Patrum* (Paris: Michel Sonnius the Elder, 1583), USTC 170674.
81 Cyprianus, *Opera* (Lyon). Uncertain identification: USTC records five different editions between 1535 and 1550.

(cont.)

No.	Quantity in warehouse	Transcription of the entry
37.	4	Loci Communes Similium et Dissimilum 8° Paris, 5 sc.[82]
38.	2	Lexicon Theologicum folio Lione, 20 sc.[83]
39.	2	Landolfo de Vita Christi Folio uno Lione (uno Venetia), 25 sc.[84]
[Fol. 3v]		
40.	1	Liber Rut Feu Aurdentii 8° Paris, 3 sc.[85]
41.	1	Omilie Feu Ardenti 8° Paris, 2 sc.[86]
42.	1	Idem in exodo 8° Paris, 1.10 sc.[87]
43.	1	Laurenzi Iustiniani Opera Folio Lione, 9 sc.[88]
44.	1	Loci Communes Teologici 8° Paris, 5 sc.[89]
45.	1	Navarra Manual de Confessori 8° Lion, 5 sc.[90]
46.	3	Primari sopra San Paolo in 8° Paris, 5 sc.[91]
47.	3	Omelie Crisologi 8° Paris, 6 sc.[92]
[Fol. 4r]		
48.	6	Rational divinorum officiorum in 8° Lione, 18 sc.[93]
49.	3	Ossi Cardinalis sopra Concili Folio Lion, 30 sc.[94]

---

82 Jean Dadré, *Loci communes similium et dissimilium* (Paris). Uncertain edition: USTC records two editions: Guillaume Julian, 1577 (USTC 170381); Michel Julian, 1582 (USTC 137730).
83 Johann Altenstaig, *Lexicon theologicum* (Lyon: Jean Symonet, 1579), USTC 112229.
84 Ludolph von Saxen, *Vita Iesu Christi* (Lyon). Uncertain identification: USTC records forty different editions between 1479 and 1577.
85 François Feu-Ardent, *Liber Ruth* (Paris: Sébastien Nivelle, 1582), USTC 170627.
86 Unidentified.
87 Fremin Capitis, *Expositio in Exodum* (Paris: Nicolas Chesneau, 1579), USTC 171492.
88 Lorenzo Giustiniani, *Opera* (Lyon: Heirs of Jacques Giunta, 1569), USTC 140624.
89 Konrad Kling, *Loci communes theologici* (Paris: Gilles Gorbin, 1565), USTC 198783.
90 Martin de Azpilcueta, *Enchiridion sive Manuale confessariorum* (Lyon). Uncertain identification: USTC records ten different editions between 1580 and 1587.
91 Petrus Lombardus, *Petri Longobardi in omnes D. Pauli epistolas* (Paris). Uncertain identification: USTC records eighteen different editions between 1535 and 1547.
92 Petrus Chrysologus, *Opus homiliarum* (Paris: Jerôme de Marnef & Guillaume Cavellat, uncertain year). Uncertain identification: USTC records three editions printed by de Marnef and Cavellat between 1574 and 1585.
93 Guillaume Durand, *Rationale divinorum officiorum* (Lyon: heirs of Jacques Giunta, 1565), USTC 158034.
94 Stanisław Hozjusz, *Opera* (Lyon: heirs of Jacques Giunta, 1564), USTC 120899.

(cont.)

No.	Quantity in warehouse	Transcription of the entry
50.	1	Omellie Taulerij 8° Lion, 5 sc.[95]
51.	6	Pandetta Evangelica in 16 Lion, 6 sc.[96]
52.	6	Omellie Peraldi in 8° Lione, 18 sc.[97]
53.	1	Opera Divi Basilij Folio Paris, 15 sc.[98]
54.	1	Omellie Jo. Noiardo primo 2° 3° 4° in 8° Lion, 8 sc.[99]
55.	1	Postille in Epistole et Evangelia 8° Paris, 2.10 sc.[100]
56.	2	Procopij in Esaiam Folio Paris, 30 sc.[101]
57.	2	Summa Armilla in 8° Lion, 6 sc.[102]
[Fol. 4v]		
58.	1	Idem [Summa Conciliorum] in 16 Lion, 2 sc.[103]
59.	4	Soti de Justitia et Jure in folio Lione, 36 sc.[104]

95 Johannes Tauler, *Homiliae seu sermones in Evangelia* (Lyon: Sébastien Honorat, 1557), USTC 206019.
96 Simon Du Corroy, *Pandecta legis evangelicae* (Lyon: Sébastien Gryphius, uncertain year). Uncertain identification: USTC records four editions printed by Gryphius between 1547 and 1552.
97 Guillaume Pérault, *Homeliae, sive Sermones* (Lyon: Charles Pesnot, 1576), USTC 141366.
98 Basilius Magnus, *Omnia Opera* (Paris: 1563). Uncertain identification: USTC records three different editions printed in Paris in 1566 by Michelle Guillard, Sébastien Nivelle, and Jean de Roigny.
99 Jean Royardes, *Homiliae in Evangelia dominicalia* (Lyon: 1573). Uncertain identification: USTC records four different editions printed in Lyon in 1573 by Symphorien Béraud, Guillaume Rouillé, Antoine Gryphe, and Charles Pesnot.
100 Antonius Broickwy von Konigstein, *Postillae, sive enarrationes in epistolarum, et euangeliorum lectiones* (Paris). Uncertain identification: USTC records seven different editions between 1544 and 1550.
101 Procopius Gazaeus, *Epitomē tōn eis ton prophētēn Ēsaian* (Paris: Nicolas Chesneau, 1580), USTC 170513.
102 Bartolomeo Fumo, *Summa aurea armilla* (Lyon: Charles Pesnot, 1583), USTC 113342.
103 Bartolomé Carranza de Miranda, *Summa conciliorum* (Lyon) Uncertain identification: USTC records four different editions between 1564 and 1587.
104 Domingo de Soto, *De Iustitia et Iure* (Lyon) Uncertain identification: USTC records four different editions between 1558 and 1582.

(cont.)

No.	Quantity in warehouse	Transcription of the entry
Section: Libri di Filosofia		
[Fol. 5r]		
60.	4	Idem [Aristoteles] Sopra Fisica in 16 Lione, 6 sc.[105]
61.	5	Aristoteles de Animalium in 16 Lione, 5 sc.[106]
62.	1	Idem Rettorica in 16 Lione, 0.10 sc.[107]
63.	2	Idem de Generatione libri duo in 8° Lione, 0.6 sc.[108]
64.	2	Idem de Sensum et sensibili in 8° Lione, 0.12 sc.[109]
65.	2	Idem de Celo in 8° Lione, 0.12 sc.[110]
66.	2	Idem de Annima 8° Lione, 0.12 sc.[111]
67.	2	Idem Phisica in 8° Lione, 0.12 sc.[112]
68.	2	Clavis Philosofie in 16 Lione, 1.10 sc.[113]
[Fol. 5v]		
69.	4	Idem [Aristoteles] Super Fisica in 16 Lione, 6 sc.[114]
70.	5	Idem [Aristoteles] de Animalium in 16, 7.10 sc.[115]

---

105 Aristoteles, *Physicorum libri VIII* (Lyon) Uncertain identification: USTC records five different editions between 1560 and 1580.
106 Aristoteles, *Libri omnes, quibus historia, partes, incessus, motus, generatioque animalium, atque plantarum naturae brevis descriptio* (Lyon: heirs of Jacques Giunta, 1560), USTC 126387.
107 Aristoteles, *Rhetoricorum artisque Poeticae libri omnes* (Lyon: heirs of Jacques Giunta, 1561), USTC 153193.
108 Aristoteles, *De generatione et corruptione libri duo* (Lyon). Uncertain identification: USTC records nine different editions between 1535 and 1559.
109 Aristoteles, *De sensu et sensili* (Lyon). Uncertain identification: USTC records eleven different editions between 1535 and 1559.
110 Aristoteles, *De caelo et mundo* (Lyon: Scipion de Gabiano, 1529), USTC 155835.
111 Aristoteles, *De anima libri tres* (Lyon). Uncertain identification: USTC records fifteen different editions between 1530 and 1559.
112 Aristoteles, *Physicorum libri octo* (Lyon). Uncertain identification: USTC records thirty different editions between 1520 and 1586.
113 Gerhard Dorn, *Clavis totius philosophiae chymisticae* (Lyon: heirs of Jacques Giunta, 1567), USTC 158205.
114 See note 111.
115 See note 112.

(cont.)

No.	Quantity in warehouse	Transcription of the entry
71.	2	Crisostomi Javelli in Philosophia in 8° Lione, 3 sc.[116]
72.	2	Idem Super Methafisica in 8° Lione et Venetia, 3 sc.[117]
[Fol. 6r]		
73.	2	Cuolibeti Adriani 6.i in 8° Lione, 6 sc.[118]
[Fol. 6v]		
74.	2	Idem [Francisco Toledo] Logica in 8° Lione, 6 sc.[119]
[Fol. 7r]		
75.	1	Thesaurus Bibliorum in 8° Lione, 2 sc.[120]
76.	10	Testamenti Novi in 16 Lione, 20 sc.[121]

Section: Libri di Legge

[Fol. 10v]		
77.	3	Andreae Alciati Commentaria in folio Lione, 3 sc.[122]
78.	2	Idem in ff. in folio Lione, 4 sc.[123]
79.	2	Idem super C. in 8° Lione, 3 sc.[124]

---

[116] Crisostomo Iavelli, *Totius rationalis philosophiae compendium* (Lyon: heirs of Jacques Giunta, 1562), USTC 120885.

[117] Crisostomo Iavelli, *In omnibus Metaphysicae libris quaesita textualia* (Lyon: Barthélemy Poncet and Gaspard Portonariis, 1559), USTC 206074.

[118] Hadrianus VI, *Hadriani sexti Quaestiones duodecim quodlibeticae* (Lyon: Guillaume Rouillé, 1546), USTC 157685.

[119] Francisco Toledo, *Commentaria in universam Aristotelis Logicam* (Lyon: Alessandro Marsili, 1579), USTC 138906.

[120] William Allott, *Thesaurus Bibliorum* (Lyon: Alessandro Marsili, 1580), USTC 156370.

[121] *Testamenti novi. Editio vulgata* (Lyon). Uncertain identification: USTC records forty two different editions between 1531 and 1582.

[122] Andrea Alciati, *Ad rescripta principum commentarii* (Lyon: Sébastien Gryphius, uncertain year). Uncertain identification: USTC records eight editions printed by Gryphius between 1530 and 1547.

[123] Andrea Alciati, *Lectura super secunda parte ff. novi in titulo de verborum obligatione edita* (Lyon: Jacques Sacon, 1519), USTC 145084.

[124] Andrea Alciati, *Index locupletissimus d. Andreae Alciati super commentariis codicis Iustiniani* (Lyon: Jacques Giunta, 1542), USTC 200397.

(cont.)

No.	Quantity in warehouse	Transcription of the entry
80.	2	Idem in Pandectas in 8° Lione, 4 sc.[125]
81.	2	Idem de Praesumptio in 8° Lione, 6 sc.[126]
82.	1	Idem Paradox in 8° Lione, 2 sc.[127]
83.	2	Allegationes Lapi in 8° Lione, 4 sc.[128]
84.	2	Arii Pinelli de bonis Maternis In 8° Lione, 4 sc.[129]
85.	2	Baldi Super Feudi in 8° Lione, 3 sc.[130]
86.	3	Belloni Super Institutiones in 8° Lione, 6 sc.[131]
87.	2	Constitutiones Burgundiae In folio Lione, 24 sc.[132]
88.	3	Centum modi argumentandi in 8° Lione, 6 sc.[133]
[Fol. 11r]		
89.	2	Alciati de verborum significatione in 8° Lione, 6 sc.[134]
[Fol. 11v]		
90.	1	Decisiones Francisci Marc. prima et 2ª Lione, 15 sc.[135]

125 Andrea Alciati, *In Digestorum seu Pandectarum librum XII* (Lyon). Uncertain identification: USTC records four different editions between 1537 and 1546.
126 Andrea Alciati, *Tractatus de praesumptionibus* (Lyon: heirs of Jacques Giunta, 1551), USTC 150986.
127 Andrea Alciati, *Paradoxorum ad Pratum, libri sex* (Lyon: Jacques Giunta, 1546), USTC 149646.
128 Lapo da Castiglionchio, *Allegationes domini Lapi* (Lyon: Jacques Giunta, 1537). SBN IT\ICCU\BVEE\020476. Not recorded in USTC.
129 Aires Pinhel, *Ad constitutiones Cod. de bonis maternis commentarij* (Lyon: heirs of Jacques Giunta, uncertain year), USTC records two editions printed by the heirs of Jacques Giunta in 1560 (USTC 152784) and 1566 (USTC 120914).
130 Baldo degli Ubaldi, *Super feudis* (Lyon: Jacques Giunta, 1522), USTC 155558.
131 Niccolò Belloni, *Super utraque parte institutionum lucubrationes* (Lyon: heirs of Jacques Giunta, 1557), USTC 152350.
132 *Consuetudines ducatus Burgundiae* (Lyon: Barthélemy Vincent, 1582), USTC 84505.
133 Nicolaas Everaerts, *Centum modi argumentandi* (Lyon: Jean Pullon and Guillaume Rouillé, 1546), USTC 149527.
134 Andrea Alciati, *De verborum significatione* (Lyon). Uncertain identification: USTC records twelve different editions between 1529 and 1582.
135 François Marc, *Decisiones aureae* (Lyon: Basile Bouquet and Giunta, 1587), USTC 142431; 162186.

(*cont.*)

No.	Quantity in warehouse	Transcription of the entry
[Fol. 12r]		
91.	4	Emblemata Alciati in 8° Lione, 4 sc.[136]
[Fol. 12v]		
92.	2	Opera Iulii Clari in folio Lione, 14 sc.[137]
93.	4	Niccas. Super Institutiones in 8° Lione, 8 sc.[138]
94.	3	Practica Rebuffi in folio Lione, 36 sc.[139]
95.	1	Quaestiones Iuridicae diversae in folio Lione, 12 sc.[140]
[Fol. 13r]		
96.	1	Rhennatus Coppin de legibus Andium in folio Lione [i.e. Paris], 6 sc.[141]
97.	1	Repetitio Guiglielmi Benedicti in folio Lione, 18 sc.[142]
98.	1	Remissiones iur. in folio Lione, 18 sc.[143]
99.	1	Text. Civile in 16 Lione Bagnato, 24 sc.[144]
100.	1	Sylv. Nuptial. in 8° Lione, 6 sc.[145]
[Fol. 13v]		
101.	2	Tractatus de Actionibus Zasij in 8° Lione, 4 sc.[146]

---

136   Andrea Alciati, *Emblemata* (Lyon). Uncertain identification: USTC records nine different editions between 1547 and 1587.
137   Giulio Claro, *Iulii Clari patritii Alexandrini Opera* (Lyon: Jeanne Giunta, 1579), USTC 141684.
138   Nicasius a Woerda, *Enarrationes in quatuor libros Institutionum imperialium* (Lyon). Uncertain identification: USTC records nine different editions between 1549 and 1566.
139   Pierre Rebuffe, *Praxis beneficiorum* (Lyon: Guillaume Rouillé, 1586), USTC 142385.
140   *Syntagma communium opinionum* (Lyon: Jeanne Giunta, 1583–1584), USTC 142062.
141   René Choppin, *De legibus Andium municipalibus libri* (Paris: Nicolas Chesneau, 1581), USTC 171614.
142   Guillaume Benôit, *Repetitio in cap. Raynutius, extra de testamentis* (Lyon). Uncertain identification: USTC records five different editions between 1544 and 1575.
143   Accursius, *Digestum vetus, seu, Pandectarum iuris ciuilis tomus sextus* (Lyon: heirs of Jacques Giunta, 1589), USTC 155251.
144   Unidentified.
145   Giovanni Nevizzano, *Sylvae Nuptialis libri sex* (Lyon). Uncertain identification: USTC records ten different editions between 1516 and 1572.
146   Johann Urlich Zasius, *In tit. instit. de actionibus enarratio* (Lyon: Jean Frellon the Younger, 1551), USTC 112912.

(cont.)

No.	Quantity in warehouse	Transcription of the entry
[Fol. 14v]		
102.	2	Io. Roberti de Animadversiones in 4° Parige, 3 sc.[147]
Section: Libri legati di legge usati		
[Fol. 15r]		
103.	1	Repetitiones Rebuffi in folio Lione in tre volumi, 36 sc.[148]
Section: Letture		
[Fol. 16v]		
104.	1	Didaci Covarruias Opera Lione, 18 sc.[149]
Libri volgari		
[Fol. 20r]		
105.	3	Vite di Poeti antichi in 8° Lione, 3 sc.[150]
[Fol. 21r]		
106.	1	Idem [Orlando Furioso] in 12 Lione, 3 sc.[151]
Section: Libri di Humanita legati in 8°		
[Fol. 66v]		
107.	2	Gramatica Eligium in 8° Lione, 3 sc.[152]

---

147 Jean Robert, *Animadversionum iuris civilis libri tres* (Paris: Gilles Beys, 1580), USTC 171584.
148 Pierre Rebuffi, *Repetitiones variae* (Lyon: Guillaume Rouillé, 1583), USTC 142051.
149 Diego Covarrubias y Leyva, *Omnia opera* (Lyon: Compagnie des libraires de Lyon, 1586), USTC 138281.
150 Jean de Notredame, *Le vite delli piu celebri et antichi primi poeti provenzali* (Lyon: Alessandro Marsili, 1575), USTC 844923.
151 Ludovico Ariosto, *Orlando Furioso* (Lyon: Guillaume Rouillé, uncertain year). Uncertain identification: USTC records six editions printed by Rouillé between 1569 and 1580.
152 Eloy Vergier, *Grammatica pro pueris* (Lyon: Sébastien Gryphius, 1547), USTC 149799.

(cont.)

No.	Quantity in warehouse	Transcription of the entry

Section: Libri di Medicina

[Fol. 67v]
108.   1   De morbo Gallico opera in folio Lione, 12 sc.[153]
[Fol. 68v]
109.   1   Opera Veghae in folio Lione, 18 sc.[154]
[Fol. 69r]
110.   1   Idem [Pract. Ioan. Vic.] in 8° Lione, 3 sc.[155]
111.   1   Practica Argenteri in medicina in 8° Paris, 2 sc.[156]

Section: Libri d'Humanita

[Fol. 70v]
112.   1   Cosmografia universale Muster in folio Lione, 15 sc.[157]
113.   1   Cornucopia in folio Paris, 12 sc.[158]
[Fol. 72v]
114.   1   Poetin divers. in folio Lione, 4 sc.[159]
[Fol. 73r]
115.   1   Plinio cum in folio Lione, 5 sc.[160]

---

153   Juan Almenar, *Morbi Gallici curandi ratio exquisitissima* (Lyon: Scipion & Jean-François de Gabiano, 1536), USTC 147126.
154   Cristóbal de la Vega, *Opera, nempe, liber de arte medendi* (Lyon: Guillaume Rouillé, uncertain year), USTC records two editions printed by Rouillé in 1576 (USTC 125453) and 1587 (USTC 142470).
155   Leonello Vittori, *Practica medicinalis* (Lyon: Jean and François Frellon, 1554), USTC 149655.
156   Giovanni Argenterio, *In artem medicinalem Galeni Commentarij tres* (Paris: Jean Poupy, 1578), USTC 170446.
157   Sebastian Münster, *La Cosmographie universelle de tout le monde* (Paris: Nicolas Chesneau, 1575), USTC 1435.
158   Niccolò Perotti, *Cornucopiae seu latinae linguae commentarii* (Paris). Uncertain identification: USTC records fourteen different editions between 1496 and 1529.
159   Unidentified.
160   Gaius Plinius Secundus, *Historiae mundi libri XXXVII* (Lyon). Uncertain identification: USTC records eleven different editions between 1548 and 1587.

(cont.)

No.	Quantity in warehouse	Transcription of the entry

[Fol. 73v]

116.	1	Polibio in 8° Lione, 2 sc.[161]

[Fol. 74v]

117.	1	[Epistolae] Plinij in 16 Lione, 3 sc.[162]

Section: Libri di Legge sciolti

[Fol. 75v]

118.	2	Lambertini de iure patronatus reale Lione, 48 sc.[163]
119.	2	Opera Rebuffi Reale Lione, 48 sc.[164]
120.	4	Tractatus de pignoribus in folio Lione, 48 sc.[165]
121.	1	Opera Menochi in folio, 24 sc.[166]
122.	1	Opera Vigelli in folio Lione, 60 sc.[167]
123.	10	Opera Iul. Clar. in folio Lione, 60 sc.[168]

---

[161] Polybius, *Polybij Megalopolitani Historiarum libri* (Lyon: Sébastien Gryphius, uncertain year). Uncertain identification: USTC records two editions printed by Gryphius in 1542 (USTC 140442) and 1554 (USTC 151543).

[162] Gaius Plinius Secundus, *Epistolarum libri X* (Lyon: Sébastien Gryphius, uncertain year). Uncertain identification: USTC records two editions printed by Gryphius between 1530 and 1551.

[163] Cesare Lambertini, *Tractatus de iure patronatus*, 3 v. (Lyon: Philippe Tinghi, 1578–1580), USTC 141614.

[164] Pierre Rebuffi, *Petri Rebuffi Tractatus varii* (Lyon: Guillaume Rouillé, 1581), USTC 141882.

[165] Antonio Negusanzio, *Tractatus de pignoribus et hypothecis* (Lyon). Uncertain identification: USTC records six different editions between 1535 and 1579.

[166] Giacomo Menochi, *Omnia quae quidem extant opera in ius canonicum & civile* (Lyon: [Compagnie des libraires], 1583), USTC 142045.

[167] Nikolaus Vigel, *Methodus universi iuris civilis* (Lyon: Heirs of Guillaume Rouillé and Pierre Roland, 1591) USTC 147961.

[168] Giulio Claro, *Opera omnia* (Lyon: Pierre Landry, 1591), USTC 147966.

(cont.)

No.	Quantity in warehouse	Transcription of the entry

Section: Libri di Teologia et Filosofia

[Fol. 77r]

124.	2	Gregorii Opera in folio Lione, 36 sc.[169]
125.	1	Cornelius Iansenius in folio Lione, 24 sc.[170]
126.	3	Opera Iavelli in folio Lione, 54 sc.[171]

Section: Libri Rossi e Negri

[Fol. 78v]

127.	2	Idem [Messali della Luna] in 4° Parigi, 24 sc.[172]
128.	2	Breviarij Romani Parigi in 8°, 10 sc.[173]

---

169 Gregorius Magnus, *Opera omnia* (Lyon). Uncertain identification: USTC records seven different editions between 1539 and 1551.
170 Cornelius Jansenius, *Commentariorum in suam concordiam* (Lyon). Uncertain identification: USTC records seventeen different editions between 1577 and 1591.
171 Crisostomo Iavelli, *Omnia opera* (Lyon, 1580) Uncertian identification: USTC records five different lyonnaise editions of Iavelli's *Opera omnia* each of which was printed in 1580.
172 Unidentified.
173 *Breviarium romanum, ex sacra potissimum scriptura confectum* (Paris). Uncertain identification: USTC records nineteen different editions printed between 1515 to 1587.

CHAPTER 17

Early Modern Shelf Lives: the Context and Content of Georg Willer's Music Stock Catalogue of 1622

Amelie Roper

It has been estimated that over 700 million books were produced in the first two centuries of European print.[1] Amongst the diverse and evolving output, it stands to reason that some, such as bibles and Latin school primers, were bestsellers, reprinted time and time again, and finding a ready market amongst those who could afford to buy books. Others appeared in only one edition, suggesting that their market was rather more limited, and, in certain cases, that they struggled to find buyers. Some could be used and re-used, their content remaining relevant long after production, whilst others, such as almanacs, were more time-critical, becoming obsolete only months after printing. Linked to this, some were intended to be retained and treasured long after their original production, whilst others, including pamphlets and broadsheets, had a more ephemeral, disposable character.[2] This breadth of production was at the heart of one of the key issues underpinning the economics of bookselling in early modern Europe: for how long should a bookseller retain unsold titles after their initial printing in the hope that they might sell? Linked to this, at what point should a decision be taken that any remaining copies of an edition had reached the end of their economical 'shelf life', and were therefore suitable only for recycling or perhaps re-sale by means of another bookseller or even a book lottery?[3]

The question of shelf life was one that any major bookseller would have had to grapple with. By 1602, the Plantin firm was dividing the stock housed in its Frankfurt warehouse into distinct categories: "minus vendibiles" or "non vendibiles" ("saleable at a loss" or "non-saleable") and "vendibiliores" ("more

---

1 Andrew Pettegree, 'How to lose money in the business of books: commercial strategies in the first age of print', *Good Impressions: the First Century of Music Printing and Publishing* (International Conference, University of Salzburg, 13–15 July 2015).
2 For further discussion of the 'disappearance' of certain types of texts, see Rudolf Hirsch, *Printing, Selling, and Reading, 1450–1550* (Wiesbaden: Harrassowitz, 1967; reprinted 1974), p. 11.
3 For further discussion of book lotteries, see Daniel Bellingradt's article within this volume.

saleable").[4] In some instances, the decision concerning a book's shelf life was a fairly straightforward one. As a general rule, the value of stock declined with age. This decline was exacerbated by the tendency of publishers to issue new and improved editions of standard works thereby rendering older ones obsolete both intellectually and financially. Similarly, any titles whose content was time critical would quickly reach the end of their useful shelf lives.

Nevertheless, some booksellers and printers felt a sense of pride in the breadth and volume of books that they stocked, a factor that encouraged retention even when it meant titles might be sold at a loss.[5] A case in point is the Wechel press in Frankfurt. As well as the manuscript catalogue submitted by Andreas Wechel to the *Bücherkommission* in 1579, printed lists of the firm's holdings survive from 1590, 1594, 1602 and 1618.[6] Ian Maclean has noted that most of the catalogue of 1594 was available in 1618, as well as some Wechel publications dating from the 1560s which were not declared in 1579. Rather than reflecting an intrinsic value in the books, this is more likely to indicate a view that nothing was to be lost by the continued advertisement of unsold stock.[7] In such circumstances, one might assume that only an acute shortage of valuable shelf space in the shop or warehouse would act as a catalyst in any decisions to discard titles.

Other factors also came into play in the management of stock, notably the agreements entered into by booksellers, printers, authors and other intermediaries at the time copies of a particular edition were acquired, and the price paid. Some might have been acquired on a sale or return basis, whilst others would have been purchased by the bookseller outright, and were thus his sole responsibility to sell. For titles purchased outright, one might assume that a bookseller would be more likely to retain those of a higher value for a longer

---

4 Ian Maclean, *Scholarship, Commerce, Religion: The Learned Book in the Age of Confessions, 1560–1630* (Cambridge, Mass.: Harvard University Press, 2012), p. 176.
5 Maclean, *Scholarship, commerce, religion*, p. 192.
6 Written in Wechel's own hand, the 1579 manuscript catalogue can be found in the Österreichisches Staatsarchiv, Haus-, Hof- und Staatsarchiv, Bücherkommission im Reich, Kasten 1 Konvolut 4, f. 34. For libraries holding the catalogues of 1590 and 1594, see VD16 ZV 19076 (USTC 706244) and VD16 ZV 21400 (USTC 706245) respectively. The 1618 catalogue is documented as VD17 23:263261B and is available in the Bodleian Library, Oxford, Broxb. 106.9. The 1602 catalogue was printed on a single sheet. A copy can be found in the Staatsarchiv Bamberg, shelfmark Eph.lit.q.14(1). For further commentary on the Wechel press, see R.J.W. Evans, 'The Wechel presses: humanism and Calvinism in central Europe, 1572–1627', *Past and present* 69, Supplement 2 (1975), and Ian Maclean, 'André Wechel at Frankfurt, 1572–1581', in *Learning and the Marketplace: Essays in the History of the Early Modern Book* (Leiden: Brill, 2009), pp. 163–225.
7 Maclean, 'The market for scholarly books and conceptions of genre in northern Europe, 1570–1630', in Maclean, *Learning and the Marketplace*, pp. 9–24: 17.

time period, in the hope that custom might be forthcoming. Titles acquired by exchange, whereby a financial settlement had already been reached in the form of payment in kind by means of books, paper or other goods of an equivalent value, might also have been retained for longer.

Decisions concerning the duration of shelf life would have been especially challenging in the highly specialist area of music printing. The market for partbooks and choir books, in particular, was small, and many were issued in only one edition and did not have any 'time critical' characteristics. As a result, there was not the natural turnover of stock present in other more mainstream areas of the market. Contrary to popular opinion, printed music was not necessarily significantly more expensive than literary texts.[8] Nevertheless, the sheer time and effort involved in getting music into print would have made booksellers more wary of discarding it, thereby compounding the difficulties in establishing a clear-cut shelf life.

Whilst very little documentation survives concerning the workings of early modern booksellers who sold music publications, or the financial transactions of printers who ventured into the specialist field of music printing, we are fortunate to have one source which sheds light on the thorny question of shelf life in the music printing industry in early modern Germany: Georg Willer's *Catalogus librorum musicalium variorum authorum* of 1622 (Figure 17.1).[9] This music stock catalogue was issued by Augsburg's famous Willer bookselling firm in the early years of the Thirty Years' War. For many years thought to have been destroyed in a fire, it was re-discovered by musicologist Richard Schaal in the 1960s.[10]

---

8   Iain Fenlon, *Music, Print and Culture in Early Sixteenth-Century Italy*, The Panizzi Lectures, 1994 (London: British Library, 1995), p. 86, suggests that printed music in Italy did not cost any more than literary texts, with retail prices of partbook editions comparable to inexpensive editions of literature or classics. Stephen Rose, 'Music printing in Leipzig during the Thirty Years' War', *Notes*, 2nd s., 61.2 (2004), pp. 323–349: 345, has also studied the cost of music printing in seventeenth-century Germany with reference to the accounts of Michael Wachsmann and his widow for the seven books they contracted out to the Leipzig printer Gregor Ritzsch in 1629 to 1630. Ritzsch charged Wachsmann 6 florins per bale for printing a catechism and 6.25 florins per bale for a partbook edition. This suggests that partbooks were only slightly more expensive than ordinary texts. By contrast, in England, where there was a small market and music printing was constrained by royal monopolies, music seems to have cost between three and four times as much to print as normal books. See Margaret Dowling, 'The printing of John Dowland's *Second Booke of Songs or Ayres*', *The Library*, 4th s., 12 (1932), pp. 365–380.

9   Bayerische Staatsbibliothek, Res/4 Cat. 45 (12). Digital version available from the Bayerische Staatsbibliothek at http://reader.digitale-sammlungen.de/resolve/display/bsb10888116.html, last accessed: 16 December 2018.

10 Sources giving the erroneous information concerning the catalogue's destruction in a

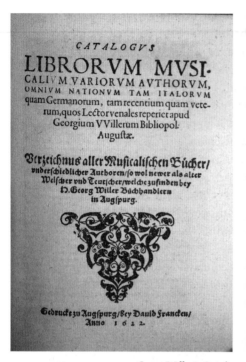
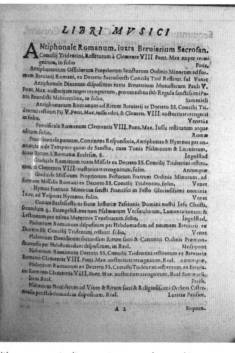

FIGURE 17.1A–1B Georg Willer's *Catalogus librorum musicalium variorum authorum* (Augsburg: David Franck, 1622), title page (a) and first page (b).
BAYERISCHE STAATSBIBLIOTHEK, RES/4 CAT. 45 (12) [URN:NBN:DE: BVB:12-BSB10888116-9]

Schaal went on to publish a short article on it, incorporating a transcription of its content.[11] However, he did not attempt to link the catalogue's content back to extant printed editions, and, as a result, the potential of this source in providing an insight into the distribution of musical repertoire has not been fully exploited. This article redresses this balance, considering the circumstances

---

fire include Wolfgang Boetticher, *Orlando di Lasso und seine Zeit, 1532–1594: Repertoire-Untersuchungen zur Musik der Spätrenaissance* (Kassel: Bärenreiter, 1958), p. 729, and Wilhelm-Martin Luther, 'Bibliographie' in Friedrich Blume (ed.), *Die Musik und Geschichte und Gegenwart* (17 vols., Kassel: Bärenreiter, 1949–1951), I, 8/9 Lieferung, col. 1832 and 1838. This information is corrected by Imogen Fellinger, 'Musikbibliographien', in *Die Musik in Geschichte und Gegenwart. Sachteil* (19 vols., Kassel and London: Bärenreiter, 1997), VI, cols. 1036–1037.

11 Richard Schaal, 'Georg Willers Augsburg Musikalien-Lagerkatalog von 1622', *Die Musikforschung*, 16 (1963), pp. 127–139. See also Richard Schaal (ed.), *Die Kataloge des Augsburger Musikalien-Händlers Kaspar Flurschütz, 1613–1628* (Wilhelmshaven: Heinrichofen's Verlag, 1974), pp. 10–11.

surrounding its production, its content and the insights it gives into the workings of one of the largest bookselling firms in early modern Europe. In so doing, we can come to a more nuanced understanding of the shelf lives of early modern music editions.

Georg Willer and the Augsburg Book Trade

It is no coincidence that the 1622 *Catalogus librorum musicalium variorum authorum* was issued by a bookseller based in Augsburg. By 1600, the free imperial city in south-west Bavaria was firmly established as one of the largest commercial centres in Germany. A period of rapid economic growth over the course of the sixteenth century had seen its population expand from 30,000 to 45,000.[12] A centre for both trade and banking, Augsburg's success was dependent on the existence of a sophisticated communications network. Situated at the crossroads of several overland trade routes, it benefitted from direct access to important Alpine passes connecting northern Italy to northern Europe.[13] It was also located at the junction of two large, navigable rivers: the Lech and the Wertach. Alongside their use for transportation, these waterways underpinned the city's thriving industrial base, providing power for mills producing textiles, wood, metals and paper.[14] In addition, Augsburg had long been part of the imperial postal network, with a new post office built outside the city walls in 1549.[15] This regular and reliable service was essential to Augsburg's economic prosperity.[16]

---

12   See Gregory Jecmen and Freyda Spira, *Imperial Augsburg: Renaissance Prints and Drawings 1475–1540* (Washington: National Gallery of Art, 2012), p. 28, and Kathy Stuart, *Defiled Trades and Social Outcasts: Honor and Ritual Pollution in Early Modern Germany* (Cambridge: Cambridge University Press, 1999), p. 33.
13   For further discussion of trade routes, see Giles Mandelbrote, 'The first printed library catalogue? A German doctor's library of the sixteenth century and its place in the history and the distribution of books by catalogue', in Fiammetta Sabba (ed.), *Le biblioteche private come paradigma bibliografico* (Rome: Bulzoni, 2008), pp. 310–311, and Andrew Pettegree, *The Book in the Renaissance* (New Haven: Yale University Press, 2010), p. 18.
14   Jecmen and Spira, *Imperial Augsburg*, p. 26.
15   Andrew Pettegree, *The Invention of News: How the World Came to Know About Itself* (New Haven: Yale University Press, 2014), p. 174. Until the establishment of the imperial post office at Leipzig in 1598, Augsburg was also the only free imperial city that formed part of the postal network. See also Wolfgang Behringer, *Im Zeichen des Merkur: Reichspost und Kommunikationsrevolution in der Frühen Neuzeit* (Göttingen: Vandenhoeck and Ruprecht, 2004), especially pp. 67–73, 84–97 and 324–331.
16   Pettegree, *The Invention of News*, pp. 168 and 178.

The city's economic growth gave rise to several wealthy and influential merchant families. From the mid-fifteenth century until the close of the Thirty Years' War, the international banking and mining interests of the Fugger family, which included claims in Latin America, made them the richest family in Europe, and it was to them that emperors, kings and popes turned for loans to fund their extravagant ways of life.[17] Their rivals, the Welsers, also had commercial interests in banking and boasted a union with the imperial family through the marriage of Philippine Welser to Archduke Ferdinand, son of Emperor Ferdinand I.[18] Both the Fuggers and the Welsers delighted in book collecting and music making and were generous patrons of the arts.[19] This patronage, combined with the availability of an efficient communications network and access to paper mills, wood-cutters and craftsmen for metal work, meant Augsburg was well-placed to flourish both in the production and distribution of printed books.

Printing with movable type reached Augsburg in 1468 and by the end of the fifteenth-century the city had become an important centre for German book production with a particular emphasis on texts in the vernacular.[20] Production was aided by the fact that anyone with the necessary capital and technical skill was free to open a print shop, as there was no requirement for guild membership. Furthermore, printers did not even need to have Augsburg citizenship, since, like the work of physicians and apothecaries, printing was included amongst the free trades.[21] In the early years of the sixteenth century, the city

---

17   Jecmen and Spira, *Imperial Augsburg*, p. 26, explains that Hans Fugger, a weaver from a small Swabian village, arrived in Augsburg in 1367. By the early sixteenth century, the family was led by Jakob the Rich, and its wealth from textiles, trading, mining and banking was without equal in the city. The Fugger company's trade routes reached as far as South America, India and Africa. See in addition Allan W. Atlas, *Renaissance Music: Music in Western Europe 1400–1600* (New York: Norton, 1998), pp. 468–469 and Mandelbrote, 'The first printed library catalogue', p. 311. The latter explains that, in 1572, Philip II of Spain asked the Fuggers for a loan of a million ducats.

18   Susan Hammond, *Editing Music in Early Modern Germany* (Aldershot: Ashgate, 2007), pp. 161–163.

19   See also Adolf Layer, *Musik und Musiker der Fuggerzeit: Begleitheft zur Ausstellung der Stadt Augsburg* (Augsburg: Himmer, 1959) and Mark Häberlein, *The Fuggers of Augsburg. Pursuing Wealth and Honor in Renaissance Germany* (Charlottesville: University of Virginia Press, 2012).

20   Pettegree, *The Book in the Renaissance*, p. 36, states that over 60% of the editions published in Augsburg in the fifteenth century were in German. This stands in sharp contrast to the dominance of Latin in the production of early printed books overall.

21   Hans-Jörg Künast, 'Augsburg's role in the German book trade in the first half of the sixteenth century', in Malcolm Walsby and Graeme Kemp (eds.), *The Book Triumphant: Print in Transition in the Sixteenth and Seventeenth Centuries* (Leiden: Brill, 2011), pp. 320–333:

made further advances in the printing industry, becoming one of the first locations north of the Alps to venture into the specialist field of mensural music printing with movable type.[22] By the beginning of the seventeenth century, it was home to a number of well-regarded music printing firms, including that of Valentin Schönig.[23] Music printing was thus embedded in Augsburg's culture of book production, albeit on a more modest scale to that of nearby Nuremberg.

Assisted by its geographic location, the city also made its mark on the book trade, in a large part due to the activities of Georg Willer (Figure 17.2). Born in Augsburg around 1515, by the early 1550s, Willer owned a bookshop and in 1553 went on to take over the established bookselling business of Johannes Rynmann and Wolfgang Präulein.[24] After his death in 1593 or 1594, his sons Elias and Georg the Younger continued the business until the early 1630s.[25] With branches in Tübingen, Ingolstadt, Freiburg im Breisgau and Vienna in addition to Augsburg, it was a firm of the highest standing, with a particular strength in the distribution of printed music.[26] Georg the Elder is known to

---

326. Printers were required to take an oath swearing that they would not print libellous or seditious literature. Nevertheless, its effect was limited, since a board of censure was not installed until 1537, the year in which Augsburg was officially reformed.

22   In 1507, the Augsburg printer Erhard Öglin printed *Melopoiae*, a choir book comprising a collection of twenty-two odes with texts by Horace and Conrad Celtis, set to music by Petrus Tritonius. In the colophon, Celtis described Öglin as "the first amongst us Germans who pressed shimmering music in metal". However, Öglin was not the only printer north of the Alps to be grappling with the challenges of printing mensural music with movable type. Also in 1507, Basel's Gregor Mewes printed *Concentus harmonici quattour missarum peritissimi m[u]sicorum Jakobi Obrechti*. See Birgit Lodes, 'Concentus, Melopoiae und Harmonie 1507: zum Geburtsjahr des Typendrucks mehrstimmiger Musik nördlich der Alpen', in Birgit Lodes (ed.), *Niveau, Nische, Nimbus: die Anfänge des Musikdruckes Nördlich der Alpen* (Tutzing: Hans Schneider, 2010), pp. 33–66, *Gregor Mewes' 'Concentus harmonici' und die letzten Messen Jakob Obrechts.* (Habilitationsschrift, University of Munich, 2002) and 'Mewes, Gregor', in *Die Musik in Geschichte und Gegenwart. Personenteil* (19 vols., Kassel: Bärenreiter, 2004), XII, col. 115–116.

23   Christoph Reske, *Die Buchdrucker des 16. und 17. Jahrhunderts im deutschen Sprachgebiet: auf Grundlage des gleichnamigen Werkes von Josef Benzing* (Wiesbaden: Harrassowitz, 2007), pp. 42–43.

24   Hans-Jörg Künast and Brigitte Schürmann, 'Johannes Rynmann, Wolfgang Präulein und Georg Willer-Drei Augsburger Buchführer des 15. und 16. Jahrhunderts', in Helmut Gier and Johannes Janota (eds.), *Augsburger Buchdruck und Verlagswesen: von den Anfängen bis zur Gegenwart* (Wiesbaden: Harrassowitz, 1997), pp. 23–40: 31.

25   This coincided with the death of Georg the Younger in the early 1630s.

26   For further background on Willer, see Schaal (ed.), *Die Kataloge des Augsburger Musikalien-Händlers Kaspar Flurschütz*, p. 10, Künast and Schürmann, 'Johannes Rynmann, Wolfgang Präulein und Georg Willer', pp. 31–32, and Karl Steiff, 'Georg Willer', in *Die Allgemeine Deutsche Biographie* (56 vols., Leipzig, 1898), XLIII, pp. 268–269.

FIGURE 17.2   Portrait of Georg Willer the Elder (ca. 1515–ca. 1594), ca. 1591
STAATS- UND STADTBIBLIOTHEK AUGSBURG, GRAPHIKSAMMLUNG
19/629

have had links with important musical institutions, including the *Münchener Hofkantorei*.[27] More generally, an increased rate of production in the field of music printing from the 1530s brought with it a greater demand for independent booksellers such as Willer, whose wider sale and distribution networks complemented those cultivated by the printers themselves.[28]

Willer's 1622 Music Stock Catalogue

Georg Willer the Elder is widely recognised for his innovative contribution to bibliography.[29] A seasoned visitor to the biannual Frankfurt book fairs, from autumn 1564 he began to publish a composite catalogue of the new books on offer.[30] This was intended for the use by the reading public and booksellers who did not attend the fair but bought their stock from those who did.[31] The catalogues were arranged by discipline: theology, law, medicine and philosophy, followed by history and geography, poetry and music.[32] The first catalogue to contain a dedicated music section appeared in autumn 1565. Whilst there is some uncertainty concerning the way in which Willer compiled the catalogues, their success cannot be disputed.[33] Issued regularly at every fair until the end

---

27   Schaal, 'Georg Willers Musikalien-Lagerkatalog von 1622', p. 127.
28   Schaal (ed.), *Die Kataloge des Augsburger Musikalien-Händlers Kaspar Flurschütz*, p. 10.
29   In spite of their primarily mercantile function, Fellinger, 'Musikbibliographien', col. 1036–1037, describes the book fair catalogues as the first, systematically-ordered bibliographies.
30   Bernhard Fabian (ed.), *Die Messkataloge des sechszehnten Jahrhunderts* (5 vols., Hildesheim: Olms, 1972–2001). Maclean, 'English Books on the Continent, 1570–1630', in Maclean, *Learning and the market place*, pp. 339–370: 342, explains that German and Latin books were included initially, and other vernaculars (French, Italian and Spanish) added in an appendix after 1570.
31   This purpose is indicated by a statement on the title page of the first catalogue, which reads "Ad exterorum Bibliopolarum, omniumque rei Litterariae studiosorum gratiam et usum" ("For the convenience and use of booksellers elsewhere and all students of literature"). For further discussion of the first book fair catalogue, see Graham Pollard and Albert Ehrman, *The Distribution of Books by Catalogue: From the Invention of Printing to A.D. 1800* (Cambridge: Roxburghe Club, 1965), pp. 75–77.
32   Maclean, 'English Books on the Continent', p. 342. For further commentary on the arrangement of Willer's book fair catalogues, see Andrew Pettegree, *The French Book and the European Book World* (Leiden: Brill, 2007), pp. 133–134.
33   Archer Taylor (rev. William P. Barlow), *Book Catalogues: Their Variety and Uses* (Winchester: St Paul's Bibliographies, 1986), p. 88, states that the catalogues summarised the volumes that Willer brought back to Augsburg from the Frankfurt fair, probably in bulk. Meanwhile, Pollard and Ehrman, *The Distribution of Books by Catalogue*, p. 77, suggests that the production of Willer's catalogues was a co-operative venture. Printers intending to go to the fair sent Willer title pages of their forthcoming works, so that he could arrange

of the sixteenth century, their production continued more sporadically until the late 1620s under the direction of Georg the Younger.[34] Following Willer's lead, similar catalogues began to be produced by other booksellers, notably the rival Augsburg firm of Portenbach and Lutz.[35] Willer's achievement also formed part of a wider culture of innovation in catalogue production in Augsburg. No fewer than three catalogues of its city library were published between 1575 and 1600, and 1572 saw Augsburg's production of one of the first known printed catalogues of a private library.[36]

The book fair catalogues of the Willer firm have long been exploited by scholars studying the dissemination of printed books. This is no less true for those with interests in the field of music printing, where researchers have been able to benefit from Albert Göhler's index and commentary on their musical content.[37] However, the *Catalogus librorum musicalium variorum authorum* of 1622 has received relatively little scholarly attention. Sixteen pages in length and existing in a single, unannotated copy in the Bayerische Staatsbibliothek, it lists a total of 355 items of printed music stocked by the Willer firm at the time of the catalogue's issue in 1622.[38] Whilst the majority of the titles listed in the catalogue can be traced back to works surviving in print, the catalogue also provides a welcome source of information on the existence of a number of lost editions which are known to have been printed, but for which no copies are

---

them in subject order. The catalogues could then be distributed to printers around Europe, and by them passed to prospective customers.

34 The last extant Willer book fair catalogue dates from 1627.

35 For further discussion of imitators of the Willer book fair catalogues, see Pollard and Ehrman, *The Distribution of Books by Catalogue*, pp. 77–79.

36 Mandelbrote, 'The first printed library catalogue?', pp. 295–311. See also David McKitterick, 'Book catalogues: their varieties and uses', in Peter Davison (ed.), *The Book Encompassed: Studies in Twentieth-Century Bibliography* (Cambridge: Cambridge University Press, 1992), pp. 161–175: 163–164, which suggests that the earliest extant catalogue for a public collection was that produced for Cambridge University Library in 1574.

37 Albert Göhler, *Verzeichnis der in den Frankfurter und Leipziger Messkatalogen der Jahre 1564 bis 1759 angezeigten Musikalien* (Hilversum: Knuf, 1901; reprinted 1965).

38 Some sources give the number of entries as 359, including Schaal, 'Georg Willers Augsburg Musikalien-Lagerkatalog von 1622', p. 127, but this is incorrect. The higher number results from extra line breaks in the original. These have led to the interpretation of some consecutive entries as multiple publications when they in fact describe a single edition. For example, lines 20 and 21 of page 8 read "Fasciculus sive Missus secundus, quinque vocum" and "Concentuum cuius modi Paduanas & Galiardas" respectively. Rather than referring to two works, this refers to one: Georg Engelmann's *Fasciculus sive missus secundus quinque vocum concentuum, cujus modi paduanas & galliardas vulgo vocant*, printed in Leipzig by Thomas Schürers Erben in 1617. RISM A/I E 694. Similar errors have been made as a result of line breaks on pages 11 and 14.

extant today.[39] Linked to this, in a number of instances, it constitutes one of only a handful of sources documenting the existence of certain little-known composers of the late-sixteenth and early-seventeenth centuries.[40]

One such case is Michael Tonsor's *Fasciculus cantionum ecclesiasticorum*, which is known to have been printed in Dillingen in 1605, but which remains lost today.[41] The 1622 catalogue enables us to refine our knowledge of this work, proving both that its printing came to fruition and that copies continued to exist in 1622. Another work, also lost today, is Adolarius Eichorn's collection of intradas, galliards and courantes, apparently printed in Nuremberg and listed twice in the catalogue.[42] Used in conjunction with the more detailed entry in the music section for the Frankfurt book fair catalogue for 1616, we learn that the work was printed the same year by Abraham Wagenmann. We are also able to gain a little more information on the otherwise elusive Eichorn, who is described as an organist in Rothenburg ob der Tauber.[43]

In contrast to the highly-structured book fair catalogues, the 1622 stock catalogue is loosely organised. Psalters and antiphoners are described first, followed by a lengthy section listing sacred and secular polyphonic music. This is arranged very roughly in alphabetical order by title. Thus, collections of songs (*cantiones*) are followed by *canzonettas*, motets, magnificats and masses. A section on psalm and hymn settings comes next, complemented by a lengthy list-

---

39   These include catalogue entries 25, 39, 66, 72, 109, 146, 149, 174, 185, 212, 214, 247, 248, 263, 264, 267, 288, 306, 311, 333, 338, 339, 340 and 341.

40   Little-known composers documented in the catalogue include Antonio Marissal (entry 26), David Oberndörffer (entry 319) and Matthäus Odontius (entry 327), all of whom do not currently have entries in the latest editions of either *The New Grove Dictionary of Music and Musicians* or in the *Personenteil* of *Die Musik in Geschichte und Gegenwart*.

41   This work appears as entry 25 in the catalogue, described as "Cantionum Ecclesiastic. fasciculus à 5 & 6 voc. per Michael Tonsorem Dillingae". The inclusion of "Ecclesiastic." enables us to distinguish this from another of Tonsor's lost works, entitled simply *Fasciculus cantionum*, and printed in Dillingen in 1600. See the works list included in Horst Leuchtmann, 'Tonsor, Michael', in *Grove Music Online* accessed via *Oxford Music Online*, http://www.oxfordmusiconline.com, last accessed: 29 May 2018. For details of the loss of this work, see also Ernest F. Schmid, *Musik an den schwäbischen Zollernhöfen der Renaissance* (London: Bärenreiter, 1962), pp. 574 and 581, which document the existence of this work in a 1623 inventory prepared after the death of Prince Johann Georg of Hohenzollern-Hechingen, as well as in an earlier inventory of 1609.

42   This work appears in duplicate in the catalogue as entries 311 and 340. Entry 340 reads "Adolarium Aichorn, Schoene außerlesne gantz newe Intrada, Galliarda, vn Courant, ohne Text, mit 4 Simmen compnirt. 4. Nürnberg".

43   See the music section of the *Catalogus Universalis Pro Nundinis Francofurtensibus Autumnalibus, De Anno M.DC.XVI* (Frankfurt: Kruger, 1616), USTC 2043307, f. D1v. Copy held in the Bayerische Staatsbibliothek, shelfmark Res/4 Cat. 44a, Beibd. 10.

ing of madrigal anthologies. At this juncture, approximately half-way through the catalogue, an overall structure becomes more difficult to discern, though short sections dedicated to specific composers and genres can be identified. These include a substantial list of works by Michael and Hieronymus Praetorius and a small grouping of lute and keyboard tablature books.[44]

Whilst the 1622 music catalogue is in itself a rarity, the production of similar documents is not as unusual as one might expect. Seven music catalogues dating from 1613 to 1628 are known to exist for Augsburg's Kaspar Flurschütz firm.[45] Their production can be linked to the highly specialist market at which most music materials were aimed. As we shall see, not only did they require careful marketing, but in some cases, they had a very long shelf life, remaining both relevant and useful to potential customers decades after their original publication. Music books thus warranted their own catalogue due to the likelihood that they would remain in stock for a number of years and their specialist market. Once printed, such catalogues could be distributed to potential customers as a means of marketing the availability of music stock. Interestingly, despite its mercantile function, the printer, David Franck, does not include vertical rules at the outer margins of the catalogue, setting it apart from others produced by Augsburg's Michael Manger with the express purpose of selling the contents.[46] However, the generous right-hand margin would have provided ample space for annotation by potential purchasers, a feature also replicated in the book fair catalogues.

Turning now to the description of the printed music editions, similarities are immediately apparent between the music stock and book fair catalogue entries. Comparison with the music section of Willer's spring 1621 fair catalogue reveals that both included title, composer, format and place of publication (Figure 17.3).[47] In the music stock catalogue, however, the titles are abridged for economy of space, with entries generally confined to one or two lines of print. In addition to the absence of dates of publication, there are no prices and no indication of the number of copies available.

---

44   Works by Michael and Hieronymus Praetorius form catalogue entries 226 to 240. Works by Melchior Franck are grouped together as catalogue entries 274 to 284. The tablature section comprises entries 342 to 346.

45   These are now preserved in the Staatsbibliothek in Berlin. See Schaal (ed.), *Die Kataloge des Augsburger Musikalien-Händlers Kaspar Flurschütz*, pp. 11–15. Schaal also includes transcriptions for all seven of the Flurschütz catalogues.

46   For details of other catalogues with this format, see Mandelbrote, 'The first printed library catalogue?', pp. 305–306.

47   The corresponding entries in the catalogue are numbers 30 to 32.

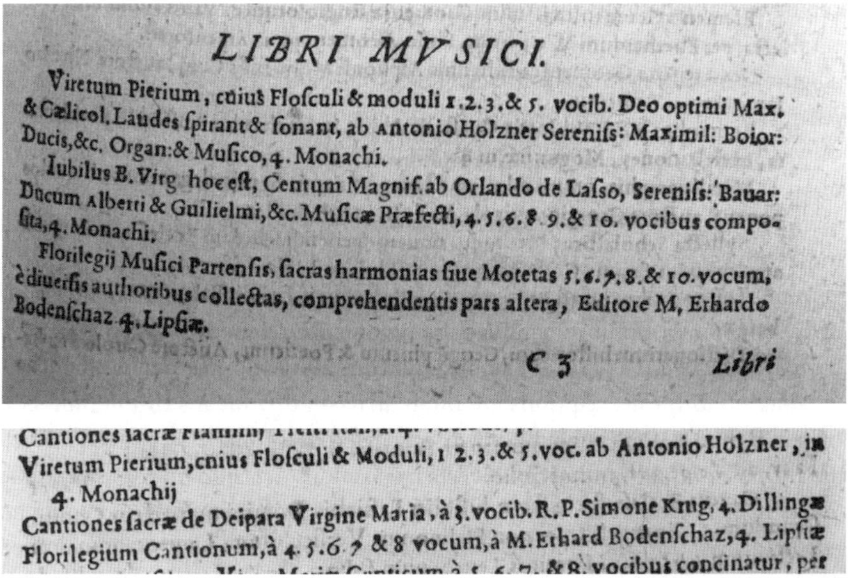

> **LIBRI MVSICI.**
>
> Viretum Pierium, cuius Flosculi & moduli 1.2.3.& 5. vocib. Deo optimi Max.
> & Caelicol. Laudes spirant & sonant, ab Antonio Holzner Serenißs: Maximil: Boior:
> Ducis,&c. Organ:& Musico, 4. Monachi.
> Iubilus B. Virg hoc est, Centum Magnif.ab Orlando de Lasso, Serenißs: Bauar:
> Ducum Alberti & Guilielmi,&c. Musicae Praefecti, 4.5.6.8.9.& 10. vocibus compo-
> sita, 4. Monachi.
> Florilegij Musici Partensis, sacras harmonias siue Motetas 5.6.7.8.& 10. vocum,
> è diuersis authoribus collectas, comprehendentis pars altera, Editore M, Erhardo
> Bodenschaz 4. Lipsiae.
>
> C 3   *Libri*

> Cantiones sacrae Fiammij [...]
> Viretum Pierium, cnius Flosculi & Moduli, 1 2.3.& 5.voc. ab Antonio Holzner, in
> 4. Monachij
> Cantiones sacrae de Deipara Virgine Maria, à 3.vocib. R.P.Simone Krug, 4.Dillingae
> Florilegium Cantionum, à 4.5.6.7 & 8 vocum, à M.Erhard Bodenschaz, 4. Lipsiae
> [...] & 8. vocibus concinatur, per

FIGURE 17.3A–3B Comparison of the music section of Willer's spring 1621 fair catalogue and the 1622 music stock catalogue. 17.3a (top): Spring 1621 book fair catalogue. 17.3b (bottom): Entries 30 to 32 of the 1622 music stock catalogue.
BAYERISCHE STAATSBIBLIOTHEK, RES/4 CAT. 45 (10) [URN:NBN:DE: BVB:12-BSB10888114-8] AND BAYERISCHE STAATSBIBLIOTHEK, RES/4 CAT. 45 (12) [URN:NBN:DE:BVB:12-BSB10888116-9].

The fact that Willer's music stock catalogue does not simply replicate the three 1621 book fair catalogue entries is significant. The second fair catalogue entry, which describes a work by Orlando Lasso, does not appear in the music catalogue at all.[48] This tendency recurs in relation to the book fair catalogue for spring 1622, which lists fifteen music editions of which only three appear in the music stock catalogue.[49] This is not merely a product of timing, since the fair catalogue of spring 1622 includes a number of additional works printed between 1619 and 1621.[50] In theory, these would have been available for description when the music stock catalogue was produced. The difference in content

---

48 Orlando Lasso, *Iubilus. B. Virginis. Hoc est. Centum Magnificat ... IV. V. VI. VII. IIX. et X. vocibus composite* (Munich: Nicolaus Heinrich, 1619). RISM A/I L 1031.
49 Entries 56, 82 and 328 in the music catalogue of 1622 also appear in the spring 1622 fair catalogue.
50 These include Gabriel Plautzio's *Flosculus vernalis* (1621), RISM A/I P 2602; USTC 2161345; Valentin Dretzel's *Sertulum musicale* (1620), RISM A/I D 3535; USTC 2160554; and Orlando Lasso's *Iubilus B. Virginis* (1619), RISM A/I L1031 (the latter also appears in the fair catalogue for spring 1621. See footnote 48).

can be explained by the distinct purposes of the catalogues. Willer's 1622 stock catalogue is not a compilation of the music sections of previous book fair catalogues, but rather functions as an inventory of the firm's music books at a particular point in time. The absence of a work suggests it had either sold out or was never stocked by the firm in the first place. Conversely, the presence of an edition indicates that it was in stock. In one discrete source, therefore, we have a snapshot both of what was available to purchase, and, indirectly, an indication of what might have sold out.

Whilst the absence of dates and prices was not unusual, the abridged nature of the entries in the 1622 catalogue is noteworthy, since it gives a clue as to the motivation of the Willer firm in producing the list at this particular point in time.[51] Shorter descriptions are often arrived at by means of the omission of qualitative details such as "newly compiled" or "diligently edited" as well as composer affiliations. This suggests a conscious decision on the part of the Willer firm to leave out the extra information that in other scenarios might pad out an entry and function as a sales pitch aimed at the discerning customer. This was not merely a strategy to save space. Whilst we cannot be certain as to whether the production of the music stock catalogue in 1622 was a one-off decision, or whether similar catalogues were produced by the firm and subsequently lost, the brevity of the entries suggests that it was primarily aimed at the book trade rather than private purchasers. This theory is supported by its loose organisation. Neither feature was especially conducive to use by a musician keen to find a specific title, but, for an experienced member of the book trade seeking to buy up music stock in bulk, the list was more than adequate.

Production of a catalogue aimed at the book trade at this particular point in time would have made sound business sense. The 1590s were a decade of recession followed by a general downturn in the European economy in the 1610s and 1620s.[52] The effects on the book trade from the 1610s are reflected in the account books of the Plantin firm, which include evidence of a retraction of credit conceded to German booksellers including the Willers.[53] This occurred in tandem with the onset of the Thirty Years' War. Shortly after its outbreak, most German

---

51   Maclean, *Scholarship, Commerce, Religion*, pp. 179–181, explains that the omission of years allowed for the reissuing of unsuccessful books, whilst the lack of prices avoided the embarrassment of stating variable discounts, which are known to have been a feature of negotiations at the fairs.
52   Mary Fulbrook, *A Concise History of Early Modern Germany* (Cambridge: Cambridge University Press, 2004), p. 51. See also David Hackett Fischer, *The Great Wave: Price Revolutions and the Rhythm of History* (New York: Oxford University Press, 1996), p. 95.
53   Maclean, *Scholarship, Commerce, Religion*, p. 219.

states devalued their currency and a period of severe inflation ensued in the form of the so-called *Kipper- und Wipper-Zeit*.[54]

The implications of such economic upheaval for merchants and tradesmen were illustrated vividly in a number of contemporary broadsheets, including one printed in Augsburg in 1621 (Figure 17.4). Entitled *Ein newe Rähterschafft* (*A new riddle*), the combination of text and image suggests that the answer to the 'riddle' of inflation was money. Against the backdrop of a country landscape, a ladder ascends diagonally toward the sky. Below, a peasant, craftsmen and merchant watch as six coins are carried skywards on the backs of children. The children are encouraged by their father at the base of ladder, who is intent on making his fortune through the debasement of money. At his feet are a money-bag and chest. The prospects for the man, however, are not good, for, in contrast to the biblical Jacob's ladder, which led to divine salvation, this ladder rests precariously on the backs of toads.[55]

The combined effect of the *Kipper- und Wipper Zeit* and outbreak of the Thirty Years' War would have encouraged the Willer firm to re-evaluate their music stock with a view to selling off as much as possible before market conditions became even more challenging. The catalogue's function was thus to encourage sales amongst members of the book trade.

This purpose is reinforced by the working practices of the Willer firm, details of which can be revealed by analysis of the catalogue. There is compelling evidence to suggest that the catalogue entries were compiled with reference to the title pages of physical copies of the books in stock at that particular moment. This is indicated by the presence of a number of distinctive features that replicate elements of the typography of the originals. The description of Hans Christoph Haiden's *Postiglion der Lieb* (Nuremberg: Paul Kauffmann, 1622), for example, abbreviates the composer's name to "J.C.H.", mirroring the title

---

54   Rose, 'Music printing in Leipzig', p. 344. See also Fischer, *The Great Wave*, p. 69, which includes a graph charting gradual increase in prices in Augsburg between 1460 and 1660. Extremely marked peaks are visible in the early years of the 1620s and 1630s.

55   For a commentary on this broadsheet, see B. Ann Tlusty, *Augsburg During the Reformation Era: An Anthology of Sources* (Indianapolis: Hackett Publishing, 2012), p. 262, and Paas, *The Kipper und Wipper inflation*, pp. 50–53. In addition to the copy held at the Herzog August Bibliothek Wolfenbüttel, shelfmark IE 187, Paas records another at the Staatsbibliothek, Bamberg, shelfmark VI G 160. Interestingly, this publication bears a striking resemblance to an additional broadsheet also printed in 1621, entitled *Newe Muentzlaitter* (*New coin-ladder*) (ibid., p. 55). A copy can be found in the Germanisches Nationalmuseum Nuremberg, shelfmark HB 24968/1363. Whilst the illustration is very similar to *Ein newe Raehterschafft*, the poet's message is more minatory. Rather than offering the hope of God's ladder, ascending into heaven, the poet reminds the reader that the ladder may well lead down to hell.

FIGURE 17.4　*Ein newe Rähterschafft* (Augsburg: Daniel Manasser, [1621]), 350 × 242 mm
HERZOG AUGUST BIBLIOTHEK WOLFENBÜTTEL, IE 187

page.[56] Meanwhile, the catalogue's entry for the *Novae cantiones sacrae* of 1590, a collection of songs by various members of the Regnart family, omits their surname, perhaps as a result of a misreading of the title page. A duplicate entry appears later in the catalogue, replicating this error and leaving out the place of publication.[57] Interestingly, this is not the only duplicate, with four other editions appearing twice, and one even in triplicate.[58] In one instance, the duplicates appear some distance from each other in the catalogue.[59] Assuming that the content was compiled by means of a shelf-by-shelf inventory of music titles, this suggests that the stockroom or warehouse had pockets of disorganisation and that multiple copies were not always stored together.

There is also evidence to suggest that the catalogue's entries were assembled by a pair of bookshop employees. One might have retrieved the items, and perhaps read out the salient details from the title pages and preliminaries, whilst the other would have acted as a scribe. Balthasar Fritsch's collection of part songs *Newe teutsche Gesang nach Art der welschen Madrigalien mit 5 Stimmen* (Leipzig: Abraham Lamberg, 1608), for example, is rendered as "Frische teutsche Gesaeng nach Art der welschen Madrigalien".[60] The composer's surname, Fritsch, has thus been recorded as "Frisch" ("fresh" or "new"). Whilst this error could have been made during the printing process, it seems more likely that the composer's surname was misheard or miscopied by Willer's staff. The latter explanation is all the more plausible given that "Frische teutsche Liedlein" and "Frische teutsche Gesänge" were common titles for song anthologies.[61]

---

56   Catalogue entry 336. See copy in London, British Library, C.197.(1.).
57   See catalogue entries 47 and 60, which describe the *Novae cantiones sacrae quatuor, quinque et sex vocum* (Douai: Jean Bogard, 1590), USTC 111011 and 405484 through to 405488. A likelihood of a misreading of the title page is confirmed by the copy of this work in the University Library, Ghent, shelfmark BHSL.RES.0601. The first names of three members of the family, Franciscus, Jacobo and Pascasius, are clearly presented on the title page. However, there is an unusually large gap before the next name, Carolo, which is followed by their surname (Regnart). The gap before Carolo led those compiling the catalogue to interpret "Pascasius" as the composer's surname, rather than as a first name. As a result, both "Carolo" and the all-important "Regnart" are omitted from the catalogue descriptions completely.
58   The additional four duplicates are catalogue entries 301 and 314, 311 and 340, 169 and 172 and 139 and 351. The work listed in triplicate is described in catalogue entries 42, 55 and 62.
59   Catalogue entries 139 and 351.
60   Catalogue entry 335.
61   For example, Georg Forster's five-part compilation entitled *Frische teutsche Liedlein*. This was published in Nuremberg by Johannes Petreius between 1539 and 1556 and reprinted subsequently.

There is also evidence to suggest that, rather than simply blindly copying details from title pages, Willer's staff had some degree of musical knowledge. A case in point is the entry at the head of page seven of the catalogue. This reads "Magnificat sex vocibus, Michaelis Hererii", and, as might be expected, is included as part of a small section dedicated to compilations of magnificats.[62] Composer and editor Michael Herrer was an Augustinian canon based at the foundation in Suben am Inn, Upper Austria, from November 1591. There he met Martin Langreder, another canon and composer of *contrafacta*.[63] This entry in fact refers to Martin Langreder's *Canticum gloriosae deiparae Virginis Mariae ... super varia (ut vocant) madrigalia* for six voices, published in Passau by Matthäus Nenninger in 1602, and edited by Herrer.[64] In the preface, Herrer explains that he has taken the works from the "vast treasure" of *contrafacta* left behind by Langreder after his death.[65]

Whilst both names appear on the title page, it is telling that Herrer, who appears to have been a more prominent musician than Langreder, is listed as the author.[66] In addition, Willer's staff also recognised that the works were magnificats, even though this description does not appear on the title page. The genre might have been inferred from their location with similar compositions in the warehouse, from a wrapper on the outside, or alternatively by leafing through to the contents list. Overall, therefore, the impression is of a catalogue compiled at speed by staff who had some knowledge of musical repertoire, and with the inclusion of only the bibliographic detail necessary for identification by experienced members of the book trade.

---

62 Catalogue entries 101 to 109.
63 Horst Leuchtmann and A. Lindsey Kirwan, 'Herrer, Michael', in *Grove Music Online* accessed via *Oxford Music Online*, http://www.oxfordmusiconline.com, last accessed: 29 May 2018.
64 RISM A/I L 608. A copy of the combined quinta and sexta vox can be found in the British Library, shelfmark C. 261. For further discussion of this work, see Horst Leuchtmann, 'Zur Biographie Michael Herrers', *Mitteilungsblatt der Gesellschaft für Bayerische Musikgeschichte* 6 (1973), pp. 121–123.
65 Horst Leuchtmann, 'Langreder, Martin', in *Grove Music Online* accessed via *Oxford Music Online*, http://www.oxfordmusiconline.com, last accessed: 29 May 2018.
66 In addition to the work discussed, according to Leuchtmann, 'Langreder, Martin', online, only one further publication is known for Langreder. This is a five-voice occasional motet, *Honora medicum ... nobili ... viro Ioanni Hiltprando ... dedicatum* (Passau: Matthäus Nenninger, 1602), RISM L 609. A copy can be found in the British Library, shelfmark B.293.

Patterns of Sale

Considering the catalogue as a whole, it is also possible to draw some conclusions concerning what sold successfully as well as what lingered on the shelves. The catalogue contains just four books on music theory and only one hymn book. In both cases, it seems likely that the affordability of their octavo format combined with their wider market appeal ensured that many editions of these types of music publication sold out. It could also simply be that there was no need to advertise these titles, as they would sell without promotion. Weight to this theory is provided by the post-mortem inventory of the Leipzig outlet of the Wittenberg bookseller Andreas Hoffmann.[67] Dated 6 December 1600, it records the existence of no fewer than 149 copies of Listenius' *Musica* and 92 of Rhau's *Enchiridion musicae practicae*, both of which were popular school and university primers on music theory, issued multiple times during the sixteenth century.[68] It seems highly probable that a major European bookseller such as Willer would have continued to have staple works such as these in stock, but that they were omitted from the catalogue because they did not need special promotion. From their absence, we may also infer that the 1622 music catalogue did not necessarily list every music book stocked at that time, but concentrated on those which they were particularly keen to ensure were sold.

Alexander Fisher has also drawn attention to the absence of one particular work from the catalogue.[69] Entitled *Siren coelestis*, this anthology of sacred concertos for two to four voices and continuo was edited by Georg Victorinus. Originally printed in Munich in 1616, it went on to be issued in a new edition in 1622.[70] Neither edition appears in the music stock catalogue. In the case of the 1622 edition, this may have been because it was still in preparation and therefore too new to have found its way onto the list. The 1616 edition, by contrast, is just the specialist type of music publication one might expect to find promoted in the catalogue, particularly given that a new edition was in the

---

67 See Albrecht Kirchhoff, 'Sortiments-Meßlager in Leipzig: Andreas Hoffmann von Wittenberg', *Archiv für Geschichte des deutschen Buchhandels*, 17 (1894), pp. 53–78: 73. This inventory is also discussed in Rose, 'Music printing in Leipzig', p. 344, who helpfully includes a transcription and translation of part of the inventory (p. 349).

68 38 editions of Listenius' *Musica* and 12 of Rhau's *Enchiridion musicae practicae* are currently listed in VD16. See http://www.vd16.de, last accessed: 16 December 2018.

69 Alexander Fisher, 'Celestial sirens and nightingales: change and assimilation in the Munich anthologies of Georg Victorinus', *Journal of Seventeenth-Century Music*, 14.1 (2008). Online only at http://www.sscm-jscm.org/v14/no1/fisher.html, last accessed: 16 December 2018.

70 RISM B/I 1616^2 and 1622^3.

pipeline, potentially rendering the old one obsolete and therefore more difficult to sell. We can infer from this that the 1616 edition had probably sold out. Rather than an uncharacteristic failure on the part of Willer to stock desirable editions, therefore, the absence of this anthology is an indication of its popularity.

Other notable works are also missing. We have already touched upon the absence of a work by Orlando Lasso which had been included in the music section of the spring 1621 book fair catalogue.[71] Only three of Lasso's works appear overall, and those of other celebrated composers are also only present in small numbers. This is particularly true of works by Italian masters. There is just one entry for Claudio Monteverdi and nothing at all for Giovanni Gabrieli.[72] These characteristics are suggestive of a more widespread trend towards the popularity of Italian music editions, borne out in the evidence of contemporary private libraries. As early as 1586, for example, the library of the Augsburg patrician and merchant Johann Heinrich Herwart is known to have included two hundred printed volumes of Italian songs.[73] Simply put, Italian music editions sold well in Germany.

Interestingly, the stock catalogue indicates that editions of Italian music printed in Germany sold less well than their counterparts printed in Italy. Gioseffo Biffi's *Primo libro delle canzonette* printed in Nuremberg in 1596, for example, remains in stock over twenty-five years after publication.[74] Conversely, his *Madrigali con duoi soprani* (Milan, 1598), and his *Della ricreatione di Posilipo libro primo* (Naples, 1606), had presumably sold out, as they are not included in the catalogue.[75] Meanwhile, Flaminio Tresti's *Sacrae cantiones seu moteta* printed in Frankfurt in 1610 also remains, despite the title page's enticing description "iam primum in Germaniae impressae" ("for the first time printed in Germany").[76] Significantly, whilst Tresti does not appear to have chosen Ger-

---

71 RISM A/I L 1031. See footnotes 48 and 50.
72 The work by Monteverdi constitutes catalogue entry 176. The edition is described simply as "Madrigali a cinque voci", printed in Antwerp. It could therefore be one of a number of editions printed by Pierre Phalèse, including RISM A/I M 3465, 3472 or 3482.
73 John Kmetz, 'Germany. Art music to 1648', in *Grove Music Online* accessed via *Oxford Music Online*, http://www.oxfordmusiconline.com, last accessed: 29 May 2018.
74 Catalogue entry 34. RISM A/I B 2632.
75 For a summary of Gioseffo Biffi's life and works, see Barbara Kimball Ansbacher, 'Biffi, Gioseffo', in *Grove Music Online* accessed via *Oxford Music Online*, http://www.oxfordmusiconline.com, last accessed: 29 May 2018.
76 Catalogue entry 29. RISM A/I T 1176. Mariangela Donà, 'Tresti, Flaminio', in *Grove Music Online* accessed via *Oxford Music Online*, http://www.oxfordmusiconline.com, last accessed: 29 May 2018, suggests that this edition may be lost. However, RISM indicates that there are copies in Staats- und Universitätsbibliothek Carl von Ossietzky, Musikabteilung,

many for the printing of any further works, a number of his editions were published in Venice and Milan in the period between 1585 and 1613. These include several books of madrigals and *canzonettas* which would have found a ready market in Germany at the time.[77] Again, these do not appear in the catalogue, so we can assume that they had probably sold out.

This suggests that, when purchasing Italian music, buyers may have preferred more 'authentic' editions printed in Italy. However, another factor contributing to their presence in the catalogue could have been the numbers of copies acquired. One might reasonably assume that the Willer firm would stock German editions, particularly those from Frankfurt and Nuremberg, in greater numbers than those from Venice, Milan or Naples. Those which did not sell could presumably be returned more easily and certainly without the need to wait until the next book fair. There may also have been a degree of market saturation. Italian printed music had the potential to permeate into German culture not only by means of purchases taking place within the German-speaking lands but also through musicians themselves crossing national boundaries and purchasing abroad. Popular as it was, there was only so much Italian-printed music that the market could absorb.

A detailed analysis of the places of publication of the catalogue entries provides a more refined understanding of music sale patterns. The dominance of Nuremberg (63 entries), Antwerp (37 entries) and Venice (24 entries) is unsurprising. As key centres for the production of printed music, it stands to reason that more of their publications would remain. The presence of no fewer than 40 Frankfurt editions is also noteworthy. It, too, was an important location for the production of printed music. However, additional factors came into play. Since it was the home of a major European book fair, it seems likely that the Willer firm would have had ready access to music printed in Frankfurt. Moreover, in 1599, Elias Willer left the family bookselling business, purchasing Sigmund Feyerabend's Frankfurt firm. He went on to operate in Frankfurt independently, leaving his brother to continue in Augsburg alone. However, in a shrewd business move, Elias retained property in Augsburg together with his citizenship, presumably as a means of maintaining strong links with its thriving

---

Hamburg, as well as the Landesbibliothek und Murhardsche Bibliothek der Stadt Kassel and the Biblioteka Jagiellońska, Krakow.

77 These include *Il primo libro de madrigali* (Venice, 1585), *Il secondo libro de madrigali* (Venice, 1587), *Vespertini concentus* (Milan, 1589), *Il terzo libro de madrigali* (Venice, 1590), *Il primo libro delle canzonette* (Venice, 1594) and *Il quarto libro de madrigali* (Venice, 1596). For further details, see the works list in Donà, 'Tresti, Flaminio', online.

book trade.[78] A combination of family ties, business relations and a successful music printing industry thus account for the prominence of Frankfurt music publications in the catalogue.

Also of significance is the presence of 22 editions printed in Leipzig. As in the case of the Frankfurt music editions, ready access to stock from the Leipzig fair may have had an influence on the inclusion of music printed there. Leipzig is thought to have produced about a tenth of all music printed in the German-speaking lands in the first half of the seventeenth century, so volume of production was undoubtedly a contributing factor.[79] It was also a question of market, or rather in some cases, lack of it. As a general rule, music printed in Leipzig in the first half of the seventeenth century was by local composers. These included Erhard Bodenschatz, Sethus Calvisius and Johann Hermann Schein, all of whom are represented in the catalogue.[80] Although the music of Calvisius and Schein was vigorously advertised at the book fairs, its main market was the more provincial one of the churches and schools of Saxony and Thuringia.[81] This is borne out by the content of the 1622 catalogue which lists a number of their older works published in Leipzig which had failed to find buyers. These include a number of pedagogical works such as Calvisius' *Tricinia auserlesene teutsche Lieder* of 1603 which were intended "to be sung, and also practised on instruments".[82]

Calvisius' pupil Bodenschatz achieved more long-lasting recognition. Amongst his anthologies were the two books of *Florilegium portense* which contained an exhaustive selection of motets for liturgical use. The first book was issued in Leipzig in 1603 under the title *Florilegium selectissimarum cantionum praestantissimorum aetatis nostrae autorum*.[83] This went on to be printed in a revised and enlarged edition in 1618, the *Florilegium Portense continens CXV selectissimas cantiones praestantissimorum aetatis nostrae autorum*.[84] The second book was then issued in 1621 as *Florilegii musici portensis*.[85] The set became such a staple in Lutheran churches that Johann Sebastian Bach was

---

78   Künast and Schürmann, 'Johannes Rynmann, Wolfgang Präulein und Georg Willer', p. 32.
79   Rose, 'Music Printing in Leipzig', pp. 323–324.
80   See entries 32, 148, 249 and 269 (Bodenschatz), 195, 208 and 259 (Calvisius) and 20, 255, 307 and 332 (Schein).
81   Rose, 'Music printing in Leipzig', p. 325.
82   Entry 259.
83   RISM B/I 1603^1.
84   RISM B/I 1618^1.
85   RISM B/I 1621^2. For full details of Bodenschatz's works, see Otto Riemer and Clytus Gottwald, 'Bodenschatz, Erhard', in *Grove Music Online* accessed via *Oxford Music Online*, http://www.oxfordmusiconline.com, last accessed: 29 May 2018.

buying and presumably using copies over a century later.[86] Interestingly, only the 1603 edition appears in the 1622 Willer catalogue.[87] The publication of the 1618 edition, which, on account of its absence, appears to have sold out by the time the catalogue was issued in 1622, would have made the 1603 edition all the more difficult to sell.

Shelf Lives

Turning now to dates of publication, it is possible to match the vast majority of the 355 items described to specific, dated printed editions and thereby to look more generally at the shelf lives of the publications. It is striking that only about a fifth of the content was printed in the period between 1615 and 1622.[88] To a certain extent, this can be explained by the fact that the catalogue was never intended as a means of promoting music that had appeared recently. It is thus not surprising that none of the works in the catalogue date from 1622. Music editions appearing that year may simply have been printed too late for inclusion. In addition, there was always the option to advertise their availability in the next book fair catalogue. Prioritising the marketing of older stock in the 1622 music catalogue therefore made sound business sense.

A further factor was the outbreak of the Thirty Years' War in 1618. Prefaces to music books issued in central Germany during this period suggest that printing was severely interrupted by the hostilities. In 1623, Burckhard Grossmann, a Jena-based merchant and editor of the musical anthology *Angst der Hellen*, complained of the devastation that the conflict had inflicted upon musical life, referring to it as "Saul's spear". After bemoaning the decline of music at court, church and in schools, he commented that:

> Saul's spear is also found in print shops ... since no one will devote himself to the requisite notes, rests, staves, and other characters, and among ten journeyman-printers, scarcely one can be found who has learned how to set or print these things or has a desire to learn this.[89]

---

86   See Rose, 'Music printing in Leipzig', p. 339, and Werner Neumann and Hans-Joachim Schulze (eds.), *Fremdschriftliche und gedruckte Dokumente zur Lebensgeschichte Johann Sebastian Bachs, 1685–1750: kritische Gesamtausgabe*, Bach-Dokumente, 2, (Kassel: Bärenreiter, 1969), pp. 199 and 294. Since there are no known editions of the *Florilegium portense* after 1621, it appears likely that Bach acquired second-hand copies.

87   Riemer and Gottwald, 'Bodenschatz, Erhard', online. Included as entry 32. RISM A/I C 263.

88   73 entries can be dated to the period 1615 to 1622. This is 21% of the content as a whole.

89   *Angst der Hellen und Friede der Seelen* (Jena: J. Weidner, 1623). RISM B/I 1623^{14}. See also

The Thirty Years' War brought death and destruction to large areas of Germany, as foreign and mercenary armies criss-crossed the Continent.[90] Combined with raging inflation, such upheavals dissuaded both booksellers and printers from undertaking partbook editions.[91] Early signs of the damage to the book trade that resulted are already in evidence in the 1622 catalogue, with only 27 of the 355 editions included dating from 1618 or afterwards, thereby suggesting that the luxury field of music printing felt the impact of the conflict keenly.

Nevertheless, its effect should not be exaggerated, for it certainly did not prevent the determined composer from getting his music published. Despite his bitter lamentation of "Saul's spear", Burckhardt Grossmann succeeded in getting his anthology of motets printed in Jena. Meanwhile in Leipzig, Johann Hermann Schein published all of his partbook collections himself from 1628, stating in 1623 that one reason for self-publishing was the "outrageous, inhuman inflation, by which piety as well as free arts and music have found themselves utterly bereft".[92] As Stephen Rose has shown, the typographical quality of printed music from the war years could be low, with cheap paper, crude type and numerous errors. Nevertheless, the persistence of music printing even in adverse circumstances testifies to the importance of music in Lutheran life, an importance also reflected in music's pervasive place in the book trade.[93]

Considering works with a longer shelf life, it is significant that Willer's 1622 catalogue lists no fewer than 29 editions printed before 1600. Of these, the earliest is Elias Nicolaus Ammerbach's organ tablature book of 1575.[94] This consists of forty vocal intabulations, together with one *praeambulum*, taken from popular international repertory.[95] Unlike his first book, the *Orgel oder Instrument Tabulatur* of 1571, there is no evidence to suggest that this publication was reprinted.[96] It thus appears that it really did remain in stock nearly fifty

---

Rose, 'Music printing in Leipzig', p. 331, from where this translation is taken. Further commentary on this work can be found in Hammond, *Editing Music*, pp. 33–34.

90 Pettegree, *The Invention of News*, p. 179.

91 Rose, 'Music printing in Leipzig', p. 339, comments that in Leipzig during the 1620s and 1630s, apart from Lamberg, few booksellers showed much interest in publishing partbook editions.

92 Schein, *Fontant d'Israel*, Leipzig, 1623. See also Rose, 'Music printing in Leipzig', p. 339.

93 Rose, 'Music printing in Leipzig', p. 347.

94 *Ein new kunstlich Tabulaturbuch, darin sehr gute Motetn und liebliche deutsche Tenores jetziger Zeit vornehmer Componisten auff die Ordel unnd Instrument abgesetzt ... auffs beste colorir uberschlagen corrigirt und in Druck verfertiget durch Nicolaum Ammorbach* (Leipzig: J. Beyer, 1575). RISM B/I 1575[17]; catalogue entry 343. USTC 644845; VD16 ZV 588.

95 Clyde William Young, 'Ammerbach, Elias Nikolaus', in *Grove Music Online* accessed via *Oxford Music Online*, http://www.oxfordmusiconline.com, last accessed: 29 May 2018.

96 *Orgel oder Instrument Tabulatur ... in Druck vorfertiget durch Eliam Nicolaum sonst Ammer-*

years after its original publication. Whilst it is possible that Willer had bought up a stock of unsold copies cheaply, other factors also came into play in terms of this title's continuing availability. Ammerbach was one of the most notable organists of St Thomas' in Leipzig, and his influence continued well beyond his lifetime. Johann Sebastian Bach is thought to have owned no fewer than three copies of the 1571 *Orgel oder Instrument Tabulatur*.[97] Moreover, German organ letter-tablature was still in use in Bach's time. He himself used it on several occasions to save space. Whether he attached sufficient importance to it to teach his pupils to read it, or whether he instead presented copies of the *Orgel oder Instrument Tabulatur* to each of his sons, William Friedemann and Carl Philip Emmanuel, cannot now be ascertained. Nevertheless, the fact that Bach was not only familiar with organ tablature but used it himself suggests that his interest in Ammerbach's work was more than purely antiquarian.[98]

More generally, this suggests that books of organ tablature continued to be both usable and relevant long after their initial production, a conclusion reinforced by the fact that the Ammerbach title forms part of a small section dedicated to lute and keyboard tablature in which four of the five editions listed date from before 1590.[99] Further weight to this argument is provided by the December 1600 post-mortem inventory of bookseller Andreas Hoffmann. As well as documenting the presence of a large number of copies of music theory books, it indicates that he held single copies of three editions of tablature.[100] Amongst these is Sixt Kargel's *Lautenbuch* published in Strasbourg in 1586, which also appears in Willer's catalogue of 1622.[101] Of all the areas of the music printing industry, tablature was the one where publications enjoyed the longest shelf life. With their distinctive notation, they were clearly aimed at a

---

bach (Leipzig: J. Berwalds Erben, 1571). RISM B/I 1571[17]; USTC 681731; VD16 ZV 527. This was reprinted in 1583 by Katharina Gerlach in Nuremberg. RISM B/I 1583[22]; USTC 681732; VD16 A 2310.

97   One of these can be found in Cambridge University Library, another in the British Library and the third in Leipzig City Library. Research has shown that the copies in Cambridge University and Leipzig City Library certainly come from Bach's collection. The British Library copy had strong links with Bach but the evidence that it was originally his property is not so conclusive. See Stanley Godman, 'Bach's copies of Ammerbach's 'Orgel oder Instrument Tabulatur' (1571)', *Music and Letters*, 38.1 (1957), pp. 21–27.

98   Godman, 'Bach's Copies', p. 23.

99   Entries 342 to 346. Aside from the editions of Ammerbach, Kargel and Paix (see footnote 104 below), the remaining edition, described in entry 346, is Johann Woltz's *Nova musices organicae tabulatura* printed in Basel in 1617. RISM B/I 1617[24]; USTC 2158770.

100 See Rose, 'Music printing in Leipzig', p. 349, and Kirchhoff, 'Sortiments-Meßlager in Leipzig', p. 73.

101 Catalogue entry 344. RISM B/I 1586[23]; USTC 780990.

very specific section of the already restricted music-buying market. Moreover, the fact that all five are described as being in the substantial folio format would have further encouraged their retention, just as it circumscribed their potential customer base.[102]

One final factor remains to be considered: the possibility that some of the older publications, amongst them the books of tablature, could be second-hand. Whilst it is possible that Willer's tablature entries refer to single, second-hand copies, this seems unlikely. Aside from the wealth of evidence attesting to their continuing relevance as valued and unsurpassed sources of repertoire, there is no indication that they were bound, a key indicator of second-hand copies.[103] Moreover, one of the four editions, Jakob Paix's *Ein schön nutz unnd gebreüchlich Orgel Tabulaturbuch* of 1583, was printed by Reinmichel in Lauingen at the expense of the Willer firm.[104] It seems highly probable that the firm would have continued to stock new rather than second-hand copies of one of their own publications.

Overall, therefore, Georg Willer's music catalogue of 1622 offers a multidimensional insight into the dissemination of printed music in the late-sixteenth and early-seventeenth centuries. A valuable counterpart to the biannual book fair catalogues, it provides a unique insight into the working practices of one of Europe's most prominent booksellers. Behind its contents lie a distinct set of day-to-day working routines informed by a knowledge of the music printing industry and its potential customers. In producing a trade-orientated catalogue for this very particular area of the market at a time when economic conditions were worsening, the Willer firm showed characteristic business acumen. Attempting to sell specialist books that had been stockpiled over a period of almost fifty years before market conditions deteriorated still further was a sound business move.

The catalogue also provides a snapshot of the types of music publications that lingered in the Willer warehouse, as well as those which sold more readily. Music editions printed in Italy together with hymn books and books on music theory emerge as bestsellers, whilst organ tablature displays an astonishingly long shelf life. Moreover, by examining what remained in stock more closely, we are able to gauge the criteria used by the Willer firm to establish which

---

102   This follows the "bigger books linger longer" theory discussed further in Owen Gingerich, *The Book Nobody Read* (London: Arrow Books, 2004), pp. 113–134.
103   For further discussion of the second-hand market, see Maclean, *Scholarship, Commerce, Religion*, pp. 192–193.
104   RISM B/I 1583[23]; USTC 645727; VD 16 ZV 25216. The imprint reads "In verlegung Georgen Willers. Getruckt bey Leonhart Reinmichel".

music publications to retain, in some cases decades after their original printing. What emerges is a carefully-considered stock management process rather than one based simply on date of publication or lack of space. This took into account such factors as how the music would be used and by whom, how relevant the repertoire was likely to be in the future, and how likely the content was to be superseded by a newer edition. Underpinned by a broader knowledge of the market and a network of business relations, these flexible criteria enabled the firm to weigh up the delicate balance between the depreciation in value of stockpiled music editions and the likelihood of a sale.

CHAPTER 18

Religion, Learning and Commerce: Daniel Delerpinière, a Protestant Bookseller in Saumur, 1661

Jean-Paul Pittion

In January 1661, Jean Baranger, *notaire royal* in the town of Saumur was called to the house and bookshop of the bookseller Daniel Delerpinière to make an inventory of his goods. Delerpinière, a widower, was about to re-marry. He had a son from his first marriage and the purpose of the inventory was to determine the value of the estate from this first marriage so that the son and heir could receive his portion, half of the estimated value of the goods and chattel, including the contents of the bookshop. The notarial deed has survived and it includes a detailed list of the "marchandises, outils et ustensiles de librairie" that were in the bookshop.[1] The list was drawn up by three of Delerpinière's Saumur colleagues, Isaac Desbordes, Jean Ribotteau and René Péan. On the basis of this archival document of some 46 folios and of other manuscript and printed material, we shall attempt to build a picture of Delerpinière's bookselling activities in the 1660s.

Daniel Delerpinière began his bookselling career in the 1620s. He was a member of the Protestant (Reformed) community of Saumur and from 1666 until his death in 1679, he was an elder of the town church in which his son, also named Daniel, was one of the *pasteurs*. The Reformed community of the town was small: on the basis of (incomplete) church records, it is estimated that it numbered probably 800 to 900 members in the middle of the century, but this figure does not take into account quite a few occasional worshippers, most of them foreign traders, merchants or visitors, and a fluctuating student population. All told, in a town with a population of between 10,000 and 12,000 inhabitants, the Reformed represented a small minority of at best ten per cent.[2] But socially and economically they belonged to the town elite,

---

1 Angers, Archives départementales de Maine et Loire, SE 69/375 (étude Baranger).
2 Philippe Chareyre, 'Les Protestants de Saumur au XVIIe siècle, religion et société', in *Saumur capitale européenne du Protestantisme au XVIIe siècle* (Fontevraud: Centre culturel de l'Ouest, 1991), pp. 27–70.

nurturing among the Catholic populace a resentment against many of those who were their "betters".

The size of the Reformed population belies the importance of Saumur as a leading cultural and intellectual centre of French Protestantism. By 1611 its Academy and its "collège d'humanités", founded in 1593 by the town Governor, the Reformed grandee Philippe Duplessis Mornay, were already flourishing. Mornay called the printer Thomas Portau to start a printing workshop in the town, and Saumur soon became established as the main centre of French Protestant publishing, already more active, by 1610, than that of La Rochelle.[3] By 1611 the town already had one well-stocked bookshop, owned by the Reformed bookseller Claude Girard. That year, the young English grandee, Thomas Wentworth, passing through the town on his "grand tour", was able to buy from it not only as many of Mornay's works as he could, but also copies of works by Montluc, Bodin and Justus Lipsius, not to forget *Il Pastor Fido* by Guarini.[4] From the military stronghold that it was in the early decades of the century, Saumur was to become the "international capital of French Protestantism". The *academie* attracted German, Scottish and English students.[5] The college was frequented mostly by the sons of the Reformed elites from the region or from Normandy and Paris. Its reputation was already such in the 1620s that the Oratorians founded a rival establishment in the town. By the middle of the century, the school of theology of the Academy where future pastors from all over the kingdom came to study and be trained, was known throughout Protestant Europe.[6]

In 1661, the year of the inventory, Delerpinière's shop had been in existence for over thirty years. It was situated in the "ville close", at the heart of the old city of Saumur, close to the church of Saint Pierre, in the central district of shops and markets. The bookshop occupied the ground floor of a three-story narrow building typical of the region. The building opened on a yard at the back of

---

3   Louis Desgraves, 'Thomas Portau, imprimeur à Saumur (1601–1623)', *Bibliothèque de l'Ecole des Chartes*, CXXVI, no. 1 (1968), pp. 63–133.
4   Letter dated 10 December 1611. See Julia Merritt (ed.), *The Papers of Thomas Wentworth, 1st Earl of Strafford, 1593–1641, from Sheffield City Libraries: A Listing and Guide to the Microfilm Collection* (Marlborough: Adam Matthew, 1994).
5   See Jean-Paul Pittion, 'Naissance de l'institution. Aux origines de l'Académie de Saumur', in *Saumur, capitale européenne du protestantisme* (Fontevraud: Abbaye royale de Fontevraud and Centre culturel de l'Ouest, 1991), pp. 71–77.
6   For a recent history of the Academy, see Pittion, 'Histoire de l'Académie', in *Registre de l'Académie Protestante de Saumur (1613–1685) édition présentation, introduction historique et notices* (Saumur: Archives municipales, 2009), freely accessible at http://archives.ville-saumur.fr/a/752/, last accessed June 2018.

which were situated a kitchen and a cellar cum store room. A room occupying part of the first floor probably served as a bedroom for an apprentice. On the top floor, a larger well-furnished room must have been the master bedroom. The shop was organised into two separate spaces: the front room with shelving, a counter and two cupboards opened directly onto a street, the rue du Mûrier. A door led to a back room opening onto an inner courtyard. The back room was used for storing books in sheets or editions in progress, together with stacks and bundles of old or damaged books to be sold by weight, old unsold and unsaleable books in bundles.

In the inventory, the books are grouped and listed by format. The three booksellers who documented the 1,800 volumes in stock were experienced bookmen. They proceeded, as was customary, shelf-by-shelf, dictating the title, the estimated value and the number of copies to the notary clerk. They made sure that different editions of the same work were identified in the inventory by place of printing and/or by format. Examples include editions of the Psalms, "2 Pseaumes in 24 Genève" (valued at 4 livres 10 sols), or editions of the classics identified by giving the editor's name, for instance "Horatius Hensii". For works in French the name of the author always appears first, but not always in the case of learned works in Latin, where the abbreviated titles can make identification tricky. The three booksellers were familiar with the production of the local presses and from those of the region, as shown by a number of entries, including the first two parts of Agrippa d' Aubigné's *Histoire Universelle*, which specifies that the two volumes are "en l'envoy de Maillé" (2 copies valued at 20 livres).[7]

The listings in the inventory follow the way the books were arranged on the shelves, i.e. by format and occasionally by size. Some in-folio editions listed as in-quartos, were shelved among them, obviously because of their smaller size. Lack of space on the shelves or careless re-shelving probably explains why some duodecimos are listed among the octavos and vice-versa, though occasionally works seem to have been grouped by author or by subject matter. Both recent editions and older second-hand ones of the same work could be available in the shop. Thus two second-hand, very "tired" copies of Pierre Charron's *Traité de la Sagesse* ("toutte frippée") that dated at the latest from 1645, were shelved amongst the octavos, while four new editions by the Elseviers—the latest published in 1656—were among the duodecimos.[8] Apart from testify-

---

7   *Histoire universelle du Sieur d'Aubigné ... Première Partie, & Les Histoires du Sieur d'Aubigné ... Tome Second* (Maillé: Jean Moussat, 1616–1618 and 1616–1620), in-2, USTC 6807826. Jean Moussat was Thomas Portau's son-in-law.
8   Pierre Charon, *Traicté de sagesse, ... Plus quelques discours chrestiens mesme aucteur, qui ont*

ing to the long-lasting fame enjoyed by Charron's work (the first edition of which appeared in 1601), this and other examples indicate that the shop dealt in second-hand as well as in new copies. It is also likely that second-hand copies of well-known works could be borrowed for a fee.

Altogether the shelves of the bookshop contained over 1,800 volumes representing some 1615 titles, thus distributed:
- in-2: 248 volumes = 172 titles, 75 % in Latin
- in-4: 429 volumes = 187 titles, 80 % in Latin
- in-8: 470 volumes = 250 titles, approximately 50 % in Latin
- in-12, in-16, in-24: 400 volumes = 106 titles 70 % in Latin

In addition, 82 in-folios, 60 in quartos and 80 octavos were listed as "vieux bouquins". According to the Dictionnaire de l'Académie of 1694, the term means "un vieux livre qui n'est guere estimé". These "vieux bouquins", different from the "frippés" second-hand copies, were probably old stock left from previous booksellers (Girard or perhaps Portau). Their individual titles are nor given in the inventory and they are valued in bulk, e.g. the 80 octavos are together valued at 12 livres.

The in-folio and in-quarto works that can be identified show a mix of older and newer editions.[9] The format in-folio was the most frequently used in the sixteenth and seventeenth centuries for learned treatises. This remained the case for the in-quartos, though the format was becoming increasingly reserved for particular genres, including plays and sermons. Among the legal works listed in the inventory, authoritative treatises of jurisprudence or of notarial practice by Pierre de L'Hommeau[10] and Jean Papon,[11] as well as classics of French legal erudition by Barnabé Brisson (1530–1591) and André Tiraqueau

---

esté trouvez après son décez, avec son portraict au naturel et l'éloge ou sommaire de sa vie (Paris: L. Feugé, 1645), in-8, USTC 6035709; Charron, De la Sagesse, trois livres (Leiden: Elsevier, 1646), in-12, USTC 1027902.

[9] This paper is a partial analysis of a source that would deserve to be fully transcribed. Most items can be identified by developing the abridged title and comparing format and date with works listed in the catalogues of major libraries and in specialized bibliographies.

[10] See Pierre de L'Hommeau, Deux livres de la jurisprudence françoise, avec belles remarques et décisions notables, tirées des lois françoises et romaines ... enrichies des plus célèbres arrests du Parlement de Paris et autres courts souveraines de France, le tout rapporté sur chacun article de la Coustume d'Anjou, par M. Pierre Delommeau, sieur du Verger (Saumur: T. Portau, 1605), 2 tomes in 1 vol. in-4, USTC 6806870 (five copies, valued at 16 livres). Note: on each occasion where more than one copy is listed in the inventory, the price estimate is intended as an overall value attributed to the group of copies, not to individual copies.

[11] One copy of Jean Papon's treatise Trias judiciel du second notaire, de Jean Papon (Lyon: J. de Tournes, 1575), in-4, 3 volumes, USTC 24918 and 61134, was valued at 6 livres.

(1480?–1558)[12] are present in older editions. But the inventory also lists the recent editions of the *Corpus juris civilis* (in two volumes valued at 22 livres, probably the Lyon 1650 edition) and of the *Corpus canonicum* (an edition in three volumes valued at 30 livres) as well as even more recent treatises of local customs.[13]

Among the medical works in-folio, the bookshop had a number of old abridgments of Galen, including a "fuscius in galenum",[14] though it had neither the Venice nor the Basel editions of the *Opera Omnia*. Available on the shelves were one copy each of the Basel edition of the works of Hippocrates, valued at 12 livres, one of Avicenna's *Opera* in four volumes and one of Mesue's *Opera* valued at 6 livres.[15] On the other hand, there were also more recent editions in French of the collected works of some leading figures of the new "ratio-

---

12 Among those by Barnabé Brisson, *Formulis et sollemnibus populi Romani verbis libri VIII* (Frankfurt am Main: J. Wechel and P. Fischer, 1592), in-4, USTC 615209 (one copy, valued at 13 livres); or by André Tiraqueau, *Semestria in Genialium dierum Alexandri ab Alexandro libros sex* (Lyon: heirs of G. Rouille, 1614), in-2, USTC 6901834 (one copy, valued at 7 livres). This was probably a re-issue by the heirs of Rouille of the 1586 edition (USTC 142394).

13 In particular *Coutume du pays et duché d'Anjou, tirée du greffe de la sénéchaussée d'Angers, avec conférence des articles des coutumes de Paris, Touraine, et le Maine* (Angers: J. Le Boullenger, 1656), in-2, (two copies, valued at 8 livres); *Les Coustumes du païs et comté du Maine, avec les commentaires de Me Julien Bodreau* (Pari: G. Alliot, 1645), in-2 (two copies, valued at 8 livres) and *Remarques et notes sommaires sur la coutume du Maine, avec un recueil des jugemens et sentences rendues au siège présidial et sénéchaussée du Mans et des arrests de la cour intervenuz sur l'interprétation d'aucuns articles, par Me Mathurin Louis, sieur des Malicottes. Enrichy des sommaires sur chaque article et de deux tables* (Le Mans: J. Olivier, 1657), in-2 (one copy, valued at 4 livres).

14 Valued at 1 livre. This must be the handbook by Leonhard Fuchs, entitled *Sex Galeni de Morborum ac symptomatum differentiis et causis libri [et Liber de curandi ratione per sanguinis missionem], pro juvanda memoria per Leonhartum Fuchsium, in tabulas digesti.— Tabula libri de curandi ratione per sanguinis missionem* (Paris: J. Dupuys, 1553), USTC 204185. Other editions by Fuchs are joint editions of Galen and Hippocrates.

15 The most recent (and first "complete") edition of Hippocrates's works was the Basel edition by Cornarius: Hippocrates, *Opera quae ad nos extant omnia, per Janum Cornarium latina lingua conscripta et recognita cum accessione Hippocratis de Hominis structura libri, antea non excuse, recens illustrata cum argumentis in singulos libros, tum indice insuper copiosissimo, per Joannem Culman num, ... nunc primum editis. Omnia quam antehac ... repurgatiora* (Basel: H. Froben & N. Episcopius, 1558), in-2, USTC 603112. I have been unable to trace an Avicenna folio edition in 4 volumes. For Mesue, the only possible edition is his *Opera quae extant omnia, ex duplici translatione, altera quidem antiqua, altera vero nova Jacobi Sylvii. Item authores omnes qui cum Mesue imprimi consueverunt ... Accesserunt his Annotationes in eundem Mesuen Joannis Manardi et Jacobi Sylvii. Adjectae sunt etiam nunc recens Andreae Marini Annotationes in simplicia cum imaginibus desideratis. Scholion item ejusdem in olea quaedam, quae omnia ... ab eodem Marino ... castigate* (Venice: V. Valgrisi, 1561), in-2, USTC 842294.

nal" Galenic medicine. André Du Laurens (1558–1609) was represented in two copies, valued at 5 livres; two copies of the works of Nicolas de La Framboisière (1560–1636) were also available, valued at 6 livres.[16] Also on offer were surgical treatises, including Paré's *Œuvres*[17] and chemical treatises, among them the works of Andreas Libavius.[18]

By the 1660s, both law and medicine were orientated towards a form of learning that was more specific and more practical than speculative. Undoubtedly, lawyers who came in the bookshop would have liked to own for consultation recent editions of local *Coutumes* (see note 13) or of *Le Praticien françois*, 3 copies of which were on offer, valued 2 livres 19 sols.[19] And surgeons as well as physicians would have been interested by the "modern" edition of Gui de Chauliac, revised by Laurent Joubert or by that of the *Chirurgie* by Pigray listed among the octavos.[20] These were works useful for practice, obviously placed on the shelves with an eye on possible professional buyers. Five lawyers, three royal officers, three physicians, one surgeon and one chemist can be identified among the 347 customers who had accounts with Delerpinière.[21] But however regular and learned potential professional customers may have been, their patronage cannot really explain the number of Latin editions in-folio or in-quarto of older legal and medical works that were still on the shelves in the 1660s. Some of the editions of these older works can also be found listed in the

---

16   A new enlarged edition of the collected works of Nicolas Abraham de La Framboisière was published in Lyon in 1644: *Les oeuvres où sont methodiquement descrites l'histoire du monde, la medecine ... et la guerison des maladies ... Avec les ars liberaux ... Derniere edition, reveuë, corrigée, & augmentée de nouveau par l'autheur d'un VIII. tome* (Lyon: J.-A. Huguetan, 1644), in-2, USTC 6905185. Earlier editions appeared in 1611 and 1631.

17   Obviously one of several editions published in Lyon, e.g. Ambroise Paré, *Les Oeuvres, reveues et corrigées en plusieurs endroicts et augmentées d'un fort ample traicté des fiebvres ... nouvellement treuvé dans les manuscrits de l'autheur* (Lyon: P. Rigaud, 1652), in-2.

18   The only in folio edition of Libavius's works that we can trace is his *Appendix necessaria Syntagmatis arcanorum chymicorum* (Frankfurt am Main: P. Kopf, 1615), in-2, USTC 2029929.

19   Jean Le Pain, *Le practicien françois, ou Livre auquel sont contenues les plus fréquentes et ordinaires questions de practique, tant en matière civile et criminelle, que bénéficiale et profane, digérées par demandes et responses* (Paris: J. Gesselin, 1626), in-8, USTC 6024381.

20   Guy de Chauliac, *Chirurgia magna, ... nunc demum suae primae integritati restituta a Laurentio Jouberto* (Lyon: S. Béraud and S. Michel, 1585), in-4 (but listed among the folios), USTC 142193 (one copy valued at 2 livres). Pierre Pigray's *Epitome des préceptes de médecine et chirurgie, avec ample déclaration des remèdes propres aux maladyes* was reprinted several times in the period, by Rouen and Lyon printers, for instance in 1642 by J. Berthelin in Rouen. One copy valued at 10 sols was among the octavos on the shelves.

21   Altogether these 343 customers owed a total of a little above 6753 livres to Delerpinière, 47 of whom we have so far been able to identify.

catalogue of the library of the Academy which contained a significant number of books formerly owned by Duplessis-Mornay.[22] All this suggests that Delerpinière had acquired some old stock from Portau's shop after it was ransacked by Royal troops in 1621 or from other older Saumur booksellers, Claude Girard and Louis Guyon. These "remainder" copies and, even more so, the batches of unspecified "vieux bouquins", awaiting disposal either on the shelves or in the back room illustrate the difficulties that booksellers of the period had, even more than those of to-day, to shift long-standing or outdated stock.

This may also explain the presence of old Latin theological works among the folios and quartos. A number of dogmatic treatises were remains of a past period of the internal theological debates that accompanied the construction of orthodoxy within the Reformed churches. This category included the works by Johannes Oecolampadius (1482–1531), Lutheran theologian Martin Chemnitz (1522–1586), Italian pastor Girolamo Zanchi (1516–1590) and Huguenot minister Daniel Chamier (1564–1621).[23] On the other hand it is less surprising to find that the bookshop had kept some well-known early works written against the Roman church, particularly given the leading role played by Duplessis Mornay in polemics against the Papacy and on the Eucharist, during the first two decades of the century. Perhaps as a reminder of more militant times, the *Théâtre de l'Antéchrist* of Nicolas Vignier, which Mornay arranged to have printed in Saumur, though a quarto edition, was placed among the folios next to a copy of "Mid(ni)stère diniquité de Duplessis" and three copies of "Du Plessis de l' Eucharistie".[24]

Nevertheless, one should not assume that all of that older stock had been left sitting on the shelves, unsold and unsaleable, since it had come into the bookshop. The presence among the in-folios of some unusual scholarly material suggests otherwise. It is striking to discover from the inventory, that the

---

22 See Clotilde Périgault, 'La Bibliothèque de l'Academie protestante de Saumur en 1685. Transcription de l'inventaire et identification bibliographique' (Unpublished dissertation, Tours, Centre d'Études Supérieures de la Renaissance, 2004).

23 Respectively indicated as "Oecolampade" (valued at 2 livres); Martin Chemnitz's "Harmonia", stocked in three copies, shelved in two different locations, and valued at 15 livres each (probably to be identified with USTC 661612); three tomes of Zanchi's works, valued at 8 livres; and "Chamier Opera", in two volumes, valued at 29 livres.

24 *Théâtre de l'Antéchrist, auquel est répondu au cardinal Bellarmin, au sieur de Rémond, à Pererius, Ribera, Viegas, Sanderus et autres qui, par leurs escrits, condamnent la doctrine des églises réformées sur ce subjet, par Nicolas Vignier* ([Saumur: T. Portau], 1610), in-4, USTC 6802650. The Mornay must be identified with the only known quarto edition of this text: *De l'Institution, usage et doctrine du sainct sacrement de l'Eucharistie en l'Église ancienne* (La Rochelle: H. Haultin, 1598), in-4, USTC 7715. Another copy of the work, probably in better condition and shelved separately, was valued at 4 livres.

bookshop kept copies of important sources for biblical scholarship, such as two copies of a "Lexicon Arabicum de Go[e]lius", valued at 15 livres, one of the "Testamentum Arabicum figuré", valued at 15 livres, several Hebrew bibles, including one copy of "Biblia Hebraica 7 vol. Stephanum" valued at 18 livres, two "Biblia Hebraica de venise" (the Bomberg edition) valued at 9 livres, and two "Biblia hébraique cum concordantia heb.", valued at 50 livres (the Basel Buxtorf edition). Or again among the quartos, one finds an unspecified Hebrew grammar (two copies valued at 1 livre), and among the octavos, "4 Herpenii grammatica heb" and the *Epitome* and *Abbreviations* of the two Buxtorf.[25] The presence of all these works testifies to the links that existed between the bookshop and the scholarly activities of the Academy. On the list of Delerpinière's customers we can identify at least six "proposants", i.e. students of theology destined to become *pasteurs*. The works by Buxtorf senior and junior, and that by Erpen may have been waiting on the shelves for them as any reader would have required a working knowledge of Hebrew. The copies of the Hebrew bibles and other scholarly works not detailed here, could only have been obtained for scholars of Hebrew and oriental languages, and prominently among them, for Louis Cappel, professor of biblical studies in the Academy and the founder of biblical criticism. His major work, the *Critica Sacra* appeared in 1655. On his death in 1558, he owed some seven livres sixteen sols to the bookshop. Apart from Cappel, few would have been sufficiently committed to Biblical scholarship to have wanted to acquire a set of the expensive editions of the Estienne or the Basel bibles. On the other hand, it is also quite possible that the copies on the shelves were for borrowing or for consultation in situ for a fee. They could also be orders from abroad awaiting shipment.[26]

Ten *pasteurs*, mostly from the region, had accounts with Delerpinière in 1661 and the bookshop kept an important and significant stock of Reformed religious works for these *pasteurs* and members of their churches. On the shelves and grouped together were numerous editions of the New Testament and of the Book of Psalms in French, in a great variety of impressions, formats and

---

25   Thomas van Erpe, *Grammatica ebraea generalis* (four copies valued at 5 livres), to be identified with either the 1627 Genevan edition by De Tournes, or more probably the 1659 Leiden edition by F. Moyard, both in-8. Johann Buxtorf, *Epitome grammaticae hebraeae ... Adjecta succincta de mutatione punctorum vocalium instructio et Psalmorum aliquot hebraicorum latina interpretatio* (Basel: L. König, 1629), in-8, USTC 2111794 (one copy valued at 10 sols); Johann Buxtorf and Johann Buxtorf Jr. (ed.), *De Abbreviaturis hebraicis liber novus et copiosus, cui accesserunt operis talmudici brevis recensio ... item bibliotheca rabbinica nova, ... editione hac secunda omnia castigatiora* (Basel: L. König, 1640), in-8, USTC 2101727 (one copy valued at 12 sols).

26   See note 33, below.

bindings, as shown by the following entries: "5 N.Test. Maroquin 12°" (valued at 15 livres); "1 idem Maroquin antique" (valued at 4 livres); "2 Bible 3 vol 12° veau" (valued at 12 livres); "4 psaumes Gros Romain en Maroquin 8°" (valued at 12 livres); "1 Bible de Sedan Maroquin" (valued at 5 livres); "4 Test. et psaumes toutte musique" (valued at 8 livres); "3 N.Test. commun" (valued at 6 livres); "1 psaumes toutte musique" (valued at 2 livres); "5 psaumes maroquin noir 24°" (valued at 6 livres 5 sols); "2 psaumes in 24 ill" [i.e. illustrated] (valued at 2 livres); "4 Test. Gros [canon] et psaumes de Sedan Maroquin" (valued at 8 livres).[27]

The bookshop also stocked numerous Reformed works of spirituality and of religious instruction. Many of these were in editions shared by the Paris booksellers, Antoine Cellier, Louis Vendôme, Olivier de Varennes and Samuel Petit. A number of them were probably printed in Saumur.[28] The inventory lists, without detailing them, 43 volumes in-24 and in-32 of "prières et autres", valued at 5 livres, as well as several copies of often reprinted Reformed works of consolation and meditation by Du Moulin and Le Faucheur.[29] The largest category of religious works available to Delerpinière's customers were volumes of French sermons in octavo. Preaching played a central role in Reformed worship and sermons usually delivered ex tempore were afterwards revised and printed to serve for the doctrinal instruction of the faithful. The different editions and the number of copies of sermons held on the shelves testify to the authority and prestige attached to the production of *pasteurs* from the Paris church at Charenton, Jean Daillé and Charles Drelincourt.[30] This also applies to the sermons of Moïse Amyraut, the leading professor of theology in the Academy of Saumur. Many copies of his sermons were available on the shelves.[31] Most

---

27 The Psalms with music are Genevan editions; the Sedan printings are by father and son Jean and Pierre Jannon. The Jannon impressions were in the handsome and highly readable typefaces designed by Jean Jannon. The Jannon editions made them much sought after and particularly suited to presentation bindings in moroccan leather.

28 See below and notes 38 and 39.

29 Pierre du Moulin, *Familière instruction pour consoler les malades. Avec plusieurs prières sur ce sujet* (Geneva: P. Aubert, 1636), in-8 (nine copies valued at 2 livres 5 s.); Michel le Faucheur, *Prières et méditations chrestiennes. Dernière éd. reveuës et augmentées* [sic] (Charenton: Louis Vendosme, [1649]), in-12 (three copies valued at 15 ss).

30 For example, for Charles Drelincourt, his *Le Saint ministere de l'évangile representé en deus sermons* (Se vend à Charenton par Louys Vendosme, demeurant à Paris ruë de la Harpe, proche le Pont S. Michel, au Sacrifice d'Abraham, 1651), in-8 (three copies, valued at 3 livres). Among many editions of Daillé, his *Vint* [sic] *sermons de Iean Daillé sur divers textes de l'Ecriture, prononcés à Charenton* (Geneva: P. Chouët, 1653), in-8 (four copies, valued at 4 livres).

31 Among others, *Sermon sur ces paroles du chapitre douzieme de l'Epistre aux Hebrieux, vers.*

of these were published in Saumur, as were most of Amyraut's other works, in Latin or in French, listed among the quartos and the octavos. By the time of the last national synod, held in Loudun a year before the inventory was made, in 1659–1660, polemical debates around Amyraut's doctrine of grace and that of his colleague Josué de la Place on original sin had abated within the French churches but controversies about their "hypothetical universalism" still continued in some universities and schools of theology of Protestant Europe. The Saumur theological production of the previous decades, mostly from the presses of the two printers to the Academy, Isaac Desbordes and Jean Lesnier continued to be of interest abroad and the copies that Delerpinière had in stock, were most likely kept in anticipation of orders from his foreign correspondents in Geneva, Leyden or London.[32]

The list of moneys owed by Delerpinière to booksellers provides names for some of these foreign booksellers with whom he regularly traded: he owed 594 livres to "Louis et Daniel Elsevier marchands libraires, Amsterdam" and 242 livres and 171 livres respectively to the two prominent Genevan publishers and booksellers Samuel and Pierre Chouet. The papers of Joseph Williamson who stayed in Saumur as tutor to several young English aristocrats show that through Williamson, Delerpinière also traded with the London bookseller Humphrey Robinson.[33] The sums owed to French correspondents were far smaller: 173 livres to the Lyon bookseller associates Jean-Antoine Huguetan and Marc-Antoine Ravaud, but only 66, 33 and 30 livres respectively to the Paris booksellers Antoine Cellier, Samuel Petit and Etienne Lucas.

It should be noted that these sums are in virtual "monnaie de compte", at least in part, as the book trade depended as much, if not more, on swap transactions as on bills of exchange or letters of credit. In a letter to Williamson of 8 October 1657, Humphrey Robinson wrote "... we had rather deal for money (with Saumur), looking at the benefit of exchange, but in Holland and Ger-

---

29 ... *prononcé a Nyort* ... (Saumur: J. Lesnier, 1656), in-8 (eight copies valued at 1 livre 5 sols), and *Le Mystere de pieté expliqué en quatre sermons, sur ces mots de la I. à Timothée, chap. 3. vs. 16* (Saumur: J. Lesnier, 1651).

32 For a quantitative survey and analysis of this production see Pittion, 'Aspects of the history of the Saumur Protestant book-trade (1601–1684)', in Charles Benson and Siobhán Fitzpatrick (eds.), *That Woman! Studies in Irish Bibliography, a Festschrift for Mary "Paul" Pollard* (Dublin: Lilliput Press for the Library Association of Ireland Rare Books Group, 2005), pp. 193–212.

33 *Calendar of State Papers, Domestic Series [of the Commonwealth], 1649–1660*, vol. IX, Nov 1655-June 1656; vol. X, 1656–May 1657 and vol. XI, June 1657-April 1658. See for instance a letter from Robinson to Williamson, dated January 15 1656–1657 and referring to a set of Calvin's works in 9 volumes received from Delerpinière.

many we had rather deal for books".[34] A 1659 catalogue of the Lyon booksellers Huguetan and Ravaud shows that they acted as intermediaries between the French and the Italian trade and provides evidence of probable swaps with Delerpinière: among learned works they offered for sale were medical and legal books in Latin and French and also "libri protestantium" listed separately and including Saumur editions.[35] It is likely also that the sums owed by Delerpinière to Cellier represent mostly some of the "Nouveaux Testamens & Pseaumes" and "Autres Livres de Dévotion" listed in Cellier's later catalogue of 1665.[36] Copies of some editions of sermons or devotional works, listed in it, bear the imprint "se vend /se vendent à Charenton". The use of this address as well as other typographical evidence, including type and printer's devices, strongly suggest that these editions were printed in Saumur and issued with variant title pages.[37] The financial and publishing relations between Delerpinière and his Saumur colleagues and Paris Protestant booksellers need to be further explored but it is already clear that they were not entirely one-sided.

Delerpinière's most important commercial partner was the Dutch bookselling and publishing firm of the Elsevier. By the 1660s, thanks first to their clandestine editions of Jansenist works, then to their large-scale copying of Paris editions of literary works and their successful small-format series of Latin and Greek classics, the Elsevier were so firmly implanted in the Paris trade that some "libraires du Palais" were reduced to being merely their factors or agents.[38] But Delerpinière could easily by-pass the Paris intermediaries,

---

34 *Calendar of State Papers, Domestic Series [of the Commonwealth], 1649–1660*, vol. XI, June 1657-April 1658.

35 *Catalogus recens librorum, qui vaenales prostant Lugduni, in officina & societate Joan. Ant. Huguetan & Marc-Ant. Ravaud, bibliopolae Lugdunensis* (Lyon: [J.-A. Huguetan and M.-A. Ravaud], 1659).

36 *Nouveaux Testamens et pseaumes, qu'ont imprimez defunt P. Des Hayes et A. Cellier, avec le prix d'iceux, tant en blanc que reliez. 1665* (Se vendent à Charenton, par ledit Cellier, demeurant à Paris, [1665]). This text is followed by: *Autres livres de dévotion, qu'a imprimez ledit Cellier* ([Charenton and Paris: A. Cellier, 1665]), copy used: Paris, Bibliothèque Mazarine, Ms 4300–25. See about this Jean-Michel Noailly, 'Le catalogue de l'imprimeur Antoine Cellier, Charenton-Paris 1665', *Psaume: bulletin de la recherche sur le psautier Huguenot*, 6 (1991), and David Muller, 'Libraires, graveurs, vendeurs d'images protestants' (Unpublished dissertation, Paris I—Panthéon Sorbonne, 1998–1999), pp. 121–123 and Annexes.

37 See for example the two variant addresses dated 1662 and 1663 on separate issues of *Recherches curieuses sur la diversité des langues et religions par toutes les principales parties du monde, par Ed. Brerewood, et mises en français par I. de La Montagne* (Saumur: J. Lesnier and Paris: O de Varennes).

38 See Henri-Jean Martin, *Livre, pouvoirs et société à Paris au XVIIe siècle (1598–1701)* (2 vols., Geneva: Droz, 1969), I, pp. 363–364 and II, pp. 643–644.

as given the long-standing relations between Saumur and the Dutch printing trade, production from the Lesnier or Desbordes presses could be directly swapped for that of Elsevier.

Two categories of books published by them feature prominently in the inventory. Firstly, of the forty or so Elsevier editions in-12, in-16 and in-24 with French titles, over half are historical or literary works of current or fashionable interest. Several important members of the local nobility were among Delerpinière's regular customers, including the marquis de Dangeau, Governor of Touraine and the Sénéchal of Saumur. Editions of "mémoires", such as the 1652 four-volume Leyden edition of the *Mémoires de Sully* or one of the Dutch editions of the *Journal du Cardinal de Richelieu* would have been the sort of works that appealed to them.[39] Older customers would have enjoyed classics of "aristocratic" literature such as *Don Quixote* or Sidney's *Arcadia*.[40] Four well-born ladies and six well-to do young "proposants" could also be found among Delerpinière's regular clientele. This elegant clientele was fond of the literature of the Parisian salons or of the Academy, as shown by the number of copies of Elsevier editions of Guez de Balzac that were on offer.[41] Also on offer were editions of recognized French classics such as Charron's works or Montaigne's *Essais*.[42] Among topical best-sellers were nine copies of Pascal's *Les Provinciales* in the pirated Dutch edition.[43]

---

39 Several Dutch editions of the *Journal de M. le cardinal, duc de Richelieu, qu'il a faict durant le grand orage de la cour en l'année 1630 jusques à 1643* are known. Typical of this production is the one dated "1652 sur la copie imprimée à Paris", in-12. The bookshop had two copies valued at 8 livres.

40 *Le Valeureux Dom Quixote de la Manche ou l'Histoire de ses grands exploits d'armes, fidèles amours et adventures estranges. Traduit fidellement de l'espagnol de Michel de Cervantes ... par Caesar Oudin ...* [part 1] (Paris: A. Coulon, 1639), in-8, USTC 6004327 (one copy valued at 2 livres); *L'Arcadie de la Comtesse de Pembrok[e], composée par messire Philippes Sidney, ... traduite en nostre langue par un gentilhomme françois ...* (Paris: R. Foüet, 1625), 3 volumes in-8, USTC 6027722 (one copy valued at 2 livres).

41 The inventory lists among other works by this author, eight copies of his *Lettres choisies* (Amsterdam: Elsevier, 1656), in-12, valued at 8 livres; 6 copies of his *Aristippe* (Leiden: J. Elsevier, 1658), in-12, valued at 7 livres, and five copies of his *Œuvres diverses* (Leiden: J. Elsevier, 1658), in-12, valued at 5 livres. Balzac's lasting fame was largely due to these new editions.

42 Together with 2 copies of the Paris 1624 quarto edition (probably "tired", valued at 2 livres 10 sols), the bookshop had one copy of the Dutch three-volume edition recently published (Amsterdam: A. Michiels, 1659), valued at 5 livres 10 sols.

43 *Les Provinciales, ou les Lettres escrites par Louis de Montalte à un provincial de ses amis et aux RR. PP. jésuites, avec la Théologie morale des dits Pères et nouveaux casuistes, représentée par leur prattique, et par leurs livres, divisée en cinq parties* (Cologne: N. Schoute [and Amsterdam: Elsevier], 1659), 2 vols in-8 (valued at 31 livres and 10 sols).

These and similar titles, present on the shelves in Elsevier editions, were attractive to a public of men and women eager to have access to fashionable or newsworthy "nouveautés". Potential buyers could keep themselves informed by reading the gazettes and the more committed among those customers who did not reside in Saumur could rely on offers made directly to them. Apart from the evidence provided by some accounts with more distant customers, we cannot be sure how much of Delerpinière's business was actually done by mail, but his two colleagues Isaac Desbordes and Jean Lesnier certainly did some, as their surviving business correspondence shows.[44]

The bookshop played an active role not only in the cultural but also in the intellectual life of Saumur and its region: one of Delerpinière's customer was the Cartesian Louis de la Forge who performed public demonstrations and dissections in the town. With an eye on the *curiosi* and *virtuosi* of the town, Delerpinière kept copies of Descartes, Gassendi and Galileo's works.[45] Though its specialised and professional holdings and its fashionable stock contributed to the reputation of the bookshop, it is doubtful whether sales of books of this type would have kept the bookshop financially secure for long, had it not been for another group of Elsevier imports, the textbooks used by the young students who studied in colleges of humanities in Saumur.

From small early beginnings, the population of "collégiens" studying humanities in Saumur grew during the century. By the 1660s we can estimate that the college attached to the Reformed Academy had some three hundred pupils and the more recent "college royal" set up by the Oratorians somewhat less. School textbooks were worth little individually, but together they guaranteed regular sales as the school population was partly renewed every year. The programmes of humanities of the two colleges differed slightly, particularly with regard to the study of Greek texts, but not to the extent of affecting the general potential of sales. It is this school clientele that accounts for the many textbooks listed in the inventory, and to begin with, for the number of works by Erasmus in small format present on the shelves, in particular his *Adagia* and his

---

44   In a letter dated June 1663 to Élie Bouhéreau, who had just finished his maîtrise at Saumur, Desbordes informs him that he has received from Holland: "La Gallerie des femmes, folio ... Menagii Poemata 12°, Comédies, La Comédie des Fâcheux, Sertorius, L'Étourdi, [le] Dépit ammbitieux [sic]", adding "le tout est à votre service et de vos amis". See J.-P. Pittion, 'Notes for a Saumur bibliography: XVIIth century documents in Marsh's Library, Dublin, Part I', *Long Room*, 3 (1971), pp. 9–22.

45   One copy of "Gassendi Opera 6 vol.", valued at 45 livres; "2 Geometrie (? gall[ic]e) Descartes", valued at 5 livres, and "1 Gallileus de sistema Mundi", valued at 3 livres, probably Galileo Galilei, *Systema cosmicum. Accessit locorum S. Scripturae cum terrae mobilitate conciliatio* (Lyon: J.A. Huguetan, 1641), in-4, USTC 6904937.

Colloquia.⁴⁶ Many copies of standard Latin classical texts were also available, for example six "Horatius" valued at 2 livres, five "Catulle Propertii" (2 livres), "Ovidii Opera" (5 livres), three "Plautus" (3 livres), 4 "Claudianii quæ extant" (2 livres 10 sols), two "Terentius Farnabii" (2 livres) and one "Cornelii Tacitii" (16 sols). There were also many copies of rhetoric textbooks, Latin dictionaries and Latin grammars.⁴⁷

The total stock of the library was estimated at 5,455 livres, but this estimate does not give any idea of what the average yearly turnover could have been. Considered individually, the professional books on the shelves were evidently the most valuable but sales of this category of works would have been very slow. The memoirs and belles-lettres editions obviously attracted a high-class clientele, but genteel customers were notoriously slow to pay their suppliers: some twenty-five customers on Delerpinière's books owed more than fifty livres (these sums were often made up of "cédules", i.e. in IOUs difficult to negotiate).⁴⁸ It is safe to assume that the bookshop's vitality depended to a large extent on exchanges with foreign booksellers that contributed to renewing the stock, and the regular sales of schoolbooks must have played an essential part in the financial stability of the bookshop.

During a career that spanned over four decades, from the profits he made in bookselling, Daniel Delerpinière also financed a number of editions that were printed mostly by his Reformed colleagues Isaac Desbordes, Jean Lesnier and René Péan. A study of his role as publisher lies outside the scope of this

---

46 Among other editions, Desiderius Erasmus, *Adagiorum epitome. Editio novissima ... repurgata ... adaucta* (Amsterdam: Elsevier, 1650), in-12, USTC 1032413 (two copies valued at 2 livres); Desiderius Erasmus, *Colloquia nunc emendatiora. Coronis apologetica pro colloquiis Erasmi ex ipsius scriptis ... collecta a P. S. Accedit ejusdem de colloquiorum utilitate dissertatio* (Amsterdam: Elsevier, 1650), in-12 and in-16, various USTC records (four copies in-12, valued at 6 livres; eight copies in-16, valued at 6 livres); Desiderius Erasmus, *Institutio principis christiani, cui adjunximus querelam pacis undique gentium ejectae et profligatae* (Leiden: A. Clouck, 1628), in-16, USTC 1011722 (three copies valued 2 livres 4 sols); *Colloques d'Érasme, fort curieusement traduits de latin en françois, pour l'usage des amateurs de la langue* [par Samuel Chappuzeau] (Leyden: A. Vingart, 1653), in-12 (two copies valued at 1 livre and 5 sols).

47 Latin grammars include four copies of Gerhardus Johannes Vossius, *Grammatica Latina* (Leiden: B. & A. Elsevier, 1644), in-8, USTC 1011922 (valued at 3 livres).

48 A few days after the inventory was closed, in an addendum to the act, Daniel Delerpinière's son, also named Daniel, and one of the *pasteurs* of Saumur agreed to accept a portion of 3,070 livres from the total of 6,753 owed to the bookshop as part of his inheritance, provided he received compensation in goods if at the end of a two year period all or part of these moneys owed were not redeemed (Archives départementales de Maine et Loire, SE 69 354 [3/4]).

article, but would reveal a firm commitment to the academy and to his church. As a bookseller as well as a publisher, Delerpinière exemplifies the mix of commerce, learning and religion that made the Saumur Protestant book-trade an international success during the seventeenth century.

PART 5

New Markets

∴

CHAPTER 19

Turning News into a Business: the Commerce of Early Newspaper Publishing

Jan Hillgärtner

When Johann Carolus petitioned the council of Strasbourg to grant him the right to publish a newspaper in 1605, he had already been active as a vendor of written newsletters. Scholars believe his move from script to print to have been motivated by economic considerations.[1] Using the printing press rather than relying on the work of scribes meant that Carolus could produce a greater output in less time. His idea would soon spread and publishers all over Germany started their own newspapers within a few years. Today, we can trace over 200 newspaper titles, established during the seventeenth century in Germany.[2] The number serves as a testament to the commercial appeal of the business and the interest it attracted amongst publishers.

Soon after the idea of a regular periodical emerged, the newspaper industry experienced strong competition between its various stakeholders. Publishers and postmasters both had an interest in publishing their own papers and from the start it was not clear who would be legally entitled to do so. In Frankfurt, one of the centres of postal exchange in the Holy Roman Empire, Johann von den Birghden started his *Frankfurter Postzeitung* in 1615. He served as Imperial Postmaster and contributed to the expansion of the postal service. Local competition arose for him in 1619 when the publisher Johann Theobald Schönwetter appealed to Ferdinand II for a privilege to publish a second newspaper in the Free Imperial City. His wish was granted by the Emperor and Schönwetter entered the market with his *Diarium Hebdomadale* in late 1619.[3] Von den

---

1 Martin Welke, 'Johann Carolus und der Beginn der periodischen Tagespresse. Ein Versuch, einen Irrweg der Forschung zu korrigieren', in Martin Welke and Jürgen Wilke (eds.), *400 Jahre Zeitung. Die Entwicklung der Tagespresse im internationalen Kontext* (Bremen: Edition Lumière, 2008), pp. 9–116.
2 Johannes Weber, 'Deutsche Presse im Zeitalter des Barock. Zur Vorgeschichte öffentlichen politischen Räsonnements', in Hans-Wolf Jäger (ed.), *'Öffentlichkeit' Im 18. Jahrhundert* (Göttingen: Wallstein, 1997), pp. 137–149.
3 Else Bogel and Elger Blühm (eds.), *Die deutschen Zeitungen des 17. Jahrhunderts. Ein Bestandsverzeichnis mit historischen und bibliographischen Angaben* (3 vols., Bremen: Schünemann Universitätsverlag, 1971), I, p. 40.

Birghden immediately took legal actions against his competitor, arguing that due to his experience as postmaster, he should have the sole right to publish a newspaper in Frankfurt.[4] The idea of a prerogative on newspaper publication by Imperial postmasters, albeit frequently re-used by fellow postmasters, did not convince the authorities to remove his competitor. He made another appeal, this time straight to the Habsburg administration in Vienna, asking that the privilege awarded to Schönwetter be revoked. Here he put forward an additional damaging argument, that the *Diarium Hebdomadale* presented anti-Habsburg sentiments. Schönwetter had his privilege annulled in April 1621, following an assessment by the Imperial fiscal expert Immendorfer who accepted von den Birghden's allegations. A few years later von Birghden would surrender his privilege when he too was accused of partial reporting, but the newspaper he started continued to flourish under the editorial control of Gerhard Vrints.[5]

In 1655, fifty years after the first newspaper appeared in Strasbourg, Timotheus Ritzsch made a pledge to John George I. He petitioned the Elector of Saxony to grant him a privilege for his newspaper. With ducal support, Ritzsch hoped to secure his position in his Leipzig hometown and to establish a monopoly for his own *Wöchentliche Zeitung*. In fact, he was the third to publish a newspaper in the Saxon city after a Justus Janson, Johann Albrecht and Mintzel unsuccessfully tried to establish their own periodicals between 1631 and 1643.[6] Ritzsch fared considerably better than his forerunners, thanks to a change in the political landscape. The Swedes took Leipzig in 1642 and Ritzsch's immediate competitor, Moritz Pörner, had his newspaper privilege revoked by Lennart Torstenson. Ritzsch emerged as the local protégé of the Swedes for news publishing and knew how to make use of his favourable position.

Ritsch's *Wöchentliche Zeitung* was published from 1643 onwards in up to four issues per week. His position was bolstered by a ten-year privilege secured in 1649 before the Peace of Westphalia brought Swedish rule in Leipzig to an end. Christoph Mühlbach, the newly appointed postmaster of Leipzig, contested Ritzsch's privilege and ultimately it was the town council had found a way to satisfy both parties. They ordered that Ritzsch could continue publishing

---

4   Wolfgang Behringer, 'Post, Zeitung und Reichsverfassung. Machtkämpfe zu Beginn des Zeitungswesens', in Klaus Beyrer and Peter Albrecht (eds.), *Als die Post noch Zeitung machte. Eine Pressegeschichte* (Giessen: Anabas, 1994), pp. 40–63.
5   Bogel and Blühm, *Die deutschen Zeitungen*, pp. 10–16.
6   Johannes Weber, 'Umriß der Zeitungsgeschichte Leipzigs im 17. Jahrhundert', in Arnulf Kutsch (ed.), *350 Jahre Tageszeitung. Forschungen und Dokumente* (Bremen: Edition Lumière, 2010), pp. 133–143.

his newspaper and that Mühlbach was entitled to twenty copies of each issue for his own distribution.

Legal battles over the privilege to print a newspaper were legion and took place in many corners of the Holy Roman Empire.[7] The sheer amount of these cases makes it abundantly clear that privileges that granted a printer or publisher the right to issue a newspaper were a valuable good. This article will describe the scope of the newspaper industry in the Holy Roman Empire during the first century of their existence. It explores the commercial appeal of newspapers to the numerous publishers who attempted to establish their own, as well as the many subsequent failures.

The data that forms the basis of this study has been gathered from the bibliography of Bogel and Blühm. It was furthermore enhanced through extensive archival work. It enables us to understand how the industry grew and why the new media attracted so many publishers and postmasters. The article argues that success in the news business was never foreordained. In the first fifty years of newspaper publishing failure was more common than success. After 1650, innovative business models became a core feature of the newspaper world. The looming competition drove publishers to create new forms of reporting and create new ways of enriching the news by adding editorial content.

Traditional narratives of print have tended to portray the emergence of the newspaper as an outright success story. And on the surface, this narrative looks convincing: the output of newspapers grew steadily over the entire century. Establishing a newspaper initially appealed predominantly to a set of well-capitalised urban printers; those with the resources to establish a network of correspondents and gather enough potential subscribers to make their product commercially viable. By the middle of the century, even printers operating in more scattered locations with German minorities such as Breslau, Danzig, Riga, Reval, Laibach or Copenhagen had taken to publishing their own periodical. Jürgen Wilke and others have taken a more sceptical view. Wilke discussed the many and frequent disruptions within the postal network, causing a drought of news for the new papers.[8] The first age of the newspaper coincided with a period of conflict, which further disrupted communications. As well as facing competition with other newspapers publishers, the co-existence

---

7 Walter Schöne, 'Drei Jahrhunderte Leipziger Presse', *Zeitungswissenschaft*, 11 (1936), pp. 506–568.
8 Jürgen Wilke, *Nachrichtenauswahl und Medienrealität in vier Jahrhunderten. Eine Modellstudie zur Verbindung von historischer und empirischer Publizistikwissenschaft* (Berlin: De Gruyter, 1984), pp. 34–54. For examples of failed newspapers see Andrew Pettegree, *The Invention of News. How the World Came to Know About Itself* (New Haven: Yale University Press, 2014).

of the newspaper with different news media such as broadsheets, pamphlets and newsletters yielded yet another challenge.[9] But this could not hold back the powerful new medium and new titles continued to appear steadily from 1605 onwards.

The First Fifty Years. Hopes and Setbacks

A conservative calculation shows that more than 24,000 newspaper issues were printed between 1609 and 1650 and these will form the basis of the following investigation.[10] Newspaper publishing blossomed at the onset of the Thirty Years War. In terms of output, Germany was the uncontested leader in newspaper publishing in the seventeenth century.[11]

Outside Germany, newspaper publishing was often restricted to specific cities such as London and Paris or a small set of important towns as was the case in the Northern and Southern, Italy and Spain. But the industry gained momentum abroad too. Outside the 'Deutsches Sprachgebiet', the newspaper flourished in The Dutch Republic and the Southern Netherlands during the first half of the seventeenth century. Publishers in Amsterdam, Delft, Arnhem, Antwerp and Bruges produced fourteen different titles in Dutch and French during the 1630s alone.[12] For Low Countries, we find that altogether 30,400 surviving issues appeared during the seventeenth century; around 22,500 issues in the Dutch Republic and 7,900 issues in the Southern Netherlands. Italian printers also produced around 30,000 newspaper issues throughout the entire seventeenth century.[13]

German newspapers output surpassed that of all other territories. German-language newspapers appeared in at least 70 towns across the Holy Roman

---

9   Johannes Arndt, 'Zeitung, Mediensystem und Reichspublizistik', in Volker Bauer and Holger Böning (eds.), *Die Entstehung des Zeitungswesens im 17. Jahrhundert. Ein neues Medium und seine Folgen für das Kommunikationssystem der Frühen Neuzeit* (Bremen: Edition Lumière, 2011), pp. 179–200.

10 For an explanation of the bibliographic method, see Jan Hillgärtner, 'Die Katalogisierung der deutschen Presse des 17. Jahrhunderts im Universal Short Title Catalogue (USTC)', *Jahrbuch für Kommunikationsgeschichte*, 16 (2014), pp. 171–185.

11 Elger Blühm, 'Deutsches Zeitungswesen im 17. Jahrhundert', in Paul Rabe (eds.), *Bücher und Bibliotheken im 17. Jahrhundert in Deutschland* (Hamburg: Hauswedell, 1980), pp. 126–134.

12 Arthur der Weduwen, *Dutch and Flemish Newspapers of the Seventeenth Century* (2 vols., Leiden / Boston: Brill, 2017).

13 I thank Nina Lamal for providing me with the figures.

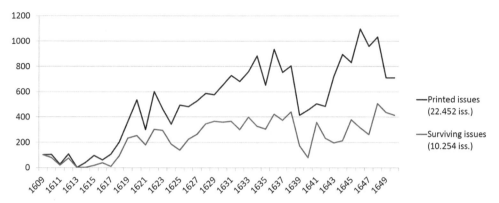

FIGURE 19.1   Newspapers published in Germany, 1609–1650

Empire, Denmark, Sweden and the Swiss Confederation. This number was possibly higher, if we consider that at least 62 German newspapers cannot be assigned to a definite place of publication.[14] For Germany, it has been estimated that throughout the century, no less than 50,000 issues have been available to readers.[15] Such estimates must be reconsidered. The extensive bibliographic and archival research which forms the foundation of this study has revealed that as many as 22,358 newspaper issues have been printed in the period between 1605 and 1650 alone. This is about half of Blühm's estimated figures for the whole century. Granted that about half of these issues are lost today, it is very likely that the actual overall number of printed newspapers and newspaper issues must have been considerably higher, especially we factor in lost or newly discovered issues. Over 2,000 previously unrecorded issues came to the attention of scholars during the 1990s.[16]

The newspaper business grew steadily, but slowly and it clearly was not a medium that took audiences by storm. The first years of newspaper publishing in Germany are practically a duopoly between two publishers and competition grew only over time.

---

14   Bogel and Blühm, *Die deutschen Zeitungen*, pp. 1–284.
15   Elger Blühm, 'Fragen zum Thema Zeitung und Gesellschaft im 17. Jahrhundert', in Elger Blühm (ed.), *Presse und Geschichte. Beiträge zur historischen Kommunikationsforschung* (Munich: Verlag Dokumentation, 1977), pp. 54–70. Scholars have debated this number, see for example the findings of Vladimir I. Simonov, 'Deutsche Zeitungen des 17. Jahrhunderts im Zentralen Staatsarchiv für Alte Akten (CGADA), Moskau', *Gutenberg Jahrbuch*, 54 (1979), pp. 210–220.
16   Johannes Weber, 'Neue Funde aus der Frühgeschichte des deutschen Zeitungswesens', *Archiv für Geschichte des Buchwesens*, 39 (1993), pp. 321–360.

The Strasbourg-based publisher Johann Carolus petitioned his local council to grant him a privilege in 1605.[17] Carolus sensed he could reach a far bigger audience with his newspaper compared to the newsletter.[18] By 1605 he had already made the switch from distributing handwritten newsletters to printer newspapers. In 1605 he started to print the *Straßburger Relation*. Julius Adolph von Söhne was the second publisher to start a newspaper, in 1609, the *Wolfenbütteler Aviso*. His role as official printer at the court of Duke Henry Julius of Brunswick-Lüneburg in Wolfenbüttel granted him unparalleled access to news coming straight from the court.[19] Nor were the benefits of this proximity limited to the production of news. His close ties to the Dukes of Braunschweig-Wolfenbüttel meant that he had access to an enviable distribution network, as he could rely on Henry Julius for the distribution of his periodical. The duke purchased newspaper copies and sent them to his diplomats and allies around Germany. Predictable and guaranteed sale of his products must have made for attractive business. Many of the early newspaper printers had ties of various nature to authorities. Their service as official printer to a ruler, a council or university meant favourable economic conditions since regular business was guaranteed. More importantly perhaps, an official appointment meant that they could paid directly by their patron, and had no need to rely on the success or failure of an edition on the retail market. Von Söhne acted on the Duke's request when he published his newspaper. For his competitors however, their ability to sell periodicals to a diverse range of subscribers was the defining factor that would make or break their business.

The idea of printed newsletters took hold after the first issues appeared in 1605 and soon, many publishers tried to run their own periodicals. The development of the newspaper trade was not without setbacks. Between 1610 and 1619, ten German language newspapers were founded within the Holy Roman Empire; only four had a lifespan of more than ten years.[20] Yet it was also at this

---

17   Johannes Weber, 'Straßburg 1605. Die Geburt der Zeitung', *Jahrbuch für Kommunikationsgeschichte*, 7 (2005), pp. 3–26.
18   Holger Böning, 'Handgeschriebene und gedruckte Zeitungen im Spannungsfeld von Abhängigkeit, Koexistenz und Konkurrenz', in Böning and Bauer (eds.), *Die Entstehung des Zeitungswesens im 17. Jahrhundert*, pp. 23–56.
19   Johannes Weber, 'Gründerzeitungen. Die Anfänge der periodischen Nachrichtenpresse im Norden des Reichs', in Peter Albrecht and Holger Böning (eds.), *Historische Presse und ihre Leser* (Bremen: Edition Lumière, 2005), pp. 9–41.
20   Bogel and Blühm, *Die deutschen Zeitungen*, pp. 8–39. Whilst Carolus' and von Söhne's newspapers probably continued to appear between 1610 and 1620, we can only trace issues of the *Straßburger Relation* for the years 1612 and 1619 and issues if the *Wolfenbütteler Aviso*

time that three remarkable and long-running newspapers appeared for the first time. These three papers account for most of the surviving issues which accelerates from a mere 61 issues in 1616 to 535 issues in 1620. These papers were based in Frankfurt, Berlin and Hamburg, and they all appeared in the second half of the 1610s. Despite initial difficulties, all three ultimately became successful and long-running newspapers.

Johann von den Birghden started his *Frankfurter Postzeitung* in 1615, the same year he began serving as Imperial Postmaster. His appointment gave him immediate access to a great amount of written news passing through Frankfurt. He presumably relied on his brother-in-law Nicolaus Hoffmann, who already owned a print shop and could provide the necessary manpower to publish the *Frankfurter Postzeitung*.[21] The Protestant von den Birghden fell out with authorities in 1627 over claims that his newspaper contained partial reporting. He had to surrender his position and the right to publish the newspaper to his Catholic successor Gerard Vrints.[22]

Christoph and Veit Frischmann started publishing the *Einkommende Ordinar- und Postzeitungen* in Berlin in 1617.[23] Like von den Birghden, Christoph Frischmann was a postmaster, albeit Berlin at that point did not enjoy the same importance as hub in the postal network as Frankfurt. The brothers too outsourced the printing to Georg Runge while retaining editorial control over the newspaper. It is unclear whether Runge benefitted from this deal. He kept on applying for a privilege but had to wait until 1621 before Elector George William granted him his wish. Over the following years, Runge petitioned for the renewal of his privilege: securing a local monopoly was his goal.[24] He might have perceived the local printer Matthias Zypsen as competition after Zypsen published a news pamphlet on the recent advances made by the Saxon army just before their crushing defeat at Nördlingen in 1634.[25] Runge's fears were well founded, as his workshop seems to have run out of work by

---

from 1610, 1612, 1615, 1618. Under the bibliographic rules laid out above, this prevents us from counting them in during the years that no copy has survived.

21 Christoph Reske, *Die Buchdrucker des 16. und 17. Jahrhunderts im deutschen Sprachgebiet. Auf der Grundlage des gleichnamigen Werkes von Josef Benzing* (Wiesbaden: Harrassowitz, 2007), p. 249.
22 Behringer, *Post, Zeitung und Reichsverfassung*, pp. 40–63.
23 Bogel and Blühm, *Die deutschen Zeitungen*, pp. 10–16.
24 Eckhard Plümacher, 'Ein unbekannter Berliner Drucker aus der Zeit des Dreißigjährigen Krieges. Matthias Zypsen. Ein Beitrag zur Frühgeschichte des Berliner Zeitungswesens', *Gutenberg Jahrbuch*, 59 (1984), pp. 163–171.
25 Anon., *Aviso Oder Grundlicher Bericht/ wie es mit den ChurSachs. Volck beschaffen ist* (Berlin: Matthias Zypsen, [1634]) [VD17 5002:735027V].

1638.[26] His heirs, nevertheless, maintained an interest in the news business and remained responsible for printing the *Einkommende Ordinar- und Postzeitungen*.

The third important newspaper was the *Wöchentliche Zeitung aus mehrerley örther*. It was published by Johann Meyer in Hamburg between 1618 and 1678.[27] Meyer was a local industrial entrepreneur with major interests in the haulage business. Like Carolus, he initially produced a handwritten newsletter that he would later turn into his *Wöchentliche Zeitung*. His professional ties to the cargo industry prevented him from printing the newspaper himself. Instead, he turned to the local printer Paul Lange and formed a cooperation that would soon enough turn sour. He complained to the council in Hamburg in 1630 that

> [I] have printed the newspaper at the workshop of Paul Lange for a long time for a high price. Learning that he [Lange, J.H.] has sold newspaper issues on his own account caused me considerable economic damage and I have not made a third in revenues of the sum that I have paid to the printer in the past two years.[28]

Meyer took matters into his own hands as a consequence of this betrayal. He opened his own print shop in the same year and passed on the newspaper to his widow and children after his death. But things were about to change in Hamburg when the Imperial Postmaster Hans Jakob Kleinhans began publishing his *Post Zeitung* in 1630.[29] In a move to squeeze the older competitor out of the market, Kleinhans had the council confirm that Ilsabe Meyer, Johann Meyer's widow, had to stop publishing the *Wöchentliche Zeitung aus mehrerley örther* but she decided to continue publication.[30] Showing considerable resilience, she and her successors managed to stay in business until at least 1678.

---

26   Reske, *Die Buchdrucker*, p. 104.
27   Reske, *Die Buchdrucker*, p. 339.
28   The original reads: "Und wie Ich [Meyer] hernacher mit großem schaden erfahren, daß er [Lange] dieselbe ändern Leüthen etzliche Zeit ehe, alß mir zukommen laßen, Und Ich fast 2 gantzen Jahren nicht ein Drittentheil so viel verkaufft und gelöset, alß mir die Unkosten und Buchdrücker Lohn zu Kosten kommen [...]". Richter-Nachlaß: SArch. Hamburg: Senat CI. VII Lit. Lb No. 16 Vol. Id (Pappkasten A4, Kopp 2.12). Cited after Reske, *Die Buchdrucker*, p. 339.
29   Astrid Blome, 'Das Intelligenzwesen in Hamburg und Altona', in Sabine Doering-Manteuffel, Josef Mancal and Wolfgang Wüst (eds.), *Pressewesen der Aufklärung. Periodische Schriften im Alten Reich* (Berlin: Akademie-Verlag, 2002), pp. 183–207.
30   Holger Böning, *Welteroberung durch ein neues Publikum. Die deutsche Presse und der Weg zur Aufklärung. Hamburg und Altona als Beispiel* (Bremen: Edition Lumière, 2002), pp. 32–33.

Despite the setbacks, all three newspapers enjoyed considerable success and encouraged more publishers to start their own newspapers. The output of these newcomers contributed to the growth of the newspaper industry in the period between 1620 and 1650. The growth in the decade following 1610 can be documented by over 1,100 surviving issues. The real boom would only happen between 1620 and 1629 when the printed output surged to over 5,100 issues. Newspaper publishing remained practically stagnant during the following two decades. The output grew only very moderately from 7,540 surviving issues in the 1630s to 7,738 for the 1640s. Two considerable changes took place between 1630 and 1650 within the newspaper industry. Many publishers tried to secure a foothold in the growing market. And those who had established their firms earlier increased the periodicity of their newspapers by switching from weekly to bi-weekly or even daily intervals. This change was the main driver behind the growth of the industry in the second quarter of the seventeenth century.

The Long and Short Story of Success and Failure

A closer look at newspapers production in the 1630s reveals how that the business continued to rest on uncertain foundations, as publishers struggled to find a sustainable business model. The highest number of new newspaper titles were concentrated in this decade, but most of them only lasted for a year or two. Narrowing our focus to this decade allows us to understand how frequently publishers went in and out of business. 61 newspaper titles were available for longer or shorter periods throughout the decade. Only three of them: Matthias Formica's *Ordentliche Zeitung*, Hans Jakob Kleinhans' *Ordinari Wochentliche Postzeittung* and Mertzenich's *Wöchentliche Niederländische Zeitung* proved durable. The first newspaper publishers played either minor roles, as in the case of Johann Carolus, or were out of business for good, like Julius Adolph von Söhne. Only 26 titles appeared for more than twelve months.

Amongst the papers that did establish a secure footing is Matthias Formica's *Ordentliche Postzeitungen*, the second newspaper to appear in Vienna. Formica came from a family of publishers and in 1615 inherited his father's workshop.[31] He started publishing newspapers in 1621 with the *Ordinari Postzeitung* and his newspapers are rather unusual in its formatting. Formica published all incoming reports under the headline "Aus Wienn". This was uncommon, as most

---

31 Reske, *Die Buchdrucker*, p. 978.

newspapers printed the news under the headline that indicated from the origin of the report.

Johann von Mertzenich's *Raporten* appeared in Cologne in 1620 and lasted until 1699.[32] It was the work of a veteran of the printing industry who looked back on at least 25 years of experience in publishing. It remains unclear whether he started printing in 1589 or 1595.[33] He was a prolific printer; before he started the *Raporten*, he had printed occasional news pamphlets, *Neue Zeitungen*.[34] In 1626 he began to reprint newspapers sourced from the Netherlands, though it is unclear on which of the Dutch newspapers he relied.[35] He often changed the title of his periodical, a common practice in the early newspaper world. Today known under its uniform title *Raporten*, his newspaper appeared without a title in late 1620. In 1625 Mertzenich added *Wochentliche Zeitung* on the title page. One year later, in 1626 it appeared as the *Niederländische Zeitung* and for 1630 we find both titles in use for his newspaper.

Most newspapers in Germany did not cease to exist with the death of the main publisher or printer. In most cases, officials extended the privilege to close family members. Ilsabe Meyer and other widows often constituted the second generation of printers. In Mertzenich's case, the privilege was removed from his widow Maria and passed on to his local competitor Arnold von Kempen, who kept the newspaper running.

Ten different newspapers had appeared in the period between 1610 and 1619. The growth of the 1620s was due to the involvement of established printers such as von Mertzenich in Cologne and other important centres of publishing such as Munich, Vienna and Zurich. In the 1630s, new newspapers appeared all over Germany. Publishers founded new periodicals in major capitals such as Hamburg and Leipzig, as well as in lesser territories such as Bremen, Danzig, Braunschweig and Stettin. This process slowed down in the following decade, when only eight new newspapers appeared.

But whilst the 1630s might have meant a spreading of the idea of newspaper printed from the centres into the peripheries, starting a newspaper presented many challenges. The vast majority of those who entered the newspaper market in the 1630s did not last as long as a year. Only thirteen of 51 newspapers appear to have lasted for as long as five years. The low survival rate of some titles distorts the image to some extent. For example, it is safe to assume that

---

32   Bogel and Blühm, *Die deutschen Zeitungen*, pp. 41–45.
33   Reske, *Die Buchdrucker*, p. 458.
34   Corinna Roeder, *Frühe Kölner Wochenzeitungen. Die Unternehmen der Offizinen Mertzenich und Kempen. 1620 bis 1685* (Cologne: Greven, 1998), p. 125.
35   Bogel and Blühm, *Die deutschen Zeitungen*, pp. 41–45.

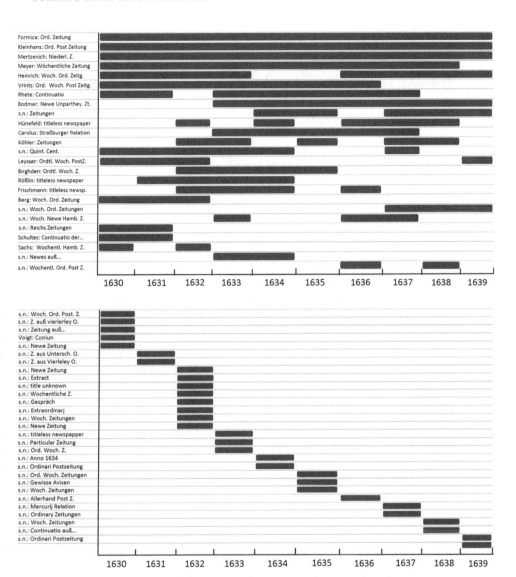

FIGURE 19.2A–B   Longevity and disruption in the newspaper business, 1630–1639

the *Straßburger Relation* appeared continuously between 1605 and at least 1667. Even so, only one issue survives between 1633 and 1637. Thirty newspaper titles alone survive in only a few stray issues, and sometimes just a single example.

Eight out of those short-lived newspapers appeared in 1632. This year was of great significance for the German public. Gustavus Adolphus's death marked a turning-point in the Swedish intervention. The fortunes in the conflict between

TABLE 19.1 Newly established newspapers, 1610–1660

Period	Newspapers founded
1610–1619	10
1620–1629	23
1630–1639	38
1640–1649	8
1650–1659	14

the Swedes and Catholic Habsburg turned after the indecisive battle at the Alte Veste close to Nuremberg in September. Adolphus had been on the march throughout Germany, taking over town after town, but was unable to secure a foothold in Nuremberg.[36] The last battle of the year, taking place in Lützen in November proved to be of great importance. The Swedes carried the day, but lost their talismanic leader. Initally there was considerable confusion in the news market whether the king was dead or alive. The event rocked the foundations of Protestant Germany; its repercussion in the printing world was a barrage of broadsheets, pamphlets, sermons and other printed material.[37] His passing caused widespread public mourning and undermined the momentum of the Swedish advance. Events like these created a desire for news, resulting in new newspaper titles. Seven out of the eight short-lived papers of 1633 appeared in the first half of the year, cashing in on the nervous exchange of letters sent between diplomats and courtiers on the death of the Swedish King. This event affected all parts of the news market. Broadsheets featuring battle

---

36   Peter H. Wilson, *Europe's Tragedy. A History of the Thirty Years War* (London: Penguin, 2009), pp. 504–507.

37   See for example the analysis of these sources by Annette Hempel, *Eigentlicher Bericht, so wol auch Abcontrafeytung: eine Untersuchung der nicht-allegorischen Nachrichtenblätter zu den Schlachten und Belagerungen der schwedischen Armee unter Gustav II. Adolf (1628/30–1632)* (Frankfurt am Main: Peter Lang, 2000); Jan Hillgärtner, 'The king is dead. German broadsheets printed on the death of Gustavus Adolphus and Charles I', in Andrew Pettegree (ed.), *Broadsheets. Single-Sheet Publishing in the First Age of Print* (Leiden / Boston: Brill, 2017), pp. 295–315; Frank Liemandt, *Die zeitgenössische literarische Reaktion auf den Tod des Königs Gustav II. Adolf von Schweden* (Frankfurt am Main: Peter Lang, 1996) and Silvia Serena Tschopp, *Heilsgeschichtliche Deutungsmuster in der Publizistik des Dreissigjährigen Krieges. Pro- und antischwedische Propaganda in Deutschland 1628 bis 1635* (Frankfurt am Main: Peter Lang, 1991).

accounts and sermons mourning the dead king further added to the barrage of media reporting the event.

The exact reasons why so many of those new newspapers failed to establish themselves are hard to establish. Many of the titles appeared anonymously and left little evidence about their fate. They disappeared as quickly as they had appeared, leaving no evidence about who published them or where they were printed. The case of one such short-lived title, however, is sufficiently well documented to allow us to acquire a broader view of this phenomenon. Two newspapers were founded in Munich in 1627 and one would outlive the other by far. The *Ordinari Zeitung*, published by Nikolaus Heinrich entered the market in the summer of this year, almost immediately to be followed by the *Gewisse und wahrhaffte Wochentliche Ordinari Zeitung*, published by Heinrich's brother-in-law Heinrich Berg.[38] Whilst Heinrich's *Ordinari Zeitung* blossomed, Berg's title survived only until 1632. Berg's father, Heinrich Berg the elder, ran one of the most important publishing houses for music printing in Munich. Adam Berg the younger took over the newspaper in 1629 and maintained it for three more years. It might have appeared that the odds were in his favour. He started the newspaper together with his mother Anna Berg and continued the tradition of publishing works by Catholic authors as well as ordinances of Maximilian I, Elector of Bavaria.[39] His last works, two monastic rules of the Carmelites, appeared in 1634.[40] Berg must have given up his newspaper in the face of local competition.

The poor survival rate for many newspapers of the time has consequences for our understanding of the early newspaper business. In Berg's case, it seems that his newspaper failed and he gave it up. When he died in 1634, his enterprise did not look attractive to his heirs. His widow, Anna Berg married the publisher Melchior Segen of Cologne. Together they showed no interest in continuing the newspaper.

---

38 Bogel and Blühm, *Die deutschen Zeitungen*, pp. 70–74.
39 An example for Benedictinan literature published by Berg is the anonymous *Fraternitatis Nominis Dei. Contra Blasphemias, Et Abusum Divini Nominis, In Ordine Praedicatorum erectae, & in Caenobio Landishuttano eiusdem Ordinis, 1626. institutae. Origo, Leges, Indugentiae, Privilegia, Preces* (Munich: Berg, 1626) [VD17 19:730753A], for instructional literature: Juan de Jesus María, *Instructio Novitiorum. Das ist Unterweisung der Novitzen / Erstlich durch den Ehrw. P. Joannem a Jesu Maria der Discalcierten Carmeliten Generaln in Latein beschriben und verteütscht* (Munich: Berg, 1633) [VD17 23:726135T].
40 Johannes Ludovicus, *Passer Solitarius Hoc Est Vita & functiones Animae contemplativae Sub Symbolo Passeris* (Munich: Berg, 1634) [VD17 12:103538E]; Teresa de Jesus, *Summarium undt kurtzer Inhalt Der Staffeln des Innerlichen Gebetts, vermittels deren die Seel zur Volkomenheit der Beschauligkeit gelangt und auffsteigt* (Munich: Berg, 1634) [VD17 12:104625L].

Bogel and Blühm speculate whether the anonymous *Wochentliche Ordinari Zeitungen* that appeared in Munich between 1638 and 1667 might be the continuation of Berg's work.[41] A closer inspection of the editorial work yields more differences than similarities. The news that constituted the reporting in each issue were usually dispatched by regular correspondents.[42] Besides this, publishers relied on re-printing news that firstly appeared in other newspapers. It was then their task to select the news for each issue and comparing newspapers from identical times often show significant differences in where the reports come from and what aspects receive coverage. For his newspaper, Berg relied on usually reports from eight places of correspondence. In every issue, he received reports from Rome and Vienna and additional reporting came from Venice and The Hague. The anonymously published *Wochentliche Ordinari Zeitungen* in contrast had an average of ten to twelve reports from Rome, Venice, Vienna, Lyon, Frankfurt and other locations. Most importantly, it received its news from the Netherlands and England via Cologne as opposed to receiving reports from The Hague as was the case in the later newspaper. The editorial differences are considerable. This makes it likely that Berg's *Wochentliche Ordinari Zeitung* was not the immediate forerunner of the latter anonymous newspaper.

Competition with his local rival Nikolaus Heinrich seems to be the most convincing reason for Berg to abandon the idea of publishing a regular newspaper. Archival evidence is scarce, meaning that we do not know exactly why Berg gave up the newspaper. It is hard to establish who subscribed to his newspaper but comparing the survival of his newspaper to that of his local competitor might indicate sales that were worse than in the case of Heinrich's *Ordinari Zeitung*. Copies of Berg's newspaper survive in the Bavarian State Library in Munich, the Salzburg Museum (former Carolino Augusteum) and the Royal Library in Stockholm. The *Ordinari Zeitung* in contrast has a wider geographical spread as numbers of the newspaper made it into the collections of the Bayerische Staatsbibliothek in Munich, the Saxon State Archive in Dresden, The Russian National Library in St Petersburg, The Czech National Museum in Prague and the Royal Library in Stockholm.[43] It is plausible to assume that the *Ordinari Zeitung*, given its wider geographical spread of readership,

---

41 Bogel and Blühm, *Die deutschen Zeitungen*, pp. 125–126.
42 For an explanation of the system of correspondents see Jürgen Wilke, 'Korrespondenten und geschriebene Zeitungen', in Johannes Arndt and Esther-Beate Körber (eds.), *Das Mediensystem im Alten Reich der Frühen Neuzeit (1600–1750)* (Göttingen: Vandenhoeck & Ruprecht, 2010), pp. 59–72.
43 Bogel and Blühm, *Die deutschen Zeitungen*, pp. 70–74.

succeeded in reaching a greater audience and enjoyed better sales when compared to Berg's newspaper.

War, Centre and Periphery in Newspaper Publishing

Globally, the newspaper flourished, but it did so to various degrees and in different locations. The Thirty Years War had positive and negative effects on the print industry as a whole and on newspaper publishing in particular. It may have brought devastation over wide parts of the Empire; yet it also stimulated a constant desire to stay abreast of the latest political occurrences.[44] Scholars have noticed the growth of the industry during the Thirty Years War, especially during the Swedish intervention between 1630 and 1635.[45] It was no accident that the influx of new titles entering the market in the period around 1630 to 1632 coincided with the beginning of the Swedish presence in Germany. Now the conflict moved inland affecting increasingly more people.

No publisher could afford to rely on a newspaper alone. It is essential to contextualise the growth of the newspaper industry against the backdrop of publishing in Germany in the first half of the seventeenth century to understand its fundamental importance in key centres. The publishing industry experienced considerable fluctuation in Wittenberg, Leipzig, Frankfurt am Main, Cologne and Jena, Germany's largest printing centres. This was especially the case in the period between 1635 and 1640 when the output stagnated at a low level.

Frankfurt's book industry suffered from the Battle of Höchst in 1622, fought between the Catholic League and the Protestant Army outside the Free Imperial City.[46] From the early sixteenth century onwards, the town has been of pivotal importance in the publishing business because of the two annual fairs and its convenient location along with easy access to Europe's most important waterway. Yet after the battle, Frankfurt's book production fell precipitately from 238 to just over 150 works published during the entire year. This meant a steep decline of over forty percent.

---

44 Johannes Weber, 'Der große Krieg und die frühe Zeitung. Gestalt und Entwicklung der deutschen Nachrichtenpresse in der ersten Hälfte des 17. Jahrhunderts', *Jarhbuch für Kommunikationsgeschichte*, 1 (1991), pp. 23–61.
45 Carsten Prange, *Die Zeitungen und Zeitschriften des 17. Jahrhunderts in Hamburg und Altona. Ein Beitrag zur Publizistik der Frühaufklärung* (Hamburg: Christians, 1978), pp. 95–100.
46 Wilson, *Europe's Tragedy*, pp. 337–338.

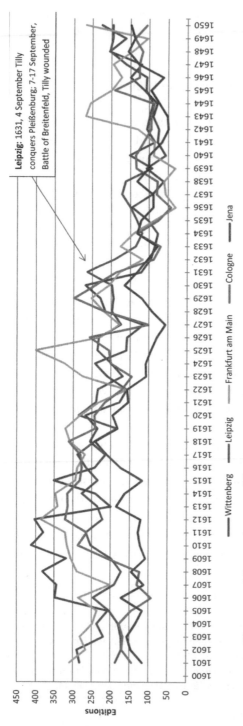

FIGURE 19.3   The output of Germany's most prolific print centres, 1600–1650

War was not necessarily adverse for news, rather it had positive effects as conflict attracted attention and increased public desire for printed sources of information. Furthermore, there was a distinct preference for ephemeral materials, not least because paper may be more difficult to come by (and thus more expensive) at a time of conflict. Cashing in on the fears of populations close to the warzone was no unknown concept as Leipzig's publishers demonstrated with the battle at Breitenfeld in 1631.[47] This one event prompted the production of some 70 broadsheets, pamphlets, *Newe Zeytungen* and other ephemeral works, all published the same year in the aftermath of the battle. This topped the production of ephemeral newsprint within the Saxon city by 27 percent, compared to the previous year.[48]

One of the remarkable things about the newspaper industry is that it emerged in towns that are not all major centres of publishing in the Holy Roman Empire. For the period between 1609 and 1650, we find that Hamburg had the most prolific newspaper industry with two different newspapers in the 1640s, some of them publishing bi-weekly issues.[49] Johann Meyer published his *Wöchentliche Zeitung* from 1618 onwards. Hans Jakob Kleinhans challenged his monopoly with his *Post Zeitung* in 1630.[50] Besides, we find around forty stray issues of a paper with an ever-changing title, published between 1632 and 1634 that might have been printed in Hamburg. The publishers within the Hanseatic town had established a strong industry, but lagged behind their competitors in Leipzig who produced almost ten times as many editions in the same period (refer to Table 19.2).[51]

Johann von den Birghden was active as a newspaper publisher with interruption between 1615 until 1627.[52] Political disagreement with the authorities led to him losing his business. Frankfurt was an important node in the postal network. The postal routes that served Antwerp and Leipzig as well as the northern route, connecting Hamburg with Augsburg, Innsbruck, Venice, Milan and Rome ran through the town. Immediate access to the postal system was crucial to von

---

47 Tschopp, *Heilsgeschichtliche Deutungsmuster*, pp. 45–50.
48 It is possible to concede that the gravity and importance of the event might have prompted readers to collect more carefully any ephemeral material about it. After all, studying the surviving broadsheets and pamphlets for said period showed that collections are skewed towards editions relating to political events rather than say administrative or academic print.
49 Bogel and Blühm, *Die deutschen Zeitungen*, pp. 87–91; 102–103.
50 Bogel and Blühm, *Die deutschen Zeitungen*, pp. 87–91.
51 The trends would stay the same, even if print production was calculated in terms of sheets rather than editions.
52 Bogel and Blühm, *Die deutschen Zeitungen*, pp. 10–16.

TABLE 19.2 Table of regional book and newspaper production, 1609–1650

Town	Newspaper issues published	Books published
Hamburg	4,071	1,453
Leipzig	1,967	8,409
Frankfurt am Main	1,830	6,628
Vienna	1,531	453
Cologne	1,454	3,956
Munich	1,250	1,098
Strasbourg	1,082	3,274
Danzig	963	585
Zurich	731	161
Wittenberg	0	7,213
Jena	0	6,308
Nuremberg	0	3,418

Birghden's success. All other towns in which newspaper publishing flourished represent nodes and hubs in the early modern news network.

Things were different in Leipzig where the almost 1,900 printed issues stem not from competition but from an increase in the regularity of publication. Here, an anonymous printer (presumably Timotheus Ritzsch) published the *Wöchentliche Zeitung* three times a week from 1643 onwards.[53] The surviving 225 issues from 1645 tell us that the paper appeared four times per week by this date. It remained so until 1650 and we do not know what happened to the paper afterwards. What is safe to say is that his *Einkommende Zeitungen*, started in 1650, was the first daily newspaper, comprising six issues per week. The towns with the greatest newspaper production were not all centres of book publications. Only Leipzig, Frankfurt and Strasbourg had a substantial book industry and produced newspapers at the same time. Cities like Wittenberg and Jena had a local printing industry that was geared towards specific needs. Wittenberg's book industry in the seventeenth century still drew on its legacy as the cradle of the Reformation. Jena's elevated position is due to the amount of academic printing.

---

[53] Bogel and Blühm, *Die deutschen Zeitungen*, pp. 131–133; Else Bogel-Hauff, 'Eine Leipziger Zeitung vor 1650', in Arnulf Kutsch and Johannes Weber (eds.), *350 Jahre Tageszeitung. Forschungen und Dokumente* (Bremen: Edition Lumière, 2010), pp. 155–160.

News and Big Business. The Period after 1650

A constant increase of published issues characterised the second half of the century. Publishers also began experimenting with the aesthetic qualities of the newspaper, leading to considerable stylistic variations. In 1664 Georg Greflinger started his *Nordischer Mercurius* in Hamburg. He strove to make the reporting as accessible as possible and intended his newspaper to be used in schools, as well as sold on the bookstalls. He took great pains to produce an appealing newspaper by summarising news and even turning news into poetry.[54] Thus he confronted sentiments shared by many of his contemporaries who maintained that news in more traditional papers was inaccessible and dry and in some cases downright incomprehensible.

Hamburg rose to pivotal importance in the news world and became the powerhouse for the advancement of the newspaper, both in terms of style and output. The introduction of journals in the world of periodicals publishing, dating to the latter half of the seventeenth century, is a case in point.[55] Nicolaus Spieringk pushed the boundaries of the newspaper genre with his *Relation aus dem Parnasso*. This was a straightforward, four-page quarto newspaper that differed little in terms of its often haphazard reports from all over the continent. He added a short section at the end of each issue in which he staged a fictitious conversation between Europe's rulers, commenting on the latest news.[56]

Despite these innovative features, the content and the style of reporting remained similar across the majority of the titles. What changed in comparison to the first half of the century is that newspaper production had now become the dominion of a small number of publishers throughout Germany. A consolidation took place in the 1650s. From this point onwards fewer publishers risked of starting their own papers. By the middle of the century, it was apparent that newspaper publishing was well-established and long lasting. It had found a place in most centres of the Holy Roman Empire. After 1650, newspaper publishing spread from the centres to the periphery and titles began to appear in Heidelberg, Konstanz, Darmstadt and Wangen im Allgäu.

Many of the publishers of the second half of the seventeenth century made news publishing the mainstay of their business; they often published more than

---

54 Elger Blühm, 'Zeitung und literarisches Leben', pp. 491–499.
55 Holger Böning, 'Aufklärung und Presse im 18. Jahrhundert', in Hans-Wolf Jäger (eds.), *'Öffentlichkeit' Im 18. Jahrhundert* (Göttingen: Wallstein, 1997), pp. 151–163.
56 Elger Blühm, 'Zeitung und literarisches Leben im 17. Jahrhundert', in Albrecht Schöne (eds.), *Stadt, Schule, Universität, Buchwesen und die deutsche Literatur im 17. Jahrhundert* (Munich: C.H. Beck, 1976), pp. 492–505.

one issue per week. Hamburg continued its tradition of fierce local competition. In the 1670s, three different newspapers regularly appeared in the city—four, if we include nearby Altona, then under Danish administration.[57] One of the town's foremost newspaper publishers, Thomas von Wiering, became active in 1675. The Deventer-born printer published his first pamphlet in Dutch in his hometown in 1662 and relocated to Hamburg before 1670.[58] He served the local publishing industry as an engraver but was also active as publisher in Hamburg between 1670 and 1675. When he established his firm, he must have decided that the best course of action was to focus his entire production on news alone. For his first title, the *Relations Courier*, he appointed the scholar Eberhard Werner Happel as editor.[59] Together they initially published three, and later four weekly issues. The newspaper was highly successful. His widow and heirs continued publishing the title after von Wiering's death in 1703 until the end of the eighteenth century. In addition, he published specialised newspapers with a narrow scope and a short life-spans. His *Türkischer Estats und Krieges-Bericht* focussed exclusively on the Second Siege of Vienna and presented one illustration per issue. The *Ausländischer Potentatien Krieges- und Stats-Beschreibung* appeared only in 1685 and presented the latest news with descriptions of Europe's royal families.[60]

Von Wiering's strong focus on news was typical of many thriving newspaper publishers during the seventeenth century. He concentrated mainly on news and frequently re-packaged the same content in various publications. News made up almost half of his surviving 281 editions. He published widely on the latest occurrences with a strong focus on news from north-eastern European, ranging from battle reports to accounts of sieges and negotiations. Von Wiering was alone in publishing news of Russia. News indirectly influenced his second most prominent genre: chronicles. From 1675 till 1703 he published an annual summary of the news, *Kürtze Chronica Der Merckwürdigsten Welt- und Wunder-Geschichten*.[61] He based his chronicles on the printed newspaper sheets and added a title page to each year's issues. The chronicles involved relatively little

---

57 Bogel and Blühm, *Die deutschen Zeitungen*, pp. 23–30; 87–91; 180–185; 206–212.
58 Reske, *Die Buchdrucker*, pp. 342–343.
59 Flemming Schock, *Die Text-Kunstkammer. Populäre Wissenssammlungen des Barock am Beispiel der 'Relationes Curiosae' von E.W. Happel* (Cologne, Böhlau, 2010), pp. 61–64.
60 Bogel and Blühm, *Die deutschen Zeitungen*, pp. 227–231; 256–261. For the editorial principles oft the *Türkischer Estats und Krieges-Bericht* see Jan Hillgärtner, 'Die erste illustrierte deutsche Zeitung? Thomas von Wierings Türckis Estats-und Krieges-Bericht', in Klaus Arnold (ed.), *Historische Perspektiven auf den Iconic Turn: Die Entwicklung der öffentlichen visuellen Kommunikation* (Cologne: Herbert von Harlem, 2016), pp. 115–142.
61 Eberhard Werner Happel, *Continuation des Couriers Historischen Kerns/ oder Kürtze*

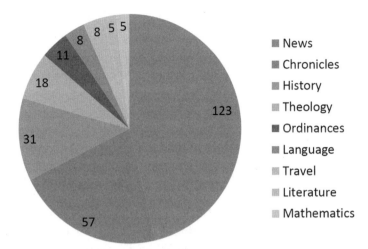

FIGURE 19.4   The publishing program of Thomas von Wiering

additional work, given that he still stocked unsold sheets and only had to add a title page. The new edition may stretch our understanding of a chronicle quite a bit, but von Wiering took it as it was. He did the same with his *Türkischer Estats- und Krieges-Bericht*.[62] In 1685, one year after the Siege of Vienna had taken place, he published the remaining newspaper sheets with a title page as *Türckischer Schau-Platz*.[63] He transformed a newspaper into a chronicle by changing its title. Von Wiering preferred the short formats and more than half of his editions appear either as pamphlets or broadsheets. This was perfectly logical given his focus on perishable content where speedy production and quick dissemination mattered.

Some, like von Wiering, geared their business almost entirely towards news publishing. For others, such as Felsecker, it was a gradual transition that would eventually see an established printer publishing a newspaper on the side. Felsecker's *Teutscher Kriegs-Curier* was first published in 1673 and lasted until 1762.[64] Felsecker must have been active as newspaper printer already at an ear-

---

Chronica Der Merckwürdigsten Welt- und Wunder-Geschichten/ welche sich im Jahr 1677. zugetragen (Hamburg: Thomas von Wiering, 1678) [VD17 23:281537S].

62 Bogel and Blühm, *Die deutschen Zeitungen*, pp. 256–258.
63 Anon., *Der Türckische Schau-Platz. Eröfnet und fürgestelt in sehr vielen nach dem Leben gezeichneten Figuren, Wobey die Türcken ... nach dem Unterscheyd ihrer Sitten/ Kleydung/ Würde/ Standt ... beschrieben werden. Wie auch der itzige Turcken-Krieg. Von seinem Beginn und Fortgang biß auff das 1685-ste Jahr* (Hamburg: Thomas von Wiering, 1685) [VD17 23:231261H].
64 Bogel and Blühm, *Die deutschen Zeitungen*, pp. 213–222.

lier stage. We learn from a petition to the Council of the Free Imperial City by Andreas Gottlieb Pilgram that Felsecker and others had publishing newspapers sometime before this.[65] Nuremberg might have been an important centre for cheap news publishing, mainly broadsheets and pamphlets, but the council decided to take a careful approach to newspapers.[66]

Before he was finally given the privilege to publish a newspaper, Felsecker published a wide range of news-related material, such as calendars: these frequently contained round-ups of the news of the past year. Some of these works were a hybrid between a calendar and a chronicle. Gottfried Achatius Bielstädt's *Alter und Neuer Zeit und Regierungs-Calender* for 1673 reported about the origins of the Anglo-Dutch war and traced the pedigree of the French kings back to the twelfth century.[67] But the calendars also differed considerably from the generally impartial and factual reporting of newspapers. Supernatural wonders occupy considerable parts of Friedrich Weißkohl's calendar when the author summarises the appearance of three black suns over Moscow in April 1672.[68]

Less than a year after starting the *Teutscher Kriegs-Curier*, Felsecker began publishing his *Verkleidete Götter-Both-Mercurius*, a periodical commonly regarded as the first journal.[69] Felsecker geared both periodicals to complement one another. The *Kriegs-Curier* reported the latest events and the *Verkleidete Götter-Both-Mercurius* offered commentary. They both share a register at the end of each year. The register referred to both publications and they were meant to be read in conjunction with each other.

In the second half of the century newspapers played an increasingly important part in their publishers' business model. Where they had previously been seen as a convenient way of occupying the presses during less busy times of

---

65 Lore Sporhan-Krempel, *Nürnberg als Nachrichtenzentrum zwischen 1400 und 1700* (Nuremberg: Verein für Geschichte der Stadt Nürnberg, 1968), pp. 122–123.

66 Sonja Schultheiß-Heinz, *Politik in der europäischen Publizistik. Eine historische Inhaltsanalyse von Zeitungen des 17. Jahrhunderts* (Stuttgart: Steiner, 2004), pp. 43–47.

67 Gottfried Achatius Bielstädt, *Alter und Neuer Der Unüberwündlichsten und Allerdurchleuchtigsten Häuser Hispanien/ Franckreich und Engellandes Nachdencklicher Zeit und Regierungs-Calender/ Auf das Jahr Christi 1674* (Nuremberg: Wolfgang Eberhard Felsecker, 1673) [VD17 27:713324Y].

68 Friedrich Weißkohl, *Alter und Neuer Von seltenen und unterschiedenen Sachen Ausgefertigter Curiositäten-Calender/ Mit Beyfügung allerhand höchst-erbaulich- und Lust-erweckenden Unterredungen von den neusten und Curioesten Sachen/ so sich im nechst-verwichnen 1672 und 73sten Jahre[n] ... zugetragen ... Auf das Jahr Christi MDCLXXIV* (Nuremberg: Wolfgang Eberhard Felsecker, 1673) [VD17 27:713292Y].

69 Johannes Weber, *Götter-Both Mercurius. Die Urgeschichte der politischen Zeitschrift in Deutschland* (Bremen: Edition Temmen, 1994), pp. 21–28.

the week, they increasingly became the commercial mainstay of publishers like Thomas von Wiering and Wolfgang Eberhard Felsecker. This was the result of a long period of evolution, as publishers searched for the best way to make money form news. The industry grew rapidly within the first three decades. It lost its momentum around 1650 and shifted towards a business in which only the specialised publishers could survive. Over the entire century, it was an enterprise requiring a great deal of trial and error, and error prevailed for most. The number of printed newspapers grew throughout the century, but this growth was not equally distributed amongst all publishers. From around the middle of the century, fewer and fewer tried their luck. Many new newspaper enterprises took off in smaller and regional towns, further away from the news centres. Those who already succeeded in business increased their output by publishing several issues per week. Furthermore, it was a small group of specialist publishers who fared best. Newspapers became a viable business for publishers such as Thomas von Wiering, who understood how to use and re-use the news for other publications, and was able to gear his entire print production towards news.

CHAPTER 20

Booksellers, Newspaper Advertisements and a National Market for Print in the Seventeenth-Century Dutch Republic

Arthur der Weduwen

On Saturday 25 May 1658, Otto Barentsz Smient placed an unusual announcement in the *Tijdinghen uyt verscheyde Quartieren* (1619–1671), a weekly newspaper published in Amsterdam. This announcement stated that:

> A young man of around 21 or 22 years old, with a good physique, dressed in grey clothes and a cape, and well-spoken, has visited booksellers in various towns to demand payment for subscription to the newspaper of Otto Smient: he has claimed to be Adriaen Smient, saying that he is a nephew of [Otto] Smient; all booksellers are therefore cautioned, not to give money to any person, unless the bill has been signed by [Otto] Smient; and if any are able to point out the same person [the impostor], they will enjoy a reward.[1]

Otto Barentsz Smient was an Amsterdam bookseller from 1636 to his death in 1689. He was part of an established family of booksellers and publishers operating in Amsterdam and Dordrecht.[2] In 1655 he acquired the oldest weekly newspaper printed in the Low Countries: the *Courante uyt Italien, Duytslandt, &c* (1618–1669). Within three years of taking over the paper, Smient and his associated booksellers became the victim of this unscrupulous impostor. Although he does not name the booksellers who were cheated, this hitherto unknown notification is of significant value for the study of the early European press. It clearly demonstrates that Smient sold his *Courante uyt Italien* to a variety of booksellers in different towns. As Smient used the *Tijdinghen*, a rival

---

1 *Tijdinghen uyt verscheyde Quartieren* [henceforth: TVQ], 21, 25 May 1658. The only surviving copy is kept at the Staats- und Universitätsbibliothek Hamburg. Accessible online, like thousands of seventeenth-century Dutch newspapers, at www.delpher.nl, last accessed on 25 February 2018.
2 M.M. Kleerkoper and W.P. van Stockum Jr., *De Boekhandel te Amsterdam voornamelijk in de 17ᵉ eeuw* (2 vols., The Hague: Martinus Nijhoff, 1914–1916), I, pp. 724–735.

Amsterdam newspaper, to warn his clientele, one must presume that the *Tijdinghen* had a similar outreach and may equally have been sold by booksellers throughout the Dutch Republic.

Archival sources detailing the distribution networks of early newspapers are extremely rare, and so particularly precious.[3] It is exactly these networks which are vital to understanding the business of periodical print and the societal impact of the newspaper in the seventeenth century. But we do have one source that sheds an unexpected light on these issues: the advertisements placed in the papers themselves. Newspapermen accepted advertisements for pragmatic reasons, to bring in vital extra income, and improve their cash flow. During the course of the seventeenth century they tell us much about the development of a consumer society, the goods and services in particular demand, and changes in taste. In the first half of the seventeenth century the advertisements placed in Dutch newspapers were overwhelmingly for books and maps. And from these notices we can learn an unexpected amount about the reach and potency of the papers themselves.

Amsterdam: Newspaper Phenomenon

Throughout the seventeenth century hundreds of news serials emerged throughout Europe. The majority were published in the Holy Roman Empire, the Low Countries and England. Many are known from only a few surviving issues: the *Arnhemsche Courant*, published weekly from at least 1619 to 1636, survives in fourteen issues. The *Courante uyt Italien, Duytsland ende Nederlandt* of Delft (1620–1643) survives in only six issues. The announcement placed by Smient in the *Tijdinghen* is likewise a chance survivor. Four newspapers appeared in Amsterdam in the 1650s; yet the *Tijdinghen* of 25 May 1658 is the only extant issue of that month.

In the first half of the seventeenth century, Amsterdam was the centre of the periodical press in the Dutch Republic. In 1618 Amsterdam became the first European city with two weekly newspapers (the *Courante* and the

---

3 Some archival sources are available for the Dutch press in the eighteenth century: see I.H. van Eeghen, 'De Amsterdamse Courant in de achttiende eeuw', *Jaarboek van het Genootschap Amstelodamum*, 44 (1950), pp. 31–58 and D.H. Couvée, 'The administration of the Oprechte Haerlemse Courant 1738–1742', *Gazette*, 4 (1958), pp. 91–110. The Noord-Hollands Archief in Haarlem now houses the archive of the Enschedé business firm, which includes extensive material on the publication of the *Oprechte Haerlemse Courant* in the eighteenth century.

Tijdinghen).[4] Several other newspapers emerged in the 1630s, and the first tri-weekly appeared in Amsterdam in 1642. By 1645 ten weekly issues of news were printed by six different publishers. This is all the more noteworthy, because almost all European news serials during this period were published without any local competition.[5]

Amsterdam dominated national news production. Until 1652, other newspapers in the Dutch Republic were either local ventures (the *Arnhemsche Courant* and the short-lived Utrecht *Nieuwe Courante uyt Italien, Duytslandt ende Nederlant*), or commercial reprints of the Amsterdam papers (the Delft *Courante uyt Italien, Duytsland ende Nederlandt*).[6] Given that the Amsterdam market was so uniquely crowded, Amsterdam newspaper publishers naturally looked for additional customers beyond their city walls. While Amsterdam undoubtedly provided a large clientele, the citizens of Leiden, Haarlem, Rotterdam and many other cities were also eager to indulge in a weekly digest of news and turned to the Amsterdam papers to fulfil this need.[7]

The sale of a newspaper was more complicated than the sale of other forms of commercial news. A pamphlet or illustrated broadsheet could be commissioned and printed during times of particular news interest; even if a pamphlet did not sell well, it remained a one-off investment. The unique feature of the newspaper—its periodicity—required much greater expenditure. Gathering news sources and maintaining correspondents was a costly business. To break even, the newspaper had to be sold regularly to hundreds of customers. All too frequently, newspaper publishers had to be prepared for several years of little or no profit.

These challenges proved too much for many publishers: most periodical ventures of the seventeenth century collapsed very soon after their inception, or disappeared after a few years. The Amsterdam newspapers, on the other hand,

---

4 Arthur der Weduwen, *Dutch and Flemish Newspapers of the Seventeenth Century, 1618–1700* (2 vols., Leiden: Brill, 2017). See also Folke Dahl, 'Amsterdam—Earliest Newspaper Centre of Western Europe', *Het Boek*, 25.3 (1939), pp. 161–198, and his *Dutch Corantos 1618–1650: A Bibliography* (The Hague: Koninklijke Bibliotheek, 1946). Now see the first issue of *The Early Modern Low Countries*, 2 (2018), on the newspaper in the Dutch Golden Age.

5 This excludes the expansion of news serials in London during the English Civil War—even if many of these news serials lasted only several weeks or months. Furthermore, two competing newspapers were published in Antwerp, Hamburg, Frankfurt and Danzig at different stages during the first half of the seventeenth century.

6 There were, however, pamphlet serials in The Hague (1648–1649) and Gouda (1649).

7 In 1622, around 100,000 inhabitants lived in Amsterdam. The total population of the Dutch Republic was around 1.6–1.8 million. Jan de Vries and Ad van der Woude, *The First Modern Economy: Success, Failure, and Perseverance of the Dutch Economy, 1500–1815* (Cambridge: Cambridge University Press, 1997), p. 64.

enjoyed extraordinary longevity. The *Courante* and the *Tijdinghen* lasted fifty-two and fifty-three years respectively; the *Ordinarise Middel-weeckse Courante* (1638–1669) and the *Ordinaris Dingsdaegsche Courante* (1640–1671), among the first mid-week papers published in Europe, lasted over thirty years. The Amsterdam newspapers could not have flourished without a sophisticated system of distribution, but the process by which this network was established and maintained has attracted very little attention.[8] More is known of the international reach of Dutch newspapers in the seventeenth century than their domestic consumption.[9] Newspapers were sent to London, Paris, Wolfenbüttel, Stockholm, Moscow and beyond, often forwarded by diplomats or mercantile agents established in the Dutch Republic. As a consequence most of the issues of early Dutch newspapers that have survived are today to be found in archives and libraries abroad.[10]

Yet the core market for Dutch newspapers obviously remained in the Dutch Republic. How newspapers reached their readers remains something of a mystery. Most recently scholars have highlighted the role of pedlars and travelling salesmen in the dissemination of current affairs publishing.[11] Early newspapers were certainly distributed by pedlars, though most of the surviving evidence pertains to the eighteenth century rather than the first flourishing of newspapers in the seventeenth.

For newspapers to establish their market the crucial role in this early era seems to have been the relationship established between the publishers and

---

8   Its potential has been recognised: see Laura Cruz, 'From shelf to maps: reconstructing booksellers networks in the seventeenth century Netherlands', in Laura Cruz and Joel Mokyr (eds.), *The Birth of Modern Europe: Culture and Economy, 1400–1800. Essays in Honour of Jan de Vries* (Leiden: Brill, 2010), pp. 61–80; B. van Selm, 'Het komt altemael aen op het distribuweeren: de boekdistributie in de republiek als object van onderzoek', in J.J. Kloek and W.W. Mijnhardt (eds.), *De Productie, Distributie en Consumptie van Cultuur* (Amsterdam: Rodopi, 1991), pp. 89–99: 89–90. See also Craig E. Harline, *Pamphlets, Printing, and Political Culture in the Early Dutch Republic* (Dordrecht: Springer, 1987), p. 83.

9   Ingrid Maier, 'Zeventiende-eeuwse Nederlandse couranten vertaald voor de Tsaar', *Tijdschrift voor Mediageschiedenis*, 12.1 (2009), pp. 27–49, and Ingrid Maier and René Vos, 'Gelezen van Londen tot Moskou: Internationale dimensies van de Oprechte Haerlemse Courant in de zeventiende eeuw', *Haerlem Jaarboek* (2005), pp. 9–32; see also Folke Dahl, *A Bibliography of English Corantos and Periodical Newsbooks, 1620–1642* (Stockholm: Almquist och Wiksell, 1953), and his 'Amsterdam—Earliest Newspaper Centre of Western Europe'.

10   Der Weduwen, *Dutch and Flemish Newspapers*, pp. 5–14; Dahl, *Dutch Corantos*.

11   Jeroen Salman, *Pedlars and the Popular Press: Itinerant Distribution Networks in England and the Netherlands 1600–1850* (Leiden: Brill, 2014), pp. 173, 215–220, and Roeland Harms,

a network of booksellers throughout the Dutch Republic.[12] The Amsterdam bookseller Cornelis Claesz is known to have worked together with printers in Dordrecht, Alkmaar, Rotterdam, Middelburg, Haarlem and Delft in the final decade of the sixteenth century.[13] The Universal Short Title Catalogue (USTC) records over 400 editions printed between 1601 and 1650 for Amsterdam publishers and booksellers by printers in other Dutch cities, including relatively distant towns like Middelburg, Zwolle and Franeker. Publishers in Leiden, The Hague and Utrecht engaged in similar practices, entrusting their publications to printers elsewhere.

These connections were valued and often based on long-lasting business relationships. In his notification of 25 May 1658, Otto Barentsz Smient was worried that an impostor was using his well-known family name to claim payment from booksellers. Collecting payments in person was a well-established practice in the book trade. The wife of Tjerck Claessen, a Leeuwarden bookseller, went on journeys as far as Rotterdam to make a payment to another publisher.[14] Reconstructing these networks in relation to the newspaper market requires attention to another development: the newspaper advertisement.

The Emergence of Advertising

To many newspaper publishers, the periodical was one of many business ventures. It was therefore only natural that they should use their newspaper as a means to advertise their other publications. Publishers hoped that subscribers could perhaps be tempted to complement their weekly newspapers by also purchasing a news pamphlet or an illustrated broadsheet of a siege or battle. Abraham Verhoeven, the first newspaper publisher in Antwerp, frequently used his own news serial, the *Nieuwe Tijdinghen*, to advertise future issues and

---

'Handel in letteren. De ambulante handel in actueel drukwerk in zeventiende-eeuws Amsterdam', *De Zeventiende Eeuw*, 23.2 (2007), pp. 216–229. See also H. Borst, 'Broer Jansz in Antwerpse ogen: de Amsterdamse courantier na de slag bij Kallo in 1638 neergezet als propagandist', *De zeventiende eeuw*, 25.1 (2009), pp. 73–89: 83–84.

12   Der Weduwen, *Dutch and Flemish Newspapers*, pp. 62–67.
13   Bert van Selm, *Een menighte treffelijcke Boecken: Nederlandse Boekhandelscatalogi in het begin van de zeventiende eeuw* (Utrecht: HES Uitgevers, 1987), p. 180.
14   Henk Borst, 'Van Hilten, Broersz. en Claessen. Handel in boeken en actueel drukwerk tussen Amsterdam en Leeuwarden rond 1639', *De zeventiende eeuw*, 8 (1992), pp. 131–138: 133.

other associated prints and maps.¹⁵ In London Nathaniel Butter and Nicholas Bourne likewise experimented with notifications for books in the early 1620s.¹⁶ The most important developments in early advertising took place in the Dutch Republic.¹⁷ The first advertisements were placed in Broer Jansz's *Tijdinghen* in 1621.¹⁸ By the mid-1630s the majority of issues of the *Tijdinghen* and Jan van Hilten's *Courante uyt Italien* carried one or two advertisements—at a time when newspapers in the Holy Roman Empire, Paris, London and Antwerp carried hardly any.¹⁹ Before 1650, over 95% of advertisements placed in the

15 Detailed in Arthur der Weduwen and Andrew Pettegree, *News, Business and the Birth of Modern Advertising: Advertisements and Public Announcements in Dutch and Flemish Newspapers, 1620–1675* (forthcoming, Leiden: Brill, 2019). See also Der Weduwen, *Dutch and Flemish Newspapers*, pp. 326–332.
16 Blanche B. Elliott, *A History of English Advertising* (London: Business Publications Ltd in association with B.T. Batsford Limited, 1962).
17 Arthur der Weduwen, 'From piety to profit: the development of newspaper advertising in the Dutch Golden Age', in Siv Gøril Brandtzaeg, Paul Goring and Christine Watson (eds.), *Travelling Chronicles: Episodes in the History of News and Newspapers from the Early Modern Period to the Eighteenth Century* (Leiden: Brill, 2018), pp. 233–253; W.P. Sautijn Kluit, 'De Amsterdamsche Courant', *Bijdragen voor Vaderlandsche Geschiedenis en Oudheidkunde*, n.s., Fifth part (1868), pp. 209–292: 220–221; Dahl, 'Amsterdam—Earliest Newspaper Centre of Western Europe', p. 183; Bert van Selm, 'Het komt altemael aen op het distribuweeren', pp. 91–92; Borst, 'Van Hilten, Broersz. en Claessen', p. 131; Dick Kranen, *Advertenties van kwakzalvers & meesters in de oprechte Haerlemse Courant, (1656–1733)* (Ede: Kranen, 2007), p. 19; Marika Keblusek, *Boeken in de Hofstad. Haagse Boekcultuur in de Gouden Eeuw* (Hilversum: Verloren, 1997), p. 102; Andrew Pettegree, *The Invention of News: How the World Came to Know About Itself* (New Haven: Yale University Press, 2014), pp. 300–301. Some topical studies of Dutch newspaper advertisements have been published: see P.C.J. van der Krogt, *Advertenties voor kaarten, atlassen, globes e.d. in Amsterdamse kranten, 1621–1811* (Utrecht: Hes & de Graaf, 1985) and Kranen, *Advertenties van kwakzalvers & meesters in de oprechte Haerlemse Courant*.
18 Few issues of Dutch newspapers have survived for the late 1610s and early 1620s. The first dozen notifications of books and prints can be found in the *Tijdinghen uyt verscheyde Quartieren* of 1 March 1621, 8 March 1621, 5 June 1621, 9 April 1622, 7 January 1623, 27 July 1624, 10 August 1624, 31 August 1624, 19 October 1624, 23 November 1624 and in the *Courante uyt Italien* of 10 August 1624 and 21 December 1624.
19 For France, Gilles Feyel, *L'Annonce et la nouvelle: La presse d'information en France sous l'Ancien Régime (1630–1788)* (Oxford: Voltaire Foundation, 2000); for England, R.B. Walker, 'Advertising in London Newspapers, 1650–1750', *Business History*, 15.2 (1973), pp. 112–130, Christine Ferdinand, 'Constructing the frameworks for desire: how newspapers sold books in the seventeenth and eighteenth centuries', and Michael Harris, 'Timely notices: the uses of advertising and its relationship to news during the late seventeenth century', both in Joad Raymond (ed.), *News, Newspapers and Society in Early Modern Britain* (London: Frank Cass, 1999), pp. 141–156 and pp. 157–174; and Michael Harris, 'Printed advertisements: some variations in their use around 1700', in Robin Myers, Michael Harris and Giles Mandelbrote (eds.), *Books For Sale: The Advertising and Promotion of Print since the Fifteenth*

Amsterdam newspapers were placed by booksellers and publishers. Initially such notifications advertised the publication of prints and books which accompanied developing news stories. Engraved maps of battles and sieges of the Thirty Years' War or the Dutch struggle against Spain were popular. By the early 1630s the range of books expanded: the advertisements promoted works of poetry, histories, accounts of explorations, political pamphlets, medicinal or mathematical tracts, academic dissertations or religious texts, such as bibles, commentaries and sermons.

The Dutch book trade dominated newspaper advertising at this stage. A case study of one particular year reveals the extent of this phenomenon. In 1639 four different newspaper publishers were active in Amsterdam. On Saturdays Jan van Hilten published his *Courante*, while Broer Jansz published the *Tijdinghen*. From at least 1635, Jansz had also published a weekly French translation of his paper, the *Nouvelles de divers Quartiers*, on Mondays. Since 1638, François Lieshout had published a weekly paper on Tuesdays, the *Ordinarise Middel-weeckse Courante*; he was joined in 1638 by Joost Broersz, a son of Broer Jansz, who started the *Courante Extra-ordinaire*.[20]

Luckily, almost all 1639 issues of the two oldest weekly newspapers, the *Courante* and the *Tijdinghen*, have survived (see Table 20.1). This was not yet twenty years after the first advertisements appeared, yet already around 80% of their issues carried at least one advertisement. The two newspapers were well known in the Dutch Republic and beyond; the print run of the *Courante* was high enough to warrant the use of two printing presses.[21]

Century (New Castle, Delaware: Oak Knoll Press and London: The British Library, 2009); for Antwerp in the eighteenth century, D. Lyna and I. van Damme, 'A strategy of seduction? The role of commercial advertisements in the eighteenth-century retailing business of Antwerp', *Business History*, 51.1 (2009), pp. 100–121; for the American colonies, Emma Hart, 'A British Atlantic world of advertising? Colonial American "for sale" notices in comparative context', *American Periodicals: A Journal of History, Criticism and Bibliography*, 24.2 (2014), pp. 110–127. A transnational approach is used in Stephen Botein, Jack R. Censer and Harriet Ritvo, 'The Periodical press in eighteenth-century English and French society: a cross-cultural approach', *Comparative Studies in Society and History*, 23.3 (1981), pp. 464–490.

20 This was to change in name to the *Ordinaris Dingsdaegsche Courant* in 1640, and continue as such until 1671.

21 Der Weduwen, *Dutch and Flemish Newspapers*, pp. 181–187; Dahl, *Dutch Corantos*; see also Borst, 'Broer Jansz in Antwerpse ogen'; Michiel van Groesen, 'A week to remember: Dutch publishers and the competition for news from Brazil, 26 August–2 September 1624', *Quaerendo*, 40 (2010), pp. 26–49, and his, '(No) news from the western front: the weekly press of the Low Countries and the making of Atlantic news', *Sixteenth Century Journal*, 44.3 (2013), pp. 739–760.

TABLE 20.1 Amsterdam newspapers, 1639

	CID	TVQ	NDQ	OMWC	CEO
Total number of issues	53	53	52	52	unknown
Extant issues	49	45	24	26	6
Issues with advertisements	39	34	2	5	1
Total number of advertisements	61	43	2	5	1
Total number of advertisers	47	33	1	4	1

Half of the yearly run of François Lieshout's *Ordinarise Middel-weeckse Courante* has survived. Lieshout was an established current affairs publisher, but he had only published his newspaper since the summer of 1638. A new newspaper generally required some time to consolidate in a competitive market. It is therefore not surprising that there are few advertisements in the surviving 1639 issues. Still, Lieshout was popular enough that Evert Kloppenburch, a prolific Amsterdam publisher, advertised at least twice; while Jan Wolfersz in Rotterdam also used the new periodical for his new edition of a journal account of an overseas voyage.[22]

Only six issues of Joost Broersz's *Courante Extra-ordinaire* have survived. This paper was not yet numbered, and it is therefore uncertain how many issues were published in 1639. Only one extant issue contains an advertisement: a news pamphlet on the English invasion of Scotland printed by Broersz himself. As a son of Broer Jansz, Joost Broersz found himself in a similar situation as Lieshout. He was well known in the Amsterdam news industry, specialising in English and Scottish current affairs, but was making his first independent steps in the periodical market. Both Broersz and Lieshout would make rapid strides: by 1645–1646, around 55% of surviving issues of their periodicals featured at least one advertisement.[23]

Twenty-four issues of the *Nouvelles de divers Quartiers* survive. These represents a very interesting case. The *Nouvelles* provided a full translation of the reports in the *Tijdinghen*, but never included the advertisements placed in the Dutch edition. The only advertisements to appear in the *Nouvelles* in 1639 were placed by Jansz himself. Why did Broer Jansz go to the trouble of publishing a

---

22 Der Weduwen, *Dutch and Flemish Newspapers*, pp. 481–486. Jan Wolfersz advertised the *Journael ghehouden op de heenreyse en wederkomste van Oost-Indien* of Zeyger van Rechteren. USTC 1515415.

23 That is, 21 out of 37 issues for Joost Broersz, and 24 out of 45 issues for François Lieshout.

French edition, but not draw on his extensive network of bookselling contacts to offset the production costs and increase his profit? The answer must lie in the intended audience for this French venture. There were certainly a considerable number of potential French-speaking customers in Dutch towns. Since the last decades of the sixteenth century, a large number of Walloon emigrants had made their way to the new state and many prospered in their new homes. They certainly represented a sizeable audience for a French-language newspaper. But it was not necessarily the case that any local bookseller had a large number of French-language titles to advertise to this market.

That said, the complete absence of advertisements is certainly very striking. The reason for this may lie elsewhere. As we will see, the identity of the advertising booksellers and publishers gives a clear indication of the scope of the market for the Dutch newspapers. The absence of advertising in the French newspaper may also give us a significant clue that a large part of the intended market for the *Nouvelles* lay outside the Dutch Republic: either in the Southern Netherlands or in France. At this point, France was served by a single newspaper, the *Gazette*; a flourishing venture but one wholly subservient to the state. In the Southern Netherlands, served by three Dutch and one French-language periodicals at this point, newspapers were also clearly closely aligned with the local state authorities.[24] It is perfectly possible that a considerable potential readership existed in these places for the Dutch newspapers, but this was far too speculative for Dutch advertisers to invest on the hope of a few sales in these more distant markets.

Scholars have long recognised the importance of the *Gazette de Leyde* and other French-language newspapers published in the Dutch Republic in offering an alternative source of news in late seventeenth and eighteenth-century France.[25] What we see here is tantalising evidence that this phenomenon may long predate the establishment of the *Gazette de Leyde* in 1677.[26]

---

24 Der Weduwen, *Dutch and Flemish Newspapers*, pp. 48–60; Paul Arblaster, *From Ghent to Aix: How they Brought the News in The Habsburg Netherlands, 1550–1700* (Leiden: Brill, 2014).

25 See, amongst others, Feyel, *L'Annonce et la nouvelle*; Henri Duranton, Claude Labrosse and Pierre Rétat (eds.), *Les Gazettes Européennes de langue française (XVIIe–XVIIIe siècles)* (Saint-Étienne: Publications de l'Université Saint-Étienne, 1992); and Charles-Henri Depezay, 'Between the French *Gazette* and Dutch French language newspapers', in Brendan Dooley (ed.), *The Dissemination of News and the Emergence of Contemporaneity in Early Modern Europe* (Farnham: Ashgate, 2010), pp. 115–135.

26 Indeed, almost all extant issues of the *Nouvelles de divers Quartiers* are today found in France—but not a single issue survives in The Netherlands.

Advertising and the Book Trade

In total, a minimum of 112 advertisements were placed in Amsterdam newspapers in 1639. One advertisement is concerned with a public sale of art; one with the sale of paper; and two others with the sale of the bookshop of the Amsterdam publisher Jan Evertsz Kloppenburch. The remaining 108 advertisements all publicised new books or prints. Publishers frequently advertised for more than one book in a single advertisement, so these 108 advertisements represent 117 books. The total documented output of books in the Dutch Republic in 1639 is at least 578 books.[27] Taking into account historical loss, it is probable that the 117 works advertised represent approximately 10% of the total annual production of the Dutch Republic.[28] This statistic is testament to the integration of newspaper advertisements in the general book market.

The genre of books advertised is diverse (see Table 20.2). Devotional texts, bibles and sermons were popular. Demand was consistently high, but the market for religious print was competitive. Short religious pamphlets went through many reprints and publishers were keen to notify readers of the latest editions. Works of literature and poetry were likewise popular; some of the most celebrated Dutch literature was published during the first half of the seventeenth century.[29] The majority of books advertised were in Dutch. Eighty-three works were published in Dutch, thirty-three in Latin, four in French, and one in German.[30] While most classical works, histories and works of jurisprudence advertised were published in Latin, the majority of religious works, items of news, literature, poetry and drama were in Dutch.

A significant proportion of the books advertised were relatively small. It was possible to calculate the length of sixty-seven books of the 1639 corpus. Printing them required an average of forty-one sheets. However, if one neglects the four largest works for their abnormally large sheet count (an average of 267 sheets), the average drops to twenty-six sheets. The average sheet count of the smallest half of the corpus is only eight sheets. These include illustrated broad-

---

27 USTC. This statistic includes 34 works advertised in 1639 newspapers which have not survived.
28 Arthur der Weduwen and Andrew Pettegree, 'Publicity and its uses. Lost books as revealed in newspaper advertisements in the seventeenth-century Dutch Republic', in Flavia Bruni and Andrew Pettegree (eds.), *Lost Books. Reconstructing the Print World of Pre-Industrial Europe* (Leiden: Brill, 2016), pp. 202–222.
29 René van Stipriaan, *Het volle leven: Nederlandse literatuur en cultuur ten tijde van de republiek (circa 1550–1800)* (Amsterdam: Prometheus, 2002).
30 The total of 121 does not match with the 117 works advertised, as several books featured more than one language.

TABLE 20.2 1639 book advertisement genres

1639 book advertisements

Classification	Titles
Religion	49
Literature/Poetry	18
History	9
News/Current Affairs	9
Classics	7
Theatre/Drama	4
Economics/Finance	4
Jurisprudence	4
Education	3
Mathematics	3
Geography/Exploration	2
Catalogues	2
Music	1
Medicine	1
Astronomy	1

sheets on the Dutch victory at the Battle of the Downs, news pamphlets, a mathematical treatise, sermons, and a Latin tract on the duties of preachers. Clearly booksellers and publishers did not only pay to see their most substantial works advertised in periodicals. The newspapers reached a sufficiently wide readership willing to purchase shorter, vernacular works. Here one sees a crucial difference between newspapers and book trade or auction catalogues, which contained a larger proportion of Latin and academic works.[31] Such catalogues were largely intended for fellow book trade professionals and serious collectors. They provide a wealth of information on the international scholarly world. Newspaper advertisements portray a more popular section of the book trade, offering a view of an industry in constant transformation.

---

31 Van Selm, *Een menighte treffelijcke Boecken*. See also Broer Jansz, *The Catalogus Universalis: a facsimile edition of the Dutch booktrade catalogues compiled and published by Broer Jansz, Amsterdam 1640–1652*, ed. H.W. de Kooker, introduction translated by A.E.C. Simoni (Utrecht: Hes & De Graaf, 1986).

Around 60% of all book advertisements placed in Amsterdam newspapers in the mid-seventeenth century were placed by Amsterdam booksellers and publishers.[32] Similarly, 62% of book advertisements in the 1639 corpus originate from Amsterdam.[33] This is not surprising; Amsterdam was the most prominent centre of book production in the Low Countries, with at least ninety-one different booksellers active in the city around 1650. This represents around 40% of the known total of 247 booksellers in the entire Dutch Republic. Publishers in Amsterdam could advertise with the Amsterdam newspapermen with relative ease: most bookshops were located close to the central Dam square, where many newspapermen had their premises.

Many prolific Amsterdam publishers were recurring advertisers. In 1639, Evert Kloppenburch advertised on at least seven occasions for five different texts. Marten Jansz Brandt, a specialist in theological works and popular orthodox religious pamphlets, appears nine times for six different books—three of which were written by the Amsterdam preacher Roelof Pietersz. Other prominent publishers include Hendrick Laurensz, Jan Evertsz Kloppenburch and Joost Hartgers. Throughout the mid-seventeenth century, these publishers make regular use of both the *Courante* and the *Tijdinghen*, and later the Tuesday newspapers as well. Each publisher had a particular niche: Hartgers specialised in Dutch literature, theatre, and accounts of voyages, while the Kloppenburchs advertised largely religious works and histories, and Laurensz promoted his medical, religious, and classical works.

Publishers used advertisements with considerable stylistic flair. On 31 December 1639 Joost Hartgers advertised in the *Courante* for an emblem book by Jan Hermansz Krul: the new *Minne-spieghel ter deughden*. Krul was a popular author in the 1630s, and was published at least twenty-six times by at least eight different printers. According to the 1639 advertisement by Hartgers it contained 'various comedies and songs, to which is added a second part, the *Wegh-Wijser der Deughden*, with many new engravings; it is enlarged by a fourth by the author, and larger than the edition published by Cornelis Danckertsz.'[34] The Danckertsz edition had been announced several months earlier in the *Courante*, and in order to draw attention to his own publication, Hartgers emphasised its superior quality. Likewise, Marten Jansz Brandt published many short works by Frans Esausz den Heussen, always described in advertise-

---

32   Table 20.6, in the appendix. See also Der Weduwen and Pettegree, *News, Business and the Birth of Modern Advertising*.
33   67 out of 108 advertisements.
34   *Courante uyt Italien* [henceforth: CID], 53, 31 December 1639.

ments as a preacher on the east side of the island of Vlieland.[35] Den Heussen's *Verdedingh, Vande Leere, Schriften, ende Observatien der Gereformeerde Kercke* was advertised by Brandt in both the *Courante* and the *Tijdinghen* as a text 'against the scandalous libel and lies of Barent Barentsz, Mennonite Bishop on West-Vlieland.'[36] In this way the advertisement could help to stoke contemporary controversy.

Advertisers often noted that their latest publication was an improved or enlarged edition, or that the work was printed in a new format or on exceptionally fine paper. When translations were advertised, usually of Latin, English or French texts, the name of the translator was sometimes supplied, with the assurance that the translation was faithful to the original publication. In addition, the practical value or application of books was accentuated. The publisher Antoni Tielemans emphasised that his *Den Sendtbrief des heylighen Apostels Jude* by Andreas Willetus was 'most useful against the temptations of Popery'.[37] When Broer Jansz advertised for a bible, complete with the psalms, he noted that it was 'most convenient for use in church', given its duodecimo format.[38] Publishers tried to engage a specific audience with their advertisements. When Joost Broersz advertised in his own newspaper for an English Bible, he printed the advertisement in both English and Dutch.[39] He ensured that his bible would be noticeable to the large English immigrant community living in the Dutch Republic. When Hendrick Tjercksz de Vries published a tract on 'Italian accounting' he highlighted that it was the third impression of a popular text, 'very convenient for all merchants, clerks, and accounts.'[40] An edition of Andreas Vesalius' *De Humani Corporis* published by Johannes Janssonius in 1642 was 'most useful for doctors and surgeons, but also for all people interested in anatomy', and a handbook of ordinances and privileges of Amsterdam printed by Jacob Pietersz Wachter was 'most useful for all lawyers and merchants.'[41] Advertisers targeted defined audiences; in so doing they provide useful evidence of the profile of the first subscribers of Dutch newspapers: merchants, lawyers, civil servants, scholars and magistrates.

---

35   Den Heussen's works were advertised by Brandt at least six times between 1638 and 1643.
36   CID 30, 23 July 1639. TVQ 31, 30 July 1639.
37   TVQ 45, 10 November 1640.
38   TVQ 10, 7 March 1643.
39   *Ordinaris Dingsdaegsche Courante* 45, 7 November 1645.
40   CID 43, 26 October 1641.
41   CID 50, 13 December 1642; CID 46, 12 November 1639 and TVQ 47, 19 November 1639.

The National Market

The greatest value of advertising to booksellers was the wide reach of the newspapers. Booksellers throughout the Dutch Republic were guaranteed the attention of a widely dispersed audience by advertising their works in the weekly papers. Extant advertisements allow us, for the first time, to define the extent of this national market quite precisely. A significant minority of advertisements in Amsterdam newspapers were sent in from other towns and cities. In 1639, 47 of 108 advertisements featured works being offered by booksellers or publishers outside of Amsterdam: ten from The Hague, seven from Rotterdam, six from Leiden, five from Haarlem and Leeuwarden, four from Utrecht and Dordrecht, two from Arnhem, and one from Hoorn, Delft, Gouda and Middelburg.[42]

These publishers often used the newspaper to advertise their most notable publications. Anthoni Jansz Tongerloo in The Hague advertised for both his known works in 1639: two separate editions of sermons by the Remonstrant minister Johannes Wtenbogaert.[43] Likewise, the Leeuwarden printer Jan Jansz de Fries advertised on 26 March 1639 for a second edition of Johan van den Sande's *Decisiones Frisicæ sive Rerum in suprema Frisiorum curia judicatarum, libri v*. This large work of jurisprudence was the only work published by De Fries in 1639, and it is likely to have been his major enterprise that year.[44]

For publishers such as Tongerloo and De Fries advertisements played a vital role in bringing new and important publications to the attention of potential purchasers throughout the Republic. But the real significance of the advertisements from our point of view is rather different. They indicate that booksellers and publishers far beyond Amsterdam had regular access to the Amsterdam newspapers. It is likely that many, like the booksellers cheated by Otto Barentsz Smient's impostor, bought newspapers for their own use, as well as onward sale. In the periodical the bookseller could discover the latest publications of his rivals. Enterprising booksellers could order books advertised, and sell them to their local clientele. Additionally, provincial booksellers were incentivised to sell the Amsterdam newspapers to their customers: it could provide extra income, and publicise their own publications to their clientele.

---

42 Six of these advertisements featured booksellers and publishers from more than one town: three from The Hague and Leiden, and one from Amsterdam and Hoorn, Amsterdam and Arnhem, and Amsterdam and The Hague.
43 Advertised in CID 8 and TVQ 8, both 19 February 1639, and in TVQ 13, 26 March 1639.
44 USTC 1023592. The *Decisiones* was almost 70 sheets long—the first edition was published in 1635 by De Fries.

Some archival evidence supports this conjecture. Tjerck Claessen was a Leeuwarden bookseller and printer from 1628 until at least 1641. A small archival collection of receipts highlights the business relationship between Claessen and Jan van Hilten.[45] Van Hilten sent Claessen twelve copies of his *Courante* each week. Claessen was able to sell these copies to local customers and the magistrates of Leeuwarden, to whom he regularly supplied books, ordinances and forms. When Van Hilten printed a special issue of his newspaper on the Dutch victory at the Downs in 1639, he despatched fifty copies to Leeuwarden, as well as twenty-five copies of an effigy of the victorious admiral, Maarten Tromp. Claessen most certainly relied on the *Courante* to keep up to date with events, and the business opportunities these events created. On 4 August 1640 Claes Jansz Visscher, a notable engraver and news publisher, advertised an engraving or illustrated broadsheet of Gelderland, portraying the route of the army of the Prince of Orange on his latest campaign. Claessen wrote to ask for copies to sell on to his customers, and was duly sent a consignment in three days.[46] The business relationship between Claessen and Van Hilten was mutually beneficent. Van Hilten could sell multiple copies of his weekly newspaper and supplementary publications through one local supplier. At the same time Claessen sold the latest periodical news of Amsterdam, generating additional profit for his business, while receiving additional information on what to stock in his shop.

The case of Claessen in Leeuwarden was far from unique. The following map and table (Figure 20.1 and Table 20.3) display the number and location of booksellers and publishers who advertised in Amsterdam newspapers between 1636 and 1645 (see also the appendix, Table 20.6, for a complete table).[47]

Between 1636 and 1645 Amsterdam newspapers carried advertisements for books and prints published in twenty-three towns, by 168 booksellers and publishers. Unsurprisingly, most advertisements were placed for economic and political centres with a large number of booksellers: Amsterdam, Leiden, The Hague, Haarlem, Utrecht and Rotterdam. Apart from Amsterdam, none of these cities were served by a local newspaper during this period. It is probable that there was little need for a local paper, given the proximity of Amsterdam

---

45 Borst, 'Van Hilten, Broersz. en Claessen', pp. 132–135.
46 Borst, 'Van Hilten, Broersz. en Claessen', p. 134.
47 The map is the result of the inspection of 97 % of all surviving issues of Amsterdam newspapers published between 1636 and 1645 (1,121 issues out of a corpus of 1,159). It includes four newspaper publishers: Jan van Hilten, Broer Jansz, his son Joost Broersz, and François Lieshout. Jan Jacobsz Bouman and Mathijs van Meininga, two other publishers active at the time, were excluded on the basis of low survival rates and a minimal number of advertisements.

TABLE 20.3 Advertising booksellers in Amsterdam newspapers, 1636–1645

Province	City	Advertising booksellers
Holland	Alkmaar	2
	Amsterdam	68
	Delft	3
	Dordrecht	4
	Enkhuizen	2
	Gouda	1
	Haarlem	7
	Heusden	1
	Hoorn	2
	Leiden	22
	Rotterdam	7
	The Hague	14
Zeeland	Middelburg	6
	Zierikzee	1
Utrecht	Utrecht	8
Friesland	Franeker	4
	Leeuwarden	5
Gelderland	Arnhem	2
Overijssel	Deventer	3
	Kampen	2
	Zwolle	1
Groningen	Groningen	1
Generality Lands	Den Bosch	1

and the business connection between the booksellers in the major towns and the Amsterdam newspaper publishers.

Yet the newspapers reached far beyond major urban centres. Franeker, with its university, boasted significant book production and consumption. Nearby Leeuwarden provided ample business as the administrative capital of Friesland. Middelburg, Enkhuizen, Hoorn, Kampen, Dordrecht and Delft were naval and commercial hubs. Even peripheral centres of the book trade, located at the frontiers of the Dutch Republic, contributed to the advertising content of the newspapers. Groningen, Arnhem, Den Bosch, Deventer and Zwolle were served by relatively few booksellers and publishers. But they were clearly familiar with the newspapers. Operating in small local markets, publishers such as Jacob van

FIGURE 20.1   Advertisers in Amsterdam newspapers, 1636–1645. Each circle represents a city or town. The number in the circle represents the number of advertising booksellers and publishers from that location. The map is an extract of Johannes Janssonius, *Belgii Foederati Nova Descriptio* (Amsterdam: Johannes Janssonius, 1658).
WIKIMEDIA COMMONS

Biesen in Arnhem or Hans Sas in Groningen would profit greatly from publicising their works on a national platform. Additionally, local readers would be exposed to the wealth of texts published in Amsterdam and the regular digest of news offered by the weekly periodicals.

These figures make clear that the Amsterdam newspapers were fully integrated into the national book market. The Dutch book trade underwent a momentous expansion in the first half of the seventeenth century. The total number of booksellers almost quadrupled between 1600 and 1650, from 68 to

247.[48] Bookselling establishments emerged in numerous towns, some with only a couple of thousand inhabitants. Between 1636 and 1645, thirty-five different cities and towns were served by at least one bookseller. Table 20.4 displays the number of booksellers and publishers active in each town at some point between 1636 and 1645.[49] The table compares the number of active booksellers and publishers to those advertising in Amsterdam newspapers.

Over two-thirds of booksellers in Leiden, The Hague, Rotterdam, Leeuwarden and Franeker used the newspapers to advertise their publications. In some towns, such as Deventer, Arnhem, Heusden and Zierikzee, all active booksellers advertised their wares in the newspapers. Of the twelve towns which do not appear in advertisements, ten only had one bookseller or publisher. In total, 52% of booksellers and publishers in the Dutch Republic advertised in Amsterdam newspapers between 1636 and 1645.

TABLE 20.4 The Dutch book trade in relation to Amsterdam newspaper advertisements, 1636–1645

Cities (34)	Active booksellers/ publishers (318)	Booksellers/publishers advertising in Amsterdam newspapers (167, 52%)	Total number of advertisements (758)
Amsterdam	114	68 (59%)	481
Leiden	33	22 (67%)	57
Utrecht	20	8 (40%)	32
Dordrecht	19	4 (21%)	18
The Hague	18	14 (78%)	37
Haarlem	13	7 (54%)	19
Hoorn	10	2 (20%)	6
Middelburg	10	6 (60%)	8
Delft	9	3 (33%)	8
Rotterdam	9	7 (78%)	27
Leeuwarden	7	5 (71%)	15
Enkhuizen	6	2 (33%)	5
Franeker	5	4 (80%)	9

---

48   J.A. Gruys and C. de Wolf, *Thesaurus Nederlandse boekdrukkers en boekverkopers tot 1700 met Plaatsen en Jaren van Werkzaamheid* (Nieuwkoop: HES & de Graaf, 1980).

49   The statistics on booksellers/publishers come from Gruys and de Wolf, *Thesaurus Nederlandse boekdrukkers en boekverkopers tot 1700*.

TABLE 20.4 The Dutch book trade in relation to Amsterdam newspaper advertisements (*cont.*)

Cities (34)	Active booksellers/ publishers (318)	Booksellers/publishers advertising in Amsterdam newspapers (167, 52%)	Total number of advertisements (758)
Gouda	5	1 (20%)	1
Groningen	5	1 (20%)	2
Alkmaar	4	2 (50%)	2
Gorinchem	4	0 (0%)	0
Kampen	4	2 (50%)	3
Deventer	3	3 (100%)	4
Zwolle	3	1 (33%)	4
Arnhem	2	2 (100%)	16
Den Bosch	2	1 (50%)	1
Zutphen	2	0 (0%)	0
Bergen op Zoom	1	0 (0%)	0
Beverwijk	1	0 (0%)	0
Harderwijk	1	0 (0%)	0
Heusden	1	1 (100%)	1
Medemblik	1	0 (0%)	0
Nijmegen	1	0 (0%)	0
De Rijp	1	0 (0%)	0
Sneek	1	0 (0%)	0
Tholen	1	0 (0%)	0
Zaandam	1	0 (0%)	0
Zierikzee	1	1 (100%)	2

Jan van Hilten and Broer Jansz

Publishers with a relatively large and well-known output could afford to advertise in more than one Amsterdam newspaper on a regular basis. Marten Jansz Brandt, Joost Hartgers, Hendrick Laurensz, the widow and heirs of Hillebrant Jacobsz van Wouw, Paulus Aertsz van Ravesteyn, and many others are regularly found advertising in several newspapers in the space of one or two weeks. These publishers had an interest in maintaining their hard-won business position, and they had the capital to invest in frequent advertising.

TABLE 20.5 The number of advertising booksellers and publishers in the newspapers of Jan van Hilten and Broer Jansz, 1636–1645

Province	City	Jan van Hilten	Broer Jansz
Holland	Alkmaar	0	2
	Amsterdam	57	40
	Delft	3	0
	Dordrecht	4	3
	Enkhuizen	2	1
	Gouda	1	0
	Haarlem	7	4
	Heusden	1	0
	Hoorn	1	1
	Leiden	11	14
	Rotterdam	5	4
	The Hague	13	4
Zeeland	Middelburg	5	2
	Zierikzee	1	0
Utrecht	Utrecht	7	3
Friesland	Franeker	4	0
	Leeuwarden	3	5
Gelderland	Arnhem	2	2
Overijssel	Deventer	3	0
	Kampen	2	1
	Zwolle	1	0
Groningen	Groningen	0	1
Generality Lands	Den Bosch	0	1

The pattern was rather different with booksellers and publishers in the smaller towns. Here, the national reach of the Amsterdam newspapers encouraged the consolidation of local monopolies. Thomas Pieter Baart was a bookseller active in Alkmaar throughout the period 1619–1636. Baart subscribed to Broer Jansz's *Tijdinghen*, which he sold on to local customers. At his death in 1636, Baart owed Jansz 154 *gulden* and 11 *stuivers* for copies of the paper supplied to him.[50] While three other booksellers were active in Alkmaar during this period, Baart

---

50   Borst, 'Broer Jansz in Antwerpse ogen', p. 83.

ensured that he was the only bookseller to act as an agent for Jansz. As such Baart and Jansz came to an effective commercial understanding: Jansz delegated the sale of his paper in and around Alkmaar to Baart, who then operated a local monopoly on the sale of periodical news. Pieter Thomasz Baart, the son of Thomas Pieter Baart, took over his father's shop after his death. On 25 July 1637, the son advertised in the *Tijdinghen* for a chronicle of the house of Egmond.[51] No advertisements from Alkmaar can be found in Jan van Hilten's *Courante*, and it seems that Broer Jansz was able to corner the local Alkmaar market.

It is very well possible that booksellers in other locations operated with similar arrangements. The following table (Table 20.5) displays the advertising connections of Jan van Hilten and Broer Jansz for the years 1636–1645. It portrays the number and location of booksellers and publishers advertising with each newspaper publisher. It is clear that Van Hilten maintained a wider network of advertisers then Jansz. Three publishers from Delft and Deventer advertised in Van Hilten's *Courante*; so did four from Franeker. None of these placed advertisements in Jansz's *Tijdinghen*. Van Hilten also had contacts in Gouda, Heusden, Zierikzee and Zwolle who do not appear in Jansz's newspaper. In larger cities, such as Amsterdam, Haarlem, The Hague, Utrecht and Middelburg, Van Hilten enjoyed a more varied clientele. For his part, Jansz enjoyed unrivalled connections in Alkmaar, Den Bosch, and Groningen. Leiden provides interesting results; out of twenty-two advertising publishers, only four advertised in the newspapers of both Van Hilten and Jansz. The rest advertised only in one or the other.

Van Hilten was twenty years old when he took over the *Courante* from his father, Caspar, in 1623. Originally from Hamburg, Van Hilten was primarily a publisher, not a printer.[52] For the first two decades of his career as a newspaper publisher, Van Hilten did not print the *Courante* himself. Instead Van Hilten dedicated himself to his publishing contacts. He had an understanding with Abraham Casteleyn, then a notable newsletter writer in Haarlem, who supplied him with exclusive news. The range of Van Hilten's sources was indeed greater than that of Broer Jansz, and Dutch playwright P.C. Hooft considered Van Hilten's *Courante* the more reliable.[53] Jansz, born in 1579, was twenty-four years older than Van Hilten.[54] Before he started the *Tijdinghen*, he was

---

51 USTC 1011715. TVQ 30, 25 July 1637.
52 See Kleerkoper and Van Stockum, *De Boekhandel te Amsterdam*, pp. 260–261.
53 Der Weduwen, *Dutch and Flemish Newspapers*, pp. 15–23. P.C. Hooft to Joost Baak, 25 August 1631, letter 474, in W. van Tricht, et. al. (eds.), *De briefwisseling van Pieter Corneliszoon Hooft*, II (Culemborg: Tjeenk Willink/Noorduijn, 1977), p. 233.
54 See Kleerkoper and Van Stockum, *De Boekhandel te Amsterdam*, pp. 322–324.

already a seasoned printer, specialising in news pamphlets and broadsheets. He prided himself on his first-hand experience at the front as a news hound: he styled himself 'former *courantier* in the Army of the Prince'. He was considered more patriotic by contemporaries and by more recent scholars of the newspapers.[55]

The two men were by no means cutthroat rivals. Van Hilten's printer, Jan Fredericksz Stam, worked together with Jansz on various publications, and Broer Jansz occasionally advertised in Van Hilten's *Courante*. Still, the business of news was not a romantic industry. In a competitive periodical market, it paid to have the better of one's competitor. Van Hilten's experience as a publisher— as opposed to Jansz's career as a printer—allowed him to maintain a wider network of correspondents and advertising booksellers. The reputation of the *Courante* may have convinced some booksellers and publishers to advertise with Van Hilten instead of Jansz. The extant advertisements pay tribute to Van Hilten's business success.

Conclusions

Before newspaper advertisements first appeared in the Dutch Republic in 1621, thousands of books were bought, sold and exchanged throughout the country. The emergence of newspapers advertisements did not fundamentally alter the Dutch print industry. The strength of the Dutch economy, the relative high rates of urbanisation and literacy and the important role of the Republic in the international market had turned the Dutch Republic, and especially Holland, into a major centre of the book trade. Still the rapid proliferation of advertisements in Amsterdam newspapers marks an important development in the history of the early press. The competitive periodical industry of Amsterdam was integrated into a wider, national market of print. Booksellers and publishers rapidly turned to the weekly papers as an additional means of promotion and exchange. The Amsterdam newspaper publishers maintained direct relations with many provincial traders. Publishers in Middelburg could expect booksellers in Utrecht or Arnhem to see the titles they advertised. Popular Amsterdam publishers highlighted their latest publications to newspaper readers in Friesland, Zeeland and Overijssel, which these readers could then request from their local bookseller.

---

55 Der Weduwen, *Dutch and Flemish Newspapers*, pp. 260–263. See also Van Groesen, '(No) news from the western front', and Borst, 'Broer Jansz in Antwerpse ogen'.

Jan van Hilten, Broer Jansz, François Lieshout and Joost Broersz were shrewd in recognising the value of the advertisement. It added a distinct feature to the periodical, otherwise largely filled with foreign diplomatic and military news. Delegating the sale of newspapers to booksellers minimised the effort required to build a network of subscribers, and to chase up overdue payments.[56] It also strengthened the commercial bonds between Amsterdam publishers and provincial booksellers. Reconstructing the distribution networks of the early press remains a challenging task, but we can say a great deal more as a result of the evidence that can be extracted from a study of advertisements.

Appendix. Booksellers and Publishers Advertising in Amsterdam Newspapers, 1636–1645

TABLE 20.6 Booksellers and publishers advertising in Amsterdam newspapers, 1636–1645

Advertisements, 1636–1645		Jan van Hilten	Broer Jansz	Joost Broersz	François Lieshout
Alkmaar	Pieter Thomas Baart		x		
	Symon Cornelisz Brekegeest		x		
Amsterdam	Jan Albertsz		x		
	Jan Banningh	x	x		
	Francois van Beusekom	x			
	Abraham Biestkens	x			
	Joan Blaeu	x	x		
	Willem Jansz Blaeu	x	x		
	Jan Jacobsz Bouman		x		
	Jacques Bourse	x			
	Marten Jansz Brandt	x	x	x	
	Joost Broersz	x	x	x	x
	Joseph Bruyningh	x			
	Claes Jansz Bruyningh				x
	Jan Bruynsz	x			
	Pieter de la Burgh	x			
	Jacob Aertsz Colom		x		

---

56 See also R.M. Wiles, *Freshest Advices: Early Provincial Newspapers in England* (Columbus: Ohio State University Press, 1965).

TABLE 20.6 Booksellers and publishers advertising in Amsterdam newspapers, 1636–1645 (*cont.*)

Advertisements, 1636–1645	Jan van Hilten	Broer Jansz	Joost Broersz	François Lieshout
Cornelis Danckertsz	×	×		×
Louis Elzevier	×			
Joost Hartgers	×	×	×	×
Hendrick Barentsz Hartogsvelt		×		
Jacob Heerman	×	×		
Jan van Hilten	×			
Rombout van der Hoeyen			×	
Henricus Hondius	×			
Dirck Cornelis Houthaeck	×	×		
Theunis Jacobsz	×	×		
Johannes Jacott	×	×		
Johannes Janssonius	×	×		
Broer Jansz	×	×		
Gerrit Jansz	×		×	
Cornelis Jansz	×	×		
Gillis Joosten	×			
Evert Kloppenburch	×	×		×
Jan Evertsz Kloppenburch	×	×		
Willem van der Laech	×			
Hendrick Laurensz	×	×		
Cornelis de Leeuw	×			
Jacob Lescaille	×			
François Lieshout	×	×		
Jan Marcusz	×	×		
Paulus Matthijsz	×			
Abraham Meindertsz			×	
Dirck Meyer	×	×	×	
Pieter Nolp	×			
Joachim Nosch		×		
Cornelis Lodewijksz van der Plasse	×			
Dirck Pietersz Pers	×	×		
Boudewijn de Preys	×			
Nicolaes van Ravesteyn	×	×		×
Jan Rieuwertsz	×			
Adriaen Roman	×			

TABLE 20.6 Booksellers and publishers advertising in Amsterdam newspapers, 1636–1645 (*cont.*)

Advertisements, 1636–1645		Jan van Hilten	Broer Jansz	Joost Broersz	François Lieshout
	Salomon Savry		×		
	Jacques vander Schuere		×		
	Pieter Jansz Slijp				×
	Otto Barentsz Smient	×			
	Jan Fredericksz Stam	×	×		
	Willem Stam	×	×		
	Thomas Stafford	×			
	Dominicus vander Stichel	×			
	Antoni Tielemans	×	×		
	Johannes Troost	×			
	Denijs Verschuere	×	×		
	Aeltje Verwou (wed. B. v. Dorsten)	×			
	Claes Jansz Visscher	×	×		
	Hendrick Tjerck de Vries	×	×		
	Jacob Pietersz Wachter	×	×		
	Pieter Walschaert	×	×	×	
	Abraham de Wees	×	×		
	Gerrit Willemsz	×			×
Arnhem	Jacob van Biesen	×	×	×	×
	Jan Jacobsz	×	×		
Bremen	Berthold Villerius	×			
Delft	Andries Cloeting	×			
	Felix van Sambix de Jonge	×			
	Jan Pietersz Waelpot	×			
Den Bosch	Jan van Dockum			×	
Deventer	Charles Hoornaert	×			
	Conraet Thomasz	×			
	Willem Willemsz	×			
Dordrecht	François Boels	×	×		×
	Michiel Feermans	×			
	Jasper Goris	×	×		
	Mathias Havius	×	×		
Emden	H. Fresenborgh	×			
Enkhuizen	Volchardt Camerlingh	×			
	Albert Wesels Kluppel	×	×		

TABLE 20.6 Booksellers and publishers advertising in Amsterdam newspapers, 1636–1645 (*cont.*)

Advertisements, 1636–1645		Jan van Hilten	Broer Jansz	Joost Broersz	François Lieshout
Franeker	Ids Alberts	×			
	Johannes Arserius	×			
	Uldrick Balck	×			
	Hans Fabiaen Duringh	×			
Gouda	Pieter Rammazeyn	×			
Groningen	Hans Sas		×		
Haarlem	Thomas Fonteyn	×	×		
	Hendrick van Marcken	×	×		
	Adriaen Roman	×	×		
	Michiel Segerman	×	×		
	Pieter Soutman	×			
	Robbert Tinneken	×		×	
	Hans van Wesbusch	×			
Hamburg	Arent Pietersz		×		
Heusden	Hendrick van Troyen	×			
Hoorn	Marten Gerbrantsz	×			
	Laurens Willemsz		×		
Kampen	Pieter van Wieringen	×	×		
	Roelof Dircksz Worst	×			
Leeuwarden	Hans Willemsz Coopman		×		
	Claude Fonteyn	×	×		
	Jan Jansz de Fries	×	×		
	Frans Hardomans		×		
	Gijsbert Sybes	×	×		
Leiden	Daniel Burchoorn		×	×	
	Willem Christiaensz		×	×	
	Abraham Commelijn		×		
	Isaac Commelijn		×		
	Adriaen Gerritsz	×			
	Frans Hackius		×		
	Frans de Heeger	×	×		
	David Jansz van Ilpendam	×	×		
	Jacob Lauwijck		×		
	Johannes Lissius	×			
	Justus Livius		×		

TABLE 20.6 Booksellers and publishers advertising in Amsterdam newspapers, 1636–1645 (*cont.*)

Advertisements, 1636–1645		Jan van Hilten	Broer Jansz	Joost Broersz	François Lieshout
	David Lopez de Haro	x			
	Jan Maire		x		
	Jacob Marcusz	x	x		
	Severyn Matthysz	x			
	Frans Moyaert	x		x	
	Paulus Aertsz van Ravesteyn	x	x		
	Jacob Roels	x			
	Felix van Sambix	x			
	Hieronimus de Vogel		x		
	Adriaen Wijngaerden			x	
	Gijsbrecht de Wit		x	x	
Middelburg	Jacob Fierens	x			
	Anthoni de Later	x			
	Michiel Roman		x		
	Zacharias Roman	x	x		
	Jacob van de Vivere	x			
	Johannes de Wilde	x			
Rotterdam	Mathijs Bastiaensz (wed.)		x		
	Arnout Leers	x		x	
	Joannes Naeranus	x	x		
	Bastiaen Wagens			x	
	Isaac van Waesbergen	x	x		
	Pieter van Waesbergen	x	x		
	Jan Wolfersz	x			x
The Hague	Balthasar van Berckenrode	x	x		
	Isaac Burchoorn	x			
	Gijsbrecht Ernst	x			
	Hendrik Hondius	x			
	Dirk Maire	x			
	Simon de Putter		x		
	Juff. Schuermans	x			
	Franck van der Spruyt	x			
	Johan Stampioen	x			
	Anthoni Jansz Tongerloo	x	x		
	Johannes Velen	x			

BOOKSELLERS, NEWSPAPER ADVERTISEMENTS AND A NATIONAL MARKET 447

TABLE 20.6 Booksellers and publishers advertising in Amsterdam newspapers, 1636–1645 (*cont.*)

Advertisements, 1636–1645		Jan van Hilten	Broer Jansz	Joost Broersz	François Lieshout
Utrecht	Jan Vely	×			
	Johannes Verhoeve	×	×		
	Hillebrant van Wouw (wed. en erf.)	×	×		
	Jan van Doorn	×	×		
	Amelis Jansz	×			
	Aegidius Roman	×			
	Esdras Willemsz Snellaert	×			
	Willem Strick	×			
	Lucas Symonsz de Vries	×			
	Jan van Waesbergen		×		
	Gijsbert van Zyl	×	×		
Zierikzee	Balthasar Dol	×			
Zwolle	Gerard Bartjens	×			×

CHAPTER 21

'Without Being Denounced or Humiliated': the Purchase of Books for Religious Communities in New Spain

Idalia Garcia

> People's mobility also facilitated the movement of objects, books, relics, sacred images and above all, ideas [...] Few empires in the world were able to offer their subjects such vast lands or conditions for travel and spreading their ideas over the world's seas.
> ANTONIO RUBIAL (2012)

∴

In October 1660, an inquisitional edict was issued at the request of the Holy Office's prosecutor, Juan de Ortega Montañés, who reported having received:

> [...] intelligence that in the fleet anchored at the fortress of San Juan de Ulúa in the port of New Veracruz, a large number of boxes had arrived containing books whose owners did not have the required licences, some of which were mere scraps of paper, while others had been wrongly drawn up, and no inventories had been presented to the Holy Office's Commissioner in the aforementioned city.[1]

This account, which may have been rather exaggerated, gives some idea of the circulation of books since colonization began at the end of the fifteenth century. The discovery of the New World opened up immense possibilities for

---

1 Archivo General de la Nación (henceforth: AGN), Indiferente Virreinal, Caja 0286, exp. 5, fol. 37r. The original reads: "Edicto inquisitorial diciendo que tiene noticias que en la flota de San Juan de Ulúa puerto de la Nueva—Veracruz, había llegado un número de cajones de libros sin que sus dueños trajesen licencia, por lo que exhorta a todos los vecinos y moradores que habitan el distrito y declaren si han traído libros para sí". Digitized document accessible at http://www.agn.gob.mx/guiageneral/, last accessed: April 2015.

extending not only the frontiers of the Spanish Empire, but also for spreading its culture, commerce and religion. Indeed, the Catholic religion was the closest ally of the conquest and evangelization of the Americas. However, it was also a great source of wealth given the fact that, since the beginning of the sixteenth century, the Crown had virtual control over the Church's finances and personnel.[2]

Moreover, the activity of priests and other members of the church provided an invaluable way to introduce indigenous peoples to the European way of life, a process that began in New Spain in 1524 with the establishment of all the religious orders that worked in this colony. The first to arrive were the Franciscans, followed by the Dominicans, Augustinians, Jesuits, Carmelites and finally the Mercedarians. The following century saw the arrival of regular orders, such as the Bethlehem Brothers also known as Hospitallers, which eventually left a deep mark upon daily life in New Spain. This was a colony administered by civil servants in the interest of the Crown, but where members of the religious orders were always active.

New Spain was a culturally diverse territory stretching from Nicaragua to the American West, and including the Philippines. It was characterized by regulated coexistence between Europeans and the indigenous population. In every corner of these lands religious orders established monasteries, convents, colleges and novitiates where their members lived and were educated, as well as schools for both the indigenous peoples and new generations of Spaniards. The early years were a time of construction and reconstruction of many religious buildings practically all over New Spain. This was later followed by a period of consolidation for all these foundations, including the development of libraries built up ever since the sixteenth century. All these collections, except those of the Jesuits, were in use right up to the passage of the Leyes de Reforma (Reform Laws) in 1859, which nationalized church property. The tragic fate of these libraries was exacerbated by the subsequent closure of the monasteries in 1860 and convents for women the following year. By the second half of the nineteenth century, many of these collections had been lost altogether, while the remainders were dispersed throughout Mexico and abroad and found their way into other libraries.

As for Jesuit libraries, the process of dispersal began as early as 1767. The expulsion of the Company of Jesus from the lands of the Spanish Crown led to the confiscation of large collections of books by the Junta de Temporalidades,

---

2 William S. Maltby, *Auge y caída del imperio español*, transl. Jesús Cuéllar Menezo (Madrid: Marcial Pons Historia, 2011), pp. 122–123.

which supervised Jesuit property and its subsequent transfer of ownership. Charles III's decrees established that these collections were to be absorbed by other institutions, such as universities and seminaries, once any material considered harmful had been expurgated. However, the process in New Spain was very disorganized resulting in considerable losses.[3] Books were reported stolen and the collections deteriorated because of the unsuitable conditions in which they were stored. Even though the king had ordered very detailed inventories of the collections to be drawn up when the Jesuits were expelled, in some places it was necessary to compile new inventories to identify these losses. This was the case for the library of the Jesuit College of Santa Maria de Parras, where separate inventories were drawn up in 1767 and again in 1784.[4]

This case is an exception, given that very few of the surviving inventories provide information on Jesuit libraries. The same can be said of the libraries of other religious orders for which little evidence remains. When investigating these libraries, we must take careful note of provenance information, such as the handwritten notes, ex-libris and stamps. These can tell us that a specific book belonged to a member of a religious order, a monastery or convent, a novitiate or a seminary. Information on the content of New Spain's libraries can also be found in two types of documentary sources. The first are the "licenses to censor" which provide information about the communal and private libraries of religious foundations. These licenses were issued to a priest so he could expurgate the books of a specific monastery or convent, or of the foundations in a specific province. One such example is the license given to Father Marcos Coronel, prior of the Monastery of Zacatecas, allowing him to expurgate the books "of the library of the said monastery and also the books used by members of that monastery".[5] The inquisitional inspections of libraries referred to in these documents were carried out every time a new Spanish index of prohibited books was published. These documents can also provide information

---

3   Carlos Alberto Martínez Tornero, 'Las Temporalidades jesuitas. Aproximación al funcionamiento administrativo después de la expulsión de la Compañía de Jesús en 1767', in *Esteban de Terreros y Pando: vizcaíno, polígrafo y jesuita. III Centenario: 1707–2007* (Bilbao: Instituto de Estudios Vascos, Universidad de Deusto, 2008), pp. 527–550: 546.

4   AGN, Temporalidades, vol. 172, exp. 6, fols. 27r–47v. "Pueblo de Parras, 1784. Expediente que instruye el reconocimiento de la Librería de esta Ocupación hecho por el actual Comisionado con el más prolijo escrutinio, expresión de valores de dichos libros; con separación de los que faltan en el día, y precio de ellos; è igualmente supernumerarios que se encontraron, como más por menor se percibe del mismo expediente" (1784). In Jesuit documents, a Jesuit institution that has been taken under the tutelage of the viceregal authorities is called "ocupación".

5   AGN, Inquisición, vol. 763, exp. 2, fol. 213r. "Inquisición de México. Año de 1716. Cuaderno de las calificaciones que remitieron los Provinciales de las Religiones de este Reino de la Nueva

about the size of collections. For example, the Franciscan Angel García Duque reported that, in 1717, he had expurgated 2,000 books belonging to the Colegio de la Santa Cruz in Querétaro.[6]

The second type of documentary source is the lists of books purchased in Europe for the libraries of religious houses, colleges and seminaries in New Spain. These lists are somewhat rarer, but they provide titles and the number of volumes which were imported to enrich the libraries of religious communities across the Atlantic. To-date, interest in the study of this evidence has been very limited. As far as I know, only two studies have been published: one by Klaus Wagner on the Dominicans of Coyoacán in Mexico City, and the other by Pedro Rueda on the Augustinians of the city of Puebla de los Angeles.[7] In her study dealing with the book trade in the eighteenth century Cristina Gómez Álvarez also mentions acquisitions by priests and other members of religious orders.[8] Both Wagner and Rueda studied orders for books to be bought in Europe. These documents are similar to one recently-found example. It was written by the Jesuit Joaquín de Donazan in the Hacienda de San José, on 29 March 1721. He sent fifty pesos through the Brother Procurator, Juan Nicolás, to Fathers Gaspar Rodero and Diego Velez, procurators in Rome, for the purchase of the following books:

> La vida de Nuestro Santo Padre Ignacio por el padre Francisco Garcia
> La vida de San Francisco Xavier por el mismo padre Garcia
> Origen de la Compañia por el padre Revade Neira
> todos los tomos de Varones Ilustres de la Compañia
> Las Platicas del Padre Juan Martinez de la Parra
> Año Virgineo por el Doctor Don Esteban Dolz del Castellar
> Un libro de Medicina por el hermano Estainefer
> La Corte Santa por el padre Causino

España, y de las Islas Filipinas, de haberse expurgado según el Nuevo Expurgatorio el año de 1707, los libros de las Librerías de los Conventos de cada Provincia, y de los Religiosos particulares de ellos".

6 "Inquisición de México. Año de 1716", fol. 208r.
7 Klaus Wagner, 'Libros para el convento de Santo Domingo de Coyoacán', *Historiografía y bibliografía americanistas*, 23 (1979), pp. 117–119; Pedro Rueda Ramírez, 'El abastecimiento de libros de la biblioteca conventual de San Agustín de Puebla de los Ángeles a través de la Carrera de las Indias (1609–1613)', *Estudios de Historia Novohispana*, 44 (2011), pp. 17–43 (the latter freely available at: http://www.revistas.unam.mx/front/, last accessed 19 May 2018).
8 Cristina Gómez Alvarez, *Navegar con libros: el comercio de libros entre España y Nueva España: una visión cultural de la Independencia 1750–1820* (Madrid: UNAM; Trama Editorial, 2011), pp. 72–74.

Las obras del padre Eusebio Nierember
Las obras de padre Luis de la Puente
Las obras del padre Aguado
Doctrina del Cardenal Bellarmino
Guerras civiles de Francia por Henrique Catherino
La Cima de Inglaterra por el padre Revade Neyra
La Coronica de San Francisco por Cornexo
Los libros de David.[9]

No more similar documents have surfaced to-date in Mexico, but this book list provides an insight into the interest shown by members of religious orders in the writings of a range of authors. Moreover, as Wagner and Rueda have pointed out, it also demonstrates interest in the works of members of one's own religious order. In this case, most of the authors are Jesuits: Roberto Bellarmino, Nicolas Causino, Juan de Esteyneffer, Francisco García, Juan Martínez de la Parra from New Spain, Juan Eusebio Nieremberg, Luis de la Puente and Pedro de Ribadeneira. The list seems modest for a Jesuit institution, but we must not forget that they were ordered for an *hacienda* (estate) and not for a college or novitiate. For this reason, the request for the *Florilegio medicinal* of Esteyneffer is not surprising, given that only the Jesuit educational institutions employed doctors.

There is other evidence of boxes of books being exported from Europe to the Viceroyalty of New Spain directly by members of religious orders. The procurators of the orders were mainly responsible for these purchases, although in some cases the task was delegated to *definidores* or by some other member of the order such as a retired preacher.[10] The procurators were members of religious orders who, both in Europe and the Americas, were responsible for providing for virtually every need in a religious province including clothing, food, money and, of course, books.[11] In the documentation we find the

---

9   AGN, Indiferente Virreinal, Caja 5284, exp. 16, fol. 83r. "Año de 1721. Memoria de los libros que se enviaron a comprar a España con los padres Gaspar Rodero y Diego Vélez que salieron de México a 2 de abril de 1721 y llegaron cincuenta pesos para dichos libros". A digital reproduction is available at http://www.agn.gob.mx/guiageneral/, last accessed January 2015.

10   "Definidores" is expressed as: "the title given in several religious orders to those who are chosen from the superiors and members of the order gathered together in a general or provincial chapter to organize the affairs of the order, the province or the congregation", as given in Nicolas Sylvestre Bergier, *Diccionario de teología* (10 vols, Madrid: Imp. D. Primitivo Fuentes, 1846), II, p. 23.

11   For instance, about money transfers see: AGN, Indiferente Virreinal, Caja 1243, exp. 3, fol. 1r.

names and positions of each one of the members involved in this export of books. However, little reference is made to the booksellers and merchants who undoubtedly participated in this transatlantic trade. This is another aspect of the market which requires further research. The reconstruction of these commercial networks will allow us to understand how the market in New Spain was supplied with the variety of European editions which circulated throughout Spanish America.

Among this body of evidence are two particularly interesting documents involving the Jesuit Francisco de Florencia who bought several books for the province of New Spain. Although neither of these two surviving documents is dated, they indicate the position held by Florencia.[12] This enables us to deduce that the purchases were made between 1669 and 1678 given that during those years Florencia was appointed procurator, initially for the curiae of Madrid and Rome and, after 1671, for all Jesuit provinces in the Americas. At the end of this period, Father Florencia returned to New Spain where he was director of two Jesuit colleges until his death.[13] During this time he also wrote several works including a history of the Jesuits in New Spain and a number of texts dedicated to the Virgin of Guadalupe.[14] This documentation is particularly important because it includes the price of each item and, although this is not in fact the only book list containing this information, such lists are quite rare. To date, I have found only three other similar documents: one about twelve boxes intended for the Monastery of Saint Francis in Mexico City in 1698, the second concerning three boxes sent to the Carmelites in 1788 and the third about another box intended for the same order in 1791.[15]

"Padre Bernardo Rolandegui de la Compañía de Jesús, Procurador General de la Provincia de México, Veracruz. Sobre haber recibido del padre Francisco Aragón, Jesuita y procurador de Filipinas, 750 pesos en doblones, puestos a embarcarlos a Cádiz y entregarlos al procurador de Indias (1700)", freely accessible at http://www.agn.gob.mx/guiageneral/, last accessed May 2015.

12 AGN, Indiferente Virreinal, Caja 5707, in particular ff. 5–6. "Memoria de los libros que ha comprado el Padre Procurador Francisco de Florencia para la provincia de Nueva España, y el costo de ellos".
13 Jason Dyck, 'La parte censurada de la Historia de la Provincia de Francisco de Florencia', *Estudios de Historia Novohispana*, 44 (2011), pp. 143–144.
14 Francisco de Florencia, *Historia de la Provincia de la Compañia de Jesus de Nueva-España: dividida en ocho libros* (Mexico: Juan Joseph Guillena Carrascoso, 1694) CCPB000052251-1; *La estrella de el Norte de Mexico aparecida al rayar el dia de la luz evangelica en este Nuevo-Mundo ... en la historia de la milagrosa imagen de N. Señora de Guadalupe de Mexico ...* (Mexico: Maria de Benavides, widow of Juan de Ribera, 1688), CCPB000052249-X.
15 AGN, Inquisición, vol. 76, exp. 6, fols. 178r–202r. "Diligencias que se hicieron por unos cajones de libros prohibidos que se detuvieron en la aduana de México y que estaban

Books Sent to Monasteries

Many books were brought to New Spain by their owners, both laymen and members of religious orders. These people crossed the Atlantic from Europe to the Americas in search of a new life; for those belonging to religious orders such travel was constant throughout the colonial period.[16] There were two ways to legally export books across the Atlantic during the period of Spanish rule; one was the regulated trade and the other was the export of a person's books along with their other personal belongings. The book trade has been studied for several decades based on the trail of papers documenting the circulation of books between Europe and the Americas. Such studies have been greatly facilitated by the enormous quantity of documentation generated by the regulations of the time, which demanded the declaration of all merchandise exchanged between Europe and America. Every box was registered at the port of departure and again on arrival at its destination.

Declarations of books being exported included details of each item contained in the boxes so that the appropriate taxes could be levied in Seville or Cadiz, and each box had to be identified with a special merchant's mark. Although books had been exempt from the *almojarifazgo* (customs duty) since 1480, they were still subject to the *avería*.[17] In other words, under Spanish rule, the book trade was not taxed, but was charged a levy to cover the expense of providing armed escorts for merchant vessels. Inventories of books included in the "Registro de navíos" (a list of merchandise) would also be examined by inquisitional inspectors who controlled the trade between Spain and the colonies. Once their authorization had been obtained and dues paid, the books could be shipped.[18] These lists were checked again on arrival at the Spanish American port, where the boxes were opened to cross-check that information.

---

destinados al Convento de San Francisco de México. Se cita la causa del Beato Sebastián de Aparicio (1698)". AGN, Inquisición, vol. 1231, exp. 14, ff. 331r–334v. "Fray Valentín de la Madre de Dios, presenta la lista de trece cajones de libros que le remite el padre Fray Ignacio de San Juan Bautista, para el uso de los Padres Carmelitas de esta Provincia de México (1788)". AGN, Inquisición, vol. 1348, ff. 5r–6r. "Fr. Valentín de la Madre de Dios solicita se le entregue un cajón de libros que remite el Reverendo Padre Fr. Ignacio de San Juan Bautista, para el uso de los Carmelitas México, 1791".

16 Antonio Rubial, 'Religiosos viajeros en el mundo hispánico en la época de los Austrias (El caso de Nueva España)', *Historia Mexicana*, 61.3 (January–March 2012), pp. 813–848: 818.
17 Details can be found in the *Recopilación de leyes de los Reinos de las Indias* (4 vols, Madrid: por Julian de Paredes, 1681), III, f. 79r, Ley XXVII, Libro VIII, Titulo XV.
18 Natalia Maillard Álvarez, 'Aproximación a la creación de las redes de distribución de libros en América a través de las fuentes españolas (segunda mitad del siglo XVI)', *Anuario de Estudios Americanos*, 71.2 (July–December 2014), pp. 479–503: 498.

It is no wonder, therefore, that Father Joseph de Vidal, Procurator General of the Jesuits in New Spain complained that "the opening of these boxes gave rise to many denunciations as well as to inconvenience and humiliation".[19]

It was perhaps in order to avoid this situation that a few members of religious orders approached the Supreme Council of the Inquisition directly for exemption from the second part of this process, and not to have to undergo the mandatory inspection. This meant that the boxes would be opened on arrival in Mexico City, but not in Veracruz. Several of these requests were indeed granted, such as the one from the Jesuit Manuel de Villabona, Procurator General of the Provinces in the Indies on April 23, 1671, in which he:

> wrote a note explaining that he was sending the colleges and houses of the Company in the Province of Mexico three boxes of books numbered one, two and three, and branded with an image of Jesus, the declaration of which he presented to us requesting that, owing to the possible damage that would be caused by their being opened, and given that they are permitted works, not ones proscribed or identified for confiscation by the Holy Office, we hereby order that ... no impediment be put in his way ... Having examined this request and being aware that the books have been inspected, we issue the following order to you and to whomever it may concern that the person transporting the aforementioned three boxes of books be allowed free passage without let or hindrance and with no tax being levied, under penalty of a fine of twenty thousand maravedíes.[20]

Requests like this one are not unusual; here we quote only this one example that was approved in Madrid by inquisitors Martín de Castellón, Antonio de Ariola and Álvaro de Valenzuela y Mendoza, and countersigned by secretary Diego Ruvalcaba. Unfortunately, in this case the list of books is missing from the file. In another document Villabona states that the boxes were sent by the Procurator Juan de Ribadeneira; he refers to the loss of a fourth box because it was impounded and kept for almost a year at the customs where "damp rotted the most valuable books", and states that the list also contained the "prices

---

19   AGN, Inquisición, Caja 1579A, exp. 1, fol. 1r. "Petición del Procurador General de la Compañía de Jesús, Joseph Vidal, para que los libros se revisen directamente en el Santo Oficio (1601)".

20   AGN, Indiferente Virreinal, Caja 1722, exp. 30, fol. 1r. "Provisión dada por el Santo Oficio de la Inquisición para que se permitiera el paso a los 3 cajones de libros que remitió Manuel de Villabona religioso de la Compañía de Jesús, a las casas y colegios de la Compañía de la Provincia de México. Madrid (1671)".

valid here".[21] This documentation also allows us to infer that the boxes were not examined as thoroughly in Spain as they were in the Spanish American ports, for no reports have been found of delay or loss of merchandise in trials held in Spain.

In contrast, in documentation from the Americas we discover evidence not only of the inspection of book lists but also the examination of the boxes themselves. I refer here to a case begun in September 1620 when Santiago de Estrada requested that the Inquisition release four boxes of books containing three hundred copies of the *Templo militante y vidas de santos* by Bartolomé de Carrasco. In response to this request, the inquisitors ordered the boxes be examined by the inspector Bartolomé Gómez, Rector of the Jesuit College of Santo Domingo de Porta Coeli, who, on the 15 of December of that same year certified that:

> [...] the four boxes of books mentioned in this memorandum were opened in my presence. Only the books listed in the said inventory were found, none of which is prohibited or included in the new index of titles to be expurgated.[22]

The other method permitted of transporting books was that they were taken by people making the voyage in order to be reunited with family members or to take up a post as a civil servant in the Indies, or when a member of a religious order was joining a community or mission. The inquisitors had to be notified about these books in a document covering what we may call "books being used". This phrase is borrowed from the very words employed by those making the declaration about the books being imported "in use or in their possession". This declaration was presented by every traveller journeying with books between the two continents, whether they were laymen or members of a religious order.

---

21   "Cartas de Manuel de Villabona a los Procuradores de Nueva España Juan Vallejo y Eugenio de Losa, con noticias personales, de negocios, en pleito en Guatemala, remisión de libros y demás. Madrid (1670)", AGN, Indiferente Virreinal, Caja 1722, exp. 31, fols 5v–6r. A digitization is freely accessible at http://www.agn.gob.mx/guiageneral/, last accessed: May 2015.

22   AGN, Indiferente Virreinal, Caja 5486, exp. 3, fols 1r–2v. "Carta que Santiago de Estrada, Notario del Santo Oficio, remite a la Inquisición de México en la que notifica el envío de cuatro cajones con trescientos libros intitulados Templo militante y vidas de Santos, escrito por Bartolome Carrasco y marcados para entregarse a Pedro Francisco Santoyo, mercader. Nueva Veracruz". The edition in question is: Bartolomé Cairasco de Figueroa's *Templo militante, triumphos de virtudes, festiuidades y vidas de Santos* (Valladolid: Luis Sánchez, 1602), USTC 5022305.

The following is an example of a document dated 21 September 1752 and compiled at the Colegio Máximo by Manuel Mariano de Iturriaga. The chest was indicated to contain the following titles:

> Ciceron en cinco tomitos
> Ovidio
> Un tomito del Padre Señeri
> Vida de San Juan Nepomuceno
> Vida de Nuestro Padre por Mateo.[23]

At the end of the document, Mariano de Iturriaga informed the Inquisition: "These are the ones I remember; if there are others, I cannot recall them". Such documents are consistent with the inquisitors' guidelines, requiring all readers to present details of the books they carried in their luggage. In some cases, the person transporting the books did not clarify if they were for personal use or for their community, as in this Franciscan case dated 1699:

> I, Friar Manuel Sánchez of the Order of our Father Saint Francis, Retired Preacher and Priest of the Province of Zacatecas, appear before Your Lordship to inform you that, having brought from the Kingdom of Castile a large box of books for preaching and instruction, Morals and Lives of Saints, together with two chests containing a few more volumes, all of which were impounded at the customs, a total of approximately one hundred and twenty folio and quarto books; and having registered the said books with the Commissioner of the city of Cadiz, as ordered by the Holy Tribunal of the city of Seville, I received a license to embark with them. In the Port of Veracruz, I declared them to the Commissioner of the said city of Veracruz, and I brought over these books together with the license. I humbly beseech Your Lordship to release the said books, box and chests into my possession, granting me the gracious favour of Your Illustrious Lordship.[24]

---

[23] AGN, Indiferente Virreinal, Caja 1007, exp. 8, fol. 13r. "Retención en las aduanas de libros, Puebla, Veracruz; manifestación de títulos prohibidos, (1752–1756)". A digitization is freely accessible at http://www.agn.gob.mx/guiageneral/, last accessed: May 2015.

[24] AGN, Indiferente Virreinal, Caja 0791, exp. 013, fol. 10r. "Fray Manuel Sánchez pide se le entregue un cajón con libros para predicar que están en la Aduana, Zacatecas (1695)". A digitization is freely accessible at http://www.agn.gob.mx/guiageneral/, last accessed: May 2015.

Two years later we find a similar case, but on this occasion the person involved does mention the titles and seems aware that the books will be used collectively:

> I, Friar Martín de Alfaro, Retired Preacher and Commissioner of the Supreme and General Inquisition, Priest and Custodian of the Province of Santiago de Jalisco in New Spain, appear before Your Illustrious Lordship and declare that in the Customs House of this City of Seville I have a case containing some books used by all of us and, so that they can be returned to me, I require an order from Your Illustrious Lordship. I trust in Your Illustrious Lordship's kindness.
>
> Nucleus Aureus = Saint Mary three volumes various sermons: Durando—five scholastic volumes, Hortus Marianus—one volume, Quinto Curcio in the vernacular one volume, Friar Isidro—sermons one volume and Learned Preacher five volumes.[25]

The export of these books was authorized by the *calificador* Juan de Curiel, because all of them were "absolutely sound". This same phrase authorizing the release of "inspected and expurgated" books can be found in other documents. For example, in the following case authorizing the export and sale of a specific title:

> I, Doctor Don Roberto Ramírez de Varrientos, doctor in canon law and canon of the holy cathedral of this city, bishop of Cadiz, Consultor, commissary judge of the Tribunal of the Inquisition of the City of Seville, do hereby grant permission on behalf of the Holy Office to Doctor Don Nuño Núñez Chacón, presbyter of this city, to transport to the Indies, province of New Spain, one hundred sets of the first and second parts of the work entitled Maiestas Gratiarum et Virtutum omnium Beatae Mariae, the author of which is the illustrious Fray Francisco Guerra, who was bishop of this city and bishopric, given that they have been expurgated and examined on my orders and he is dispatching them to be sold in those kingdoms, granted at Navidad de Cadiz on 16 June 1665 = Transported in four boxes, numbered and marked on the outside.[26]

---

25 AGN, Inquisición, vol. 178, exp. 18, fol. 258r. "Licencia para que se le entreguen en la aduana al Padre Fray Martín de Alfaro, del Orden de San Francisco, dos cajones de libros (1701)".

26 AGN, Indiferente Virreinal, Caja 0791, exp. 013, fol. 8r. "Nuño Núñez Chacón, Presbítero de Cádiz, para enviar 100 juegos de libros a la Nueva España (1665)". A digitization is freely accessible at http://www.agn.gob.mx/guiageneral/, last accessed: May 2015. Fran-

In May 1786, Friar Pedro Pérez, Procurator General of the Dominicans in the Province of Mexico requested the release of ten boxes sent from Spain by Matías Hernández. Seven may have been for the Monastery of Santo Domingo in Mexico City and the other three for the Provincial, Friar Ignacio Gentil. Unfortunately, only a receipt for the first box survives. To judge from the information contained in that receipt, these books must have been intended for the community of Dominicans. The content is as follows:

    2 Richart Diccionario de las Ciencias Eclesiasticas 6 tomos.
    1 Historia de las Ordenes Monasticas Militares 8 tomos.
    1 Natal Alexandro sus obras 15 tomos.
    1 dicho Alexandro 15 tomos.
    2 Billuart Theologia 3 tomos.
    1 Benedicto XIV Opera omnia 6 tomos.
    1 Ydem Bullario 2 tomos.
    1 Richardt analisis conciliorum en francez 5 tomos.
    1 Diccionario Historia Natural por Bomar 12 tomos.
    1 Bibliotheca de los Padres por Tricalet en Francez 8 tomos.
    2 Billuart Teologia 3 tomos.
    2 Tomo 2º y 4º de Contenson.
    1 Apologia de la Religion Christiana en Francez 2 tomos.
    1 La certitud del christianismo 1 tomo Octavo.
    1 Jamin Pensamientos Theologicos.
    1 Natal Alexandro sus obras 15 tomos.
    1 Historia de las Ordenes Monasticas y Militares 8 tomos.
    1 Biblioteca de los Padres por Fricalet en Francez.
    1 Misal Dominicano Romano.
    1 Benedicto XIV Opera Omnia 6 tomos.
    1 Ydem 12 tomos Roma.
    1 Ydem Sinodo 2 tomos Vitela.
    2 Ydem Bullario 2 tomos.
    1 serpertaculo de la naturaleza 16 tomos.
    2 tomos 1º y 3º del contemon cumpto. 4 tomos.
    2 dichos teologia 4 tomos.
    1 colectario en papel.
    2 Constituciones.

---

    cisco Guerra, *Maiestas gratiarum ac virtutum omnium deiparae Virginis, Mariae; auctore ... D. FR. Francisco Guerra, ordinis minorum, provinciae conceptionis episcopo Gadicensi, regioque consiliario. Tomus primus-secundus* (Hispali: Johannes de Ribera, 1659).

1 Sancti Joanes Chrisostomi 13 tomos.
2 San Bernardo Opera.
1 Sancti Barili Opera.
1 Benedicto la Opera Omnia.
1 Ydem Bulario.
1 Santo Tomas de Villanueva
2 Pouguet Ynstituciones Catholicas
1 San Leon Magno.
1 Amort Theologia 4 tomos
1 Ydem Yndulgenzias
1 Ydem demostracio critico
1 Ydem Moral
1 Ydem de Revelaciones.
1 Ydem Privilegio.
1 Ydem Controbersia.
1 Ydem casos consiencia.
1 Ydem Etica Christiana.
1 Ydem Divino Amore.
1 Santo Tomas de Villanueva.
1 Patuzi de seda Ynterni.
1 San Didimi de Trinitati.
1 Concordia Patrium Grecorum
1 Sermones de Cheminau en francez.
1 Lopez Lucerna Mistica.
1 Año espiritual en francez.
1 Cathecismo ad Ordinandus.
9 Misales de Santo Domingo
1 Juego de Breviarios completos.
50 Oficios de Difuntos.[27]

From the information provided by just this one box we can appreciate the importance and the value of this purchase. The Monastery of Santo Domingo in Mexico City was one of the principal Dominican houses in New Spain and needed substantial numbers of books, having a novitiate as well as being the point of reference for travellers on their way to the Philippines. The initial construction of the monastery was concluded in 1532; however, owing to structural

---

27   AGN, Inquisición, vol. 1207, exp. 6, fols. 264r–264v. "Fray Pedro Pérez Procurador General de la Provincia de Procuradores de México, presenta la memoria que ampara 10 cajones de libros (1786)".

problems in 1552 a rebuilding programme was begun, culminating in 1575 with four cloisters, as well as a magnificent library "which was a room one hundred and four feet long and thirty-four feet wide, higher than all others, with nine skylights high up in the walls to light it".[28]

These books were destined to become part of a rich collection which must have included thousands of volumes. The immensity of the collection is suggested by the length of the expurgation process carried out in 1716. The Dominicans initially requested two months but were forced to request a further three to finish the task because of "the very large numbers of books".[29] The extensive inventory of the library, compiled in 1810, has not yet been studied in detail. On the basis of this list Ignacio Osorio Romero has established that the library contained 2,407 titles in 6,008 volumes.[30] As it transpires from the analysis of this book list, this was a collection intended to provide the theological education typical of the Dominican order. Among the authors represented in the list are the Dominican Noel Alexandre, Saint Augustine, John Chrysostom, Saint Bernard, Thomas of Villanueva, Leo the Great, Benedict XIV, Giovanni Vincenzo Patuzzi, José López Ezquerra, Charles René Billuart, the Jesuit Pierre Poussines, Juan de Palafox y Mendoza, François Aimé Pouget, and several works by Eusebio Amort, as well as breviaries, missals, and handbooks for funerals.

Other interesting cases which can be documented are those of authors who themselves organized the export of their own works. For example, towards the end of the seventeenth century, the Bachelor of Law, Juan García de la Yedra, Lawyer for the Royal Councils and Commissioner of the Holy Office, wrote:

> On behalf of the Holy Office of the Inquisition I grant permission to the Reverend Master, Father Friar Juan Riquelme, priest of the regular observance of Our Father Saint Francis, *Calificador* of the Holy Office, regular *Definidor* for this province of Andalucía, and public notary of his order, to export from this city and send to the kingdoms of Mexico with Don Manuel Pezana in one of the ships of the present fleet under the orders of General Don Manuel de Velasco, Knight of the Order of Santiago, two hundred printed books: *Crisis en defensa de las obras de la Venerable Madre*

---

28   Pedro Álvarez y Gasca, *La Plaza de Santo Domingo. Siglo XVI* (Mexico City: INAH, 1971), pp. 69–72.
29   "Inquisición de México. Año de 1716", fol. 148r.
30   Ignacio Osorio Romero, *Historia de las bibliotecas novohispanas*, (Mexico City: SEP, Dirección General de Bibliotecas, 1986), p. 174.

Maria de Jesus de Ágreda, as witnessed by the necessary licences and permits, dated Cadiz, 4 June 1699.³¹

Unfortunately, in many cases like those already mentioned, the book lists are not accompanied by surviving explanatory documentation, perhaps because this has been lost or wrongly filed during various reorganizations of the archives. There is no way to know for sure about this possibility, only when you find the missing relationship between two documents in the Archive. For example, evidence indicates that books had been acquired for the monastery of Saint John the Baptist, Coscomatepec in Veracruz; however, no list of these titles is known to survive to-date. Some dispatches were authorized by Inquisitor Flores:

> Miguel Rodríguez, resident of San Juan de Coscomatepec, is carrying in his mule train three boxes of books for the Monastery of the Discalced Carmelites of this city, sent by Friar Cristóbal de la Cruz, procurator of the same order in Seville. May Our Lord preserve Your Lordship for many years. New Spain, 29 October 1622. Doctor Juan Marsial Flores.³²

In other cases, we find lists of books and petitions which are not related. For example, an undated document contains a request for the release of seventy boxes of books by Fray Joseph de Vera, *definidor* of the Province of San Nicolás de Tolentino in Michoacán, on behalf of his Provincial General. However, the list of books attached to this file does not correspond to the ones sent to the Augustinians, but to two boxes of books "all printed in Madrid" ordered for his own use by Juan Francisco de Campos, Canon Theologian of Puebla Cathedral.³³ In most of the cases where we have precise information about the titles,

---

31   AGN, Indiferente Virreinal, Caja 0791, exp. 013, fol. 5r. "Fray Juan de Richeline envía 200 cuadernos impresos en defensa de la obra de María de Jesús Agueda a Manuel Bezaña, Andalucía (1699)". A digitization is freely accessible at http://www.agn.gob.mx/guiageneral/, last accessed: May 2015. The edition being transported is: Juan Riquelme (O.F.M.), *Manifestum defensorium primae ex tribus partis Operis Venerabilis Matris Mariae a Iesu de Agreda, inscripti: Mistica Ciudad de Dios* (Cádiz: Cristóbal de Requena, 1697), CCPB000617065-X.

32   AGN, Indiferente Virreinal, Caja 5501, exp. 75, 1 fol. "Envío de 3 cajones de libros para el convento de los Carmelitas Descalzos, por parte de Fray Cristóbal de la Cruz, procurador de la misma orden por conducto de Miguel Rodríguez". A digitization is freely accessible at http://www.agn.gob.mx/guiageneral/, last accessed: May 2015.

33   AGN, Indiferente Virreinal, Caja 5702, exp. 57, 2r. "Carta que hace Fray José de Vera de la

this is usually owing to the fact that both the request and the list of books are combined in one document as is the case with the following example which documents the purchase of books for the Order of Carmen. In February of 1776, the Procurator General Friar Cristóbal de la Santísima Trinidad submitted a request to the Inquisition for permission to send the books, to be transported by Pedro de Campos from Veracruz to the Provincial, Friar Sebastián de San Antonio. The list consists of two inscriptions.[34] One is "These items in box number 1 are marked in the margin", and the books that correspond are:

2 juegos de Orsi de a 4 tomos de Potestate Romani Pontifici
12 juegos de a 4 tomos Labarre Sermones
1 juego en dos tomos Antoine Teologia moral
1 juego en dos tomos Frautwein contra Fretonio

The other is "These were contained in box number 2 marked as above", and the books listed are as follows:

3 juegos de a 2 tomos Bocanegra Sermones
3 juegos de a 18 tomos Croyset Año Cristiano
3 Ydem de a 2 tomos Discursos Espirituales
3 Ydem de a tomo Ylusiones del Corazon
3 Ydem de a tomo Retiro Espiritual

As the document itself shows, these books were for a private library, that of the Provincial, rather than for an institution. Among them, can be found works by the preacher Giuseppe Agostino Orsi, the Jesuit Paul Gabriel Antoine, Nicholas de Labarre, Jean Croiset, and Francisco Alexandro Bocanegra, containing theological writings and material for sermons. These are titles that could be found in religious libraries all over New Spain and, although we are here dealing with a private library, these books would eventually, on the death of their owner, be incorporated into an institutional collection. Indeed, such a procedure was often set out in the regulations governing the collective life of these communities. For example, the Franciscans established that "All deceased friars' books

---

provincia de San Nicolás Tolentino perteneciente a los Agustinos de Michoacán en ella se habla de 70 cajones de libros que van a remitir al padre provincial. Contiene una lista de libros que trajeron en el navío de Santa Fe. Sin lugar".

34 AGN, Inquisición, vol. 1181, exp. 5, fol. 159r. "Memoria de los libros que en dos cajones conduce de la Veracruz don Pedro de Campos para el Reverendo Padre Provincial del Carmen, Fray Sebastián de San Antonio (1776)".

become after their death the property of the general Congregation, thenceforth being available in the communities' libraries in the Province, according to these libraries' needs and with no exceptions being made".[35] Some books were exchanged between monasteries in the same province when one institution needed more than another or when the books were duplicated. On some occasions, books were sold by the monasteries, as we can see below:

> This book was bought by Don Joseph Flores in the library of the Monastery of our Father Santo Domingo in Mexico City from the Very Reverend Father librarian Friar Miguel Doliba who has permission from the Very Reverend Father provincial to sell duplicates as they are of no use to the said library and, because this book bears a stamp, I add this note on 18 May 1748.[36]

All the books sold in this way were recorded as part of an administrative process in order to avoid confusion and misapprehension. In this context, we can understand the annotations of Francisco Antonio de la Rosa Figueroa, archivist and librarian of the Franciscan Province of the Holy Gospel in Mexico City, who drew up an alphabetical catalogue of the library of the Monastery of San Francisco in Mexico City and its subsequent expurgation.[37] Thanks to this process, the Franciscan was able to determine which volumes were duplicated in the library of which he was in charge and thus decide whether to donate them to monasteries which had poorer resources.

> I have set aside from N.M.R.P. Prov. fr. Joseph de la Vallina this book, together with 16 others from the library of this monastery in Mexico City for the monastery of San Pedro Atocpa—signed 19 August 1753. Fr. Franco. Ant. de la Rosa Figueroa. Librarian.[38]

---

35   "Concerning books", *Estatutos Generales de Barcelona para la familia cismontana de la Regular obseruancia de Nuestro Padre San Francisco, vltimamente reconocidos y con mejor metodo dispuestos en la Congregacion general celebrada en a ciudad de Segouia el año del Señor de 1621* (Madrid: Tomas Iunti, 1622), USTC 5013554, p. 23, n. 3.

36   Note on the front cover of Niccolò Toppi, *Biblioteca napoletana et apparato a gli huomini illustri in lettere di Napoli* (Naples: Antonio Bulifon, 1678), quoted by José Herrera Peña, *La biblioteca de un reformador* (Michoacán: Universidad Michoacana de San Nicolás de Hidalgo, 2005), pp. 69–70.

37   Francisco Morales, "Impresos y manuscritos en lenguas indígenas en la antigua Biblioteca de San Francisco de México", *Estudios de Cultura Náhuatl*, 26 (1996), pp. 367–397: 370–371.

38   Note on the front cover of Calistus Placentinus, *Enarrationes evangeliorvm a septvagesima vsqve ad octavam Paschae, iuxta sensum literalem Praemissis svppvtationibus temporum*

The presence of these annotations in books conserved in monastery libraries is an indication that this action was an accepted practice and did not give rise to any suspicion or concern in the Holy Office. This is not surprising, because these libraries were always under strict inquisitional scrutiny. Indeed, much evidence, both from books and documents, bears witness to the inspections made of the libraries in order to remove any prohibited books and to carry out expurgation. Anything expurgated had to be noted down in the book itself so: "This book has been censored in accordance with the new index of 1632".[39] In this way, an expurgated book can be differentiated from a book that has not been inspected. Documents have been found giving information about how these inspections were conducted. They were very well organized. They required a censor to be appointed, a permit to be issued, and a final report to be submitted, containing the list of all prohibited books discovered.

Books were bought for all the libraries of the religious foundations, urban and rural, large or small, which were dedicated to religious education, missionary activity or spiritual retreat, whether communal or private. All these acquisitions show that members of religious orders in New Spain had access to the same written material as their European counterparts and were subject to the same restrictions. Nonetheless, the imposition of these restrictions was laborious, bureaucratic and frustrating for the individuals involved. Two examples describe situations which gave rise to certain differences of opinion between the port authorities, the inquisitors and the members of religious orders in charge of importing books. The first involves the Franciscans and 12 boxes of books which they purchased in 1698. The boxes contained "approximately 100 books" listed under unusual titles such as "Various Treatises". These titles were considered rather ambiguous and suspicious by captain Pedro de Licona, syndic of the Franciscan monastery in Veracruz, who decided not to release the books until the inquisitorial authorities were able to reach a decision about them. From their description in the list, we might assume that some of the books would be collections of printed material or something similar. In fact, the Franciscans were not being completely open. There were other things in the boxes: images and books supporting the attempt to have Sebastián of Aparicio canonized.

---

    totius vitae D. Iesu, & descriptionibus Palestinae; adiuncta etiam tabella, vt quando, & vbi ea gesta sint quae narrantur, facilius intelligi posit per Calistim Placentium (Lyon: Pierre Landry, 1573), USTC 156120, copy used: BNMx RFO 226.07 PLA.e. 1573.

39   Handwritten note on the front cover of Antonio Possevino, *De nuae militis galli* (Lyon: Jean Baptiste Buysson, 1593), USTC 146338, copy used: Mexico City, Jesuit Community, Library Eusebio Francisco Kino, 21665.

Objects of devotion were also sent together with books for the Province of the Holy Gospel. The boxes were dispatched to the viceregal capital in Pascual de Iglesias's mule train, where they were set aside for delivery. The items intended for the Province were handed over to the Procurator General, Friar Buenaventura de Armaolea, and those supporting the cause of the Venerable Aparicio went to Friar Sebastián de Moya. Another purchase that ran into problems was a remittance of three boxes containing books which the Procurator General of the Order of Carmen in New Spain, Ignacio de Juan Bautista, had sent for the Carmelites in that colony. The books should have been delivered to the Monastery of the Santo Desierto by Father Valentín de la Madre de Dios who signed the request in 1788. However, the administrator in Veracruz, Pedro Corbalán, decided to hold the books because he believed that the paperwork was incorrect.[40] The Carmelites argued in their favour and finally the books were released without further complications.

An examination of these lists shows that both documents appear to comply with the legal requirements of the times, making the unwillingness of the authorities to hand over these books somewhat difficult to understand. The reason appears to be their excessive bureaucratic zeal rather than any desire to protect religious purity. A great deal remains to be discovered about these purchases of books by religious communities; material which attests to an active culture of the buying of books in the Spanish American colonies.

---

40   AGN, Patronato Indiano 188, exp. 5, fol. 85r–85v. "Expediente sobre trece cajones de libros venidos de Castilla, para la Religión del Carmen (1788)".

CHAPTER 22

Advertising and Selling in Cromwellian Newsbooks

Jason McElligott

⁂

The advertisements in a newspaper are more full of knowledge in respect to what is going on in a state or community than the editorial columns are.[1]

∴

It is possible to trace the proto-history of advertising to the market stalls and shops of ancient Greece and Rome, but commercial advertising probably first emerged in the north of Italy during the fifteenth and sixteenth centuries. In its earliest form this advertising probably amounted to no more than the erection of written or visual signs over shops and stalls. Later, traders began to issue business tokens which served to advertise their enterprises. Advertising also developed in the Netherlands and some of the more economically advanced cities of northern Europe during the same period. However, advertising remained rare until the invention of printing. From this date forwards, businesses could, in theory at least, attract a larger number of customers through the use of relatively cheap printed advertisements. These printed advertisements tended to be posted-up in public places where they could be read by, or to, large numbers of people. As urban communities grew in terms of population numbers, social complexity and geographical size it began to make sense to try to create a central location where potential customers could peruse commercial notices. As such, the father of the famous French essayist, Montaigne, established the world's first office for advertisements in Paris in the late sixteenth century.[2] Following this French example, in March 1611, James I granted letters patent to Sir

---

1 Henry Ward Beecher, *Proverbs from Plymouth Pulpit: The Press* (1887). This paper is based on a study of every single newsbook which appeared in London between 1 January 1649 and 1 January 1660. See Jason McElligott, 'The Newsbooks of Interregnum England' (Unpublished MA dissertation, University College Dublin, 1996).
2 Henry Sampson, *A History of Advertising from the Earliest Times* (London: Chatto and Windus, 1874), pp. 19–29.

Arthur George and Sir Walter Cope, which gave them "absolute full and free license, power and authority" for the term of 21 years, to set up

> a publique office, room or place of resort or repaire of people for the notice of borrowing and lending of moneys, for the better knowledge of buying, selling or exchanging of lands, tenements or hereditaments, leases or any other goods or chattels whatsoever.

Sir Arthur and Sir Walter duly established an office which contained a "Publique Register for generall Commerce" near Durham House in the Strand, but the venture soon folded as a result of the patent's stipulation that no man was to pay "any more for such search or entry, then shall please himself".[3]

In December 1637, Charles I granted a patent to Captain Robert Innes to establish an "Office of Intelligence". This was to be a place to which

> masters or others having lost goods, women for satisfaction whether their husbands be living or dead, parents for lost children, or any others for discovering murders or robberies, and for all bargains and intelligences

might resort. As was the case with the patent granted in 1611, Captain Innes was hampered by the restriction that he was not to charge any fee for his service.[4] Perhaps this restriction explains why, by the time of his death in 1643, Innes had not acted upon his patent. Soon after his death, Innes's widow sold the patent to a certain Oliver Williams, who will feature prominently later in this article.

The next attempt to establish an office for advertisements came in 1648 when Samuel Hartlib petitioned parliament to be appointed Superintendent-General of an "Office of Addresse" with the power to charge two or three pence for each entry. This proposal earned the fulsome praise of the political economist William Petty who believed such an office was necessary because

---

[3] J.B. Williams, *A History of English Journalism to the Foundation of the Gazette* (New York, Bombay and Calcutta: Longmans, Green and Co., 1908), pp. 158–160.

[4] Samuel Hartlib, *A Further Discoverie of the Office of Publick Addresse for Accommodations* (1648), republished in *The Harleian Miscellany; or, a collection of scarce, curious, and entertaining pamphlets and tracts, as well in manuscript as in print, found in the late Earl of Oxford's Library, interspersed with historical, political, and critical notes* (London: printed for Robert Dutton, 1810), VI, pp. 159–170.

> the present [economic] condition of men is like a field, where a battle hath been lately fought where we see many legs, and arms, and eyes lying here and there, which for want of a union, and a soul to quicken and enliven them, are good for nothing, but to feed ravens and infect the air.[5]

Despite this endorsement, Hartlib's proposal was rejected by the House because of his demand that he be provided with £200 per year and a "convenient great house" for use as an office.[6] Less than a year later, however, the then most prominent journalist on the side of Parliament, Henry Walker, successfully established an 'Office of Entries' in London. The erection of this office was a defining moment in the history of English advertising not only because Walker obtained the right to charge for his services, but because he announced the fact in his weekly newsbook, *Perfect Occurrences*:

> There is an office of Entries to be erected on Monday next for great profit and ease of the Citys of London and Westminster and parts adjacent ... [where] ... for 4d any person may both search and record his entry and have notice of ... what is desired.[7]

The early years of the Commonwealth saw the establishment of offices modelled upon Henry Walker's "Office of Entries". For example, in April 1650, a Mr Adolphus Speed established a primitive accommodation agency known as "The Office of Generall Accomodations by Addresse" in King Street. A few months later, a merchant named Henry Robinson set up an office which registered servants for work.[8] The number of such offices seems to have reached a peak in 1655. In that year, *Perfect Proceedings* carried an advertisement for an "Office for Generall Accomodation" at the house of Edward Tooly in Basinghall Street. This office provided lists of solicitors, employees and lodgings and a service to

---

5 Sir William Petty, *The Advice of WP. to Mr Samuel Hartlib, for the advancement of some particular parts of learning* (1648), reprinted in *The Harleian Miscellany* (1810), VI, pp. 141–158.
6 Samuel Hartlib, *A Further Discoverie*, pp. 160–162.
7 *Perfect Occurrences*, no. 137, 10–17 August 1649, p. 1220.
8 See Adolphus Speed, *A General Accomodation by Addresse* ([London]: s.n., 1650), ESTC R206323, and Henry Robinson, *The Office of Adresses and Encounters: Where all people of each Rancke and Quality may receive directions and advice for the most cheap and speedy way of attaining whatsoever they can lawfully desire* (London: Matthew Simmons, 1650), ESTC R203369.

all ministers, widdoes and others that have studies of books to sell at secondhand, [who] may at the said office give in a catalogue of their books, and such as want any books scarce to come by, may upon their repair to the said office, view the said catalogues and very probably know where to be supplied.[9]

In May 1655, *A Perfect Account* instructed those interested in acquiring "the great house at Hammersmith" to "see Mr Robinson at the Office of Addresses behind the Exchange".[10] Four months later, *The Weekly Intelligencer* advertised an "Office of Addresses for the West Indies", where members of the public could send a letter to the West Indies for 3d. For a small extra fee this office, which was located at the Phoenix in Seething Lane, would write one's letter and act as "a holding place for return letters" which, the advertiser remarked, "are often lost".[11] It is intriguing to note how common it was for these offices and agencies to be advertised in the London newsbooks. Indeed, in several cases these offices and agencies would be lost to history were it not for their appearance as paid inserts in serial publications.

Advertisements in Serials

The first English corantoes (serials which dealt exclusively with foreign news) appeared in August 1621. However, it was not until three years later that a paid advertisement first appeared in an English coranto. This notice, contained in *The continuation of the weekly news*, advertised a map which illustrated that title's account of the recent siege of the Dutch city of Breda.[12] The next seven years saw a small number of advertisements appear in printed news sheets, but in 1632 all licences to print corantoes were revoked in response to complaints by the Spanish ambassador about the inclusion of items relating to internal Spanish affairs.[13] In November 1641 serial quarto pamphlets of domestic and foreign news first appeared in London, and rapidly established themselves as an important factor in Civil War and Interregnum print culture. The

---

9   *Perfect Proceedings*, no. 304, 19–26 July 1655, p. 4828.
10 *A Perfect Account*, no. 229, 23–30 May 1655, p. 8.
11 *The Weekly Intelligencer*, 18–25 September 1655, p. 39.
12 Joseph Frank, *The Beginnings of the English Newspaper, 1620–1660* (Cambridge, Mass.: Harvard University Press, 1961), p. 11.
13 James Playstead Wood, *The Story of Advertising* (New York: Ronald Press Co., 1958), p. 32.

history, politics and literary culture of these newsbooks have been much examined by scholars since the appearance of Joad Raymond's seminal *The Invention of the Newspaper* (1996).[14] There has, however, been relatively little attention paid to the commercial basis of the newsbook business, the economic realities which underpinned the regular appearance of a title over a period of time. One way to understand the business nature of the newsbooks (and throw light on the broader economic, social and cultural history of England) is to examine the growth of paid advertising. This developed slowly and fitfully during the 1640s, but developed significantly during the 1650s. In fact, the first advertisement of the Civil War period appeared in July 1646, a full five years after the first newsbooks were published. This was carried in Samuel Pecke's *A Perfect Diurnall*, and made reference to "a booke now in presse entitled *Magnalia Dei Anglicana, or England's Parliamentary Chronicle*". By the end of the year Pecke had carried three further book notices.[15] From 1647, both Henry Walker's *Perfect Occurrences* and Richard Collings' *Kingdome's Weekly Intelligencer* began to include occasional advertisements for books, but the inclusion of advertisements in the newsbooks remained rare until the closing months of 1649, and these were almost exclusively connected with the book trade.

The small number of advertisements in the newsbooks of the 1640s can be explained by the economic displacement caused by two civil wars and the availability of other means of advertising, such as handbills and posters, or notices at the back of books and pamphlets which listed other printed matter for sale in the premises from which a particular item had been purchased. However, the fact that the majority of newsbooks were short-lived and had small circulations may have made many of them an unattractive medium for advertising. One might expect that the more established titles such as *Perfect Occurrences* or *The Kingdomes Weekly Intelligencer* would have attracted advertisements, yet the forceful and explicit advocacy of political opinions in these and other titles must have discouraged many potential advertisers. By contrast, the increasingly nation-wide distribution of the newsbooks and the gradual return to peace and stability which occurred during the Interregnum led to an

---

14   Joad Raymond, *The Invention of the Newspaper: English Newsbooks, 1641–1649* (Oxford: Clarendon Press, 1996).
15   *A Perfect Diurnall*, no. 156, 20–27 July 1646, p. 156, quoted in Roger P. McCutcheon, 'The beginnings of book-reviewing in English periodicals', *Papers of the Modern Languages Association*, 37 (1922), pp. 691–706: 698–699; Joshua J. McEvilla, 'A catalogue of book advertisements from English serials: printed drama, 1646–1668', *Papers of the Bibliographical Society of America*, 107.1 (2013), pp. 10–48.

unprecedented growth in newspaper advertising. The number of newspaper advertisements soared from less than a dozen in 1649, to more than 900 in 1659.

117 different newsbook titles were published in England between 1 January 1649 and 1 January 1660. Of these, only 29 titles contained any advertisements. The vast majority of titles—very many of which were short-lived—carried no advertisements. Of those titles which did carry paid notices, only 11 newsbooks carried more than fifty advertisements. In total, there were 3,839 advertisements in English newsbooks between 1 January 1649 and 1 January 1660.[16] The largest number of advertisements appeared in Marchamont Nedham's officially-sanctioned *Mercurius Politicus* (1251 ads), *The Publick Adviser* (990), and *The Publick Intelligencer* (755).[17] Advertising was, therefore, concentrated overwhelmingly in a number of market-leading titles. Before 1655, advertisements usually only appeared in every second or third issue of *Politicus*. During the first half of 1655, however, the number of advertisements in *Mercurius Politicus* began to climb and by late summer it was carrying between half a dozen and ten inserts per issue. Following the uncertainty occasioned by the suppression of the rest of the press in August 1655 and the creation of a state-sponsored monopoly under the control of Marchamont Nedham, the number of advertisements in *Mercurius Politicus* fell dramatically. In fact, for a full five weeks after Cromwell's order was issued *Politicus* did not attract one single paying advertisement. Similarly, *The Publick Intelligencer*, which began life after the August suppression as a second title under Nedham's control, only attracted its first advertisement one full month after it first appeared on the streets of London. Thereafter, the number of advertisements in both of Nedham's newsbooks remained low for over a year. As a rule, while *Politicus* carried only one or two advertisements, *The Publick Intelligencer* frequently appeared without any inserts whatsoever.

---

16 Elizabeth L. Furdell, 'Grub Street commerce: Advertisements and politics in the early-modern British press', *The Historian*, 63.1 (2000), pp. 35–52; R.B. Walker, 'Advertising in London newspapers, 1650–1750', *Business History*, 15.2 (1973), pp. 112–130.

17 In decreasing order, the other advertisements appeared in *Occurrences from Forraigne Parts* (106 ads), *A Perfect Account* (102), *The Weekly Intelligencer* (90), *A Perfect Diurnal* (88), *A Particular Advice* (83), *The Weekly Information* (69), *The Weekly Post* (67), *The Faithfull Scout* (54), *The Loyal Scout* (47), *Perfect Proceedings* (46), *Mercurius Fumigosus* (15), *Mercurius Democritus* (8), and *Certain Passages* (5). There were three ads in both *An Exact Accompt* and *The Moderate*. There were two ads in *The Diary*, *Perfect Weekly Account*, and the *True and Perfect Dutch Diurnal*. The following titles contained only one insert: *Mercurius Aulicus, Mercurius Jocosus, The French Intelligencer, The Loyal Messenger, The Moderate Intelligencer, The Modest Narrative, The Weekly Account*, and the 1652 edition of *Mercurius Pragmaticus*.

It was only after November 1656 that the volume of advertising in *Politicus* once again attained pre-September 1655 levels. From this point onwards the number of advertisements in Nedham's titles grew steeply. In 1658, the number of advertisements per issue regularly rose above 10 for the first time, and during 1659 *Mercurius Politicus* and *The Publick Intelligencer* sometimes carried as many as twenty advertisements per issue.[18] For example, in early June 1659 issue no. 570 of *Mercurius Politicus* contained notices about a runaway servant named Richard from Cheapside, a horse lost in Bexley in Kent, a plant nursery in Westchester, and no fewer than seventeen separate books and pamphlets. These included advertisements for James Harrington's *The Commonwealth of Oceana*; an English-Italian dictionary; an "Astrological Discourse" about the effect of a forthcoming conjunction of Saturn and Mars; a tract on the medicinal virtues of tobacco; and several religious books and pamphlets, including two attacks on the leading Presbyterian Richard Baxter.[19] The men who paid for these insertions were a mixture of prominent and less well-known booksellers from different religious and political backgrounds.[20] The editorial and news sections of the newsbooks were controlled and regulated during the 1650s, but it seems that all who could afford to pay were welcome to advertise their wares.

A notice in a newspaper cost a standard 6d, but soon after Marchamont Nedham gained a monopoly over the press in 1655, he increased the tariff to half a crown (2 shillings and 6 pence).[21] During the Interregnum printers began, as a result of the growth in the number of newsbook advertisements, to group all advertisements together on the final page of their eight-page newsbooks. The exception to this was the printer Thomas Newcombe, who always placed the advertisements in Nedham's *Mercurius Politicus* and *The Publick Intelligencer* on pages twelve and/or thirteen of these sixteen-page titles. As the decade progressed printers began to use italic and bold fonts to draw attention to inserts. In 1653, Elizabeth Alsop placed a thick black border around an advertisement for a religious book. Five years later, Thomas Newcombe used an identical border on two separate occasions to draw attention to a book advertisement.[22] A much more common way of drawing attention to an advertisement, however,

---

18   See, for example, *The Publick Intelligencer*, no. 181, 13–20 June 1659, and *Mercurius Politicus*, no. 570, 2–9 June 1659.
19   *Mercurius Politicus*, no. 570, 2–9 June 1659, unpaginated, but page 12 and 13 of this issue.
20   Jason McElligott, 'Licensing, censorship and the book trade', in Laura Lunger Knoppers (ed.), *The Oxford Handbook of Literature and the English Revolution* (Oxford: Oxford University Press, 2012), pp. 141–142.
21   Frank, *The Beginnings of the English Newspaper*, p. 246; Williams, *A History of English Journalism*, p. 166.
22   *Mercurius Politicus*, no. 421, 17–24 June 1658, p. 13; no. 422, 24 June–1 August 1658, p. 646.

was by way of inserting a small woodcut illustration of a pointing hand into the left-hand margin beside the insert. In 1652, Robert Wood carried an illustration of a diamond necklace and locket which had been lost by their owner, but the extra costs involved in producing the necessary woodcut ensured that such illustrations were exceedingly rare.[23] The only other illustration to appear beside an advertisement was a small crest which was used on twelve separate occasions to advertise a particular brand of lozenges in *The Faithful Scout* and *The Weekly Post* during 1655.[24]

Before 1659, the use of headlines in advertisements was confined solely to *Mercurius Politicus*. In that year, however, with the emergence of new newsbooks in the wake of the fall of the Protectorate, headlines which read "An Advertisement" appeared forty times in *The Loyall Scout, The Weekly Post*, and *The Weekly Intelligencer*. On three separate occasions the printer of *The Loyall Scout* and *The Weekly Post* divided his adverts into two separate sections and grouped those advertisements for quack physicians together under the headline "Physical Advertisements".[25] Most advertisements ran to between four and six lines of text. However, almost 5% of advertisements were significantly longer than this norm. Of these hundred or so advertisements, about one-third took up a third of a page, one-eight took up half a page and the remaining number filled three-quarters of a page. The longest insert of the decade, which ran to 30 lines of text, appeared in *The Loyall Scout* for the services of an "astrological physician".[26]

The breakdown of advertisements by publisher is instructive. Marchamont Nedham's titles (63.1%) carried nearly five times more inserts than his nearest rival, George Horton (13.2%). Oliver Williams accounted for 9.2% of the total number, Richard Collings for 4.4%, and John Crouch for 1.2%. Bernard Alsop's *A Perfect Account* carried only 14 advertisements (0.6%). The use of advertising was a distinctly London-based phenomenon. Only 3% of the total number of advertisements were either placed by, or referred to, some service outside the capital. This figure is even more striking if one considers that 90% of the population lived outside London. The vast majority of these advertisements directed to audiences outside London concerned runaway apprentices, or lost and stolen goods. This reflects the fact that while it made sense to inform magistrates or horse-shippers across the country to be on the lookout for runaways or

---

23   *The Faithful Scout*, no. 64, 2–9 April 1652, p. 499.
24   Both of these titles were owned by Robert Wood.
25   *The Loyall Scout*, no. 25, 14–21 October 1659, p. 205; *The Weekly Post*, no. 25, 18–25 October 1659, p. 205.
26   *The Loyall Scout*, 15–22 July 1659, p. 101.

stolen goods, the itinerant pedlars and the small retail shops which accounted for the majority of provincial commerce did not feel the need to advertise in the London-based newsbooks.[27]

The advertisements which appeared in the newsbooks can be divided into six distinct categories. The first, and by far the most numerous category, consists of 2,303 book advertisements. This figure represents almost 60% (actually 59.99%) of the total number of 3,839 advertisements.[28] In addition, there were 710 (18%) inserts advertising various commercial goods, services or activities. Another major category is the 591 advertisements (15%) for various quack physicians and magical 'cures'. Lost, found, and stolen advertisements accounted for 4%, and a general category of 'personal' adverts for 3.6%. Notices informing the public about runaway servants and apprentices comprised slightly less than 2% of the total.

Books. Book advertisements accounted for almost 60% of the total number of paid notices in London newsbooks during the Interregnum. They were relatively rare before 1653, but thereafter increased slowly. In December 1653, for example, *A Perfect Account* carried a notice by the bookseller John Sweeting at "the Angel in Popes Head Alley" advertising five plays in one volume by Richard Brown; an edition of letters written by John Donne; and poems by Donne and John Quarles. The same issue also informed readers that Philemon Stephens at "the Gilded Lion in Pauls Churchyard" had recently published *'Thomas Campanella his Discourse touching the Spanish Monarchy'*.[29] In July 1655, one issue of *The Perfect Diurnall* carried six separate notices of books being sold by eight booksellers in different locations across London.[30] However, the history of book advertisements during the Interregnum is (as with newsbook advertising more generally) largely that of the newsbooks controlled by Marchamont Nedham.

Across the decade as a whole, religious books accounted for just under 60% of the total number of book advertisements. The other categories of books were (in descending order of appearance): politics (circa 120 items), history, medicine, Greek or Latin classics, legal texts, plays, dictionaries, crime stories or news, poetry, gardening, and maps. The categorization of early modern texts

---

27   For example, *The Publick Intelligencer*, no. 105, 19–26 October 1657, p. 45.
28   Christine Ferdinand, 'Constructing the framework of desire: How newspapers sold books in the seventeenth and eighteenth centuries', in Joad Raymond (ed.), *News, Newspapers, and Society in Early-Modern Britain* (London: Taylor & Francis, 1999), pp. 157–175.
29   *A Perfect Account*, no. 152, 30 November–7 December 1653, pp. 1213, 1216.
30   *The Perfect Diurnall*, no. 291, 2–6 July 1655, p. 4484.

is often problematic, as a text could be both historical *and* political, or might even be religious, political *and* historical in nature.[31] For the purposes of this article, however, a simplified categorization is employed in order to give modern readers a general sense of the different types of books advertised. This categorization is intended to be indicative rather than scientific. The relatively small number of books dealing with political matters were mainly officially sanctioned texts such as Marchamont Nedham's *Case of the Commonwealth truly Stated*, or an edition of Hugo Grotius's *The Authority of the Highest powers about sacred things*. The diversity and number of historical books advertised during the decade is striking, and speaks to the widespread popularity of this genre and its perceived importance in promoting critical thought and rhetorical skills.[32] A proper understanding of history also had political and religious implications. Advertisements included *The History of the United Provinces; The History of the East Indies; The History of Stonehenge; The Compleat History of the Monarchy of China; An epitomy of the Civil Wars in France during the reign of Charles the ninth*; and Oliver Cromwell's favourite book, *The History of the World* by Sir Walter Raleigh. There were also more than 30 advertisements for English, Dutch, Latin and French dictionaries. On a less academic note, a large number of books on gardening and fishing were published, as were a significant number of cookery books. These cookery books included: *The Art of Cookery; The French Cook; The Art of Cookery refined*; and *Health's Improvements: or, rules Comprizing and discovering the nature, Method, and manner of preparing all sorts of food used in this nation*.[33] Scholars have detected political sub-texts in some of the recreational books of the 1650s, but there is no sense that any of the advertised cookery books or outdoor manuals were marketed as anything other than factual sources of entertainment and leisure reading.[34]

One cannot pretend that these advertisements present an accurate account of the books which the men and women of the 1650s bought and read, yet they do, at the very least, give some indication of the type of books which booksellers felt it worthwhile to advertise. In addition, they demonstrate that there were a

---

31   Ian Green, *Print and protestantism in early-modern England* (Oxford: Oxford University Press, 2000), pp. 1–21.
32   Kate Loveman, *Samuel Pepys and His Books: Reading, Newsgathering, and Sociability, 1660–1703* (Oxford: Oxford University Press, 2015), pp. 166–167.
33   *Mercurius Politicus*, no. 204, 4–11 May 1654, p. 3476; no. 205, 11–18 May 1654, p. 3492; no. 255, 26 April–3 May 1655, p. 16; no. 431, 26 August–2 September 1658, p. 775; *The Weekly Intelligencer*, no. 326, 4–11 April 1654, p. 216.
34   Laura Lunger Knoppers, 'Opening the Queen's closet: Henrietta Maria, Elizabeth Cromwell, and the politics of cookery', *Renaissance Quarterly*, 60 (Summer 2007), 464–495: 464–469.

large number of booksellers in 1650s London who recognised the potential of advertising, and had the money to pay for this service. Unfortunately, in the absence of any surviving booksellers' accounts, it is impossible to tell whether publishers experienced a substantial increase in sales after their products were advertised in the newsbooks.

Commerce. A significant feature of 1650s newsbook advertising was the gradual growth in the number of inserts advertising commercial goods, products and services. For example, in 1658 readers were informed that

> the best writing Ink for deeds and Records is made and sold by Tho. Roth, Stationer, at the Lamb at the east-End of Paul's near the school.[35]

There were fewer than half a dozen commercial advertisements in 1649 and this figure remained more or less constant until 1657. In that year, however, the number of such advertisements in *Mercurius Politicus* and *The Publick Intelligencer* grew to sixty. 1657 also saw the publication of two new serial titles devoted entirely to advertising, *The Publick Adviser* and *The Weekly Information*. Between them these titles attracted almost 700 commercial advertisements. Both of these newsbooks divided their commercial advertisements into four main categories. The most numerous were those which gave notice of the arrival of various ships' cargoes into London port. The other categories were lands or houses for sale, rent or let; jobs offered or sought; and the various carrier services which operated from London to the main provincial towns.[36] By September 1657, however, both of these newsbooks had disappeared and *Mercurius Politicus* and *The Publick Intelligencer* once again became the only domestic newsbooks available in England. In 1658 there were slightly more than sixty commercial advertisements in *Mercurius Politicus* and *The Publick Intelligencer*. This figure is almost identical to the number of commercial inserts which had appeared in the two titles during the previous year. During 1659, however, the number of commercial advertisements rose to 160. This figure is twenty-seven times greater than the number of such advertisements which had appeared in 1649.

Cures. Logically, medical cures and medicines could be examined under the heading of commercial goods, products and services described above. How-

---

35 *The Publick Intelligencer*, no. 141, 30 August–6 September 1658, p. 793.
36 See Dorian Gerhold's use of advertisements in 'The development of stage coaching and the impact of turnpike roads, 1653–1840', *Economic History Review*, 67.3 (2014), pp. 818–845.

ever, they are described here separately because the range of cures offered in the newsbooks is both fascinating and instructive of the neuroses of the seventeenth century. Apparently, many people were expected to believe the wildest claims so long as the quack in question could provide (or at least claimed to be able to provide) a list of patients whom he or she had cured. For example, in 1655 Daniel Border's *Faithful Scout* wrote:

> I am requested to give intelligence, that the Gentlewoman so famous for the cure of all Cancers in the Breast, although of many years continuance, is now resident in the City of London, and hath lately performed that great and excellent cure of *Mrs Farrow* in Gun-powder Alley who had a Cancer in her breast of 12 years standing, whom the Colledge of Physitians hath concluded incurable. The said Gentlewoman hath also several choice and approved Receits for all manners of Diseases whatsoever, wholly desiring the benefit of the lame and sick, and not her own gain: And therefore desires to give this publique notice, that all persons whatsoever may repair to *Mr Webs* house at the sign of the Horse-shoe in three Fox Court in Long lane.[37]

Judging by the large number of advertisements, these cures seem to have been a very profitable business. Inevitably, such profits meant that there was fierce competition between the various practitioners. Often this competition took the form of copyright infringement and piracy. In 1659 Edmund Buckworth, Edward Maynard and Robert Brown (among others) were producing lozenges which they claimed could cure all manner of diseases. Each man claimed that his was the original and best product. So it was that Buckworth took out a series of advertisements which complained of "divers pretenders who counterfeit the same [lozenges], to the prejudice and disparagement of the said gentleman [himself] and the abuse of the people".[38] By contrast, Maynard notified the public that he had begun to seal his lozenges in bags and write his name on the package. Robert Brown went one better by sealing his "chymical pectored lozenges to cure distempers" in a paper bag and printing his coat of arms on the paper that contained them.[39] This is a strikingly early example of the intersection of advertising, branding, and claims of the infringement of commercial copyright.

---

37   *The Faithful Scout*, no. 237, 20–27 July 1655, p. 1891.
38   *The Weekly Intelligencer*, no. 2, 10–17 May 1659, p. 15.
39   *The Weekly Intelligencer*, no. 18, 30 August–6 September 1659, p. 143; no. 20, 13–20 September 1659, p. 155.

Lost, Found and Stolen. In his magnificent book, *The Restoration Newspaper*, James Sutherland remarked that Restoration gentlemen seemed to be forever losing watches.[40] By contrast, the newsbooks of the Interregnum carried only one advertisement for a lost watch. Lost horses, on the other hand, accounted for fifty-one of the ninety lost property notices. Even if a gentleman was careful enough to avoid losing his horse, he had a good chance of having it stolen. Of the fifty-seven advertisements concerning the theft of property the vast majority, no fewer than forty-seven, were appeals for information as to the whereabouts of stolen horses. The decade also saw nine advertisements for lost bags, five for a lost hawk,[41] one for a lost dog and one for a lost parakeet.[42] The two advertisements of the 1650s for lost children retain their emotional power more than 350 years later. In June 1652, *The Weekly Intelligencer* carried a notice from Simon Reynolds in "Barnsby-Street, at the Signe of the White-Hart" who had

> lost a Child on Saturday in the Evening, being the fifth of June, Aged about 4 yeers, in a light coloured Coat, and a black silk Cap: If any can give Intelligence concerning him, he will give them thanks, and a good reward.[43]

Three years later, *The Faithful Scout* informed readers of a

> child (by name, *Ann Rowland*) that is lost, having a coloured fluff Coat, with a plain Holland Quoif, and a yellow string under the chin, aged two years and a half; her Parents live in Grubstreet, next to the Flying-horse.[44]

These advertisements suggest that some newsbooks were circulated, read and commented upon sufficiently widely for parents to believe that there was a chance that they might help to reunite them with their lost children.

Personal. Some of the advertisements categorized under the loose heading of 'personal advertisements' while organizing this data can provide fascinating insights into the private lives and domestic affairs of quite humble citizens. For example, the 1650s saw almost a dozen advertisements placed by estranged

---

40 James Sutherland, *The Restoration Newspaper and Its Development* (Cambridge: Cambridge University Press, 1986), p. 84.
41 *A Particular Advice*, no. 47, 9–16 December 1659, p. 526.
42 For comparison, see Sarah H. Meacham, 'Pets, status, and slavery in the late-eighteenth-century Chesapeake', *The Journal of Southern History*, 77.3 (2011), pp. 521–554.
43 *The Weekly Intelligencer*, no. 76, 1–8 June 1652, p. 486.
44 *The Faithful Scout*, no. 237, 20–27 July 1655, p. 1893.

husbands concerning the behavior of errant wives; in 1659 an English settler in Ireland, Richard Smith, notified the readers of *The Publick Intelligencer* that his wife, Sarah, had committed adultery and escaped to England with a certain Captain Richard Edmonds.[45] By contrast, not one woman in the entire country felt it necessary to use the newsbooks to appeal for the return of an estranged husband. This anomaly is perhaps explained by the fact that the men who notified the country that they were cuckolds were not issuing an appeal for a reconciliation: they were giving notice that they would not be responsible for any debts accumulated by their estranged wives.

Two of the most unusual advertisements of the entire decade concerned the disappearance of a young girl named Sarah Mayne. In 1655 Henry Walker ran the following notice:

> If anyone can discover a young Gentlewoman twixt 12 and 13 years of age, fair complexioned, that was stolen the 19th of September last by one *Mr William Glascock* (who is since indited) [he] shall have 100 pound for his payns, or giving notice where they have been any time since, shall be well rewarded by *Mrs Morgan* at *Mr Confets* house neer Kings gate, Holborn.[46]

Almost eighteen months after her disappearance, Sarah Mayne had still not been returned, and her parents inserted a notice in *Mercurius Politicus* to the effect that

> whereas in September 1654, one *Sarah Mayne*, being then but Twelve years of age, and heir to a great Estate, was stoln away out of the Tuition of *David Morgan* Esquire, and Dorothy his Wife, mother of the said Sarah, and hath been ever since concealed in the hands of evil-minded people, with design to have the marrying of her, when of Age to consent, which she will very shortly be; Therefore all Justices of Peace and others are desired to take notice, that her Guardians are not thereto consenting, and to secure such as shall attempt it, to answer the Law: There be severall persons stand indicted at the Upper-Bench for stealing her away.[47]

History does not record what became of young Sarah Mayne. In the same year that she disappeared, the family of Joan Hele, "a rich heir of great quality in the West" inserted a lengthy notice in *Mercurius Politicus* to the effect that they

---

45   *The Publick Intelligencer*, no. 183, 27 June–4 July 1659, p. 557.
46   *Perfect Proceedings*, no. 291, 19–26 April 1655, p. 16.
47   *Mercurius Politicus*, no. 302, 20–27 March 1656, p. 6057.

had finally succeeded, after more than forty hearings, in obtaining an annulment of the marriage between their daughter and a certain Mr Chamberlain, "a pretended Nobleman's son, though indeed a vintners son of a very inconsiderable fortune".[48]

Runaways. There were ninety-five advertisements appealing for the return of runaway servants and apprentices during the decade. These advertisements usually contained a physical description, details of the reward offered, and the master's address to which the runaway could be returned. Most runaways stole money or valuables, or both, from their masters before absconding. In July 1655 Thomas Simson stole a horse, £10 and a watch before escaping from his master, John Cook, an inn-keeper in York.[49] George Norton, an apprentice to Israel Pownoll of Portsmouth, helped himself to "about £26 of his master's money",[50] while Charles Billingsby, an apprentice surgeon, disappeared with the enormous sum of £40.[51] Many of the runaway apprentices and servants were extremely young. For example, Thomas Simson was only fourteen years of age when he ran away from his master.[52] It is also striking how many servants of foreign origin absconded from their places of employment. "A Negro boy" owned by Lord Willoughby of Parham was "about 14 years of age" when he absconded.[53] In August 1655, Mr Edmund Rolse of Rochester offered a reward of 40 shillings for the return of "Robert Davers a tall young black man [who] ran away from his master". In 1658, *Mercurius Politicus* reported that two servants, both of whom were "proper blackmen", had absconded. The following year brought reports that an eighteen-year-old Indian servant, and a young French servant who "speaks English well" had fled their places of work.[54]

The number of foreigners in seventeenth-century England was small. Yet these youths account for nearly 15% of the total number of advertisements

---

48 *Mercurius Politicus*, no. 242, 25 January–1 February 1654, p. 5096. See Mark S. Dawson, 'First impressions: Newspaper advertisements and early-modern English body imaging, 1651–1750', *Journal of British Studies*, 50.2 (2011), pp. 277–306, and Marissa C. Rhodes, 'Domestic vulnerabilities: Reading families and bodies into eighteenth-century Anglo-Atlantic wet nurse advertisements', *Journal of Family History*, 40.1 (2015), pp. 39–63.
49 *The Perfect Diurnall*, no. 291, 2–6 July 1655, p. 4484.
50 *Mercurius Politicus*, no. 592, 27 October–3 November 1659, p. 840.
51 *The Publick Intelligencer*, no. 207, 12–19 December 1659, p. 952.
52 *The Publick Intelligencer*, no. 141, 30 August–6 September 1658, p. 9.
53 *Mercurius Politicus*, no. 275, 13–20 September 1655, p. 5528.
54 *Perfect Proceedings*, no. 306, 2–9 August 1655, p. 16; *Mercurius Politicus*, no. 408, 18–25 March 1658, p. 407; *The Publick Intelligencer*, no. 168, 14–21 March 1659, p. 300; no. 164, 14–21 February 1659, p. 237.

placed for runaway servants and apprentices. These children and young adults must have had particularly pressing reasons for absconding, as it is unlikely that a fugitive foreign child would have got very far in seventeenth-century England without being noticed. Some runaways may have suffered nothing more serious than a severe case of homesickness, but it is probable that others absconded as a result of violence, bullying or intimidation from their workmates or employers. Indeed, there is some evidence to suggest that violence was a common experience for many apprentices. For example, in November 1660 an apprentice stationer named Oliver Hunt took the unusual step of petitioning the Secretary of State, Lord Nicholas, to ask that his master, Peter Cole, be called "to account for misuse in beating him, not allowing him to go out, and thereby alluring him to desert".[55] One should be careful of repeating Lawrence Stone's assertion that all apprentices were "exposed to almost limitless sadism from their masters".[56] It was, after all, in a master's best interests to ensure that his staff were healthy and contented. This should not blind one to the evidence that many youths were deeply unhappy as apprentices or servants.[57]

Newsbooks and Offices of Intelligence

Thus far the history of advertising has been presented as two separate strands: the offices of intelligence and the newsbooks. In May 1657 these strands became entwined, albeit temporarily, when Marchamont Nedham issued a prospectus advertising "The Offices of Publick Advice". These eight Offices—one each in east Smithfield, Lombard Street, Whitefriars, Southwark, Westminster, The Strand, Barbican, and Holborn—were designed to be "a constant means of promoting and quickening all manner of dealings, and intercourse betwixt man and man upon any occasion". The advertisements which were paid for in these offices, and were presumably displayed to the public in these premises, were to be published weekly in Nedham's *The Publick Adviser*, a new 16-page newsbook which would be "sold every Tuesday morning at any Stationers shop".[58]

---

55 Mary Anne Everett Green (ed.), *Calendar of State Papers Domestic: Charles II, 1660–1* (London: Her Majesty's Stationery Office, 1860), XXII, p. 380.
56 Lawrence Stone, *The Family, Sex and Marriage in England, 1500–1800* (London: Penguin, 1990), p. 120.
57 Michael MacDonald, *Sleepless Souls: Suicide in Early-Modern England* (Oxford: Oxford University Press, 1990), p. 252.
58 *The Office of Publick Advice newly set up in several Places in and about London and Westminster, by authority* (London: Thomas Newcombe, 1657), ESTC R211957; *The Publick Intelligencer*, no. 83, 18–25 May 1657, p. 1373; Williams, *A history of English journalism*, p. 169.

Not only was *The Publick Adviser* the first English newspaper devoted solely to advertising, but it was also the first to charge differential rates for inserts. The standard charge for all inserts had been 6d, but after September 1655 Nedham's monopoly on the newsbooks meant that he could raise the price to 2s 6d. It now cost five shillings to advertise a book, and eight shillings to give notice of a runaway servant or apprentice. Merchants advertising the arrival of ships' cargoes were charged six shillings, but the price went up one penny for every ton of cargo over 100 tonnes. Similarly, it cost five shillings to advertise lands up to the value of £30, and one penny extra per pound thereafter. The negative effect of these fairly substantial tariff increases on advertisers may have been offset by the fact that *The Publick Adviser*, unlike other newsbooks, carried advertisements not merely for one week but for a total of "four weeks together in the same book".

The first issue of *The Publick Adviser* contained a preface to readers that explained the purpose of such a unique venture and asked them to refrain from passing judgement upon it for the moment because "at first so great and exquisite an Account cannot be expected, as were to be wished". Despite these words of caution, the first issue carried sixty-five advertisements and must have been considered a success by the publisher. In the second issue, which contained 62 advertisements, Nedham wrote that the Offices were "now sufficiently made known to the people, and do begin to come in use and practice". However, Nedham soon faced a major difficulty which threatened the viability of his new venture.[59]

Nedham's difficulty went by the name of Oliver Williams, the Anabaptist gunsmith who, in 1643, bought the patent granted by Charles I for an "Office of Intelligence" from the widow of Robert Innes. On the day that the second issue of *The Publick Adviser* appeared on the streets, Williams issued a broadsheet *Prohibition to all persons who have set up any Offices called by the names of Addresses, Publique Advice or Intelligence*.[60] In this broadsheet Williams claimed that his patent had been validated by an order of the Council of State in 1653 which had confirmed all grants issued by Charles I. As such Nedham was, according to Williams, acting unlawfully both in erecting such offices and charging for his services. In response to this "foolish paper", Nedham insinuated that Williams had procured his patent "in an irregular way", and claimed,

---

59   *The Publick Adviser*, no. 1, 19–26 May 1657, pp. 1–2; no. 2, 26 May–2 June 1657, p. 32; no. 6, 22–29 June 1657, p. 96; no. 14, 17–24 August 1657, p. 236.
60   Oliver Williams, *A Prohibition to all persons who have set up any Offices called by the names of Addresses, Publique Advice or Intelligence* (London: printed for the author, [26 May] 1657), ESTC R211937.

not entirely accurately, that his Office was "a new invention never practised before". While Nedham acknowledged that Williams' patent had indeed been confirmed by the Council of State, he claimed "it reaches not at all to the Offices of Publick Advice, it being a business quite of another nature". Nedham warned that his offices were "erected upon a justifiable ground of authority according to law; as he [Williams] and others shall finde".[61]

Despite this strong warning, Williams soon erected six "Offices of Intelligence": one each in St Katherines, Threadneedle Street, Holborn Court, Holborn, Charing Cross and Southwark. In the first week of trading these offices attracted an impressive total of sixty-eight advertisements which were then published in *The Weekly Information from the Office of Intelligence*.[62] Despite Williams' determination to press ahead with his project only one issue of this newsbook ever appeared.[63] It is likely that Nedham was able to use his position as the official propagandist of the regime to persuade the authorities to suppress his commercial rival. Certainly, it is clear that when Nedham's own *The Publick Adviser* folded after a run of only three months it was solely as a result of harsh commercial realities rather than interference by the authorities. This is suggested by the fact that within six weeks of establishing his new venture, Nedham was forced to close his offices in Westminster and Barbican, "which by experience have [been] found useless". Six weeks later, a further three offices were closed for "several good and weighty reasons". By the time *The Publick Adviser* was discontinued in September 1657 only three of the eight original offices were still trading.[64] Although the closure of the "Offices of Publick Advise" was a set-back for Marchamont Nedham, it was by no means a disaster. During 1658, *Mercurius Politicus* and *The Publick Intelligencer* ran 274 and 186 advertisements respectively: 460 in total for the year. During the first four and a half months of 1659, these two titles carried 236 advertisements. Trial and error seem to have proved that a network of advertising offices was less profitable and more troublesome than taking in paid advertisements at the business premises of Thomas Newcombe, the man who printed both of Nedham's newsbooks.

---

61   *The Publick Intelligencer*, no. 82, 11–18 May 1657, p. 1357; no. 88, 22–29 June 1657, p. 1449.
62   *The Weekly Information*, no. 1, 13–20 July 1657.
63   J.G. Muddiman (aka J.B. Williams), *The King's journalist, 1659–1689: Studies in the reign of Charles II* (London: Bodley Head, 1923), pp. 13–14.
64   *The Publick Adviser*, no. 6, 22–29 June 1657, p. 96; no. 12, 3–10 August 1657, p. 212.

Restoration and Beyond

The commercial future seemed bright for Nedham in 1659, but his spirited defence of the Protectorate ensured that he was sacked as editor of both titles upon the return of the Rump Parliament in May of that year. The Baptist preacher John Canne edited both titles until he too was expelled and Nedham returned to his old post in August. During Canne's three and a half months as editor, the two newsbooks ran 170 advertisements. During the final four months of the year Nedham succeeded in securing 152 inserts. As we have seen, the crises of 1655 (which culminated in the rule of the Major Generals) had a detrimental effect on the presence of advertising in newsbooks, but now the number of paid inserts in the newsbooks grew despite the severe political turmoil. During 1659, *Mercurius Politicus* and *The Publick Intelligencer* attracted a total of 558 paying advertisements: an increase of 21% over the number for the previous year. It is not clear precisely how much an advertisement cost in 1659 (were customers charged a standard 2s 6d or the higher, variegated rates pioneered by the short-lived *The Public Adviser*?) Whatever the exact price, it does seem likely that by 1659 paid inserts had become an integral component of the economics of news production and dissemination. It certainly seems clear that many people with commodities or services to sell had recognized the potential benefits of serial publications by the end of the decade. If the use of advertising is one indication of the existence of a profitable, capitalized industry which is both sensitive to the desires of customers and tries to manufacture new cravings for non-essential commodities, then the growth of paid notices in the London newsbooks of the 1650s is significant; it provides us with a sense of the commercialised, market-sensitive (dare one say 'capitalist'?) nature of the newsbooks and the wider book-trade.

One indication of the increased prominence, usefulness and importance of newsbook advertising might be the fact that in November 1659 the Secretary to the Lord General Fleetwood felt obliged to place an advertisement in both of Nedham's newsbooks informing the public that a pamphlet purporting to be *The Lord General Fleetwood's answer to the Humble representation of Colonel Morley* was a "meer fiction". One week later, an advertisement appeared in *The Publick Intelligencer* to the effect that "a book lately printed of 18 sermons pretended to be preached by Dr Usher, the late Archbishop of Armagh and Primate of Ireland, at Oxford 1640" was neither authorized nor authentic.[65] Here, in

---

65 *Mercurius Politicus*, no. 594, 10–17 November 1659, p. 873; *The Publick Intelligencer*, no. 202, 7–14 November 1659, p. 860, and no. 203, 14–21 November 1659, p. 888.

the context of a dramatic collapse in censorship (and with little prospect of redress at law), advertisements in newsbooks seem to have acquired the status of sites of public notice and record. One might reasonably have expected the volume of newsbook and newspaper advertising to have increased after 1660, but the determined efforts of the newly restored monarchy to regulate the public realm of printed news and debate meant that the history of journalism for much of the three decades after the Restoration is that of the anaemic two-page *The London Gazette*. This newspaper did carry advertisements, but their number was severely limited by the available space. Many of the defining features of these Restoration notices would have been familiar to readers of the 1650s, and this should come as no surprise because the printer of *The London Gazette*, Thomas Newcombe, had learned the trade of serial production while working on Nedham's newsbooks. It was really only from the late 1680s, when *The London Gazette* lost decisively its monopoly, that the number of newspaper advertisements began to track significantly upwards. Throughout the first half of the eighteenth century, the quantity of advertisements increased significantly across the newspaper industry of Britain and Ireland. However, the categories and types of advertisements appearing in these newspapers were strikingly similar to those which had first appeared in Nedham's newsbooks. Nedham's influence (and that of his colleague Thomas Newcombe) also extended to the language, typography and lay-out of eighteenth-century newspaper advertisements across Britain and Ireland.[66] Nedham has long been recognised as an important figure in the history of English journalism and political polemic, but it is now possible to appreciate his pioneering role in the development of newspaper advertising.

---

66   See, for example, George Faulkner's *The Dublin Journal*, no. 2588, 24–28 December 1751.

PART 6

Modern Book Market

CHAPTER 23

Book Bitch to the Rich—the Strife and Times of the Revd. Dr. Thomas Frognall Dibdin (1776–1847)

John A. Sibbald

The Regency period in Britain witnessed an extraordinary upsurge in the collecting of books and manuscripts, driven by a new enthusiasm for the antique and the bibliographically distinctive, and in particular for the 'fourteeners', that is to say, incunabula, books in black-letter and the products of the early presses both at home and abroad.[1] The trend which had begun in the second half of the eighteenth century, had, by the turn of the nineteenth century, truly become a frenzy, climaxing with the great Roxburghe Sale in 1812.[2] This period of early nineteenth-century book collecting has been described as 'heroic' and 'fabulous'.[3] Vast sums of money were spent in assembling private libraries. The auction rooms regularly saw records tumbling.[4]

---

1 Archer Taylor, *Book Catalogues: Their Varieties and Uses* (New York: Frederic C. Beil, 1987), p. 101. Peter Danckwerts points out in his Introduction to the 2004 reprint of the first edition of *Bibliomania*, Dibdin's own enthusiasm for black-letter was more "because Blackletter texts had been largely ignored by early scholars, and because they represent English literature and English History". Thomas F. Dibdin, *The Bibliomania, or, book madness: containing some account of the history, symptoms, and cure of this fatal disease: in an epistle addressed to Richard Heber, Esq.; edited by Peter Danckwerts* (Richmond: Tiger of the Stripe, 2004), p. xiv. Textual references to Dibdin's *Bibliomania* are normally to this modern edition; the abbreviated reference is given as Dibdin, *Bibliomania*. On a few occasions, a reference is made to the earlier editions of 1811 and 1842; this is always indicated by adding the date within brackets.

2 "A growing interest in old books on account of the age made itself felt in the later eighteenth century and developed rapidly in the early nineteenth century". Taylor, *Book Catalogues*, p. 101. The starting point is seen as the Askew sale of 1775. "The fact is, Dr Askew's sale has been considered as a sort of aera in bibliography. Since that period, rare and curious books in Greek and Latin literature have been greedily sought after, and obtained at most extravagant prices". Dibdin, *Bibliomania*, p. 50. Anthony Askew (bap. 1722, d. 1774), physician and book collector, "his library of almost 7000 books was auctioned over twenty days in February and March the following year and fetched nearly £4,000; among the principal purchasers were George III, Louis XV, and the British Museum". M.J. Mercer, 'Askew, Anthony (bap. 1722, d. 1774)', *Oxford Dictionary of National Biography* (Oxford: Oxford University Press, 2004; online edition, May 2005) [henceforth: *ODNB online*], last accessed 7 November 2017.

3 E.J. O'Dwyer, *Thomas Frognall Dibdin: Bibliographer & Bibliomaniac Extraordinary. 1776–1847* (Pinner: Private Libraries Association, [1967]), p. 7.

4 "Books grow scarcer every day, and the love of literature, and of possessing rare and interest-

Ubiquitous in the role of 'Master of Ceremonies', either directly acquiring books or manuscripts on behalf of his clients or indirectly though his publications setting out the norms for collecting, is the Reverend Doctor Thomas Frognall Dibdin (1776–1847).[5] Dibdin, even if he didn't actually coin the term, attributed the frenzy to 'Bibliomania' and spent a large part of his working life promoting it as such.[6] He claimed that the astronomical sums paid by collectors at the Roxburghe sale were a direct result of the interest his writings had excited in "old books never known before".[7] Amongst the book trade, he became an authority in his own lifetime. He comments "The booksellers used to quote me in their catalogues" and, even to-day, some still do.[8]

Dibdin has been described as "the chronicler of what was in retrospect, the golden age of book collecting".[9] He knew personally and wrote about many of the most important British collectors of books and manuscripts "whose collections now for the most part are dispersed, and secure in both national and institutional libraries on both sides of the Atlantic".[10] But Dibdin's interests extended far beyond the collections with which he was personally connected. He travelled extensively, providing accounts of the libraries, both private and institutional, and the collectors, booksellers, binders, printers, and others he encountered. He also travelled abroad on behalf of his clients and, in preparation of his *A bibliographical, antiquarian and picturesque tour in France and Germany*, spent nine months on the continent visiting libraries both private and institutional.[11] His works are crammed with detail not only about contemporary buying and selling but with a huge amount of information about earlier

---

ing works, increases in equal ratio. Hungry bibliographers meet, at sales, with well-furnished purses, and are resolved upon sumptuous fare. Thus the hammer vibrates, after a bidding of forty pounds, where formerly it used regularly to fall at four!". Dibdin, *Bibliomania*, p. 51.

5 William Jerdan, *Men I have known* (London: Routledge, 1866), p. 169.
6 "Dibdin was prompted to write *Bibliomania* by the appearance of a poem of the same name ... by John Ferriar, a distinguished Manchester physician. Ferriar, who worked with the mentally ill, would have been better placed to pass a medical judgement upon the existence of the book disease than Dibdin, but his poem is no more a medical treatise than Dibdin's book". Danckwerts, 'Introduction', p. x.
7 O'Dwyer, *Dibdin*, p. 21.
8 O'Dwyer, *Dibdin*, p. 14.
9 Victor E. Neuburg (ed.), *Thomas Frognall Dibdin: Selections* (Metuchen, N.J. and London: Scarecrow Press, 1978), p. 2.
10 Neuburg, *Selections*, p. 2.
11 Thomas F. Dibdin, *A bibliographical, antiquarian and picturesque tour in France and Germany* (3 vols., London: printed for the author by W. Bulmer and W. Nicol, Shakespeare Press, 1821).

FIGURE 23.1   *The Revd. T.F. Dibdin*, engraved by James Thomson after Thomas Phillips, from Dibdin's *Continental tour*, 2nd ed. 1829
PRIVATELY OWNED

sales, the conduct of auctions, buyers, prices and the book trade, much of it apparently gleaned from his own enviable collection of annotated sale catalogues.[12] The purpose of this paper, therefore, is chiefly to open the door of Dibdin's store cupboard for those unfamiliar with its rich and diverse contents.

The only substantial source of information about Dibdin's life is to be found in his own *Reminiscences of a literary life*, published in 1836.[13] He was born in Calcutta in 1776, the elder son of Thomas Dibdin (c. 1731–1780), a naval captain and later merchant venturer. His mother, Elizabeth Compton (d. c. 1780) was his father's second wife. His uncle was the famous song writer Charles Dibdin (bap. 1745, d. 1814).[14] Both his parents dying when he was four, he was brought up by his maternal uncle, William Compton, and educated in Reading. His schoolmaster there, John Man, "would now and then purchase old books by the sackful" and allowed the young Dibdin free access to his own library.[15] There he claims to have caught the "electric spark of bibliomania" when his attention was caught by the small octavo edition of Sandby's Horace 'with cuts', although he could not read a word of the text.[16] He waited until becoming an undergraduate before making his first purchases, which were Thomson's *Castle of Indolence*, Newton's Milton, Warburton's Pope and Theobald's Shakespeare.

---

12 "... but, thanks to what must have been an impressive collection of auction catalogues, he can look back over sixty years and more to tell us who bought what, when, and how much they paid". Dankwerts, 'Introduction', p. xv. "His sale catalogues were especially enviable. He possessed the first English example, that of the library of Lazarus Seaman (1676), sold in lot 30 with numerous others bound in six quarto volumes, which Richard Heber did well to secure for £8 2s. 6d. Many of the greatest auction catalogues—Farmer, Mead, Roxburghe, Steevens, Girardot de Préfond, La Vallière, Crevenna—he owned on Large Paper". Alan N.L. Munby, 'Dibdin's reference library', in R.W. Hunt, I.G. Philip and R.J. Roberts (eds.), *Studies in the Book Trade in Honour of Graham Pollard* (Oxford: Oxford Bibliographical Society, 1975), pp. 280–281.

13 O'Dwyer, *Dibdin*, p. 8. Thomas F. Dibdin, *Reminiscences of a literary life* (2 vols., London: John Major, 1836).

14 Jon A. Gillaspie, 'Dibdin, Charles (bap. 1745, d. 1814)', ODNB online, last accessed 7 November 2017.

15 T.F. Dibdin, *Reminiscences*, I, p. 50. "I was allowed to go into my master's private room whenever I pleased. It was sufficiently well filled with books. A large arm-chair was near the fire place, with a set of Hume and Smollett's History of England, with cuts, close at hand. I was for ever taking down these volumes ...". Dibdin, *Reminiscences*, I, p. 50.

16 Dibdin, *Reminiscences*, I, pp. 50–51. Horace, *Quinti Horatii Flacci Opera* (2 vols., London: William Sandby, 1749). Retaining his affection for this edition he later described it in his *Introduction to the Greek and Latin Classics* (2 vols., London: Longman, Hurst Rees and Orme, 1808), I, p. 420 "I have always considered this work as a very pleasant and respectable production ... The plates are numerous, and many of them conceived and executed with great taste".

The above were my first book purchases, at a Mr. Collins's, in Change-alley, near my uncle's residence, in Walbrook. They were put up in the window at marked prices, and I think I was upwards of a week fluttering about that same window, in the agonising hesitation of purchasing or not. I disdained to let the shopman carry them home, but took them triumphantly under my arm, and deposited them in a trunk.[17]

He matriculated, as a commoner, at St John's College, Oxford, where he was conscious of the disadvantage of not having received a public school education and proper pre-entrance tuition.[18] He passed his examination in 1797, but did not take his degree until 1801. He was awarded his MA, along with BD and DD degrees in 1825. Initially he pursued a career in law, firstly in London, where instead of being called to the Bar, he moved to Worcester, where he found the practice of law no less uncongenial and unsuccessful.[19] Abandoning the law, he turned to the Church, describing it as of all the professions, as the one "... in which all the acquirements of education, of eloquence, and of delivery are called up to show their mastery over the mind and heart of man ...".[20] The Church provided him with a stipend, occupying him only on Sundays while he pursued his other careers as author, bibliographer, cataloguer, traveller and book amanuensis to the rich and powerful.[21] In the period after

---

17 Dibdin, *Reminiscences*, I, p. 85.
18 "I had scarcely entered upon my studies, or joined my class, before I began to be conscious of my comparative backwardness; or rather of my premature entrance upon college life. Two years of stiff and steady discipline with a private tutor should have preceded it". Dibdin, *Reminiscences*, I, pp. 80–81.
19 "To say the truth, I had no thorough love of my profession at heart—at least of its technical parts. Declarations, pleas, rejoinders and surrejoinders had no hold either of my judgment or fancy. They seemed to me to be a vast compound of wordy nothingness—as an effort to conceal the truth, and to substitute mysticism for plain matter of fact". Dibdin, *Reminiscences*, I, p. 153.
20 Dibdin, *Reminiscences*, I, p. 160.
21 Dibdin, *Reminiscences*, I, p. 220. His preferments included "the preachership of Archbishop Tenison's chapel in Swallow Street, London, the evening lectureship of Brompton Chapel, preacherships at Quebec and Fitzroy chapels, the vicarage at Exning near Newmarket in Suffolk (1823), the rectory of St Mary's, Bryanston Square, in Marylebone, Middlesex (1824), and from 1831 until his death a royal chaplaincy-in-ordinary. This last position apparently saved him from arrest for debt in 1836". John V. Richardson Jr., 'Dibdin, Thomas Frognall (1776–1847)', *ODNB online*, last accessed 7 November 2017. Of the period during the preparation of the catalogue of the Spencer Library at Althorp, Neuburg comments "We may, however, speculate upon the attention he paid to his clerical duties at this time. It must have been scant enough, with long periods spent outside London". Neuburg,

the Roxburghe sale, when the market for rare books began to decline, with 'bibliophobia' replacing 'bibliomania', it was to the Church that he turned his attentions, reinventing himself as a remarkably successful writer of devotional works.[22] Indeed, his final work published in 1844 was a small collection of sermons amounting to a mere thirty pages.[23]

In all, Dibdin produced over forty-six publications, a number of which ran to more than one edition.[24] Indeed some are still in print, or at least, in reprint today. Subsequent editions of his works, too, had a habit of almost unstoppable expansion. The first edition of *Bibliomania* starts off at a modest 99 pages but by the time of the 'new and improved' third edition in 1842, it had expanded to over 680 pages.[25] His *Introduction to the knowledge of rare and valuable editions of the Greek and Latin classics*, the work which catapulted Dibdin into public awareness and which allegedly sold out in six weeks, grew beyond its original 76 pages in the first edition of 1802 to 920 in the fourth edition of 1827.[26] Even by the third edition of 1808, the author "in order that it might not be swelled to an inconvenient size" removed certain sections from the previous edition of 1804 along with "many references to catalogues, and the specification of prices for which rare books have been sold" although, exhibiting some commercial

---

Selections, p. 11. Thomas F. Dibdin, *Horae bibliographicae cantabrigiensis* (New Castle, DE: Oak Knoll Books, 1989), p. 18 where the Introduction by Renato Rabaiotti notes references to complaints about Dibdin's literary activities diverting him from his duties at St Mary's, Bryanston Square, when an anonymous complaint to the Bishop of London grew into a full-scale whispering campaign.

22 "By 1831 the book trade was sharing the general business depression arising out of the Reform Bill agitation, a situation aggravated in the case of the antiquarian trade by an epidemic of cholera which made people wary of handling any possible source of infection". O'Dwyer, *Dibdin*, p. 29. "By the 1820s he auctioned his drawings and took, as he said, 'a final leave of bibliography' to pursue his clerical career more seriously". Richardson, 'Dibdin, Thomas Frognall'.

23 Thomas F. Dibdin, *The Old Paths: being two sermons preached on the first and second Sundays in Advent, in the District Church of St. Mary, Bryanston Square* (London: T. Taylor, 1844).

24 Richardson, 'Dibdin, Thomas Frognall'.

25 Thomas F. Dibdin, *Bibliomania; or book-madness; containing some account of the history, symptoms, and cure of this fatal disease in an epistle addressed to Richard Heber, Esq.* (London: Longman, Hurst and Orme, 1809); *Bibliomania; or, book-madness; a bibliographical romance. Illustrated with cuts ... New and improved ed., to which are now added preliminary observations* (2 vols., London: Henry G. Bohn, 1842).

26 Thomas F. Dibdin, *An introduction to the knowledge of rare and valuable editions of the Greek and Roman classics: being, in part, a tabulated arrangement from Dr. Harwood's view, etc.* (Gloucester: Payne, 1802); (2 vols., London: Harding and Lepard, 1827). Neuburg notes the work is additionally useful in that "it demonstrates the range of material available to the scholar in the early nineteenth century". Neuburg, *Selections*, p. 3.

savvy, this latter was partly to avoid readers complaining "of the total inutility" of the previous edition.²⁷

Many of Dibdin's publications were lavishly, even extravagantly produced. "The pinnacle of Dibdin's career, in terms of his reputation as a bibliophile and as a producer of some of the finest, most complicated book publications of his day, was his publication of the *Bibliographical Decameron*".²⁸ De Ricci praises the *Bibliotheca Spenceriana*, replete with plates, illustrations and facsimiles, as "the handsomest and most elaborate catalogue of a private library yet issued".²⁹ Dibdin's bibliographer William A. Jackson, who in other aspects of Dibdin's output has been one of his fiercest critics, nevertheless has the highest regard for the physical production of his books, commenting:

> The typographic merits of many of his publications, particularly in the fine paper copies, can hardly be exaggerated. Some of them are among the finest productions of M'Creery, Bensley, Bulmer and Nichols, and those printers must have been driven nearly distracted by his demands for still more proofs, more India paper vignettes, and more color insertions.³⁰

---

27 Dibdin, *An introduction to the knowledge of rare and valuable editions of the Greek and Roman classics: being, in part, a tabulated arrangement from Dr. Harwood's view, etc.* (London: Longman, Hurst and Orme, 1808), *Introduction*, pp. vi–vii.

28 David A. Stoker, 'Thomas Frognall Dibdin' in William Baker & Kenneth Womack (eds.), *Nineteenth-Century British Book-Collectors and Bibliographers* (Detroit, MI: Gale Research, 1997), p. 76. A view clearly shared by Dibdin as he writes "I look upon the whole period of the conception, concoction, and publication of the Decameron as the sunniest period of my life". Dibdin, *Reminiscences*, II, p. 595. Thomas F. Dibdin, *The bibliographical Decameron; or ten days pleasant discourse upon illuminated manuscripts, and subjects connected with early engraving, typography and bibliography* (3 vols., London: for the author, by W. Bulmer and Co., Shakespeare Press, 1817).

29 Seymour de Ricci, *The Book Collector's Guide: A Practical Handbook of British and American Bibliography* (Philadelphia: The Rosenbach Company, 1921), p. 75. It has been held "to set the pattern for the modern bibliophile owner's catalogue". Taylor, *Book Catalogues*, p. 9. "Its principal value lay in Dibdin's careful establishment of the principle of first-hand examination of books, an important advance in the study of bibliography". Richardson, 'Dibdin, Thomas Frognall'. Thomas F. Dibdin, *Bibliotheca Spenceriana; or a descriptive catalogue of the books printed in the fifteenth century, and of many valuable first editions in the library of George John Earl Spencer* (4 vols., London: for the author, by W. Bulmer and Co., Shakespeare Press, 1814–1815).

30 William A. Jackson, *An Annotated List of the Publications of the Reverend Thomas Frognall Dibdin, D.D.: Based Mainly on Those in the Harvard College Library with Notes of Others* (Cambridge, Mass.: The Houghton Library, 1965), p. 11. "Dibdin's career as bibliographical author and maker of books is inseparable from the new confidence of English printers at the turn of the nineteenth century". Ina Ferris, *Book-Men, Book Clubs, and the Romantic Literary Sphere* (Basingstoke: Palgrave Macmillan, 2015), p. 49.

Dibdin estimated that he spent some twenty thousand pounds alone on the production of the *Bibliographical Decameron*, *Bibliotheca Spenceriana*, the *Aedes Althorpianae*, and the *Bibliographical tour*.³¹ In addition to the cost of travelling some nine months abroad accompanied by his illustrator George Lewis in preparation of the *Bibliographical tour*, Dibdin reckons the cost of the plates at almost £5,000, with a further £3,000 for paper, printing, copperplate printing and boards.³² Even after the sale of original drawings, he calculates his losses at over £400.³³ His projected *History of the University of Oxford* envisaged an outlay of £6,330 on the plates alone, without taking into account the costs of paper, printing and promotion.³⁴ These were huge sums of money and "the expense must have been horrific for a man of Dibdin's limited means".³⁵ It has been estimated that a 'responsible' middle-class family might live comfortably at this period on £200 a year.³⁶

All of these, as well as other works by him were initially offered for sale on a subscription basis, whereby the subscriber was usually required to put up a third of the price in advance. A.N.L. Munby has drawn attention to the fact that Dibdin's papers would provide ample documentation for a study of the production and marketing of books by subscription.³⁷ For the *Decameron*, he received £1,093 in advance.³⁸ There was generally a substantial mark-up for

---

31 Dibdin, *Reminiscences*, I, p. viii. Thomas F. Dibdin, *Aedes Althorpianae; or an account of the mansion, books, and pictures, at Althorp; the residence of George John Earl Spencer ... To which is added a supplement to the Bibliotheca Spenceriana* (2 vols., London: W. Nicol, successor to W. Bulmer and Co., Shakespeare Press, 1822). Thomas F. Dibdin, *A bibliographical, antiquarian and picturesque tour in France and Germany* (3 vols., London: for the author, by W. Bulmer and W. Nicol. Shakespeare Press, 1821).

32 Dibdin, *Reminiscences*, II, p. 654. At p. 657 he provides a breakdown of the sums paid out to the individual artists who contributed illustrations. Anthony Lister, 'A bibliomaniac abroad', *Antiquarian Book Monthly Review* [Oxford: ABMR Publications], Part 1 in vol. XI, number 8, issue 124 (1984), pp. 300–305; Part 2 in vol. XVI, number 9, issue 125 (1984), pp. 346–349.

33 Dibdin, *Reminiscences*, II, p. 663.

34 Dibdin, *Reminiscences*, II, p. 854.

35 Danckwerts, 'Introduction', p. xxi. Rabaiotti in the Introduction to Dibdin, *Horae*, p. 15. "Any single one of the major publishing projects he had seen through up until this time had involved him in expenditures exceeding the entire earnings available to him in several hypothetical lifetimes on a clergyman's stipend".

36 Marc Vaulbert Chantilly, 'Property of a distinguished poisoner: Thomas Griffiths Wainewright and the Griffiths family library', in Robin Myers, Michael Harris and Giles Mandelbrote (eds.), *Under the Hammer: Book Auctions Since the Seventeenth Century* (New Castle: Oak Knoll Press, 2001), pp. 111–142: 121.

37 Munby, 'Dibdin's reference library', p. 283.

38 Dibdin, *Reminiscences*, II, p. 600.

large paper copies.³⁹ The subscription lists and references quoted in the *Reminiscences* indicate he was usually well supported by the book trade.⁴⁰ Advance trade orders for the *Aedes Althorpianae* amounted to 54 large paper copies at 12 guineas and 217 on small paper at 6 guineas.⁴¹ A consortium of booksellers even tried to buy out the remaining stock of 320 copies of the ordinary paper edition of the *Decameron* for £2,000.⁴² Dibdin shrewdly resisted this approach and estimated that in the long run he gained several hundred pounds.⁴³ The *Bibliographical tour* saw booksellers not only in London subscribing enthusiastically in advance with two firms ordering over 100 copies each, but also from the provinces and even abroad—though he reckoned an extra guinea on each copy would have seen him recover about £900 instead of the loss he made of £400.⁴⁴ His translation of *The Imitation of Christ* attracted no less than 600 advance subscribers.⁴⁵ Presumably it must have given the author some gratification to find his own works trading for high prices when they went out of print such as the £52.10s. and £40 he records as being paid for large paper copies of *The Bibliomania*.⁴⁶

---

39 For example, *Bibliotheca Spenceriana*: 5 guineas and 12 guineas on large paper: *Aedes Althorpianae*: £6. 16s. 6d. and 12 guineas; *Bibliographical Decameron*: £7. 17s. 6d. and 15 guineas; *Bibliographical tour*: 9 guineas and 16 guineas. John Windle and Karma Pippin, *Thomas Frognall Dibdin: A Bibliography* (Newcastle, DE: Oak Knoll Press, 1999), pp. 76, 85, 100 and 127.
40 Although relationships with the book trade were not always as happy as the accounts of various booksellers in his various works might suggest. He was convinced Payne & Foss elbowed him out of overseeing the sale of the Heber library at a time when the resulting fees would have removed the then threat of his bankruptcy. "Dibdin certainly had many enemies in the book trade who could, if necessary, have revealed a good deal of damaging information about his past history of tangled financial dealings with booksellers and publishers". Arnold Hunt, 'The Sale of Richard Heber's library', in Myers, Harris and Mandelbrote (eds.), *Under the Hammer*, pp. 143–171: 152–153.
41 Dibdin, *Reminiscences*, II, p. 569.
42 Trade subscriptions alone for the large paper copy had amounted at some stage to 52 copies. Windle and Pippin, *Bibliography*, p. 99.
43 Dibdin, *Reminiscences*, II, p. 625.
44 Out of an edition of 100 copies on large paper and 900 on ordinary, the trade, including foreign booksellers, initially subscribed to 54 large paper copies and 391 on ordinary paper. Dibdin, *Reminiscences*, II, pp. 660 and 663.
45 Thomas à Kempis, *The imitation of Christ; in three books by Thomas à Kempis. Translated from the Latin original ascribed to Thomas à Kempis; with an introduction and notes by the Rev. Thomas Frognall Dibdin, D.D.* (London: for the author by William Nicol, at the Shakespeare Press, published by William Pickering and John Major, 1828). Dibdin, *Reminiscences*, II, p. 829.
46 Dibdin, *Reminiscences*, I, p. 325.

Reflecting on the publication of these costly productions and apparently with no sense of modesty, false or otherwise, he remarks "Perhaps the personal history of literature exhibits not many instances of greater courage and daring"; although, with expenditure on such an heroic scale we may perhaps look more kindly on his claim that the work his publications gave to others amounted to "a species of Patriotism which might challenge the approbation of the wise and good".[47] It has been suggested that 'bibliomania' was not the only condition to afflict Dibdin and that his recklessly extravagant publishing, always hoping to recover the losses on the previous publication, almost amounted to an addiction.[48] There is perhaps, too, just a hint of the addict's self-justification when Dibdin says:

> The other source of consolation is, that if I have been occasionally generous at the expense of prudence, in the remuneration given to artists, I have in many instances done good—by having cheered a sinking heart, and excited a praiseworthy spirit of emulation.[49]

Alas, Dibdin died in poverty, having had to sell his own library and only escaping arrest for debt on one occasion by claiming privilege as one of His Majesty's Chaplains in Ordinary.[50] Despite the opportunities that must have strewn the

---

47 Dibdin, *Reminiscences*, I, pp. viii & ix.
48 "It is not clear that Dibdin was afflicted by true bibliomania, or even that such ailment exists, but it does seem he suffered from an addiction to publishing in a manner which was recklessly extravagant. He was like a compulsive gambler who, having won, bets again in the hope of repeating his success; when he loses, he bets again in the hope of recouping his losses". Danckwerts, 'Introduction', p. xxiii.
49 Dibdin, *Reminiscences*, II, p. 589.
50 Despite the generosity of Earl Spencer who had insured Dibdin's life for £1,000, he died leaving his widow, a helpless invalid, and daughter in financial distress as he possibly had already raised money on this during his lifetime. O'Dwyer, *Dibdin*, p. 4. N. Barker, *The Publications of the Roxburghe Club: An Essay* (Cambridge: printed for presentation to members of the Roxburghe Club, 1964), p. 27. His reference library came under the hammer for the first time in 1817. "Increasingly severe pecuniary difficulties dogged him until his death in 1847, and certainly he never formed a second library on this scale. Such books as he retained after 1817 or acquired later were sold off piecemeal". Munby, 'Dibdin's reference library', p. 282. Munby reproduces a list of buyers and the sale catalogue, of which he could trace only four extant copies (British Library, the Bodleian, Harvard University Library and at the Grolier Club, New York) and which comprised 770 lots. The catalogue includes conditions of sale—no purchaser to advance less than 1s, and to pay down 5s in the pound in part payment, the lots to be taken away at the expense of the buyer within three days and the remainder of the purchase-money to be absolutely paid on or before delivery. Dibdin was a Chaplain in Ordinary to King William IV and to Queen Victoria. Neuburg, *Selections*, p. 6.

path of his commercial life, and his unique position at the centre of a rising market, ultimately his abilities as a man of business were found sadly wanting.[51]

The successful publication of the *Introduction to the classics* not only caught the public's attention, it also and most profitably introduced Dibdin to George John, second Earl Spencer (1758–1834). Spencer owned one of the most valuable private libraries in the country.[52] He became Dibdin's life-long patron, appointing him at one time his librarian and obtaining Church patronage for him. The subsequent publication of his *Bibliomania* in 1809 confirmed the author firmly in the eye of the book-collecting public. Written in less than a month, "a remarkable feat when one considers the mass of information it contains", "it marks the first full flowering of Dibdin's love affair with books".[53]

It has been described as "an anthem to the printed book, a warning to the unwary about the perils of obsessive book-collecting and the confessions of a rabid book-collector".[54] He identifies the condition of bibliomania as having

> ... almost uniformly confined its attacks to the male sex, and among these, to people in the higher and middle classes of society, while the artificer, labourer and peasant have escaped wholly uninjured. It has raged chiefly in palaces, castles, halls, and gay mansions ...[55]

Female book-collectors appear thin on the ground at this period, the exception being Frances Mary Richardson Currer (1785–1861) of Eshton Hall, England's earliest female bibliophile to whom Dibdin dedicates the *Northern tour* and whom he places at the head of all female collectors in Europe.[56] She recipro-

---

51 "Dibdin bought and sold books on quite a large scale ... His search for early printed books for his patron Earl Spencer, must occasionally have left him with duplicates or imperfect copies from which Spencer's copies had been 'improved' ...". Munby, 'Dibdin's reference library', p. 282. Lister, 'A bibliomaniac abroad', pp. 300–305 gives a detailed account of Dibdin's purchases during his tour of Northern France, part of Rhineland and Austria in preparation for the *Bibliographical tour*.

52 "He is a prime example of the wealthy aristocratic bibliophile during the bibliomania of the early years of the nineteenth century". Clare A. Simmons, 'George John Spencer, Second Earl Spencer' in William Baker and Kenneth Womack (eds.), *Nineteenth-Century British Book-Collectors*, p. 413. Spencer's prime concern in building his collection was to acquire first editions of the Greek and Latin classics and to establish a complete collection of Aldines. The library, with later additions by other members of the family, was purchased by Enriqueta Augustina Rylands, widow of the Manchester cotton magnate John Rylands. She presented the library in its entirety to Manchester as a memorial to her husband. The Spencer collection formed the core of the John Rylands Library, opened in 1900.

53 Danckwerts, 'Introduction', p. xxi. Windle and Pippin, *Bibliography*, p. 35.

54 Danckwerts, 'Introduction', p. vii.

55 Dibdin, *Bibliomania*, pp. 14–15.

56 Thomas F. Dibdin, *A bibliographical, antiquarian and picturesque tour in the Northern*

cates the compliment by subscribing to no less than eight large paper copies and one on ordinary paper.[57] He recast *Bibliomania* in the form of a dialogue with the object of relieving "the dryness of the didactic style by the introduction of *Dramatis Personae*".[58] The style which nowadays seems flowery and contrived is as unpalatable to the modern reader as his similarly lugubrious efforts in the *Bibliographical Decameron*.[59] The *mise en page* challenges the reader's eye.[60] The chief interest, as in so many of Dibdin's publications, lies in the footnotes. He has been described as "history's most voluminous exponent of foot-note authorship as a literary genre in itself".[61] Dibdin himself admits that the characters are there primarily as "pegs to hang notes on".[62]

---

counties of England, and in Scotland (2 vols., London: for the author by C. Richards, 1838). Seymour De Ricci, *English Collectors of Books & Manuscripts (1530–1930) and Their Marks of Ownership* (Cambridge: Cambridge University Press, 1930), pp. 141–143. Dibdin considered that her country house library was, in its day, surpassed only by those of Earl Spencer, the Duke of Devonshire, and the Duke of Buckingham. She was a close friend of Richard Heber and Charlotte Brontë used her surname for her pseudonym, 'Currer Bell'. Colin Lee, 'Currer, Frances Mary Richardson (1785–1861)', ODNB online, last accessed 7 November 2017. *Northern tour*, II, p. 1086. Of the 5,655 owners recorded by Alston, only 192 are women (although it should not be assumed, of course, that they were necessarily collectors as distinct from owners, for example widows of book-collecting spouses, or mere owners of bookcases). Robin C. Alston, *Inventory of Sale Catalogues of Named and Attributed Owners of Books Sold by Retail or Auction 1676–1800* (2 vols., Yeadon: privately printed for the author, 2010), I, p. 17.

57   Windle and Pippin, *Bibliography*, p. 185.
58   Thomas F. Dibdin, *Bibliomania or book-madness: a bibliographical romance in six parts* (London: printed for the author, 1811), p. vii.
59   "I scarcely know how its precise plan originated; but the sale of the *Valdarfer Boccaccio* seemed to have *decameronised* every thing else. I thought if I could bring together a few ladies and gentlemen of a less equivocal character than those introduced by "Il Maestro Joanne Boccaccio"—and make them discourse upon subjects less equivocal than many of those started by that most original Italian writer—I might do good: the more especially if I could bring certain topics to bear upon the fine arts, typography, and bibliography". Dibdin, *Reminiscences*, II, pp. 595–596.
60   "Occluding transparency and jamming reading's linear progression (the orderly left-to-right movement of the English reader's eye as it proceeds across and down the page), the … pages [of the *Decameron*] constitute a baroque space of overflowing forms". Ferris, *Book-Men*, p. 62.
61   Rabaiotti in the Introduction to Dibdin, *Horae*, p. 19. In his parody of Dibdin's *Library companion or, the young man's guide, and the old man's comfort, in the choice of a library* (London: for Harding, Triphook, and Lepard and J. Major, 1824), entitled 'The street companion; or the young man's guide and the old man's comfort, in the choice of shoes. By the Rev. Tom Foggy Dribble', *London magazine and review*, 1 (Jan 1825), pp. 73–77, Thomas De Quincey, in one passage, has a footnote to a footnote on a footnote to a footnote. William E.A. Axon, 'De Quincey and T.F. Dibdin', *The Library*, 2nd s., 8 (1907), pp. 267–274: 269.
62   Dibdin, *Bibliomania* (1842), p. xii.

Figure 23.2 provides a typical example. It comes from volume three of the *Bibliographical Decameron*. The characters are discussing the sale of the library of the book collector and bookseller James Edwards (1756–1816) in London in 1815.[63] Lot 812 is Luther's translation of the Bible, printed at Wittenberg in 1541.[64] Dibdin records the presence of Luther's signature and annotations along with those of his fellow reformers Johannes Bugenhagen, Philipp Melanchthon, and Georg Major.

It sold for £89. 5s. to George Hibbert (1757–1837), a Jamaica trade merchant, opponent of the abolition of the slave trade and book collector, after a tussle with the most omnivorous of all British book collectors, Richard Heber (1774–1833).[65] Dibdin wonders why such a book which "must always excite the deepest and most lively emotion in the breast of every Protestant" was not acquired by the British Museum or Lambeth Palace Library. Clearly the British Museum took the point and acquired it when it reappeared at the sale of Hibbert's library in 1829.[66] The British Library copy of the Hibbert sale catalogue records the purchaser as Henry Hervey Baber (bap. 1775, d. 1869), Keeper of

---

63   Page Life, 'Edwards, James (1756–1816)', *ODNB online*, last accessed 7 November 2017.
64   Dibdin, *Bibliographical Decameron*, III, pp. 123–124. *Biblia: das ist: die gantze heilige schrifft: Deudsch auffs new zugericht* (Wittenberg: Hans Lufft, 1541). Bernhard Fabian (ed.), *Handbuch deutscher historischer Buchbestände in Europa: eine Übersicht über Sammlungen in ausgewählten Bibliotheken* (12 vols., Hildesheim: Olms-Weidmann, 1997–2001), X, p. 45, no. 1.24. Philip R. Harris, *A History of the British Museum Library 1753–1973* (London: British Library, 1998), p. 71. There is no listing for it in the British Library purchase register for 1827–1833 DH5/1, but the Library advises that this particular register is by no means an exhaustive list of all Library purchases for this period. The author is grateful to the Rare Book Department of the British Library for this information and confirming the identity of Baber as the purchaser. The book featured in the exhibition "Germany: Memories of a Nation", The British Museum, London, 16 October 2014–1 January 2015. Dibdin's conclusion that this was Luther's very own copy is probably wrong. Susan Reed, Curator of German Studies at the British Library refers to the existence of other copies similarly inscribed (see Neil MacGregor, *Germany: Memories of a Nation* (London: Allen Lane, 2014), chapter 6, pp. 100–101). Indeed the British Library holds two such. She notes "This is a deluxe edition, so they may have done some signed copies to circulate or give to particular people". Further evidence of Luther's awareness of his 'celebrity' status and the promotional value of his signature is offered in Andrew Pettegree, *Brand Luther. 1517, Printing and the Making of the Reformation* (New York: Penguin, 2015), p. 181, where the author cites a letter from Luther to Georg Spalatin in early March 1521 with which he enclosed some copies of Cranach's early engraved portrait of himself, which at Cranach's request he had also autographed.
65   David Hancock, 'Hibbert, George (1757–1837)', and Arthur Sherbo, 'Heber, Richard (1774–1833)', *ODNB online*, last accessed 7 November 2017.
66   *A Catalogue of the Library of G. H.* (London: W. Nicol, 1829).

124 NINTH DAY.

a different result had attended the fate of a *few* of the rarer and more precious articles! However, let the *Vellum Livy*

> SALE OF MR. EDWARDS'S LIBRARY.
>
> Luther's translation of the Bible after his final revision. His own copy, which he used till his decease. This copy must always excite the deepest interest and most lively emotions in the breast of every Protestant. The manuscript notes prefixed to each volume seem to introduce us to the closet and acquaintance of a bright assemblage of Reformers. We find Luther exhibiting in the privacy of retirement the same unshaken confidence in the Deity under the persecutions he was suffering, as he nobly evinced in public. In a *manuscript note* in the second volume he transcribes the verse of the 23rd Psalm: 'Etiam quum ambularem per vallem lethalis umbræ, non timerem malum, quia tu mecum es,' and then adds a passage strongly indicative of his own exalted ideas of faith. He appears to have bequeathed this copy to BUGENHAGEN, who, on the 19th of May, 1556, wrote in it a pious distich and some religious sentiments, in which he denies the necessity of profane learning. The illustrious MELANCTHON was its next possessor. He writes a remarkable passage relative to the final consummation of all things, and intimates his belief that the end of the world is not far distant, adding " may Jesus Christ, the Son of Almighty God, preserve and protect his poor flock, scriptum manu Philippi, 1557." The same year it passed into the hands of GEORGE MAJOR, another Reformer, who has written in it a compendious exposition of his faith, signed with his name. In this version Luther omits the contested verse in St. John's Epistle, relative to the three heavenly witnesses.'

After such a description, it might not, perdie, have been a very forced or a very fanciful conclusion, that, either the British Museum, or the Archiepiscopa Library at Lambeth, would have stretched forth its potent arm to select this BIBLICAL GEM for the archives of one of these collections. But ' Dis aliter visum est.' Two private individuals, of less potency, but of equal spirit, resolved to compete with each other for the possession of the same: and these were my good friends Mr. R. Heber and Mr. G. Hibbert. Their contest was equally vigorous and glorious—and in such a fight, victor and vanquished almost partake of the same bibliomaniacal immortality. But the *latter* was the fortunate champion, at the reasonable sum of . . . . 89*l*. 5*s*. 0*d*.

> 821 Evangelia Quatuor, Græce, folio. A magnificent manuscript upon vellum of the tenth century, most elaborately executed. The subject of each page is designated at the top in letters of gold. Bound in blue velvet, with bronze-gilt medallions of the birth of our Saviour and the adoration of the Magi on the sides. *Purchased by Mr. Payne for Dr. Burney*, ... 210 0 0

FIGURE 23.2   *The Bibliographical Decameron*, vol. III, p. 123

Printed Books.[67] Despite the then current sharp decline in book prices at auction, it went for the remarkable sum of £267.11s. The description in the Hibbert sale catalogue is lifted almost verbatim from the *Bibliographical Decameron*, confirming Dibdin's own observation that "The booksellers used to quote me in their catalogues".[68]

Dibdin describes bibliomania as a preoccupation with:

I. Large paper copies
II. Uncut copies
III. Illustrated copies
IV. Unique copies
V. Copies printed on vellum
VI. First editions
VII. True editions
VIII. A general desire for black-letter

While he facetiously refers to the above as 'symptoms', they are to a large extent not only the preoccupations of contemporary collectors, but for the most part also his own. Under these headings he writes what amounts to more of a manifesto than simply a *vade mecum* for the book collector of the Regency period.[69]

Despite *Bibliomania's* warnings about obsessive book-collecting, Dibdin's own preoccupation with some of these criteria comes close to the obsessive. His preoccupation with 'Large Paper', or its closely analogous 'Uncut' or 'Tall paper' condition is evident in the litany of references to his own copies in this format. He observes "The want of margin is a serious grievance of complaint by collectors ...".[70] This preoccupation extends beyond the bibliographical and enters his vocabulary as a term of general approbation. Of the kitchen fireplaces at Dirleton Castle in East Lothian, he writes "The breasts of these chimneys tell us that a whole ox (whether of the "large paper" description, is another question) might be roasted in each of them".[71] Mr Kerr, his host at a dinner of the Maitland Club is "always a sort of large-paper hospitality man".[72]

Equally obsessive is his preoccupation, one might also say fetish, with copies printed on vellum where the very material seems to act as a kind of bibliographical aphrodisiac. Recalling the period when he was compiling the *Introduction*

---

67 P.R. Harris, 'Baber, Henry Hervey (bap. 1775, d. 1869)', *ODNB online*, last accessed 7 November 2017.
68 O'Dwyer, *Dibdin*, p. 14.
69 Dibdin, *Bibliomania*, pp. 56–74.
70 Dibdin, *Bibliomania*, p. 6, note (48).
71 Dibdin, *Northern tour*, II, p. 981.
72 Dibdin, *Northern tour*, II, p. 771.

FIGURE 23.3 *Bibliomania*, 1811
PRIVATELY OWNED

to the classics, he writes "At that time, I could have undertaken a "journey to Mecca" to see a first Homer, or a first Plato printed upon vellum".[73] He is let off relatively lightly having to journey only as far as Glasgow to see the Plato of 1513 on vellum in the Hunterian Library, where the 'pure yet ardent embrace' with which he clasps it to his bosom must have given rise to mixed emotions, one suspects, on the part of his guide, 'Moral Will', the Revd. Dr. Fleming (1794–1866), Professor of Oriental Languages and assistant Librarian at Glasgow University Library.[74] Pursuing his metaphor almost a little too far he asks, presumably rhetorically, "Can such happiness be imparted from an intercourse with rare and curious tomes?". More prosaically he remarks elsewhere "Three hundred guineas would not procure such another copy".[75]

Dibdin's works abound with biographical detail and sketches of collectors and members of the book trade. Neuburg emphasises the importance of this source material:

> Many are to be found in the pages of DNB, but in general, justice has not been done to these booksellers and literary antiquarians of the late eighteenth and early nineteenth centuries. Their activities and achievements, extraordinarily difficult to summarize, represent an important element in cultural and intellectual history.[76]

The thought too seems to have struck Dibdin as he makes Lysander in the *Bibliographical Decameron* say "The rise and progress of the Bookselling trade has always struck me as no very incurious or uninteresting feature in the annals of literature; especially in this country".[77]

One such who did not make it into the DNB's Pantheon is 'Poor Sancho the black'.[78] Taking his mother's name, William Leech Osborne turned his father's

---

73 Dibdin, *Reminiscences*, I, p. 206.
74 Plato, *Apanta ta tou Platonos. Omnia Platonis opera* (Venice: Aldo Manuzio and Andrea Torresano, 1513), USTC 849832. Copy at Glasgow University Library, Hunterian Sp. Coll. Bh3-e.16. Dibdin, *Reminiscences*, I, p. 193. Dibdin, *Northern tour*, II, p. 724. For Dr Fleming see *Fasti Ecclesiae Scoticanae: the succession of ministers in the Church of Scotland from the Reformation. New edition* (Edinburgh: Oliver & Boyd, 1915–), VII, p. 354.
75 Dibdin, *Introduction* (1808), II, p. 133.
76 Neuburg, *Selections*, p. 20.
77 Dibdin, *Bibliographical Decameron*, III, p. 434.
78 But his father Charles Ignatius Sancho (?1729–1780) will be found there as the first African to be given an obituary in the British press and the only Afro-Briton to vote in the elections of 1774 and 1780. Vincent Carretta, 'Sancho, (Charles) Ignatius (1729?–1780)', *ODNB online*, last accessed 7 November 2017.

grocery shop at 20 King Charles Street, Westminster, into a printing and bookselling business. Dibdin provides a typically characteristic vignette:

> The son, our sooty bibliopolist, had a most ardent passion for books: and especially for English topography and black letter ... Alas, poor Sancho! He happened, unluckily, to have an ardent attachment to pursuits of a more mischievous nature than that of black letter lore—and, withal, thought that these pursuits could only be substantially enjoyed with a glass of Champagne and Madeira, and with cherries at a guinea a pound! But he has paid the forfeit of his temerity. He died of a brain fever, and his property was meted out to his creditors under a commission of bankruptcy.[79]

At the other end of the spectrum, so to speak, or as Dibdin might put it "For glossy jet is paired with shining white" is the book collector 'Milk White' Gosset.[80] The Revd. Dr. Isaac Gosset (1745–1812) is described as "a small man, sickly and deformed ... Despite his short stature, which forced him to stand in the pulpit on two hassocks, he was a noted preacher at the Trinity Chapel in Conduit Street and elsewhere".[81] Gosset became Dibdin's neighbour in Kensington. Dibdin explains his appellation derives not from his colour or his clothes, but for his love of vellum.[82] Gosset was a familiar figure in the salerooms of the London book auctioneers. From his customary seat beside the rostrum he kept up a sort of running commentary on the lots as they were put up, his constant use of the phrase 'a pretty copy' causing amusement.[83] Dibdin described him as "at times vastly gay and cheerful during the sale, and he may be said to have

---

79   Dibdin, *Bibliographical Decameron*, III, p. 438. Carretta has the family premises at Charles Street, Westminster, but Dibdin has William at Mews Gate premises previously occupied by Thomas Payne before he moved to Pall Mall. Dibdin, *Bibliographical Decameron*, III, p. 437.
80   Dibdin, *Bibliographical Decameron*, III, p. 438.
81   Marc Vaulbert de Chantilly, 'Gosset, Isaac (1745–1812)', ODNB *online*, last accessed 7 November 2017.
82   "This must not be understood with reference to the colour of his complexion, or of his clothes—but to his love of books, 'bound in vellum'". Dibdin, *Bibliographical Decameron*, III, p. 5. Dibdin points out that being familiar with his library he saw "no violent predilection for this 'milk white' tint; and the 'cliquant' of an epithet is, we know, oftentimes as thoughtlessly reverberated as the epithet itself is precipitately bestowed".
83   See Vaulbert de Chantilly, 'Gosset, Isaac'. Heber was described as very much under Gosset's wing, occupying the seat on the Doctor's right at all the book auctions in London. Alan N.L. Munby, 'Father and son: the Revd. Reginald Heber's vain attempt to stem the rising tide of his son Richard's bibliomania', *The Library*, 5th s., 31.3 (1976), pp. 181–187: 182.

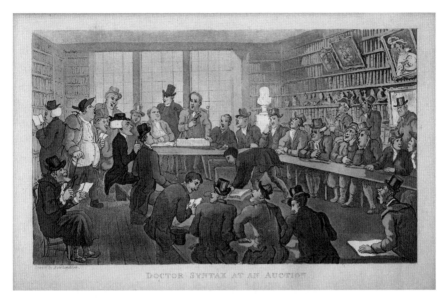

FIGURE 23.4 *Dr Syntax at an auction*, by Thomas Rowlandson
PRIVATELY OWNED

dealt around his jibes and jokes in manner the most felicitous imaginable".[84] Dibdin casts Gosset as Lepidus in the second edition of *Bibliomania*.[85]

In between come a host of other colourful characters which animate even further Rowlandson's already lively depictions of the salerooms of the period, such as George Nicol (1740?–1828), the bookseller and publisher who organized the sale of books owned by the late third duke of Roxburghe, for which he wrote the catalogue and oversaw the highly successful auction of books many of which whose acquisition he had been involved in.[86] There is the bookseller James Edwards (1756–1816) who

> travelled diligently and fearlessly abroad: was now exploring the book-gloom of dusty monasteries, and at other times marching in the rear or front of Bonaparte's armies in Italy ... and may be fairly said to have carried out his concerns upon a scale as original as it was bold and successful.[87]

---

84 Dibdin, *Bibliographical Decameron*, III, p. 5.
85 Dibdin, *Reminiscences*, I, p. 295.
86 Dibdin, *Bibliographical Decameron*, III, p. 49. Vivienne W. Painting, 'Nicol, George (1740?–1828)', ODNB online, last accessed 7 November 2017.
87 Dibdin, *Bibliographical Decameron*, III, pp. 16–17. Edwards is portrayed as Rinaldo in *Bibliomania*. Dibdin notes that those who were less favourably inclined towards Edwards

Unlike most other booksellers introduced to us by Dibdin, Edwards died a rich man, leaving instructions that his coffin was to be made out of his library shelves.[88] There is poor Mr Lunn who, according to Dibdin, "had undoubtedly more zeal than prudence, and more pretension than knowledge". Having amassed a stock of foreign literature, he became a victim of the fall in prices following the peace. As 'a somewhat desperate speculation' he had bought up all the Wetstein Greek Testaments in Holland, and "suffered severely for his temerity, for his shelves long groaned beneath the weight of the Dutch critic". His stock was eventually sold for the benefit of his creditors and, with an interesting footnote on credit terms, Dibdin recounts that to benefit his widow and daughters "Liberal time was allowed for making good the purchases, and the result of the sale proved more fortunate than had been predicted".[89]

Both the *Bibliographical Decameron* and the expanded editions of *Bibliomania* devote much space to the sale of books by public auction.[90] Dibdin's works list literally scores of catalogues, both English and foreign (although mainly French), giving information about the circumstances of the sale, prices achieved, and history of ownership. The *Bibliomania* especially recommends sixteen catalogues as guides to the market value of books.[91] Taylor emphasizes the value of the catalogues of private libraries of the early nineteenth century as source material because of the preoccupation of the age with incunabula and black-letter. Arguably, the same could, presumably, be said of the sale catalogues of the period. Dibdin also includes references to numerous trade stock catalogues of which Taylor comments:

---

described his enunciation as "affectingly soft, and that he had too much of the air and grimace of a Frenchman"—a gibe that must in 1817 in the aftermath of the Napoleonic wars have been particularly wounding. Dibdin, *Bibliographical Decameron*, III, p. 439.

88   Michael F. Suarez and Michael L. Turner (eds.), *The Cambridge History of the Book in Britain*, vol. v, *1695–1830* (Cambridge: University Press, 2009), p. 719. Dibdin, *Bibliographical Decameron*, III, p. 16. Neuburg, *Selections*, p. 20.

89   Dibdin, *Bibliographical Decameron*, III, pp. 438–439.

90   Dibdin, *Bibliographical Decameron*, III, pp. 1–181. Dibdin, *Bibliomania* (1842), pp. 103–139.

91   Du Fresne (i.e. Trichet du Fresne, Paris, 1662): Cordes (Paris, 1643); Heinsius (2 vols., Leiden, 1682); Baluze (3 vols., Paris, 1719); Colbert (3 vols., Paris, 1728); Rothelin (Paris, 1746); De Boze (Paris, 1745 and 1753); Préfond (Paris, 1757); Pompadour (Paris, 1765); Gaignat (2 vols., Paris, 1769); Gouttard (Paris, 1780); Bünau (3 vols in 7 parts, Leipzig, 1750–1756); Soubise (Paris, 1788); La Vallière (9 vols., Paris, 1783–1788); Crevenna (6 vols., Amsterdam, 1775–1776); Lamoignon (3 vols., Paris, 1791–1792). Dibdin, *Bibliomania* (1811), p. 95. As footnotes to pp. 96–133, Dibdin provides details of these catalogues, and of over ninety other private and public collections, claiming, somewhat disingenuously, "Such an attempt is quite novel". Taylor, *Book Catalogues*, pp. 187–188.

Booksellers' recommendations of titles to make up a select general library are a variety of dealers' catalogues as yet unexplored by either bibliographers or students of intellectual history. Their value as a summary of what someone with more or less competence thought a cultivated man ought to read is obvious.[92]

He points out that they differ greatly in scope, and have, of course, a more immediately commercial intention from such lists as provided by Dibdin's *Library companion* and similar works.[93]

Dibdin's works also provide interesting detail about the conduct of sales, terms of credit, the times and costs of sales. For example, in the revised edition of the *Bibliomania*, Lisardo attends an auction at 12.30pm and departs at 3pm, paying for his purchases on departure with a banker's draft.[94] He estimates the costs of the 1817 sale of the library of Justin, Comte de MacCarthy Reagh (1744–1811), which included a Gutenberg Bible on vellum (the Grenville copy now in the British Library), at £200 per £1,000 including the government tax.[95]

The eighteenth and early nineteenth centuries saw libraries coming to the market outstanding both in terms of quality and quantity, and Dibdin regularly records the time that it took to disperse these huge collections.[96] At the height of the book bubble, Dibdin estimates that between November 1806 and November 1807 just three London auction houses alone disposed of 149,200 volumes in the course of thirty-nine sales.[97] But the torrent had begun earlier in the pre-

---

92 Taylor, *Book Catalogues*, p. 148.
93 Thomas F. Dibdin, *The Library Companion* (London, Printed for Harding, Triphook and Lepard, 1824), pp. xxv–vii. Taylor, *Book Catalogues*, p. 148.
94 Dibdin, *Bibliomania* (1811), pp. 160–184. Dibdin records numerous sales as taking place in the evening, but the later eighteenth century saw a move towards sales starting in the early afternoon. Was this a reflection of changing meal times, or a move towards the greater convenience of booksellers rather than of private individuals? Nigel Ramsay, 'English book collectors and the salerooms in the eighteenth century' in Myers, Harris and Mandelbrote (eds.), *Under the Hammer*, pp. 89–110: 103.
95 Dibdin, *Bibliomania*, p. 157 note 274. Dibdin, *Bibliographical Decameron*, III, p. 162.
96 "… the effective criteria of the great collectors were not so much literary as physical". John Carter, *Taste & Technique in Book-Collecting* (Cambridge: University Press, 1948), p. 14.
97 The auction houses were Leigh & Sotheby, King & Lochée, and Stewart. "Such has been the circulation of books, within the foregoing period, by the hands of three Auctioneers only; and the prices which a great number of useful articles [i.e. lots] brought is a sufficient demonstration that books are esteemed for their intrinsic value, as well as for the adventitious circumstances which render them rare or curious. But posterity are not to judge of the prevalence of knowledge in these times by the criterion of, what are technically called, book-sales only. They should be told that, within the same twelve months, thousands and tens of thousands of books of all sorts have been circulated by the London

vious century. The library of Thomas Rawlinson's (1681–1725) took nine years to disperse.[98] Describing Rawlinson's profile as a collector, Dibdin wrote:

> This Thomas Rawlinson ... was ... most desperately addicted to book-hunting. Because his own house was not large enough, he hired London House, in Aldersgate Street, for the reception of his library; and here he used to regale himself with the sight and the scent of innumerable black letter volumes, arranged in 'sable garb', and stowed perhaps 'three deep', from the bottom to the top of his house.[99]

The sale of the Mead library along with prints, drawings and antiquities in 1754 occupied some seventy-one days between November 1754 and April 1757.[100] Richard Rawlinson's (1690–1755) library, which contained over 20,000 volumes, took some fifty days in 1756.[101] The sale of the library of Martin Folkes (1690–

Booksellers: and that, without travelling to know the number disposed of at Bristol, Liverpool, York, Manchester, or Exeter, it may be only necessary to know that one distinguished House alone, established not quite a furlong from the railings of St. Paul's Cathedral, sold not far short of two hundred thousand volumes within the foregoing period". He contemplates that if the market continues to expand, "the book-fairs of Leipsic shall be forgotten in the superior splendour of those of London!". Dibdin, *Bibliomania* (1842), pp. 456–458. Dibdin reckons the number of volumes by multiplying lot (article) numbers by 3 (Dibdin, *Bibliomania* (1842), p. 370). See also Taylor, *Book Catalogues*, p. 75 where a note refers to the 1754 Osborne and Shipton catalogue of libraries from Viscount Coke and others containing nearly two hundred thousand volumes. Alston estimates that Osborne during his career as a bookseller re-distributed over two million books and that those re-distributed by Baker and Leigh (the founders of Sotheby's) and James Christie would certainly have exceeded this figure. Alston, *Inventory of Sale Catalogues*, I, p. 5.

98   Dibdin, *Bibliographical Decameron*, III, pp. 52. Dibdin, *Bibliomania*, p. 32.
99   Dibdin, *Bibliomania*, p. 32.
100 Dibdin, *Bibliomania*, p. 35. Richard Mead (1673–1754), physician, was a major collector of both books and art. He had a separate room built at the foot of the garden of his house on Great Ormond Street which housed his library and collections, which were among the largest of his time. Mead's collection of books and manuscripts was second only to that of Hans Sloane. His books numbered some 10,000 volumes, including 146 incunabula and many fine bindings. His library was especially rich in the classics and in works of medicine and natural philosophy. Mead aimed to find the best editions of canonical works. Anita Guerrini, 'Mead, Richard (1673–1754)', *ODNB online*, last accessed 7 November 2017.
101 Dibdin, *Bibliomania*, p. 40. Richard Rawlinson, topographer and bishop of the nonjuring Church of England, "was one of the greatest collectors of the eighteenth century and his lasting monument is the vast accumulation of 5,000 manuscripts which have furnished material for all manner of historical, theological, and literary studies since they came to rest in the Bodleian in 1756". Mary Clapinson, 'Rawlinson, Richard (1690–1755)', *ODNB online*, last accessed 7 November 2017.

1754), President of the Royal Academy and friend of Newton, was announced to commence on 2 March 1776 and continue for forty days (Sundays excepted) with the catalogue priced 6d "to be had at most considerable places in Europe, and all the booksellers of Great Britain and Ireland".[102] The Roxburgh sale in 1812, held in the dining room of the Duke's house in St James Square, lasted forty-three days. The first seven parts of the Heber sale amounting to 80,000 volumes in 39,354 lots, began in 1834 and lasted one hundred and forty-four days, with ultimately a total of three years required to complete the dispersal of that immense collection. Dibdin provides numerous examples along with summaries of many other sales taking place over similarly extended periods.

Such prolonged sales raise interesting questions about marketing and potential buyer fatigue. How effective was the network of newspaper advertisements, newspaper reporting of sales, and the distribution of catalogues to interested parties, bookshops and coffee houses in sustaining buyers' attention?[103] What effect did sales over such prolonged periods have on prices achieved? Did other copies of the same works achieve more successful prices when they were offered at smaller sales? To what extent did extended credit operate for buyers of numerous lots? What effects did having to inventory such mountains of books, sometimes in crammed and difficult physical circumstances, such as those of the Heber collections, have on the presentation of information in the sale catalogues?[104] How did the inclusion or omission of bibliographical detail

---

102   Dibdin, *Bibliomania*, p. 36.
103   Dibdin comments on the proliferation of newsprint "There is at present, such an hunger and thirst after information, that the reading man looks towards his weekly Journal, or Register, or Chronicle, with the same eagerness, and certainty that he used to anticipate his monthly supplies of mental food. Hence he has his *Literary Gazette*, or *Literary Chronicle*, or *Somerset House Chronicle*!—to which may be probably added one or two of the many two-penny publications that are also weekly distributed, and of which the aggregate total is scarcely to be credited". Dibdin, *Library companion*, pp. xiv–xv. In a footnote on p. xv, he notes "The fact is, however, that upwards of one hundred thousand of them are circulated per week; among which, the *Mechanic's Magazine*, the *Mirror*, the *Lancet*, and *the Chemist*, take the lead". While albeit not a sale catalogue, but a large catalogue of dealer's stock, Taylor refers to a catalogue issued by the London firm of Osborne & Shipton in 1754 being sent to the most eminent coffee houses in and near London with a note on its title page "for Gentlemen's Perusal, who are earnestly desired not to take them away: for, as this Sale will continue for Two Years, they will always be an amusement to Gentlemen". Taylor, *Book Catalogues*, p. 75.
104   Heber owned two houses in London, a country house, Hodnet Hall in Shropshire, and lodgings crammed with books in Brussels, Antwerp, Ghent, Malines, Nuremberg and Leiden. Hunt, 'Sale of Richard Heber's Library', pp. 146–147. Dibdin wrote of his first visit to the Pimlico House "I looked around me with amazement. I had never seen rooms, cupboards, passages and corridors so chocked, so suffocated with books. Treble rows were

influence potential buyers?[105] Perhaps a project which organized and analysed the price and other relevant data to be found on the pages of Dibdin's publications could add significantly to our understanding of some of these issues.

Dibdin's last great gamble on an already declining market for such works was the publication in 1838 of *A bibliographical antiquarian and picturesque tour in the Northern counties of England and in Scotland*, after which he issued nothing of substance, turning instead to works of devotion and sermons. This work shows that Dibdin did not confine his attentions to England. Initially Dibdin appears to have been less convinced of North Britain's claims to share the rampant southern enthusiasm for the printed book. In *Bibliomania* Dibdin has Lorenzo declaring "Of Scotland—I know nothing in commendation respecting the Bibliomania".[106] Dibdin notes that the catalogues of Messrs Constable, Laing and Blackwood "are a sufficient demonstration that the cause of the Bibliomania flourishes in the city of Edinburgh" but remains unde-

---

here, double rows were there. Hundreds of slim quartos—several upon each other—were longitudinally placed over thin and stunted duodecimos, reaching from one extremity of a shelf to another. Up to the very ceiling the piles of volumes extended; while the floor was strewed with them, in loose and numerous heaps". Dibdin, *Reminiscences*, I, pp. 436–437. Dibdin's proposal for preparing the sale catalogue envisaged no less than six assistants. Hunt, 'Sale of Richard Heber's Library', p. 148.

105   Dibdin prepared or had a hand in several sale catalogues; see Windle and Pippin, *Bibliography*, nos. A21, A22, A32, A36 and A43. He clearly valued the inclusion of bibliographical information as likely to have a positive effect. "I love to hear that the bibliographical labour bestowed upon a catalogue has answered the end proposed, by sharpening the appetites of the purchasers". Dibdin, *Bibliomania* (1842), p. 123. He comments on poorly printed sale catalogues: "Slips in typography have sometimes nearly as awkward an effect as in ethics" and instances a misprint in the catalogue of the sale of the Talleyrand Library: "For 'See a MS. Note at the beginning' we read 'See a MS. not eat the beginning'". Dibdin, *Bibliographical Decameron*, III, p. 136. However, the trend in the late eighteenth and early nineteenth centuries appears to have tended to a more abbreviated style of cataloguing. Hunt raises the possibly that this was because catalogues were for the benefit of experienced booksellers whereas early and mid-eighteenth century catalogues may have been aimed at private individuals. Hunt, 'Sale of Richard Heber's Library', pp. 105–106. "Gentlemen no longer bid in person at auction sales but relied on their agent to bid on their behalf". Arnold Hunt, 'Bibliotheca Heberiana' in Robin Myers and Michael Harris (eds.), *Antiquaries, Book Collectors and the Circles of Learning* (Winchester: St Paul's Bibliographies, 1996), pp. 83–112: 96, noting also that in the decline of the era of bibliomania, it was becoming increasingly difficult for those outside London to obtain sale catalogues. In advance of the penny post, the expense of postage was also a hindrance. "Evidence to the Select Committee on Postage in 1838 suggested many booksellers would have sent out circulars had postage been cheaper". Suarez and Turner, *Cambridge History of the Book*, vol. V, p. 376.

106   Dibdin, *Bibliomania* (1842), p. 415.

cided as to "Whether they have such desperate bibliomaniacs in Scotland, as we possess in London, and especially of the book auction species—is a point which I cannot take upon me to decide". *En passant*, he notes with approval Walter Scott's interest in black-letter, but with a somewhat breathtaking dismissal of the Scottish Enlightenment, he concludes "I am fearful that there are too many politico-economical, metaphysical, and philosophical miasmata, floating in the atmosphere of Scotland's metropolis, to render the climate there just now favourable to the legitimate cause of the Bibliomania".[107]

The *Northern tour* finds Dibdin in rather more expansive mode, with some 600 or so pages of volume two devoted to a country whose book-collecting interests he appeared previously happy to gloss over in a couple of footnotes. As the title proclaims, the work is not exclusively devoted to the bibliographical, but very much in the genre of Defoe, Pennant, Johnson, Young and similar precursors. There is, nevertheless, a lot of interesting detail about libraries, collectors, booksellers, binders and the newly fashionable book clubs, such as the Bannatyne and Maitland.

He is, though, not always complimentary about the places he visits. Of the university town of St Andrews in Fife, he writes:

---

107 Dibdin greatly admired Scott, whom he calls "this second Shakespeare". Dibdin, *Reminiscences*, II, p. 758. He characterises Scott as "Sir Tristram" in *Bibliomania* with a popularity "blazing into extraordinary reputation, and the author of two poems, "*The Lay of the Last Minstrel*" and "*Marmion*", which can perish only with our language". *Reminiscences*, I, p. 296. He records seeing the original MS of *Marmion* on the premises of Scott's publisher Robert Cadell and includes a facsimile of a page of the MS in the *Northern tour*, II, p. 531. Dibdin, *Bibliomania* (1842), p. 415. Scott's interest in mediaeval English literature had been kindled by the discovery of Percy's *Reliques* at the age of thirteen and the realisation that the editor "considered such works as worthy of 'sober research, grave commentary, and apt'. Scott's response underlines Percy's originality in treating the ballads with the seriousness of scholarship". Arthur Johnston, *Enchanted Ground: The Study of Medieval Romance in the Eighteenth Century* (London: University of London Athlone Press, 1964), p. 17. Scott owned some ten works by Dibdin, including *Specimen of a digested catalogue of rare, curious, and useful books* (1808) and *Specimen of an English De Bure* (1810), (Windle and Pippin, nos. A10 of which only 40 copies were printed and A12 of which only 50) and both inscribed to Scott, and an inscribed copy of the 1809 edition of *Bibliomania*. Scott appears in the list of subscribers for an octavo copy of Dibdin's edition of Ames and Herbert's *Typographical antiquities* (2 vols., London: William Miller, 1810–1819), p. 531. For information about Scott's library, now held at Abbotsford and managed by the Faculty of Advocates, see the Faculty's website: http://www.advocates.org.uk/faculty-of-advocates/the-advocates-library/abbotsford (last accessed: 29 December 2018).

FIGURE 23.5   *The Gateway to St Andrews*, from Dibdin's *Northern Tour*
PRIVATELY OWNED

> There is, perhaps, no spectacle, upon a small scale, of the perishableness of human institutions and earthly fabrics, more decided and more desolate than that of St Andrew's:—the once metropolitan see, and ecclesiastical law giver of Scotland.[108]

He continues:

> You enter St Andrew's under a Gateway ... The street before you, half a mile in length, is the longest in the town. It is broad, but very indifferently paved, and the houses have a low and mean aspect.[109]

To re-enforce the picture he adds in a footnote: "In Pennant's time this street was "grass-grown", presenting such a "dreary solitude, that it formed the perfect idea of having been laid waste by the pestilence"".

He commends, though, the University Library, which he estimates to have about 35,000 volumes, for its 'noble alphabetical catalogue' executed in folio in 1826 by the university printer Robert Tullis, a copy of which he was given by Principal Haldane (1772–1854).[110] He notes that by this time St. Andrews, like other Scottish universities entitled to claim under the Copyright Act a copy of every work printed in the United Kingdom, has commuted this right to an annual grant enabling the acquisition of what it considered to be 'the more eligible publications'.[111] He has a fit of the vapours, though, on discovering that the St Andrews' manuscript copy of Andrew of Wyntoun's *Orygynale Cronykil of*

---

108 Dibdin, *Northern tour*, II, p. 865.
109 Dibdin, *Northern tour*, II, pp. 874–875.
110 Dibdin, *Northern tour*, II, p. 918, with Dibdin wrongly giving the year as 1827. *Catalogus librorum in Bibliotheca Universitatis Andreanae, secundum literarum ordinem dispositus* ([St Andrews, Fife]: impensis Academiae Andreanae: typis Roberti Tullis, Academiae Typographi, 1826). For Robert Haldane, Principal of St Mary's College and Professor of Mathematics, see *Fasti Ecclesiae Scoticanae*, VII, p. 423. R.N. Smart, *Biographical Register of the University of St Andrews, 1747–1897* (St Andrews: University of St Andrews Library, 2004), p. 364.
111 The 1709 Copyright Act of Queen Anne entitled "An Act for the encouragement of learning by vesting the copies of printed books in the authors or purchasers of such copies. During the times therein mentioned" (cited either as 8 Ann. c. 21 or as 8 Ann. c. 19), gave publishers copyright protection provided they entered their titles before publication in the Stationers' Register and sent nine copies of each book, also before publication, to Stationers' Hall to be forwarded to the nine privileged libraries. These were initially the Bodleian Library (Oxford), Cambridge University Library, Sion College (London), the Advocates Library (Edinburgh), and the Universities of St Andrews, Edinburgh, Glasgow and Aberdeen. It was replaced by the 1842 Copyright Act.

Scotland is bound in a mere 'calf half-binding'. "I had fainted" he says "but for the opportune and friendly interposition of the Librarian" who brought him round with an assurance "that the present work should be clothed in morocco".[112] Perhaps taking into account the cost of rebinding the *Chronicle*, the library ordered, and rather late in the day, only a small paper copy of the *Tour*. A question, perhaps, of balancing the books?

The *Northern tour* provides a description of booksellers, binders and engravers in Edinburgh where there are several in Princes Street including that of Thomas George Stevenson (1809?–1893) whose shop he describes as being now "the only existing 'cask' in this city which preserves the true ancient Wynkn de Worde 'odour'".[113] He meets a number of distinguished collectors such as Thomas Thomson (1768–1852), President of the Bannatyne Club, the antiquary James Maidment (bap. 1793, d. 1879) and the author and judge Lord Cockburn (1779–1854). There are accounts of the University, Advocates' and Signet Libraries with reference to some of their more distinguished contents.

In Glasgow he visits the University Library and the Hunterian Museum. He is full of praise for the work of Robert and Andrew Foulis whom he compares favourably with the work of Didot, Bodoni, Bensley and Bulmer:

> ... there is that about the Foulis-type which always gladdens my eyes, and warms my heart:—a just proportion—an elegant form: and upon paper, in these degenerate days of cotton-mania, we must never expect to see again.[114]

He notes their early sojourn in Paris returning to London "carrying along with them no less than six or seven hogsheads of books".[115] Widely entertained by enthusiastic bibliophiles, he comments, rather prudishly, that dinners in Edinburgh and Glasgow 'usually' terminated in the grossest intoxication.[116]

---

112   Dibdin, *Northern tour*, II, p. 920. The librarian seems to have been as good as his word and the offending 'calf-half' was replaced by one of full brown, morocco, gilt—possibly even by the local binder Melville Fletcher who Dibdin met and found had been a pupil of Charles Lewis, the foremost London binder of his day. Dibdin misspells "Fletcher" as "Flecher" in the Index to the *Northern tour*. Also see the *Scottish Book Trade Index*, freely accessible at http://www.nls.uk/catalogues/scottish-book-trade-index, last accessed: 29 December 2018. I am most grateful to Mr Daryl Green, formerly of the University of St Andrews Library (currently Magdalen College, Oxford), for confirmation that the volume had been rebound.
113   Dibdin, *Northern tour*, II, p. 503. *Scottish Book Trade Index*.
114   Dibdin, *Northern tour*, II, pp. 760–761.
115   Dibdin, *Northern tour*, II, p. 763.
116   Dibdin, *Northern tour*, II, p. 772. Rabaiotti discusses Dibdin's moralising streak in his Intro-

Although the *Scots Times* in 1836 could wax lyrical over Dibdin, "Is there a lover of books in merry England or Broad Scotland who feels no interest in Dr Dibdin?", not everyone was captivated.[117] With that particular irascibility that a Scotchman reserves for an Englishman who has erred and strayed onto territory that he considers to be his own particular fiefdom, comes W.B.D.D. Turnbull snapping and snarling on the heels of the *Northern tour* as he corrects a number of the author's infelicities with such comments as "O Doctor, Doctor! What blunders are you after now" and "Dr Dibdin is garrulous, ergo, an ass!". Dibdin he finds 'slovenly'.[118] He sarcastically observes "Dr Dibdin's brains seem to be in their 'ordinary way of confusion'" and scorns with a "Dear delightful Dr Dibdin!" the author's moral concerns over the unisex arrangements for 'stitching' and 'thumping' in the workshops of the Edinburgh binders Messrs Henderson & Bisset.[119]

In the *Northern tour* Dibdin journeys as far as Perth, having reached Scotland by way of York and Newcastle and returning by way of Sunderland, having covered, he reckons, some 1700 miles, by various means including a daring twenty miles by rail on the Hexham Railway Company line to Carlisle of which, being Dibdin, he provides a highly dramatized account.[120]

It is also Scotland, or more precisely a Scotchman, even if one born in London, who provides Dibdin with the zenith of his commercial career, in the form of John Ker, third Duke of Roxburghe (1740–1804).[121] Known as the 'Book Duke',

---

duction to Dibdin's *Horae*. Dibdin, *Horae*, pp. 21–22. See also below for his concerns over the unisex arrangements for 'stitching' and 'thumping' in the workshops of the Edinburgh binders Messrs Henderson & Bisset.

117 O'Dwyer, *Dibdin*, p. 7.
118 William Barclay David Donald Turnbull (1811–1863), archivist and antiquary, and founder of the Abbotsford Club, named in honour of Sir Walter Scott, the aim of which was to publish original works and reissues relevant to Scottish history. "A learned, industrious, and careful scholar, Turnbull's scholarly caution did not extend beyond the pages of his works; his biographer, Eyton, ascribed to him 'an ardent temperament, cherishing strong prejudices, which impelled him to the expression of his opinions in unmitigated terms, and on several important occasions to a hasty and incautious course of action' (Eyton, 5)". Francis Edwards, 'Turnbull, William Barclay David Donald (1811–1863)', *ODNB online*, last accessed 20 June 2018. He was the author of *Notes, chiefly correctory, on Dr. Dibdin's tour through Scotland* (s.l., 1838). Of Turnbull, Dibdin remarks "I have never yet had the courage to request a catalogue raisonné of his Christian names". Dibdin, *Northern tour*, II, p. 616.
119 "I do hope ... that their premises will be exchanged for rooms where the lungs may have a more healthful atmosphere to breathe in—where the women who stitch may be separated from the men who thump". Dibdin, *Northern tour*, II, p. 632.
120 Dibdin, *Northern tour*, I, p. 405.
121 Brian Hillyard, 'Ker, John, third duke of Roxburghe (1740–1804)', *ODNB online*, last accessed 7 November 2017.

the sale of his libraries from Floors Castle in Scotland and his London home at 13 St James's Square (where he kept his main library) has gone down in the history of book collecting as the high point of bibliomania during the Regency period.[122] The sale has been described as "the first great sale of modern times" and "also the last manifesto of a closing era of taste".[123] Dibdin vividly describes 'The Roxburghe Fight' as he calls it in several of his works.[124] The sale in London in 1812 was in two parts, the first beginning 18 May and occupying forty-two days and the second 13 July, a further four days, the 9,353 lots bringing a total of £23,397.10s.6d.[125] The sale saw £2,260 paid for the Valdarfer Boccaccio of 1471, then thought to survive in only one copy—a record price for a single book not surpassed until Bernard Quaritch paid £4,950 for the 1459 Mainz Psalter at the Syston Park sale in 1884.[126]

Under Dibdin's inspiration a coterie of fellow collectors and bibliophiles dined together on 16 June, the eve of the sale of the Boccaccio. The diners decided that this occasion should not be forgotten and so they dined again together the next year on 17 June, the anniversary of the sale, and again the year after. These celebrations gave rise to the Roxburghe Club whose members still dine together each year on, or about, that memorable day.[127]

---

122 Jerdan, *Men I have known*, p. 169.
123 Carter, *Taste and technique*, p. 14.
124 Dibdin, *Bibliographical Decameron*, III, p. 49.
125 There was a further sale the following year at Kelso (Hillyard, 'Ker, John, third duke of Roxburghe').
126 Giovanni Boccaccio, *Decamerone* (Venice: Christophorus Valdarfer, 1471), USTC 996798. Copies in the British Library, Manchester, Milan and Paris. The successful purchaser was George Spencer, then Marquess of Blandford (later the 5th Duke of Marlborough) against fierce competition from his cousin and fellow bibliomaniac, George John, 2nd Earl Spencer. When financial difficulties forced Marlborough to sell his library seven years later, Spencer acquired the Valdarfer Boccaccio for only £918. The volume passed to Mrs Enriqueta Rylands when she purchased the Spencer Collection from the 2nd Earl's grandson in 1892, and hence to the John Rylands Library. Details of this copy are discussed by Julianne Simpson, Rare Books and Maps Manager at the John Rylands Library, at https://rylandscollections.wordpress.com/tag/valdarfer-boccaccio/ (11 June 2012), last accessed on 7 November 2017.
127 The founding of the Roxburghe Club "forms a watershed in the history of book-collecting and in the widest sense, of bibliography. It looks back at the 'heroic' period of book-collecting of which it was the culmination; it looks forward over the development in the study and collection of books which has taken place since". Nicolas Barker, *Roxburghe Club*, p. 1. At the first anniversary dinner in 1813 "It was proposed and concluded for each Member of the Club to reprint a scarce piece of ancient lore to be given to the Members, one copy being on vellum for the Chairman, and only as many copies as Members ...".

"Posterity has, for the most part, been unkind and even condescending to the memory of the Revd. Thomas Frognall Dibdin".[128] He has been described as 'the world's worst bibliographer'.[129] Jackson, his first bibliographer, says of him "The most exasperating of bibliographers—hardly a statement he makes can be accepted without checking".[130] The first edition of the *Dictionary of National Biography* refers to him as "an ignorant pretender without the learning of a schoolboy, who published a quantity of books swarming with errors of every description".[131] Its successor, the *Oxford Dictionary of National Biography*, offers a more measured account of Dibdin's life and work, concluding:

> ... his main contribution seem to have been his zealous enthusiasm in promoting book collecting generally among the aristocracy, as well as putting forth the principle of first-hand examination of books in the compilation of bibliographies.[132]

There is a certain sterility about many of Dibdin's compilations.[133] Dibdin was not a scholar. Where a scholarly assessment of a work was required, such as in the *Introduction to the classics*, he borrowed heavily on the work of others, for the most part restricting his own opinions to matters of type, layout and illustration. He certainly valued scholarship and was an enthusiastic supporter, under the guise of black-letter, of the school that wanted to look back to earlier

---

Barker, *Roxburghe Club*, p. 6. Lists of members of the Club from 1812 and its publications can be found on the Club's website http://www.roxburgheclub.org.uk/membership/, last accessed: 29 December 2018.
128 Neuburg, *Selections*, p. 2.
129 O'Dwyer, *Dibdin*, p. 7.
130 Jackson, *Annotated list*, p. 10.
131 Sir Leslie Stephen (ed.), *Dictionary of National Biography* (London: Smith Elder, 1908), V, p. 912. The author of the article, Henry Luard, speaking of the Spencer catalogue, states "He could not even read the characters of the Greek books he describes; and his descriptions are so full of errors that it may be doubted if a single one is really accurate". He dismisses the *Bibliographical tour* in the following harsh terms "the style is flippant, and at times childish, and the book abounds with follies and errors. It would have been (it has been said) 'a capital volume, if there had been no letterpress'". Even if he was careless, clearly Dibdin had sufficient mastery of Greek to gain him entry to Oxford. Cf. Dibdin, *Bibliomania*, p. xviii and Dibdin, *Reminiscences*, I, p. 81, where he claimed to be able to master Xenophon "with comparative ease" even if Demosthenes "required closer grappling with".
132 Richardson, 'Dibdin, Thomas Frognall'.
133 "It is not, however, originality ... that we find in Dibdin's pages; it is the sheer extent of his output, providing us as it does with a starting point for a view of his contemporaries who wrote about books and book collecting ...". Neuburg, *Selections*, p. 24.

periods of English literature as an important influence on later writers.[134] But then the same accusation of sterility could equally be levelled at many of Dibdin's patrons whose feverish competition to assemble vast collections of books mirror Dibdin's own huge compilation of facts. "It was the sheer desirability of books that captivated Dibdin and many of his contemporaries".[135] Even if we are grateful to his patrons for preserving many works that might otherwise have been lost, their efforts often appeared to serve no purpose other than the self-indulgence of ownership arising out of the possession of deep pockets. Moreover, unlike their predecessors, who tended to think in terms of eventual public ownership of their books, they did not on the whole even leave their vast collections for the benefit of posterity.[136]

Ultimately, what are we to make of the Reverend Doctor? Is there more than just the infatuation with large paper, printing on vellum, binding in morocco with all edges gilt: the addiction to the thrill of the chase, borne along on a tsunami of his own unleashing? There are probably a number of reasons why interest in Dibdin persists.

He was writing at a time which saw the public appearance at auction of a huge number of important books of the early period, and he has much interesting information on their prior history and ownership. He helped to form a number of important libraries that ultimately entered public collections, such as the Spencer collection later acquired for the John Rylands Library in Manchester. Despite his self-proclaimed struggle "to avoid a prolixity which might be wearisome and a brevity which might be superficial or obscure", his works are valuable as a source of information about the practices of the book trade and the auction houses.[137] The detail he provides about his own works, give us first-

---

134 "Thus aspects of Earlier English literature which had been the object of conscious rebellion in the previous century, or which had interested only a few pedants, or which had been read and enjoyed and occasionally imitated, began to attract attention after 1760". Johnston, *Enchanted Ground*, pp. 2–3. Scott was interested in acquiring the de Worde Malory at the Roxburghe sale for his intended, but subsequently abandoned, edition of the *Morte Darthur*. Johnston, *Enchanted Ground*, p. 191.
135 Neuburg, *Selections*, p. 22.
136 Carter, *Taste and Technique*, pp. 13–14. As Neuberg points out there were exceptions. One such was Francis Douce (1757–1834) for whom "Scholarship was the justification, then, for book collecting, as Douce saw it, and in him the scholar and collector were combined. When he died, his collection of books, manuscripts, prints and coins was bequeathed to the Bodleian Library". Another was Richard Heber. Although Heber's library was dispersed by auction, in his lifetime his "reputation was that of bibliophile and student of English literature. In this role he made both his library and his knowledge readily available to contemporaries". Neuburg, *Selections*, p. 19.
137 Dibdin, *Reminiscences*, I, p. viii.

hand insight into the publishing and book-selling practices of the period.[138] The Roxburghe Club, the world's oldest and most prestigious bibliophilic society, remains an enduring memorial to Dibdin's inspiration, enthusiasm and conviviality.

We need to balance our modern perspective of Dibdin as "a Regency amateur in the hard new world of Victorian professionalism" with his value as a source of the cultural history of his period.[139] His preoccupation with the rich and aristocratic might tempt dismissal as a mere 'book bitch to the rich'—the subscription list for his *Reminiscences* includes one royal duke, nine of the more ordinary variety, two marquesses, six earls, two viscounts, assorted bishops and numerous distinguished wealthy collectors.[140] Nevertheless, Dibdin prompts the modern reader to reflect seriously on the relationship between that of collecting and bibliography.[141] A kinder *sobriquet* is probably that given him by his contemporary, the journalist and antiquary William Jerdan (1782–1869), who in contemplating Dibdin's role in the 'book madness' of the period, calls him 'the Beau Brummell of the folly'.[142] "His chatter may sometimes repel, but a profound sense of purpose underlay all his work: it was the book which mattered".[143]

---

138 "Working closely with printers, compositors, and correctors, Dibdin became a familiar figure in printing quarters vividly recalling its workaday milieu in his Reminiscences …". Ferris, *Book-Men*, p. 54.
139 Dibdin, *Bibliomania*, p. xxiv.
140 "It is customary to decry the abilities of Thomas Frognall Dibdin, and certainly his snobbery, prolixity, facetiousness and inaccuracy invite ridicule. Nevertheless his enthusiasm infected a whole generation of collectors with bibliomania …". Munby, 'Dibdin's reference library', p. 279.
141 "Dibdin stimulates a continuing discussion of the subject; for, even when he is wrong, he never allows us for a moment to forget that the printed word is at the heart of the problem". Neuburg, *Selections*, p. 4.
142 Jerdan, *Men I have known*, p. 172. Of his account of book-collectors and book auctions Dibdin wrote "They may serve, as well to awaken curiosity in regard to yet further interesting memoranda respecting scholars, as to shew the progressive value of books, and the increase of the disease called Bibliomania. Some of the most curious volumes in English literature have, in these notes, been duly recorded; nor can I conclude my laborious, though humble task, without indulging a fond hope that this account will be consulted by all those who make book-collecting their amusement". Dibdin, *Bibliographical Decameron*, III, p. 461.
143 Neuburg, *Selections*, p. 24. I am most grateful to Mr. John Stevenson, Mr. Julian Russell and Dr. Murray Simpson who read this paper in draft and for their invaluable comments. Mr. Trevor Kyle kindly helped with the illustrations.

CHAPTER 24

Lost in Transaction: 'Discollecting' Incunabula in the Nineteenth and Twentieth Centuries

Falk Eisermann

Introduction

Libraries, archives, museums and other public institutions all over the world currently own about half a million copies of incunabula. Many of these were acquired during the nineteenth and early twentieth centuries from the antiquarian booktrade. One major player on the acquisition market at that time, especially in the decades around 1900, was the Royal (later Prussian State) Library, today Staatsbibliothek zu Berlin—Preußischer Kulturbesitz. This chapter will mainly focus on the library's incunabula acquisitions in the first decades of the past century, following the founding of the Gesamtkatalog der Wiegendrucke (GW) in 1904.[1] During this period Berlin's fifteenth-century collection expanded due to a process which can only be called an acquisitional frenzy of extraordinary dimensions. Partly due to the contemporaneous library practice of deaccessioning surplus stock followed by duplicate sales, and the ongoing dissolution of institutional collections, the book market at the time was awash with incunabula. Many new items came to Berlin directly from institutional owners, others, especially valuable ones, turned up in the book trade and were subsequently bought by the Staatsbibliothek.

Or they were not. My interest in the subject of the library's history of buying—and sometimes selling, but that is not the subject here—incunabula first arose from reviewing an archival file that contains the correspondence

---

1 *Gesamtkatalog der Wiegendrucke*, 12 vols. (to be continued), vols. 1–8 (Leipzig: Hiersemann, 1925–1940), 2nd rev. ed. vols. 1–7 (Stuttgart/New York: Hiersemann, 1968); vol. 8 ff. (Stuttgart: Hiersemann, 1978–). GW numbers without preceding letter 'M' can be looked up in the printed volumes as well as in the database; for the 'M' numbers see www.gesamtkatalogderwiegendrucke.de. All online resources quoted in this article have last been seen on 19 December 2018. The present chapter is a sequel to my article 'The Gutenberg galaxy's dark matter: lost incunabula, and ways to retrieve them', in Flavia Bruni and Andrew Pettegree (eds.), *Lost Books. Reconstructing the Print World of Pre-Industrial Europe* (Leiden/Boston: Brill, 2016), pp. 31–54. My thanks, as always, to Christine Magin for her support, and to Paul Needham, who almost let his morning coffee go cold in order to meet my deadline.

between the GW and the Munich antiquarian book dealers Julius and Ida Halle; here it will be called the 'Halle file'. This file, which is kept without shelfmark in the GW's archives, has to the best of my knowledge never been researched or published. It mostly deals with general enquiries and day-to-day incunabula business; yet it also contains a considerable amount of information on rare, sometimes unique, fifteenth-century books and broadsides that were offered to the Berlin library, and often sent to the GW editors for inspection. However, none of these rare incunabula were ultimately acquired by the Staatsbibliothek and most of them subsequently disappeared from bibliographical view. Among the incunabula thus lost in transaction was at least one extremely important, if not spectacular, item from the earliest years of printing. Before dealing with the file itself, I will briefly outline how the Staatsbibliothek's shopping spree manifested itself in the period up to about 1930.

Shopping Sprees and Other Forms of Collection Building

As of now, the Staatsbibliothek has neither a copy-specific catalogue of its incunabula collection, nor a comprehensive history of its acquisition history regarding fifteenth-century books and broadsides.[2] Some fifteenth-century books became part of the private library of the Brandenburg electors long before the Royal Library was officially founded in 1661. Probably the first and certainly the most famous acquisition was Martin Luther's copy of the Hebrew Bible printed by Gershom Soncino in Brescia in 1494.[3] After Luther's death the copy had remained in the family and was sold by his grandchildren to the future elector towards the end of the sixteenth century. Since 2015 this copy is listed in the UNESCO Memory of the World heritage programme.[4]

The acquisitional and historical documentation for the first two centuries of the library's existence is fragmentary. The most decisive change in the manage-

---

2   The most important contribution in this regard remains Ursula Altmann, 'Die Inkunabelsammlung', in Horst Kunze (ed.), *Deutsche Staatsbibliothek 1661–1961. Geschichte und Gegenwart* (Leipzig: VEB Verlag für Buch- und Bibliothekswesen, 1961), pp. 381–403.
3   GW 4200; Staatsbibliothek, 8° Inc 2840. Stephen G. Burnett, 'Luthers hebräische Bibel (Brescia, 1494)—Ihre Bedeutung für die Reformation', in Irene Dingel and Henning P. Jürgens (eds.), *Meilensteine der Reformation. Schlüsseldokumente der frühen Wirksamkeit Martin Luthers* (Gütersloh: Gütersloher Verlagshaus, 2014), pp. 62–69; Christoph Mackert, 'Luthers Handexemplar der hebräischen Bibelausgabe von 1494—Objektbezogene und besitzgeschichtliche Aspekte', in Dingel and Jürgens, *Meilensteine*, pp. 70–78.
4   See http://blog.sbb.berlin/drei-weitere-stuecke-der-staatsbibliothek-jetzt-im-unesco-register-memory-of-the-world/.

ment and build-up of the incunabula collection occurred during Ernst Voulliéme's (1862–1930) time in office. Voulliéme compiled the first inventory of the Staatsbibliothek's incunabula and became one of the founding fathers of the GW.[5] In a 1916 paper comprising only eight pages and modestly titled 'New Incunabula Acquisitions of the Royal Library', he announced a rapid and substantial growth of the collection that had taken place during the short period following the publication of the 1914 supplement to his inventory.[6] Since then, Voulliéme writes, with some understatement, the library had been able to "make a series of lucky acquisitions".[7] Lucky indeed: The most substantial portion consisted of no fewer than 230 items from the duplicate stocks of the Munich Royal Library, mainly German and Italian incunabula with an emphasis on editions from printing houses in Augsburg, Strasbourg and Venice. Voulliéme describes these as "enough useful items to fill gaps", hinting towards the plan to accumulate a comprehensive collection of fifteenth-century typography for the purposes of the GW.[8] Fifteen editions were acquired from the Royal Lyceum at Konitz, today Chojnice in Poland, among them a vellum copy of the first Aldine Aristotle.[9] A 1485 *Missale Basiliense*, the first book printed by Nikolaus Kessler in Basel, was acquired from the Mariengymnasium in Stettin (Szczecin, Poland); together with almost 4,000 incunabula and tens of thousands of other rare books it was destroyed in the final days of World War II.[10] From the Church Library at Neuruppin the Staatsbibliothek bought a copy of what had until then been an unrecorded edition of the *Missale Havelbergense*.[11]

5   Ernst Voulliéme, *Die Inkunabeln der Königlichen Bibliothek und der anderen Berliner Sammlungen. Ein Inventar* (Leipzig: Harrassowitz, 1906); four supplements covering the additions from 1907–1926 were published in 1907, 1914, 1922, and 1927, respectively. The post-World War II status of the collection is documented in Anneliese Schmitt, *Die Inkunabeln der Deutschen Staatsbibliothek zu Berlin* (Berlin: Akademie-Verlag, 1966). About Voulliéme see the obituary by Max Joseph Husung, 'Ernst Voulliéme', *Zentralblatt für Bibliothekswesen*, 48 (1931), pp. 189–192; Anneliese Schmitt, '"Los! ... Die Schreibereien sind aber langweilig, also Taten!" 100 Jahre Gesamtkatalog der Wiegendrucke und 100 Jahre Berliner Inkunabelkatalog im Spiegel der Briefe von Ernst Voulliéme an Konrad Haebler', *Gutenberg Jahrbuch* (2006), pp. 179–187.
6   Ernst Voulliéme, 'Neue Inkunabel-Erwerbungen der Königlichen Bibliothek', *Zentralblatt für Bibliothekswesen*, 33 (1916), pp. 47–54.
7   Voulliéme, 'Inkunabel-Erwerbungen', p. 47: "eine Reihe glücklicher Erwerbungen".
8   Voulliéme, 'Inkunabel-Erwerbungen', p. 47: "genug brauchbare Stücke zur Auffüllung von Lücken". The items are listed on pp. 48–50.
9   GW 2334.
10 GW M24254. Werner Schochow, *Bücherschicksale. Die Verlagerungsgeschichte der Preußischen Staatsbibliothek. Auslagerung, Zerstörung, Entfremdung, Rückführung* (Berlin: de Gruyter, 2003).
11 GW M24408.

New to incunabula bibliography were also several broadsides with coin regulations for the Saxonian territories, bought from the State Archives at Weimar.[12] A further six incunabula hitherto not present in the Royal Library were donated from the estate of Dr Georg August Freund (1836–1914), a collector of gastronomical and dietetic works.[13] In addition, more than forty items came from the trade, but Voulliéme did not disclose the vendors' names.[14] Voulliéme's article concluded with a number of examples of 'in-house collection building'; among other things he reported the discovery of a rare Bohemian *Psalterium* in the stacks of the Staatsbibliothek and Konrad Haebler's finding of two vellum copies of a 1487 Strasbourg indulgence in a binding.[15] At the same time, the only complete copy of the *Rituale Caesaraugustanum* printed in Valencia or Hijar about 1486 was donated by the Association of the Friends of the Library.[16]

Voulliéme's 1916 article provides a summary of the varying sources and methods of collection enhancement that were possible even during World War I; or perhaps they were possible only due to the precarious economical and social conditions in wartime Germany. Even Voulliéme, as efficient and prudent as any Prussian library official was supposed to be, must have felt how unusual these transactions were. Yet the 1914–1916 campaign was not a unique event in the history of the Berlin Royal Library. Similar bulk acquisitions had been conducted before, comprising incunabula from ecclesiastical libraries in Lower Saxony, such as the *Ministerialbibliotheken* in Uelzen and Celle, acquired in 1896 and 1911, respectively, and from school libraries and public collections in Thuringia, e.g. the library of the Heiligenstadt Gymnasium and the Royal Library at Erfurt, the latter including 645 incunabula.[17]

---

12   GW 10387–10394.
13   For Konitz, Stettin, Neuruppin, Weimar and the Freund collection see Voulliéme, 'Inkunabel-Erwerbungen', pp. 50–51. On Freund see also the information in http://d-nb.info/gnd/11753708X.
14   Voulliéme, 'Inkunabel-Erwerbungen', p. 47.
15   Voulliéme, 'Inkunabel-Erwerbungen', pp. 53–54. GW M36275 (*Psalterium*), and GW M12900 (indulgences).
16   GW M38259. Konrad Haebler, 'Zur Druckertätigkeit des Alfonso Fernandez de Cordoba. Nach einer Neuerwerbung der Königlichen Bibliothek', *Zentralblatt für Bibliothekswesen*, 32 (1915), pp. 196–202.
17   Altmann, 'Die Inkunabelsammlung', pp. 392–393.

The Halle File

Let us now turn to the Halle file, which sheds light on other aspects of acquisitioning and, crucially, non-acquisitioning during that—incunabulistically speaking—highly significant period. The file consists of 109 items of correspondence, mostly one- or two-page letters, including the odd postcard or telegram. Sixty or so letters were sent by the book dealer and addressed to the "Kommission für den Gesamtkatalog der Wiegendrucke"; all others are answers and enquiries by members of the GW staff. Almost all GW letters were signed by Max Joseph Husung, head of the incunabula department from 1927 until his removal from office by the Nazi authorities on 24 September 1933.[18] Halle's letters are preserved in the original, the GW's in carbon copies. The file begins with a Halle letter dated 27 September 1924 (Figure 24.1) and ends abruptly on 25 June 1931; these dates, however, clearly mark neither the beginning nor the end of the exchange, and it is very likely that parts of the correspondence have not survived.[19]

Isaak (later Julius) Halle, born in 1864, was a nephew and former apprentice of the famous Munich antiquarian Ludwig Rosenthal.[20] With his wife Ida, Julius founded his own business at Ottostraße 3a in Munich in 1889. Unlike his uncle and other members of the legendary Rosenthal family, little is known about his life; there is no biographical or other study about him or his company.[21] Julius died on 9 December 1927, and Ida took over and subsequently

---

18   Friedhilde Krause and Rolf Volkmann, *Max Joseph Husung. Porträt eines bedeutenden Einbandforschers und Bibliophilen* (Hannover: Laurentius, 1993); Horst Kunze, 'Max Joseph Husung und die Bibliophilie', *Bibliothek und Wissenschaft*, 29 (1996), pp. 327–332.

19   The contents are hitherto quoted 'Halle file' plus number and date.

20   Reinhard Wittmann, 'Münchens Jüdische Antiquariate—Glanz und Zerstörung', *Münchner Beiträge zur jüdischen Geschichte und Kultur*, 2 (2009), pp. 23–42: 38–39; for the larger context see also Wittmann, *Hundert Jahre Buchkultur in München* (Munich: Hugendubel, 1993); Ernst Fischer, *Verleger, Buchhändler & Antiquare aus Deutschland und Österreich in der Emigration nach 1933. Ein biographisches Handbuch* (Elbingen: Verband deutscher Antiquare, 2011), p. 117 (on Ida Halle). Archival material on the history of Halle's company, including business and biographical data, tax details, and also the correspondence between Jacques Rosenthal and Julius and Ida Halle, along with a complete series of annotated Rosenthal sales catalogues from 1895 to 1935 is preserved in the Municipal Archive (Stadtarchiv), Munich. This material has not yet been sufficiently catalogued, and I have not been able to inspect it for the purposes of the present chapter. My thanks to Anton Löffelmeier (Stadtarchiv München) for the relevant information.

21   *Die Rosenthals. Der Aufstieg einer jüdischen Antiquarsfamilie zu Weltruhm. Mit Beiträgen von Elisabeth Angermair et al.* (Vienna, Cologne, Weimar: Böhlau, 2002); on Halle pp. 81, 83, 115.

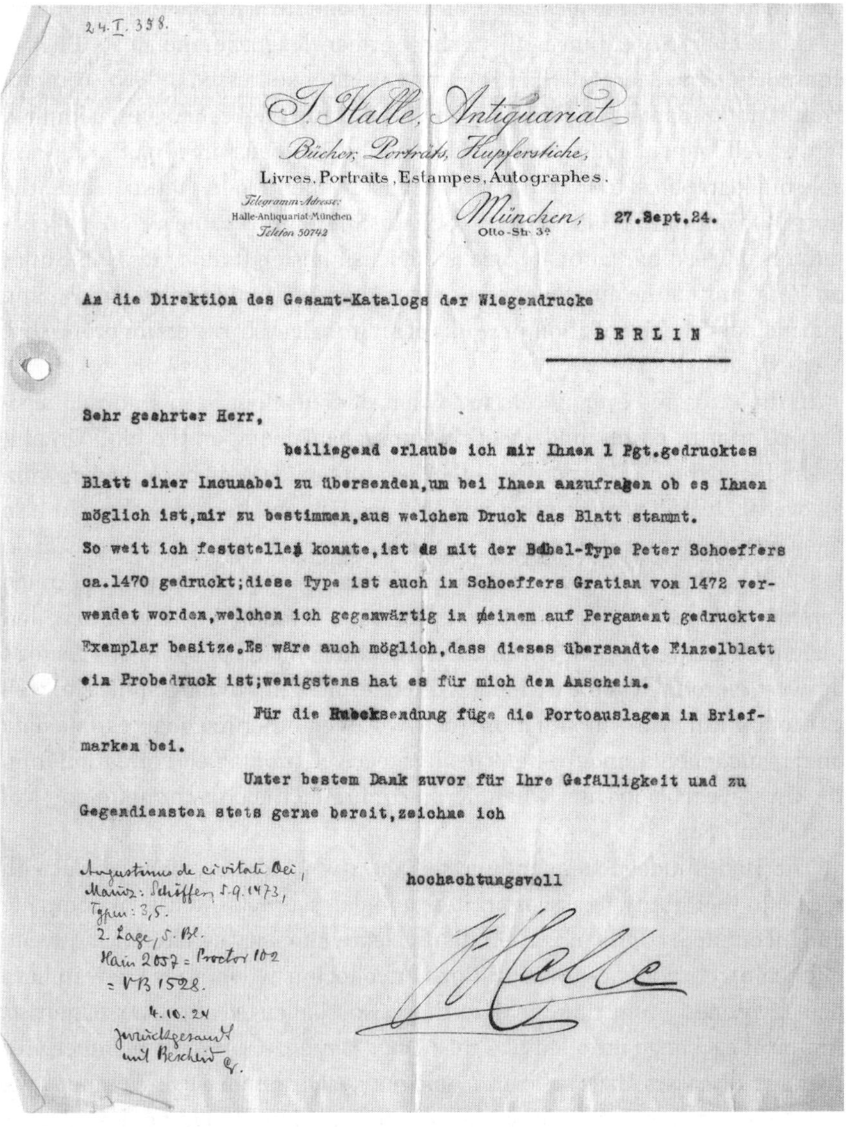

24.I. 358.

J. Halle, Antiquariat

Bücher, Porträts, Kupferstiche,

Livres, Portraits, Estampes, Autographes.

Telegramm-Adresse: Halle-Antiquariat-München

Telefon 50742

München, 27.Sept.24.

Otto-Str. 3a

An die Direktion des Gesamt-Katalogs der Wiegendrucke

B E R L I N

Sehr geehrter Herr,

beiliegend erlaube ich mir Ihnen 1 Pgt.gedrucktes Blatt einer Incunabel zu übersenden,um bei Ihnen anzufragen ob es Ihnen möglich ist,mir zu bestimmen,aus welchem Druck das Blatt stammt.
So weit ich feststellen konnte,ist es mit der Bibel-Type Peter Schoeffers ca.1470 gedruckt;diese Type ist auch im Schoeffers Gratian von 1472 verwendet worden,welchen ich gegenwärtig in meinem auf Pergament gedruckten Exemplar besitze.Es wäre auch möglich,dass dieses übersandte Einzelblatt ein Probedruck ist;wenigstens hat es für mich den Anschein.

Für die Rücksendung füge die Portoauslagen in Briefmarken bei.

Unter bestem Dank zuvor für Ihre Gefälligkeit und zu Gegendiensten stets gerne bereit,zeichne ich

hochachtungsvoll

J. Halle

Augustinus de civitate Dei,
Mainz: Schöffer 5.9.1473,
Typen: 3,5.
2. Lage, 5. Bl.
Hain 2057 = Proctor 102
= VB 1528.
4.10.24
zurückgesandt
mit Bescheid

FIGURE 24.1 Halle's first surviving letter to the GW, 27 September 1924
STAATSBIBLIOTHEK ZU BERLIN—PREUẞISCHER KULTURBESITZ, GW ARCHIVE

worked hard to earn her nickname "die teure Halle", which of course is a tongue-in-cheek characterization both in the German language and in its English equivalent ("the dear Halle").[22] The first GW letter addressed to "Sehr verehrte Frau Halle" is dated 24 February 1928.[23] The company's catalogues, compiled by the well-known bibliographer Ernst Schulte Strathaus (1881–1968), are valuable bibliographical tools to this day. It must be mentioned that soon after the forced closing of the Halle business Schulte Strathaus became a close collaborator of the leading National Socialist 'Reichsminister' Rudolf Hess; his duties on Hess' staff in the aptly named Braunes Haus in Munich between 1934 and 1941 included the 'acquisition' of works of art from Jewish owners for prominent Nazis.[24]

In the 1920s and ever since, the GW has of course not been a normal business partner or correspondent of antiquarians. Relying on the bibliographical and typographical expertise of the Gesamtkatalog staff, book dealers from all over the world were sending not only acquisition offers to Berlin, but also many enquiries regarding rarities, or items considered as such, as they still do to this day. They also often made originals available to the GW without much ceremony. Some of these enquiries were, just like today, time-consuming and tedious to answer, as evident in the tone and subtexts of some of Husung's answers. Nevertheless the exchanges often resulted in a bibliographical as well as economical 'win-win' situation: the GW gained otherwise inaccessible data on rare incunabula, and the book dealers received profitable information from the GW, especially in cases when Berlin confirmed the rarity or uniqueness of particular items.

The Halles indeed frequently asked the GW to identify incunabula with regard to their rarity, to assign printers and dates, or to send lists of complete and incomplete copies of certain items, clearly nursing the ulterior motive to offer complete volumes to institutions or collectors whom they knew to have defective ones. From time to time they also challenged the GW's expertise. A typical exchange unrolled like this: On 3 May 1926, GW staff member Carl Wehmer discusses Halle's recent catalogue 59. Of number 134, Wehmer says, the GW has never seen a copy; the collation of number 142 he describes as incomplete and the date given in the catalogue as hardly possible; according

---

22   Wittmann, 'Münchens Jüdische Antiquariate', p. 38.
23   Halle file, no. 56.
24   Jan-Pieter Barbian, *Literaturpolitik im NS-Staat. Von der Gleichschaltung bis zum Ruin* (Frankfurt am Main: Fischer Taschenbuch-Verlag, 2010), chapter 3.3; Andreas Heusler, *Das braune Haus. Wie München zur "Hauptstadt der Bewegung" wurde* (Munich: DVA, 2008).

to Wehmer's assessment, no. 280a contains an interesting date, but a dubious collation. Could Halle please check against his copies the accompanying GW descriptions of no. 134 and above all no. 280a, the latter representing an edition having just been catalogued in Berlin for inclusion in a forthcoming GW volume?[25] Help arrives quickly: The next day—time and again, the file demonstrates how effective the mail used to be—Halle sends the three incunabula to Berlin; Husung returns them a week later, admitting that Halle's collation of no. 280a had indeed been correct.[26]

Back and forth the letters fly; yet the exchange is always strictly business, with no small talk or indication of any kind of personal contact or exchange. In fact, it is not without frictions which are mainly due to Husung's formal, sometimes almost abrasive manner. A comprehensive analysis of the file has to be reserved for future studies; for now I will focus on what I consider its most important aspect: the primary, in some cases the only available documentation of hitherto undescribed fifteenth-century editions.

Lost in Transaction

On 14 November 1927, Halle reports that among their old papers they have found a description of an incunable not in GW, namely an edition of the medical compilation *Articella* (Figure 24.2). This 94-leaf octavo, published by the de Gregoriis company in Venice on 4 June 1481, had been sold by Julius Halle almost twenty-five years earlier to Leo Olschki in Florence.[27] Apparently this was the only surviving copy of this edition, and as far as I know it has not been seen or mentioned in any bibliographical context except the GW database since 1903. Thus the rudimentary description in the Halle file remains the only available record. Allowing for errors or falsifications, the 1481 *Articella* must be considered one of the earliest dated works by the de Gregoriis brothers, and only the second edition of the text altogether. Given its unusual format (octavo) it

---

25   Halle file, no. 14.
26   Halle file, nos. 15, 16.
27   Halle file, no. 41; GW 02678ION. On Olschki, see *Die Rosenthals*, pp. 115–118; Bernard M. Rosenthal, 'Cartel, Clan, or Dynasty? The Olschkis and the Rosenthals 1859–1976', *Harvard Library Bulletin*, 25 (1977), pp. 381–398. For Rosenthal aficionados it might be mentioned that the original typescript of Bernard's paper, a carbon copy numbered "21 of 50 copies", is preserved among the papers of the famous German paleographer Bernhard Bischoff in the library of the Monumenta Germaniae Historica, Munich, and can be viewed online at http://www.mgh-bibliothek.de//dokumente/b/b037067.pdf.

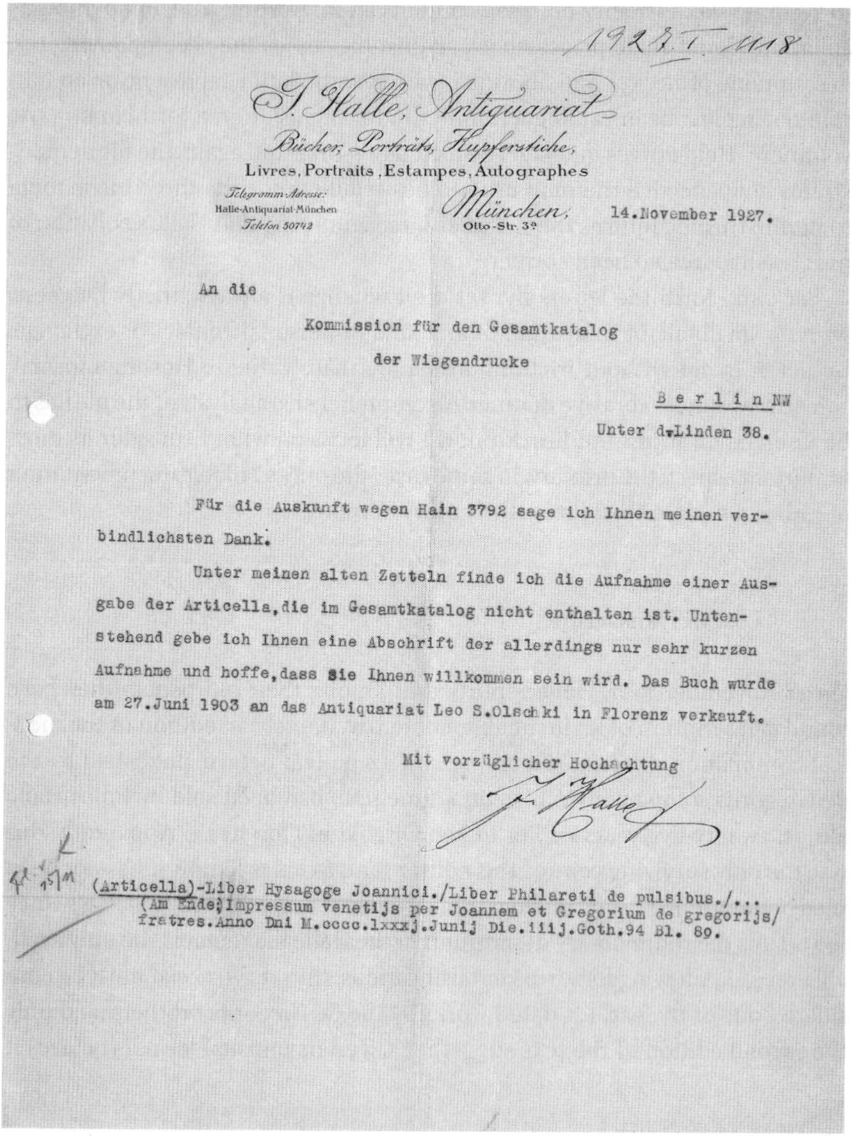

1927 T 1118

J. Halle, Antiquariat
Bücher, Porträts, Kupferstiche,
Livres, Portraits, Estampes, Autographes

Telegramm-Adresse:
Halle-Antiquariat-München
Telefon 50742

München, Otto-Str. 3a   14. November 1927.

An die

Kommission für den Gesamtkatalog
der Wiegendrucke

Berlin NW
Unter d. Linden 38.

Für die Auskunft wegen Hain 3792 sage ich Ihnen meinen verbindlichsten Dank.

Unter meinen alten Zetteln finde ich die Aufnahme einer Ausgabe der Articella, die im Gesamtkatalog nicht enthalten ist. Untenstehend gebe ich Ihnen eine Abschrift der allerdings nur sehr kurzen Aufnahme und hoffe, dass Sie Ihnen willkommen sein wird. Das Buch wurde am 27. Juni 1903 an das Antiquariat Leo S. Olschki in Florenz verkauft.

Mit vorzüglicher Hochachtung

J. Halle

(Articella)-Liber Hysagoge Joannici./Liber Philareti de pulsibus./...
(Am Ende:) Impressum venetijs per Joannem et Gregorium de gregorijs/ fratres. Anno Dni M.cccc.lxxxj. Junij Die. iiij. Goth. 94 Bl. 8o.

FIGURE 24.2 Letter from Halle to the GW announcing an unrecorded *Articella* edition, 14 November 1927
STAATSBIBLIOTHEK ZU BERLIN—PREUẞISCHER KULTURBESITZ, GW ARCHIVE

has to be considered an important 'missing link' in the editorial and textual history of the *Articella*, and thus certainly merits inclusion in a future 'Incunabula Most Wanted' list.[28]

Six weeks later, in a letter accompanied by nine slips of bibliographical descriptions, Ida Halle notifies the GW of a *Sammelband* she had just acquired "in an old library".[29] The volume contains, the writer says, eight Nuremberg schoolbooks, "of which no less than six are hitherto unknown". The dealers ask for 5000 Reichsmark, or a duplicate exchange. Husung has the volume sent to Berlin on 4 January 1928; when after nearly two weeks it still has not reached the GW, a slightly agitated exchange follows. Its arrival is finally confirmed on 16 January, accompanied by a request to Halle to please address future deliveries more carefully.[30] Soon thereafter, Husung returns the volume with a succinct analysis: The Staatsbibliothek will not acquire it, given that only three of its parts, not six as assumed by Halle, are to be considered unique, and these were already known to be the property of the Benedictine monastery of Lambach in Austria, whence Halle obviously had gotten the *Sammelband*.[31] This is actually one of the few provenance-related remarks in the file. The important volume finally found its way into the Bavarian State Library; it should be mentioned in this context that the Lambach and Halle provenances were not recorded in the print version of the Bavarian State Library's incunabula catalogue.[32]

---

28   Another *Articella* octavo printed by the de Gregoriis brothers is recorded as GW 0268310N, originally dated for typographical reasons [c. 1500]. However, the original GW entry was based on an incomplete copy in the Biblioteca Comunale at Assisi lacking the colophon, and it is in fact very likely that this copy belongs to a rare *Articella* post-incunable, namely the de Gregoriis octavo dated 21 June 1502. This edition is absent from EDIT16, but four copies are listed by Jon Arrizabalaga, *The Articella in the Early Press, c. 1476–1534* (Cambridge: Wellcome Unit for the History of Medicine; Barcelona: CSIC Department of History of Science, 1998; online: http://hdl.handle.net/10261/34330), pp. 50–51 no. 7. The GW record has been updated accordingly.

29   Halle file, no. 45 (3 January 1928).

30   Halle file, nos. 46–51.

31   Halle file, no. 52.

32   *Bayerische Staatsbibliothek. Inkunabelkatalog (BSB-Ink)*, 7 vols. (Wiesbaden: Reichert, 1988–2009); online version: http://inkunabeln.digitale-sammlungen.de/. The volume in question, shelfmark 4 Inc. c.a. 1361d, contains BSB-Ink A-261,1 (a text in three parts, separately described as GW 1078+1113+1201; seven to ten copies of the individual parts are known), D-263,1 (GW 8904, two copies), E-95,1 (GW 9406, unique), N-57,2 (GW M26111, four copies), O-53,1 (GW 1220, three copies), P-715,1 (GW M35042, two copies), P-874,1 (GW 11089, unique), and V-286,1 (GW M51043, unique).

Another example: In 1931, three unrecorded, apparently unique broadsides were sent to Berlin, among them an "Einblattdruck, der heilige Ambrosius", which the GW subsequently assigned to Johann Amerbach in Basel, c. 1495.[33] Later on, after it had become clear that the broadside must have been printed by Johann Petri and that it was connected to his monumental Ambrosius edition of 1506,[34] perhaps serving as a kind of advertisement, the imprint analysis was changed. Thus the broadside does not show up in the GW or in other incunabula bibliographies. The second item, a curious leaf called *Titel des türkischen Kaisers Baiazet II. an Johann Albrecht I. König von Polen*, now assigned [Munich: Johann Schobser, c. 1500], provoked a controversial exchange about its dating (Figure 24.3).[35] For obvious reasons, Halle had the keen wish to make it an incunable and to assign it to Schobser's Augsburg press, active from 1485 to 1499. However, the GW considered 1501 as the most likely publication date. The third item, an illustrated broadside with Latin prayers to St Nicholas, had already been pointed out to the GW by the Munich dealer Emil Hirsch (1866–1954), who had subsequently sold it to Halle.[36] Images of all three broadsides are kept in the GW's photo archives; the originals, however, vanished after 1931.

The three cases described previously were interesting items, but the most spectacular news had already been delivered the year before. In January 1930, Ida Halle informs Husung about an extraordinary item from her stock, her pièce de résistance: the first edition of the *Ars moriendi*, printed in the German vernacular by Johann Mentelin at Strasbourg.[37] Due to its outstanding features—printer, early date, uniqueness, language, the first printed book in small octavo—the dealer asks for the considerable amount of 16,000 Reichsmark, about 70,000 Euro in today's currency, a sum of enormous purchasing power in 1930. Husung confirms that he already knows about the *Ars* from Karl Schorbach (1851–1939), the leading authority on Mentelin, and regrets that the Staatsbibliothek will not be able to acquire it; would Frau Halle still please send it for cataloguing purposes?[38] Ida does so on 4 February; a fortnight later

---

33 Halle file, nos. 104, 105 (3 February and 7 February).

34 USTC 742721 and 640312 (duplicate entry); VD16 A 2177.

35 Halle file, nos. 106–109; GW M47125. Piotr Tafiłowski, 'List Bajezida II do Jana Olbrachta', in *Szlachta polska i jej dziedzictwo. Księga na 65 lat Prof. dr. hab. Jana Dzięgielewskiego* (Warsaw: Oficyna Wydawnicza Aspra-JR, 2013), pp. 169–176.

36 Halle file, no. 106; GW M27913. For the renowned Hirsch, see Fischer, *Verleger*, pp. 139–140; *Die Rosenthals*, esp. pp. 147–151.

37 Halle file, nos. 86–92, 94, 96–99. GW 0261410.

38 Karl Schorbach, *Der Strassburger Frühdrucker Johann Mentelin (1458–1478). Studien zu seinem Leben und Werke* (Mainz: Verlag der Gutenberg-Gesellschaft, 1932), appendix, pp.*2–*3 no. 2.

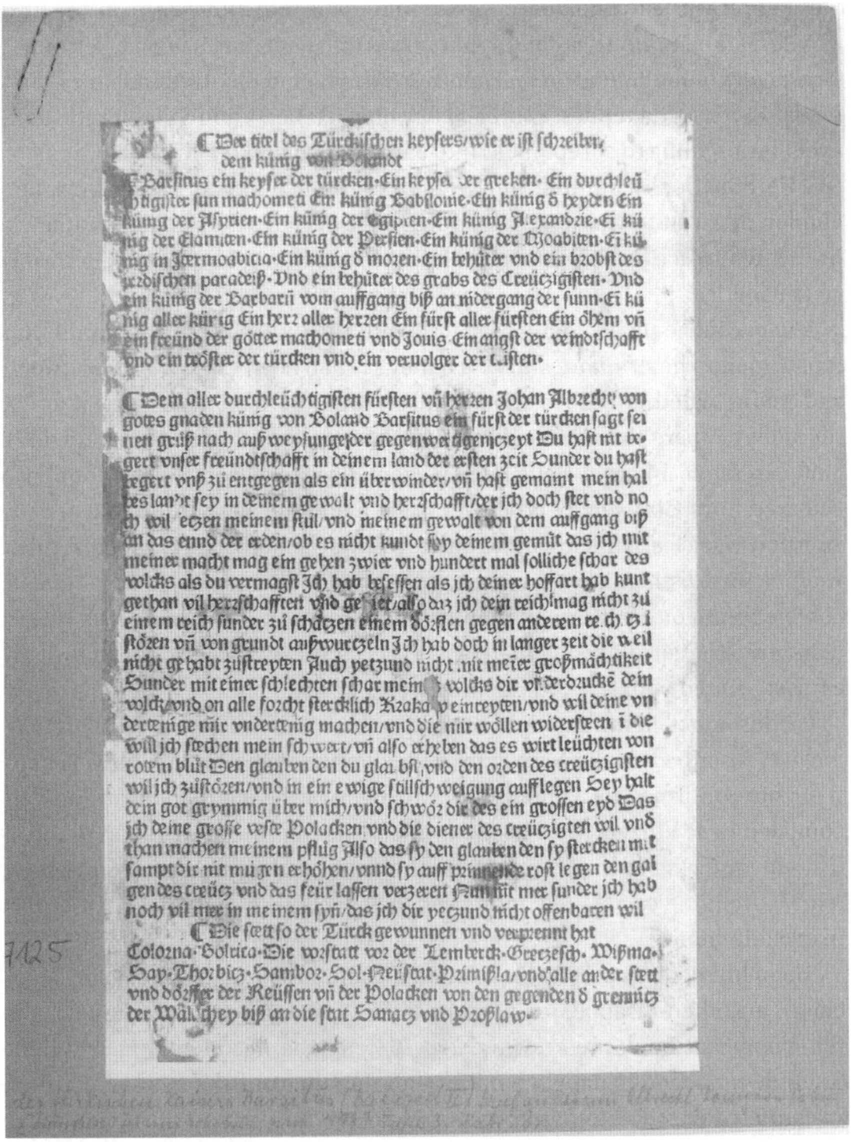

Der titel des Türckischen keysers/wie er ist schreiben
dem künig von Bolandt
Barsitus ein keyser der türcken·Ein keyser der greken· Ein durchleü
chtigister sun machometi Ein künig Babilonie·Ein künig d heyden Ein
künig der Asyrien·Ein künig der Egipten·Ein künig Alexandrie·Ei kü
nig der Elamiten·Ein künig der Persien·Ein künig der Moabiten·Ei kü
nig in Iermoabicia·Ein künig d moren·Ein behüter vnd ein brobst des
erdischen paradeiß·Vnd ein behüter des grabs des Creüczigisten·Vnd
ein künig der Barbarii vom auffgang biß an nidergang der sunn·Ei kü
nig aller künig Ein herr aller herren Ein fürst aller fürsten Ein öhem vñ
ein freünd der götter machometi vnd Jouis Ein angst der veindtschafft
vnd ein tröster der türcken vnd ein veruolger der [illegible]isten·

Dem aller durchleüchtigisten fürsten vñ herren Johan Albrecht von
gotes gnaden künig von Boland Barsitus ein fürst der türcken sagt sei
nen gruß nach auß weysunge der gegenwertigen zeyt Du hast mit be·
gert vnser freündtschafft in deinem land der ersten zeit Sunder du hast
begert vnß zü entgegen als ein überwinder/vñ hast gemaint mein hal
bes landt sey in deinem gewalt vnd herrschafft/der ich doch stet vnd no
ch wil setzen meinem stül/vnd meinem gewalt von dem auffgang biß
an das ennd der erden/ob es nicht kundt sey deinem gemüt das ich mit
meiner macht mag ein gehen zwier vnd hundert mal solliche schar des
volcks als du vermagst Ich hab besessen als ich deiner hoffart hab kunt
gethan vil herrschafften vnd ge[illegible]iet/also daz ich dein reich mag nicht zü
einem reich sunder zü schätzen einem dörflen gegen anderem [illegible]
stören vñ von grundt außwurtzeln Ich hab doch in langer zeit die weil
nicht gehabt züstreyten Auch yetzund nicht mit meiner großmächtikeit
Sunder mit einer schlechten schar meines volcks dir vñ der drucke dein
volck/vnd on alle forcht sterckhlich Kraka[illegible] eintreyten/vnd wil deine vn
dertenige mir vndertenig machen/vnd die mir wöllen widersteen [illegible] die
will ich stechen mein schwert/vñ also erheben das es wirt leüchten von
rotem blüt Den glauben den du glaubst/vnd den orden des creüczigisten
wil ich züstören/vnd in ein ewige stillschweigung aufflegen Sey halt
dein got grymmig über mich/vnd schwör dir des ein grossen eyd Das
ich deine grosse veste Polacken vnd die diener des creüczigten wil vnd
than machen meinem pflüg Also das sy den glauben den sy stercken mit
sampt dir nit mügen erhöhen/vnnd sy auff prinnende rost legen den gal
gen des creücz vnd das feür lassen verzeren Nun nit mer sunder ich hab
noch vil mer in meinem syñ/das ich dir yeczund nicht offenbaren wil

Die stett so der Türck gewunnen vnd verprennt hat
Colozna·Golcica·Die vorstatt vor der Lemberck·Grezesch·Wißma·
Say·Thorbicz·Sambor·Sol·Neüstat·Primißla/vnd alle ander stett
vnd dörffer der Reüssen vñ der Polacken von den gegenden d grenitz
der Walachey biß an die stat Sanacz vnd Proßlaw·

FIGURE 24.3 Broadsheet *Titel des türkischen Kaisers*, imprint: [München: Johann Schobser, c. 1500]; whereabouts of unique copy unknown
STAATSBIBLIOTHEK ZU BERLIN—PREUßISCHER KULTURBESITZ, GW ARCHIVE

Husung returns the book and provides the date "not after 1468". In the next couple of weeks, he tries to talk Ida into a trade-off, but has on offer only a paper copy of the *Hypnerotomachia Poliphili*, which did not fool anyone.[39] In a recent auction, Ida replies, a similar copy only fetched 3,300 Swiss francs; however, she is willing to accept "beautiful early illustrated French, Italian, Spanish and German books, but only of adequate value". Echoing an earlier letter and employing an all-too familiar sale strategy, she declares the Staatsbibliothek to be the right place for this important imprint, which would otherwise probably go to America.

The exchange peters out in May 1930 with the GW enquiring about the current owner of the *Ars moriendi*, which they say had been "formerly at Göttweig", and asking whether the Austrian monks should be named as owners in GW "in order to spare them difficulties". Ida replies curtly that the book is still in her possession, and that Halle must be named as its owner, as it had not been acquired from Göttweig.[40] Wherever Halle made the acquisition, the copy in question was clearly identical with the one that Schorbach had seen at Göttweig. It was distinguished by a rather strange-looking, and perhaps forged, contemporaneous(?) German manuscript note on the first page: "Dis ist von den alerersten getrukten büchlen eins. m.cccc.xxxxxv" ("This is one of the very earliest printed books. 1455") (Figure 24.4).[41]

Of this exact item, a couple of images have survived in the GW's photo archive, inscribed "Halle München". The identity of the Halle/Göttweig copy is further confirmed by a manuscript catalogue of the incunabula at Göttweig compiled by P. Vinzent Werl in 1843, which lists the *Ars moriendi* on p. 497 as "Nummer 1312 (schwarz)/1055 (rot)" with the imprint information "Strassburg, Ioa. Mentellin.—c. 1465–68"; moreover, the catalogue also quotes the German manuscript note.[42]

Thus, Mentelin's *Ars moriendi* entered the GW as owned by "Halle (München)" and then disappeared without trace. No later documents referring to this important book are known. After 1930, it was not offered in any Halle or other catalogues I have seen. Perhaps it was part of the stock evacuation Ida initiated immediately after the Nazi takeover, just before she emigrated to Switzerland in 1933. Apparently it was not on offer in the 1935 Berlin auction in which Halle's leftover stock was sold by Paul Graupe, one of the few remaining Jewish antiquarians provided, until 1936, with a special permission to trade

---

39   GW 7223, the Berlin paper copy is Inc 4508a = 4° Ren. 21,5.
40   Halle file, nos. 96–99.
41   Schorbach, *Frühdrucker*, p. *3, and image of fol. 1a at pl. IVa.
42   Information provided by P. Franz Schuster OSB, Göttweig, to the GW, 27 February 2013.

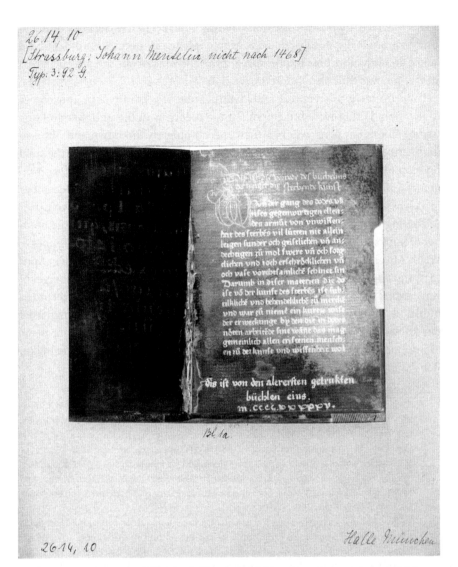

FIGURE 24.4 *Ars moriendi* [German]. [Strasbourg: Johann Mentelin, not after 1468], fol. 1a; whereabouts of unique copy unknown
STAATSBIBLIOTHEK ZU BERLIN—PREUßISCHER KULTURBESITZ, GW ARCHIVE

books.⁴³ This early octavo, one of the oldest imprints in the German vernacular, typographically closely related to Mentelin's first German Bible of 1466, and hence an item of utmost importance for the early history of the printing press altogether, was thus also lost in transaction.⁴⁴

Unfortunately, the recovery and identification of very rare or unique copies of incunabula that were once upon a time recorded in the antiquarian book trade, seldom happens, whereas 'new', i.e. completely unknown and hitherto undescribed incunabula are frequently found.⁴⁵ By chance, during the final revision of this paper, the unique copy of Nicolaus Perottus, *Rudimenta grammatices*, published by the Compagnia del Drago in Florence on 3 December 1500, was rediscovered in the library of the Fondazione Giorgio Cini in Venice.⁴⁶ According to the GW's records, this item passed through a considerable number of bookshops during the past century. First mentioned in 1930 at Täuber & Weil's, Munich, it was in the hands of Heinrich Rosenthal at Luzern on 15 April 1937, and appeared in lists published from 1957 to 1959 by Menno Hertzberger of Amsterdam.⁴⁷ Only six Compagnia del Drago incunabula have been recorded until now, none of them from the year 1500. The Cini finding has both increased our knowledge of this small Florentine workshop, and added another piece of information regarding the transmission of Perottus' bestseller in the Italian Renaissance.⁴⁸

43   Auction catalogue: Paul Graupe, *Die Bestände der Firma J. Halle, München, i. L.* [in liquidation, FE], vol. 1: *Manuskripte, Inkunabeln, Holzschnittbücher, Chroniken und Topographien, Kostüme und Uniformen ... Versteigerung am 24. und 25. Mai 1935* (Berlin: n. pr., 1935); Chris Coppens, 'Der Antiquar Paul Graupe (1881–1953)', *Gutenberg-Jahrbuch* (1987), pp. 255–264; Patrick Golenia, Kristina Kratz-Kessemeier, and Isabelle le Masne de Chermont, *Paul Graupe (1881–1953). Ein Berliner Kunsthändler zwischen Republik, Nationalsozialismus und Exil* (Cologne, Weimar, Vienna: Böhlau, 2016), focus on Graupe's activities as an art dealer.
44   For the 1466 Mentelin Bible, see GW 4295.
45   To give but one example: Luigi Carpaneto, 'Un incunabolo delle collezione Olschkiana ritrovato?', *La Bibliofilía*, 88 (1986) pp. 212–213; the edition in question is GW M18252: Johannes Lichtenberger: *Pronosticazione*. Modena: Dominicus Roccociola, [not after 1500]. According to the Olschki catalogue quoted by Carpaneto, the copy under discussion was printed on vellum, which would make it unique among all recorded copies of Lichtenberger's widespread prognostication. For an important late medieval manuscript sold by Halle in 1918 which only recently was rediscovered in the University Library, Bonn, see Christoph Cluse, 'Aus dem wiederentdeckten Trierer Zinsregister von 1347–1496', *Aschkenas*, 26 (2016), pp. 69–90.
46   Venice, Fondazione Giorgio Cini, G 536. My thanks go to Ilenia Maschietto of the Fondazione Cini for providing images and information about this copy, which was identified as GW M31154 by Oliver Duntze (GW, Berlin) in March 2016.
47   Regarding the copy's former whereabouts see the GW manuscript image provided at http://gesamtkatalogderwiegendrucke.de/docs/M31154.htm.
48   Franz Josef Worstbrock, 'Niccolò Perottis Rudimenta grammatices. Über Konzeption und

Conclusion

For the time being, we have to close this case study, and will conclude with remarks aiming at the general topic of this volume. During my preliminary research I tried to widen my knowledge of antiquarian booktrade practices by reading the autobiographies of a couple of antiquarians. This is a curious literary genre which certainly has the occasional highlight, but which in general does not impress me very much. One learns little if anything about how rare books, especially incunabula, were discovered and identified during the daily acquisition routines, and how they circulated in the trade.[49] That kind of information is generally considered a business secret, and hence autobiographers are not inclined to disclose such details to their readers; the books in question rather focus on the experiences, personal views, and achievements of their individual authors. One recent example is *Books, Friends, and Bibliophilia*, the memoirs of the famous Dutch dealer Anton Gerits. I found this a rather chatty and sometimes dull work. However, one learns quite a bit about dealer psychology, competition, and certainly a lot about ego issues. One paragraph from the preface, written by the American bibliographer Joseph Rosenblum, deserves special attention:

> Mr. Gerits notes that booksellers have been complaining for decades, if not centuries, about the problem of finding good books. But no imprints of the fifteenth or even nineteenth centuries are being published any longer (one hopes), and an increasing number have been institutionalized, never to emerge again (like the aunts in Arsenic and Old Lace).[50]

As we have seen, it is a gross misapprehension to assume that books owned by institutions never re-emerge. On the contrary: as someone who is concerned with the documentation of all surviving specimens of fifteenth-century print-

---

Methode einer humanistischen Grammatik', in Wolfram Ax (ed.), *Von Eleganz und Barbarei. Lateinische Grammatik und Stilistik in Renaissance und Barock* (Wiesbaden: Harrassowitz, 2001), pp. 59–78; Marianne Pade and Camilla Plesner Horster (eds.), *Niccolò Perotti: The Languages of Humanism and Politics. Contributions from the Conference 'Un umanista romano del secondo Quattrocento. Niccolò Perotti', held at the Istituto Storico Italiano per il Medio Evo and the Danish Academy in Rome, 4–5 June 2009* (Internet publication, Aarhus/Copenhagen, 2011); online: http://www.renaessanceforum.dk/rf_7_2011.htm.

49 For a similar observation, see Piet J. Buijnsters, 'The Antiquarian Book Trade in the Netherlands during the Second World War', *Quaerendo*, 36 (2006), pp. 251–292: 251.

50 Joseph Rosenblum, 'Preface', in Anton Gerits, *Books, Friends, and Bibliophilia. Reminiscences of an Antiquarian Bookseller* (New Castle, DE: Oak Knoll Press, 2004), p. viii.

ing, editions and copies alike, I find it increasingly difficult to keep trace of just the important items that indeed, and regrettably, do re-emerge from institutions at any given time and are often enough subsequently lost in transaction. In the past two decades, scores of owners of once glorious book collections, most of them originally conceived as permanent, did away with all or some of their incunabula: most recently the Otto Schäfer collection at Schweinfurt, preceded by the Donaueschingen and Sigmaringen court libraries, or Amsterdam's Bibliotheca Philosophica Hermetica, to name just a few prominent examples. In some instances the deaccessioning process made the headlines, as was the case with the London Law Society, and one could, amongst others, name the Southwark Diocesan Archives, Washington Cathedral and Los Angeles Law Libraries, Wigan Public Library, the Biblioteca Internazionale di Gastronomia in Lugano, and a number of theological seminaries in the United States.[51] Selling duplicate copies of incunabula and other rare books used to be a common procedure in past centuries, but is generally frowned upon today.[52] Some institutions, even major ones such as the Vatican, still do it every now and then, mostly in order to raise funds for new acquisitions, but they rarely advertise the fact. "When special collections libraries and historical societies de-accession books, they often hope to keep a low profile, since the very act of removing long-held rarities from a collection can rankle donors, scholars, fellow librarians, even the bibliophilic public".[53] From my point of view such

---

51   Rebecca Rego Barry, 'Historic collection of rare books slated for auction despite criticisms' in the *Fine Books & Collections* blog https://www.finebooksmagazine.com/fine _books_blog, published on 20 May 2013. See for example Richard J. Janet, 'The decline and fall of St. Mary's of the Barrens: a case study in the contraction of an American Catholic religious order—part one', *Vincentian Heritage Journal*, 22 (2001), pp. 153–181, and Janet, 'The decline and fall of St. Mary's of the Barrens: a case study in the contraction of an American Catholic religious order—part two', *Vincentian Heritage Journal*, 25 (2005), pp. 1–30. The sale of the library, including a large number of incunabula originally donated by Estelle Doheny (1875–1958), took place at Christie's, New York, on 14 December 2001.

52   Georg Leyh, 'Dubletten-Austausch', *Zentralblatt für Bibliothekswesen*, 39 (1922), pp. 321–323, and Karl Schottenloher, 'Verwertung der Dubletten', *Zentralblatt für Bibliothekswesen*, 40 (1923), pp. 378–382; more recently Bettina Wagner, 'Dublettenauktionen der Münchener Hofbibliothek in der ersten Hälfte des 19. Jahrhunderts', *Aus dem Antiquariat* (2006/2), pp. 89–97; Maria Marten, 'Die Last der Dubletten. Bücherabgaben der Königlichen Bibliothek zu Hannover als Instrument fürstlicher Landespolitik und ihre sammlungsgeschichtliche Erschließung', *Zeitschrift für Bibliothekswesen und Bibliographie*, 58 (2011), pp. 256–266.

53   Rebecca Rego Barry, 'Deaccession & auction rare books' in the *Fine Books & Collections* blog, published on 3 March 2014. As recently as 2003 a massive book swap took place between the Vatican Library and Massimo de Caro, who later became infamous for his Galileo forging and for the looting of the Girolamini library in Naples, including a number

secrecy is problematic indeed, whereas the policy itself is no major cause for concern as long as transactions are thoroughly documented and made public, such as the exchanges between Cambridge University Library and the British Library that were recently described by John Goldfinch in a volume aptly titled *Incunabula on the Move*.[54] Yet mostly these transactions are never made public and thus contribute to muddling the bibliographical record.

For libraries that still have the means to acquire such costly material, buying incunabula is a routine. Anyone participating in the discussion about preserving cultural heritage, or anyone reading, like me, book dealers' and auction catalogues as an occupational habit, will be aware of the chances and risks underlying each and every change of ownership. By deciding to acquire a particular item for an institution, one hopes to preserve a small portion of the cultural heritage, even when its provenance documentation is patchy, which is too often the case. On the other hand, the decision not to acquire certain items may lead to their disappearance altogether, as we have seen. Whatever one does: historical information can and will get lost in transaction.

of incunabula such as the 1499 *Hypnerotomachia Poliphili* and a copy of the 1465 Lactantius; see the comprehensive account by Nick Wilding, 'Forging the Moon', *Proceedings of the American Philosophical Society*, 160 (2016), pp. 37–72: 57 ff. Wilding states that of the six copies of *Hypnerotomachia* owned by the Vatican before 1934, only three remain; moreover, "the online notes by the former Director of the Printed Books Department, Father William Sheehan, C.S.B., to the digital incunabula catalogue have been purged"; the deletion happened "at some point between 2012 and 2014" (p. 59).

54 John Goldfinch, 'Movements of incunabula between the former British Museum Library and the University Library in Cambridge', in Ed Potten and Satoko Tokunaga (eds.), *Incunabula on the Move. The Production, Circulation and Collection of Early Printed Books* (Cambridge: Bibliographical Society, 2014), pp. 101–129.

Modern Authors' Index

Allen, Robert   78
Armstrong, Elizabeth   212–213
Aubert, Vilhelm   157n6

Barwick, George Frederick   277, 280
Baudrier, Henri Louis   197
Beavan, Iain   261
Bland, Mark   128
Blome, Astrid   169n40
Blühm, Elger   399, 401, 410
Bogel, Else   399, 410
Brayman Hackel, Heidi   128
Bühler, Curt   297
Buning, Marius   15

Ciccarello, Domenico   17

Darnton, Robert   123
De Ricci, Seymour   495
Dondi, Cristina   73n4, 75, 82–83

Eeghen, Isabella Henrietta van   160n13, 162–163n22
Eisenstein, Elizabeth   2, 6, 10

Febvre, Lucien   85
Fisher, Alexander   371
Fontaine, Laurence   45
Frymire, John   223, 228

Gascon, Richard   195n55
Genette, Gérard   226
Gering, Traugott   25n4
Gerits, Anton   537
Giddens, Eugene   111–112
Giesecke, Michael   36n18
Gilmont, Jean-François   85–86
Göhler, Albert   362
Goinga, Hannie van   163n22–23
Goldfinch, John   539
Gómez Álvarez, Cristina   451
Gültlingen, Sybille von   182

Harris, Michael   154n1
Harris, Neil   73n4, 82–83
Hellinga, Lotte   10–11

Hillgärtner, Jan   2
Hoftijzer, Paul   89–90

Ingram, Elizabeth Morley   125

Jackson, William A.   495, 519
Johns, Adrian   6

Kruseman, Arie Cornelis   89–90
Künast, Hans-Jörg   277

Lowry, Martin   181n3
Luard, Henry   519n131
Luborsky, Ruth Samson   125

Maclean, Ian   11, 86n27, 354
Mandelbrote, Giles   112–114
Martin, Henri-Jean   85
Muldrew, Craig   45
Munby, Alan Noel Latimer   496, 498n50

Neddermeyer, Ute   82–83
Nuovo, Angela   56, 73, 327

Orenstein, Nadine   90

Pettas, William   194n52
Piccard, Gerhard   37n23, 39n29

Rabaiotti, Renato   494n21
Raven, James   10
Raymond, Joad   471
Reed, Susan   501n64
Rhodes, Dennis   247–248, 252
Robijntje Miedema, Nine   144–145
Rose, Stephen   376
Rosenblum, Joseph   537
Rueda, Pedro   450–451

Schaal, Richard   355–356
Schlumbohm, Jürgen   45
Scholderer, Victor   25n6
Schorbach, Karl   532, 534
Sherman, William H.   123
Simpson, Julianne   518n126
Slights, William E.   126

Sombart, Werner   36n17
Stehlin, Karl   43n39
Steinbrink, Matthias   43n37, 45
Stone, Peter   157
Sutherland, James   479

Taylor, Archer   508
Taylor, Gary   113–114
Tordi, Domenico   330

Verde, Armando F.   56
Voullième, Ernst   524–525

Wagner, Klaus   75, 451–452
Weiss, Adrian   111–112, 119
Werl, P. Vinzent   534
Wilding, Nick   539n53
Wilke, Jürgen   399

Zamprogna, Roberto   254

Subject Index

Academies 325–326, 328, 381, 386–387, 392
Advertising and advertisements 129–133, 164–165, 174, 272–274, 420–447, 467–486
   cost of 473
   of books 429–447, 475–477
   of lotteries 154n1, 158n10, 164–176
Antiquarian book trade and booksellers 489–539
   prices 505, 531
Auctions 162, 166, 489, 501, 503, 507–512, 517–518
Authors and authorship 224–225, 370, 374–375, 431
   Dibdin, Thomas 494–500
   Erasmus 296, 299, 318–319, 321
   Jesuit authors 452
   Luther, Martin 225, 228–229, 276–300
   Wujek, Jakub 224, 228–229, 232–236

Banks and bankers 49, 57, 206, 358
Bestsellers 312, 372–373
Bibliomania 489–521
Book fairs 17, 35
   Frankfurt 17, 46, 247–248, 250, 361–366, 373, 411
   Leipzig 374, 510n97
   London 510n97
   Lyon 8, 193–194
   Medina del Campo 194
   Recanati 327
Bookselling and book trade, early modern 17, 303–321, 516
   agents 57–60, 254–255
   bankruptcy 273
   booksellers, early modern 82, 255–256, 262–267, 261–275, 378, 380–394, 437, 439–440, 442–447
   chapmen 264–267, 423
   cross-confessional 223–245, 298
   general dealers 264–267
   high-end items 227
   international trade 15–16, 58, 66, 292–294, 296, 313, 339–352, 372, 389–393
   market saturation 373
   networks 357
   prices 72–87, 233n22, 272, 275, 453
   retail 56
   saleability 353–354, 375, 377
   sale accounts 255–259
   sale conditions 354
   sale outlets 57, 61–62, 275
   second-hand 176–177, 317, 383
   trans-Atlantic 448–466
Bookshops 60–62, 112–115, 119, 122–123, 261, 267–275, 308, 310–313, 359
   iconographic representations 113–115, 119
   inventories 304, 330
   non-book items on sale 270
   organisation 381–383
   stock 17, 111–112, 114, 119, 272, 309–321, 331, 354, 364, 372, 375–376, 379, 382–392
Branding 11, 19, 289–290, 299
Buying (also see collectors and collecting; readers and reading)
   abroad 77
   antiquarian market 493
   browsing 111–135
   buying habits, early modern 56, 75–77, 80–82, 448–466
   buying habits, modern 522–525
   customer-base 51, 56
   customers 111–113, 119, 123, 256, 270, 320, 327, 385, 387, 392–393, 432–433, 434, 448–466

Catalogues
   auction catalogues, modern 492n12, 501, 503
   book fair catalogues, early modern 361–362, 364–366, 372, 375
   stock catalogues, early modern 11–12, 121, 353–379
   compilation of 367, 369
Censorship 217, 241, 243
   expurgation 450–451, 456, 458, 461, 464–465
   prohibited books 304–306, 318–320
   Index of Antwerp 305

SUBJECT INDEX   543

Index of the University of Louvain
    305
Roman Index   305
Tridentine Index   305–306
Collectors and collecting   11–12, 73, 75–77,
    81–82, 85, 211–212, 449–450, 461, 463–
    464, 489–521, 522–539

Debt and credit   44–51, 57, 63–65, 189,
    193–194, 270, 327, 366, 387, 389–390,
    393
Distribution   10, 26, 241n37, 247, 296, 315–
    316, 359, 372–373, 399, 410, 415, 420–
    423, 433–436, 440
    shipments   317, 410, 454–456, 462, 466

Genres and typologies of texts
    bibles   13, 20, 30, 75, 210
    books of hours   13
    broadsheets   31
    calendars and almanacs   418
    canon and civil law   15, 31, 184–188, 253,
        332, 383–384
    catechisms   20
    cheap print   31, 38n27, 265, 273
    classics   334
    dictionaries   208–222
    literature and poetry   332
    liturgy   30–31, 49, 52
    mathematics   334
    medicine   332, 384–385
    music   13, 14, 335, 353–379
    newspapers   2–3, 13, 397–447, 467–
        486
    occasional publications   137–141, 408–
        409, 413, 416, 426
    Reformation *Flugschriften*   2–3
    religious guidebooks   136–153
    sermons   223–245, 278, 280, 388
    theology   30
Guild systems
    Basel   35–36, 43
    Dutch Republic   91–92, 161, 175
    Florence   56
    London, Stationers' Company   15

Humanist publishing programmes   18, 181,
    208–222

Illustrations and illustrated books   13, 93–
    95, 125, 367–368, 434
    engravings   90, 93–94
    woodcuts   227–230, 233–235, 474
Incunabula   23–71, 522–539

Libraries, early modern   12, 372, 386, 450,
    461, 464, 523
Loss and survival   295, 362–363, 401, 406–
    407, 409, 421, 427, 429, 523–524,
    529–537
Lotteries   154–177
    as sale strategies   3, 157, 176–177, 353
    locations (international)   154, 156,
        159
    locations (Amsterdam)   163, 168–171,
        175–176
    organisation   164–165, 171, 174–175
    organisers (Amsterdam)   166–172
    regulations (Amsterdam)   170

Materiality of production
    colophon   297
    layout   235–239, 278–289
    print runs   9, 38n27, 80, 183, 196, 240–
        241, 426
    title-pages   239, 277–292, 297
    types   228–229, 277
Merchant companies
    Florence   61

News and newspaper publishing   397–447,
    467–486
    failure   409, 422
    growth of the industry   399, 401–402,
        405, 415, 418–419
    places of correspondence   410
    success   403–406, 413–414

Paper   185, 196, 432, 503
    influence on book prices   257, 295
    large-paper copies   492n12, 497, 500,
        503, 520
    mills   26, 196, 357–358
    purchase of   44, 46
    quality or type of   9, 376
    paper trade   26–27, 157, 160, 165–166,
        271
Patronage   242, 358, 402

Payments (also see Buying; Debt and credit;
    Sale strategies)   8, 17, 44, 47, 49, 58, 61,
        65–66, 193–194, 257, 387, 389, 393, 420,
        424, 442, 451
Postal networks   357, 403, 413–414
Printing and printing industry
    colour   5
    failure and bankruptcy   2, 4, 23–54, 409,
        422
    family enterprises   16, 246–260
    financial capital   42, 44
    for educational purposes   25, 209, 219,
        371, 392
    for the locality   10, 18, 42
    in the fifteenth century   3, 23–54, 358
    investments and assets   191, 195, 198–207
    involvement in other trades   17, 188–190,
        196–197, 203–207
    itinerant   7, 23, 36, 62
    jobbing printers   41–42
    organisation of the industry   35–36, 85–
        86, 88–92, 161
    output patterns   1, 6, 23–54, 182–186, 224,
        229, 262, 400, 411–412
    printing materials   51, 85, 195–196,
        330
    Reformation   2–3, 18–20, 276–300
    shift from manuscript   4, 9, 25, 55–57,
        72–73
    spread of   3
    success   10, 18–20, 403–406, 413–
        414
    technology   4
    types   52–54, 196, 228–229, 376
    typesetters   59
Printing societies and companies
    Basel   37, 40–41
    Lyon   15, 182, 184–188, 190–194, 196–199,
        202–207
    Paris   15
    Venice   58, 60–61, 67–71, 247–248, 250,
        252
Privileges and licenses to print   14–15
    Brussels   309
    Dutch Republic   88–108
        application of   94
        as sale strategies   99–101, 103, 106
        conditions   96
        issued by   94–99
        request of   92–96
        revocation of   98–99
        validity of   102–103
    France   15
    Germany   295, 297–299, 397–398, 406
    Italy, Venice   15, 252

Readers and reading (also see Buying)   10,
    122–123
    editing and correcting   214–221
    readership   228, 233, 239, 241–243, 275,
        320, 332, 335, 364, 385, 392, 428, 430,
        432–434, 448–466, 474
    reading practices   147–149, 273, 324

Sale and commercial strategies   4, 161
    advertisements as marketing strategies
        111–135, 429–432
    barter   17, 41, 161, 246–260, 355, 389–
        391
    catalogues and booklists   121, 366–367
    circulating libraries   271
    counterfeiting   181–182, 276–300
    customisation   5, 9
        copies on large paper   492n12, 497,
            500, 503, 520
        copies on vellum   5, 503, 505–506,
            509, 518n127, 520, 524–525, 536n45
    gift-copies   9
    imitations   143–146, 181, 208–209, 221,
        229, 410
    mail orders   272–273, 392
    re-issues   239, 241, 366n51, 417
    sale catalogues   366–367
    serialisation   11
    specialisation   13, 359, 411, 415–417
Slow-sellers   176–177, 241, 353, 378, 386
Sources and methodologies for the history of
    the book
    account books   45, 82
    advertisements   272–274, 421, 475–477
    annotated copies   147–149, 212–222, 235,
        464–465
    bibliographic structure   119–132, 226–228
    bookshop inventories   63, 304
    censorship records   303–321
    criminal records   46–50, 249, 252, 274,
        327
    historic wages   46, 77–80, 84

SUBJECT INDEX

letters and correspondences, early modern   227–228n12, 231n21, 247–248, 250–251, 389, 392
letters and correspondences, modern   526–534
lists of books purchased   451–466
memoirs   306
modern sale and antiquarian catalogues   528
output analysis   23–54, 182–186, 262, 411–412
paratext   111–135, 214, 241–243, 329
printing and bookselling contracts   190–193, 237, 330, 355n8
privileges   88–108
probate inventories   187–207, 269–270, 330, 371, 377, 380–394
rental records   62, 188, 191, 198–199, 201
sale accounts   255–259
sheet count   39–40, 83–84, 185, 429
stratification of copies   410–411, 423

tax records   39, 198
text-encoding   115
trade directories   262–263, 265, 267, 269, 273

Translations
    advertisements of   432
    in bookshops   313, 315–316, 328, 334
    in the marketplace   9, 88, 92–93, 101, 103, 103n58, 145–146n19, 223, 225–226, 229, 236, 497
    of news   426–427
    sales of   501

Warehouses
    locations   16, 60
    overstocked   1, 159–162, 176–177, 241, 260, 386
    shared   184, 193, 195, 206
    stock   7, 100, 331–333, 340–352, 353, 369

Alphabetical Index

Aberdeen 158, 261n3
Accademia Veneziana 9
Accursius 31
Agli, Tommaso di Iacopo degli 63
Albert VII, Archduke of Austria 95
Albertus Magnus 315
Aldine editions 11–12, 524
    Hypnerotomachia Poliphili 534, 539n53
Alfaro, Martín de 458
Aliprandi, Laurent 194
Alkmaar 424, 439–440
almojarifazgo (customs duty) 454
Alsop, Bernard 474
Alsop, Elizabeth 473
Amadori, Marco 328
Amadori, Pellegrino 329
Amerbach, Johann 7, 27, 35, 53–54, 532
Americas 448–466
Amman, Jost 233–235
Ammerbach, Elias Nicolaus 376–377
Amsterdam 92, 96, 100, 102, 156, 158–177, 420–424, 426–427, 429, 431, 433–434, 436–439, 441–442, 536
    Courante Extra-ordinaire 426–427
    Courante uyt Italien ... 420–422, 425–426, 431, 434, 440–441
    lottery locations 163, 168–171, 175–176
    Nouvelles de divers Quartiers 426–427
    Ordinarise Middelweeckse Courante 426–427
    Tijdinghen uyt verscheyde Quartieren 420–422, 425–427, 431, 439–440
Amyraut, Moïse 388–389
Andrews, John 121
    Andrew's Resolution 121
    Sovereign Salve 121
Angrisano, Gian Giacomo 256–259
Anna Jagiellon, Queen of Poland 242
Anne of Denmark, Queen consort of Scotland 247
Anselmo, Aurelio 249–250
Antoninus Florentinus 30
Antonio di Niccolò di Lorenzo 62–63
Antwerp 13, 16, 373, 413, 422n5
    Nieuwe Tijdinghen 424
Apollonius, Levinus 315

Aretino, Pietro 250, 313
Ariosto, Ludovico 313
    Orlando furioso 9, 13
Armaolea, Buenaventura de 466
Arnhem 101, 433, 435–437
    Arnhemsche Courant 421
Arrigo di Gherardo 59–60, 62–63, 65–66
Articella 529–531
Askew, Anthony 489n2
Aubigné, Agrippa d' 382
Augsburg 278, 284–289, 290, 292–294, 355–379, 413
Augustinians 449, 451, 462
    Puebla de Los Angeles 451
Aulus Gellius 215
Aurelius Augustinus (St Augustine) 30, 32
Australse Compagnie 95
avería (levy) 454
Avicenna 384
Aylmer, John 127

Baart, Pieter Thomasz 440
Baart, Thomas Pieter 439
Baber, Henry Hervey 501
Bach, Johann Sebastian 374, 377
Badia Fiesolana 57–59, 62
    Don Arcangelo da Vicenza 57
    Don Gregorio di Matteo 57
Badius, Josse 181
Ballard, Robert 14
Baranger, Jean 380
Barbarigo, Pier Francesco 11
Barradas, Sebastião 252
Bartholomeus Brixiensis 31
Bartolo di Fruosino 58–59, 64
Bartolomeo di Andrea di Lapo da Prato 64
Barzizza, Gasparino 25, 27–29, 44, 52
Basel 6, 23–54, 247, 283–284, 299, 331, 359n22, 384, 532
    Carthusian Library 28
    Grosse Gesellschaft (trade consortium) 43n38
    Kundschaften 50
    Liber diversorum 50
    Schillingsteuer (tax) 39
    University 25

ALPHABETICAL INDEX 547

University Library 28
Urteilsbücher 47, 50
Verbotsbuch 50
Vergichtbücher 44, 48–51, 54
Baudartius, William 102–103, 106
Baudouin, François 320
Beatus Rhenanus 27
Beccadelli, Antonio 313
Bede, the Venerable 310
Belcari, Tommaso 65
Bella di Giovanni da Colonia 62
Benedetto di Giovanni 64
Benedictis, Nicholas de 298
Béraud, Symphorien 181n1
Berg, Adam 409
Berg, Anna 409
Berg, Heinrich I 409
Berg, Heinrich II 409–411
Berlaimont, Noël de 309, 313
Berlin 403, 522, 528–529, 531, 534
    Einkommende Ordinar- und Postzeitungen
    403, 414
    Royal Library 522–523, 525
    Staatsbibliothek 522–523, 531
Besançon, Didier 199
Białobrzeski, Marcin 228, 241–242
Bichi, Metello 252
Biel, Friedrich (variant names: Fadrique de Basilea, Federigo Aleman) 29–30, 44
Biese, Jacob van 435–436
Biffi, Gioseffo 372
Birghden, Johann von den 397–398, 403, 413–414
Birkowski, Fabian 237
Birr, Anton 213
Bischoff, Andreas 43, 47
Bischoff, Bernhard 529n27
Bischöffin, Barbara 47
Bleau, Joan 102
Blickling Hall, Norfolk 211–212
    copy of *Thesaurus Linguae Latinae* 212–222
Bloom, Michael 299
Boccaccio, Giovanni, *Decameron* 63, 497, 500n59, 518
Bodenschatz, Erhard 374
Boethius, Anicius Manlius Severinus 31
Boillon, Martin 184
Bolard, Fleury 197–198, 203

Bologna 331
Bonifacius VIII, pope 31, 140
Bonomini, Giampiero of Cremona 57, 61
Borchers, Albrecht 172
Borchers, Johannes 172
Borders, Daniel 478
Bosse, Abraham, *La Galerie du Palais* 112
Bourne, Nicholas 425
Bozon, Pierre 196
Bracciolini, Poggio 319
Brandt, Marten Jansz 431–432, 438
Braubach, Peter 281–282
Brescia 297, 298n40
Bridges, John 127
Brink, Jan Gerritsz ten 171
Brisson, Barnabé 383
Britain (also see England and Scotland) 156, 489–521
Brobstlin, Ulrich 47
Broeck, Laurentius vander 308
Broersz, Joost 426–427, 432, 440
Brogiotti, Francesco 254
Brongers, Hendrik Jr. 166, 171
Brontë, Charlotte 500n56
Brown, John 264
Bruno, Giordano 247
Brussels 303–321
    Council of Troubles 303–321
    State Archives 306
Buchanan, George 209n5
Buiksloot 169, 171
Bulgarini, Bellisario 82–83, 85
Buonafé, Leonardo di Giovanni 63
Burgos 16, 28, 30
Busleyden, Guilielmus 307
Bussi, Giovanni Andrea 73
Butter, Nathaniel 425
Bytner, Jan 237

Caccini, Matteo di Biagio 64, 66
Cadiz 457–458
Caetani, Enrico 143
Calcutta 492
Calvisius, Sethus 374
Cambridge University Library 539
Campana, Francesco di Giovanni 64
Campano, Giovanni Antonio 328
Campos, Juan Francisco de 462
Campos, Pedro de 463

Canisius, Petrus 312
Canne, John 485
Cappel, Louis 387
Capponi, family of bankers 206
Cardon, Jacques 254
Carmelites 449, 453, 463, 466
Carocci, Vincenzo 328
Carolus, Johann 397, 402
Carrasco, Bartolomé de 456
Cartolari, Baldassarre 327
Casas, Bartolomé de las, *The Spanish Colony* 125–126
Casteleyn, Abraham 440
Castellion, Sébastien 319
Castelvetro, Giacomo 247
Castiglione, Baldassarre 313
Catholic Church 143
Cavellat, Pierre jr 254
Cavendish, Margaret, *World's Olio* 133
Celle, Ministerialbibliothek 525
Cellier, Antoine 389–390
Cesarini, Giuliano 26
Cezary, Franciszek młodszy 152
Cezary, Franciszek 150–152
Chamier, Daniel 386
Chanlockfoot 265
Chaponay, Humbert de 205
Chaponay, Nicolas de 205
Charenton 388, 390
Charles I, King of England 468
Charles V, Holy Roman Emperor 281
Charles VIII, King of France 205
Charron, Pierre 382–383
Chauliac, Gui de 385
Chellini, Raffaele 62
Chemnitz, Martin 386
Chojnice (Konitz), Royal Lyceum 524
Chouet, Pierre 389
Chouet, Samuel 389
Christie's (New York) 538n51
Christopher Columbus 73, 75–77
Churchyard, Thomas 131–132
Cicero, Marcus Tullius 28, 63
Ciepielik, Gabriel Eliasz 147
Cimino, Giambattista 256
Cione di Damiano di Matteo 59n18, 62
Ciotti, family of printers-publishers 246–260
    Ciotti, Francesco 17, 246–250, 253–260

Ciotti, Francesco Maria (possible variant name for Francesco C.) 259n36–260
Ciotti, Giovanni Battista 246–252
Ciotti, Giovanni Battista jr 259n36
Ciotti, Giovanni 248
Ciotti, Girolamo 259n36
Ciotti, Sebastiano 246–247
Ciotti, Simone 246–247
Cirillo, Decio 253
Claessen, Tjerck 434
Claesz, Cornelis 424
Clement VIII (Pope) 140
Cluny 7
Cochelet, Anastasius 95
Cockburn, Henry Thomas 516
Colle Valdelsa 62
Collings, Richard 471, 474
Cologne 145, 247, 331, 406, 409
    Niederländische Zeitung 406
    Raporten 406
Colón, Hernando 72–73, 75–82
Colijn, Michiel 96, 102–103
Comenius, Johann Amos, *Orbis Sensualium Pictus* 113, 123
Compagnia di Venezia 58–61, 63, 66
Compagnie d'Ivry 182, 187, 190, 193–194, 199
Compagnie des Libraires 182, 184–187, 190, 193, 196–198, 206–207
    Compagnie des Textes 187, 191–192
    Compagnie des Lectures 187, 191–192
Compton, Elizabeth 492
Compton, William 492
Congregation of the Index 249
Conradus de Usin de Openen, ser 59
Constance 286, 415
COPAC 211
Cope, sir Walter 468
Copyright Act (1709) 515n111
Copyright Act (1842) 515n111
Corbalán, Pedro 466
Cornelis, Willem 95
Coronel, Marcos 450
Corsini, Antonio 61, 68
Corvin, Anton 227
Costantini, Giovanni Battista 330
Cotton, Antoine de 201
Council of Trent 143, 312
Counter Reformation 224

ALPHABETICAL INDEX

Cranach, Lucas   14, 19, 286, 289–290, 295, 501n64
Crantz, Martin   28
Cristóbal de la Santísima Trinidad   463
Crocus, Cornelius   314
Cromerus, Martinus   312
Crouch, John   474
Crul, Cornelis   320
Cruz, Cristóbal de la   462
Csombor, Márton   143
Cupar   273
Curiandrus, Abelius   101
Curiel, Juan de   458

Daillé, Jean   388
Dale, Jan van den   314
Dąmbski, Stanisław Kazimierz   147
Danckertsz, Cornelis   431
Daniel, Samuel, *Delia*   129
Danzig   422n5
Darmstadt   415
David, Heinrich   43
David, Konrad   43
Davies, John, *Wits Bedlam*   117
De Caro, Massimo   538n51
De Franceschi, Francesco   249
De Franceschi, Giacomo   249
De Franceschi, Giovanni Antonio   249, 253
De Gregori brothers   529, 531n28
De Gregorio, Pietro   257
De La Court, Pierre   97–99
Delerpinière, Daniel   380–394
Delft   421, 424, 433, 435, 440
    Courante uyt Italien ...   421
Della Cornia, Fulvio   323
Den Bosch   435
Denmark   401
Derrere, Alessis   189
Desbordes, Isaac   380, 389, 392–393
Despauterius, Johannes   313
Deventer   435, 437, 440
Dibdin, Charles   492
Dibdin, Thomas   492
Dibdin, rev. Thomas Frognall   489–521
    Aedes Althorpianae   496–497
    Bibliographical Decameron   495–496, 500–501, 503, 505, 508
    Bibliographical tour   490, 496–497

Bibliomania   494, 497, 499–500, 503, 508–509, 512
Bibliotheca Spenceriana   496
    Northern tour   499, 512–517
Didier, Marguerite   201
Dillingen   363
Dioscorides Pedanius   315
Dodo, Jean   203
Doheny, Estelle   538n51
Doliba, Miguel   464
Dominicans   449, 451, 459–461, 464
    Coyoacán, Mexico City   451
Donatus   31
Donthers, Cornelis   312
Dordrecht   95, 420, 424, 433, 435
Döring, Christian   295
Douce, Francis   520n136
Drelincourt, Charles   388
Drusius, Johannes   101
Du Laurens, André   385
Du Moulin, Pierre   388
Duns Scotus, Johannes   64
Duple (or Dubbue), Carlo di Ridolfo   62
Duplessis Mornay, Philippe   381, 386
Durret, François   196, 203
Durret, Huguet   196
Dutch Republic   88–108, 154–177, 400, 420–447
    Bills of Lading   94
    First Stadtholder Period   99
    Provincial States   91
    States General   91, 94–95, 99, 101–102
    States of Holland   96–98, 100, 102
    Synod of South Holland   97
    Triple Alliance   99
Du Val, Antoine   312

Early English Books Online (EEBO), Text Creation Partnership   115
Eck, Johannes   227, 283, 296
Edgeworth, Maria   270
Edict of Nantes   211
Edinburgh   261–262, 273, 516–517
    National Library of Scotland   247, 263
Edwards, James   501, 507–508
Egenolff, Christoph   14
Eichelberg, Jacob   48
Eichorn, Adolarius   363
Eilenburg   1n3

Ellys, Sir Richard   211–212
Elsevier firm   382, 390–392
   Elsevier, Daniel   389
   Elsevier, Louis   95, 389
Elwe, Jan Barend   173, 175
Emenes, Johannes van   165–166, 169
England   2, 15, 99, 111–135, 154, 158, 355n8, 517
Enkhuizen   435
Erasmus   23, 27, 101, 296, 299, 313, 317, 392
Erfurt   227n10, 294
Estienne, family of printers-publishers   211–212
   Estienne, Henri I   317
   Estienne, Henri II   212–213, 215, 221
   Estienne, Robert   18, 208–222
      Thesaurus Linguae Latinae   208–222
Estrada, Santiago de   456
Europe   88, 154–159, 161, 451–454
Eyens, Jasperus   308

Fabriano   251
Fabricius, Georg   313, 319
Farina, Giovanni Antonio   256
Farnese, Pier Luigi   322
Farri, Domenico   13
Fazello, Tommaso   255
Felsecker, Wolfgang Eberhard   417–419
Fernando Álvarez de Toledo, Duke of Alba   304–306
Ferrara   250, 298
Ferrini, Giovanni di Lazzaro   67, 69
Feyerabend, Sigmund   373
Fichet, Guillaume   28
Ficino, Marsilio   61, 63
Fife   266–275
   Fife Chapman Society   266–267
Flach, Martin   36
Florence   16, 55–71, 80, 297, 298n40, 331, 529, 534
   cartolai   56, 62
   Catasto   62
   Garbo, via del   61, 67, 69–70
   Sant'Apollinare, parish   62
   Spinelli bank   57
Flores, Joseph   464
Flores, Juan Marsial   462
Flurschütz, Kaspar   364
Folkes, Martin   510
Forge, Louis de la   392

Formica, Matthias   405
Foulis, Andrew   516
Foulis, Robert   516
Fowler, William   247–248
France   14–16, 28, 99, 208, 428
   Gazette   428
Francesco della Fontana   58n15
Franciscans   449, 451, 453, 457–458, 463, 465
   Querétaro, College of Santa Cruz   451
Francisco de Florencia   453
Franeker   435, 437, 440
Frankfurt am Main   12, 14, 16, 247, 353–354, 372–374, 397–398, 403, 411, 413–414, 422n5
   Diarium Hebdomadale   397–398
   Frankfurt Fair   17, 46, 247–248, 250, 361
   Frankfurter Postzeitung   397, 403
Frederick the Wise, Elector of Saxony   12, 286, 289
Freiburg im Breisgau   359
Freund, Georg August   525
Friburger, Michael   28
Fries, Jan Jansz de   433
Frischmann, Christoph   403
Frischmann, Veit   403
Fritsch, Balthasar   369
Froben, Johannes   23, 27, 299
Froschauer, Hans   278
Fugger, family of bankers   293, 358
Fünffinger, Hans   49

Gabiano, family of printers-publishers   181–207
   estates   191, 198–201
   Gabiano, Ange de   197
   Gabiano, Balthazar de   182
   Gabiano, Balthazar II de   190, 198
   Gabiano, Barthélemy de   190, 198
   Gabiano, Catherine de   205
   Gabiano, Henri de   190, 198
   Gabiano, Hugues de   197, 205
   Gabiano, Jean-Barthélemy de   193–194
   Gabiano, Luxembourg de   14, 182, 187–207
Gabrieli, Giovanni   372
Gaffuri, Francesco di messer Cristoforo   60, 65–70
Galen   315, 384
Gallo, Pietro Paolo   256–257

ALPHABETICAL INDEX

García de la Yedra, Juan   461
García Duque, Angel   451
Gardane, Antonio   14
Gaspar von Dinslaken   66
Gdacjusz, Adam   242n39
Geneva   210, 212–213, 220–221, 389
   Bibliothèque de Genève   213
Gentil, Ignacio   459
George, sir Arthur   468
George, Duke of Saxony   1, 298
George John, Earl Spencer   499, 518n126
George Spencer, Duke of Marlborough
   518n126
Gering, Ulrich   28
Gerits, Anton   537
Germany   522–539
German Peasants' War   276
Gesamtkatalog der Wiegendrucke (GW)   30,
   522–539
Giolito de Ferrari, Gabriele   13
Giolito de Ferrari, Giovanni   17
Giovanni di Niccolò di Lorenzo ('El Guazza')
   60–70
Girard, Claude   381, 386
Giuliano di Giovanfrancesco da Modena   57
Giunta, family of printers-publishers   16,
   194, 205, 250, 252
   branches and warehouses   16
   Giunta, Bernardo jr   248, 250, 252
   Giunta, Jacques   184, 205
   Giunta, Leonardo   327
Glasgow   261n3, 262, 505, 516
   Hunterian Museum   516
   University Library   505, 516
Godfrey, Robert   119
Gómez, Bartolomé   456
Gosset, rev. Isaac   506–507
Göttweig   534
Gouda   422n6, 433, 440
Göy, Peter   308
Grande Compagnie des libraires   191
Grandon, Antoine   203
Graupe, Paul   534
Greflinger, Georg   415
Grimma   1n3
Grodzicki, Stanislaw   226, 244
Groningen   435–436
Grossmann, Burckhard   375–376
Gruneweg, Martin   143

Grynaeus, Simon   309, 315
Grzegorz of Żarnowiec   228, 233
Gualzelli, Chimenti di Taddeo   61–62
Guarini, Battista   248
Gubbio   259–260
Guérin, Jacques   315
Guerra, Domenico and Giovanni Battista   13
Guidetti, Guidetto   64
Guillelmus Parisiensis   226
Gustavus II Adolphus, King of Sweden
   407–408
Gutenberg, Johannes   4, 5
   Bible   509
Gutierrez, Andrés   28, 30
Gutknecht, Jobst   291, 293, 295
Guyon, Louis   386
Gylgenstein, Conrat ('Hablützel')   47

Haarlem   424, 433–434, 440
Haebler, Konrad   525
Hagen, Johannes vander   308
Haguenau   281–283
Haiden, Christopher   367
Halle, Ida   523, 526, 528, 531–532, 534
Halle, Julius (Isaak)   523, 526–527, 529–530,
   532
Hamburg   403–404, 413, 415–416, 422n5,
   440
   Ausländischer Potentiaten Krieges- und
      Stats-Beschreibung   416
   Kürtze Chronica ...   416
   Nordischer Mercurius   415
   Post Zeitung   404, 413
   Relation aus dem Parnasso   415
   Relations Courier   416
   Türkischer Estats und Krieges-Bericht
      416–417
   Wöchentliche Zeitung   404, 413
Hamont, Michiel van   308–321
Happel, Eberhard Werner   416
Harington, John   9
Hartgers, Joost   431, 438
Hartlib, Samuel   468–469
Harvey, Gabriel, *The Trimming of Thomas
   Nashe*   129–132
Haultin, Pierre   203
Head, Richard
   English Rogue Continued, The   114
Heath, Robert   115

Heber, Richard 492n12, 500n56, 501, 520n136
  library 497n40
  sale 511
Heidelberg 415
Heidfeld, Johann 92
Heinrich, Nikolaus 409–410
Henry Julius, Duke of Brunswick-Lüneburg 402
Herborn 92
Hermans, Theodoricus 308
Hernández, Matías 459
Herrer, Michael 370
Hertzberger, Menno 536
Herwart, Johann Heinrich 372
Hess, Rudolph 528
Heusden 437, 440
Heussen, Frans Esausz den 431
Heynlin, Johannes 27, 30
Hibbert, George 501, 503
Hilten, Jan van 425–426, 434, 440–442
Hippocrates 384
Hirsch, Emil 532
Hirsinger, Frydlin and Elsin 46
Hoffmann, Andreas 371
Hoffman, Nicolaus 403
Holonius, Gregorius 314
Holtrop, Willem 165
Höltzel, Hieronymus 289, 295
Holy Roman Empire 154, 223, 228, 276–300, 397–419
Hommius, Festus 100
Hoorn 433, 435
Hortensius, Lambertus 103, 106–107
Horton, George 474
Hospitallers 449
Houwaert, Jan Baptist 314
Huguetan, Jacques 184
Huguetan, Jean 181, 184
Huguetan, Jean-Antoine 389–390
Hungary 154
Husung, Max Joseph 526, 528–529, 531–532, 534
Hutton, George 269

Incunabula Short Title Catalogue (ISTC) 30
Ingolstadt 359
Innes, capt. Robert 468
Innsbruck 413
Inquisition 249–250, 252
Iohannes Dominichus 64
Isabella Clara Eugenia of Spain 95
Italy 7, 220, 254–255, 357, 372–373, 378, 400
Iturriaga, Manuel Mariano de 457

Jacobus de Voragine 30
Jadwiga of Poland 139
Jakob von Kilchen 43
James VI and I, King of Scotland and England 247, 467
Jansenists 390
Janssoon, Jan 101, 432
Jansz, Broer 13, 425–426, 432, 439–442
Jansz, Pieter 171, 173
Januszowski, Jan 241
Jena 375–376, 414
Jenson, Nicolas 56, 58–61, 66–67, 70
Jerdan, William 521
Jesuits 323–324, 449–453, 455–456
  Parras, College of Santa Maria 450
  Santo Domingo de Porta Coeli 456
  Zacatecas, monastery 450
Joaquín de Donazan 451
Jodocus of Erfurt 31
Johannes Andreae 31
Johannes Cratonus 63
Johannes Teutonicus 31
John Chrysostom 310
John Ker, Duke of Roxburghe 507, 517
John George I, Elector of Saxony 398
John George II, Elector of Saxony 102
John of Cologne 57–61, 66–67, 70
John the Steadfast, Elector of Saxony 295
Jones, Richard 121
Jonson, Ben 124, 131–132
  Every Man out of His Humour 124
  Sejanus 132
Joubert, Laurent 385
Juan Bautista, Ignacio de 466
Junta de Temporalidades 449–450
Juste, family of typefounders 196
Justinian, emperor 31

Kalisz 239
Kampen 435
Kargel, Sixt 377
Karnkowski, Stanisław 242
Kazimierz 139, 142

ALPHABETICAL INDEX

Kempen, Arnold von   406
Kettilby, Walter   121
Kingsbarns   267, 269
Kirkcaldy   267–268
Kleinhans, Hans Jakob   404–405
Kleparz   139, 142
Kloppenburch, Evert   427, 431
Kloppenburch, Jan Evertsz   429, 431
Klug, Joseph   19, 280
Koberger, Anton   7, 54
Koczowicz, Andrzej   147
König, Frans Christiaan Hermanus Nathanael   164, 171
Kraiński, Krzysztof   228
Krakow   136–153, 224, 229, 233, 237, 239
    bishops   147
    churches and places of pilgrimage   141–143, 150–152
    Drukarnia Akademicka   152
    Jubilee Year   140–141, 147, 150
    Przewodnik   136–153
    tailors' guild   147
Królewiec   224, 229, 241
Krul, Jan Hermansz   431

La Framboisière, Nicolas de   385
Lambach   531
Landino, Cristoforo   65
Lange, Paul   404
L'Angelier, Abel   9
Langreder, Martin   370
La Rochelle   381
Lasso, Orlando   365, 372
Łaszczów   241
Lauerman, Cornelis   313–314
Lauingen   378
Laurensz, Hendrik   100, 431, 438
Laurentius, Jacobus   100
Lautte, Jean   316
Lech   357
Leeuwarden   433–435, 437
Le Faucheur, Michel   388
Leiden   389, 433–434, 437
    Gazette de Leyde   428
Leipzig   1–2, 18–19, 298–299, 355n8, 357n15, 371, 374, 376–377, 398, 411–414
    Wöchentliche Zeitung   398, 414
LeMaire, Jacob   95
Lemplin, Jacob   46

Leopold I, Holy Roman Emperor   102–103n58
Le Rouge, Jacques   56
Le Roy, Adrien   14
Lesnier, Jean   389, 392–393
Leszno   237, 241
Lewes, Robert, *The Merchants Map*   115
Lewis, George   496
L'Hommeau, Pierre de   383
Libavius, Andreas   385
Licona, Pedro de   465
Liebkind, Albertus   57
Lieshout, François   426–427, 440
Liesvelt, Ferdinand   308
Linacre, Thomas   209n5
Lisbon   16
Listenius, Nicolaus   371
Lodge, Thomas, *Wits Misery*   113
Loe, Jan van der   309
Loersfeld, Johann   294
London   15, 116, 158, 273, 296, 389, 422n5, 425, 469–470, 493, 497, 501, 509, 512n105, 513, 516, 518
    A Perfect Account   470, 474–475
    A Perfect Diurnall   471, 475
    British Library   501n64, 539
    British Museum   501
    Kingdome's Weekly Intelligencer   471
    Lambeth Palace Library   501
    Mercurius Politicus   472–474, 477, 480–481, 484–485
    Perfect Occurrences   471
    The Faithful Scout   474, 478–479
    The London Gazette   486
    The Loyall Scout   474
    The Publick Adviser   472, 477, 482–484
    The Publick Intelligencer   472–473, 477, 480, 484–485
    The Weekly Information   477, 484
    The Weekly Intelligencer   470, 474, 479
    The Weekly Post   474
Lotter, Melchior   19, 284
Louis de Blois   308–309
Louvain, Françoise de   9
Low Countries   303–321, 400, 420–447
Lublin   239
Lucas, Etienne   389
Ludwig von Elchingen   47

Lupoto 73
Lufft, Hans 20
Luther, Martin 19, 225, 227–229, 276–300, 501, 523
   Hauspostille 225, 228–231
Luzern 536
Lyon 7–8, 14–16, 181–207, 208, 213, 298, 331, 339, 384, 389–390
   consulat 204–205
   fairs 190, 194

MacCarthy-Reagh, Justin, Comte de 509
Machiavelli, Niccolò 313
Maciejowski, Bernard, bishop of Krakow 140–141, 228n14
Mâcon 7
Madiis, Francesco de 75, 82
Madrid 16, 453, 455, 462
Maidment, James 516
Maittaire, Michel 211–212
   Annales typographici 211
   Stephanorum historia 211
Malecki, Hieronim 229, 231
Malegonelle, Antonio di Piero 65
Maler, Matthes 294
Malleus maleficarum 313
Mameranus, Nicolaus 309
Man, John 492
Manchester 499
   John Rylands Library 499n52, 518n126, 520
Manger, Michael 364
Manthen, Johannes 58–59
Manutius, Aldus 11–13, 81n17, 181–182, 298–299
Maringo, Giovanni Battista 253
Marino, Giambattista 248, 252
Marprelate, Martin 127
Marseille 45
Martelli, Braccio 65
Martelli, Francesco 61, 68
Martelli, Niccolò 59
Martelli, Niccolò 59
Martin, Louis 196
Martinozzi, Angiolo 73
Martin's Month's Mind 126–127
Maximilian I, Elector of Bavaria 409
McTurk, James 265
Mead, Richard 510n100

Medici, bank 26, 206
Medina del Campo 16
   fairs 194
Meltinger, Ulrich 43, 45–46, 49
Mentelin, Johann 532, 534–536
Mercedarians 449
Mertzenich, Johann von 405–406
Mertzenich, Maria von 406
Mesue 63, 384
Metsius, Laurentius 307
Meurier, Gabriel 313
Meurs, Aert 94
Mewes, Gregor 359n22
Mexico 449, 451–452, 455, 459
Mexico City 451, 453, 455, 459–460, 464
Meyer, Ilsabe 404, 406
Meyer, Johann 404, 413
Middelburg 424, 433, 435, 440
Milan 145, 373, 413
Minima Societas (Venice) 249
Misintis, Bernardinus de 297–298
Młodzianowski, Tomasz 243–244
Molina, Gaspard 189
Molino, Domenico 248
Montaigne, Michel de 467
Montanari, Domenico 256
Montano, Benito Arias 305–306
Montcher, Jean 196
Monteverdi, Claudio 372
Montora, Francesco 256
Mortimer, William 158n9
Moya, Sebastián de 466
Mucante, Gioanni Paolo 143
Muerman, Jacob van 174–175
Mühlbach, Christoph 398–399
Münchener Hofkantorei 361
Munich 361, 362, 371, 409–410, 523, 526, 532, 536
   Bayerische Staatsbibliothek 362, 531
   Gewisse und wahrhaffte Wochentliche Ordinari Zeitung 409–410
   Ordinari Zeitung 409–410
   Royal library 524
   Wochentliche Ordinari Zeitungen 410
Münster, Sebastian 319
Murmellius, Johannes 313
Myszkowski, Piotr 242

Nadler, Jörg   294
Naples   250, 254–257
　　Girolamini Library   538n51
Narr, Peter   47
Nazis   526, 528, 534
Nedham, Marchamont   472–476, 482–486
Nelli, Antonio   57, 59–61, 63, 68, 70–71
Nenninger, Matthäus   370
Neuruppin, Church Library   524
Newcombe, Thomas   473, 484, 486
New Spain   448–466
Niccolò di Giovanni tedesco   63
Niccolò Tedeschi   31, 34, 185
Nicol, George   507
Nicolás, Juan   451
Nieman, Jan Frederik   164n26
Niger, Franciscus   28, 30
Noir, Nicolas   201
Noir, Pierre   201
Nonio, Tobia   328
Nördlingen   403
Núñez Chacón, Nuño   458
Nuremberg   7, 45, 227n10, 278, 289–291, 293, 295, 372–373
　　Teutscher Kriegs-Curier   417–418
　　Verkleidete Götter-Both-Mercurius   418

Oddi, Sforza   328–329
Oecolampadius, Johannes   386
Öglin, Erhard   359n22
Olschki firm   536n45
Olschki, Leo   529
Orlandi, Angelo   253
Orr, Andrew   273
Ortega Montañes, Juan de   448
Orvieto   329–330
Osnabrück   156
Otmar, Silvan   278, 284, 286
Ovid   313
Oxford, St John's College   493

Padua   62
Paix, Jakob   378
Palermo   250–260
Palladio, Andrea   146
Panizza, Valente   328
Pannartz, Arnold   2
Paoli, Giovanni Gualberto di ser Paolo   65
Papal States   322

Papon, Jean   383
Paracelsus   315
Paré, Ambroise   315, 385
Paris   9, 14–16, 27–28, 30, 103, 208, 220, 296, 331, 339, 389–390, 416
　　Bibliothèque Nationale de France   12
　　Sorbonne   27, 210n7, 217, 219
　　University   28, 296
Pasini, Antonio   326–327
Pasini, Luciano   18, 326–339
Paulini, Leonardo   254–259
Paulus III, Pope   322
Payne, Robert   125–126
Péan, René   380, 393
Pecke, Samuel   471
Pellini, Pompeo   328
Peloso, Paolo   256
Pérez, Pedro   459
Perottus, Nicolaus   536
Pers, Pietersz   92
Perth   517
Perugia   18, 322–352
　　academies   325–326
　　Accademia degli Insensati   325–326, 328–329
　　Archivio di Stato   330
　　University   323–324
Pesnot, Louis   203
Petit, Samuel   389
Petrarca, Francesco   313
Petri, Adam   283
Petri, Johannes   27, 532
Petty, William   468
Pezana, Manuel   461
Philippines   449, 460
Piccolomini, Enea Silvio (Pope Pius II)   26
Pietersz, Dirk   92
Pietersz, Jacob   432
Pigot's Directory (1820)   273
Pigot's Directory (1825)   263, 265, 267, 269
Pigray, Pierre   385
Pilgram, Andreas Gottlieb   418
Piotrkowczyk, Andrzej   233
Pisa   62, 64
　　University   56
Place, Josué de la   389
Plantin, Christopher   305–307, 309, 315, 317, 320
　　firm   353, 366

Frankfurt warehouse   353
Polyglot Bible   305
Plato   61, 505
Pliny the Elder   219
Plutarch   64
Poland   136–153, 223–245
Poliziano, Angelo   297
Polyander   95
Pörner, Moritz   398
Porteau, Thomas   381
Porte, Aymon de la   184, 196
Porte, Hugues de la   192, 199, 201–203, 205
Portenbach and Lutz, printing firm   362
Portonariis, Vincenzo   17, 184
Poznań   233, 239
Praetorius, Hieronymus   364
Praetorius, Michael   364
Präulein, Wolfgang   359
Ptolemy   315
Pucci, Benedetto   251
Pulci, Luigi   63

Quaritch, Bernard   518

Rabatta family   62
Raleigh, Walter   125–126
Ramírez de Varrientos, Roberto   458
Ramminger, Melchior   286, 294
Rampazetto, Francesco   13
Ravaud, Marc-Antoine   389–390
Ravesteyn, Johannes van   100
Ravesteyn, Paulus Aertsz van   438
Ravisius Textor, Joannes   313
Rawlinson, Richard   510
Rawlinson, Thomas   510
Reading   492
Recanati, fair   327
Reformation   19, 223
Regnault, Antoine   203
Regnault, Guillaume   202–203
Reinmichel, Leonhart   378
Rej, Mikołaj   229–230, 233, 235, 239, 244
Return from Parnassus, The   113–114, 123
Reulx, Joachim de   308
Rhau, Georg   20, 371
Rhau-Grunenberg, Johannes   19
Ribotteau, Jean   380
Ricciardo di Marco d'Anghiari   64
Richardson Currer, Frances Mary   499

Richel, Bernhard   26, 31–32, 34, 41
Ridolfi, Giovanbattista   56
Rigogli, Bartolomeo   64
Rihel, Wendelin   280, 282
Ripoli press   61–62
Riquelme, Juan   461
Ritzsch, Gregor   355n8
Ritzsch, Timotheus   398
Robinson, Clement
  Handful of Pleasant Delights, A   115, 133
Robinson, Henry   469–470
Robinson, Humphrey   389
Rodero, Gaspar   451
Rodríguez Dávalos, Antonio   314
Rome   16, 55, 140, 143–146, 255–256, 323, 325, 331, 413, 453
  Mirabilia Urbis Romae   143–146
Romero, Ignacio Osorio   461
Roos, Jan   164, 171
Roos, Gerbrand   164, 171, 173–175
Rosa Figueroa, Francisco Antonio de la   464
Rosenthal, Bernard   529n27
Rosenthal, Heinrich   536
Rosenthal, Ludwig   526
Rossi, Lorenzo de'   298
Rothenburg ob der Tauber   363
Rotterdam   424, 427, 433–434, 437
Rouillé, Guillaume   196, 205
Roxburghe Club   518
Roxburghe Sale   489–490, 511, 518, 520n134, 521
Runge, Georg   403
Ruppel, Berthold   25–26, 31, 34, 39, 41
Ruscelli, Girolamo   315
Rusch, Adolf   7, 64
Rychłowski, Franciszek   239–241
Rylands, Enriqueta Augustina   499n52, 518n126
Rylands, John   499
Rynmann, Johannes   359

Sachse, Melchior   294
Sacon, Jacques   196
Salamanca   16, 331
Salviani, Baldo   328
Salviati, family of bankers   206
San Antonio, Sebastián de   463
Sánchez, Manuel   457
Sande, Johan van den   433

ALPHABETICAL INDEX 557

San Nicolás de Tolentino, Michoacán   462
Santiago de Compostela   145
Sarpi, Paolo   250
Sartorius, Johannes   313
Sas, Hans   436
Saumur   380–394
    Académie de Saumur   381, 386–387, 389
Schäfer, Otto   538
Schalekamp, Mathijs   170
Schedel, Krzysztof   239
Schein, Johann Hermann   374, 376
Schellink, Josse   309, 312
Schirlentz, Nicolas   20
Schmid, Michel   44
Schönig, Valentin   359
Schönwetter, Johann Theobald   397–398
Schulte Strathaus, Ernst   528
Schuurmann, Dirk   169–170
Schweinfurt   538
Scotland   154, 158, 261–275, 512–513, 515, 517–518
    National Records of Scotland   274
Scoto, Girolamo   328
Scott, George   269–272
Scott, sir Walter   270, 513
Scottish Book Trade Index (SBTI)   263–264, 269
Seaman, Lazarus   492n12
Segen, Melchior   409
Senneton, Claude   196, 199, 201–203, 205
Senneton, Jacques   196, 199, 201
Senneton, Jean   196, 199, 201
Seville   16, 458, 462
Shakespeare, William
    First Folio   113, 133
Short-Title Catalogue (STC)   133
Sicily   248, 250–260
Siebeneicher, Jakub   141, 147
Sigismund III Vasa, King of Poland and Grand Duke of Lithuania   237
Sistema Bibliotecario Nazionale (SBN)   339
Sixtus IV, Pope   2, 31, 33
Skarga, Piotr   226, 228, 237–240, 244
Slovenia   154
Smient, Otto Barentsz   420–421, 424
Soldoyer, Nicolas   306
Söhne, Julius Adolph von   402
Sorelli, Luigi   254

Southern Netherlands   400, 428
Spain   30, 247, 449, 459
Spalatin, Georg   12, 501n64
Spangenberg, Johann   227
Speed, Adolphus   469
Spencer Library   493n21
Spenser, Edmund
    Faerie Queen   129
Spieringk, Nicolaus   415
Spina, Francesco   61
Spir, Adam von, and Margret   46
Spirito, Lorenzo   316
Stam, Jan Friedricksz   441
St Andrews   267–273, 513–515
    University Library   515
Stanislaus of Szczepanów, bishop of Krakow   139
Stationers' Company   15, 247
Stationers' Register   515n111
Stefan Batory, King of Poland   242
Steinacher, Jacob   44, 47–49, 51
Steiner, Heinrich   289, 294
Stettin, Mariengymnasium   524
Stevenson, Thomas George   516
Stigliani, Tommaso   248
Stradom   142
Strasbourg   7, 25, 37, 46, 280, 282, 377, 397–398, 402, 414, 524–525, 532
    Straßburger Relation   402, 407
Strozzi, Girolamo di Carlo   56
Stürmer, Wolfgang   294
Suarez, Francisco   249
Suigus, Jacobinus   298
Suyderwoude, Pieter Jacobsz van   92
Sweden   401
Sweynheym, Konrad   2
Swiss Confederation   401
Sydney, Philip
    Arcadia   129

Tacuino, Giovanni   327
Tassoni, Alessandro   252
Täuber & Weil's   536
Tavernier, Melchior   103
Taylor, John   118–119
Terentius Afer, Publius   313
Terracina, Laura   13
Tertroode, Fredericus Johannes van   173, 175
Tesori, Pier Matteo   329

The Hague   422n6, 433–434, 437, 440
Thirty Years' War   355, 366–367, 375–376, 400, 411, 426
Thomas a Kempis   312
Thomas Aquinas   30, 249
Thomson, Thomas   516
Thornhill   264
Tielemans, Antoni   432
Tinghi, Philippe   203, 213
Tintinassi, Rosato   330
Tiraqueau, André   383
Tombe, Petrus Van   308
Tongerloo, Anthoni Jansz   433
Tonsor, Michael   363
   Fasciculus cantionum ecclesiasticorum   363
Tooly, Edward   469
Torcy, Nicolaus   308
Torresano, Andrea   11
Tortenson, Lennart   398
Toruń   241
Tour, Catherine de la   197, 203–206
Tournai   306
Tresti, Flaminio   372
Treviso, Biblioteca Municipale   254
Triangoli, Carlo   259
Tromp, Maarten   434
Trot, Barthelemy   182
Trots, Franciscus   308
Trzecieski, Andrzej   242
Tübingen   359
Tullis, Robert   515
Turnbull, William Barclay David Donald   517

Ubaldini, ser Antonio di messer Benedetto   63
Uelzen, Ministerialbibliothek   525
Ugelheimer, Peter   59, 66
Ulhart, Philip   290, 292
UNESCO, Memory of the World   523
Unglerowa, Helena   224n4
Universal Short Title Catalogue (USTC)   30, 80–81, 309–310, 339, 424
Ursinus   100
Utrecht   102, 433–434, 440

Valentín de la Madre de Dios   466
Valgrisi, Vincenzo   13

Valori, Filippo di Bartolomeo   60–61, 66, 68–69
Vatican Library   538n51
Veer, Ellert de   101
Velez, Diego   451
Venice   14–16, 28, 55–56, 65, 208–209, 221, 246–252, 255, 298, 331, 373, 413, 529
   Fondazione Giorgio Cini, Library   536
   Merceria   6
   Rialto   247
   St Mark's   247
Venturi, Francesco   59
Vera, Joseph de   462
Veracruz   448, 455, 457, 462–463, 465–466
   Coscomatepec   462
Vérard, Antoine   5
Verhasselt, Merten   320
Verhoeven, Abraham   13, 424
Vergilius, Publius Maro   63
Vermandel, Hendrik   171
Vervoort, Frans   309
Vesalius, Andreas   315, 432
Vetter, Daniel   237
Victorinus, Georg   371
   Siren coelestis   371–372
Vienna   359, 405
   Ordentliche Postzeitungen   405
   Ordinari Postzeitung   405
Vignier, Nicolas   386
Vilnius   241
Vincent, Antoine   196, 199, 201–202, 205
Vincent, Simon   184
Vinols, Antoine de   201
Viperano, Giovanni Antonio   324
Visscher, Claes Jansz   434
Vives, Juan Luis   313
Vivien, Georges   316
Vorselman, Gheeraert   316
Vossius, Gerard   102, 104–105
Vries, Cornelis de   165–166
Vries, Hendrick Tjercksz de   432
Vrints, Gerard   403
Vroede, Gislenus de   307

Wachsmann, Michael   355n8
Wagenaer, Jan Lucasz   93
Wagenmann, Abraham   363
Walker, Henry   469, 471, 480
Wangen im Allgäu   415

Warsaw, Biblioteka Narodowa   147, 150n26
Wechel, André   86n27, 354
Weege, Johannes   166–168, 171, 173, 175
Wehmer, Carl   528–529
Weimar, State Archives   525
Welser, family of bankers   293, 358
Wenssler, Michel   6–7, 23–35, 37–41, 43, 45–54
   creditors   46–50
   Haus zem Lufft   23, 39
Wentworth, Thomas   381
Wertach   357
West Indies Company   96n27
Westminster   469
Wiering, Thomas von   416–417, 419
Wijnands, Wijnand   166, 171
Willetus, Andreas   432
Willer firm   353–379
   branches   359
   fair catalogue (spring 1621)   363–365
   stock catalogue (1622)   355–356, 361–379
   Willer, Elias   359, 373
   Willer, Georg I   355–356, 359–379
   Willer, Georg II   359, 362
Williams, Oliver   474, 483–484
Williamson, Joseph   389
Wirzbięta, Macjej   229
Wits ABC   116–117

Witt, Johan de   97–99
Wittenberg   1, 12, 18–20, 276–300, 371, 411, 414
Witzel, Georg   224n4
Wolfenbüttel   402
   Wolfenbütteler Aviso   402
Wolfersz, Jan   427
Wolrab, Jan   233
Wood, Robert   474
Wouw, Hillebrant Jacobsz van   438
Wtenbogaert, Johannes   433
Wujek, Jakub   224, 228–229, 232–236, 239–240

Ysenhut, Lienhart   41

Zanchi, Girolamo   386
Zanobi di Mariano   57, 64, 66
Zapparrata, Mariano   254–255
Zaragoza   16
Zenaro, Zaccaria   327
Zierikzee   437, 440
Ziletti, Francesco   328
Zocchi, Giuseppe   62n30
Zschekapürlin, Ludwig   43, 48
Zwolle   435, 440
Zypsen, Matthias   403